BUSINESS ETHICS

ETHICAL DECISION MAKING AND CASES

NINTH EDITION

O. C. Ferrell
University of New Mexico

John Fraedrich
Southern Illinois University—Carbondale

Linda Ferrell
University of New Mexico

SOUTH-WESTERN
CENGAGE Learning·

Australia · Brazil · Japan · Korea · Mexico · Singapore · Spain · United Kingdom · United States

SOUTH-WESTERN
CENGAGE Learning

Business Ethics, Ninth Edition
O.C. Ferrell, John Fraedrich,
and Linda Ferrell

Vice President of Editorial/Business:
Jack W. Calhoun

Publisher: Erin Joyner

Senior Acquisition Editor: Michele Rhoades

Managing Developmental Editor: Joanne
Dauksewicz

Editorial Assistant: Tamara Grega

Marketing Manager: Jon Monahan

Senior Marketing Communications Manager:
Jim Overly

Marketing Coordinator: Julia Tucker

Content Project Manager: Joseph Malcolm

Production Manager: Kim Kusnerak

Media Editor: Rob Ellington

Rights Acquisition Director: Audrey
Pettengill

Rights Acquisition Specialist, Text and Image:
Deanna Ettinger

Manufacturing Planner: Ron Montgomery

Senior Art Director: Tippy McIntosh

Internal Designer, Production
Management, and Composition:
PreMediaGlobal

Cover Designer: Red Hangar Design Ltd

Cover Image(s): Red Hangar Design, LLC

For product information and technology assistance, contact us at
Cengage Learning Customer & Sales Support, 1-800-354-9706
For permission to use material from this text or product,
submit all requests online at **www.cengage.com/permissions**
Further permissions questions can be emailed to
permissionrequest@cengage.com

Library of Congress Control Number: 2011939723

ISBN-13: 978-1-111-82516-4

ISBN-10: 1-111-82516-5

South-Western
5191 Natorp Boulevard
Mason, OH 45040
USA

Cengage Learning products are represented in Canada by
Nelson Education, Ltd.

For your course and learning solutions, visit **www.cengage.com**

Purchase any of our products at your local college store or at our preferred online store **www.cengagebrain.com**

Printed in the United States of America
1 2 3 4 5 6 7 15 14 13 12 11

To Doug Brown.
                    —O.C. Ferrell

To Debbie, Anna, and Lael.
                    — John Fraedrich

To Ernest Rodriguez Naaz.
                    —Linda Ferrell

BRIEF CONTENTS

©LA Nature Graphics, Shutterstock

CONTENTS

PREFACE

Business Ethics: Ethical Decision Making and Cases was introduced over 20 years ago and was the first textbook to use a managerial framework to teach business ethics. Today, this book is used in more business ethics classes than any other text. The Ninth Edition builds on this record of success and provides an enhanced teaching package to help teach the fastest-growing business course in the last two decades. Business ethics courses continue to increase as there is greater recognition of the link between good ethics and business success. This dramatic increase has occurred as a result of understanding that ethical conduct is an important part of an effective business strategy. No longer is ethics considered merely an independent personal decision; rather, managers are held responsible both within and outside their company for building an ethical organizational culture. Now that ethics has been linked to financial performance, there is recognition that business ethics courses are as important as other functional areas such as marketing, accounting, finance, and management.

The Ninth Edition has been extensively updated to reflect rapid advances in academic understanding as well as managerial best practices in business ethics. This real world approach prepares students to enter the business world understanding how ethical decision making occurs as well as how to improve their understanding of the importance of business ethics in their careers. Throughout the book, up-to-date examples are used to make foundational concepts come to life. Students will face many ethical challenges in their careers, and our approach helps them to understand risk and be prepared to address ethical dilemmas. One approach to business ethics education is to include only a theoretical foundation related to ethical reasoning. Our method is to provide a balanced approach that includes the concepts of ethical reasoning as well as the organizational environment that influences ethical decision making.

The mass media has provided many examples of corporations and industries that have failed to achieve adequate ethical performance in their decision making processes. Often ethical misconduct comes to light when firms have been involved in legal violations. When these violations become a detriment to stakeholders and the economy, then legislation is passed to make what should be good ethical decisions into legal requirements. Examples include the Federal Sentencing Guidelines for Organizations (FSGO), the Sarbanes-Oxley Act, and more recently the Dodd-Frank Wall Street Reform and Consumer Protection Act.

This type of legislation is being developed on a global basis, with the U.K. Anti-bribery Act as the most stringent anti-bribery legislation in the world. Therefore, students need to understand that ethical decision making must take into account many elements, including requirements that stem from attempts to legalize ethics. On the other hand, it is hoped that most businesses rise above the minimum requirements of this legislation and see business ethics as good for the bottom line of the firm as well as society.

Using a managerial framework, we explain how ethics can be integrated into strategic business decisions. This framework provides an *overview of the concepts, processes, mandatory, core, and voluntary business practices* associated with successful business ethics programs. Some approaches to business ethics are excellent as exercises in intellectual reasoning, but they cannot deal with the many actual issues and considerations that people in business organizations face. Our approach supports ethical reasoning and the value of individuals being able to face ethical challenges and voice their concerns about appropriate behavior. Employees in organizations are ultimately in charge of their own behavior and need to be skillful in making decisions in gray areas where the appropriate conduct is not always obvious.

We have been diligent in this revision to provide the most relevant examples of how the lack of business ethics has challenged our economic viability and entangled countries and companies around the world. This book remains the market leader because it *addresses the complex environment of ethical decision making in organizations and pragmatic, actual business concerns.* Every individual has unique personal principles and values, and every organization has its own set of values, rules, and organizational ethical culture. Business ethics must consider the organizational culture and interdependent relationships between the individual and other significant persons involved in organizational decision making. Without effective guidance, a businessperson cannot make ethical decisions while facing a short-term orientation, feeling organizational pressure to perform well and seeing rewards based on outcomes in a challenging competitive environment.

By focusing on individual issues and organizational environments, this book gives students the opportunity to see roles and responsibilities they will face in business. The past decade has reinforced the value of understanding the role of business ethics in the effective management of an organization. Widespread misconduct reported in the mass media every day demonstrates that businesses, governments, non-profits, and institutions of higher learning need to address business ethics.

Our primary goal has always been to enhance the awareness and the ethical decision-making skills that students will need to make business ethics decisions that contribute to responsible business conduct. By focusing on these concerns and issues of today's challenging business environment, we demonstrate that the study of business ethics is imperative to the long-term well-being of not only businesses, but also our economic system.

PHILOSOPHY OF THIS TEXT

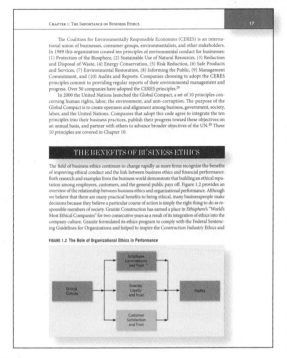

The purpose of this book is to help students improve their ability to make ethical decisions in business by providing them with a framework that they can use to identify, analyze, and resolve ethical issues in business decision making. Individual values and ethics are important in this process. By studying business ethics, students begin to understand how to cope with conflicts between their personal values and those of the organization.

Many ethical decisions in business are close calls. It often takes years of experience in a particular industry to know what is acceptable. We do not, in this book, provide ethical answers but instead attempt to prepare students to make informed ethical decisions. First, we do not moralize by indicating what to do in a specific situation. Second, although we provide an overview of moral philosophies and decision-making processes, we do not prescribe any one philosophy or process as best or most ethical. Third, by itself, this book will not make students more ethical nor will it tell them how to judge the ethical behavior of others. Rather, its goal is to help students understand and use their current values and convictions in making business decisions and to encourage everyone to think about the effects of their decisions on business and society.

Many people believe that business ethics cannot be taught. Although we do not claim to teach ethics, we suggest that by studying business ethics a person can improve ethical decision making by identifying ethical issues and recognizing the approaches available to resolve them. An organization's reward system can reinforce appropriate behavior and help shape attitudes and beliefs about important issues. For example, the success of some campaigns to end racial or gender discrimination in the workplace provides evidence that attitudes and behavior can be changed with new information, awareness, and shared values.

CONTENT AND ORGANIZATION

In writing *Business Ethics*, Ninth Edition, we strived to be as informative, complete, accessible, and up to date as possible. Instead of focusing on one area of ethics, such as moral philosophy or social responsibility, we provide balanced coverage of all areas relevant to the current development and practice of ethical decision making. In short, we have tried to keep pace with new developments and current thinking in teaching and practices.

The first half of the text consists of ten chapters, which provide a framework to identify, analyze, and understand how businesspeople make ethical decisions and deal with ethical issues. Several enhancements have been made to chapter content for this edition. Some of the most important are listed in the next paragraphs.

Part One, "An Overview of Business Ethics," includes two chapters that help provide a broader context for the study of business ethics. Chapter 1, "The Importance of Business Ethics," has been revised with many new examples and survey results to describe issues and concerns important to business ethics. Chapter 2, "Stakeholder Relationships, Social Responsibility, and Corporate Governance," has been significantly reorganized and updated with new examples and issues. This chapter was reorganized and expanded to develop an overall framework for the text.

Part Two, "Ethical Issues and the Institutionalization of Business Ethics," consists of two chapters that provide the background that students need to identify ethical issues and understand how society, through the legal system, has attempted to hold organizations responsible for managing these issues. Chapter 3, "Emerging Business Ethics Issues," has been significantly reorganized and updated and provides expanded coverage of business ethics issues. Reviewers requested more detail on key issues that create ethical decisions. Within this edition, we have increased the depth of ethical issues and have updated the following new issues: abusive and intimidating behavior, lying, bribery, corporate intelligence, environmental issues, intellectual property rights, and privacy. Chapter 4, "The Institutionalization of Business Ethics" examines key elements of core or best practices in corporate America today along with legislation and regulation requirements that support business ethics initiatives. The chapter is divided into three main areas: voluntary, mandated, and core boundaries.

Part Three, "The Decision-Making Process" consists of three chapters, which provide a framework to identify, analyze, and understand how businesspeople make ethical decisions and deal with ethical issues. Chapter 5, "Ethical Decision Making and Ethical Leadership," has been revised and updated to reflect current research and understanding of ethical decision making and contains a new section on ethical leadership. Chapter 6, "Individual Factors: Moral Philosophies and Values," has been updated and revised to explore the role of moral philosophies and moral development as individual factors in the ethical decision-making process. This chapter now includes a new section on white-collar crime. Chapter 7, "Organizational Factors: The Role of Ethical Culture and Relationships," considers organizational influences on business decisions, such as role relationships, differential association, and other organizational pressures, as well as whistle-blowing.

Part Four, "Implementing Business Ethics in a Global Economy," looks at specific measures that companies can take to build an effective ethics program, as well as how these programs may be affected by global issues. Chapter 8, "Developing an Effective Ethics Program," has been refined and updated with corporate best practices for developing effective ethics programs. Chapter 9, "Managing and Controlling Ethics Programs," offers a framework for auditing ethics initiatives as well as the importance of doing so. Such audits can help companies pinpoint problem areas, measure their progress in improving conduct, and even provide a "debriefing" opportunity after a crisis. Finally, Chapter 10, "Business Ethics in a Global Economy" is completely revised to reflect the complex and dynamic events that almost caused a global depression. This chapter will help students understand the major issues involved in making decisions in a global environment.

Part Five consists of 20 cases in the text that bring reality into the learning process. Eight of these cases are new to the ninth edition, and the remaining twelve have been revised and updated. In addition, five shorter cases are available on the Instructor's Companion website:

- Apple Inc.'s Ethical Success and Challenges
- Toyota: Challenges in Maintaining Integrity
- The Container Store: An Employee-centric Retailer
- The Ethics Program at Eaton Corporation
- Barrett-Jackson Auction Company: Family, Fairness, and Philanthropy

The companies and situations portrayed in these cases are real; names and other facts are not disguised; and all cases include developments up to the end of 2011. By reading and analyzing these cases, students can gain insight into ethical decisions and the realities of making decisions in complex situations.

TEXT FEATURES

Many tools are available in this text to help both students and instructors in the quest to improve students' ability to make ethical business decisions.

- Each chapter opens with an outline and a list of learning objectives.
- Immediately following is "An Ethical Dilemma" that should provoke discussion about ethical issues related to the chapter. The short vignette describes a hypothetical incident involving an ethical conflict. Questions at the end of the "Ethical Dilemma" section focus discussion on how the dilemma could be resolved.

CASE 1
Monsanto Attempts to Balance Stakeholder Interests

CASE 2
Starbucks' Mission: Social Responsibility and Brand Strength

CASE 3
Walmart: The Future Is Sustainability

CASE 4
BP Struggles to Resolve Sustainability Disaster

CASE 5
New Belgium Brewing: Ethical and Environmental Responsibility

CASE 6
Coping with Financial and Ethical Risks at American International Group (AIG)

CASE 7
Microsoft Manages Legal and Ethical Issues

CASE 8
Countrywide Financial: The Subprime Meltdown

CASE 9
Enron: Questionable Accounting Leads to Collapse

CASE 10
Home Depot Implements Stakeholder Orientation

CASE 11
The Fraud of the Century: The Case of Bernard Madoff

CASE 12
Insider Trading at the Galleon Group

CASE 13
GlaxoSmithKline Experiences High Costs of Product Quality Issues

CASE 14
Hospital Corporation of America: Learning from Past Mistakes?

CASE 15
The Coca-Cola Company Struggles with Ethical Crises

CASE 16
Recreational Equipment Incorporated (REI): A Responsible Retail Cooperative

CASE 17
Better Business Bureau: Protecting Consumers and Dealing with Organizational Ethics Challenges

CASE 18
The American Red Cross Faces Organizational Challenges

CASE 19
Nike: Managing Ethical Missteps—Sweatshops to Leadership in Employment Practices

CASE 20
Best Buy Fights against Electronic Waste

- New to this edition, each chapter has a contemporary real world debate issue. These debate issues have been found to stimulate thoughtful discussion relating to content issues in the chapter. Topics of the debate issues include Google and consumer privacy, the universal health care debate, the contribution of ethical conduct to financial performance, the Consumer Financial Protection Bureau, and new legislation concerning whistle-blowing.
- At the end of each chapter are a chapter summary and an important terms list, both of which are handy tools for review. Also included at the end of each chapter is a "Resolving Ethical Business Challenges" section. The vignette describes a realistic drama that helps students experience the process of ethical decision making. The "Resolving Ethical Business Challenges" minicases presented in this text are hypothetical; any resemblance to real persons, companies, or situations is coincidental. Keep in mind that there are no right or wrong solutions to the minicases.

The ethical dilemmas and real-life situations provide an opportunity for students to use concepts in the chapter to resolve ethical issues.

Each chapter concludes with a series of questions that allow students to test their EQ (Ethics Quotient).

- Cases. In Part Five, following each real-world case are questions to guide students in recognizing and resolving ethical issues. For some cases, students can conduct additional research to determine recent developments because many ethical issues in companies take years to resolve.

EFFECTIVE TOOLS FOR TEACHING AND LEARNING

Instructor's Resource Manual.   The *Instructor's Resource Manual* contains a wealth of information. Teaching notes for every chapter include a brief chapter summary, detailed lecture outline, and notes for using the "Ethical Dilemma" and "Resolving Ethical Business Challenges" sections. Detailed case notes point out the key issues involved and offer suggested answers to the questions. A separate section provides guidelines for using case analysis in teaching business ethics. Detailed notes are provided to guide the instructor in analyzing or grading the cases. Simulation role-play cases, as well as implementation suggestions, are included. For others involved in attempting to simulate more of the actual constructs students will face in their business careers we suggest accessing http://www.businessreality.org/.

Role-Play Cases.   The ninth edition provides six behavioral simulation role-play cases developed for use in the business ethics course. The role-play cases and implementation methods can be found in the *Instructor's Resource Manual* and on the website. Role-play cases may be used as a culminating experience to help students integrate concepts covered in the text. Alternatively, the cases may be used as an ongoing exercise to provide students with extensive opportunities for interacting and making ethical decisions.

Role-play cases simulate a complex, realistic, and timely business ethics situation. Students form teams and make decisions based on an assigned role. The role-play case complements and enhances traditional approaches to business learning experiences because it (1) gives students the opportunity to practice making decisions that have business ethics consequences; (2) re-creates the power, pressures, and information that affect decision making at various levels of management; (3) provides students with a team-based experience that enriches their skills and understanding of group processes and dynamics; and (4) uses a feedback period to allow for the exploration of complex and controversial issues in business ethics decision making. The role-play cases can be used with classes of any size.

Test Bank and Exam View.   The *Test Bank* provides multiple-choice and essay questions for each chapter and includes a mix of objective and application questions. *ExamView*, a computerized version of the Test Bank, provides instructors with all the tools they need to create, author/edit, customize, and deliver multiple types of tests. Instructors can import questions directly from the test bank, create their own questions, or edit existing questions.

Instructor's Resource CD-ROM.   This instructor's CD provides a variety of teaching resources in electronic format, allowing for easy customization to meet specific instructional needs. Files include Word files of the Test Bank, along with its computerized version, *ExamView;* Lecture PowerPoint® slides; and Word and PDF files from the Instructor's Resource Manual.

Videos.   A DVD is also available to support the Ninth Edition. The segments can be used across several chapters, and the Video Guide (which appears at the end of the Instructor Manual) contains a matrix intended to show the closest relationships between the videos and chapter topics. The Video Guide also includes summaries of each video as well as teaching guidelines and issues for discussion.

Instructor Companion Site.   The Instructor Companion Site includes a complete Instructor Manual, Word files from both the Instructor Manual and Test Bank, and PowerPoint slides for easy downloading.

CourseMate.   This unique student website makes course concepts come alive with interactive learning, study, and exam preparation tools supporting the printed text. CourseMate delivers what you need, including an interactive eBook, an interactive glossary, quizzes, videos, KnowNOW blogs, and more. The site contains links to companies and organizations highlighted in each chapter; links to association, industry, and company codes of conduct; case website links; company and organizational examples; and academic resources, including links to business ethics centers throughout the world and the opportunity to sign up for weekly abstracts of relevant *Wall Street Journal* articles. Four Ethical Leadership Challenge scenarios are available for each chapter. Training devices, including Lockheed Martin's Gray Matters ethics game, are also available.

WebTutor™.   Whether you want to Web-enable your class or teach entirely online, WebTutor provides customizable text-specific content within your course system. This content-rich, web-based teaching and learning aid reinforces chapter concepts and acts as an electronic student study guide. WebTutor provides students with interactive chapter review quizzes, critical-thinking, writing-improvement exercises, flashcards, PowerPoints, and links to online videos.

Additional Teaching Resources.   O.C. Ferrell and Linda Ferrell are leading the Bill Daniels Business Ethics Initiative at the University of New Mexico. This initiative is part of a four state initiative to develop teaching resources to support principle-based ethics education. Their publically accessible website contains original cases, debate issues, videos, interviews, and PowerPoint modules on select business ethics topics, as well as other resources such as articles on business ethics education. It is possible to access this website at http://danielsethics.mgt.unm.edu.

ACKNOWLEDGMENTS

A number of individuals provided reviews and suggestions that helped to improve this text. We sincerely appreciate their time and effort.

Donald Acker
Brown Mackie College

Donna Allen
Northwest Nazarene University

Suzanne Allen
Walsh University

Carolyn Ashe
University of Houston–Downtown

Laura Barelman
Wayne State College

Russell Bedard
Eastern Nazarene College

B. Barbara Boerner
Brevard College

Judie Bucholz
Guilford College

Greg Buntz
University of the Pacific

Julie Campbell
Adams State College

Robert Chandler
University of Central Florida

April Chatham-Carpenter
University of Northern Iowa

Leslie Connell
University of Central Florida

Peggy Cunningham
Dalhousie University

Carla Dando
Idaho State University

James E. Donovan
Detroit College of Business

Douglas Dow
University of Texas at Dallas

A. Charles Drubel
Muskingum College

Philip F. Esler
University of St. Andrews

Joseph M. Foster
Indiana Vocational Technical College—Evansville

Terry Gable
Truman State University

Robert Giacalone
University of Richmond

Suresh Gopalan
West Texas A&M University

Mark Hammer
Northwest Nazarene University

Charles E. Harris, Jr.
Texas A&M University

Kenneth A. Heischmidt
Southeast Missouri State University

Neil Herndon
Educational Consultant

Walter Hill
Green River Community College

Jack Hires
Valparaiso University

David Jacobs
American University

R. J. Johansen
Montana State University–Bozeman

Edward Kimman
Vrije Universiteit

Janet Knight
Purdue North Central

Anita Leffel
University of Texas at San Antonio

Barbara Limbach
Chadron State College

Nick Lockard
Texas Lutheran College

Terry Loe
Kennesaw State University

Nick Maddox
Stetson University

Isabelle Maignan
ING Bank

Phylis Mansfield
Pennsylvania State University–Erie

Robert Markus
Babson College

Randy McLeod
Harding University

Francy Milner
University of Colorado

Ali Mir
William Paterson University

Debi P. Mishra
Binghamton University, State University of
New York

Patrick E. Murphy
University of Notre Dame

Lester Myers
University of San Francisco

Cynthia Nicola
Carlow College

Carol Nielsen
Bemidji State University

Lee Richardson
University of Baltimore

William M. Sannwald
San Diego State University

Zachary Shank
Albuquerque Technical Vocational Institute

Cynthia A. M. Simerly
Lakeland Community College

Karen Smith
Columbia Southern University

Filiz Tabak
Towson University

Debbie Thorne
Texas State University–San Marcos

Wanda V. Turner
Ferris State College

Gina Vega
Salem State College

William C. Ward
Mid-Continent University

David Wasieleski
Duquesne University

Jim Weber
Duquesne University

Ed Weiss
National-Louis University

Joseph W. Weiss
Bentley University

Jan Zahrly
University of North Dakota

We wish to acknowledge the many people who assisted us in writing this book. We are deeply grateful to Jennifer Jackson for her work in organizing and managing the revision process. We would also like to thank Jennifer Sawayda and Jessica Talley for all their assistance in this edition. We are also indebted to Melanie Drever, Barbara Gilmer, and Gwyneth V. Walters for their contributions to previous editions of this text. Debbie Thorne, Texas State University–San Marcos, provided advice and guidance on the text and cases. Finally, we express appreciation to the administration and to our colleagues at the University of New Mexico and Southern Illinois University at Carbondale for their support.

We invite your comments, questions, or criticisms. We want to do our best to provide teaching materials that enhance the study of business ethics. Your suggestions will be sincerely appreciated.

– O. C. Ferrell
– John Fraedrich
– Linda Ferrell

PART 1

An Overview of Business Ethics

© LA Nature Graphics, Shutterstock

CHAPTER 1

THE IMPORTANCE OF BUSINESS ETHICS

CHAPTER OBJECTIVES

- To explore conceptualizations of business ethics from an organizational perspective

- To examine the historical foundations and evolution of business ethics

- To provide evidence that ethical value systems support business performance

- To gain insight into the extent of ethical misconduct in the workplace and the pressures for unethical behavior

AN ETHICAL DILEMMA*

John Peters had just arrived at the Memphis branch offices of Bull Steins (BS) brokerage firm. BS is one of the top 50 firms in the industry with a wide range of financial products. Five years prior, John had graduated from Midwest State University and started work at Marell and Pew Brokerage. While at Marell and Pew, he had learned that in finance, one must follow both the letter and the spirit of the law. BS started courting John after he had worked at Marell

for four years because he had a good reputation and an investment portfolio worth approximately $100 million with some 400 investors.

A hard worker, John acquired his clients through various networking avenues, including family, the country club, cocktail parties, and serving on boards of charitable organizations. He called one client group the Sharks. These were investors who took risks, made multiple transactions every month, and looked for short-term, high-yield investments. The second group he called the Cessnas because most of them owned twin-engine planes. This group was primarily employed in the medical field but included a few bankers and lawyers. He called the final group the Turtles because they wanted stability and security. This group would normally trade only a few times a year.

John was highly trained and was not only comfortable discussing numbers with bankers and medical billing with physicians, but he also had the people skills to convey complex financial products and solutions in understandable terms to his Turtles, who were primarily older and semiretired. This was one of the main reasons Al Dryer had wanted to hire him. "You've got charisma, John, and you know your way around people and financial products," Dryer explained.

At Marell and Pew, Skyler had been John's trainer. Skyler had been in the business for 15 years and had worked for three of the top brokerage firms in the world. Skyler quickly taught John some complicated tricks of the trade. For example, "Your big clients [Sharks and Cessnas] will like IPOs [initial public offerings], but you have to be careful about picking the right ones," Skyler said. "Before suggesting one, look at who is on their board of directors and cross-reference them with other IPO boards in the last 5 to 7 years. Next, cross-check everyone to see where the connections are, especially if they have good ties to the SEC (Securities and Exchange Commission). Finally, you want to check these people and the companies they have been associated with. Check every IPO these people were involved in and what Moody's ratings were prior to the IPO. As you know, Moody's is one of two IPO rating companies in the United States, and they're hurting for revenue because of the financial downturn. If you see a bias in how they rate because of personal relations to the IPO people, you've got a winner," Skyler smiled.

During his five years at the company, Skyler had taught John about shorting, naked shorting, and churning. She explained shorting by using an example. "If I own 1,000 shares at $100/share and you think the stock is going to tank (go down), you 'borrow' my shares at $100/share, sell them, and the next week the stock goes down to $80/share. You call your broker and buy back the 1,000 shares

at $80 and give me my 1,000 shares at $80/share. Do you see what happened?" Skyler asked. "You borrowed my shares and sold them for $100,000. The following week, when the company stock fell to $80, you repurchased those 1,000 shares for $80,000 and gave them back to me. In the meantime, you pocketed the difference of $20,000." Skyler went on, "Naked short selling is the same as shorting but you don't pay any money for the stock. There is a three-day grace period between buying and selling. That means you have at least three days of *free money*!"

Al Dryer instructed John to wait to resign from Marell and Pew until late on Friday so that BS could send out packets to each of his accounts to explain that he was switching companies. John thought about this, but was told by others this was standard practice. "But what about the noncompete clause I signed? It says I can't do that," said John to a few brokers not associated with either firm. Their response was, "It's done all the time." On Friday John did what BS asked, and there were no negative consequences for either John or the firm. Six months went by and John's portfolio increased to $150 million. Other brokers began imitating John's strategy. For example, for his Sharks, John would buy and sell at BS and call some of his buddies to do the same thing using money from the Sharks. Another tactic involved selling futures contracts without providing evidence that he held the shares sold (naked shorting). While much of what he was doing was risky, John had become so successful that he guaranteed his Turtles against any loss.

Several years later John was buying and selling derivatives, a form of futures contract that gets its value from assets such as commodities, equities (stocks), bonds, interest rates, exchange rates, or even an index of weather conditions. While his risk-taking Shark group had expanded threefold, John's Cessna pool had all but dried up. However, his Turtles had grown dramatically to an average worth of $500,000. The portfolio he managed had topped $750 million, a lot more than he had when he started at BS ($500 million in Sharks and $250 million for Turtles).

"This year is going to be better than last year," said John to some of the brokers at BS. But expenses were rising fast. John's expense account included country club memberships, sports tickets, and trips for clients. Instead of charging the firm, John always paid for these out of his own pocket. He was indirectly letting his clients know that it was his money he was spending on them; the clients were grateful for his largess, and those who would have grumbled about delays in the delivery of securities purchased were less apt to do so. John saw a great opportunity to make his heavy hitters happy. Unbeknownst to them, he would buy and sell stocks for these clients and later surprise them with the profits.

By this time, John was training new hires at BS, which would have taken a lot of his personal and professional time if he had done it right. For example, because John was a senior partner, he had to sign off on every trade they made; he needed to budget an hour a day just to sign the four other brokers' trades. But John also had a lot of other things on his mind. He had decided to get married and adopt children. His soon-to-be wife, Leslie, quit her job to be a full-time mom and was designing their new 18,000-square-foot home. With all these activities going on at once, John was not paying much attention to the four new brokers and their training.

Then one Monday morning, John received a call from the SEC asking about some trades made by the four new brokers. "It appears to us there may be some nonpublic information your brokers have concerning several IPOs," the agent said. "If they do have such information, this could be considered insider information. John, I'm calling you as a courtesy because we go way back to our college days, but I have to know," said the agent. John thanked him and went straight to the new brokers and asked them about the IPO. One of the new brokers replied, "John, you told us that in order to excel in this business, you need to be an expert on knowing exactly where things become legal and illegal. You said, 'Trust me, I've been doing this for 15 years, and I've never had a problem.' We just did what you've taught us."

John knew that if they did have insider information, he would probably be found partially responsible because he was supposed to be training them. At the very least, the SEC would start checking his trades over the past several years. He also knew that, when subjected to scrutiny, some of his past trades might be deemed questionable as well.

What should John do?

QUESTIONS | EXERCISES

1. What are John's ethical issues?
2. Are there any legal considerations for John?
3. Discuss the implications of each decision John has made thus far and may make in the future to handle his situation.

*This case is strictly hypothetical; any resemblance to real persons, companies, or situations is coincidental.

The ability to recognize and deal with complex business ethics issues has become a significant priority in twenty-first–century companies. In recent years, a number of well-publicized scandals resulted in public outrage about deception and fraud in business and a subsequent demand for improved business ethics and greater corporate responsibility. The publicity and debate surrounding highly visible legal and ethical lapses at a number of well-known firms, including AIG, Countrywide Financial, and Fannie Mae, highlight the need for businesses to integrate ethics and responsibility into all business decisions.

Highly visible business ethics issues influence the public's attitudes toward business and can destroy trust. Ethical decisions are a part of everyday life for those who work in organizations. Ethics is a part of decision making at all levels of work and management. Business ethics is not just an isolated personal issue; policies and informal communications for responsible conduct are embedded in an organization's operations. This means that ethical or unethical conduct is the province of everyone who works in an organizational environment.

Making good ethical decisions is just as important to business success as mastering marketing, finance, and accounting decisions. While education and training emphasize functional areas of business, business ethics is often viewed as easy to master, something that happens with little effort. In fact, ethical behavior requires understanding and identifying real-life issues, areas of risk, and approaches to making choices in an organizational environment. Some approaches to business ethics look only at its philosophical dimensions and the social consequences of decisions. This approach fails to address the complex organizational environment of businesses and pragmatic business concerns. By contrast, our approach is managerial and reflects how business ethics is practiced in the business world.

It is important to learn how to make decisions in the internal environment of an organization to achieve goals and career advancement. But business does not exist in a vacuum. The decisions of people in business have implications for shareholders, workers, customers, and society. Ethical decisions must take these stakeholders into account, for unethical conduct can negatively affect society as a whole. Our approach focuses on the practical consequences of decisions and on positive outcomes that have the potential to contribute to both business success and society at large. The field of business ethics deals with questions about whether specific business practices are acceptable. For example, should a salesperson omit facts about a product's poor safety record in a sales presentation to a client? Should an accountant report inaccuracies that he or she discovered in an audit of a client, knowing the auditing company will probably be fired by the client for doing so? Should an automobile tire manufacturer intentionally conceal safety concerns to avoid a massive and costly tire recall? Regardless of their legality, others will certainly judge the actions taken in such situations as right or wrong, ethical or unethical. By its very nature, the field of business ethics is controversial, and there is no universally accepted approach for resolving its issues.

A Josephson Institute of Ethics Report Card survey of teens showed that 89 percent feel that being an ethical person is more important than being rich. However, of those surveyed, 59 percent admitted to cheating on a test within the last year. One-third admitted to using the Internet to plagiarize an assignment. One-fourth of the students surveyed admitted to lying on some of the survey questions.[1]

If today's students are tomorrow's leaders, unethical behavior seems poised to become more common. Perhaps even more distressing, an Arizona State University survey of state educators revealed that 50 percent admitted to cheating on state tests, either accidentally or intentionally. One percent admitted to changing answers on their students' tests or encouraging certain students to avoid the tests altogether.[2]

Before we get started, it is important to state our philosophies regarding this book. First, we do not moralize by telling you what is right or wrong in a specific situation. Second, although we provide an overview of group and individual decision-making processes, we do not prescribe any one philosophy or process as the best or most ethical. Third, by itself, this book will not make you more ethical, nor will it tell you how to judge the ethical behavior of others. Rather, its goal is to help you understand and use your current values and convictions when making business decisions so that you think about the effects of those decisions on business and society. In addition, this book will help you understand what businesses are doing to improve their ethical conduct. To this end, we aim to help you learn to recognize and resolve ethical issues within business organizations. As a manager, you will be responsible for your decisions and the ethical conduct of the employees you supervise. The framework we develop in this book therefore focuses on how organizational ethical decisions are made and on ways companies can improve their ethical conduct.

In this chapter, we first develop a definition of business ethics and discuss why it has become an important topic in business education. We also discuss why studying business ethics can be beneficial. Next, we examine the evolution of business ethics in North America. Then we explore the performance benefits of ethical decision making for businesses. Finally, we provide a brief overview of the framework we use for examining business ethics in this text.

BUSINESS ETHICS DEFINED

The term *ethics* has many nuances. It has been defined as "inquiry into the nature and grounds of morality where the term morality is taken to mean moral judgments, standards and rules of conduct."[3] Ethics has also been called the study and philosophy of human conduct, with an emphasis on determining right and wrong. *The American Heritage Dictionary* offers these definitions of ethics: "The study of the general nature of morals and of specific moral choices; moral philosophy; and the rules or standards governing the conduct of the members of a profession."[4] One difference between an ordinary decision and an ethical one lies in "the point where the accepted rules no longer serve, and the decision maker is faced with the responsibility for weighing values and reaching a judgment in a situation which is not quite the same as any he or she has faced before."[5] Another difference relates to the amount of emphasis that decision makers place on their own values and accepted practices within their company. Consequently, values and judgments play a critical role when we make ethical decisions.

Building on these definitions, we can begin to develop a concept of business ethics. Most people would agree that high ethical standards require both businesses and individuals to conform to sound moral principles. However, some special aspects must be considered when applying ethics to business. First, to survive, businesses must earn a profit. If profits are realized through misconduct, however, the life of the organization may be shortened. Competitors in particular are quick to point out a company's misconduct. For instance, in the battle between Microsoft's Bing search engine and Google, Google accused Microsoft Corp. of copying its Internet search engine results. Recognizing the damage this could do to its reputation, Microsoft quickly defended its reputation and claimed that Google's accusations were little more than a publicity stunt.[6] Second, businesses must balance their desire for profits against the needs and desires of society. Maintaining this balance often requires compromises or trade-offs. To address these unique aspects of the business world, society has developed rules—both legal and implicit—to guide businesses in their efforts to earn profits in ways that do not harm individuals or society as a whole.

Most definitions of business ethics reference rules, standards, and moral principles regarding what is right or wrong in specific situations. For our purposes, **business ethics** comprises the principles, values, and standards that guide behavior in the world of business. **Principles** are specific and pervasive boundaries for behavior that are universal and absolute. Principles often become the basis for rules. Some examples of principles include freedom of speech, fundamentals of justice, and civil rights. **Values** are used to develop norms that are socially enforced. Integrity, accountability, and trust are examples of values. Investors, employees, customers, interest groups, the legal system, and the community often determine whether a specific action is right or wrong, ethical or unethical. Although these groups are not necessarily right, their judgments influence society's acceptance or rejection of a business and its activities.

WHY STUDY BUSINESS ETHICS?

A Crisis in Business Ethics

As we've already mentioned, ethical misconduct has become a major concern in business today. The Ethics Resource Center conducted the National Business Ethics Survey (NBES) of about 3,000 U.S. employees to gather reliable data on key ethics and compliance outcomes and to help identify and better understand the ethics issues that are important to employees. The NBES found that 49 percent of employees reported observing at least one type of misconduct. Approximately 63 percent reported the misconduct to management, an increase from previous years.[7] Largely in response to the financial crisis, business decisions and activities have come under greater scrutiny by many different constituents, including consumers, employees, investors, government regulators, and special interest groups. For instance, regulators are looking carefully at Countrywide Financial to see whether its top executives purposely misled investors about the risks of certain securities it was selling. One lawsuit alleges that Countrywide and top executives like former CEO Angelo Mozilo misled investors by portraying its investments as low risk.[8] Such misconduct has lowered consumer trust in business. Figure 1.1 shows the percentage of respondents who say that they trust a variety of businesses in various industries. Notice that the levels of consumer trust in most industries is declining. Banks have some of the lowest ratings, indicating that

FIGURE 1.1 Americans' Trust in Business Sectors (percentage of respondents who say they trust companies in the following categories)

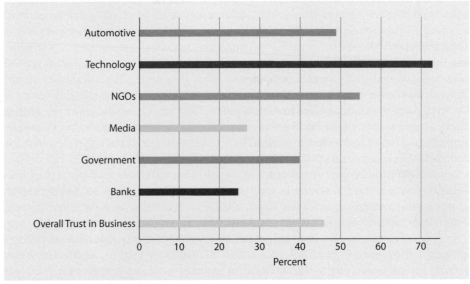

Source: "2011 Edelman Trust Barometer Findings," Edelman Trust Barometer, http://www.edelman.com/trust/2011/uploads/Edelman%20Trust%20Barometer%20Global%20Deck.pdf (accessed February 15, 2011).

the financial sector has not been able to restore its reputation since the 2008–2009 recession. Most significant is the fact that less than half of all respondents surveyed have an overall trust in business. There is no doubt that negative publicity associated with major misconduct has lowered the public's trust in business.[9]

Specific Issues

Misuse of company resources, abusive behavior, harassment, accounting fraud, conflicts of interest, defective products, bribery, and employee theft are all problems cited as evidence of declining ethical standards. For example, BP has received negative publicity for a number of ethical issues, particularly after the 2010 *Deepwater Horizon* explosion and Gulf Coast disaster. Shortly after BP's announcement that it is committed to becoming the safest offshore energy operator, the public learned that a safety regulator had ordered BP to fix safety lapses on three of its rigs in the North Sea. Such an incident makes one question the extent of BP's commitment.[10] Other ethical issues relate to recognizing the interest of communities and society. For instance, Walmart dropped plans to build a Supercenter near a Civil War site after two years of fighting with historians and residents. This is not the first instance in which Walmart battled with communities about building around areas with historical significance. However, in this case, Walmart listened to stakeholder concerns and decided to move to a new location.[11] Although large companies like Walmart have significant power, pressures from society and government still limit what they can do.

Ethics plays an important role in the public sector as well. In government, several politicians and some high-ranking officials have experienced significant negative publicity, and some have had to resign in disgrace over ethical indiscretions. Former House Majority Leader Tom DeLay received a three-year prison sentence for money laundering and conspiracy charges. DeLay was accused of channeling $190,000 of corporate money into the Republican National Committee to help elect Republicans to the Texas Legislature.[12] The DeLay scandal demonstrates that ethical behavior must be proactively practiced at all levels of society.

Every organization has the potential for unethical behavior, as the FBI realized after discovering that several of its agents had cheated on a test. A Justice Department investigation revealed that several FBI agents, including some supervisors and a legal advisor, cheated on a test about FBI procedures for the surveillance of Americans. According to the investigation, certain agents took the test together, got the answer sheets in advance, and even took advantage of a design flaw in their computers to reveal the answers. The FBI announced that it would take disciplinary action against those agents found guilty of misconduct.[13]

Even sports can be subject to ethical lapses. Former Atlanta Falcons quarterback Michael Vick spent 18 months in prison after authorities found out he had been operating a dogfighting ring. Vick was released by the Atlanta Falcons and signed on with the Philadelphia Eagles. Although Vick has seemingly turned over a new leaf, many sports fans were outraged that he was reaccepted into the NFL.[14] In Japan, another ethical dilemma in sports occurred when as many as 13 sumo wrestlers were suspected of fixing matches. Guilty verdicts could seriously jeopardize the sport, thus reiterating the importance of ethics in maintaining the integrity of an industry.[15]

Whether they are made in the realm of business, politics, science, or sports, most decisions are judged either right or wrong, ethical or unethical. Regardless of what an individual believes about a particular action, if society judges it to be unethical or wrong, whether correctly or not, that judgment directly affects the organization's ability to achieve its business goals. For this reason alone, it is important to understand business ethics and recognize ethical issues.

The Reasons for Studying Business Ethics

Studying business ethics is valuable for several reasons. Business ethics is not merely an extension of an individual's own personal ethics. Many people believe that if a company hires good people with strong ethical values, then it will be a "good citizen" organization. But as we show throughout this text, an individual's personal values and moral philosophies are only one factor in the ethical decision-making process. True, moral rules can be applied to a variety of situations in life, and some people do not distinguish everyday ethical issues from business ones. Our concern, however, is with the application of principles and standards in the business context. Many important ethical issues do not arise very often in the business context, although they remain complex moral dilemmas in one's own personal life. For example, although abortion and the possibility of human cloning are moral issues in many people's lives, they are not an issue in most business organizations.

Professionals in any field, including business, must deal with individuals' personal moral dilemmas because such dilemmas affect everyone's ability to function on the job. Normally, a business does not establish rules or policies on personal ethical issues such as sex or the use of alcohol outside the workplace; indeed, in some cases, such policies would be illegal. Only when a person's preferences or values influence his or her performance on the job do an individual's ethics play a major role in the evaluation of business decisions.

> "Having sound personal ethics may not be sufficient to enable you to handle the ethical issues that arise in a business organization."

Just being a good person and, in your own view, having sound personal ethics may not be sufficient to enable you to handle the ethical issues that arise in a business organization. It is important to recognize the relationship between legal and ethical decisions. Although abstract virtues linked to the moral high ground of truthfulness, honesty, fairness, and openness are often assumed to be self-evident and accepted by all employees, business-strategy decisions involve complex and detailed discussions. For example, there is considerable debate over what constitutes antitrust, deceptive advertising, and violations of the Foreign Corrupt Practices Act. A high level of personal moral development may not prevent an individual from violating the law in a complicated organizational context where even experienced lawyers debate the exact meaning of the law. Some approaches to business ethics assume that ethics training is for people whose personal moral development is unacceptable, but that is not the case. Because organizations are culturally diverse and personal values must be respected, ensuring collective agreement on organizational ethics (that is, codes reasonably capable of preventing misconduct) is as vital as any other effort that an organization's management may undertake.

Many people who have limited business experience suddenly find themselves making decisions about product quality, advertising, pricing, sales techniques, hiring practices, and pollution control. The values they learned from family, religion, and school may not provide specific guidelines for these complex business decisions. In other words, a person's experiences and decisions at home, in school, and in the community may be quite different from his or her experiences and decisions at work. Many business ethics decisions are close calls. In addition, managerial responsibility for the conduct of others requires knowledge of ethics and compliance processes and systems. Years of experience in a particular industry may be required to know what is acceptable. For example, when are highly disparaging advertising claims unethical? H&R Block claimed that it had found errors in two out of three tax returns prepared by Jackson Hewitt, thus implying that Jackson Hewitt customers had been shortchanged due to incompetence. Disputes over the accuracy of claims like this are complex and, in this case, Jackson Hewitt sued H&R Block over the advertising campaign.[16]

Studying business ethics will help you begin to identify ethical issues when they arise and recognize the approaches available for resolving them. You will also learn more about the ethical decision-making process and about ways to promote ethical behavior within your organization. By studying business ethics, you may also begin to understand how to cope with conflicts between your own personal values and those of the organization in which you work.

THE DEVELOPMENT OF BUSINESS ETHICS

The study of business ethics in North America has evolved through five distinct stages—(1) before 1960, (2) the 1960s, (3) the 1970s, (4) the 1980s, and (5) the 1990s—and continues to evolve in the twenty-first century (see Table 1.1).

Before 1960: Ethics in Business

Prior to 1960, the United States endured several agonizing phases of questioning the concept of capitalism. In the 1920s, the progressive movement attempted to provide citizens with a "living wage," defined as income sufficient for education, recreation, health, and retirement. Businesses were asked to check unwarranted price increases and any other practices that would hurt a family's living wage. In the 1930s came the New Deal, which specifically blamed business for the country's economic woes. Business was asked to work more closely with the government to raise family income. By the 1950s, the New Deal had evolved into

TABLE 1.1 Timeline of Ethical and Socially Responsible Concerns

1960s	1970s	1980s	1990s	2000s
Environmental issues	Employee militancy	Bribes and illegal contracting practices	Sweatshops and unsafe working conditions in third-world countries	Cybercrime
Civil rights issues	Human rights issues	Influence peddling	Rising corporate liability for personal damages (for example, cigarette companies)	Financial misconduct
Increased employee-employer tension	Covering up rather than correcting issues	Deceptive advertising	Financial mismanagement and fraud	Global issues, Chinese product safety
Changing work ethic	Disadvantaged consumers	Financial fraud (for example, savings and loan scandal)	Organizational ethical misconduct	Sustainability
Rising drug use	Transparency issues			Intellectual property theft

Source: Adapted from "Business Ethics Timeline," *Ethics Resource Center*, http://www.ethics.org/resources/business-ethics-timeline.asp (accessed May 27, 2009). Copyright © 2006, Ethics Resource Center (ERC). Used with permission of the ERC, 1747 Pennsylvania Ave. N.W., Suite 400, Washington, DC, 2006, www.ethics.org.

President Harry S Truman's Fair Deal, a program that defined such matters as civil rights and environmental responsibility as ethical issues that businesses had to address.

Until 1960, ethical issues related to business were often discussed within the domain of theology or philosophy. Individual moral issues related to business were addressed in churches, synagogues, and mosques. Religious leaders raised questions about fair wages, labor practices, and the morality of capitalism. For example, Catholic social ethics, which were expressed in a series of papal encyclicals, included concern for morality in business, workers' rights, and living wages; for humanistic values rather than materialistic ones; and for improving the conditions of the poor. Some Catholic colleges and universities began to offer courses in social ethics. Protestants and other religions also developed ethics courses in their seminaries and schools of theology and addressed the issue of morality and ethics in business. The Protestant work ethic encouraged individuals to be frugal, work hard, and attain success in the capitalistic system. Such religious traditions provided a foundation for the future field of business ethics. Each religion applied its moral concepts not only to business but also to government, politics, the family, personal life, and all other aspects of life.

The 1960s: The Rise of Social Issues in Business

During the 1960s American society witnessed the development of an anti-business trend, as many critics attacked the vested interests that controlled the economic and political aspects of society—the so-called military–industrial complex. The 1960s saw the decay of inner cities and the growth of ecological problems such as pollution and the disposal of toxic and nuclear wastes. This period also witnessed the rise of consumerism—activities undertaken by independent individuals, groups, and organizations to protect their rights as consumers. In 1962 President John F. Kennedy delivered a "Special Message on Protecting the Consumer Interest" in which he outlined four basic consumer rights: the right to safety, the right to be informed, the right to choose, and the right to be heard. These came to be known as the **Consumers' Bill of Rights.**

The modern consumer movement is generally considered to have begun in 1965 with the publication of Ralph Nader's *Unsafe at Any Speed,* which criticized the auto industry as a whole, and General Motors Corporation (GM) in particular, for putting profit and style ahead of lives and safety. GM's Corvair was the main target of Nader's criticism. His consumer protection organization, popularly known as Nader's Raiders, fought successfully for legislation that required automobile makers to equip cars with safety belts, padded dashboards, stronger door latches, head restraints, shatterproof windshields, and collapsible steering columns. Consumer activists also helped secure passage of consumer protection laws such as the Wholesome Meat Act of 1967, the Radiation Control for Health and Safety Act of 1968, the Clean Water Act of 1972, and the Toxic Substance Act of 1976.[17]

After Kennedy came President Lyndon B. Johnson and the "Great Society," a series of programs that extended national capitalism and told the business community that the U.S. government's responsibility was to provide all citizens with some degree of economic stability, equality, and social justice. Activities that could destabilize the economy or discriminate against any class of citizens began to be viewed as unethical and unlawful.

The 1970s: Business Ethics as an Emerging Field

Business ethics began to develop as a field of study in the 1970s. Theologians and philosophers had laid the groundwork by suggesting that certain moral principles could be applied to business activities. Using this foundation, business professors began to teach and write about corporate **social responsibility,** an organization's obligation to maximize its positive impact on stakeholders and minimize its negative impact. Philosophers increased their involvement, applying ethical theory and philosophical analysis to structure the discipline of business ethics. Companies became more concerned with their public images, and as social demands grew, many businesses realized that they had to address ethical issues more directly. The Nixon administration's Watergate scandal focused public interest on the importance of ethics in government. Conferences were held to discuss the social responsibilities and ethical issues of business. Centers dealing with issues of business ethics were established. Interdisciplinary meetings brought together business professors, theologians, philosophers, and businesspeople. President Jimmy Carter attempted to focus on personal and administrative efforts to uphold ethical principles in government. The Foreign Corrupt Practices Act was passed during his administration, making it illegal for U.S. businesses to bribe government officials of other countries.

By the end of the 1970s, a number of major ethical issues had emerged, including bribery, deceptive advertising, price collusion, product safety, and ecology. *Business ethics* became a common expression. Academic researchers sought to identify ethical issues and describe how businesspeople might choose to act in particular situations. However, only limited efforts were made to describe how the ethical decision-making process worked and to identify the many variables that influence this process in organizations.

The 1980s: Consolidation

In the 1980s, business academics and practitioners acknowledged business ethics as a field of study, and a growing and varied group of institutions with diverse interests promoted it. Business ethics organizations grew to include thousands of members. Five hundred courses in business ethics were offered at colleges across the country, with more than 40,000 students enrolled. Centers for business ethics provided publications, courses, conferences, and seminars. Business ethics was also a prominent concern within such leading companies as General Electric, Chase Manhattan, General Motors, Atlantic Richfield, Caterpillar, and S. C. Johnson & Son, Inc. Many of these firms established ethics and social policy committees to address ethical issues.

In the 1980s, the **Defense Industry Initiative on Business Ethics and Conduct** (DII) was developed to guide corporate support for ethical conduct. In 1986 18 defense contractors drafted principles for guiding business ethics and conduct.[18] The organization has since grown to nearly 50 members. This effort established a method for discussing best practices and working tactics to link organizational practice and policy to successful ethical compliance. The DII includes six principles. First, the DII supports codes of conduct and their widespread distribution. These codes of conduct must be understandable and cover their more substantive areas in detail. Second, member companies are expected to provide ethics training for their employees as well as continuous support between training periods. Third, defense contractors must create an open atmosphere in which employees feel comfortable reporting violations without fear of retribution. Fourth, companies need to perform extensive internal audits and develop effective internal reporting and voluntary disclosure plans. Fifth, the DII insists that member companies preserve the integrity of the defense industry. And sixth, member companies must adopt a philosophy of public accountability.[19]

The 1980s ushered in the Reagan–Bush era, with the accompanying belief that self-regulation, rather than regulation by government, was in the public's interest. Many tariffs and trade barriers were lifted, and businesses merged and divested within an increasingly global atmosphere. Thus, while business schools were offering courses in business ethics, the rules of business were changing at a phenomenal rate because of less regulation. Corporations that once were nationally based began operating internationally and found themselves mired in value structures where accepted rules of business behavior no longer applied.

The 1990s: Institutionalization of Business Ethics

The administration of President Bill Clinton continued to support self-regulation and free trade. However, it also took unprecedented government action to deal with health-related social issues such as teenage smoking. Its proposals included restricting cigarette advertising, banning cigarette vending machine sales, and ending the use of cigarette logos in connection with sports events.[20] Clinton also appointed Arthur Levitt as chairman of the Securities and Exchange Commission in 1993. Levitt unsuccessfully pushed for many reforms that could have prevented the accounting ethics scandals exemplified by Enron and WorldCom.[21]

The **Federal Sentencing Guidelines for Organizations** (FSGO), approved by Congress in November 1991, set the tone for organizational ethical compliance programs in the 1990s. The guidelines, which were based on the six principles of the DII,[22] broke new ground by codifying into law incentives to reward organizations for taking action to prevent misconduct, such as developing effective internal legal and ethical compliance programs.[23] Provisions in the guidelines mitigate penalties for businesses that are striving to root out misconduct and establish high ethical and legal standards.[24] On the other hand, under FSGO, if a company lacks an effective ethical compliance program and its employees violate the law, it can incur severe penalties. The guidelines focus on firms taking action to prevent and detect business misconduct in cooperation with government regulation. At the heart of the FSGO is the carrot-and-stick approach; that is, by taking preventive action against misconduct, a company may avoid onerous penalties should a violation occur. A mechanical approach using legalistic logic will not suffice to avert serious penalties. The company must develop corporate values, enforce its own code of ethics, and strive to prevent misconduct. We will provide more detail on the FSGO's role in business ethics programs in Chapter 4 and Chapter 8.

The Twenty-First Century: A New Focus on Business Ethics

Although business ethics appeared to become more institutionalized in the 1990s, new evidence emerged in the early 2000s that more than a few business executives and managers had not fully embraced the public's desire for high ethical standards. After George W. Bush became President in 2001, highly visible corporate misconduct at Enron, WorldCom, Halliburton, and the accounting firm Arthur Andersen caused the government and the public to look for new ways to encourage ethical behavior.[25] Accounting scandals, especially falsifying financial reports, became part of the culture of many companies. Firms outside the United States, such as Royal Ahold in the Netherlands and Parmalat in Italy, became major examples of global accounting fraud. Although the Bush administration tried to minimize government regulation, there appeared to be no alternative to developing more regulatory oversight of business.

Such abuses increased public and political demands to improve ethical standards in business. To address the loss of confidence in financial reporting and corporate ethics, in 2002 Congress passed the **Sarbanes–Oxley Act,** the most far-reaching change in organizational control and accounting regulations since the Securities and Exchange Act of 1934. The new law made securities fraud a criminal offense and stiffened penalties for corporate fraud. It also created an accounting oversight board that requires corporations to establish codes of ethics for financial reporting and to develop greater transparency in financial reports to investors and other interested parties. Additionally, the law requires top executives to sign off on their firms' financial reports, and they risk fines and long prison sentences if they misrepresent their companies' financial positions. The legislation further requires company executives to disclose stock sales immediately and prohibits companies from giving loans to top managers.[26]

The 2004 and 2008 amendments to the FSGO require that a business's governing authority be well informed about its ethics program with respect to content, implementation, and effectiveness. This places the responsibility squarely on the shoulders of the firm's leadership, usually the board of directors. The board is required to provide resources to oversee the discovery of risks and to design, implement, and modify approaches to deal with those risks.

The Sarbanes–Oxley Act and the FSGO have institutionalized the need to discover and address ethical and legal risk. Top management and the board of directors of a corporation are accountable for discovering risk associated with ethical conduct. Such specific industries as the public sector, energy and chemicals, health care, insurance, and retail have to discover the unique risks associated with their operations and develop ethics programs that will prevent ethical misconduct before it creates a crisis. Most firms are developing formal and informal mechanisms that effect interactive communication and transparency about issues associated with the risk of misconduct. Business leaders should consider that the greatest danger to their organizations lies in *not* discovering any serious misconduct or illegal activities that may be lurking.

> "Business leaders should consider that the greatest danger to their organizations lies in *not* discovering any serious misconduct or illegal activities that may be lurking."

Unfortunately, most managers do not view the risk of an ethical disaster as being as important as the risk associated with fires, natural disasters, or technology failure. In fact, ethical disasters can be significantly more damaging to a company's reputation than risks that are managed through insurance and other methods. The great investor Warren Buffett has stated that it is impossible to eradicate all wrongdoing in a large organization and that one can only hope that the misconduct is small and is caught in time. Buffett's fears were realized in 2008 when the financial system collapsed because of pervasive, systemic use of instruments such as credit default swaps, risky debt such as subprime lending, and corruption in major corporations.

In 2009 Barack Obama became president in the middle of a great recession caused by a meltdown in the global financial industry. Many firms, such as AIG, Lehman Brothers, Merrill Lynch, and Countrywide Financial, had engaged in ethical misconduct in developing and selling high-risk financial products. President Obama was able to lead the passage of legislation to provide a stimulus for recovery. His legislation to improve health care and to provide more protection for consumers focused on social concerns. Congress passed legislation regarding credit card accountability, improper payments related to federal agencies, fraud and waste, and food safety. The Dodd–Frank Wall Street Reform and Consumer Protection Act addressed some of the issues related to the financial crisis and recession. The Dodd–Frank Act was the most sweeping financial legislation since the Sarbanes–Oxley Act and possibly since laws put into effect during the Great Depression. It was designed to make almost every aspect of the financial services industry more ethical and responsible. This very complex law required regulators to create hundreds of rules to promote financial stability, improve accountability and transparency, and protect consumers from abusive financial practices.

The basic assumptions of capitalism are under debate as countries around the world work to stabilize markets and question those who manage the money of individual corporations and nonprofits. The financial crisis caused many people to question government institutions that provide oversight and regulation. As societies work to create change for the better, they must address issues related to law, ethics, and the required level of compliance necessary for government and business to serve the public interest. Not since the Great Depression and President Franklin Delano Roosevelt has the United States seen such widespread government intervention and regulation—something that most deem necessary, but which is nevertheless worrisome to free market capitalists.

DEVELOPING AN ORGANIZATIONAL AND GLOBAL ETHICAL CULTURE

Legally based compliance initiatives in organizations are usually designed to help establish cultural initiatives that make ethics a part of organizational values. Ethical culture is positively related to workplace confrontation over ethics issues, reports to management of observed misconduct, and the presence of ethics hotlines.[27] To develop more ethical corporate cultures, many businesses are communicating core values to their employees by creating ethics programs and appointing ethics officers to oversee them. The ethical component of a corporate culture relates to the values, beliefs, and established and enforced patterns of conduct that employees use to identify and respond to ethical issues. The term **ethical culture** can be viewed as the character of the decision-making process that employees use to determine whether their responses to ethical issues are right or wrong. Ethical culture is the component of corporate culture that captures the values and norms that an organization defines as appropriate conduct. The goal of an ethical culture is to minimize the need for enforced compliance of rules and maximize the use of principles that contribute to ethical reasoning in difficult or new situations. An ethical culture creates shared values and support for ethical decisions and is driven by top management.

Globally, businesses are working more closely together to establish standards of acceptable behavior. We are already seeing collaborative efforts by a range of organizations to establish goals and mandate minimum levels of ethical behavior, from the European Union, the North American Free Trade Agreement (NAFTA), the Southern Common Market (MERCOSUR), and the World Trade Organization (WTO) to, more recently, the Council on Economic Priorities' Social Accountability 8000 (SA 8000), the Ethical Trading Initiative, and the U.S. Apparel Industry Partnership. Some companies will not do business with organizations that do not support and abide by these standards. Many companies demonstrate their commitment toward acceptable conduct by adopting globally recognized principles emphasizing human rights and social responsibility. For instance, the Global Sullivan Principles (GSP) are based on the activism of Reverend Leon Sullivan. Sullivan's activism was a response to South African apartheid, during which he encouraged companies to withdraw their investments from South Africa. Sullivan's activism inspired him and other interested citizens to develop requirements for companies concerning employee rights and workplace conditions. These standards include non-segregation, equal and fair compensation, programs to move minorities into management ranks, and other human rights measures. Over one hundred companies have adopted the Sullivan Principles, and this landmark code has inspired a multitude of organizations to formulate their own codes of conduct.[28] The Global Sullivan Principles are discussed in greater detail in Chapter 10.

The Coalition for Environmentally Responsible Economies (CERES) is an international union of businesses, consumer groups, environmentalists, and other stakeholders. In 1989 this organization created ten principles of environmental conduct for businesses: (1) Protection of the Biosphere, (2) Sustainable Use of Natural Resources, (3) Reduction and Disposal of Waste, (4) Energy Conservation, (5) Risk Reduction, (6) Safe Products and Services, (7) Environmental Restoration, (8) Informing the Public, (9) Management Commitment, and (10) Audits and Reports. Companies choosing to adopt the CERES principles commit to providing regular reports of their environmental management and progress. Over 50 companies have adopted the CERES principles.[29]

In 2000 the United Nations launched the Global Compact, a set of 10 principles concerning human rights, labor, the environment, and anti-corruption. The purpose of the Global Compact is to create openness and alignment among business, government, society, labor, and the United Nations. Companies that adopt this code agree to integrate the ten principles into their business practices, publish their progress toward these objectives on an annual basis, and partner with others to advance broader objectives of the UN.[30] These 10 principles are covered in Chapter 10.

THE BENEFITS OF BUSINESS ETHICS

The field of business ethics continues to change rapidly as more firms recognize the benefits of improving ethical conduct and the link between business ethics and financial performance. Both research and examples from the business world demonstrate that building an ethical reputation among employees, customers, and the general public pays off. Figure 1.2 provides an overview of the relationship between business ethics and organizational performance. Although we believe that there are many practical benefits to being ethical, many businesspeople make decisions because they believe a particular course of action is simply the right thing to do as responsible members of society. Granite Construction has earned a place in *Ethisphere*'s "World's Most Ethical Companies" for two consecutive years as a result of its integration of ethics into the company culture. Granite formulated its ethics program to comply with the Federal Sentencing Guidelines for Organizations and helped to inspire the Construction Industry Ethics and

FIGURE 1.2 The Role of Organizational Ethics in Performance

©Cengage Learning 2013

> "The reputation of a company has a major effect on its relationships with employees, investors, customers, and many other parties."

Compliance Initiative. To ensure that all company employees are familiar with Granite's high ethical standards, the firm holds six mandatory training sessions annually, conducts ethics and compliance audits, and uses field compliance officers to make certain that ethical conduct is taking place throughout the entire organization.[31] Among the rewards for being more ethical and socially responsible in business are increased efficiency in daily operations, greater employee commitment, increased investor willingness to entrust funds, improved customer trust and satisfaction, and better financial performance. The reputation of a company has a major effect on its relationships with employees, investors, customers, and many other parties.

Ethics Contributes to Employee Commitment

Employee commitment comes from employees who believe their future is tied to that of the organization and from employee willingness to make personal sacrifices for the organization.[32] The more a company is dedicated to taking care of its employees, the more likely it is that the employees will take care of the organization. Issues that may foster the development of an ethical culture for employees include the absence of abusive behavior, a safe work environment, competitive salaries, and the fulfillment of all contractual obligations toward employees. An ethics and compliance program can support values and appropriate conduct. Social programs that may improve the ethical culture range from work–family programs to stock ownership plans to community service. Home Depot associates, for example, participate in disaster-relief efforts after hurricanes and tornadoes, rebuilding roofs, repairing water damage, planting trees, and clearing roads in their communities. Because employees spend a considerable number of their waking hours at work, a commitment by an organization to goodwill and respect for its employees usually increases the employees' loyalty to the organization and their support of its objectives. The software company SAS has topped *Fortune*'s "100 Best Places to Work for" list for two consecutive years thanks to the way it values its employees. During the 2008–2009 recession, founder Charles Goodnight refused to lay off workers and instead asked his employees to offer ideas on how to reduce costs. By actively engaging employees in cost-cutting measures, SAS was able to cut expenses by 6 to 7 percent. SAS is also unusual in that its annual turnover rate is four percent, versus the 20 percent industry average.[33]

Employees' perceptions that their firm has an ethical culture leads to performance-enhancing outcomes within the organization.[34] A corporate culture that integrates strong ethical values and positive business practices has been found to increase group creativity and job satisfaction and decrease turnover.[35] For the sake of both productivity and teamwork, it is essential that employees both within and among departments throughout an organization share a common vision of trust. The influence of higher levels of trust is greatest on relationships within departments or work groups, but trust is a significant factor in relationships among departments as well. Programs that create a work environment that is trustworthy make individuals more willing to rely and act on the decisions of their coworkers. In such a work environment, employees can reasonably expect to be treated with full respect and consideration by their coworkers and superiors. Trusting relationships between upper management and managers and their subordinates contribute to greater decision-making efficiencies. One survey found that when employees see values such as honesty, respect, and trust applied frequently in the workplace, they feel less pressure to compromise ethical standards, observe less misconduct, are more satisfied with their organizations overall, and feel more valued as employees.[36]

The ethical culture of a company seems to matter to employees. According to a report on employee loyalty and work practices, companies viewed as highly ethical by their employees were six times more likely to keep their workers.[37] Also, employees who view their company as having a strong community involvement feel more loyal to their employers and feel more positive about themselves.

Ethics Contributes to Investor Loyalty

Ethical conduct results in shareholder loyalty and can contribute to success that supports even broader social causes and concerns. Former Walmart CEO Lee Scott has stated, "As businesses, we have a responsibility to society. We also have an extraordinary opportunity. Let me be clear about this point, there is no conflict between delivering value to shareholders and helping solve bigger societal problems. In fact, they can build upon each other when developed, aligned, and executed right."[38]

Investors today are increasingly concerned about the ethics, social responsibility, and reputation of companies in which they invest, and various socially responsible mutual funds and asset management firms help investors purchase stock in ethical companies. Investors are also recognizing that an ethical culture provides a foundation for efficiency, productivity, and profits. Investors know, too, that negative publicity, lawsuits, and fines can lower stock prices, diminish customer loyalty, and threaten a company's long-term viability. Many companies accused of misconduct have experienced dramatic declines in the value of their stock when concerned investors divested. Warren Buffett and his company Berkshire Hathaway command significant respect from investors because of their track record of financial returns and the integrity of their organizations. Buffett says, "I want employees to ask themselves whether they are willing to have any contemplated act appear the next day on the front page of their local paper—to be read by their spouses, children and friends—with the reporting done by an informed and critical reporter." The high level of accountability and trust Buffett places in his employees translates into investor trust and confidence.[39] At the same time, even Buffett must remain constantly alert for ethical misconduct. This became clear when David Sokol, the leading contender to succeed Buffett, resigned after committing what many believed to be a conflict of interest. This ethical conflict highlights a potential need for more oversight at Berkshire Hathaway to ensure compliance with company standards.[40]

When TIAA-CREF investor participants were asked if they would choose a financial services company with strong ethics or higher returns, surprisingly, 92 percent of respondents said they would choose ethics while only 5 percent chose higher returns.[41] Investors look at the bottom line for profits or the potential for increased stock prices or dividends. But they also look for any potential flaws in the company's performance, conduct, and financial reports. Therefore, gaining investors' trust and confidence is vital to sustaining the financial stability of the firm.

Ethics Contributes to Customer Satisfaction

It is generally accepted that customer satisfaction is one of the most important factors in a successful business strategy. Although a company must continue to develop and adapt products to keep pace with customers' changing desires and preferences, it must also seek to develop long-term relationships with its customers and stakeholders. Patagonia, Inc., has engaged in a broad array of ecological, socially responsible, and ethical behaviors over many years to better connect with its target markets. The company has donated approximately $40 million to environmentally oriented causes. Employees can volunteer for environmental

DEBATE ISSUE   TAKE A STAND

Does Being Ethical Result in Better Performance?

While research suggests that more ethical businesses have better performance, there is also an alternate view. Many businesspeople think that ethics and social responsibility require resources that do not contribute to profits and that time spent in ethics training could be better used for other business activities. One viewpoint is that when companies push the edge, pay minor fines for misconduct, or are not caught in wrongdoing, they may end up being more profitable than companies with a strong ethical culture. Many financial companies became extremely profitable when taking high-risk opportunities with limited transparency about the nature of the complex products they were selling. To gain competitive advantage, a firm needs to be able to reach markets and make sales. If a firm is too ethical, it might lose competitive advantages. On the other hand, *Ethisphere*'s World's Most Ethical Companies index indicates that since 2005, more ethical companies have had the best financial performance.

1. Ethical businesses are the most profitable.
2. The most ethical businesses are not always the most profitable.

groups and earn up to one month's pay. The entire clothing line was sourced using organic cotton beginning in 1996. In addition, the company is currently creating the Patagonia National Park to protect wildland ecosystems and biodiversity in Chile and Argentina. All new facilities are being built with LEED certification, demonstrating a commitment to green building and the environment.[42]

For most businesses, both repeat purchases and an enduring relationship of mutual respect and cooperation with customers are essential for success. By focusing on customer satisfaction, a company continually deepens the customer's dependence on the company, and as the customer's confidence grows, the firm gains a better understanding of how to serve the customer so that the relationship may endure. Successful businesses provide an opportunity for customer feedback, which can engage the customer in cooperative problem solving. As is often pointed out, a happy customer will come back, but a disgruntled customer will tell others about his or her dissatisfaction with a company and discourage friends from dealing with it.

Trust is essential to a good long-term relationship between a business and consumers. The Millennium Poll of 25,000 citizens in 23 countries found that almost 60 percent of people focus on social responsibility ahead of brand reputation or financial factors when forming impressions of companies.[43] As social responsibility becomes more important for companies, corporate social responsibility may be viewed as a sign of good management and may, according to one study, indicate good financial performance. However, another study indicates that the reverse may be true, and companies who have good financial performance are able to spend more money on social responsibility.[44] Google would be an example of such a company. Google shows extreme care for its employees at its Googleplex headquarters in Mountain View, California. Investment in employee satisfaction and retention involves providing bicycles for efficient travel between meetings, lava lamps, massage chairs, shared work cubicles to allow for intellectual stimulation and idea generation, laptops for every employee, pool tables, volleyball courts, outdoor seating for brainstorming, snack rooms packed with various snacks and drinks, and more.[45]

When an organization has a strong ethical environment, it usually focuses on the core value of placing customers' interests first. Putting customers first does not mean that the interests of employees, investors, and local communities should be ignored, however. An ethical culture that focuses on customers incorporates the interests of all employees, suppliers, and other interested parties in decisions and actions. Employees working in an ethical environment support and contribute to the process of understanding customers' demands and concerns. Ethical conduct toward customers builds a strong competitive position that has been shown to positively affect business performance and product innovation.

Ethics Contributes to Profits

A company cannot nurture and develop an ethical culture unless it has achieved adequate financial performance in terms of profits. Businesses with greater resources—regardless of their staff size—have the means to practice social responsibility while serving their customers, valuing their employees, and establishing trust with the public. Ethical conduct toward customers builds a strong competitive position that has been shown to positively affect business performance and product innovation.[46] When Intel discovered a design flaw in one of its chips, it recognized the need to put stakeholders ahead of profits. Even though it cost the company $1 billion in repairs and delays, the company halted shipments so it could fix the problem. By acting responsibly to ensure that it offered a quality product, Intel may be more profitable in the long run than if it had simply ignored the problem and gotten caught after the product introduction.[47] Every day, business newspapers and magazines offer new examples of the consequences of business misconduct. It is worth noting, however, that most of these companies have learned from their mistakes and recovered after they implemented programs to improve ethical and legal conduct.

Ample evidence shows that being ethical pays off with better performance. As indicated earlier, companies that are perceived by their employees as having a high degree of honesty and integrity have a much higher average total return to shareholders than do companies perceived as having a low degree of honesty and integrity.[48] Figure 1.3 compares publicly

FIGURE 1.3 *Ethisphere*'s 2010 World's Most Ethical Companies versus S&P 500 and FTSE 100

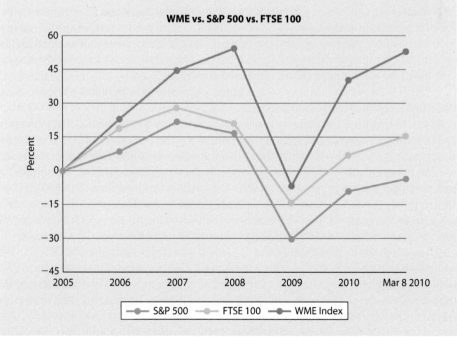

Source: "*Ethisphere*'s 2010 World's Most Ethical Companies," *Ethisphere*, Quarter 01, p. 28.

traded companies in *Ethisphere*'s 2010 World's Most Ethical Companies index with companies from the S&P 500 and the FTSE 100 indexes. The World's Most Ethical Companies index was developed through methodology designed by a committee of leading attorneys, professors, and organization leaders. As Figure 1.3 indicates, between 2005 and 2010, the companies in this index outperformed the other indexes of publicly traded companies. These results provide strong evidence that corporate concern for ethical conduct is becoming a part of strategic planning toward obtaining the outcome of higher profitability. Rather than being just a function of compliance, ethics is becoming an integral part of management's efforts to achieve competitive advantage.

OUR FRAMEWORK FOR STUDYING BUSINESS ETHICS

We have developed a framework for this text to help you understand how people make ethical decisions and deal with ethical issues. Table 1.2 summarizes each element in the framework and describes where each topic is discussed in this book.

In Part One, we provide an overview of business ethics. This chapter has defined the term *business ethics* and explored the development and importance of this critical business area. In Chapter 2, we explore the role of various stakeholder groups in social responsibility and corporate governance.

Part Two focuses on ethical issues and the institutionalization of business ethics. In Chapter 3, we examine business issues that lead to ethical decision making in organizations. In Chapter 4, we look at the institutionalization of business ethics, including both mandatory and voluntary societal concerns.

In Part Three, we delineate the ethical decision-making process and then look at both individual factors and organizational factors that influence decisions. Chapter 5 describes the ethical decision-making process from an organizational perspective. Chapter 6 explores individual factors that may influence ethical decisions in business, including moral philosophies and cognitive moral development. Chapter 7 focuses on organizational dimensions including corporate culture, relationships, and conflicts.

In Part Four, we explore systems and processes associated with implementing business ethics into global strategic planning. Chapter 8 discusses the development of an effective ethics program. In Chapter 9, we examine issues related to implementing and auditing ethics programs. Finally, Chapter 10 considers ethical issues in a global context. In addition, we provide an appendix that describes the ethical and social responsibility considerations of sustainability.

We hope that this framework will help you to develop a balanced understanding of the various perspectives and alternatives available to you when making ethical business decisions. Regardless of your own personal values, the more you know about how individuals make decisions, the better prepared you will be to cope with difficult ethical decisions. Such knowledge will help you improve and control the ethical decision-making environment in which you work.

It is your job to make the final decision in an ethical situation that affects you. Sometimes that decision may be right; sometimes it may be wrong. It is always easy to look back with hindsight and know what one should have done in a particular situation. At the time, however, the choices might not have seemed so clear. To give you practice making ethical decisions, Part Five of this book contains a number of cases. In addition, each chapter begins with a vignette, "An Ethical Dilemma," and ends with a minicase, "Resolving Ethical Business Challenges," that involves ethical problems. We hope these will give you a better sense of the challenges of making ethical decisions in the real business world.

TABLE 1.2 Our Framework for Studying Business Ethics

Chapter	Highlights
1. The Importance of Business Ethics	• Definitions
	• Reasons for studying business ethics
	• History
	• Benefits of business ethics
2. Stakeholder Relationships, Social Responsibility, and Corporate Governance	• Stakeholder relationships
	• Stakeholder influences in social responsibility
	• Corporate governance
3. Emerging Business Ethics Issues	• Recognizing an ethical issue
	• Honesty, fairness, and integrity
	• Ethical issues and dilemmas in business: abusive and disruptive behavior, lying, conflicts of interest, bribery, corporate intelligence, discrimination, sexual harassment, environmental issues, fraud, insider trading, intellectual property rights, and privacy
	• Determining an ethical issue in business
4. The Institutionalization of Business Ethics	• Mandatory requirements
	• Voluntary requirements
	• Core practices
	• Federal Sentencing Guidelines for Organizations
	• Sarbanes–Oxley Act
5. Ethical Decision Making and Ethical Leadership	• Ethical issue intensity
	• Individual factors in decision making
	• Organizational factors in decision making
	• Opportunity in decision making
	• Business ethics evaluations and intentions
	• The role of leadership in a corporate culture
	• How leadership styles influence ethical decisions
	• Habits of strong ethical leaders
6. Individual Factors: Moral Philosophies and Values	• Moral philosophies, including teleological development philosophies and cognitive moral deontological, relativist, virtue ethics, and justice philosophies
	• Stages of cognitive moral development

(continued)

TABLE 1.2 Our Framework for Studying Business Ethics *(continued)*

Chapter	Highlights
7. Organizational Factors: The Role of Ethical Culture and Relationships	• Corporate culture
	• Interpersonal relationships
	• Whistle-blowing
	• Opportunity and conflict
8. Developing an Effective Ethics Program	• Ethics programs
	• Codes of ethics
	• Program responsibility
	• Communication of ethical standards
	• Systems to monitor and enforce ethical standards
	• Continuous improvement of ethics programs
9. Implementing and Auditing Ethics Programs	• Implementation programs
	• Ethics audits
10. Business Ethics in a Global Economy	• Global Culture and Cultural Relations
	• Economic Foundations of Business Ethics
	• Multinational Corporations
	• Global Cooperation
	• Global Ethics Issues

SUMMARY

This chapter has provided an overview of the field of business ethics and introduced the framework for the discussion of business ethics. Business ethics comprises principles and standards that guide behavior in the world of business. Investors, employees, customers, interest groups, the legal system, and the community often determine whether a specific action is right or wrong, ethical or unethical.

Studying business ethics is important for many reasons. Recent incidents of unethical activity in business underscore the widespread need for a better understanding of the factors that contribute to ethical and unethical decisions. Individuals' personal moral philosophies and decision-making experience may not be sufficient to guide them in the business world. Studying business ethics will help you begin to identify ethical issues and recognize the approaches available to resolve them.

The study of business ethics has evolved through five distinct stages. Before 1960, business ethics issues were discussed primarily from a religious perspective. The 1960s saw the emergence of many social issues involving business and the concept of social conscience as well as a rise in consumerism, which culminated with Kennedy's Consumers' Bill of Rights. Business ethics began to develop as an independent field of study in the 1970s, with academics and practitioners exploring ethical issues and attempting to understand how individuals and organizations make ethical decisions. These experts began to teach and write about the idea of corporate social responsibility, an organization's obligation to maximize its positive impact on stakeholders and to minimize its negative impact. In the 1980s, centers of business ethics provided publications, courses, conferences, and seminars, and many companies established ethics committees and social policy committees. The Defense Industry Initiative on Business Ethics and Conduct was developed to guide corporate support for ethical conduct; its principles had a major impact on corporate ethics.

However, less government regulation and an increase in businesses with international operations raised new ethical issues. In the 1990s, government continued to support self-regulation. The FSGO sets the tone for organizational ethics programs by providing incentives for companies to take action to prevent organizational misconduct. The twenty-first century ushered in a new set of ethics scandals, suggesting that many companies had not fully embraced the public's desire for higher ethical standards. The Sarbanes–Oxley Act therefore stiffened penalties for corporate fraud and established an accounting oversight board. The current trend is away from legally based ethical initiatives in organizations and toward cultural initiatives that make ethics a part of core organizational values. The ethical component of a corporate culture relates to the values, beliefs, and established and enforced patterns of conduct that employees use to identify and respond to ethical issues. The term *ethical culture* describes the component of corporate culture that captures the rules and principles that an organization defines as appropriate conduct. It can be viewed as the character of the decision-making process that employees use to determine whether their responses to ethical issues are right or wrong.

Research and anecdotes demonstrate that building an ethical reputation among employees, customers, and the general public provides benefits that include increased efficiency in daily operations, greater employee commitment, increased investor willingness to entrust funds, improved customer trust and satisfaction, and better financial performance. The reputation of a company has a major effect on its relationships with employees, investors, customers, and many other parties, and thus has the potential to affect its bottom line.

Finally, this text introduces a framework for studying business ethics. Each chapter addresses some aspect of business ethics and decision making within a business context. The major concerns are ethical issues in business, stakeholder relationships, social responsibility and corporate governance, emerging business ethics issues, the institutionalization of business ethics, understanding the ethical decision-making process, moral philosophies and cognitive moral development, corporate culture, organizational relationships and conflicts, developing an effective ethics program, implementing and auditing the ethics program, and global business ethics.

IMPORTANT TERMS FOR REVIEW

business ethics	principles	values
Consumers' Bill of Rights	social responsibility	Defense Industry Initiative on Business Ethics and Conduct
Federal Sentencing Guidelines for Organizations	Sarbanes–Oxley Act	ethical culture

RESOLVING ETHICAL BUSINESS CHALLENGES*

Frank Garcia was just starting out as a salesperson with Acme Corporation, a medical supplies company. Acme's corporate culture was top-down, or hierarchical. Because of the competitive nature of the medical supplies industry, few mistakes were tolerated. Otis Hillman was a buyer for Thermocare, a national hospital chain. Frank's first meeting with Otis was a success, resulting in a $500,000 contract. This sale represented a significant increase for Acme and led to an additional $1,000 bonus for Frank.

Some months later, Frank called on Thermocare, seeking to increase the contract by $500,000. "Otis, I think you'll need the additional inventory. It looks as if you didn't have enough at the end of last quarter," said Frank.

"You may be right. Business has picked up. Maybe it's because of your product, but then again, maybe not. It's still not clear to me whether Acme is the best for us. Speaking of which, I heard that you have season tickets to the Cubs!" replied Otis.

Frank thought for a moment and said, "Otis, I know that part of your increases is due to our quality products. How about we discuss this over a ball game?"

"Well, OK," Otis agreed.

By the seventh-inning stretch, Frank convinced Otis that the additional inventory was needed and offered to give Thermocare a pair of season tickets. When Frank's boss, Amber, heard of the sale, she was very pleased. "Frank, this is great. We've been trying to get Thermocare's business for a long time. You seem to have connected with their buyer." As a result of the Thermocare account, Frank received another large bonus check and a letter of achievement from the vice president of marketing.

Two quarters later, Frank had become one of the top producers in the division. At the beginning of the quarter, Frank ran the numbers on Thermocare's account and found that business was booming. The numbers showed that Otis's business could probably handle an additional $750,000

worth of goods without hurting return on assets. As Frank went over the figures with Otis, Otis's response was, "You know, Frank, I've really enjoyed the season tickets, but this is a big increase." As the conversation meandered, Frank soon found out that Otis and his wife had never been to Cancun, Mexico. Frank had never been in a situation like this before, so he excused himself to another room and called Amber about what he was thinking of doing.

"Are you kidding?" responded Amber. "Why are you even calling me on this? I'll find the money somewhere to pay for it."

"Is this OK with Acme?" asked Frank.

"You let me worry about that," Amber told him.

When Frank suggested that Otis and his wife be his guests in Cancun, the conversation seemed to go smoothly. In Cancun, Otis decided to purchase the additional goods, for which Frank received another bonus increase and another positive letter from headquarters.

Some time later, Amber announced to her division that they would be taking all of their best clients to Las Vegas for a thank-you party. One of those invited was Thermocare. When they arrived, Amber gave each person $500 and said, "I want you to know that Acme is very grateful for the business that you have provided us. As a result of your understanding the qualitative differences of our products, we have doubled our production facilities. This trip and everything that goes with it for the next few days is our small way of saying thank you. Every one of you has your salesperson here. If there is anything that you need, please let him or her know, and we'll try to accommodate you. Have a good time!"

That night Otis saw Frank at dinner and suggested to him that he was interested in attending an "adult entertainment" club. When Frank queried Amber about this, she said, "Is he asking you to go with him?"

"No, Amber, not me!"

"Well, then, if he's not asking you to go, I don't understand why you're talking to me. Didn't I say we'd take care of their needs?"

"But what will Acme say if this gets out?" asked Frank.

"Don't worry. It won't," said Amber.

QUESTIONS | EXERCISES

1. What are the potential ethical issues faced by Acme Corporation?

2. What should Acme do if there is a desire to make ethics a part of its core organizational values?

3. Identify the ethical issues of which Frank needs to be aware.

4. Discuss the advantages and disadvantages of each decision that Frank could make.

*This case is strictly hypothetical; any resemblance to real persons, companies, or situations is coincidental.

CHECK YOUR EQ

Check your EQ, or Ethics Quotient, by completing the following. Assess your performance to evaluate your overall understanding of the chapter material.

1. Business ethics focuses mostly on personal ethical issues.	Yes	No
2. Business ethics deals with right or wrong behavior within a particular organization.	Yes	No
3. An ethical culture is based upon the norms and values of the company.	Yes	No
4. Business ethics contributes to investor loyalty.	Yes	No
5. The trend is away from cultural or ethically based initiatives to legal initiatives in organizations.	Yes	No
6. Investments in business ethics do not support the bottom line.	Yes	No

ANSWERS 1. No. Business ethics focuses on organizational concerns (legal and ethical—employees, customers, suppliers, society). 2. Yes. That stems from the basic definition. 3. Yes. Norms and values help create an organizational culture and are key in supporting or not supporting ethical conduct. 4. Yes. Many studies have shown that trust and ethical conduct contribute to investor loyalty. 5. No. Many businesses are communicating their core values to their employees by creating ethics programs and appointing ethics officers to oversee them. 6. No. Ethics initiatives create consumer, employee, and shareholder loyalty and positive behavior that contribute to the bottom line.

CHAPTER 2

STAKEHOLDER RELATIONSHIPS, SOCIAL RESPONSIBILITY, AND CORPORATE GOVERNANCE

©LA Nature Graphics, Shutterstock

CHAPTER OBJECTIVES

- To identify stakeholders' roles in business ethics
- To define social responsibility
- To examine the relationship between stakeholder orientation and social responsibility
- To delineate a stakeholder orientation in creating corporate social responsibility
- To explore the role of corporate governance in structuring ethics and social responsibility in business
- To list the steps involved in implementing a stakeholder perspective in social responsibility and business ethics

CHAPTER OUTLINE

AN ETHICAL DILEMMA*

Carla knew something was wrong when Jack got back to his desk. He had been with Aker & Aker Accounting (A&A) for 17 years, starting right after graduation and progressing through the ranks. Jack was a strong supporter of the company, and that was why Carla had been assigned to him. Carla had been with A&A for two years. She had graduated in the top 10 percent of her class and passed the CPA exam on the first try. She had chosen A&A over one of the "Big Four" firms because A&A was the biggest and best

firm in Smallville, Ohio, where her husband, Frank, managed a locally owned machine tools company. She and Frank had just purchased a new home when things started to turn strange with her boss.

"What's the matter, Jack?" Carla asked.

"Well, you'll hear about it sooner or later. I've been denied a partner's position. Can you imagine that? I have been working 60- and 70-hour weeks for the last 10 years, and all that management can say to me is 'not at this time,'" complained Jack.

Carla asked, "So what else did they say?"

Jack turned red and blurted out, "They said maybe in a few more years. I've done all that they've asked me to do. I've sacrificed a lot, and now they say a few more years. It's not fair."

"What are you going to do?" Carla asked.

"I don't know," Jack said. "I just don't know."

Six months later, Carla noticed that Jack was behaving oddly. He came in late and left early. One Sunday Carla went into the office for some files and found Jack copying some of the software that A&A used in auditing and consulting. A couple of weeks later at a dinner party, Carla overheard a conversation about Jack doing consulting work for some small firms. On Monday morning she asked him if what she had heard was true.

Jack responded, "Yes, Carla, it's true. I do have a few clients that I work for on occasion."

"Don't you think there's a conflict of interest between you and A&A?" asked Carla.

"No," said Jack. "You see, these clients are not technically within the market area of A&A. Besides, I was counting on that promotion to help pay some extra bills. My oldest son decided to go to a private university, which is an extra $25,000 each year. Plus our medical plan at A&A doesn't cover some of my medical problems—and you don't want to know the cost of those. The only way I can afford to pay for these things is to do some extra work on the side."

"But what if A&A finds out?" Carla asked. "Won't they terminate you?"

"I don't want to think about that. Besides, if they don't find out for another six months, I may be able to start my own company."

"How?" asked Carla.

"Don't be naive, Carla. You came in that Sunday. You know."

Carla realized that Jack had been using A&A software for his own gain. "That's stealing!" she said.

"Stealing?" Jack's voice grew calm. "Like when you use the office phones for personal long-distance calls? Like when you decided to volunteer to help out your church and copied all those things for them on the company machine? If I'm stealing, you're a thief as well. But let's not get into this discussion. I'm not hurting A&A and, who knows, maybe within the next year I'll become a partner and can quit my night job."

Carla backed off from the discussion and said nothing more. She couldn't afford to antagonize her boss and risk bad performance ratings. She and Frank had bills, too. She also knew that she wouldn't be able to get another job at the same pay if she quit. Moving to another town was not an option because of Frank's business. She had no physical evidence to take to the partners, which meant that it would be her word against Jack's, and he had 17 years of experience with the company.

QUESTIONS | EXERCISES

1. Identify the ethical issues in this case.
2. Imagine that you are Carla. Discuss your options and what the consequences of each option might be.
3. Imagine that you are Jack. Discuss your options and what the consequences of each option might be.
4. Discuss any additional information you feel you might need before making your decision.

*This case is strictly hypothetical; any resemblance to real persons, companies, or situations is coincidental.

Business ethics issues, conflicts, and successes revolve around relationships. Building effective relationships is considered one of the most important areas of business today. A business exists because of relationships between employees, customers, shareholders or investors, suppliers, and managers who develop strategies to attain success. In addition, an organization usually has a governing authority, often called a board of directors, that provides oversight and direction to make sure that the organization stays focused on its objectives in an ethical, legal, and socially acceptable manner. When unethical acts are discovered in organizations, in most instances knowing cooperation or complicity has facilitated the acceptance and perpetuation of the unethical conduct.[1] Therefore, relationships are associated not only with organizational success but also with organizational misconduct.

A stakeholder framework helps identify the internal stakeholders, such as employees, boards of directors, and managers, and the external stakeholders, such as customers, special interest groups, regulators, and others who agree, collaborate, and engage in confrontations on ethical issues. Most ethical issues exist because of conflicts in values and belief patterns about right and wrong among and within stakeholder groups. This framework allows an organization to identify, monitor, and respond to the needs, values, and expectations of different stakeholder groups.

The formal system of accountability for and control of ethical and socially responsible behavior is corporate governance. In theory, the board of directors provides oversight for all decisions and use of resources. Ethical issues relate to the role of the board of directors, relationships with shareholders, internal control, risk management, and executive compensation. Ethical leadership is associated with appropriate corporate governance.

In this chapter, we first focus on the concept of stakeholders and examine how a stakeholder framework can help us understand organizational ethics. Then we identify stakeholders and the importance of a stakeholder orientation. Using the stakeholder framework, we explore the concept of social responsibility, including the various dimensions of social responsibility. Next, we examine corporate governance as a dimension of social responsibility and ethical decision making to provide an understanding of the importance of oversight in responding to stakeholders. Finally, we provide the steps for implementing a stakeholder perspective on social responsibility and ethical decisions in business.

STAKEHOLDERS DEFINE ETHICAL ISSUES IN BUSINESS

In a business context, customers, investors and shareholders, employees, suppliers, government agencies, communities, and many others who have a "stake" or claim in some aspect of a company's products, operations, markets, industry, and outcomes are known as **stakeholders.** These groups are influenced by business, but they also have the ability to influence businesses; thus, the relationship between companies and their stakeholders is a two-way street.[2] Sometimes activities and negative press generated by special interest groups can force a company to change its practices. For example, consumer groups have been lobbying to improve the nutritional value of food products targeted at children. Cereal manufacturers such as Post Foods and General Mills have responded by cutting the sugar levels in their cereals that focus on the youth market (Fruity Pebbles, Cocoa Pebbles, Lucky Charms, Trix, and others) to 9 grams or less per serving. At the same time, the U.S. Department of Agriculture has recommended a limit of 48 grams of sugar for children with a 2,200 calorie-a-day intake.[3]

Many firms experienced conflicts with key stakeholders and consequently damaged their reputations and shareholder confidence during the global financial crisis. While many threats to reputations stem from uncontrollable events and the business environment, ethical misconduct is more difficult to overcome than poor financial performance. Stakeholders who are most directly affected by negative events will have a corresponding shift in their perceptions of a firm's reputation. On the other hand, firms sometimes receive negative publicity for misconduct that can destroy trust and tarnish their reputations, making it more difficult to retain existing customers and attract new ones.[4] To maintain the trust and confidence of its stakeholders, CEOs and other top managers are expected to tell the truth and act in a responsible manner. Providing untruthful or deceptive information to stakeholders is, if not illegal, certainly unethical, and can result in a loss of trust. Mark Hurd, former CEO of Hewlett-Packard, lost the confidence of his board of directors and departed from the company. Hurd was under an internal investigation as a result of an alleged relationship with a former contractor. Although Hurd was found not to have violated the company's sexual harassment policy, investigators did find that he had committed other violations, including irregularities in expense reimbursements.[5]

The financial crisis was based on a failure to consider the ramifications of unethical decision making affecting all stakeholders, including society and the economic system. The foundation of the crisis was subprime loans, which involved lending money to people who could not possibly repay their loans. Many companies engaged in providing fictitious financial information. Loan companies were making low-documentation or no-documentation loans. Individuals' data were manipulated to allow loans to qualify. For example, incomes could be increased to three to four times their actual level, and appraisal values of homes were incorrectly represented to allow loan packages to attain approval.

Ethical misconduct and decisions that damage stakeholders will generally impact the company's reputation in terms of both investor confidence and consumer confidence. As investor perceptions and decisions begin to take their toll, shareholder value will drop, exposing the company to consumer scrutiny that can increase the damage. According to a recent Edelman trust survey, the bottom three industries in terms of trust were insurance, banks, and financial services, whereas technology, automotive, and telecommunications were among the most trusted industries.[6] Reputation is a factor in consumers' perceptions of product attributes and corporate image, and it can lead to consumer willingness to purchase goods and services at profitable prices. For example, Toyota suffered significant damage to its reputation as a result of problems with sudden acceleration until a 10-month-long study by the National Highway Traffic Safety Administration found that driver error was mostly to blame, not faulty electronics. During the quarter prior to the NHTSA report, Toyota's profits dropped 39 percent.[7] Some scandals, or perceived wrongdoing, may lead to boycotts and aggressive campaigns to dampen sales and earnings. When Dallas city officials passed an initiative that sent natural gas-powered taxis to the front of the line at Dallas Love Field, traditional energy taxi drivers claimed "foul play". The taxi drivers saw this as an attempt to support Texas's natural gas industry, not general support for alternative fuel. For Super Bowl XLV, traditional taxi drivers planned a boycott that would make it difficult for tourists to move around the city to make public their concerns about the favoritism shown toward natural gas taxis.[8]

New reforms intended to improve corporate accountability and transparency suggest that stakeholders including regulatory agencies, local communities, attorneys, and public accounting firms can play a major role in fostering responsible decision making.[9] Stakeholders apply their values and standards to many diverse issues, including working conditions, consumer rights, environmental conservation, product safety, and proper information disclosure, that may or may not directly affect an individual stakeholders own welfare. We can assess the level of social responsibility that an organization bears by scrutinizing its effects on the issues of concern to its stakeholders.[10]

Stakeholders provide resources that are more or less critical to a firm's long-term success. These resources may be both tangible and intangible. Shareholders, for example, supply capital; suppliers offer material resources or intangible knowledge; employees and managers grant expertise, leadership, and commitment; customers generate revenue and provide loyalty and positive word-of-mouth promotion; local communities provide infrastructure; and the media transmits positive corporate images. When individual stakeholders share similar expectations about desirable business conduct, they may choose to establish or join formal communities that are dedicated to better defining and advocating these values and expectations. Stakeholders' abilities to withdraw these needed resources gives them power over businesses.[11]

> "Stakeholders provide resources that are more or less critical to a firm's long-term success."

Identifying Stakeholders

We can identify two different types of stakeholders. **Primary stakeholders** are those whose continued association is absolutely necessary for a firm's survival. These include employees, customers, investors, and shareholders, as well as the governments and communities that provide necessary infrastructure. Some firms take actions that can damage relationships with primary stakeholders. Figure 2.1 indicates that, after experiencing some declines in 2007, strong ethical corporate cultures are back on the rise. Ethical corporate cultures are important because they are linked to positive relationships with stakeholders. By the same token, concern for stakeholders' needs and expectations is necessary to avoid ethical conflicts.

Secondary stakeholders do not typically engage in transactions with a company and therefore are not essential to its survival. They include the media, trade associations, and special interest groups like the American Association of Retired People (AARP), a special interest group that works to support retirees' rights such as health care benefits. Both primary and secondary stakeholders embrace specific values and standards that dictate what constitutes acceptable and unacceptable corporate behaviors. It is important for managers to recognize that while primary groups may present more day-to-day concerns, secondary groups cannot be ignored or given less consideration in the ethical decision-making process.[12] Table 2.1 shows a select list of issues important to various stakeholder groups and identifies how corporations impact these issues.

Figure 2.2 offers a conceptualization of the relationship between businesses and stakeholders. In this **stakeholder interaction model,** there are reciprocal relationships between the

FIGURE 2.1 After Declining, Strength of Ethical Culture Is On the Rise Again

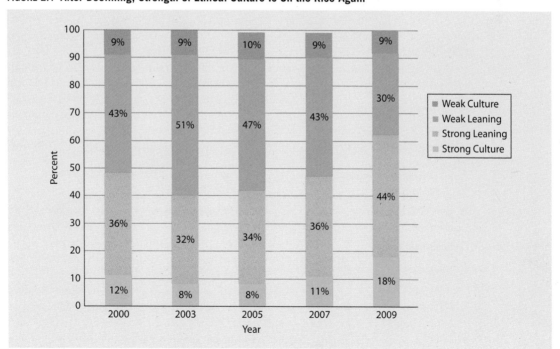

Note: Due to rounding, some numbers do not equal 100 percent.

Source: "2009 National Business Ethics Survey: Ethics in the Recession," (Arlington, VA: Ethics Resource Center, 2009): p. 14.

TABLE 2.1 Examples of Stakeholder Issues and Associated Measures of Corporate Impacts

Stakeholder Groups and Issues	Potential Indicators of Corporate Impact on These Issues
Employees	
1. Compensation and benefits	• Ratio of lowest wage to national legal minimum or to local cost of living
2. Training and development	• Changes in average years of training of employees
3. Employee diversity	• Percentages of employees from different genders and races
4. Occupational health and safety	• Standard injury rates and absentee rates
5. Communications with management	• Availability of open-door policies or ombudsmen
Customers	
1. Product safety and quality	• Number of product recalls over time
2. Management of customer complaints	• Number of customer complaints and availability of procedures to answer them
3. Services to disabled customers·	• Availability and nature of measures taken to ensure services to disabled customers
Investors	
1. Transparency of shareholder communications	• Availability of procedures to inform shareholders about corporate activities
2. Shareholder rights	• Frequency and type of litigation involving violations of shareholder rights
Suppliers	
1. Encouraging suppliers in developing countries	• Prices offered to suppliers in developed countries in comparison to countries' other suppliers
2. Encouraging minority suppliers	• Percentage of minority suppliers
Community	
1. Public health and safety protection	• Availability of emergency response plan
2. Conservation of energy and materials	• Data on reduction of waste produced and comparison to industry
3. Donations and support of local organizations	• Annual employee time spent in community service
Environmental Groups	
1. Minimizing the use of energy	• Amount of electricity purchased; percentage of "green" electricity
2. Minimizing emissions and waste	• Type, amount, and designation of waste generated
3. Minimizing adverse environmental effects of goods and services	• Percentage of product weight reclaimed after use

FIGURE 2.2 Interactions between a Company and Its Primary and Secondary Stakeholders

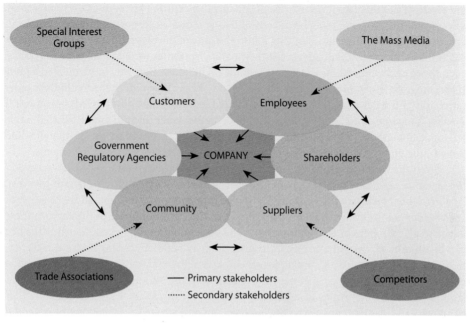

Source: Adapted from Isabelle Maignan, O. C. Ferrell, and Linda Ferrell, "A Stakeholder Model for Implementing Social Responsibility in Marketing." *European Journal of Marketing* 39 (2005): 956–977. Used with permission.

firm and a host of stakeholders. In addition to the fundamental input of investors, employees, and suppliers, this approach recognizes other stakeholders and explicitly acknowledges the dialogue that exists between a firm's internal and external environments. Corporate social responsibility actions that put employees at the center of activities gain the support of both external and internal stakeholders.[13]

A Stakeholder Orientation

The degree to which a firm understands and addresses stakeholder demands can be referred to as a **stakeholder orientation.** This orientation comprises three sets of activities: (1) the organization-wide generation of data about stakeholder groups and assessment of the firm's effects on these groups; (2) the distribution of this information throughout the firm; and (3) the responsiveness of the organization as a whole to this information.[14]

Generating data about stakeholders begins with identifying the stakeholders that are relevant to the firm. Relevant stakeholder communities should be analyzed on the basis of the power that each enjoys, as well as by the ties between them and the company. Next, the firm should characterize the concerns about the business's conduct that each relevant stakeholder group shares. This information can be derived from formal research, including surveys, focus groups, Internet searches, and press reviews. For example, Best Buy obtains input on social and environmental responsibility issues from company representatives, suppliers, customers, and community leaders. Shell has an online discussion forum where website visitors are invited to express their opinions on the company's activities and their implications. Employees and managers can also generate this information informally as they carry out their daily activities. For example, purchasing managers know about suppliers' demands, public relations executives are tuned into the media, legal counselors are aware of the regulatory environment, financial executives are connected to investors, sales representatives are in touch with customers, and human resources advisers communicate directly with employees. Best Buy found that one of the biggest barriers to selling new electronics was the fact that buyers felt their older electronics were too valuable to replace, even though they longed for the new technology. Therefore, Best Buy implemented a "Buy Back" program. Customers who purchase the "Buy Back" Program can bring in their older purchases and receive a gift card equal to the redemption value of their older products.[15] Finally, companies should evaluate their impact on the issues that are important to the various stakeholders they have identified.[16] While shareholders desire strong profitability and growth, societal stakeholders have needs that extend beyond these two requirements.[17]

Given the variety of employees involved in the generation of information about stakeholders, it is essential that the information they gather be circulated throughout the firm. The firm must facilitate the communication of information about the nature of relevant stakeholder communities, stakeholder issues, and the current impact of the firm on these issues to all members of the organization. The dissemination of stakeholder intelligence can be organized formally through activities such as newsletters and internal information forums.[18] In particular, companies should utilize these activities to communicate the company's code of conduct to employees. Such communication informs employees about appropriate and inappropriate conduct within the organization. Research suggests that employees in organizations with ethical codes of conduct are less accepting of potential misconduct toward stakeholders.[19] However, ethical codes are of little use if they are not effectively communicated throughout the firm.

> "Employees in organizations with ethical codes of conduct are less accepting of potential misconduct toward stakeholders."

A stakeholder orientation is not complete unless it includes activities that address stakeholder issues. For example, many Chinese manufacturers and companies that use Chinese suppliers have been under attack in recent years over concerns about product safety. From lead-tainted toys at Mattel, melamine-tainted dairy products, and potentially deadly generic drugs (a highly lucrative, $75 billion-a-year business that employs over five million Chinese people), China has faced serious allegations and criticism over its lack of oversight and concern for consumer welfare.[20]

The responsiveness of an organization as a whole to stakeholder intelligence consists of the initiatives that the firm adopts to ensure that it abides by or exceeds stakeholder expectations and has a positive impact on stakeholder issues. Such activities are likely to be specific to a particular stakeholder group (for example, family-friendly work schedules) or to a particular stakeholder issue (for example, pollution reduction programs). These responsiveness processes typically involve the participation of the concerned stakeholder groups. Kraft, for example, includes special interest groups and university representatives in its programs so that the company may become sensitized to present and future ethical issues.

A stakeholder orientation can be viewed as a continuum in that firms are likely to adopt the concept to varying degrees. To gauge a given firm's stakeholder orientation, it is necessary to evaluate the extent to which the firm adopts behaviors that typify both the generation and dissemination of stakeholder intelligence and the responsiveness to this intelligence. A given organization may generate and disseminate more intelligence about some stakeholder communities than others and respond accordingly.[21]

SOCIAL RESPONSIBILITY AND THE IMPORTANCE OF A STAKEHOLDER ORIENTATION

From the perspective of social responsibility, business ethics embodies values, norms, and expectations that reflect concerns of major stakeholders, including consumers, employees, shareholders, suppliers, competitors, and the community. In other words, these stakeholders have concerns about what is fair, just, or in keeping with respect for stakeholders' rights.

Many business people and scholars have questioned the role of ethics and social responsibility in business. Legal and economic responsibilities are generally accepted as the most important determinants of performance. "If this is well done," say classical theorists, "profits are maximized more or less continuously and firms carry out their major responsibilities to society."[22] Some economists believe that if companies address economic and legal issues they are satisfying the demands of society, and that trying to anticipate and meet additional needs would be almost impossible. Milton Friedman has been quoted as saying that "the basic mission of business [is] . . . to produce goods and services at a profit, and in doing this, business [is] making its maximum contribution to society and, in fact, being socially responsible."[23] Even with the business ethics scandals of the twenty-first century, Friedman suggests that although those individuals guilty of wrongdoing should be held accountable, the market is a better deterrent to wrongdoing than new laws and regulations.[24] Thus, Friedman would diminish the role of stakeholders such as the government and employees in requiring that businesses demonstrate responsible and ethical behavior.

This Darwinian form of capitalism has been exported to many developing countries, such as Russia, and is associated with a "Wild West" economy where anything goes in business. Friedman's capitalism is a far cry from that of Adam Smith, one of the founders of capitalism. Smit developed the concept of the invisible hand and explored the role of self-interest in economic systems; however, he went on to explain that the "common good is associated with six psychological motives and that each individual has to produce for the common good, with values such as Propriety, Prudence, Reason, Sentiment and promoting the happiness of mankind."[25] These values could be correlated with the needs

DEBATE ISSUE   TAKE A STAND

Is It Acceptable to Promote a Socially Irresponsible but Legal Product to Stakeholders?

When you think of cheating, you may think of irresponsible behavior in the classroom. But Noel Biderman has created a company called Avid Life Media (based in Toronto) that is dedicated to another form of cheating.

Avid Life Media is owner of six website brands, including Cougar Life and Hot or Not. One of its more controversial brands is Ashley Madison, the motto of which is "Life is Short. Have an Affair." The website has over 8.5 million members. The company encourages married men and women to spend less than a minute to register on the largest website to openly promote infidelity. The company employs hundreds of programmers, designers, and marketers and has conducted a private placement for investors. While many stakeholders would say that the purpose of the website is wrong, there is nothing illegal about this business. But the fact that the website helps people engage in cheating on their spouses—including providing an email address to which one's spouse would never have access—has many people concerned. They consider facilitating secrecy for socially questionable conduct to be wrong.[26]

1. There is nothing wrong in providing a legal service that many people desire.
2. From a stakeholder perspective, it is wrong to provide socially irresponsible services.

and concerns of stakeholders. Smith established normative expectations for motives and behaviors in his theories about the invisible hand.

In the twenty-first century, Friedman's form of capitalism is being replaced by Smith's original concept of capitalism (or what is now called enlightened capitalism), which reemphasizes stakeholder concerns and issues. This shift may be occurring faster in developed countries than in those still being developed. The involvement of the government in owning a majority interest in General Motors and AIG for a period of time, and its minority ownership of large banks such as Citigroup, changed the face of capitalism in the United States. The government's $819 billion stimulus package, passed in 2009, has increased its reach and provided funding to reshape energy, health care, and education policy. Theodore Levitt, a renowned business professor, once wrote that although profits are required for business just like eating is required for living, profit is not the purpose of business any more than eating is the purpose of life.[27] Norman Bowie, a well-known philosopher, extended Levitt's sentiment by noting that focusing on profit alone can create an unfavorable paradox that causes a firm to fail to achieve its objectives. Bowie contends that when a business also cares about the well-being of stakeholders, it earns the trust and cooperation that ultimately reduce costs and increase productivity.[28]

It should be obvious from this discussion that ethics and social responsibility cannot be just reactive approaches to issues as they arise. Only if firms make ethical concerns a part of their foundation and incorporate ethics into their business strategies can social responsibility as a concept be embedded in daily decision making the way it is, for instance, at Herman Miller, an office furniture company known for its social responsibility initiatives. The company is one of a few office furniture producers in the world that are certified by the Business and Institutional Furniture Manufacturers Association for their low emission products.[29] A description of corporate social responsibility should include rights and duties, consequences and values—all of which refer to specific strategic decisions. The ethical component of business strategy should be capable of providing an assessment of top management, work group, and individual behavior as it relates to ethical decisions. Table 2.2 lists CR Magazine's best companies in terms of corporate citizenship and social responsibility.

TABLE 2.2 CR's Best Corporate Citizens

1	Hewlett-Packard Co.
2	Intel Corp.
3	General Mills, Inc.
4	International Business Machines Corp.
5	Kimberly-Clark Corp.
6	Abbott Laboratories
7	Bristol-Myers Squibb
8	Coca-Cola Co.
9	Gap, Inc.
10	Hess Corporation

Source: *CR's 100 Best Corporate Citizens 2010*,
http://www.thecro.com/files/CR100Best.pdf (accessed August 9, 2011).

SOCIAL RESPONSIBILITY AND ETHICS

The terms *ethics* and *social responsibility* are often used interchangeably, but each has a distinct meaning. In Chapter 1, we defined *social responsibility* as an organization's obligation to maximize its positive impact on stakeholders and to minimize its negative impact. For example, one of Google's founders, Larry Page, has promised to dedicate 1 percent of Google's profits, 1 percent of its equity, and significant employee time to "Google.org" or "DotOrg" to tackle global issues such as climate change, poverty, pandemics, etc. The company already gives tens of millions of dollars to charity each year.[30] General Electric pledged to decrease pollution and double its research and development spending on cleaner technologies.[31] Walmart has also joined the growing ranks of green companies. It has a number of environmentally friendlier stores, which reduce energy consumption and pollution. Walmart hopes to take what it learns from these stores and use that in all of the new stores that it builds.[32] Many other businesses have tried to determine what relationships, obligations, and duties are appropriate between their organizations and various stakeholders. Social responsibility can be viewed as a contract with society, whereas business ethics involves carefully thought-out rules or heuristics of business conduct that guide decision making.

> "Social responsibility can be viewed as a contract with society."

If social responsibility is considered an important corporate concern, then it does need quantitative credibility. Employee satisfaction, consumer loyalty, and other stakeholder concerns can all be quantified to some extent. However, some of the values and other dimensions of social responsibility are more qualitative. The International Organization for Standardization (ISO) established ISO 26000, which is a corporate social responsibility regulation meant to promote a common understanding in the area of social responsibility. ISO 26000 cannot be used for certification purposes but is intended as a guideline. Organizations that adopt this guideline must take into account societal, environmental, cultural, legal, political, economic, and organizational diversity while adhering to international norms of behavior.[33] ISO 14000 is an environmental regulation standard any business can adopt to help it reduce its carbon footprint, pollution, and waste.[34] Many U.S. firms are choosing to reduce their carbon footprint by purchasing renewable energy, especially solar and wind power. Experts estimate that wind energy could meet up to 20 percent of the energy needs in the U.S. by 2020. The United States is second only to China in wind power generation.[35] While corporate responsibility needs quantitative credibility, significant aspects of it are more qualitative in nature: employee satisfaction, customer motivations, company values, and ethical decision-making processes, for instance. To some extent, all of these can be broken down into quantitative data, but the essence of them cannot. These variables also shift constantly, making yesterday's survey irrelevant today.[36]

There are four levels of social responsibility—economic, legal, ethical, and philanthropic—and these can be viewed as steps (see Figure 2.3).[37] At the most basic level, companies have a responsibility to be profitable so that they can provide a return on investment to their owners and investors, create jobs for the community, and contribute goods and services to the economy. Of course, businesses are also expected to obey all relevant laws and regulations. Business ethics, as previously defined, comprises principles and standards that guide behavior in the world of business. Philanthropic responsibility refers to activities that are not required of businesses but that promote human welfare or goodwill. Ethics, then, is one dimension of social responsibility.

FIGURE 2.3 Steps of Social Responsibility

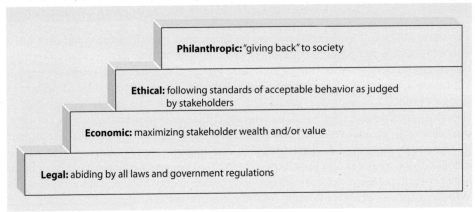

Source: Adapted from Archie B. Caroll, "The Pyramid of Corporate Social Responsibility: Toward the Moral Management of Organizational Stakeholders," *Business Horizons* (July–August 1991): 42, Figure 3.

The term **corporate citizenship** is often used to express the extent to which businesses strategically meet the economic, legal, ethical, and philanthropic responsibilities placed on them by their various stakeholders.[38] Corporate citizenship has four interrelated dimensions: strong sustained economic performance, rigorous compliance, ethical actions beyond what the law requires, and voluntary contributions that advance the reputation and stakeholder commitment of the organization. A firm's commitment to corporate citizenship indicates a strategic focus on fulfilling the social responsibilities that its stakeholders expect of it. Corporate citizenship involves acting on the firm's commitment to the corporate citizenship philosophy and measuring the extent to which it follows through by actually implementing citizenship initiatives. Table 2.3 lists some of the world's most ethical

TABLE 2.3 A Selection of the World's Most Ethical Companies

Trader Joe's	Salesforce.com, Inc.
Xerox	Barrett Jackson Auction Company
Nike	Patagonia
Dow Corning Corporation	Hewlett-Packard Company
Ford Motor Company	ARAMARK
General Electric	Caterpillar
PepsiCo	International Paper
Whole Foods Market	AstraZeneca
Aflac	Google
General Mills	IKEA
Best Buy	Gap
Starbucks	UPS
Target	

Source: "2010 World's Most Ethical Companies," *Ethisphere*, Q4, 30–31.

companies, all of which have demonstrated their commitment to stakeholders. As Chapter 1 demonstrated, many of these companies have superior financial performance compared to the indexes of other publically traded firms.

Reputation is one of an organization's greatest intangible assets with tangible value. The value of a positive reputation is difficult to quantify, but it is very important. A single negative incident can influence perceptions of a corporation's image and reputation instantly and for years afterward. Corporate reputation, image, and brands are more important than ever and are among the most critical aspects of sustaining relationships with constituents including investors, customers, financial analysts, media, and government watchdogs. It takes companies decades to build a great reputation, yet just one slip can cost a company dearly. Although an organization does not control its reputation in a direct sense, its actions, choices, behaviors, and consequences influence stakeholders' perceptions of it.

CORPORATE GOVERNANCE PROVIDES FORMALIZED RESPONSIBILITY TO STAKEHOLDERS

Most businesses, and often many courses taught in business programs, operate under the assumption that the purpose of business is to maximize profits for shareholders—an assumption manifest, for example, in the 1919 decision of the Michigan Supreme Court, which ruled in the case of *Dodge v. Ford Motor Co.*[39] that a business exists for the profit of shareholders, and the board of directors should focus on that objective. In contrast, the stakeholder model places the board of directors in the position of balancing the interests and conflicts of a company's various constituencies. External control of the corporation resides not only with government regulators but also with key stakeholders including employees, consumers, and communities, which exert pressure for responsible conduct. Mandates for stakeholder interests have been institutionalized in legislation that provides incentives for responsible conduct. And shareholders have been pushing for more power in the boardroom, as many feel their interests have not been well represented in the resolution of issues such as executive compensation.

Today, the failure to balance stakeholder interests can result in a failure to maximize shareholders' wealth. Money managers sometimes engage in risky trading that can lead to large losses, as evidenced in the conduct of Allen Stanford and Bernard Madoff.[40] Most firms are moving more toward a more balanced stakeholder model as they see that this approach will sustain the relationships necessary for long-term success.

Both directors and officers of corporations are fiduciaries for the shareholders. Fiduciaries are persons placed in positions of trust that act on behalf of the best interests of the organization. They have what is called a duty of care, or a *duty of diligence,* to make informed and prudent decisions.[41] Directors have a duty to avoid ethical misconduct and to provide leadership in decisions to prevent ethical misconduct in the organization.

Directors are not generally held responsible for negative outcomes if they have been informed and diligent in their decision making. However, questions arose about the role of directors when firms such as Countrywide Financial engaged in misconduct, such as granting subprime loans to customers who could not afford them. The case of Countrywide illustrates the obligation that board members have to request information, conduct research, use accountants and attorneys, and obtain the services of ethical compliance consultants to ensure that the corporations in which they have an interest are being run in an ethical manner. The National Association of Corporate Directors, a board of directors trade group, has helped to formulate a guide for boards to help them do a better job of governing corporate America.[42]

Directors share a *duty of loyalty,* which means that all their decisions should be in the best interests of the corporation and its stakeholders. Conflicts of interest exist when a director uses the position to obtain personal gain, usually at the expense of the organization. For example, before the Sarbanes–Oxley Act in 2002, directors could give themselves and their officers interest-free loans. Scandals at Tyco, Kmart, and WorldCom are all associated with officers receiving personal loans that damaged the corporation.

Officer compensation packages present a challenge for directors, especially those on the board who are not independent. Directors have an opportunity to vote for others' compensation in return for their own increased compensation. Following the global financial crisis, many top executives at failed firms received multimillion dollar bonuses in spite of the fact that their companies required huge government bailouts simply to stay afloat. General Motors garnered significant criticism after paying 96 percent of its U.S. salaried workforce bonuses between 4 and 16 percent, with less than 1 percent receiving bonuses of at least 50 percent of their salaries at the time. General Motors still owes the U.S. government $27 billion of the $50 billion in bailout funds provided in 2009.[43]

Directors' knowledge about the investments, business ventures, and stock market information of a company creates issues that could also violate their duty of loyalty. Insider trading of a firm's stock has very specific rules, and violations can result in serious punishment. The obligations of directors and officers for legal and ethical responsibility interface and fit together based on their fiduciary relationships. Ethical values should guide decisions and buffer the possibility of illegal conduct. One study found that a firm's sales margin will be damaged by the unethical treatment of stakeholders.[44] With increased pressure on directors to provide oversight for organizational ethics, there is a trend toward directors receiving training to increase their competency in ethics programs development, as well as in other areas such as accounting. Automated systems to monitor and measure the occurrence of ethical issues within organizations are increasingly being used to assist in this oversight process.

To remove the opportunity for employees to make unethical decisions, most companies have developed formal systems of accountability, oversight, and control that are known as **corporate governance.** *Accountability* refers to how closely workplace decisions are aligned with a firm's stated strategic direction and its compliance with ethical and legal considerations. *Oversight* provides a system of checks and balances that limit employees' and managers' opportunities to deviate from policies and strategies aimed at preventing unethical and illegal activities. *Control* is the process of auditing and improving organizational decisions and actions. Table 2.4 lists examples of major corporate governance issues.

A clear delineation of accountability helps employees, customers, investors, government regulators, and other stakeholders understand why and how the organization identifies and achieves its goals. Corporate governance establishes fundamental systems and processes for preventing and detecting misconduct, for investigating and disciplining, and for recovery and continuous improvement. Effective corporate governance creates a compliance and ethics culture in which employees feel that integrity is at the core

TABLE 2.4 Corporate Governance Topics

Executive Compensation
Enterprise-Wide Risk Management
Short- and Long-Term Strategies
Board Composition and Structure
Shareholder Relations
CEO Selection, Termination, and Succession Plans
Role of the CEO in Board Decisions
Auditing, Control, and Integrity of Financial Reporting
Compliance with Government Regulation and Reform
Organizational Ethics Programs

Source: "Corporate Alert: Top 10 Topics for Directors in 2011," December 6, 2010, http://www.corpgov.deloitte.com/binary/com.epicentric.
contentmanagement.servlet.ContentDeliveryServlet/USEng/Documents/Board%20Governance/Top%2010%20Topics%20for%20Directors%20in%20
2011_Akin_120610.pdf (accessed February 15, 2011).

of competitiveness.[45] Even if a company has adopted a consensus approach for decision making, there should be oversight and authority for delegating tasks, making difficult and sometimes controversial decisions, balancing power throughout the firm, and maintaining ethical compliance. Governance also provides mechanisms for identifying risks and planning for recovery when mistakes or problems occur.

The development of stakeholder orientation should interface with the corporation's governance structure. Corporate governance also helps to establish the integrity of all relationships. A governance system that does not provide checks and balances creates opportunities for top managers to put their own self-interest before those of important stakeholders. For example, while many people lost their investments during the recent financial crisis some CEOs were actually able to make a profit from it. Some directors even tweaked performance targets in order to make goals easier to achieve so that they could receive more bonus money. Bonuses have become a very contentious issue since they are the part of an executive's pay most tied to performance. Many people are asking why executives continue to receive bonuses as their companies fail; the fact is, most of the time executive bonuses are tied to targets other than stock prices.[46] Concerns about the need for greater corporate governance are not limited to the United States, and reforms in governance structures and issues are occurring all over the world.[47] Table 2.5 outlines some of the changes we have seen in corporate governance over the past 25 years.

Corporate governance normally involves strategic decisions and actions by boards of directors, business owners, top executives, and other managers with high levels of authority and accountability. Although in the past these people have been relatively free from scrutiny, changes in technology, consumer activism, and government attention, as well as the recent ethical scandals and other factors, have brought new attention to such issues as transparency, executive pay, risk and control, resource accountability, strategic direction, stockholder rights, and other decisions made for the organization.

TABLE 2.5 Changes in Corporate Governance

40% of boards split the CEO and Chair functions

Boards are getting smaller, with an average of 11 members (5:1 ratio independent: non-independent)

74% of boards have mandatory retirement rules for directors

Almost all boards conduct annual board performance evaluations

71% limit the time that board members can serve on outside boards

21% of new directors are women, although 10% of boards have no women directors

Over 50% of CEOs in the S&P 500 do not serve on outside boards

Important characteristics in directors: strong financial background, industry background, and international experience

Average board member retainer: $20,00 in 1986 ($40,000 in today's dollars) and $80,000 in 2010

Average total director compensation has risen to $215,000 in 2010

Source: Julie Hembrock Daum, "How Corporate Governance Changed from 1986–2010," *Business Week*, http://www.businessweek.com/print/managing/content/nov2010/ca2010118_316346.htm (accessed February 15, 2011).

Views of Corporate Governance

To better understand the role of corporate governance in business today, we must consider how it relates to fundamental beliefs about the purpose of business. Some organizations take the view that as long as they are maximizing shareholder wealth and profitability, they are fulfilling their core responsibilities. Other firms, however, believe that a business is an important member, even a citizen, of society, and therefore must assume broad responsibilities that include complying with social norms and expectations. From these assumptions, we can derive two major approaches to corporate governance: the shareholder model and the stakeholder model.[48]

The **shareholder model of corporate governance** is founded in classic economic precepts, including the goal of maximizing wealth for investors and owners. For publicly traded firms, corporate governance focuses on developing and improving the formal system for maintaining performance accountability between top management and the firms' shareholders.[49] Thus, a shareholder orientation should drive a firm's decisions toward serving the best interests of investors. Underlying these decisions is a classic agency problem, in which ownership (that is, investors) and control (that is, managers) are separate. Managers act as agents for investors, whose primary goal is increasing the value of the stock they own. However, investors and managers are distinct parties with unique insights, goals, and values with respect to the business. Managers, for example, may have motivations beyond stockholder value, such as market share, personal compensation, or attachment to particular products and projects. Because of these potential differences, corporate governance mechanisms are needed to align investor and management interests. The shareholder model has been criticized for its somewhat singular purpose and focus because there are other ways of "investing" in a business. Suppliers, creditors, customers, employees, business partners, the community, and others also invest their resources into the success of the firm.[50]

The **stakeholder model of corporate governance** adopts a broader view of the purpose of business. Although a company certainly has a responsibility for economic success and viability to satisfy its stockholders, it must also answer to other stakeholders, including employees, suppliers, government regulators, communities, and special interest groups with which it interacts. Due to limited resources, companies must determine which of their stakeholders are primary. Once the primary groups have been identified, managers must then implement the appropriate corporate governance mechanisms to promote the development of long-term relationships.[51] This approach entails creating governance systems that consider stakeholder welfare in tandem with corporate needs and interests. Patagonia, Yahoo!, and Google all use the stakeholder model of corporate governance to direct their business activities.

Although these two approaches seem to represent the ends of a continuum, the reality is that the shareholder model is a more restrictive precursor to the stakeholder orientation. Many businesses have evolved into the stakeholder model as a result of government initiatives, consumer activism, industry activity, and other external forces.

The Role of Boards of Directors

For public corporations, boards of directors hold the ultimate responsibility for their firms' success or failure, as well as for the ethics of their actions. This governing authority is being held responsible by the 2004 and 2007 amendments to the Federal Sentencing Guidelines for Organizations (FSGO) for creating an ethical culture that provides leadership, values, and compliance. The members of a company's board of directors assume legal responsibility for the firm's resources and decisions, and they appoint its top executive officers. Board members have a fiduciary duty, meaning that they have assumed a position of trust and confidence that entails certain responsibilities, including acting in the best interests of those they serve. Thus, board membership is not intended as a vehicle for personal financial gain; rather, it provides the intangible benefit of ensuring the success of both the organization and the people involved in the fiduciary arrangement. The role and expectations of boards of directors assumed greater significance after the accounting scandals of the early 2000s, and the global financial crisis has motivated many stakeholders to demand greater accountability from boards.[52]

Despite this emphasis on greater accountability for board members, many continue to believe that current directors do not face serious consequences for corporate misconduct. Although directors may be sued by shareholders, the SEC does not usually pursue corporate directors for misconduct unless it can be proven that they acted in bad faith. For instance, the SEC brought civil charges against three directors from DHB Industries for allegedly ignoring red flags indicating misconduct in the company. According to the accusations, these directors tried to hide the fraud by hiring two separate firms to perform audits, perhaps in the hope that one of the firms would sign off on the company. Because the SEC saw indications of corruption within the board, it filed a lawsuit against the directors. However, this type of action tends to be the exception rather than the norm.[53]

The traditional approach to directorship has assumed that board members manage the corporation's business, but research and practical observation have shown that boards of directors rarely, if ever, perform the management function.[54] Boards meet only a few times a year, which precludes them from managing effectively. In addition, the complexity of modern organizations mandates full attention on a daily basis. Therefore, boards of directors are concerned primarily with monitoring the decisions made by executives on behalf of the company. This function includes choosing top executives, assessing their performance, helping to set strategic direction, and ensuring that oversight, control, and accountability mechanisms are in place. Thus, board members assume ultimate authority for their organization's effectiveness and subsequent performance.

Perhaps one of the most challenging ethical issues that boards of directors must deal with is compensation. When considering executive pay raises, directors may put their own self-interest above the interests of shareholders.[55] Then there is the compensation that directors themselves receive. Directors at the nation's top 200 firms are paid a median of $228,000. Trends show that director compensation is rising, with analysts predicting that 50 percent of boards could see pay raises of up to 15 percent in a one-year period. Proponents argue that such high compensation for part-time work is necessary; after all, directors have a difficult job, and good pay is needed to attract top-quality talent. On the other hand, critics believe this level of compensation could cause a conflict of interest for directors. Some speculate that compensation over $200,000 makes directors more complacent, as they become less concerned with "rocking the boat" and more concerned with maintaining their high-paying positions.[56] Clearly, the debate over director accountability continues to rage.

Greater Demands for Accountability and Transparency

Just as improved ethical decision making requires more of employees and executives, so too are boards of directors experiencing a greater demand for accountability and transparency. In the past, board members were often retired company executives or friends of current executives, but the trend today is toward "outside directors" who have little vested interest in the firm before assuming the director role. Inside directors are corporate officers, consultants, major shareholders, and others who benefit directly from the success of the organization. Directors today are increasingly chosen for their expertise, competence, and ability to bring diverse perspectives to strategic discussions. Outside directors are also thought to bring more independence to the monitoring function because they are not bound by past allegiances, friendships, a current role in the company, or some other issue that may create a conflict of interest.

> "Directors today are increasingly chosen for their expertise, competence, and ability to bring diverse perspectives to strategic discussions."

Many of the corporate scandals uncovered in recent years might have been prevented if each of the companies' boards of directors had been better qualified, more knowledgeable, and less biased. Shareholder involvement in changing the makeup of boards has always run into difficulties. Most boards are not true democracies, and most shareholders have a minimal ability to impact decision making because they are so dispersed. The concept of board members being linked to more than one company is known as **interlocking directorate.** The practice is not considered illegal unless it involves a direct competitor.[57] A survey by *USA Today* found that corporate boards have considerable overlap. More than 1,000 corporate board members sit on four or more boards, and of the nearly 2,000 boards of directors in the United States, more than 22,000 of their members are linked to boards of more than one company. For example, of the 1,000 largest companies, one-fifth share at least one board member with another top 1,000 firm. This overlap creates the opportunity for conflicts of interest in decision making and limits the independence of individual boards of directors. In some cases, it seems that individuals earned placement on multiple boards of directors because they gained a reputation for going along with top management and never asking questions. Such a trend may foster a corporate culture that limits outside oversight of top managers' decisions.

Although labor and public pension fund activities have waged hundreds of proxy battles in recent years, they have rarely had much effect on the target companies. Now shareholder activists are attacking the process by which directors themselves are elected. Shareholders at Saks are not the only ones to vote to change board election rules. Resolutions at hundreds of companies require that candidates for director gain a majority of votes before they can join the board. It is hoped that this practice will make boards of directors more attentive and accountable.[58]

Executive Compensation

One of the biggest issues that corporate boards of directors face is **executive compensation.** In fact, most boards spend more time deciding how much to compensate top executives than they do ensuring the integrity of the company's financial reporting systems.[59] How executives are compensated for their leadership, organizational service, and performance has become a controversial topic. Indeed, 70 percent of respondents in a *Bloomberg* national poll indicated they believe large bonuses should be temporarily banned for officers at companies that received federal bailout money, while only 7 percent reported believing that such bonuses were still appropriate as an incentive tool.[60] U.S. lawmakers subpoenaed the names of American International Group (AIG) executives who received $165 million in bonuses after the company was bailed out by the government. The firm stated that it decided to make the unpopular payments because many of them were contractually required. Nevertheless, the move seemed arrogant and out of touch to many lawmakers and stakeholders, and former AIG CEO Edward Liddy requested that the executives return their bonuses. Since then, AIG has revamped its bonus system to better align pay with performance, and cut its 2010 bonuses by $20 million.[61]

Many people believe that no executive is worth millions of dollars in annual salary and stock options, even if he or she has brought great financial return to investors. Their concerns often center on the relationship between the highest-paid executives and median employee wages in the company. If this ratio is perceived as too large, then critics believe that either employees are not being compensated fairly or high executive salaries represent an improper use of company resources. According to the AFL-CIO, the average executive pay of an S&P 500 index company is over $9 million. Executive bonuses can reach into the hundreds of thousands. Add to this the fact that companies received nearly a billion dollars in government bailout money—money that came from taxpayers.[62] Understandably, many stakeholders are angry about this situation. The business press is now usually careful to support high levels of executive compensation only when it is directly linked to strong company performance.

Although the issue of executive compensation has received much attention in the media of late, some business owners have long recognized its potential ill effects. In the early twentieth century, for example, J. P. Morgan implemented a policy that limited the pay of top managers in the businesses that he owned to no more than 20 times the pay of any other employee.[63]

Other people argue that because executives assume so much risk on behalf of the company, they deserve the rewards that follow from strong company performance. In addition, many executives' personal and professional lives meld to the point that they are on call 24 hours a day. Because not everyone has the skill, experience, and desire to take on the pressure and responsibility of the executive lifestyle, market forces dictate a high level of compensation. When the pool of qualified individuals is limited, many corporate board members feel that offering large compensation packages is the only way to attract and retain top executives, thus ensuring that their firms are not left without strong leadership. In an era when top executives are increasingly willing to "jump ship" for other firms that offer higher pay, potentially lucrative stock options, bonuses, and other benefits, such thinking is not without merit.[64]

Executive compensation is a difficult but important issue for boards of directors and other stakeholders to consider because it receives much attention in the media, sparks shareholder concern, and is hotly debated in discussions of corporate governance. One area for board members to consider is the extent to which executive compensation is linked to company performance. Plans that base compensation on the achievement of several performance goals, including profits and revenues, are intended to align the interests of owners with those of management. Amid rising complaints about excessive executive compensation, an increasing number of corporate boards are imposing performance targets on the stock and stock options they include in their CEOs' pay packages. For example, in 2009 Ford Motor Co. gave CEO Alan Mulally a grant of stock options and restricted shares valued at $16 million. By 2011 these options were valued at more than $200 million. More than 90 percent of CEOs in the S&P 500 stock index received stock or stock options in a one-year period. These options have grown to more than $3 billion above the initial grant valuations.[65]

The SEC proposed that companies disclose how they compensate lower-ranking employees as well as top executives. This proposal was part of a review of executive pay policies that addressed the belief that many financial corporations have historically taken on too much risk. The SEC believes that compensation may be linked to excessive risk-taking.[66]

> "The SEC believes that compensation may be linked to excessive risk-taking."

Another issue is whether performance-linked compensation encourages executives to focus on short-term performance at the expense of long-term growth.[67] Shareholders today, however, may be growing more concerned about transparency than short-term performance and executive compensation. One study determined that companies that divulge more details about their corporate governance practices generate higher shareholder returns than less transparent companies.[68]

IMPLEMENTING A STAKEHOLDER PERSPECTIVE

An organization that develops effective corporate governance and understands the importance of business ethics and social responsibility in achieving success should also develop some processes for managing these important concerns. Although there are many different approaches to this issue, we provide some basic steps that have been found effective in utilizing the stakeholder framework to manage responsibility and business ethics. The steps include (1) assessing the corporate culture, (2) identifying stakeholder groups, (3) identifying stakeholder issues, (4) assessing organizational commitment to social responsibility,

(5) identifying resources and determining urgency, and (6) gaining stakeholder feedback. These steps include getting feedback from relevant stakeholders in formulating organizational strategy and implementation.

Step 1: Assessing the Corporate Culture

To enhance organizational fit, a social responsibility program must align with the corporate culture of the organization. The purpose of this first step is to identify the organizational mission, values, and norms that are likely to have implications for social responsibility. Relevant existing values and norms are those that specify the stakeholder groups and stakeholder issues deemed most important by the organization. Very often, relevant organizational values and norms can be found in corporate documents such as the mission statement, annual reports, sales brochures, and websites. For example, Terracycle states that its mission is "to find a meaningful use for waste materials." And indeed Terracycle has been a pioneer in taking waste materials and transforming them into consumer products. The company's efforts have kept thousands of tons of waste out of landfills. In 2010 Terracycle received the Silver Edison Green Award for its work in creating recycled products and fashions.[69]

Step 2: Identifying Stakeholder Groups

In managing this stage, it is important to recognize stakeholder needs, wants, and desires. Many important issues gain visibility because key constituencies such as consumer groups, regulators, or the media express an interest. When agreement, collaboration, or even confrontations exist on an issue, there is a need for a decision-making process, such as a model of collaboration to overcome adversarial approaches to problem solving. Managers can identify relevant stakeholders who may be affected by or may influence the development of organizational policy.

Stakeholders have some level of power over a business because they are in the position to withhold organizational resources, at least to some extent. Stakeholders have the most power when their own survival is not really affected by the success of the organization and when they have access to vital organizational resources. For example, most consumers of shoes do not need to buy Nike shoes. Therefore, if they decide to boycott Nike, they endure only minor inconveniences. Nevertheless, consumer loyalty to Nike is vital to the continued success of the sport apparel giant. A proper assessment of the power held by a given stakeholder community includes an evaluation of the extent to which that community can collaborate with others to pressure the firm.

Step 3: Identifying Stakeholder Issues

Together, steps 1 and 2 lead to the identification of the stakeholders who are both the most powerful and the most legitimate. The level of stakeholders' power and legitimacy determines the degree of urgency in addressing their needs. Step 3, then, consists of understanding the main issues of concern to these stakeholders. Conditions for collaboration exist when problems are so complex that multiple stakeholders are required to resolve the issue, and adversarial approaches to problem solving are clearly inadequate.

For example, obesity in children is becoming an issue across groups and stakeholders.[70] The United States is the most obese nation in the world with almost 40 percent of its population obese or overweight, the result being a huge rise in health problems.

While Americans have traditionally not supported government health care plans, increasing health care costs are causing some stakeholders to reconsider their stance. Currently, six out of 10 people put off going to the doctor because of the high cost, with a quarter saying that someone in their family has had trouble paying off medical bills. The majority of people appear to support health care reform, although consumers are divided as to the best method for reform. One poll revealed that while 21 percent believe the new health care law passed under the Obama administration will make the system better, 23 percent feel it could make it worse (the rest remained undecided). However, over half of respondents support funding for healthcare reform, demonstrating that the issue is important to a variety of stakeholders.[71] Stakeholder concerns have pushed the government into taking action on this important issue.

Step 4: Assessing Organizational Commitment to Social Responsibility

Steps 1 through 3 are geared toward generating information about social responsibility among a variety of influences in and around an organization. Step 4 brings these three first stages together to arrive at an understanding of social responsibility that specifically matches the organization of interest. This general definition will then be used to evaluate current practices and to select concrete social responsibility initiatives. Firms such as Starbucks have selected activities that address stakeholder concerns. Starbucks has formalized its initiatives in official documents such as annual reports, web pages, and company brochures. Starbucks is concerned with the environment and integrates policies and programs throughout all aspects of its operations to minimize its environmental impact. The company also has many community-building programs that help it to be a good neighbor and contribute positively to the communities where its partners and customers live, work, and play.[72]

Step 5: Identifying Resources and Determining Urgency

The prioritization of stakeholders and issues and the assessment of past performance lead to the allocation of resources. Two main criteria can be considered: the level of financial and organizational investments required by different actions, and the level of urgency when prioritizing social responsibility challenges. When the challenge under consideration is viewed as significant and when stakeholder pressures on the issue can be expected, the challenge can be considered urgent. For example, Facebook has encountered a severe backlash concerning its privacy settings. Privacy experts have filed complaints against Facebook for changing its privacy policies and limiting what information users can keep private, causing Facebook to scale back some of its initiatives that were intended to create a more open network.[73] Internet privacy has become such an issue that regulators are proposing a "Do Not Track" list and a social networkers' bill of rights.[74]

Step 6: Gaining Stakeholder Feedback

Stakeholder feedback can be generated through a variety of means. First, stakeholders' general assessment of a firm and its practices can be obtained through satisfaction or reputation surveys. Second, to gauge stakeholders' perceptions of a firm's contributions to specific issues, stakeholder-generated media such as blogs, websites, podcasts, and newsletters can be assessed. Third, more formal research may be conducted using focus groups, observation, and surveys. Many watchdog groups have utilized the web to inform consumers and to publicize their messages. For example, Consumer Watchdog, a California-based group that keeps an eye on everything from education to the oil industry, publicly applauded the decision of Google co-founder Larry Page to become the company's chief executive officer. Long a critic of Google's activities, the watchdog organization expressed hope that Page would take consumer issues like Internet privacy seriously.[75]

CONTRIBUTIONS OF A STAKEHOLDER PERSPECTIVE

While we provide a framework for implementing a stakeholder perspective, balancing stakeholder interests requires good judgment. When businesses attempt to provide what consumers want, broader societal interests can create conflicts. Consider that the cheapest car in the world is the Tata Nano, made in India. The Nano has a starting price of $2,900, but it also has only a small two-cylinder, 35-horsepower engine that could be suicidal on a modern expressway. Furthermore, the car has poor crash protection and no air bags. The Nano's manufacturer cuts many corners to be cheap, including using three lug nuts instead of four to hold the wheel to the axle. After launching the car, Tata had to beef up the heat shield for the exhaust and add a fuse to the electrical system when several cars caught on fire.[76] There are a number of ethical, social responsibility, and stakeholder issues with the Nano. Many consumers may be only able to afford a $2,900 car. On the other hand, stakeholders concerned with auto safety may object to a car that is potentially dangerous to drive. In the United States, regulatory authorities will not allow it to be sold as equipped in India. It is clear that balancing stakeholder interests can be a challenging process.

We feel that this chapter provides a good overview of the issues, conflicts, and opportunities of understanding more about stakeholder relationships. The stakeholder framework helps recognize issues, identify stakeholders, and examine the role of boards of directors and managers in promoting ethics and social responsibility. Finally, we believe that a stakeholder perspective can create a more ethical and reputable organization.

SUMMARY

Business ethics, issues, and conflicts revolve around relationships. Customers, investors and shareholders, employees, suppliers, government agencies, communities, and many others who have a stake or claim in some aspect of a company's products, operations, markets, industry, and outcomes are known as stakeholders. They are both influenced by and have the ability to affect businesses. Stakeholders provide both tangible and intangible resources that are more or less critical to a firm's long-term success, and their relative ability to withdraw these resources gives them power. Stakeholders define significant ethical issues in business.

Primary stakeholders are those whose continued association is absolutely necessary for a firm's survival, while secondary stakeholders do not typically engage in transactions with a company and thus are not essential to its survival. The stakeholder interaction model suggests that there are reciprocal relationships between a firm and a host of stakeholders. The degree to which a firm understands and addresses stakeholder demands can be expressed as a stakeholder orientation and includes three sets of activities: (1) the generation of data across the firm about its stakeholder groups and the assessment of the firm's effects on these groups, (2) the distribution of this information throughout the firm, and (3) the responsiveness of every level of the firm to this intelligence. A stakeholder orientation can be viewed as a continuum in that firms are likely to adopt the concept to varying degrees.

Although the terms *ethics* and *social responsibility* are often used interchangeably, they have distinct meanings. Social responsibility in business refers to an organization's obligation to maximize its positive impact and minimize its negative impact on society. There are four levels of social responsibility—economic, legal, ethical, and philanthropic—and they can be viewed as a pyramid. The term *corporate citizenship* is often used to communicate the extent to which businesses strategically meet the economic, legal, ethical, and philanthropic responsibilities placed on them by their various stakeholders.

From a social responsibility perspective, business ethics embodies standards, norms, and expectations that reflect the concerns of major stakeholders including consumers, employees, shareholders, suppliers, competitors, and the community. Only if firms include ethical concerns in their foundational values and incorporate ethics into their business strategies can social responsibility as a value be embedded in daily decision making.

Most businesses operate under the assumption that the main purpose of business is to maximize profits for shareholders. The stakeholder model places the board of directors in the position of balancing the interests and conflicts of the various constituencies. Both directors and officers of corporations are fiduciaries for the shareholders. Directors have a duty to avoid ethical misconduct and to provide leadership in decisions to prevent ethical misconduct in their organizations. To remove the opportunity for employees to make unethical decisions, most companies have developed formal systems of accountability, oversight, and control known as corporate governance. Accountability refers to how closely workplace decisions are aligned with a firm's stated strategic direction and its compliance with ethical and legal considerations. Oversight provides a system of checks and balances that limit employees' and managers' opportunities to deviate from policies and strategies intended to prevent unethical and illegal activities. Control is the process of auditing and improving organizational decisions and actions.

There are two perceptions of corporate governance, which can be viewed as a continuum. The shareholder model is founded in classic economic precepts, including the maximization of wealth for investors and owners. The stakeholder model adopts a broader view of the purpose of business that includes satisfying the concerns of other stakeholders, from employees, suppliers, and government regulators to communities and special interest groups.

Two major elements of corporate governance that relate to ethical decision making are the role of the board of directors and executive compensation. The members of a public corporation's board of directors assume legal responsibility for the firm's resources and decisions. Important issues related to corporate boards of directors include accountability, transparency, and independence. Boards of directors are also responsible for appointing top executive officers and determining their compensation, a controversial topic. Concerns about executive pay may center on the often-disproportionate relationship between executive pay and median employee wages in the company.

An organization that develops effective corporate governance and understands the importance of business ethics and social responsibility in achieving success should develop some processes for managing these important concerns. Although there are many different approaches, we have identified steps that have been found effective in utilizing the stakeholder framework to manage responsibility and business ethics. These steps are: (1) assessing the corporate culture, (2) identifying stakeholder groups, (3) identifying stakeholder issues, (4) assessing organizational commitment to social responsibility, (5) identifying resources and determining urgency, and (6) gaining stakeholder feedback.

IMPORTANT TERMS FOR REVIEW

stakeholder	primary stakeholder
secondary stakeholder	stakeholder interaction model
stakeholder orientation	corporate citizenship
reputation	corporate governance
shareholder model of corporate governance	stakeholder model of corporate governance
interlocking directorate	executive compensation

RESOLVING ETHICAL BUSINESS CHALLENGES*

Karl was getting pressure from his boss, parents, and wife about the marketing campaign for Bounce Corporation's new web browser–based game called "Breakaway." He had been working for Bounce for about two years, and the Breakaway game was his first big project. After Karl and his wife, Lisa, graduated from college, they decided to go back to their hometown of Austin, Texas. Karl's father knew the president of Bounce, which enabled Karl to get a job in the company's marketing department. Bounce is a medium-sized company with about 1,000 employees, making it one of the main employers in Austin. Bounce develops browser–based social networking games.

Within the social networking game industry, competition is fierce. Games typically have a short life cycle before the "next big thing" arrives. One of the key strategies in the industry is providing unique, visually stimulating games using simple story lines, fast action, and participant interaction. The target market for Bounce's social networking game products are adults between the ages of 18 and 44. Males constitute 75 percent of the market.

When Karl first started with Bounce, his task was to conduct market research on the types of games that players wanted. His research showed that the market was looking for more action (violence), distinct character roles, multiple levels of difficulty, and in-game rewards. Further research showed that certain tasks and scenarios were more pleasing than others. As part of his research, Karl observed people in online role-playing games; he found that many players became hypnotized by a game and would buy credits via credit card or PayPal to advance more quickly. Research suggested that many target consumers exhibited the same symptoms as compulsive gamblers. Karl's research results were well received by the company, which developed several new games based on it. These new games were instant hits with the market.

In his continuing research, Karl found that the consumer's level of intensity increased as the game's intensity level increased. Several reports later, Karl suggested that target consumers might be willing, at strategic periods, to purchase credits for more energy or stamina to complete tasks in the game. For example, a player who wanted to quickly move through the tasks required to complete a level would have to buy credits; to finish the "boss" levels within the game, credits were almost a necessity. When the idea was tested, Karl found that it did increase game productivity.

Karl also noticed that social networking games that gave positive reinforcements to the consumer, such as encouraging messages after a completed task, were played much more frequently than others. He reported his findings to Will, Bounce's president, who asked Karl to apply that information to the development of new games. Karl suggested having the games reward game players with special discounts on in-game items when specific goals were achieved. Players could then use the discounts to buy items at strategic points to increase their chances of advancing to the next level. By inserting the opportunity to buy certain items at a discount, these games generated more credit input than output, and game productivity increased dramatically. These innovations were quite successful, giving Bounce a larger share of the market and Karl a promotion to product manager.

Karl's newest assignment was the Breakaway game, a fast-paced scenario in which the goal was to destroy the enemy before being destroyed. Karl expanded the game's appeal with two notable additions. First, the game employed 3-D technology, which gave players the ability to connect their computers to HDTV sets to play the game. Second, keeping in mind that most of the consumers were male, Karl incorporated a female character who, at each level, removed a piece of her clothing and taunted the player. A win at the highest level left her nude. Test market results suggested that the two additions increased profitability per game dramatically.

Several weeks later, Will asked about the Breakaway project. "I think we've got a real problem, Will," Karl told him. "Maybe the nudity is a bad idea. Some people will be really upset about it." Will was displeased with Karl's response.

Word got around fast that the Breakaway project had stalled. During dinner with his parents, Karl mentioned the Breakaway project, and his dad said something that affected Karl. "You know, son, the Breakaway project will bring in a great deal of revenue for Bounce, and jobs are at stake. Some of your coworkers are upset about your stand on this project. I'm not telling you what to do, but there's more at stake here than just a computer game."

The next day Karl had a meeting with Will about Breakaway. "Well," Will asked, "what have you decided?"

Karl answered, "I don't think we should go with the nudity idea."

Will answered, "You know, Karl, you're right. The U.S. market just isn't ready to see full nudity in a social networking game played within a web browser. That's why I've contacted an Internet provider who will take our game and sell it on the Internet as a stand-alone adult product. I've also checked out the foreign markets and found that we can sell the game to the Mexican market if we tone down

the violence. The Taiwanese joint venture group has approved the version we have now, but they would like you to develop something that is more graphic in both areas. You see, they already have similar versions of this type of game now, and their market is ready to go to the next level. I see the Internet market as secondary because we can't package the 3-D capabilities into the stand-alone Internet product. Maybe soon we'll be able to tap into it at that level, but not now. So, Karl, do you understand what you need to be doing on Breakaway?"

QUESTIONS | EXERCISES

1. What are the ethical and legal issues at stake in this scenario?
2. What are Karl's options?
3. Discuss the acceptability and commercial use of sex, violence, and gambling in the United States.
4. Is marketing sex, violence, and gambling acceptable in other countries if these things do not conflict with local cultures?

*This case is strictly hypothetical; any resemblance to real persons, companies, or situations is coincidental.

CHECK YOUR EQ

Check your EQ, or Ethics Quotient, by completing the following. Assess your performance to evaluate your overall understanding of the chapter material.

		Yes	No
1.	Social responsibility in business refers to maximizing the visibility of social involvement.	Yes	No
2.	Stakeholders provide resources that are more or less critical to a firm's long-term success.	Yes	No
3.	Three primary stakeholders are customers, special interest groups, and the media.	Yes	No
4.	The most significant influence on ethical behavior in an organization is the opportunity to engage in unethical behavior.	Yes	No
5.	The stakeholder perspective is useful in managing social responsibility and business ethics.	Yes	No

ANSWERS 1. No. Social responsibility refers to an organization's obligation to maximize its positive impact on society and minimize its negative impact. 2. Yes. These resources are both tangible and intangible. 3. No. Although customers are primary stakeholders, special interest groups and the media are usually considered secondary stakeholders. 4. No. Other influences such as corporate culture have more impact on ethical decisions within an organization. 5. Yes. The six steps to implement this approach were provided in this chapter.

PART 2

© Sissy Borbely, Shutterstock

Ethical Issues and the Institutionalization of Business Ethics

CHAPTER 3

EMERGING BUSINESS ETHICS ISSUES

CHAPTER OBJECTIVES

- To define ethical issues in the context of organizational ethics

- To examine ethical issues as they relate to the basic values of honesty, fairness, and integrity

- To delineate misuse of company resources, abusive and intimidating behavior, lying, conflicts of interest, bribery, corporate intelligence, discrimination, sexual harassment, environmental issues, fraud, insider trading, intellectual property rights, and privacy as business ethics issues

- To examine the challenge of determining an ethical issue in business

CHAPTER OUTLINE

AN ETHICAL DILEMMA*

As Jackie sat waiting to talk to the president of Sing & Dance Records (SDR), she started to wonder whether the meeting would destroy her musical career before it even got started. Because she was an up-and-coming star recently hired by SDR and didn't know the unwritten rules of the company, the chain-of-command philosophy, and the employees and studio musicians around her very well, the wait was making her more and more uneasy. Given how well things had started, it was painful for her to recall the circumstances that had led her to this place.

Jackie had been lured to SDR after winning third place in a national talent competition. Considering how long some performers wait to land at a major record label, if they ever do so at all, she had attracted SDR's attention remarkably quickly. Jackie had a sultry voice and she wrote her own music. Music industry insiders expected big things from her soon. The opportunity at SDR seemed like a dream come true. The possibility of a lucrative recording contract, the chance to be close to her old neighborhood, and a romantic encounter with

Curtis (her future manager at SDR) made it nearly impossible for Jackie to say no.

In the beginning, Curtis had been very charming. He convinced Jackie to work with SDR by telling her about the label's industry connections, the bands it represented, and the resources it employed to boost its performers. Curtis had helped her find a nice house, had assisted with her move, and eventually had become more than her manager. As the months slipped by their relationship became close to the point where they began to discuss living together. Then Jackie started hearing rumors about Curtis and Leslie.

Leslie, who had come to SDR six months before Jackie, worked in the record label's legal department, and in a just a few months, she had become head of that department amidst rumors that Curtis had helped her get the promotion because of their personal relationship. The rumors became so intense that Jackie confronted Curtis and discovered that the stories were true. Devastated, Jackie ended her relationship with Curtis in a heated confrontation, but the professional aspect of their relationship proved more difficult to untangle.

Because of Curtis's contacts in the music industry and at SDR, Jackie couldn't afford to drop him as her manager. Days passed with little contact between the two of them, and then one afternoon Curtis stopped by the recording studio. He apologized for his behavior, and Jackie accepted his apology. But when he visited the next day, he began to make sexual advances toward Jackie. She made a joke of it to defuse the situation, but several days later he repeated the same behavior and made several suggestive remarks to her just out of earshot of her band members.

Jackie's face turned red as she said, "Curtis, you pig, you've crossed the line. Do that again, and I'll report you to Legal!"

A few more weeks went by, and then Jackie got a phone call in the studio from Curtis in which he made even more sexually suggestive comments. Every few days, he would stop by or call and remind her of some private experience they had had together. He would taunt her, saying, "Jackie, you know you want it."

Eventually, Jackie went to SDR's legal department to complain formally about Curtis, his sexual advances, and the hostile environment that he had created. The person she met with at Legal was Leslie.

After Jackie had described the situation in detail, she said, "Leslie, I need you to help me. I can't lay the vocal tracks down for my album because what he's doing shakes me up so much. He's undermining my position with my fellow musicians, he's not sharing my album with the label executives, and at the same time he's telling me that I could change all of that if I wanted to!"

Leslie responded, "Jackie, I've heard what you've said, but I have had people come to me with some very disturbing reports about you, too. For example, you and Curtis were supposedly sleeping together, and he is your manager. If that was the case, you should have reported it immediately, but you didn't. You have no tangible evidence except for your word. Even if I believed you, the allegations that you had been sexually active with Curtis could be construed as making all of what you've said mutual or consensual. If that was the case, I would have to discipline you because of this label's superior–employee ethics code, and a letter would go into your permanent file that could ruin your chances of working at another major record label for years to come. From my perspective, we can call this an informal and confidential meeting that is not to be repeated, or you can continue this formally and take your chances. It's your call, Jackie, but you should know that I am disinclined to support your accusations."

In shock, Jackie mumbled a thank-you to Leslie and left her office. The next day Curtis stopped by, smiled, and said, "Your album's status review is next week, and it doesn't look good. I've told you before that it's all about who you know in the music industry, and I have friends at all the majors."

Jackie said, "Curtis, why are you doing this to me? I'm not in love with you anymore. We have no future together. Doesn't that tell you something?"

Curtis smiled and said, "It tells me that you're not interested in a permanent relationship, which is good, because neither am I. And you know that if you want your album to be pitched to the radio stations, or if you want to headline your own tour someday, it all starts with me."

So now here Jackie was, waiting to meet with the president of the record label. As she got up from her chair, she weighed her alternatives and what had led her here. She knew that each record label had its own individual code of ethics, but she hadn't known the reality of the code at SDR until it was too late.

QUESTIONS | EXERCISES

1. Keeping in mind the facts and timeline of this situation, discuss Jackie's situation in terms of its legal and ethical issues.

2. Discuss Jackie's alternatives and the possible professional and private outcomes of her situation.

3. Is Curtis in violation of sexual harassment and/or sexual discrimination laws in the United States?

4. Certainly Curtis has damaged Jackie's performance level; however, has he also created a legally hostile work environment?

*This case is strictly hypothetical; any resemblance to real persons, companies, or situations is coincidental.

Stakeholders' ethical concerns determine whether specific business actions and decisions are perceived as ethical or unethical. In the case of the government, community, and society, what was merely an ethical issue can soon become a legal debate and eventually law. Most ethical conflicts in which there are perceived dangers turn into litigation. Additionally, stakeholders often raise ethical issues when they exert pressure on businesses to make decisions that serve their particular agendas, as when corporate shareholders demand that managers make decisions that boost short-term earnings, thus maintaining or increasing the value of the stock they own in that firm. For example, some U.K. stakeholders believe that Kraft Foods acted irresponsibly when it purchased confectioner Cadbury PLC. Before purchasing Cadbury, Kraft told the Summerdale community that the company would not cut the plant's 400 jobs. The company repeated the pledge on the day it bought Cadbury. The following week, Kraft announced it would close the plant. The community charged Kraft with reneging on its promises and blatantly telling falsehoods to mollify the community's fears.[1]

People make ethical decisions only after they recognize that a particular issue or situation has an ethical component; therefore, a first step toward understanding business ethics is to develop ethical issue awareness. Ethical issues typically arise because of conflicts among individuals' personal moral philosophies and values, the values and culture of the organizations in which they work, and the values of the society in which they live. The business environment presents many potential ethical conflicts. A company's efforts to achieve its organizational objectives may clash with its employees' attempts to fulfill their own personal goals. Similarly, consumers' need for safe and quality products may inhibit a manufacturer's ability to earn adequate profits. The desire of an oil company like BP or Chevron to create a profitable and dependable supply of oil and gas may conflict with the needs of many stakeholders. The fact that BP repeatedly placed profits over the safety of employees and the environment culminated in the 2010 *Deepwater Horizon* explosion, which released 206.2 million gallons of oil into the Gulf of Mexico.[2] Chevron continues to fight an order to pay $8.6 billion to clean up oil pollution in the Ecuadorian rainforest after local residents won a lawsuit against the company.[3]

In this chapter, we consider some of the ethical issues that are emerging in business today, including how these issues arise from the demands of specific stakeholder groups. In the first half of the chapter, we explain certain universal ethical concepts that pervade business ethics, such as honesty, fairness, and integrity. The second half of the chapter explores a number of emerging ethical issues, including misuse of company resources, abusive and intimidating behavior, lying, conflicts of interest, bribery, corporate intelligence, discrimination, sexual harassment, environmental issues, fraud, financial misconduct, insider trading, intellectual property rights, and privacy. We also examine the challenge of determining an ethical issue in business. Because of the global financial meltdown, there are certain practices and products that have or will become issues and will either be defined as illegal or unethical in the coming years. It is important that you understand that what was once a legal activity can become an ethical issue, resulting in well-known practices becoming illegal.

RECOGNIZING AN ETHICAL ISSUE

Although we have described a number of relationships and situations that may generate ethical issues, in practice it can be difficult to recognize specific ethical issues. Failure to acknowledge such obscured ethical issues is a great danger in any organization, particularly if business is treated as a game in which ordinary rules of fairness do not apply. Sometimes people who take this view are willing to do things that are not only unethical but also illegal so that they can maximize their own positions or boost the profits of their organizations. Those involved in the marketplace have an additional set of values related to profit, increased revenue, earnings per share, sales, return on assets, and/or return on investment that they must address. All or part of these objectives come into play within business and impact what people choose to do and how they justify their actions. In one's home life, one does not have the profit motive with which to contend. To be clear, businesspeople do not have a unique set of values from others; rather, the values they have are weighted differently when doing business activities because of the additional responsibilities associated with the marketplace.

Business decisions, like personal decisions, involve an unsettled situation or dilemma. Just because an activity is considered an ethical issue does not mean the behavior is necessarily unethical. An ethical issue is simply a situation, a problem, or even an opportunity that requires thought, discussion, or investigation before a decision can be made. And because the business world is dynamic, new ethical issues are emerging all the time. Table 3.1 defines specific ethical issues identified by employees in the National Business Ethics Survey (NBES). Abusive behavior and lying to employees are personal in nature, but these activities are sometimes committed by individuals in the belief that they are furthering organizational goals. Falsifying time or expenses, safety violations, and abuse of company resources are issues that directly relate to the firm's agenda. Table 3.1 compares the percentage of employees who observed specific types of misconduct over the past two National Business Ethics Surveys.

Employees could engage in more than one form of misconduct; therefore, each type of misconduct represents the percentage of employees who witnessed that particular act. Although Table 3.1 documents many types of ethical issues that exist in organizations, it is impossible to list every conceivable ethical issue. Any type of manipulation or deceit, or even just the absence of transparency in decision making, can create harm to others. For example, collusion is a secret agreement between two or more parties for a fraudulent, illegal, or deceitful purpose. "Deceitful purpose" is the relevant phrase in regard to business ethics, as it suggests trickery, misrepresentation, or a strategy designed to lead others to believe something less than the whole truth.

TABLE 3.1 Specific Types of Observed Misconduct

Behavior	2009 (%)	2007 (%)
Company resource abuse	23	n/a
Abusive behavior	22	21
Lying to employees	19	20
E-mail or Internet abuse	18	18
Conflicts of interest	16	22
Discrimination	14	12
Lying to outside stakeholder	12	14
Employee benefit violations	11	n/a
Health or safety violations	11	15
Employee privacy breach	10	n/a
Improper hiring practices	10	10
Falsifying time or expenses	10	n/a

Source: From 2009 National Business Ethics Survey: An Inside View of Private Sector Ethics, Copyright © 2009, Ethics Resource Center (ERC). Used with permission of the ERC, 2345 Crystal DR. Ste 201, Arlington, VA 22202, www.ethics.org.

Honesty

Honesty refers to truthfulness or trustworthiness. To be honest is to tell the truth to the best of your knowledge without hiding anything. Confucius defined several levels of honesty. The shallowest is called *Li,* which relates to the superficial desires of a person. A key aspect of *Li* is a striving to convey feelings that outwardly are or appear to be honest, but that are ultimately driven by self-interest. The second level is *Yi,* or righteousness, where a person does what is right based on reciprocity. The deepest level of honesty is called *Ren,* and it is based on an understanding of and empathy toward others. The Confucian version of Kant's Golden Rule is to treat your inferiors as you would want your superiors to treat you. As a result, virtues such as familial honor and reputation for honesty become paramount.

Issues related to honesty also arise because business is sometimes regarded as a game governed by its own rules rather than those of society as a whole. Author Eric Beversluis suggests that honesty is a problem because people often reason along these lines:

1. Business relationships are a subset of human relationships that are governed by their own rules, which, in a market society, involve competition, profit maximization, and personal advancement within the organization.

2. Business can therefore be considered a game people play, comparable in certain respects to competitive sports such as basketball or boxing.

3. Ordinary rules and morality do not hold in games like basketball or boxing. (What if a basketball player did unto others as he would have them do unto him? What if a boxer decided it was wrong to try to injure another person?)

4. Logically, then, if business is a game like basketball or boxing, ordinary ethical rules do not apply.[4]

This type of reasoning leads many people to conclude that anything is acceptable in business. Indeed, several books have compared business to warfare—for example, *The Guerrilla Marketing Handbook* and *Sun Tsu: The Art of War for Managers.* The common theme in these books is that surprise attacks, guerrilla warfare, and other warlike tactics are necessary to win the battle for consumer dollars. An example of this mentality at work can be seen in Larry Ellison, the CEO of Oracle. Ellison's warlike mentality is demonstrated by his decision to sell PeopleSoft's technology and let most of its 8,000 employees go. PeopleSoft CEO Craig Conway stated that "Ellison has followed a page straight out of Genghis Khan." Indeed, Ellison has frequently quoted the thirteenth-century Mongol warlord, saying things such as, "It's not enough that we win; everyone else must lose."[5] Ellison was ordered to donate $100 million to charity and pay another $22 million to the attorneys who sued him for alleged stock-trading abuses. Ellison argues that he acted in good faith and in the best interests of Oracle and Oracle's shareholders.[6]

This business-as-war mentality may foster the idea that honesty is unnecessary in business. In addition, an intensely competitive environment creates the potential for companies to engage in questionable conduct. For example, as competition in the market for beer intensified, MillerCoors and Anheuser-Busch increasingly created advertising and offered products that appealed to younger consumers, even though marketing to minors under the age of 21 is illegal.

Many argue, however, that business is not in fact a game like basketball or boxing; because people are not economically self-sufficient, they cannot withdraw from the game of business. Therefore, business ethics must not only make clear what rules apply in the game of business, but must also develop rules appropriate to the involuntary nature of participation in it.

Because of the economic motive, many in business are tempted to engage in the opposite of honesty—dishonesty. *Dishonesty* can be broadly defined as a lack of integrity, incomplete disclosure, and an unwillingness to tell the truth. Lying, cheating, and stealing are actions usually associated with dishonest conduct. The causes of dishonesty are complex and relate to both individual and organizational pressures. Many employees lie to help achieve performance objectives. For example, they may be asked to lie about when a customer will receive a purchase. Lying can be defined as (1) untruthful statements that result in damage or harm; (2) "white lies," which do not cause damage but instead function as excuses or a means of benefitting others; and (3) statements that are obviously meant to engage or entertain without malice. These definitions will become important in the remainder of this chapter.

> "Dishonesty can be broadly defined as a lack of integrity, incomplete disclosure, and an unwillingness to tell the truth."

Fairness

Fairness is the quality of being just, equitable, and impartial. Fairness clearly overlaps with concepts of justice, equity, equality, and morality. There are three fundamental elements that seem to motivate people to be fair: equality, reciprocity, and optimization. In business, **equality** is about how wealth or income is distributed between employees within a company, a country, or across the globe.

Reciprocity is an interchange of giving and receiving in social relationships. Reciprocity occurs when an action that has an effect upon another is reciprocated with an action that has an approximately equal effect. Reciprocity is the return of favors that are approximately equal in value. For example, reciprocity implies that workers be compensated with wages that are approximately equal to their effort. An ethical issue regarding reciprocity for business is the amount CEOs and other executives are paid in relation to their employees. Is a 263 to 1 pay ratio an example of ethical reciprocity? That is the wage differential between a CEO and an average worker in the United States.[7]

Optimization is the trade-off between equity (that is, equality or fairness) and efficiency (that is, maximum productivity). Discriminating on the basis of gender, race, or religion is generally considered to be unfair because these qualities have little bearing upon a person's ability to do a job. The optimal way to hire is to choose the employee who is the most talented, most proficient, most educated, and most able. Ideas of fairness are sometimes shaped by vested interests. One or both parties in the relationship may view an action as unfair or unethical because the outcome was less beneficial than expected.

Integrity

Integrity is one of the most important and oft-cited elements of virtue, and refers to being whole, sound, and in an unimpaired condition. In an organization, it means uncompromising adherence to ethical values. Integrity is connected to acting ethically; in other words, there are substantive or normative constraints on what it means to act with integrity. An organization's integrity usually rests on its enduring values and unwillingness to deviate from standards of behavior.

At a minimum, businesses are expected to follow all applicable laws and regulations. In addition, organizations should not knowingly harm customers, clients, employees, or even other competitors through deception, misrepresentation, or coercion. Although businesspeople often act in their own economic self-interest, ethical business relations should be grounded in honesty, integrity, fairness, justice, and trust. Buyers should be able to trust sellers; lenders should be able to trust borrowers. Failure to live up to these expectations or to abide by laws and standards destroys trust and makes it difficult, if not impossible, to continue business exchanges.[8] These virtues become the glue that holds business relationships together, making everything else more effective and efficient.

ETHICAL ISSUES AND DILEMMAS IN BUSINESS

As mentioned earlier, stakeholders define a business's ethical issues. An **ethical issue** is a problem, situation, or opportunity that requires an individual, group, or organization to choose among several actions that must be evaluated as right or wrong, ethical or unethical. An **ethical dilemma** is a problem, situation, or opportunity that requires an individual, group, or organization to choose among several wrong or unethical actions. There is not a right or ethical choice in a dilemma, only less unethical or illegal choices as perceived by any and all stakeholders.

A constructive next step toward identifying and resolving ethical issues is to classify the issues that are relevant to most business organizations. Table 3.2 reflects the most important ethical issues to shareholders. In this section, we classify ethical issues in relation to misuse of company resources, abusive or intimidating behavior, lying, conflicts of interest, bribery, corporate intelligence, discrimination, sexual harassment, environmental issues, fraud, insider trading, intellectual property rights, and privacy issues.

TABLE 3.2 Shareholder Issues

1. Better interaction and positioning with shareholders

2. Protest votes in director elections

3. Long-term value creation

4. Risk oversight and review risk management processes

5. Expanding roles for women

6. Cost reduction risks in response to the economic crisis and social responsibility

7. Compensation, new disclosure rules, and public image

8. Financial regulatory reform

9. Compliance, risk, and governance processes

10. Economic recovery and the U.S. fiscal outlook

Source: Rick Lash, "Leadership Trends for 2010," *Bloomberg Businessweek*, February 16, 2010, http://www.businessweek.com/managing/content/feb2010/ca20100211_634699_page_2.htm (accessed April 29, 2011); Gary Larkin, "Top 10 Issues Facing Directors in 2010," *The Conference Board*, January 8, 2010, http://tcbblogs.org/governance/2010/01/08/top-10-issues-facing-directors-in-2010/ (accessed April 29, 2011).

Misuse of Company Resources

Although different companies have different viewpoints and policies with regard to the use of company resources, the misuse of these resources has been identified by the Ethics Resource Center as the leading form of observed misconduct in organizations. Very often the enforcement of company policies in this area can be lax as employees find that their coworkers believe they are entitled to certain company resources. Misconduct can range from unauthorized use of equipment and computers to embezzling of company funds. In the retail arena, internal employee theft is a much larger problem than customer shoplifting. Time theft costs can be difficult to measure but are estimated to cost companies hundreds of billions of dollars annually. It is widely believed that the average employee "steals" 4.25 hours per week with late arrivals, leaving early, long lunch breaks, inappropriate sick days, excessive socializing, and engaging in personal activities such as online shopping and watching sports while on the job.[9] All of these activities add up to lost productivity and profits for the employer.

Using company computers for personal business is one of the most common ways employees misuse company resources. While it may not be acceptable for employees to sit in the lobby chatting with relatives or their stock brokers, these same employees can go online and do the same thing, possibly unnoticed by others. Typical examples of using a computer to abuse company time include sending personal emails, shopping, downloading music, doing personal banking, surfing the Internet for information about sports or romance, or visiting social networking sites such as Facebook. It has been found that March Madness, the NCAA basketball tournament, is one of the most significant periods during which employees engage in time theft. Many firms block websites where employees can watch sports events.

Because misuse of company resources is such a widespread problem, many companies, such as Boeing, have implemented official policies delineating the acceptable use of company resources. Boeing's policy states that the use of company resources is acceptable when it does not result in "significant added costs, disruption of business processes, or any other disadvantage to the company."[10] This policy further states that the use of company resources for noncompany purposes is only acceptable when an employee receives explicit permission to do so. This kind of policy is in line with that of many companies, particularly larger firms that can easily lose millions of dollars and thousands of hours of productivity to these activities.

Abusive or Intimidating Behavior

Abusive or **intimidating behavior** is the most common ethical problem for employees, but what does it mean to be abusive or intimidating? These terms can refer to many things—physical threats, false accusations, being annoying, profanity, insults, yelling, harshness, ignoring someone, and unreasonableness—and their meaning can differ from person to person. It is important to understand that within each term there is a continuum. For example, behavior that one person might define as yelling could be another's definition of normal speech. The lack of civility in our society has been a concern, and it is as common in the workplace as elsewhere. The productivity level of many organizations has been damaged by time spent unraveling problematic relationships.

Is it abusive behavior to ask an employee to complete a project rather than be with a family member or relative in a crisis situation? What does it mean to speak profanely? Is profanity only related to specific words or terms that are, in fact, common in today's business world? If you are using words that seem acceptable to you but that others consider profanity, have you just insulted, abused, or disrespected them?

Within the concept of abusive behavior or intimidation, intent should be a consideration. If the employee was trying to convey a compliment, then he or she probably simply made a mistake. What if a male manager asks his female subordinate if she has a date for tonight because she is dressed so nicely? When does the way a word is said (voice inflection) become important? There is also the problem of word meanings by age and within cultures. Is it okay to say "honey" to an employee, fellow employee, employee friend, and/or your superior, and does it depend on gender or location? For example, if you were to call a friend that worked with you "honey" in southern Illinois, Arkansas, or Kentucky, do you have the same acceptability factor as you would in northern Illinois, Michigan, or Minnesota? Does abusive behavior vary by gender? It is possible that the term *honey* could be acceptable speech in some environments, and be construed as being abusive or intimidating in other situations. The fact that we live in a multicultural environment and do business and work with many different cultural groups and nationalities adds to the depth of the ethical and legal issues that may arise.

Bullying is associated with a hostile workplace where someone (or a group) considered a target is threatened, harassed, belittled, verbally abused, or overly criticized. Bullying may create what is referred to as a "hostile environment," but the concept of a hostile environment is generally associated instead with sexual harassment. Regardless, bullying can cause psychological damage that may result in health-endangering consequences to the target. For example, workplace bullying is strongly associated with sleep disturbances. The more frequent the bullying, the higher the risk of sleep disturbance. Other physical symptoms include depression, fatigue, increased sick days, and stomach problems.[11] As Table 3.3 indicates, bullies can use a mix of verbal, nonverbal, and manipulative threatening expressions to damage workplace productivity. Bullying happens more than people realize. One in three American workers has been the victim of bullying, and 20 percent of bullying is technically harassment, which is illegal. Additionally, corporate bullies often target employees who excel at their jobs and are popular with their coworkers.[12]

> "Bullying can cause psychological damage that may result in health-endangering consequences to the target."

TABLE 3.3 Actions Associated with Bullies

1. Spreading rumors to damage others
2. Blocking others' communication in the workplace
3. Flaunting status or authority to take advantage of others
4. Discrediting others' ideas and opinions
5. Use of e-mails to demean others
6. Failing to communicate or return communication
7. Insults, yelling, and shouting
8. Using terminology to discriminate by gender, race, or age
9. Using eye or body language to hurt others or their reputations
10. Taking credit for others' work or ideas

Source: Cathi McMahan, "Are You a Bully?" *Inside Seven*, California Department of Transportation Newsletter, June 1999, 6.

The concept of bullying in the workplace is now considered a legal issue. Some suggest that employers take the following steps to minimize workplace bullying:

- They should have policies in place that make it clear that bullying behaviors will not be tolerated.
- The employee handbook should emphasize that workers must treat each other with respect.
- Employers should encourage employees who feel bullied to report the conduct, and handle complaints much as discriminatory harassment complaints are handled.[13]

Employees should ask the following questions to determine whether or not bullying is occurring at their workplace:

- Is your boss asking obviously impossible things from you without training, and stating that the completed work is never good enough?
- Are surprise meetings called without your knowledge?
- Have others at work told you to stop working, talking, or socializing with them?
- Are you never left alone to do your job without interference?
- Do people feel justified screaming or yelling at you in front of others, and are you punished if you scream back?
- Do human resource officials tell you that your harassment isn't illegal, and that you have to work it out between yourselves?
- Do many people in your organization verify that your torment is real, but do nothing about it?[14]

Bullying can also occur between companies that are in intense competition. Even respected companies such as Intel have been accused of monopolistic bullying. One of Intel's competitors, Advanced Micro Devices (AMD), claimed in a lawsuit that Intel used financial incentives and threats in order to stop AMD from gaining market share. AMD alleged that Intel was preventing the company from being competitive through practices such as paying computer makers rebates for using Intel chips and selling chips below cost. Intel reached an agreement with AMD to pay $1.25 billion to end all legal disputes, antitrust litigation, and patent license suits.[15] However, Intel's actions landed it in trouble in the European Union, where courts found the company guilty of antitrust violations and anticompetitive behavior regarding AMD. Intel was fined a record $1.45 billion, a penalty it continues to fight in court.[16] In many cases, the alleged misconduct can have not only monetary and legal implications but can also threaten reputation, investor confidence, and customer loyalty.

Lying

Earlier in this chapter, we discussed the definitions of **lying** and how lying relates to distorting the truth. We mentioned three types of lies, one of which is joking without malice. The other two can become very troublesome for businesses: lying by commission and lying by omission. *Commission lying* is creating a perception or belief by words that intentionally deceive the receiver of the message; for example, lying about being at work, expense reports, or carrying out work assignments. Commission lying also entails intentionally creating "noise" within the communication that knowingly confuses or deceives the receiver. *Noise* can be defined as technical explanations that the communicator knows the receiver does not understand. It can be the intentional use of communication forms that make it difficult for the receiver to actually hear the true message. Using legal terms or terms relating to unfamiliar processes and systems to explain what was done in a work situation facilitate this type of lie.

Lying by commission can involve complex forms, procedures, contracts, words that are spelled the same but have different meanings, or refuting the truth with a false statement. Forms of commission lying include puffery in advertising. For example, saying that a product is "homemade" when it is made in a factory is lying. "Made from scratch" in cooking technically means that all ingredients within the product were distinct and separate and were not combined prior to the beginning of the production process. One can lie by commission by showing a picture of the product that does not reflect the actual product. This happens frequently in business. For example, many fast-food chains purchase iceberg lettuce for their products but use romaine lettuce in their advertising because they feel it is prettier or more appealing than shredded iceberg lettuce.

Omission lying is intentionally not informing others of any differences, problems, safety warnings, or negative issues relating to the product, service, or company that significantly affect awareness, intention, or behavior. A classic example of omission lying is the tobacco manufacturers' decades-long refusal to allow negative research about the effects of tobacco to appear on cigarettes and cigars. Another example is the behavior of FreeCredit-Report.com, a company that promotes itself as a way for consumers to check their credit scores. Many customers do not realize that FreeCreditReport.com is a credit-monitoring service that costs $14.95 per month and that they will be charged if they do not cancel the service within 30 days. When lying damages others, it can be the focus of a lawsuit. For example, prosecutors and civil lawsuits often reduce misconduct to lying about a fact, such as financial performance, that has the potential to damage others. CEOs at AIG, Lehman Brothers, Fannie Mae, and Freddie Mac were scrutinized to see if they had told the truth about the financial conditions of their companies.

The point at which a lie becomes unethical in business is based on the context of the statement and its intent to distort the truth. A lie becomes illegal if it is determined by the courts to have damaged others. Some businesspeople may believe that one must lie a little or that the occasional lie is sanctioned by the organization. The question you need to ask is whether lies are distorting openness and transparency and other values that are associated with ethical behavior.

Conflicts of Interest

A **conflict of interest** exists when an individual must choose whether to advance his or her own interests, those of the organization, or those of some other group. The three major bond rating agencies—Moody's, Standard & Poor's, and Fitch Ratings—analyze financial deals and assign letters (such as AAA, B, CC) to represent the quality of bonds and other investments. Prior to the financial meltdown, these rating agencies had significant conflicts of interest. The agencies earned as much as three times more for grading complex products than for corporate bonds. They also competed with each other for rating jobs, which contributed to lower rating standards. Additionally, the companies who wanted the ratings were the ones paying the agencies. Because the rating agencies were highly competitive, investment firms and banks would "shop" the different agencies for the best rating. Conflicts of interest were inevitable.

> "To avoid conflicts of interest, employees must be able to separate their private interests from their business dealings."

To avoid conflicts of interest, employees must be able to separate their private interests from their business dealings. Organizations must also avoid potential conflicts of interest when providing products. The U.S. General Accounting Office has found conflicts of interest when the government has awarded bids on defense contracts. The conflicts of interest usually relate to hiring friends, relatives, or retired military officers to enhance the probability of getting a contract.[17]

Bribery

Bribery is the practice of offering something (usually money) in order to gain an illicit advantage. The key issue regarding whether or not something is considered bribery is whether the act is illicit or contrary to accepted morality or convention. Bribery is therefore defined as an unlawful act, but it can also be a business ethics issue because it can be defined differently in varying situations and cultural environments. For example, there is something called active corruption or **active bribery,** meaning that the person who promises or gives the bribe commits the offense. **Passive bribery** is an offense committed by the official who receives the bribe. It is not an offense, however, if the advantage was permitted or required by the written law or regulation of the foreign public official's country, including case law.

Small **facilitation payments** made to obtain or retain business or other improper advantages do not constitute bribery payments for U.S. companies in some situations. Such payments are often made to induce public officials to perform their functions, such as issuing licenses or permits. In the United Kingdom, these facilitation payments are illegal. In most developed countries, it is generally recognized that employees should not accept bribes, personal payments, gifts, or special favors from people who hope to influence the outcome of a decision. However, bribery is an accepted way of doing business in other countries, which creates challenging situations for global businesses. Bribes have been associated with the downfall of many managers, legislators, and government officials. The

World Bank estimates that more than $1 trillion is paid annually in bribes, adding more than 10 percent to the cost of doing business in certain countries.[18]

When a government official accepts a bribe, it is usually from a business that seeks some favor—perhaps a chance to influence legislation that affects it. Giving bribes to legislators or public officials, then, is a business ethics issue. Under the U.S. Foreign Corrupt Practices Act (FCPA), it is illegal for individuals, firms, or third parties doing business in American markets to "make payments to foreign government officials to assist in obtaining or retaining business."[19] Since 2007, companies have paid billions of dollars in fines to the Department of Justice for bribery violations. The law does not apply only to American firms, but to all firms transacting business within the United States. For instance, in 2010 Alcatel-Lucent, a French telecommunications company, paid $137 million to settle U.S. charges that it had bribed foreign government officials.[20]

Corporate Intelligence

Many issues related to corporate intelligence have surfaced in the last few years. Defined broadly, **corporate intelligence** is the collection and analysis of information on markets, technologies, customers, and competitors, as well as on socioeconomic and external political trends. There are three distinct types of intelligence models: a passive monitoring system for early warning, tactical field support, and support dedicated to top-management strategy.

Corporate intelligence (CI) involves an in-depth discovery of information from corporate records, court documents, regulatory filings, and press releases, as well as any other background information about a company or its executives. Corporate intelligence is a legitimate inquiry into meaningful information that can be used in staying competitive. Corporate intelligence, like other areas in business, can be abused if due diligence is not taken to maintain legal and ethical methods of discovery. Computers, LANs (local-area networks), and the Internet have made the theft of trade secrets very easy. Proprietary information like secret formulas, manufacturing schematics, merger or acquisition plans, and marketing strategies all have tremendous value.[21] Today, theft of trade secrets costs companies as much as $300 billion per year.[22] If discovered, corporate espionage can lead to heavy fines and prison sentences. For instance, former engineer Xiang Dong Yu was sentenced to 70 months in prison and fined $12,500 for allegedly stealing trade secrets from Ford Motor Co. The U.S. Attorney's office claimed that Yu had copied 4,000 documents containing confidential information before he left the company.[23] A lack of security and proper training allows one to use a variety of techniques to gain access to a company's vital information. Some techniques for accessing valuable corporate information include physically removing hard drives and copying the information they contain to other machines, hacking, dumpster diving, social engineering, bribery, and hiring away key employees.

Hacking is considered one of the top three methods for obtaining trade secrets. Currently, there are thousands of websites that offer free downloadable and customizable hacking tools that require no in-depth knowledge of protocols or Internet protocol addressing. Hacking has three categories: system, remote, and physical. **System hacking** assumes that the attacker already has access to a low-level, privileged-user account. **Remote hacking** involves attempting to remotely penetrate a system across the Internet. A remote hacker usually begins with no special privileges and tries to obtain higher level or administrative access. Several forms of this type of hacking include unexpected input, buffer overflows, default configurations, and poor system administrator practices. Remote hacking activity against businesses and financial institutions is increasing, with hackers even penetrating the computer network of the company that runs the Nasdaq Stock Market.[24] **Physical hacking** requires that the CI agent enter a facility personally. Once inside, he or she can find a vacant or unsecured workstation with an employee's login name and password. Next, the CI agent searches for memos or unused letterheads and inserts the documents into the corporate mail system. CI agents could also gain physical access to a server or telephone room, look for remote-access equipment, note any telephone numbers written on wall jacks, and place a protocol analyzer in a wiring closet to capture data, user names, and passwords.

Social engineering is another popular method of obtaining valuable corporate information. The basic goals are the same as hacking. **Social engineering** is the tricking of individuals into revealing their passwords or other valuable corporate information. Tactics include casual conversations with relatives of company executives and sending e-mails claiming to be a system administrator and asking for passwords under the guise of "important system administration work." Another common social engineering trick is **shoulder surfing,** in which someone simply looks over an employee's shoulder while he or she types in a password. **Password guessing** is another easy social engineering technique. If a person can find out personal things about someone, he or she might be able to use that information to guess a password. For example, a child's name, birthdays, anniversaries, and Social Security numbers are all common passwords and are easy to guess.

Dumpster diving is messy but very successful for acquiring trade secrets. Once trash is discarded onto a public street or alley, it is considered fair game. Trash can provide a rich source of information for any CI agent. Phone books can give a hacker names and numbers of people to target and impersonate. Organizational charts contain information about people who are in positions of authority within the organization. Memos provide small amounts of useful information and assist in the creation of authentic-looking fake memos.

Whacking is wireless hacking. To eavesdrop on wireless networks, all a CI agent needs is the right kind of radio and to be within range of a wireless transmission. Once tapped into a wireless network, an intruder can easily access anything on both the wired and wireless networks because the data sent over networks are usually unencrypted. If a company is not using wireless networking, an attacker can pose as a janitor and insert a rogue wireless access node into a supposedly secure hard-wired network.

Phone eavesdropping is yet another tool for CI agents. A person with a digital recording device can monitor and record a fax line. By playing the recording back an intruder can reproduce an exact copy of a message without anyone's knowledge. Even without monitoring a fax line, a fax sent to a "communal" fax machine can be read or copied. By picking up an extension or by tapping a telephone, it is possible to record the tones that represent someone's account number and password using a tape recorder. The tape recording can then be replayed over the telephone to gain access to someone else's account.

Discrimination

Although a person's racial and sexual prejudices belong to the domain of individual ethics, racial and sexual discrimination in the workplace create ethical issues within the business world. **Discrimination** on the basis of race, color, religion, sex, marital status, sexual orientation, public assistance status, disability, age, national origin, or veteran status is illegal in the United States. Additionally, discrimination on the basis of political opinions or affiliation with a union is defined as harassment. Discrimination remains a significant ethical issue in business despite decades of legislation attempting to outlaw it.

A company in the United States can be sued if it (1) refuses to hire an individual, (2) maintains a system of employment that unreasonably excludes an individual from employment, (3) discharges an individual, or (4) discriminates against an individual with respect to hiring, employment terms, promotion, or privileges of employment as they relate to the definition of discrimination. Between 75,000 and 100,000 charges of discrimination are filed annually with the **Equal Employment Opportunity Commission** (EEOC).[25]

Race, gender, and age discrimination are major sources of ethical and legal debate in the workplace. Once dominated by European American men, the U.S. workforce today includes significantly more women, African Americans, Hispanics, and other minorities, as well as disabled and older workers. These groups have traditionally faced discrimination and higher unemployment rates and been denied opportunities to assume leadership roles in corporate America. For example, there are only six African American chairs/CEOs of Fortune 500 companies.[26]

Another form of discrimination involves discriminating against individuals on the basis of age. The **Age Discrimination in Employment Act** specifically outlaws hiring practices that discriminate against people between the ages of 49 and 69, as well as those that require employees to retire before the age of 70. The act prohibits employers with 20 or more employees from making employment decisions, including decisions regarding the termination of employment, on the basis of age or as a result of policies requiring retirement after the age of 40. Despite this legislation, charges of age discrimination persist in the workplace. Age discrimination complaints filed with the EEOC have increased 17 percent since the start of the recession, and the number of unemployed older workers increased 330 percent between 2000 and 2010.[27] Given the fact that nearly one-third of the nation's workers will be 55 years old or over by 2016, many companies need to change their approach toward older workers.[28]

To help build workforces that reflect their customer base, many companies have initiated **affirmative action programs,** which involve efforts to recruit, hire, train, and promote qualified individuals from groups that have traditionally been discriminated against on the basis of race, gender, or other characteristics. Such initiatives may be imposed by federal law on an employer that contracts or subcontracts for business with the federal government, as part of a settlement agreement with a state or federal agency, or by court order.[29] For example, Safeway, a chain of supermarkets, established a program to expand opportunities for women in middle- and upper-level management after settling a sex-discrimination lawsuit.[30] However, many companies voluntarily implement affirmative action plans in order to build a more diverse workforce. Although many people believe that affirmative action requires the use of quotas to govern employment decisions, it is important to note that two decades of Supreme Court rulings have made it clear that affirmative action does not permit or require quotas, reverse discrimination, or favorable treatment of unqualified women or minorities. To ensure that affirmative action programs are fair, the Supreme Court has established standards to guide their implementation: (1) There must be a strong reason for developing an affirmative action program; (2) affirmative action programs must apply only to qualified candidates; and (3) affirmative action programs must be limited and temporary and therefore cannot include "rigid and inflexible quotas."[31]

Discrimination can also be an ethical issue in business when companies use race or other personal factors to discriminate against specific groups of customers. Many companies have been accused of using race to deny service or to charge higher prices to certain ethnic groups. For example, four airlines settled lawsuits alleging discrimination against passengers of perceived Arab, Middle Eastern, or Southeast Asian descent. United, American, Continental, and Delta all denied any violations but agreed to spend as much as $1.5 million to train staff on respecting civil rights.[32]

Sexual Harassment

Sexual harassment is a form of sex discrimination that violates Title VII of the Civil Rights Act of 1964. Title VII applies to employers with 15 or more employees, including state and local governments. **Sexual harassment** can be defined as any repeated, unwanted behavior of a sexual nature perpetrated upon one individual by another. It may be verbal, visual, written, or physical and can occur between people of different genders or those of the same gender. Displaying sexually explicit materials "may create a hostile work environment or constitute harassment, even though the private possession, reading, and consensual sharing of such materials is protected under the Constitution."[33] The EEOC receives between 11,000 and 14,000 charges of sexual harassment annually.[34]

Even the United Nations, an organization whose mission is to protect human rights globally, has dealt with a series of sexual harassment cases. Many U.N. employees who have made or faced accusations claim that the system is poorly equipped to handle complaints, resulting in unfair, slow, and arbitrary rulings. For example, one employee who claimed she was harassed for years in Gaza saw her superior cleared by one of his colleagues.[35]

To establish sexual harassment, an employee must understand the definition of a **hostile work environment,** for which three criteria must be met: the conduct was unwelcome; the conduct was severe, pervasive, and regarded by the claimant as so hostile or offensive as to alter his or her conditions of employment; and the conduct was such that a reasonable person would find it hostile or offensive. To assert a hostile work environment, an employee need not prove that it seriously affected his or her psychological well-being nor that it caused an injury; the decisive issue is whether the conduct interfered with the claimant's work performance.[36]

Sexual harassment includes unwanted sexual approaches (including touching, feeling, or groping) and/or repeated unpleasant, degrading, or sexist remarks directed toward an employee with the implied suggestion that the target's employment status, promotion, or favorable treatment depend on a positive response and/or cooperation. It can be regarded as a private nuisance, unfair labor practice, or, in some states, a civil wrong (tort) that may be the basis for a lawsuit against the individual who made the advances and against the employer who did not take steps to halt the harassment. The law is primarily concerned with the impact of the behavior and not its intent. An important facet of sexual harassment law is its focus on the victim's reasonable behaviors and expectations.[37] However, the definition of "reasonable" varies from state to state, as does the concept of expectations. In addition, an argument used by some in defense of what others term sexual harassment is the freedom of speech granted by the First Amendment.

> "An important facet of sexual harassment law is its focus on the victim's reasonable behaviors and expectations."

The key ethical issues associated with sexual harassment are dual relationships and unethically intimate relationships. A **dual relationship** is defined as a personal, loving, and/or sexual relationship with someone with whom you share professional responsibilities. **Unethical dual relationships** are those where the relationship could potentially cause a direct or indirect conflict of interest or a risk of impairment to professional judgment.[38] Another important factor in these cases is intent. If the sexual advances in any form are considered mutual, then consent is created. The problem is that unless the employee or employer gets something in writing before the romantic action begins, consent can always be questioned, and when it comes to sexual harassment, the alleged perpetrator must prove mutual consent.

To avoid sexual misconduct or harassment charges a company should take at least the following steps:

1. *Establish a statement of policy* naming someone in the company as ultimately responsible for preventing harassment at the company.

2. *Establish a definition of sexual harassment* that includes unwelcome advances, requests for sexual favors, and any other verbal, visual, or physical conduct of a sexual nature; that provides examples of each; and that reminds employees that the list of examples is not all-inclusive.

3. *Establish a nonretaliation policy* that protects complainants and witnesses.

4. *Establish specific procedures for prevention* of such practices at early stages. However, if a company puts these procedures in writing, they are expected by law to train employees in accordance with them, measure their effects, and ensure that the policies are being enforced.

5. *Establish, enforce, and encourage* victims of sexual harassment to report the behavior to authorized individuals.

6. *Establish a reporting procedure.*

7. *Make sure that the company has timely reporting requirements to the proper authorities.* Usually, there is a time limitation (ranging from six months to a year) to file a complaint for a formal administrative sexual charge. However, the failure to meet a shorter complaint period (for example, 60 to 90 days) so that a rapid response and remediation may occur and to help to ensure a harassment-free environment could be a company's defense against charges that it was negligent.

Once these steps have been taken, a training program should identify and describe forms of sexual harassment and give examples, outline the grievance procedures, explain how to use the procedures and discuss the importance of them, discuss the penalty for violation, and train employees about the essential need for a workplace that is free from harassment, offensive conduct, or intimidation. A corporation's training program should cover such issues as how to spot sexual harassment; how to investigate complaints, including proper documentation; what to do about observed sexual harassment, even when no complaint has been filed; how to keep the work environment as professional and non-hostile as possible; how to teach employees about the professional and legal consequences of sexual harassment; and how to train management to understand follow-up procedures on incidents.

Environmental Issues

Environmental issues are becoming significant concerns within the business community. The environment involves our physical surroundings, including the natural world and its resources. As the Earth's population continues to grow, reaching more than 7 billion people, our use of natural resources to satisfy needs such as food, shelter, transportation, and especially energy for a mobile society presents increasingly urgent questions. Our interaction with plant and animal species—particularly wildlife habitats—has become an area of critical concern. Environmental concerns are creating ethical issues for individuals, organizations, and public policymakers. The desire for sustainable business means that social responsibility, ethics, and special initiatives must be used to implement effective changes.

In Appendix A, we define sustainability from a strategic business perspective as the potential for the long-term well-being of the natural environment, including all biological entities, as well as for mutually beneficial interactions among nature and individuals, organizations, and business strategies.

Air pollution refers to gases and particulates in the air that can linger or be carried long distances by surface winds. Air pollution has three types of sources: stationary sources such as factories and power plants; mobile sources such as cars, trucks, planes, and trains; and natural sources such as windblown dust and volcanic eruptions. The **Kyoto Protocol**, one example of the world's growing concern about global warming, is an international treaty on climate change committed to reducing emissions of carbon dioxide and five other greenhouse gases and to engaging in emissions trading if member signatories maintain or increase emissions of these gases. The objective is to stabilize greenhouse gas concentrations in the atmosphere at a level that would prevent dangerous climate changes. Most scientists believe that concentrations of greenhouse gases and other air pollutants are contributing to the gradual heating of the earth, a process known as global warming. Some current estimates indicate that, if these objectives are not successfully and completely implemented, the predicted global temperature increase could be between 1.4°C to 5.8°C. Possible massive tidal surges and extreme weather patterns are in store for our planet in the future if countries do not restrict specific gases emanating from business activities. The United States is one of the only countries not to sign the protocol.

Water pollution results from the dumping of raw sewage and toxic chemicals into rivers and oceans, from oil and gasoline spills, and from the burial of industrial wastes in the ground where they may filter into underground water supplies. Fertilizers and pesticides used in farming and grounds maintenance also drain into water supplies with each rainfall. When these chemicals reach the oceans, they encourage the growth of algae that use up all the nearby oxygen, thus killing the sea life. According to the Environmental Protection Agency (EPA), more than one-third of the nation's rivers, lakes, and coastal waters are not safe for swimming or fishing as a result of contaminated runoff. Pollutants come from a variety of sources, and many of them have unknown side effects on people and wildlife.

Buildings are rarely considered major pollution sources. Yet 33 percent of major U.S. energy consumption, 33 percent of major greenhouse gas emissions, and 30 percent of raw material use are the result of buildings.[39] Two competitive certification groups authorize schools, houses, and commercial buildings as "green." These two rival groups, Green Globes and Leadership in Energy and Environmental Design (LEED), are vying for leadership in government adoption of environmental rules that determine whether a building can be called green. There is concern about stakeholder relationships between the two groups. Green Globes is led by a former timber company executive and received much of its seed money from timber and wood products companies. LEED is a nonprofit organization with fewer ties to business interests. Already two states, Maryland and Arkansas, have adopted Green Globes as an alternative to LEED, giving officials an alternative for government-funded construction. The Clinton Presidential Library in Little Rock as well as 7 World Trade Center, the first tower rebuilt near Ground Zero in New York, were certified by Green Globes.[40]

Waste management, the disposal of waste in an environmentally responsible manner, appears to be growing globally. American consumers are the world's biggest producers of trash; they contribute an average of 222 million tons of waste annually, which strains limited landfill space.[41] One waste management technique is **recycling**. Recycling is the reprocessing of materials, especially steel, aluminum, paper, glass, rubber, and some plastics for reuse. Consumers currently consider recycling to be the most important thing they can do to live "greener" lives, as Figure 3.1 demonstrates. However, the recycling process itself uses large amounts of energy. An even bigger problem for the future is that, as the world becomes more capitalistic, more people will buy more things using plastics that are made from oil and that do not degrade easily. Businesses and consumers need to make drastic changes to cut back on energy consumption and waste.

With concerns about pollution growing, many countries and businesses are moving toward sources of **alternative energy**. Although all energy sources require energy and give rise to some degree of pollution from manufacture of the technology, alternative energy sources are considered "green" because they are perceived to lower carbon emissions and create less pollution. Examples of alternative energies include wind power, solar power, geothermal power, hydropower, biofuels, and nuclear power.

Wind power, advocated by some high-profile individuals such as oil tycoon T. Boone Pickens, is gaining widespread support in the United States and has already taken off in several European countries. For instance, one-fifth of Denmark's electricity needs are supplied by wind farms.[42] Because the United States is home to the Great Plains—one of the greatest sources of wind energy in the world—experts believe that wind energy could meet as much as 20 percent of the nation's energy needs.

Solar power, another popular alternative energy source, uses light and heat from the sun to generate electricity. Some California Walmarts already use solar energy to power their stores, and the Obama administration pledged to add solar panels to the roof of the White House to set an example for the rest of the country.[43]

Geothermal power comes from the natural heat inside the Earth, which is extracted by drilling into steam beads. One bonus of geothermal energy is that it can provide a constant

FIGURE 3.1 Consumers' Favorite Green Practices

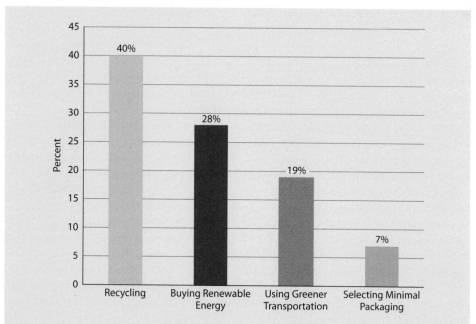

Source: "Environmentally Friendly Choices," *USA Today Snapshots*, March 3, 2009, from Green Seal and Enviromedia Social Marketing survey of 1,000 adults by Opinion Research Corp.

supply of energy every day. Some IKEA stores have started to use geothermal power to meet their energy needs.

Hydropower uses moving water or steam as a source of power. Although water is a renewable resource, hydropower disrupts aquatic life through the creation of dams. The Three Gorges Dam in China has resulted in reducing greenhouse gases for the country, although there are other environmental issues associated with the dam.[44]

Biofuels are fuels derived from organic materials like corn, sugarcane, vegetable oil, algae, and even trash. Although biofuels have been successful in places like Brazil, they remain controversial in the United States. While Brazil uses biofuels made largely from sugarcane, American biofuels are produced from corn. Some people believe that corn-based ethanol is raising the prices and diminishing the quantity of a critical food supply.

Nuclear power is a controversial form of alternative energy. Some organizations have specifically classified nuclear power as green energy because it is pollution free and because uranium is an abundant resource. However, environmental organizations claim that nuclear energy is inefficient, does not cut CO_2 emissions, and creates harmful nuclear waste. The 2011 nuclear crisis in Japan increased stakeholder concerns about the safety of nuclear power. However, nuclear energy is France's main source of power and has reduced the country's nitrogen oxide and other emissions by 70 percent.[45]

Many firms use environmentally friendly practices to demonstrate their commitment to social responsibility. Many companies make contributions to environmental protection organizations, sponsor cleanup events, promote recycling, redesign manufacturing processes to reduce waste and pollution, use more alternative energy sources, and generally reevaluate the effects of their products on the natural environment. Some companies are even becoming involved politically. For example, Exxon Mobil's CEO, Rex Tillerson, encouraged the U.S. Congress to enact a tax on greenhouse gas emissions in order to fight global warming.[46] Companies that do not recognize the potential impact of green programs on future profits and corporate reputation may pay later.

Fraud

When an individual engages in deceptive practices to advance his or her own interests over those of his or her organization or some other group, he or she is committing fraud. In general, **fraud** is any purposeful communication that deceives, manipulates, or conceals facts in order to create a false impression. Fraud is a crime and convictions may result in fines, imprisonment, or both. Global fraud costs organizations more than $2.9 trillion a year; the average company loses about 5 percent of annual revenues to fraud and abuses committed by its own employees.[47] Table 3.4 indicates what senior executives view as the biggest risks to companies. In recent years, accounting fraud has become a major ethical issue, but as we will see, fraud can also relate to marketing and consumer issues as well.

Accounting fraud usually involves a corporation's financial reports, in which companies provide important information on which investors and others base decisions that may involve millions of dollars. If the documents contain inaccurate information, whether intentionally or not, then lawsuits and criminal penalties may result. Dell agreed to pay $100 million to settle Securities and Exchange Commission charges concerning alleged accounting fraud. The company said that their growing profit margins were due to reduced costs, but records showed that Dell executives had discussed "cooking the books" to hit the company's financial goals. The SEC stated that if Dell had honestly reported to investors, almost every quarterly statement would have shown a loss.[48]

TABLE 3.4 Fraud and Misconduct Risk

Misappropriation of assets (e.g. theft of cash, inventory, or intellectual property)	35%
Other illegal or unethical acts (e.g. bribery, corruption, market rigging, or conflicts of interest)	31%
Fraudulent financial reporting (e.g. intentional misstatement of revenue, assets, or liabilities)	14%
All three are an equal threat	20%

Source: "The 2007 Oversight Systems Report on Corporate Fraud," Ethics World, http://www.ethicsworld.org/ethicsandemployees/PDF%20links/ Oversight_2007_Fraud_Survey.pdf (accessed March 12, 2009).

The field of accounting has changed dramatically over the last decade. The profession used to have a club-type mentality, and those who became certified public accountants (CPAs) were not concerned about competition. Now CPAs advertise their skills and short-term results in an environment in which competition has increased and overall billable hours have significantly decreased because of technological innovations. Additionally, accountants are permitted to charge performance-based fees rather than hourly rates, a rule change that encouraged some large accounting firms to promote tax-avoidance strategies for high-income individuals because the firms can charge 10 to 40 percent of the amount of taxes saved.[49]

Pressures on accountants today include time, reduced fees, client requests to alter opinions concerning financial conditions or lower tax payments, and increased competition. Other issues that accountants face daily involve compliance with complex rules and regulations, data overload, contingent fees, and commissions. An accountant's life is filled with rules and data that have to be interpreted correctly, and because of such pressures and the ethical predicaments they spawn, problems within the accounting industry are on the rise.

As a result, accountants must abide by a strict code of ethics that defines their responsibilities to their clients and to the public interest. The code also discusses the concepts of integrity, objectivity, independence, and due care. Despite the standards that the code provides, the accounting industry has been the source of numerous fraud investigations in recent years. Congress passed the Sarbanes–Oxley Act in 2002 to address many of the issues that could create conflicts of interest for accounting firms auditing public corporations. The law generally prohibits accounting firms from providing both auditing and consulting services to the same firm. Additionally, the law specifies that corporate boards of directors must include outside directors with financial knowledge on the company's audit committee.

Marketing fraud—the process of dishonestly creating, distributing, promoting, and pricing products—is another business area that generates potential ethical issues. False or misleading marketing communications can destroy customers' trust in a company. Lying, a major ethical issue involving communication, is a potentially significant problem. In both external and internal communications, it causes ethical predicaments because it destroys trust. The SEC charged three former executives at IndyMac Bancorp with fraud for misleading investors. The executives were accused of hiding information about IndyMac's financial condition during the recession. The executives did not receive any financial benefit because of their actions, but did not disclose important information to their investors in the hope of returning the failing bank to profitability.[50] Misleading marketing can also cost consumers hard-earned money.

False or deceptive advertising is a key issue in marketing communications. One set of laws common to many countries concerns deceptive advertising—that is, advertisements that are not clearly labeled as advertisements. In the United States, Section 5 of the Federal Trade Commission (FTC) Act addresses deceptive advertising. Abuses in advertising can range from exaggerated claims and concealed facts to outright lying, although improper categorization of advertising claims is the critical point. Courts place false or misleading advertisements into three categories: puffery, implied falsity, and literal falsity.

Puffery can be defined as exaggerated advertising, blustering, and boasting upon which no reasonable buyer would rely and is not actionable under the Lanham Act. For example, in a lawsuit between two shaving products companies, the defendant advertised that the moisturizing strip on its shaving razor was "six times smoother" than its competitors' strips, while showing a man rubbing his hand down his face. The court rejected the defendant's argument that "six times smoother" implied that only the moisturizing strip on the razor's head was smoother. Instead, the court found that the "six times smoother" advertising claim implied that the consumer would receive a smoother shave from the defendant's razor as a whole, a claim that was false.[51]

Implied falsity means that the message has a tendency to mislead, confuse, or deceive the public. Advertising claims that use implied falsity are those that are literally true but imply another message that is false. In most cases, accusations of implied falsity can be proved only through time-consuming and expensive consumer surveys, the results of which are often inconclusive. An example of implied falsity might be a company's claim that its product has twice as much of an ingredient in its product, implying that it works twice as well, when in reality the extra quantity of the ingredient has no effect over performance. The characterization of an advertising claim as **literally false** can be divided into two subcategories: *tests prove* (*establishment claims*), in which the advertisement cites a study or test that establishes the claim; and *bald assertions* (*nonestablishment claims*), in which the advertisement makes a claim that cannot be substantiated, as when a commercial states that a certain product is superior to any other on the market. Another form of advertising abuse involves making ambiguous statements in which the words are so weak or general that the viewer, reader, or listener must infer the advertiser's intended message. These "weasel words" are inherently vague and enable the advertiser to deny any intent to deceive. The verb *help* is a good example (as in expressions such as "helps prevent," "helps fight," "helps make you feel").[52] Consumers may view such advertisements as unethical because they fail to communicate all the information needed to make a good purchasing decision or because they deceive the consumer outright.

Labeling issues are even murkier. For example, the Federal Drug Administration (FDA) now regulates tobacco and has banned all flavored cigarettes. Several weeks after the new cigarette rules went into effect, a California importer started selling Djarum-brand clove "kreteks" from Indonesia. Kreteks are the shape and size of cigarettes and have cigarette filters. However, importers argue the product is a "cigar" because the wrapper is a homogenized leaf, the tobacco is air-cured, and the finished product comes in boxes of 12, not 20. If kreteks are defined as cigars, they become legal, but if the FDA calls them cigarettes, then they are illegal.[53]

Advertising and direct sales communication can also mislead consumers by concealing the facts within the message. For instance, a salesperson anxious to sell a medical insurance policy might list a large number of illnesses covered by the policy but fail to mention that it does not include some commonly covered illnesses. Indeed, the fastest-growing area of fraudulent activity is in direct marketing, which uses the telephone and impersonal media to communicate information to customers, who then purchase products via mail, telephone, or the Internet.

Consumer Fraud

Consumer fraud occurs when consumers attempt to deceive businesses for their own gain. Shoplifting, for example, accounts for 35 percent of the losses at the largest U.S. retail chains, although this figure is still far outweighed by the nearly 43 percent of losses perpetrated by store employees, according to the National Retail Security Survey. Together with vendor fraud and administrative error, retail shrinkage costs U.S. retailers $35.5 billion annually (1.44 percent of total sales).[54]

Consumers engage in many other forms of fraud against businesses, including price tag switching, item switching, lying to obtain age-related and other discounts, and taking advantage of generous return policies by returning used items, especially clothing that has been worn (with the price tags still attached). Such behavior by consumers affects retail stores as well as other consumers who, for example, may unwittingly purchase new clothing that has actually been worn.

Consumer fraud involves intentional deception to derive an unfair economic advantage by an individual or group over an organization. Examples of fraudulent activities include shoplifting, collusion or duplicity, and guile. *Collusion* typically involves an employee who assists the consumer in fraud. For example, a cashier may not ring up all merchandise or may give an unwarranted discount. *Duplicity* may involve a consumer staging an accident in a grocery store and then seeking damages against the store for its lack of attention to safety. A consumer may purchase, wear, and then return an item of clothing for a full refund. In other situations, a consumer may ask for a refund by claiming a defect. *Guile* is associated with a person who is crafty or understands right/wrong behavior but uses tricks to obtain an unfair advantage. The advantage is unfair because the person has the intent to go against the right behavior or result. Although some of these acts warrant legal prosecution, they can be very difficult to prove, and many companies are reluctant to accuse patrons of a crime when there is no way to verify wrongdoing. Businesses that operate with the philosophy that "the customer is always right" have found that some consumers will take advantage of this promise and have therefore modified return policies to curb unfair use.

> "Consumer fraud involves intentional deception to derive an unfair economic advantage by an individual or group over an organization."

Financial Misconduct

The failure to understand and manage ethical risks played a significant role in the financial crisis. The difference between bad business decisions and business misconduct can be hard to determine, and there is a thin line between the ethics of using only financial incentives to gauge performance and the use of holistic measures that include ethics, transparency, and responsibility to stakeholders. From CEOs to traders and brokers, all-too-tempting lucrative financial incentives existed for performance in the financial industry.

The global recession was caused in part by a failure on the part of the financial industry to take appropriate responsibility for its decision to utilize risky and complex financial instruments. Loopholes in regulations and the failures of regulators were exploited. Corporate cultures were built on rewards for taking risks rather than rewards for creating value for stakeholders. Ethical decisions were based more on what was legal rather than what was the right thing to do. Unfortunately, most stakeholders, including the public, regulators, and the mass media, do not always understand the nature of the financial risks taken on by banks and other institutions to generate profits. The intangible nature of financial products makes it difficult to understand complex financial transactions. Problems in the subprime mortgage markets sounded the alarm for the most recent recession.

Ethics issues emerged early in subprime lending, with loan officers receiving commissions on securing loans from borrowers with no consequences if the borrower defaulted on the loan. "Liar loans" were soon developed to create more sales and higher personal compensation for lenders. Lenders would encourage subprime borrowers to provide false information on their loan applications in order to qualify for and secure the loans. Some appraisers provided inflated home values in order to increase loan amounts. In other instances consumers were asked to falsify their incomes to make the loans more attractive to the lending institutions. The opportunity for misconduct was widespread. Top managers and even CEOs were complacent about the wrongdoing as long as profits were good. Congress and President Clinton encouraged Fannie Mae and Freddie Mac to support home ownership among low-income people by giving out home mortgages. Throughout the early 2000s, in an economy with rapidly increasing home values, the culture of unethical behavior was not apparent to most people. When home values started to decline and individuals were "upside down" on their loans (owing more than the equity of the home), the failures and unethical behavior of lending and borrowing institutions became more obvious.

The top executives or CEOs are ultimately responsible for the repercussions of their employees' decisions. Top executives at Merrill Lynch awarded $3.6 billion in bonuses shortly before the company's merger with Bank of America in 2008.[55] A combined $121 million went to four top executives, in spite of the fact that Merrill Lynch had to be rescued from bankruptcy by the government. Two ethics issues are at play in this situation. First, paying out the bonuses at all; and second, rushing their distribution in order to complete the job before Bank of America's takeover. Risk management in the financial industry is a key concern, including paying bonuses to executives who failed in their duties. Unfortunately, at the same time that the industry was focused on its own bottom line, regulatory agencies and Congress were not proactive in investigating early cases of financial misconduct and the systemic issues that led to the crisis. The legal and regulatory systems were more focused on individual misconduct rather than systemic ethical failures.

> "The top executives or CEOs are ultimately responsible for the repercussions of their employees' decisions."

This widespread financial misconduct has led to a call for financial reform. The U.S. Treasury Secretary, Timothy Geithner, is trying to change how the government goes about overseeing risk-taking in financial markets. He is pushing for stricter rules on financial management and controls on hedge funds and money market mutual funds. He believes that the United States needs greater openness and transparency, greater oversight and enforcement, and clearer, more commonsense language in its financial system.[56] The Dodd–Frank Wall Street Reform and Consumer Protection Act was passed in 2010 to increase accountability and transparency in the financial industry and to protect consumers from deceptive financial practices. The act established a new Consumer Financial Protection Bureau (CFPB) to protect consumers from unsafe financial products. The CFPB was provided with supervisory power over the credit market. Its responsibility includes making financial products and services easier to understand, curtailing unfair lending and credit card practices, and ensuring the safety of financial products before their launch into the market. The Dodd–Frank Wall Street Reform and Consumer Protection Act also gives federal regulators more power over large companies and financial institutions to prevent them from engaging in risky practices, or becoming "too big to fail." The act also holds CEOs responsible for the behavior of their companies. Large financial firms must retain at least half of top executives' bonuses for at least three years. The goal is to tie compensation to the outcomes of the executives' decisions over time.[57] We will discuss the Dodd–Frank Act and the Consumer Financial Protection Bureau in detail in Chapter 4.

Insider Trading

An insider is any officer, director, or owner of 10 percent or more of a class of a company's securities. There are two types of **insider trading:** illegal and legal. *Illegal insider trading* is the buying or selling of stocks by insiders who possess information that is not yet public. This act, which puts insiders in breach of their fiduciary duty, can be committed by anyone who has access to nonpublic material, such as brokers, family, friends, and employees. In addition, someone caught "tipping" an outsider with nonpublic information can also be found liable. To determine if an insider gave a tip illegally the SEC uses the *Dirks test,* which states that if a tipster breaches his or her trust with the company and understands that this was a breach, he or she is liable for insider trading.

Legal insider trading involves legally buying and selling stock in an insider's own company, but not all the time. Insiders are required to report their insider transactions within two business days of the date the transaction occurred. For example, if an insider sold 10,000 shares on Monday, June 12, he or she would have to report the sale to the SEC by Wednesday, June 14. To deter insider trading, insiders are prevented from buying and selling their company stock within a six-month period, thereby encouraging insiders to buy stock only when they feel the company will perform well over the long term.

Insider trading is often done in a secretive manner by an individual who seeks to take advantage of an opportunity to make quick gains in the market. An interview with inside trader Kenneth T. Robinson reveals why individuals may engage in insider trading. Robinson acted as a middleman by taking tips about corporate mergers from a friend and then passing them on to another friend, who bought stock on behalf of all three men. Robinson did this for many years without being caught until he traded in his own name and helped federal authorities connect the dots. Robinson believed that his personal trade would not cause trouble because it was not in the millions of dollars. In other words, he felt that he would never be discovered. He now faces charges of securities fraud and conspiracy. Surveys have revealed that people who get involved in this type of activity often feel superior to others and are blind to the possibility of being discovered or facing consequences.[58]

Intellectual Property Rights

Intellectual property rights involve the legal protection of intellectual property such as music, books, and movies. Laws such as the Copyright Act of 1976, the Digital Millennium Copyright Act, and the Digital Theft Deterrence and Copyright Damages Improvement Act of 1999 were designed to protect the creators of intellectual property. However, with the advance of technology, ethical issues still abound for websites. For example, until it was sued for copyright infringement and subsequently changed its business model, Napster.com allowed individuals to download copyrighted music for personal use without providing compensation to the artists.

A decision by the Federal Copyright Office (FCO) helped lay the groundwork for intellectual property rules in a digital world. The FCO decided to make it illegal for web users to hack through barriers that copyright holders erect around material released online, allowing only two exceptions. The first exception was for software that blocks users from finding obscene or controversial material on the web, and the second was for people who want to bypass malfunctioning security features of software or other copyrighted goods they have purchased. This decision reflects the fact that copyright owners are typically being favored in digital copyright issues.[59]

However, digital copyrights continue to be a controversial issue in the United States and across the world, and existing laws are often difficult to enforce. Almost a quarter of all Internet traffic involves copyrighted material, including illegally downloaded or uploaded music, movies, and television shows.[60] As China has grown into an economic powerhouse, the market for pirated goods of all types, from DVDs to pharmaceuticals and even cars, has become a multibillion dollar industry.[61] China's government has thus far proven weak in protecting intellectual property, and the underground market for such pirated goods—which are sold all over the world—has grown at a rapid pace. While intellectual property rights infringement always poses a threat to companies that risk losing profits and reputation, it can also threaten the health and well-being of consumers. For example, illegally produced medications, when consumed by unknowing consumers, can cause sickness and even death. Research on software piracy has shown that high levels of economic well-being and an advanced technology sector are effective deterrents to software piracy.[62] Perhaps as China's economy moves forward piracy will become less of a problem, but for now it poses a major threat.

Privacy Issues

Consumer advocates continue to warn consumers about new threats to their privacy, especially within the health care and Internet industries. As the number of people using the Internet increases, the areas of concern related to its use increase as well. Some **privacy issues** that must be addressed by businesses include the monitoring of employees' use of available technology and consumer privacy. Current research suggests that even when businesses use price discounts or personalized services, consumers remain suspicious. However, certain consumers are still willing to provide personal information despite the potential risks.[63]

A challenge for companies today is meeting their business needs while protecting employees' desire for privacy. There are few legal protections of an employee's right to privacy, which allows businesses a great deal of flexibility in establishing policies regarding employee privacy while using company equipment on company property. From computer monitoring and telephone taping to video surveillance and GPS satellite tracking, employers are using technology to manage their productivity and protect their resources.

Electronic monitoring allows a company to determine whether productivity is being reduced because employees are spending too much time on personal activities. Having this information can enable the company to take steps to remedy the situation. Many employers have policies that govern personal phone and Internet use on company time. Additionally, some companies track everything from phone calls and Internet history to keystrokes and the time employees spend at their desks.[64] One study has found that 42 percent of full-time employees with a company-assigned e-mail account "frequently use" it for personal communications, while another 29 percent "sometimes" do. Another survey found that 89 percent of workers say they have sent e-mail from work to an outside party that contained jokes, gossip, rumors, or disparaging remarks, while 14 percent had sent messages that contained confidential or proprietary information, and 9 percent of respondents admitted to sending sexual, romantic, or pornographic text or images.[65] Instituting practices that show respect for employee privacy but do not abdicate the employer's responsibility helps create a climate of trust that promotes opportunities for resolving employee–employer disputes without lawsuits.

There are two dimensions to consumer privacy: consumer awareness of information collection and a growing lack of consumer control over how companies use the personal information that they collect. For example, many are not aware that Google, Inc., reserves the right to track every time you click on a link from one of its searches.[66] Online purchases and even random web surfing can be tracked without a consumer's knowledge. A survey by the Progress and Freedom Foundation found that 96 percent of popular commercial websites collect personally identifying information from visitors.[67]

Personal information about consumers is valuable not only to businesses but also to criminals. More than 11 million Americans have been victims of identity theft. Personal information is stolen and sold online. Although some of this information comes from sources such as social networking profiles, poorly protected corporate files are another major source. U.S. organizations report hundreds of security breaches annually.[68]

Companies are working to find ways to improve consumers' trust in their websites. For example, an increasing number of websites display an online seal from the Better Business Bureau, available only to sites that subscribe to certain standards. A similar seal is available through TRUSTe, a nonprofit global initiative that certifies those websites that adhere to its principles. (Visit http://e-businessethics.com for more on Internet privacy.)

DEBATE ISSUE   TAKE A STAND

Is Google Violating Users' Privacy?

With two billion Google searches a day, Google is the preferred search engine for many consumers. Much of its popularity is due to the superior services it offers. Although Google does not charge for its services, critics point out that Google's services may actually be costing users their right to privacy. Google keeps all of its users' search queries forever, although after 18 months these queries become "anonymized." In other words, they cannot be traced back to the user. Google maintains that it uses these searches responsibly to refine its search engine. It also has privacy disclosures fully visible on its main page. On the other hand, the Third Party Doctrine and the Patriot Act allow the government access to users' Internet information without a judge's oversight for national security purposes. Google has been subpoenaed in the past by investigators for user information. Even anonymized data have been used to track a specific person or computer.[69]

1. Google's storage of user data is legitimate and does not constitute a violation of user privacy.

2. Google should not store users' data as this data can be misused or accessed by the government.

THE CHALLENGE OF DETERMINING AN ETHICAL ISSUE IN BUSINESS

Most ethical issues that concern a business will become visible through stakeholder concerns about an event, activity, or the results of a business decision. The mass media, special interest groups, and individuals, through the use of blogs, podcasts, and other individual-generated media, often generate discussion about the ethical nature of a decision. Another way to determine whether a specific behavior or situation has an ethical component is to ask other individuals in the business how they feel about it and whether they view it as ethically challenging. Trade associations and business self-regulatory groups such as the Better Business Bureau often provide direction for companies in defining ethical issues. Finally, it is important to determine whether the organization has adopted specific policies on the activity. An activity approved of by most members of an organization, if it is also customary in the industry, is probably ethical. An issue, activity, or situation that can withstand open discussion between many stakeholders, both inside and outside the organization, probably does not pose ethical problems.

However, over time, problems can become ethical issues as a result of changing societal values. For instance, products manufactured by Kraft Foods, Inc., such as Kraft

Macaroni and Cheese, Chips Ahoy! cookies, Lunchables, Kool-Aid, Fruity Pebbles, and Oreos, have been staples in almost every home in the United States for decades without becoming subjects of public debate; but when parents, schools, and politicians became more aware that the United States has the most overweight people in the world, things changed.[70] Additionally, since 1980 the rate of obesity in children and adolescents has more than tripled.[71] As a result, Congress proposed legislation focused on the advertising of unhealthy food products to children. Kraft realized that it had encountered an ethical situation regarding the advertising of many of its foods. Some consumer groups might perceive Kraft's $90 million annual advertising budget, which was primarily directed at children, as unethical. Because ignoring the situation could be potentially disastrous, Kraft decided to stop advertising some of its products to children and instead market healthier foods.

Once stakeholders trigger ethical issue awareness and individuals openly discuss it and ask for guidance and the opinions of others, one enters the ethical decision-making process, which we examine in Chapter 5.

SUMMARY

Stakeholders' concerns largely determine whether business actions and decisions are perceived as ethical or unethical. When government, communities, and society become involved, what was merely an ethical issue can quickly become a legal one. Shareholders can unwittingly complicate the ethical conduct of business by demanding that managers make decisions to boost short-term earnings, thus maintaining or increasing the value of their stock.

A first step toward understanding business ethics is to develop ethical issue awareness; that is, to learn to identify which stakeholder issues contain an ethical component. Characteristics of the job, the corporate or local culture, and the society in which one does business can all create ethical issues. Recognizing an ethical issue is essential to understanding business ethics and therefore to creating an effective ethics and compliance program that will minimize unethical behavior. Businesspeople must understand the universal moral constants of honesty, fairness, and integrity. Without embracing these concepts, running a business becomes very difficult.

Fairness is the quality of being just, equitable, and impartial, and it overlaps with concepts of *justice, equity, equality,* and *morality.* The three fundamental elements that motivate people to be fair are equality, reciprocity, and optimization. Equality relates to how wealth is distributed between employees, within a company or a country or globally; reciprocity relates to the return of favors that are approximately equal in value; and integrity relates to a person's character and is made up of two basic parts, a formal relation that one has to oneself and a person's set of terminal, or enduring, values from which he or she does not deviate.

An ethical issue is a problem, situation, or opportunity that requires an individual, group, or organization to choose among several actions that must be evaluated as right or wrong, ethical or unethical. By contrast, an ethical dilemma has no right or ethical solution.

Abusive or intimidating behavior can include physical threats, false accusations, being annoying, profanity, insults, yelling, harshness, ignoring someone, and unreasonableness. Bribery is the practice of offering something (usually money) in order to gain an illicit advantage. A conflict of interest occurs when an individual must choose whether to advance his or her own interests, those of the organization, or those of some other group. Corporate intelligence is the collection and analysis of information on markets, technologies, customers, and competitors, as well as on socioeconomic and external political trends. There are three intelligence models: passive, tactical, and top-management. The tools of corporate intelligence are many. One tool is hacking, which can be accomplished through systemic, remote, and physical means; another is social engineering, in which someone is tricked into revealing valuable corporate information. Other techniques include dumpster diving, whacking, and phone eavesdropping.

Another ethical/legal issue is discrimination, which is illegal in the United States when it occurs on the basis of race, color, religion, sex, marital status, sexual orientation, public-assistance status, disability, age, national origin, or veteran status. Additionally, discrimination on the basis of political opinions or affiliation with a union is defined as harassment. Sexual harassment is a form of sex discrimination. To help build workforces that reflect their customer base, many companies have initiated affirmative action programs. Environmental issues such as air, water, and waste are becoming ethical concerns within business. In general, fraud is any purposeful communication that deceives, manipulates, or conceals facts in order to create a false impression. There are several types of fraud: accounting, marketing, and consumer.

An insider is any officer, director, or owner of 10 percent or more of a class of a company's securities. There are two types of insider trading: legal and illegal. Intellectual property rights involve the legal protection of intellectual property such as music, books, and movies. Consumer advocates continue to warn consumers about new threats to their privacy.

IMPORTANT TERMS FOR REVIEW

honesty	remote hacking	environmental issues
fairness	physical hacking	air pollution
equality	social engineering	Kyoto Protocol
reciprocity	shoulder surfing	water pollution
optimization	password guessing	recycling
integrity	dumpster diving	alternative energy
ethical issue	whacking	fraud
ethical dilemma	phone eavesdropping	accounting fraud
abusive or intimidating behavior	discrimination	marketing fraud
lying	Equal Employment Opportunity Commission	puffery
conflict of interest		implied falsity
bribery	Age Discrimination in Employment Act	literally false
active bribery		labeling issue
passive bribery	affirmative action program	consumer fraud
facilitation payment	sexual harassment	insider trading
corporate intelligence	hostile work environment	intellectual property rights
hacking	dual relationship	privacy issue
system hacking	unethical dual relationship	

RESOLVING ETHICAL BUSINESS CHALLENGES*

Joseph Freberg had been with Alcon for 18 months. He had begun his career right out of college with a firm in the Southeast called Cala Industrial, which specialized in air compressors. Because of the quality of his work with Cala he had been lured away to Alcon, located in Omaha, Nebraska, as a sales manager. Joseph's first six months were hard. Working with older salespeople, trying to get a handle on his people's sales territories, and settling into the corporate culture of a new firm took 16-hour days, six days a week. During those six months, he also bought a house, and his fiancée, Ellen, furnished it, deciding almost everything from the color of the rugs to the style of the curtains.

Ellen had taken a brokerage job with Trout Brothers and seemed to be working even more hours than Joseph. But the long days were paying off. Ellen was now starting to handle some large accounts and was being noticed by the "right" crowd in the wealthier areas of Omaha.

Expenditures for the new home had exceeded Joseph and Ellen's anticipated budget, and the plans for their wedding seemed to be getting more and more elaborate. In addition, Ellen was commuting from her apartment to the new home and then to her job, and the commute killed her car. As a result, she decided to lease something that exuded success.

"Ellen, don't you think a Mercedes is a little out of our range? What are the payments?" inquired Joseph.

"Don't worry, darling. When my clients see me in this—and when we start entertaining at the new house once we're married—the payments on the car will seem small compared with all the money I'll be making," Ellen reassured him as she ran her fingers through his hair and gave him a peck on the cheek.

By the time of their wedding and honeymoon, Joseph and Ellen's bank statement looked like a bullfighter's cape—red. "Don't worry, Joseph, everything will turn out okay. You've got a good

job. I've got a good job. We're young and have drive. Things will straighten out after a while," said Ellen as she eyed a Rolex in a store window.

After the wedding, things did settle down—to a hectic pace, given their two careers and their two sets of parents 1,000 miles away in either direction. Joseph realized that Alcon was a paternal type of organization, with good benefits and tremendous growth potential. He identified whom to befriend and whom to stay away from in the company. His salespeople seemed to tolerate him, sometimes calling him "Little Joe" or "Joey" because of his age, and they were producing—slowly climbing up the sales ladder to the number-one spot in the company.

While doing some regular checkup work on the sales personnel, Joseph found out that Carl had been giving kickbacks to some of his buyers. Carl's sales volume accounted for a substantial amount of the company's existing clientele sales, and he had been a trainer for the company for several years. Carl also happened to be the vice president's son-in-law. Joseph started to check on the other reps more closely and discovered that, although Carl seemed to be the biggest offender, three of his 10 people were doing the same thing. The next day, Joseph looked into Alcon's policy handbook and found this statement: "Our company stands for doing the right thing at all times and giving our customers the best product for the best prices." There was no specific mention of kickbacks, but everyone knew that kickbacks ultimately reduce fair competition, which eventually leads to reduced quality and increased prices for customers.

Talking to a few of the old-timers at Alcon, Joseph learned that there had been only sporadic enforcement of the "no kickback" policy. It seemed that when times were good it became unacceptable and when times were bad it slipped into the acceptable range. And then there was his boss, Kathryn, the vice president. Joseph knew that Kathryn had a tendency to shoot the bearer of bad news. He remembered a story that he had heard about a sales manager coming in to see Kathryn to explain an error in a bid that one of his salespeople had made. Kathryn called in the entire sales staff and fired the salesperson on the spot. Then, smiling, she told the sales manager: "This was your second mistake, so I hope that you can get a good recommendation from personnel. You have two weeks to find employment elsewhere." From then on, the office staff had a nickname for Kathryn—"Jaws."

In an attempt to solve the problem he was facing, Joseph broached the subject of kickbacks at his monthly meeting with Carl. Carl responded, "You've been in this business long enough to know that this happens all the time. I see nothing wrong with this practice if it increases sales. Besides, I take the money out of my commission. You know that right now I'm trying to pay off some big medical bills. I've also gotten tacit clearance from above, but I wouldn't mention that if I were you." Joseph knew that the chain-of-command structure in the company made it very dangerous to go directly to a vice president with this type of information.

As Joseph was pondering whether to do nothing, to bring the matter into the open and state that it was wrong and that such practices were against policy, or to talk to Kathryn about the situation, his cell phone rang. It was Ellen. "Honey, guess what just happened. Kathryn, your boss, has decided to use me as her new broker. Isn't that fantastic?"

What should Joseph do?

QUESTIONS | EXERCISES

1. What are Joseph's ethical problems?
2. Imagine that you are Joseph. Discuss your options.
3. As Joseph, what other information do you feel you need before making your decision?
4. Discuss in which business areas the ethical problems lie.

*This case is strictly hypothetical; any resemblance to real persons, companies, or situations is coincidental.

CHECK YOUR EQ

Check your EQ, or Ethics Quotient, by completing the following. Assess your performance to evaluate your overall understanding of the chapter material.

		Yes	No
1.	Business can be considered a game people play, like basketball or boxing.	Yes	No
2.	Key ethical issues in an organization relate to fraud, discrimination, honesty and fairness, conflicts of interest, and technology.	Yes	No
3.	Only 10 percent of employees observe abusive behavior in the workplace.	Yes	No
4.	Fraud occurs when a false impression exists, which conceals facts.	Yes	No
5.	Putting one's own interests ahead of the organization's is the most commonly observed type of misconduct.	Yes	No

ANSWERS 1. **No.** People are not economically self-sufficient and cannot withdraw from the game of business. 2. **Yes.** See pages 00–00 regarding these key ethical issues and their implications for the organization. 3. **No.** According to Table 3.1, 21 percent of employees observe abusive behavior in the workplace. 4. **No.** Fraud must be purposeful rather than accidental, and exists when deception and manipulation of facts are concealed to create a false impression that causes harm. 5. **Yes.** The most observed form of misconduct in Table 3.1 is putting one's own interests ahead of the company.

CHAPTER 4

THE INSTITUTIONALIZATION OF BUSINESS ETHICS

CHAPTER OBJECTIVES

- To distinguish between the voluntary and mandated boundaries of ethical conduct
- To provide specific mandated requirements for legal compliance in specific subject matter areas related to competition, consumers, safety, and the environment
- To specifically address the requirements of the Sarbanes–Oxley legislation and implementation by the Securities and Exchange Commission
- To describe the passage of the Dodd–Frank Wall Street Reform and Consumer Protection Act along with some of its major provisions
- To provide an overview of regulatory efforts that provide incentives for ethical behavior
- To provide an overview of the recommendations and incentives for developing an ethical corporate culture contained in the Federal Sentencing Guidelines for Organizations
- To provide an overview of highly appropriate core practices and their relationship to social responsibility

CHAPTER OUTLINE

Managing Ethical Risk through Mandated and Voluntary Programs

Mandated Requirements for Legal Compliance
> *Laws Regulating Competition*
> *Laws Protecting Consumers*
> *Laws Promoting Equity and Safety*
> *Laws Protecting the Environment*

Gatekeepers and Stakeholders
> *Accountants*
> *Risk Assessment*

The Sarbanes–Oxley Act
> *Public Company Accounting Oversight Board*
> *Auditor and Analyst Independence*
> *Whistle-Blower Protection*
> *Cost of Compliance*

Dodd–Frank Wall Street Reform and Consumer Protection Act
> *New Financial Agencies*
> *Consumer Financial Protection Bureau*
> *Whistle-Blower Protection*

Laws That Encourage Ethical Conduct

Federal Sentencing Guidelines for Organizations

Highly Appropriate Core Practices
> *Voluntary Responsibilities*
> *Cause-Related Marketing*
> *Strategic Philanthropy*
> *The Importance of Institutionalization in Business Ethics*

AN ETHICAL DILEMMA*

Myron had just graduated from West Coast University with both chemistry-pharmacy and business degrees and was excited to work for

Producto International (PI). He loved having the opportunity to discover medicinal products around the world. His wife, Quan, was also enthusiastic about her job as an import-export agent for a subsidiary of PI.

Producto International was the industry leader, with headquarters in Paris. Worldwide, hundreds of small firms were competing with PI; however, only six had equivalent magnitude. These six had cornered 75 percent of world sales. So many interrelationships had developed that competition had become "managed." However, this did not constitute any illegal form of monopolistic behavior as defined by the European Union.

Myron's first assignment was in India and involved the export of betel nuts to South and perhaps North America. It is estimated that more than 20 million people chew betel nuts in India alone. The betel nut tree is one of the world's most popular plants, and its leaf is used as a paper for rolling tobacco. The betel nut is also mashed or powdered with other ingredients and rolled up in a leaf and sold as candy. Myron quickly found that regular use of the betel nut stains the mouth, gums, and teeth a deep red, which in Asia is desirable.

As Myron was learning more about the betel nut, he came across the following report from the People's Republic of China: "Studies show that the chewing of the spiced betel nut can lead to oral cancer. According to research, 88 percent of China's oral cancer patients are betel nut chewers. Also, people who chew betel nuts and smoke are 90 times more likely to develop oral cancer than nonusers." Myron found that the betel nut primarily affects the central nervous system. It increases respiration while decreasing the workload on the heart (a mild high). Myron also found that demand for it was starting to emerge in the United States as well as in other developed countries.

While Myron was working on the betel nut, David, Myron's boss, also wanted him to work on introducing khat (pronounced "cot") into Asia. Khat is a natural stimulant from a plant grown in East Africa and southern Arabia. Fresh khat leaves, which typically are chewed like tobacco, produce a mild cocaine- or amphetamine-like euphoria. However, the effect is much less intense than that produced by either of those substances, with no reports of a rush sensation or paranoia,

for example. Chewing khat produces a strong aroma and generates intense thirst. Casual users claim that khat lifts spirits, sharpens thinking, and, when its effects wear off, generates mild lapses into depression similar to those observed among cocaine users. The body appears to have a physical intolerance to khat due in part to limitations in how much can be ingested by chewing. As a result, reports suggest that there are no physical symptoms accompanying withdrawal. Advocates of khat use claim that it eases symptoms of diabetes, asthma, and disorders of the stomach and the intestinal tract. Opponents claim that khat damages health, suppresses appetite, and prevents sleep. In the United States, khat has been classified as a schedule IV substance by the Drug Enforcement Agency (DEA); freshly picked khat leaves (that is, picked within 48 hours of harvest) are classified as a schedule I narcotic, the most restrictive category used by the DEA.

After doing his research, Myron delivered his report to David and said, "I really think that, given the right marketing to some of the big pharmaceutical companies, we should have two huge revenue makers."

"That's great, Myron, but the pharmaceutical market is only secondary to our primary market—the two billion consumers to whom we can introduce these products."

"What do you mean, David?" Myron asked.

"I mean that these products are grown legally around the world, and the countries we are targeting have no restrictions on these substances," David explained. "Why not tailor the delivery of the product by country? For example, we find out which flavors people want the betel nut in, in North and South America or the Middle East. The packaging and branding will have to change by country. Pricing strategies will need to be developed relative to our branding decisions, and of course quantity usages will have to be calculated. For example, single, multiple, and super-value sizes need to be explored. The same can be done for khat. Because of your research and your business background, I'm putting you on the marketing team for both. Of course, this means that you're going to have to be promoted and at least for a while live in Hong Kong. I know Quan will be excited. In fact, I told her this morning that she would be working on the same project in Hong Kong. Producto International tries to be sensitive to the dual-career family problems that can occur. Plus you'll be closer to relatives. I told Quan that with living allowances and all of the other things that go with international placement, you two should almost triple your salaries! You don't have to thank me, Myron. You've worked hard on these projects, and now you deserve to have some of the benefits."

Myron went back to his office to think about his and Quan's future. He had heard of another employee who had rejected a similar offer, and that person's career had languished at PI. Eventually, that individual left the industry, never to be heard from again.

QUESTIONS | EXERCISES

1. Identify the social responsibility issues in this scenario.
2. Discuss the advantages and disadvantages of each decision that Myron could make.
3. Discuss the issue of marketing products that are legal but have addictive properties.

*This case is strictly hypothetical; any resemblance to real persons, companies, or situations is coincidental.

T o understand the institutionalization of business ethics, it is important to understand the voluntary and legally mandated dimensions of organizational practices. In addition, there are core practices sometimes called best practices that most responsible firms—those trying to achieve acceptable conduct—embrace and implement. The effective organizational practice of business ethics requires that all three dimensions (legal, voluntary, and core practices) be integrated into an ethics and compliance program. This integration creates an ethical culture that can effectively manage the risks of misconduct. Institutionalization relates to legal and societal forces that provide both rewards and punishment to organizations based on stakeholder evaluations of specific conduct. Institutionalization in business ethics relates to established laws, customs, and expected organizational programs that are considered normative in establishing reputation. This means that deviations from expected conduct are often considered ethical issues and therefore of concern to stakeholders. Institutions provide requirements, structure, and societal expectations that reward and sanction ethical decision making. For example, institutions such as federal regulatory agencies establish rules for appropriate conduct and even suggest core practices for ethical cultures.

In this chapter, we examine the boundaries of ethical conduct and focus on voluntary and core practices and mandated requirements for legal compliance—three important areas in developing an ethical culture. In particular, we concentrate on compliance in specific areas related to competition, consumers, safety, and the environment. We consider the requirements of the Sarbanes–Oxley legislation, its implementation by the Securities and Exchange Commission (SEC), and how its implementation has affected companies. We also examine the Dodd–Frank legislation and its rules affecting the finance industry. We provide an overview of the Federal Sentencing Guidelines for Organizations (FSGO), along with recommendations and incentives for developing an ethical corporate culture. The FSGO, the Sarbanes–Oxley Act and Dodd–Frank legislation, and industry trade associations, as well as societal expectations, support core practices. Finally, we examine voluntary responsibilities and look at how cause-related marketing and strategic philanthropy can be an important core competency in managing stakeholder relationships.

MANAGING ETHICAL RISK THROUGH MANDATED AND VOLUNTARY PROGRAMS

Table 4.1 provides an overview of the three dimensions of institutionalization. **Voluntary practices** include the beliefs, values, and voluntary contractual obligations of a business. All businesses engage in some level of commitment to voluntary activities to benefit both internal and external stakeholders. Google, Inc., works hard to give its employees a positive work environment through its benefits package. In addition to being a famously great place to work, Google offices offer such amenities as swimming pools, gyms, volleyball courts, ping-pong tables, and dance classes. The company even allows employees to bring their dogs to work.[1] Most firms engage in **philanthropy**—giving back to communities and causes. There is strong evidence to suggest that both the law and a sense of ethics increase voluntary corporate social responsibility practices. In addition, research has demonstrated that when both ethical and legal responsibilities are respected through core practices, economic performance benefits.[2]

Core practices are documented best practices, often encouraged by legal and regulatory forces as well as industry trade associations. The **Better Business Bureau** is a leading self-regulatory body that provides directions for managing customer disputes and reviews advertising cases. Core practices are appropriate and common practices that help ensure compliance with legal requirements and societal expectations. Although these practices are not enforced, there are consequences for not engaging in them when misconduct occurs. For example, the Federal Sentencing Guidelines for Organizations (FSGO) suggest that the governing authority (board of directors) be responsible for and assess an organization's ethical and compliance activities. No reporting or investigation is required by government regulatory bodies, but there are incentives for the firms that effectively implement this recommendation. For example, if misconduct occurs, firms may have opportunities to avoid serious punishment. On the other hand, if the board has made no effort to oversee ethics and compliance, its failure could increase and compound the level of punishment the company will suffer. In this way, in institutionalizing core practices the government provides organizations with the opportunity to structure their own approaches and only takes action if violations occur. **Mandated boundaries** are externally imposed boundaries of conduct, such as laws, rules, regulations, and other requirements. Antitrust and consumer protection laws create boundaries that must be respected by companies.

Organizations need to maintain an ethical culture and manage stakeholder expectations for appropriate conduct. They achieve these ends through corporate governance, compliance, risk management, and voluntary activities. The development of these drivers of an ethical culture has been institutionally supported by government initiatives and the

TABLE 4.1 Voluntary Boundary, Core Practices, and Mandated Boundaries of Ethical Decisions

Voluntary boundary	A management-initiated boundary of conduct (beliefs, values, voluntary policies, and voluntary contractual obligations)
Core practice	A highly appropriate and common practice that helps ensure compliance with legal requirements, industry self-regulation, and societal expectations
Mandated boundary	An externally imposed boundary of conduct (laws, rules, regulations, and other requirements)

Source: Adapted from the "Open Compliance Ethics Group (OCEG) Foundation Guidelines," v1.0, Steering Committee Update, December 2005, Phoenix, AZ.

FIGURE 4.1 Elements of an Ethical Culture

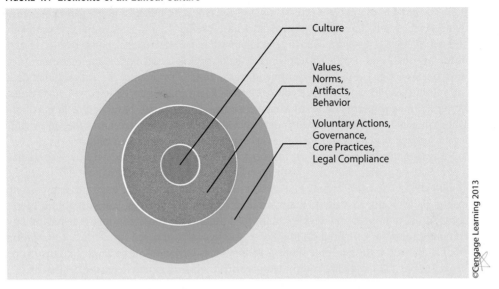

Culture

Values,
Norms,
Artifacts,
Behavior

Voluntary Actions,
Governance,
Core Practices,
Legal Compliance

demands of stakeholders. The compliance element represents areas that must conform to existing legal and regulatory requirements. Established laws and regulatory decisions leave limited flexibility to organizations in adhering to these standards. Corporate governance (as discussed in Chapter 2) is structured by a governing authority that provides oversight as well as checks and balances to make sure that the organization meets its goals and objectives for ethical performance. Risk management analyzes the probability or chance that misconduct could occur based on the nature of the business and its exposure to risky events. Voluntary activities often represent the values and responsibilities that firms accept in contributing to stakeholder needs and expectations.

Figure 4.1 depicts the key elements of an organizational culture. These elements include values, norms, artifacts, and behavior. An ethical culture creates an environment in which to structure behavior that is then evaluated by stakeholders. Values are broad and are viewed as long-term enduring beliefs about issues such as integrity, trust, openness, diversity, and individual respect and responsibility. Norms dictate and clarify desirable behaviors through principles, rules, policies, and procedures. For example, norms could provide guiding principles for anti-bribery issues, sustainability, and conflicts of interest. Artifacts are visible, tangible external symbols of values and norms. Websites, codes of ethics, rituals, language, and physical settings are artifacts. These three elements have different impacts on behaviors. Organizational decisions on such issues as governance, codes of ethics, ethics training, and legal compliance are shaped by the ethical culture.

MANDATED REQUIREMENTS FOR LEGAL COMPLIANCE

Laws and regulations are established by governments to set minimum standards for responsible behavior—society's codification of what is right and wrong. Laws regulating business conduct are passed because some stakeholders believe that business cannot be trusted to do what is right in certain areas, such as consumer safety and environmental protection. Because public policy is dynamic and often changes in response to business abuses and consumer demands for safety and equality, many laws have been passed to resolve specific problems and issues. But the opinions of society, as expressed in legislation, can change over time, and different courts and state legislatures may take diverging views. For example, the thrust of most business legislation can be summed up as follows: Any practice is permitted that does not substantially lessen or reduce competition or harm consumers or society. Courts differ, however, in their interpretations of what constitutes a "substantial" reduction of competition. Laws can help businesspeople determine what society believes at a certain time, but what is legally wrong today may be perceived as acceptable tomorrow, and vice versa.

Instructions to employees to "just obey the law" are meaningless without experience and effective training in dealing with specific legal risk areas. One area that illustrates the complexity of the law is patents. Large technology companies have begun to aggressively defend their patents in order to maintain their strategic advantages. Lawsuits among direct competitors in hardware and software have shifted to the mobile industry as technology companies fight to come out on top. For example, Nokia accused Apple, Inc., of violating 10 of its patents with the Apple iPhone. Patent issues have become so important that some firms, such as IBM and Qualcomm, have created their own patent licensing businesses.[3]

Laws are categorized as either civil or criminal. **Civil law** defines the rights and duties of individuals and organizations (including businesses). **Criminal law** not only prohibits specific actions—such as fraud, theft, or securities trading violations—but also imposes fines or imprisonment as punishment for breaking the law. The primary difference between criminal and civil law is that the state or nation enforces criminal laws, whereas individuals (generally, in court) enforce civil laws. Criminal and civil laws are derived from four sources: the U.S. Constitution (constitutional law), precedents established by judges (common law), federal and state laws or statutes (statutory law), and federal and state administrative agencies (administrative law). Federal administrative agencies established by Congress control and influence business by enforcing laws and regulations to encourage competition and to protect consumers, workers, and the environment. The Consumer Financial Protection Agency was established after the latest financial crisis, which resulted in many consumers losing their homes. State laws and regulatory agencies also exist to achieve these objectives.

The primary method of resolving conflicts and serious business ethics disputes is through lawsuits in which one individual or organization uses civil laws to take another individual or organization to court. However, businesses often want to avoid lawsuits if possible because of the high costs involved. One example is when Starbucks accused Kraft of breaching the terms of an agreement to sell Starbucks products outside Starbucks cafes. Kraft claimed that the agreement never expired, but Starbucks claimed that Kraft had failed to market its packaged coffee products properly. The firms tried to work out the issues without a costly lawsuit.[4] To avoid lawsuits and maintain the standards necessary to reduce risk and create an ethical culture, both legal and organizational standards must be enforced. When violations of organizational standards occur, the National Business Ethics Survey (NBES) notes that many employees do not feel that their company has a strong ethics program. On the other hand, when managers make it an issue to discuss ethics with their employees, misconduct appears to decline. Figure 4.2 demonstrates how talking about ethics at the highest levels of an organization correlates with a reduction in observed ethical misconduct. It is therefore important for a company to have a functioning ethics program in place long before an ethical disaster strikes.

FIGURE 4.2 Percentage of U.S. Workforce Perceiving Top Management Talks about Ethics and NOT Observing Misconduct (NBES Survey 2000–2009)

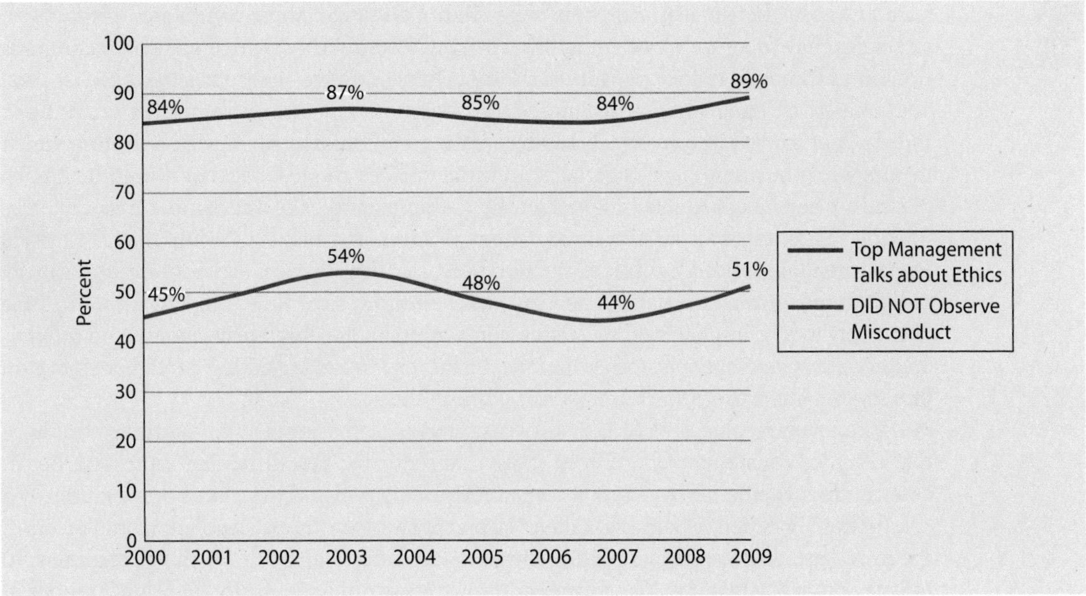

Source: 2009 National Business Ethics Survey, p. 40.

The role of laws is not so much to distinguish what is ethical or unethical as to determine the appropriateness of specific activities or situations. In other words, laws establish the basic ground rules for responsible business activities. Most of the laws and regulations that govern business activities fall into one of five groups: (1) regulation of competition, (2) protection of consumers, (3) promotion of equity and safety, (4) protection of the natural environment, and (5) incentives to encourage organizational compliance programs to deter misconduct, which we will examine later.

Laws Regulating Competition

The issues surrounding the impact of competition on business's social responsibility arise from the rivalry among businesses for customers and profits. When businesses compete unfairly, legal and social responsibility issues can result. Intense competition sometimes makes managers feel that their company's very survival is threatened. In these situations, managers may begin to see unacceptable alternatives as acceptable, and they may begin engaging in questionable practices to ensure the survival of their organizations. Both Intel and Microsoft have been hit with fines amounting to billions of dollars for alleged antitrust activity in Europe. The European Union is famous for being tough on companies suspected of antitrust activities. For instance, Google came under investigation for allegedly manipulating search engine results so that its paid services were placed higher than those of rivals—a possible violation of the European Union's antitrust laws.[5] Being aware of antitrust laws is important for all large corporations around the world.

Size frequently gives some companies an advantage over others. Large firms can often generate economies of scale (for example, by forcing their suppliers to lower their prices) that allow them to put smaller firms out of business. Consequently, small companies and even whole communities may resist the efforts of firms like Walmart, Home Depot, and Best Buy to open stores in their vicinity. These firms' sheer size enables them to operate at such low costs that small, local firms often cannot compete. Some companies' competitive strategies may focus on weakening or destroying a competitor, which can harm competition and ultimately reduce consumer choice. Many countries have laws that restrict such anticompetitive behavior. For instance, China's economic planning agency is attempting to move closer toward international laws by creating new rules against price collusion, which occurs when businesses get together and inflate prices above what they would be if each business priced its products independently.[6] Other examples of anticompetitive strategies include sustained price cuts, discriminatory pricing, and bribery. While the U.S. Justice Department aggressively enforces the Foreign Corrupt Practices Act prohibiting bribery of foreign government officials, the U.K. has even more sweeping antibribery laws. These laws apply to all companies doing business in Britain and prohibit bribes to foreign officials and private businesspeople. Other nations, including China, are taking a tougher stance on bribery and are prosecuting companies caught in the act.[7]

The primary objective of U.S. antitrust laws is to distinguish competitive strategies that enhance consumer welfare from those that reduce it. The difficulty of this task lies in determining whether the intent of a company's pricing policy is to weaken or even destroy a competitor.[8] President Obama has taken a strong position on antitrust violations and reversed the previous administration's policy, which made it more difficult for the government to pursue antitrust violations. The former administration brought a historically low number of antitrust cases to trial.[9] President Obama attempted to follow Europe's model for antitrust cases, which marks a return to a historic norm after eight years of noninterventionism.[10]

Intense competition may also lead companies to resort to corporate espionage. Corporate espionage is the act of illegally taking information from a corporation through computer hacking, theft, intimidation, sorting through trash, and impersonation of organizational members. Estimates show corporate espionage may cost companies nearly $50 billion annually. Unauthorized information collected includes that regarding patents in development, intellectual property, pricing strategies, customer information, unique manufacturing and technological operations, marketing plans, research and development, and future plans for market and customer expansion.[11] Big Lots filed a lawsuit against the research firm Retail Intelligence Group for allegedly inducing store managers to reveal valuable trade secrets. The two companies eventually settled the lawsuit, with Retail Intelligence Group promising that it would no longer contact employees working for Big Lots.[12] Determining an accurate amount for corporate espionage losses is difficult because most companies do not report such losses for fear that the publicity will harm their stock price or encourage further break-ins. Espionage may be carried out by outsiders or by employees—executives, programmers, network or computer auditors, engineers, or janitors who have legitimate reasons to access facilities, data, computers, or networks. They may use a variety of techniques for obtaining valuable information, such as dumpster diving, whacking, and hacking, as discussed in Chapter 3.

Laws have been passed to prevent the establishment of monopolies, inequitable pricing practices, and other practices that reduce or restrict competition among businesses. These laws are sometimes called **procompetitive legislation** because they were enacted to encourage competition and prevent activities that restrain trade (Table 4.2). The Sherman Antitrust Act of 1890, for example, prohibits organizations from holding monopolies in their industry, and the Robinson–Patman Act of 1936 bans price discrimination between retailers and wholesalers.

TABLE 4.2 Laws Regulating Competition

Sherman Antitrust Act, 1890	Prohibits monopolies
Clayton Act, 1914	Prohibits price discrimination, exclusive dealing, and other efforts to restrict competition
Federal Trade Commission Act, 1914	Created the Federal Trade Commission (FTC) to help enforce antitrust laws
Robinson–Patman Act, 1936	Bans price discrimination between retailers and wholesalers
Wheeler–Lea Act, 1938	Prohibits unfair and deceptive acts regardless of whether competition is injured
Lanham Act, 1946	Protects and regulates brand names, brand marks, trade names, and trademarks
Celler–Kefauver Act, 1950	Prohibits one corporation from controlling another where the effect is to lessen competition
Consumer Goods Pricing Act, 1975	Prohibits price maintenance agreements among manufacturers and resellers in interstate commerce
FTC Improvement Act, 1975	Gives the FTC more power to prohibit unfair industry practices
Antitrust Improvements Act, 1976	Strengthens earlier antitrust laws; gives Justice Department more investigative authority
Foreign Corrupt Practices Act, 1977	Makes it illegal to pay foreign government officials to facilitate business or to use third parties such as agents and consultants to provide bribes to such officials
Trademark Counterfeiting Act, 1980	Provides penalties for individuals dealing in counterfeit goods
Trademark Law Revision Act, 1988	Amends the Lanham Act to allow brands not yet introduced to be protected through patent and trademark registration
Federal Trademark Dilution Act, 1995	Gives trademark owners the right to protect trademarks and requires them to relinquish those that match or parallel existing trademarks
Digital Millennium Copyright Act, 1998	Refines copyright laws to protect digital versions of copyrighted materials, including music and movies
Controlling the Assault of Non-Solicited Pornography and Marketing Act (CAN-SPAM), 2003	Bans fraudulent or deceptive unsolicited commercial e-mail and requires senders to provide information on how recipients can opt out of receiving additional messages
Fraud Enforcement and Recovery Act, 2009	Strengthens provisions to improve the criminal enforcement of fraud laws, including mortgage fraud, securities fraud, financial institutions fraud, commodities fraud, and fraud related to the federal assistance and relief program

©Cengage Learning 2013

In law, however, there are always exceptions. Under the McCarran–Ferguson Act of 1944, for example, Congress exempted the insurance industry from the Sherman Antitrust Act and other antitrust laws. Insurance companies were allowed to join together to set insurance premiums at specific industry-wide levels. However, even actions that take place under this legal "permission" could still be viewed as irresponsible and unethical if they neutralize competition and if prices no longer reflect the true costs of insurance protection.

What is legal is not always considered ethical by some interest groups. Major League Baseball has an antitrust exemption dating back to 1922. MLB is the only major sport that has such a sweeping antitrust exemption, although the major effect it has on the game these days is that sports teams cannot relocate without MLB's permission.[13]

Laws Protecting Consumers

Laws that protect consumers require businesses to provide accurate information about their products and services and to follow safety standards (Table 4.3). The first **consumer protection law** was passed in 1906, partly in response to a novel by Upton Sinclair. *The Jungle* describes,

TABLE 4.3 Laws Protecting Consumers

Pure Food and Drug Act, 1906	Prohibits adulteration and mislabeling of foods and drugs sold in interstate commerce
Federal Hazardous Substances Labeling Act, 1960	Controls the labeling of hazardous substances for household use
Truth in Lending Act, 1968	Requires full disclosure of credit terms to purchasers
Consumer Product Safety Act, 1972	Created the Consumer Product Safety Commission to establish safety standards and regulations for consumer products
Fair Credit Billing Act, 1974	Requires accurate, up-to-date consumer credit records
Consumer Goods Pricing Act, 1975	Prohibits price maintenance agreements
Consumer Leasing Act, 1976	Requires accurate disclosure of leasing terms to consumers
Fair Debt Collection Practices Act, 1978	Defines permissible debt collection practices
Toy Safety Act, 1984	Gives the government the power to recall dangerous toys quickly
Nutritional Labeling and Education Act, 1990	Prohibits exaggerated health claims and requires all processed foods to have labels showing nutritional information
Telephone Consumer Protection Act, 1991	Establishes procedures for avoiding unwanted telephone solicitations
Children's Online Privacy Protection Act, 1998	Requires the FTC to formulate rules for collecting online information from children under age 13
Do Not Call Implementation Act, 2003	Directs the FCC and the FTC to coordinate so that their rules are consistent regarding telemarketing call practices including the Do Not Call Registry and other lists, as well as call abandonment
Credit Card Accountability Responsibility and Disclosure Act, 2009	Implemented strict rules on credit card companies regarding topics such as issuing credit to youth, terms disclosure, interest rates, and fees
Dodd–Frank Wall Street Reform and Consumer Protection Act (2010)	Promotes financial reform to increase accountability and transparency in the financial industry, protects consumers from deceptive financial practices, and establishes the Bureau of Consumer Financial Protection

among other things, the atrocities and unsanitary conditions of the meatpacking industry in turn-of-the-century Chicago. The outraged public response to this book and other exposés of the industry resulted in the passage of the Pure Food and Drug Act. Similarly, Ralph Nader had a tremendous impact on consumer protection laws with his book *Unsafe at Any Speed.* His critique of and attack on General Motors' Corvair had far-reaching effects on cars and other consumer products. Other consumer protection laws emerged from similar processes.

Large groups of people with specific vulnerabilities have been granted special levels of legal protection relative to the general population. For example, children and the elderly have received proportionately greater attention than other groups. American society has responded to research and documentation showing that young consumers and senior citizens encounter difficulties in the acquisition, consumption, and disposition of products. Special legal protection provided to vulnerable consumers is considered to be in the public interest.[14] For example, the Children's Online Privacy Protection Act (COPPA) requires commercial Internet sites to carry privacy policy statements, obtain parental consent before soliciting information from children under the age of 13, and provide an opportunity to remove any information provided by children using such sites. Critics of COPPA argue that children aged 13 and older should not be treated as adults on the web. In a study of children ages 10 to 17, nearly half indicated that they would give their name, address, and other demographic information in exchange for a gift worth $100 or more. Internet safety among children is another major topic of concern. Research has shown that filtering and age verification are not effective in making the Internet safer, and businesses, regulators, and parents are all trying to figure out how to better protect children from dangers ranging from online predators to pornography.[15]

Seniors are another highly vulnerable demographic. New laws have taken aim at financial scams directed at seniors, such as free lunch seminars. The state of Arkansas has taken the lead on this issue, conducting police sweeps of suspected scams, increasing fines, and amending laws to impose increased penalties for those who prey on the elderly. Older people are the most vulnerable group when it comes to financial scams as they rely on their savings for retirement security.[16] The role of the FTC's Bureau of Consumer Protection is to protect consumers against unfair, deceptive, or fraudulent practices. The bureau, which enforces a variety of consumer protection laws, is divided into five divisions. The Division of Enforcement monitors compliance with and investigates violations of laws, including unfulfilled holiday delivery promises by online shopping sites, employment opportunities fraud, scholarship scams, misleading advertising for health care products, high-tech and telemarketing fraud, data security, and financial practices.

The Food and Drug Administration regulates food safety, human drugs, tobacco, dietary supplements, vaccines, veterinary drugs, medical devices, cosmetics, products that give off radiation, and biological products. It has the power to authorize the marketing of these products as well as to ban those deemed unsafe for the public.[17] For example, the FDA was considering a ban against certain drinks that contained alcohol and caffeine. One of these drinks, Four Loko, contained as much alcohol as four cans of 12-ounce beers, which was combined with the equivalent of five cups of coffee. The concern was that these caffeinated alcoholic beverages would slow drinkers' perceptions of how drunk they were getting. The FDA issued warning letters to four manufacturers, who subsequently announced they would discontinue the drinks.[18]

Laws Promoting Equity and Safety

Laws promoting equity in the workplace were passed during the 1960s and 1970s to protect the rights of minorities, women, older persons, and persons with disabilities; other legislation has sought to protect the safety of all workers (Table 4.4). Of these laws, probably

TABLE 4.4 U.S. Laws Promoting Equity and Safety

Equal Pay Act of 1963	Prohibits discrimination in pay on the basis of sex
Equal Pay Act of 1963 (amended)	Prohibits sex-based discrimination in the rate of pay to men and women doing the same or similar jobs
Title VII of the Civil Rights Act of 1964 (amended in 1972)	Prohibits discrimination in employment on the basis of race, color, sex, religion, or national origin
Age Discrimination in Employment Act, 1967	Prohibits discrimination in employment against persons between the ages of 40 and 70
Occupational Safety and Health Act, 1970	Designed to ensure healthful and safe working conditions for all employees
Title IX of Education Amendments of 1972	Prohibits discrimination based on sex in education programs or activities that receive federal financial assistance
Vocational Rehabilitation Act, 1973	Prohibits discrimination in employment because of physical or mental handicaps
Vietnam Era Veterans Readjustment Act, 1974	Prohibits discrimination against disabled veterans and Vietnam War veterans
Pension Reform Act, 1974	Designed to prevent abuses in employee retirement, profit-sharing, thrift, and savings plans
Equal Credit Opportunity Act, 1974	Prohibits discrimination in credit on the basis of sex or marital status
Age Discrimination Act, 1975	Prohibits discrimination on the basis of age in federally assisted programs
Pregnancy Discrimination Act, 1978	Prohibits discrimination on the basis of pregnancy, childbirth, or related medical conditions
Immigration Reform and Control Act, 1986	Prohibits employers from knowingly hiring a person who is an unauthorized alien
Americans with Disabilities Act, 1990	Prohibits discrimination against people with disabilities and requires that they be given the same opportunities as people without disabilities
Civil Rights Act of 1991	Provides monetary damages in cases of intentional employment discrimination

©Cengage Learning 2013

the most important to business is Title VII of the Civil Rights Act, originally passed in 1964 and amended several times since. Title VII specifically prohibits discrimination in employment on the basis of race, sex, religion, color, or national origin. The Civil Rights Act also created the Equal Employment Opportunity Commission (EEOC) to help enforce the provisions of Title VII. Among other things, the EEOC helps businesses design affirmative action programs. These programs aim to increase job opportunities for women and minorities by analyzing the present pool of employees, identifying areas where women and minorities are underrepresented, and establishing specific hiring and promotion goals, along with target dates for meeting those goals.

Other legislation addresses more specific employment practices. The Equal Pay Act of 1963 mandates that women and men who do equal work must receive equal pay. Wage differences are allowed only if they can be attributed to seniority, performance, or qualifications. The Americans with Disabilities Act of 1990 prohibits discrimination against people with disabilities. Despite these laws, inequities in the workplace still exist. According to the U.S. Women's Bureau, women earn an average of 80 cents for every dollar that men earn. The disparity in wages is higher for African American women (69 cents for every dollar a white man earns) and Hispanic women (60 cents for every dollar).[19]

Congress has also passed laws that seek to improve safety in the workplace. By far the most significant of these is the Occupational Safety and Health Act of 1970, which mandates that employers provide safe and healthy working conditions for all workers. The **Occupational Safety and Health Administration** (OSHA), which enforces the act, makes regular surprise inspections to ensure that businesses maintain safe working environments.

Even with the passage and enforcement of safety laws, many employees still work in unhealthy or dangerous environments. Safety experts suspect that companies underreport industrial accidents to avoid state and federal inspection and regulation. The current emphasis on increased productivity has been cited as the main reason for the growing number of such accidents. Competitive pressures are also believed to lie behind the increases in manufacturing injuries. Greater turnover in organizations due to downsizing means that employees may have more responsibilities and less experience in their current positions, thus increasing the potential for accidents. Overworked employees are often cited as a primary factor in careless accidents, both in the United States and in other countries. For instance, in Korea cab drivers are often required to work 24-hour shifts. One analysis determined that drowsiness has caused over 27 percent of Korean commercial driver crashes on the highway within a three-year period. Similar findings on the dangers of drowsiness have been reported in the United States.[20]

Laws Protecting the Environment

Environmental protection laws have been enacted largely in response to concerns over business's impact on the environment, which began to emerge in the 1960s. **Sustainability** has become a buzzword in recent years, yet many people may not even think about what it means. According to the UN's World Commission on the Environment and Development, sustainable means "meeting the present needs without compromising the ability of future generations to meet their own needs."[21] The environment and sustainability are more important topics than ever. Thirty-five percent of people say that they are more interested in environmental issues than previously and expect companies to be more environmentally responsible than they used to be.[22] Consumer interest in sustainability is so great that many firms have even made being green a competitive issue. For example, General Electric has an Ecomagination report that allows consumers to see all the green measures it has taken. It has also implemented green marketing social media campaigns on YouTube and Flickr to spread awareness of its green initiatives.

Many people have questioned the cost-benefit analyses often used in making business decisions. Such analyses try to take into account all factors in a situation, represent them with dollar figures, calculate the costs and benefits of the proposed action, and

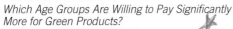

FIGURE 4.3 The Green Consumer

Which Age Groups Are Willing to Pay Significantly More for Green Products?

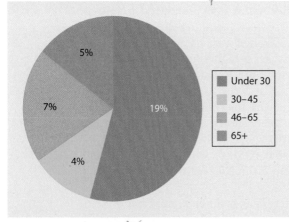

- Under 30
- 30–45
- 46–65
- 65+

5%
7%
19%
4%

Base: 2,000 internet users aged 18+

Source: Mintel, Green Marketing—US—April 2010, http://academic.mintel.com. libproxy.unm.edu/sinatra/oxygen_academic/search_results/show&/display/id=482522 (accessed January 23, 2011).

determine whether an action's benefits outweigh its costs. The problem, however, is that it is difficult to arrive at an accurate monetary valuation of environmental damage or physical pain and injury. In addition, people outside the business world often perceive such analyses as inhumane. Figure 4.3 indicates the importance of green products to consumers. Even though not everyone buys green products frequently, 73 percent of American consumers want companies to support environmental causes.[23]

The **Environmental Protection Agency** (EPA) was created in 1970 to coordinate environmental agencies involved in enforcing the nation's environmental laws. The major areas of environmental concern relate to air, water, and land pollution. Large corporations are being encouraged to establish pollution-control mechanisms and other policies favorable to the environment. Otherwise, these companies could deplete resources and damage the health and welfare of society by focusing only on their own economic interests. For example, 3M voluntarily stopped making Scotchguard, a successful product for 40 years with $300 million in sales, after tests showed that it did not decompose in the environment.[24]

Increases in toxic waste in the air and water, as well as noise pollution, have prompted the passage of a number of laws (Table 4.5). Many environmental protection laws have resulted in the elimination or modification of goods and services. For instance, leaded gasoline was phased out during the 1990s by the EPA because catalytic converters, which reduce pollution caused by automobile emissions and are required by law on most vehicles, do not work properly with leaded gasoline. Increased Corporate Average Fuel Economy (or CAFE) standards are forcing companies to figure out ways for their cars to get better gas mileage. For many carmakers, a major part of this strategy involves increased production and sales of hybrid vehicles, as well as improving electric car and hydrogen fuel-cell technology.

The harmful effects of toxic waste on water life and on leisure industries such as resorts and fishing have raised concerns about proper disposal of these wastes. Few disposal sites meet EPA standards, so businesses must decide what to do with their waste until disposal sites become available. Some firms have solved this problem by illegal or unethical measures: dumping toxic wastes along highways, improperly burying drums containing toxic chemicals, and discarding hazardous waste at sea. However, trying to pinpoint who is responsible for environmental degradation is not always easy, especially when it involves different countries. For example, an Ecuadorian judge ordered the gas giant Chevron to pay $9.5 billion to clean up oil pollution in the Ecuadorian rainforest. The original lawsuit was filed in 1993 by 30,000 plaintiffs against Texaco, which was acquired by Chevron in 2001. This could mean that Chevron is liable for the damages, but Chevron claims that a 1998 agreement that Texaco signed with Ecuador absolves it of liability. Additionally, Chevron officials are crying foul, claiming that the government colluded with the plaintiffs in the ruling. Chevron appealed to U.S. courts to block

TABLE 4.5 Laws Protecting the Environment

Clean Air Act, 1970	Established air-quality standards; requires approved state plans for implementation of the standards
National Environmental Policy Act, 1970	Established broad policy goals for all federal agencies; created the Council on Environmental Quality as a monitoring agency
Coastal Zone Management Act, 1972	Provides financial resources to the states to protect coastal zones from overpopulation
Federal Water Pollution Control Act, 1972	Designed to prevent, reduce, or eliminate water pollution
Noise Pollution Control Act, 1972	Designed to control the noise emission of certain manufactured items
Federal Insecticide, Fungicide and Rodenticide Act, 1972	Provides federal control of pesticide distribution, sale, and use
Endangered Species Act, 1973	Provides a program for the conservation of threatened and endangered plants and animals and the habitats in which they are found
Safe Drinking Water Act, 1974	Established to protect the quality of drinking water in the United States; focuses on all waters actually or potentially designed for drinking use, whether from above ground or underground sources; establishes safe standards of purity and requires all owners or operators of public water systems to comply with primary (health-related) standards
Energy Policy and Conservation Act, 1975	Requires auto dealers to have "gas mileage guides" in their showrooms
Toxic Substances Control Act, 1976	Requires testing and restricts use of certain chemical substances to protect human health and the environment
Resource Conservation and Recovery Act, 1976	Gives the EPA authority to control hazardous waste from the "cradle to grave"; includes the generation, transportation, treatment, storage, and disposal of hazardous waste, as well as a framework for the management of nonhazardous waste
Comprehensive Environmental Response, Compensation, and Liability Act, 1980	Created a tax on chemical and petroleum industries and provides broad federal authority to respond directly to releases or threatened releases of hazardous substances that may endanger public health or the environment
Emergency Planning and Community Right-to-Know Act, 1986	The national legislation on community safety, designed to help local communities protect public health, safety, and the environment from chemical hazards
Oil Pollution Act, 1990	Streamlined and strengthened the EPA's ability to prevent and respond to catastrophic oil spills; a trust fund financed by a tax on oil is available to clean up spills when the responsible party is incapable of doing so or unwilling to do so
Pollution Prevention Act, 1990	Focuses industry, government, and public attention on reducing the amount of pollution through cost-effective changes in production, operation, and raw materials use

©Cengage Learning 2013

(continued)

TABLE 4.5 Laws Protecting the Environment *(continued)*

Food Quality Protection Act, 1996	Amended the Federal Insecticide, Fungicide and Rodenticide Act and the Federal Food Drug and Cosmetic Act; the requirements include a new safety standard—reasonable certainty of no harm—that must be applied to all pesticides used on foods
Energy Policy Act, 2005	Addresses the way energy is produced in the United States in terms of energy efficiency, renewable energy, oil and gas, coal, Tribal energy, nuclear matters and security, vehicles and motor fuels, hydrogen, electricity, energy tax incentives, hydropower and geothermal energy, and climate change technology
Energy Independence and Security Act, 2007	Established a plan for moving the United States toward a more sustainable future, with steps that include the phasing out of the incandescent light bulb

the penalty.[25] Congress regularly evaluates legislation to increase the penalties for disposing of toxic wastes. Disposal issues remain controversial because, although everyone acknowledges that the wastes must go somewhere, no community wants them dumped in its own backyard.

One solid-waste problem is the result of rapid innovations in computer hardware, which render machines obsolete after just 18 months. Today, hundreds of millions of computers have reached obsolescence and tens of millions of these are expected to end up in landfills. Cell phones are another problem, with billions destined for landfills. Computers and cell phones both contain such toxic substances as lead, mercury, and polyvinyl chloride, which can leach into the soil and contaminate groundwater when disposed of improperly. Websites like electronicsrecycling.org help consumers find locations to recycle their phones and computers. The Environmental Protection Agency hosts its own electronics recycling program, which collects around 67 million pounds of electronics a year. Stores like Staples and Best Buy offer limited recycling programs, and companies like Dell and Samsung are all seeking to extend the availability of recycling for their products.[26]

GATEKEEPERS AND STAKEHOLDERS

Trust is the glue that holds businesses and their stakeholders together. Trust creates confidence and helps to forge relationships of reliance between businesses and stakeholders. Trust also allows businesses to depend upon one another as they make transactions or exchange value. Ethics helps create the foundational trust between two parties in a transaction. There are many people who must trust and be trusted to make business work properly. Sometimes these parties are referred to as *gatekeepers*. Gatekeepers include accountants, who are essential to certifying the accuracy of financial information, as well as lawyers, financial rating agencies, and even financial reporting services. All of these groups are critical in providing information that allows stakeholders to gain an understanding of the financial position of an organization. Most of these gatekeepers operate with professional codes of ethics and face legal consequences, or even disbarment, if they fail to operate within agreed-upon principles of conduct. Therefore, there is a strong need for gatekeepers to uphold ethical standards and remain independent through using standard methods and procedures that can be audited by other gatekeepers, the regulatory system, and investors.

Accountants

Accountants measure and disclose financial information, with an assurance of accuracy, to the public. Managers, investors, tax authorities, and other stakeholders who make resource allocation decisions are all groups who use the information provided by accountants. Accountants make certain basic assumptions about their clients. One assumption is that the corporation is an entity that is separate and distinct from its owners, and that it will continue to operate as such in the future. Another assumption is that a stable monetary system (such as the dollar) is in place and that all necessary information concerning the

> "Gatekeepers such as lawyers, financial rating agencies, and even financial reporting services must have high ethical standards."

business is available and presented in an understandable manner. Accountants have their own set of rules, one of which is that, if there is a choice between equally acceptable accounting methods, they should use the one that is least likely to overstate or misdirect. During the 2008–2009 financial meltdown, many people lost trust in accountants and auditors because a few made unscrupulous decisions.

Some accountants have not been adhering to their responsibilities to stakeholders. For example, Arthur Andersen was once a standard bearer for integrity. But at Andersen, growth became the priority, and its emphasis on recruiting and retaining big clients came at the expense of quality and independent audits. The company linked its consulting business in a joint cooperative relationship with its audit arm, which compromised its auditors' independence, a quality crucial to the execution of a credible audit. The firm's focus on growth generated a fundamental change in its corporate culture, one in which its high-profit consulting business was regarded as more important than providing objective auditing services. This situation presented a conflict of interest and posed a problem when partners had to decide how to treat questionable accounting practices discovered at some of Andersen's largest clients. Ultimately, Arthur Andersen was dissolved because of its ties to the Enron scandal. Gatekeepers such as lawyers, financial rating agencies, and even financial reporting services must have high ethical standards. These groups must be trusted by all stakeholders, and most operate with professional codes of ethics.

Risk Assessment

Another critical gatekeeper group in the financial meltdown was risk assessors of financial products. The top three companies in the world that independently assess financial risks are Standard & Poor's, Moody's, and Fitch. They assess risk and express it through letters ranging from "AAA," which is the highest grade, to "C," which is junk. Different rating services use the same letter grades, but use various combinations of upper- and lowercase letters to differentiate themselves.

As early as 2003, financial analysts and the three global rating firms suspected that there were some major problems with the way their models were assessing risk. In 2005 Standard & Poor's realized that its algorithm for estimating the risks associated with debt packages was flawed. As a result, it asked for comments on improving its equations. In

2006–2007 many governmental regulators and others started to realize what the rating agencies had known for years: their ratings were not very accurate. One report stated that the high ratings given to debt were based on inadequate historical data, and that businesses were "ratings shopping" to obtain the best rating possible. Investment banks were among some of the worst offenders, paying for ratings and therefore causing conflicts of interest. The amount of revenue these three companies annually receive is approximately $5 billion.

Further investigations uncovered many disturbing problems. Moody's, Standard & Poor's, and Fitch had all violated a code of conduct "that required analysts to consider only credit factors, not the potential impact on Moody's, or an issuer, an investor or other market participant."[27] These companies had also become overwhelmed by an increase in the volume and sophistication of the securities they were asked to review. Finally, faced with less time to perform the due diligence expected of them, analysts began to cut corners.

SEC Chairman Mary Schapiro believes that the SEC must take more drastic measures to implement oversight for credit-rating firms—a group that was largely blamed for not catching risky activity in the financial sector sooner. Part of the problem, as Schapiro sees it, is that credit rating firms are paid by the securities that they rank. This creates a conflict of interest problem and can affect the reliability of the ratings.[28] No organization is exempt from criticism over its level of transparency. While large financial firms have been the target of most of the public's anger over risk taking and executive pay, even nonprofits are now being scrutinized more carefully.[29]

THE SARBANES–OXLEY (SOX) ACT

In 2002, largely in response to widespread corporate accounting scandals, Congress passed the Sarbanes–Oxley Act to establish a system of federal oversight of corporate accounting practices. In addition to making fraudulent financial reporting a criminal offense and strengthening penalties for corporate fraud, the law requires corporations to establish codes of ethics for financial reporting and to develop greater transparency in financial reporting to their investors and other stakeholders.

Supported by both Republicans and Democrats, the Sarbanes–Oxley Act was enacted to restore stakeholder confidence after accounting fraud at Enron, WorldCom, and hundreds of other companies resulted in investors and employees losing much of their savings. During the resulting investigations, the public learned that hundreds of corporations had not reported their financial results accurately. Many stakeholders came to believe that accounting firms, lawyers, top executives, and boards of directors had developed a culture of deception to ensure investor approval and gain a competitive advantage. As a result of public outrage over the accounting scandals, the Sarbanes–Oxley Act garnered nearly unanimous support not only in Congress but also from government regulatory agencies, the president, and the general public. When President George W. Bush signed the Sarbanes–Oxley Act into law, he emphasized the need for new standards of ethical behavior in business, particularly among the top managers and boards of directors responsible for overseeing business decisions and activities.

At the heart of the Sarbanes–Oxley Act is the **Public Company Accounting Oversight Board,** which monitors accounting firms that audit public corporations and establishes standards and rules for auditors in accounting firms. The law gave the board investigatory and disciplinary power over auditors and securities analysts who issue reports about corporate performance and health. The law attempts to eliminate conflicts of interest by prohibiting accounting firms from providing both auditing and consulting services to the same client companies without special permission from the client firm's audit committee; it also places limits on the length of time lead auditors can serve a particular client. The Sarbanes–Oxley Act requires corporations to take greater responsibility for their decisions and to provide leadership based on ethical principles. Additionally, the law modifies the attorney-client relationship to require lawyers to report wrongdoing to top managers and/or the board of directors. It also provides protection for "whistle-blowing" employees who might report illegal activity to authorities. This "whistle-blower" protection was strengthened with the passage of the Dodd–Frank Act several years later.

> "The Sarbanes–Oxley Act requires corporations to take greater responsibility for their decisions and to provide leadership based on ethical principles."

On the other hand, SOX has raised a number of concerns. The complex law imposed additional requirements and costs on executives. Additionally, the new act has caused many firms to restate their financial reports to avoid penalties. Big public companies spent thousands of hours and millions of dollars annually to make sure that someone was looking over the shoulder of key accounting personnel at every step of every business process, according to Financial Executives International. Perhaps the biggest complaint is that in spite of Sarbanes–Oxley, financial executives were able to discover new loopholes that allowed them to engage in the misconduct that contributed to the global financial crisis.

Public Company Accounting Oversight Board

SOX aims to promote transparency, reduce conflict of interest, and increase accountability. For instance, one of its provisions called for the establishment of a board to oversee the audit of public companies in order to protect the interests of investors and further the public interest in the preparation of informative, accurate, and independent audit reports for companies. The Public Company Accounting Oversight Board has faced several challenges throughout the years, including a lawsuit claiming that the board was unconstitutional. The lawsuit made it all the way to the Supreme Court. The court ruled in favor of the board. The board must also overcome obstacles with foreign auditing firms. Although Sarbanes–Oxley requires registration from all auditors listed on the U.S. public market including foreign auditors, several countries, such as the European Union and China, do not allow inspections of their auditing firms.[30]

Auditor and Analyst Independence

The Sarbanes–Oxley Act also seeks to eliminate conflicts of interest among auditors, security analysts, brokers, dealers, and the public companies they serve in order to ensure enhanced financial disclosures of public companies' true conditions. To accomplish auditor independence, Section 201 prohibits registered public accounting firms from providing both non-audit and audit services to a public company. National securities exchanges and registered securities associations have already adopted similar conflict-of-interest rules for security analysts, brokers, and dealers who recommend equities in research reports. Such independence enables the Sarbanes–Oxley Act to better ensure compliance with the requirement for more detailed financial disclosures representing public companies' true condition. For example, registered public accounting firms are now required to identify all material correcting adjustments to reflect accurate financial statements. Also, all material off-balance-sheet transactions and other relationships with unconsolidated entities that affect current or future financial conditions of a public company must be disclosed in each annual and quarterly financial report. In addition, public companies must also report "on a rapid and current basis" material changes in the financial condition or operations.

Whistle-Blower Protection

Employees of public companies and accounting firms are also accountable to report unethical behavior. The Sarbanes–Oxley Act intends to motivate employees through whistle-blower protection that prohibits the employer from taking certain actions against employees who lawfully disclose private employer information to parties in a judicial proceeding involving a fraud claim, among others. Whistle-blowers are also granted a remedy of special damages and attorneys' fees. Unfortunately, this law did not protect certain whistle-blowers from being penalized prior to the financial crisis. Whistle-blowers at Lehman Brothers, Madoff Securities, and Stanford Financial Group (which also operated a Ponzi scheme) warned auditors and government officials of misconduct at the company. Some whistle-blowers were fired or, after losing lawsuits filed against the offending company, were forced to pay large sums in back pay and attorney's fees.[31] These cases prompted a provision for stronger whistle-blower protection in the Dodd–Frank Act, discussed in the next section.

Cost of Compliance

The national cost of compliance of the Sarbanes–Oxley Act can be extensive and can include internal costs, external costs, and auditor fees. For example, Section 404 requires companies to document both the results of financial transactions and the processes they have used to generate them. A company may have thousands of processes that have never been written down. Writing down the processes is time consuming and costly.[32] Also, because the cost of compliance is so high for many small companies, some publicly traded companies have even considered delisting themselves from the U.S. Stock Exchange.

However, studies have shown that although compliance costs were high shortly after Sarbanes–Oxley was passed, they have declined over the years. Companies have reported that their compliance costs have decreased 50 percent from their level when the laws were put into effect. One reason why the costs may be decreasing is that companies have more experience with Sarbanes–Oxley, and therefore require less time to complete the process. While 61 percent of respondent companies believed that the costs of Sarbanes–Oxley exceeded its benefits during the first year, today approximately 70 percent believe the benefits outweigh the costs.[33]

DODD–FRANK WALL STREET REFORM AND CONSUMER PROTECTION ACT

In 2010 President Obama signed into law the Dodd–Frank Wall Street Reform and Consumer Protection Act. It was heralded as "a sweeping overhaul of the financial regulatory system . . . on a scale not seen since the reforms that followed the Great Depression."[34] The new law seeks to improve financial regulation, increase oversight of the industry, and prevent the types of risk-taking, deceptive practices, and lack of oversight that led to the 2008–2009 financial crisis.[35] It contains sixteen provisions that include increasing the accountability and transparency of financial institutions, creating a bureau to educate consumers in financial literacy and protect them from deceptive financial practices, implementing additional incentives for whistle-blowers, increasing oversight of the financial industry, and regulating the use of complex derivatives.

Response to the law was split along party lines, with vocal opponents as well as proponents. Critics have several concerns, including claims that the rules on derivatives are too burdensome, the belief that such wide-scale changes will create chaos in the regulatory system, and the fear that the government will gain too much power.[36] Other companies, such as JPMorgan, claim that they support the law in general but oppose certain provisions.[37] The following sections will describe some of the most notable provisions of the Dodd–Frank Act.

New Financial Agencies

One of the provisions of the Dodd–Frank Act instituted the creation of two new financial agencies, the Office of Financial Research and the Financial Stability Oversight Council. The Office of Financial Research is charged with improving the quality of financial data available to government officials and creating a better system of analysis for the financial industry.[38] The Financial Stability Oversight Council (FSOC) is responsible for maintaining the stability of the financial system in the United States through monitoring the market, identifying threats, promoting market discipline among the public, and responding to major risks that threaten stability.[39] FSOC has the authority to limit or closely supervise financial risks, create stricter standards for banking and nonbanking financial institutions, and disband financial institutions that present a serious risk to market stability.[40] The addition of these two new agencies is intended not only to improve information collecting and oversight, but also to close the types of loopholes that allowed financial industries to engage in risky and deceptive conduct prior to the financial crisis.

Consumer Financial Protection Bureau

Another agency that the Dodd–Frank Act created was the **Consumer Financial Protection Bureau (CFPB),** an independent agency within the Federal Reserve System that "regulate[s] the offering and provision of consumer financial products or services under the Federal consumer financial laws."[41] One of the problems leading up to the 2008–2009 financial crisis was the fact that average investors often did not understand the complex financial products they were purchasing. The CFPB aims to protect consumers from this problem in the future. The government has granted the agency supervisory power over credit markets as well as the authority to monitor lenders and ensure that they are in compliance with the law.[42] The CFPB also has the responsibility to curtail unfair lending and credit card practices, enforce consumer financial laws, and check the safety of financial products before their launch into the market.[43]

The CFPB is not without its critics. Several financial firms and legislators believe that the bureau has too much power. Criticism has been levied against President Obama for bypassing Senate approval in appointing White House advisor Elizabeth Warren to oversee the creation of the bureau, and lawmakers in opposition to the CFPB are attempting to curb the bureau's powers, possibly through budget cuts. Additionally, financial institutions are concerned that the bureau's powers could lead to strict sanctions.[44] On the other hand, two-thirds of Americans agree that some type of financial reform is needed.[45] To protect against misconduct at all levels, the CFPB has oversight powers over institutions often accused of questionable dealings, such as payday lenders and debt collectors.[46] The goal of the CFPB is to create a more equitable and transparent financial environment for consumers.

Whistle-blower Bounty Program

It is clear that the whistle-blower provisions implemented in Sarbanes–Oxley were not enough to prevent the massive misconduct occurring at business institutions before the financial crisis. To encourage more employees to come forward when they witness misconduct, the Dodd–Frank law instituted a whistle-blower bounty program. Whistle-blowers who report financial fraud to the Securities and Exchange Commission and Commodities Exchange Commission are eligible to receive 10 percent to 30 percent of fines and settlements if their reports result in convictions of more than $1 million in penalties.[47]

While this will likely encourage more people to step forward, there are some challenges that will need to be considered for the program to be a success. For instance, the SEC will almost certainly be flooded with tips, some of which will come from people who just want the money. Still, the SEC is optimistic that half the tips it receives will result in payouts, suggesting that the number of credible whistle-blower complaints will increase dramatically.[48]

LAWS THAT ENCOURAGE ETHICAL CONDUCT

Violations of the law usually begin when businesspeople stretch the limits of ethical standards, as defined by company or industry codes of conduct, and then choose to engage in schemes that either knowingly or unwittingly violate the law. In recent years, new laws and regulations have been passed to discourage such decisions—and to foster programs designed to improve business ethics and social responsibility (Table 4.6). The most important of these are the Federal Sentencing Guidelines for Organizations (FSGO), the Sarbanes–Oxley Act, and the Dodd–Frank Act. One of the goals of these acts is to require employees to report observed misconduct. The development of reporting systems has advanced, with most companies having some method for employees to report observed misconduct. However, while reported misconduct is up, a sizable percentage of employees still do not report misconduct, as Figure 4.4 shows.

TABLE 4.6 Institutionalization of Ethics through the U.S. Sentencing Guidelines for Organizations

1991	*Law:* U.S. Sentencing Guidelines for Organizations created for federal prosecutions of organizations. These guidelines provide for just punishment, adequate deterrence, and incentives for organizations to prevent, detect, and report misconduct. Organizations need to have an effective ethics and compliance program to receive incentives in the case of misconduct.
2004	*Amendments:* The definition of an effective ethics program now includes the development of an ethical organizational culture. Executives and board members must assume the responsibility of identifying areas of risk, providing ethics training, creating reporting mechanisms, and designating an individual to oversee ethics programs.
2007–2008	*Additional definition of a compliance and ethics program:* Firms should focus on due diligence to detect and prevent misconduct and to promote an organizational culture that encourages ethical conduct. More details are provided, encouraging the assessment of risk and outlining appropriate steps in designing, implementing, and modifying ethics programs and training that will include all employees, top management, and the board or governing authority. These modifications continue to reinforce the importance of an ethical culture in preventing misconduct.
2010	*Amendments:* Chief compliance officers are directed to make their reports to their firm's board rather than to the general counsel. Companies are encouraged to create hotlines, perform self-audit programs, and adopt controls to detect misconduct internally. More specific language has been added to the word *prompt* in regards to what it means to promptly report misconduct. The amendment also extends operational responsibility to all personnel within a company's ethics and compliance program.

Source: "U.S. Sentencing Guidelines Changes Become Effective November 1," FCPA Compliance and Ethics Blog, November 2, 2010, http://tfoxlaw.wordpress.com/2010/11/02/us-sentencing-guidelines-changes-become-effective-november-1/ (accessed March 15, 2011).

FIGURE 4.4 Percentage of Employees Who Do Not Report Observed Misconduct

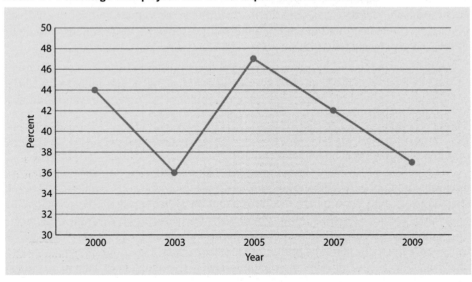

Source: 2007 National Business Ethics Survey, p. 17.

FEDERAL SENTENCING GUIDELINES FOR ORGANIZATIONS

As mentioned in Chapter 1, Congress passed the FSGO in 1991 to create an incentive for organizations to develop and implement programs designed to foster ethical and legal compliance. These guidelines, which were developed by the U.S. Sentencing Commission, apply to all felonies and class A misdemeanors committed by employees in association with their work. As an incentive, organizations that have demonstrated due diligence in developing effective compliance programs to discourage unethical and illegal conduct may be subject to reduced organizational penalties if an employee commits a crime.[49] Overall, the government philosophy is that legal violations can be prevented through organizational values and a commitment to ethical conduct.

The commission delineated seven steps that companies must implement to demonstrate due diligence:

1. A firm must develop and disseminate a code of conduct that communicates required standards and identifies key risk areas for the organization.

2. High-ranking personnel in the organization who are known to abide by the legal and ethical standards of the industry (such as an ethics officer, vice president of human resources, general counsel, and so forth) must have oversight over the program.

3. No one with a known propensity to engage in misconduct should be put in a position of authority.

4. A communications system for disseminating standards and procedures (ethics training) must also be put into place.

5. Organizational communications should include a way for employees to report misconduct without fearing retaliation, such as an anonymous toll-free hotline or an ombudsman. Monitoring and auditing systems designed to detect misconduct are also required.

6. If misconduct is detected, then the firm must take appropriate and fair disciplinary action. Individuals both directly and indirectly responsible for the offense should be disciplined. In addition, the sanctions should be appropriate for the offense.

7. After misconduct has been discovered, the organization must take steps to prevent similar offenses in the future. This usually involves making modifications to the ethical compliance program, conducting additional employee training, and issuing communications about specific types of conduct.

The government expects these seven steps for compliance programs to undergo continuous improvement and refinement.[50]

These steps are based on the commission's determination to emphasize compliance programs and to provide guidance for both organizations and courts regarding program effectiveness. Organizations have flexibility about the type of program they develop; the seven steps are not a checklist requiring that legal procedures be followed to gain certification of an effective program. Organizations implement the guidelines through effective core practices that are appropriate for their firms. The programs they put into effect must be capable of reducing the opportunity that employees have to engage in misconduct.

FIGURE 4.5 Employees Who Feel Better Prepared Are More Likely to Report

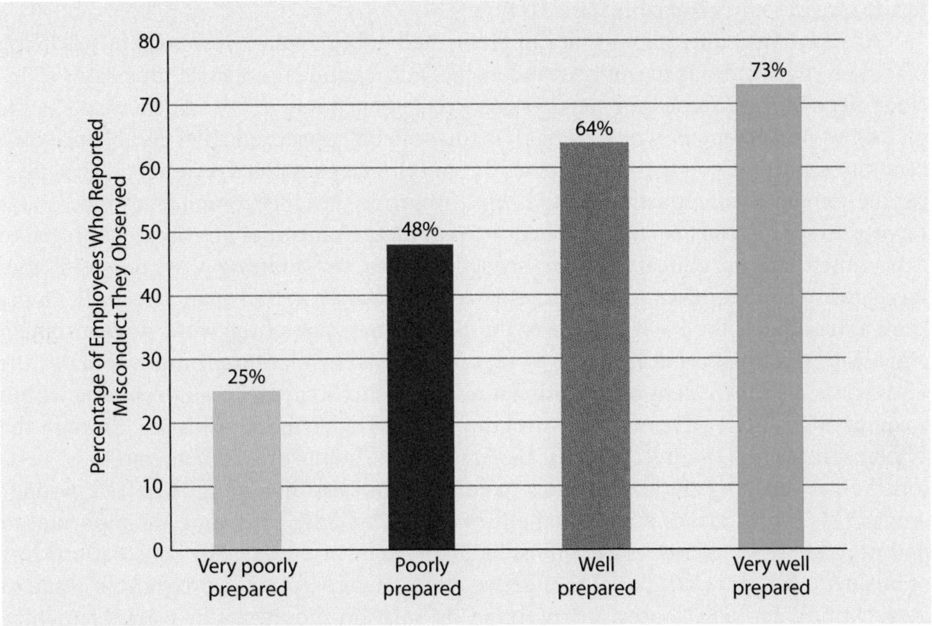

Source: *Research Brief from the 2009 NBES* (Arlington, VA: Ethics Resource Center, 2010), 19.

A 2004 amendment to the FSGO requires that a business's governing authority be well informed about its ethics program with respect to content, implementation, and effectiveness. This places the responsibility squarely on the shoulders of the firm's leadership, usually the board of directors. The board must ensure that there is a high-ranking manager accountable for the day-to-day operational oversight of the ethics program; provide for adequate authority, resources, and access to the board or an appropriate subcommittee of the board; and ensure that there are confidential mechanisms available so that the organization's employees and agents may report or seek guidance about potential or actual misconduct without fear of retaliation. Finally, the board is required to oversee the discovery of risks and to design, implement, and modify approaches to deal with those risks. Figure 4.5 demonstrates that prepared employees are more likely to respond to various ethical and legal risks. If board members do not understand the nature, purpose, and methods available to implement an ethics program, the firm is at risk of inadequate oversight and ethical misconduct that may escalate into a scandal.[51]

A 2005 Supreme Court decision held that the federal sentencing guidelines were not mandatory but should serve only as recommendations for judges to use in their decisions. Some legal and business experts believe that this decision might weaken the implementation of the FSGO, but most federal sentences have remained in the same range as before the Supreme Court decision. The guidelines remain an important consideration in developing an effective ethics and compliance program.[52]

The 2007–2008 amendments to the FSGO extend the required ethics training to members of the board or governing authority, high-level personnel, employees, and the organizations' agents. This change applies not only oversight but mandatory training to all levels of the organization. Merely distributing a code of ethics does not meet the training requirements. The 2007 and 2008 amendments now require most governmental contractors to provide ethics and compliance training.

As new FSGO amendments are implemented, more explicit responsibility is being placed on organizations to improve and expand ethics and compliance provisions to include all employees and board members, as was demonstrated in four amendments to the guidelines implemented in 2010. The first amendment concerned chief compliance officers who report misconduct to the general counsel. The guidelines recommend simplifying the complexity of reporting relationships by having the chief compliance officer make reports directly to the board or to a board committee. Companies are also encouraged to extend their internal ethical controls through hotlines, self-auditing programs, and other mechanisms so that misconduct can be detected internally rather than externally. In the third amendment, the FSGO added more specific language of the word *prompt* to help employees recognize what it means to report an ethical violation promptly. Finally, the FSGO amended the extent of operational responsibility to apply to all personnel within a company's ethics and compliance program.[53] The Department of Justice, through the Thompson Memo (Deputy Attorney General Larry Thompson's 2003 memo to U.S. Attorneys), advanced general principles to consider in cases involving corporate wrongdoing. This memo makes it clear that ethics and compliance programs are important to detecting the types of misconduct most likely to occur in a particular corporation's line of business. If it does not have an effective ethics and compliance program in place to detect ethical and legal lapses, a firm found in violation should not be treated leniently. Additionally, the prosecutor generally has wide latitude in determining when, whom, and whether to prosecute violations of federal law. U.S. attorneys are directed that charging for even minor misconduct may be appropriate when the wrongdoing was perpetuated by a large number of employees in a particular role—for example, sales staff or procurement officers—or was condoned by upper management. Without an effective program to identify an isolated rogue employee involved in misconduct, a firm may suffer serious consequences in terms of regulatory issues, enforcement, and sentencing.[54] Therefore, there is general agreement both in law and administrative policy that an effective ethics and compliance program is necessary to prevent misconduct and reduce the legal consequences if it does occur.

HIGHLY APPROPRIATE CORE PRACTICES

The focus of core practices is on developing structurally sound organizational practices and structural integrity for financial and nonfinancial performance measures, rather than on an individual's morals. Although the Sarbanes–Oxley Act and the Dodd–Frank Act provide standards for financial performance, most ethical issues relate to nonfinancials such as marketing, human resource management, and customer relations. Abusive behavior, lying, and conflict of interest are still three significant issues.

A group called the Integrity Institute has developed an integrated model that attempts to standardize the measurement of nonfinancial performance. Methodologies have been developed to assess communications, compensation, social responsibility, corporate culture, leadership, risk, and stakeholder perceptions, as well as the more subjective aspects of earnings, corporate governance, technology, and other important nonfinancial areas. The model exists to establish a standard that can predict the sustainability and success of an organization. The Integrity Institute uses measurement to an established standard as the basis for certification of integrity.[55] The Institute is one of the first to attempt such a model.

The majority of executives and board members want to measure nonfinancial performance, but no standards currently exist. The Open Compliance Ethics Group (oceg. org) has developed benchmarking studies that are available to organizations wanting to conduct self-assessments to determine the elements of their ethics programs. Developing organizational systems and processes is a requirement of the regulatory environment, but organizations are given considerable freedom in developing ethics and compliance programs. Core practices do exist and can be identified in every industry. Trade associations' self-regulatory groups and research studies often provide insights into the expected best core practices. An important priority is for each firm to assess its legal and ethical risk areas, and then to develop structures to prevent, detect, and quickly correct any misconduct.

Consider McDonald's approach to answering critics about nutritional guidance. The company began an initiative to provide nutritional information on its product packaging worldwide, becoming the first in its industry to do so. McDonald's has been seeking to build trust and loyalty among consumers, something that the company proclaims is highly important to it. McDonald's also offers new healthier products, such as oatmeal and apple slices in children's meals. The company withdrew its supersize meals after a damaging portrayal of the company in the film *Super Size Me*. The product sizes available at McDonald's are small, medium, and large, but upgrading to a bigger-portion size remains inexpensive.[56]

Voluntary Responsibilities

Voluntary responsibilities fall into the category of a business's contributions to its stakeholders. Businesses that address their voluntary responsibilities provide four major benefits to society. They:

1. Improve quality of life and help make communities places where people want to do business, raise families, and enjoy life. Thus, improving the quality of life in a community makes it easier to attract and retain employees and customers.

2. Reduce government involvement by providing assistance to stakeholders.

3. Develop employee leadership skills. Many firms, for example, use campaigns by the United Way and other community service organizations as leadership- and skill-building exercises for their employees.

4. Help create an ethical culture and values that can act as a buffer to organizational misconduct.[57]

The most common way that businesses demonstrate their voluntary responsibilities is through donations to local and national charitable organizations. In 2010 the Giving USA Foundation reported charitable contributions of $291 billion. Individual donations were $212 billion, and corporations gave $15.3 billion.[58] For example, Wells Fargo & Co. contributes around $100 million annually in community grants to non-profits and schools, and $45 million and 100,000 volunteers to Habitat for Humanity and other housing nonprofits. The company also purchases green energy, and it has a website devoted to financial education. Its employees have donated hundreds of

> "The most common way that businesses demonstrate their voluntary responsibilities is through donations to local and national charitable organizations."

thousands of hours to charities around the nation.[59] Indeed, many companies have become concerned about the quality of education in the United States after realizing that the current pool of prospective employees lacks many basic work skills. Recognizing that today's students are tomorrow's employees and customers, firms such as Kroger, Campbell Soup Co., American Express, Apple, Xerox, and Coca-Cola have donated money, equipment, and employee time to help improve schools in their communities and throughout the nation.

The Walmart Foundation, the charitable giving branch of Walmart Inc., donated $624 million in 2010 to charities and communities across the globe, and it is the largest corporate cash contributor in the nation.[60] The money supported a variety of causes such as child development, education, the environment, and disaster relief. Walmart officials believe that the company can make the greatest impact on communities by supporting issues and causes that are important to its customers and associates in their own neighborhoods. By supporting communities at the local level, Walmart encourages customer loyalty and goodwill.[61]

Cause-Related Marketing

The first attempts by organizations to coordinate organizational goals with philanthropic giving emerged with cause-related marketing in the early 1980s. **Cause-related marketing** ties an organization's product(s) directly to a social concern through a marketing program.

With cause-related marketing, a percentage of a product's sales is usually donated to a cause that appeals to the target market. Yoplait, for example, generates proceeds for the Susan G. Komen for the Cure cause with its Save Lids to Save Lives program. Susan G. Komen for the Cure is a nonprofit organization that raises funds to fight breast cancer. Yoplait has created an annual philanthropic program that encourages consumers to send in pink Yoplait yogurt lids. For every lid sent in, Yoplait donates 10 cents to Susan G. Komen for the Cure, with a guaranteed donation of $500,000. Within 12 years, the program has resulted in more than $25 million in contributions.[62]

Cause-related marketing can also affect buying patterns. For such a campaign to be successful, consumers must sympathize with the cause, the brand and cause must be perceived as a good fit, and consumers should be able to transfer their feelings about the cause to their brand perceptions and purchase intentions. Surveys reveal that 85 percent of consumers view a brand more favorably if it contributes to a cause they care about, and 80 percent indicate their willingness to switch to a brand that supports a worthwhile cause if its price and quality are equal to its competitors'.[63] This finding lends support to the idea that cause-related marketing can help to bolster a firm's reputation.

Cause-related marketing has its weaknesses too, however. For instance, consumers may perceive a company's cause-related campaign as merely a publicity stunt, especially if they cannot understand the link between the campaign and the company's business practices. Also, cause-related campaigns are often of short duration, so consumers may not adequately associate the business with a particular cause. Strategic philanthropy is more holistic, as it ties the company's philanthropic giving to its overall strategy and objectives.

Strategic Philanthropy

Strategic philanthropy is the synergistic and mutually beneficial use of an organization's core competencies and resources to deal with key stakeholders so as to bring about organizational and societal benefits. It uses the profit motive, but argues that philanthropy must have at least a long-term positive impact. For example, Gentle Giant Moving Company, a

U.S. moving company with offices in eight states, has made it a priority to incorporate philanthropy and social responsibility into its business strategy. In addition to its goal to become the best movers in the industry, Gentle Giants values customer satisfaction so much that it provides a 100 percent money-back guarantee if customers are not happy with its service. The company has established a charitable foundation that supports youth leadership development, housing assistance and homeless prevention, and green initiatives to make its practices more eco-friendly. Founder Peter O'Toole also cares for his employees and works to instill in them the type of values that Gentle Giant embodies. The company's successful integration of strategic philanthropy into its organizational practices has won it numerous awards, including a spot on *The Wall Street Journal*'s "Top Small Workplaces," a Better Business Bureau International Torch Award for Marketplace Ethics, and the Better Business Bureau Local Torch Award for Excellence (which it won four times).[64]

Home Depot directs much of the money it spends on philanthropy toward affordable housing, at-risk youth, the environment, and disaster recovery. Since 2008, Home Depot has been working with Habitat for Humanity on a five-year, $30 million initiative to provide funding for at least 5,000 energy-efficient homes. After the 2010 earthquake in Haiti, Home Depot and the Home Depot Foundation donated thousands of dollars, including a $100,000 contribution to the Red Cross, for earthquake relief and recovery.[65] These organizations demonstrate how companies can successfully incorporate voluntary responsibilities into their business strategies.

THE IMPORTANCE OF INSTITUTIONALIZATION IN BUSINESS ETHICS

Institutionalization involves embedding values, norms, and artifacts in organizations, industries, and society. In the United States and many other countries, institutionalization involves legislation that is often finalized through Supreme Court decisions. Therefore, this chapter provides an overview of legal as well as cultural institutions that work both outside and inside the organizational environment to support and control ethical decision making in organizations.

As discussed in Chapter 2, those in charge of corporate governance should be especially mindful of the institutions, including mandated requirements for legal compliance as well as core practices and voluntary actions, that support ethics and social responsibility. While voluntary conduct, including philanthropic activities, is not required to run a business, the failure to understand highly appropriate and common practices, referred to as core practices, provides the opportunity for unethical conduct.

It is important to recognize that the institutionalization of business ethics has advanced rapidly over the last 20 years as stakeholders have recognized the need to improve business ethics. The government has stepped in when scandals and misconduct have damaged consumers, investors, and other key constituents important for businesses. More recently, gatekeepers such as lawyers, financial rating agencies, and even financial reporting services have been questioned as some of their decisions seem to have contributed to major scandals involving companies like AIG, Countrywide Financial, and Lehman Brothers. Legislation and amendments related to the Federal Sentencing Guidelines for Organizations, the Sarbanes–Oxley Act, and the Dodd–Frank Act, have attempted to develop and enforce ethical practices that will support trust in business.

SUMMARY

To understand the institutionalization of business ethics, it is important to understand the voluntary and legally mandated dimensions of organizational practices. Core practices are documented best practices, often encouraged by legal and regulatory forces as well as by industry trade associations. The effective organizational practice of business ethics requires all three dimensions to be integrated into an ethics and compliance program. This integration creates an ethical culture that can effectively manage the risks of misconduct. Institutionalization in business ethics relates to established laws, customs, and the expectations of organizational ethics programs that are considered a requirement in establishing reputation. Institutions reward and sanction ethical decision making by providing structure and reinforcing societal expectations. In this way, society as a whole institutionalizes core practices and provides organizations with the opportunity to take their own approach, only taking action if there are violations.

Laws and regulations are established by governments to set minimum standards for responsible behavior—society's codification of what is right and wrong. Civil and criminal laws regulating business conduct are passed because society—including consumers, interest groups, competitors, and legislators—believes that business must comply with society's standards. Such laws regulate competition, protect consumers, promote safety and equity in the workplace, protect the environment, and provide incentives for preventing misconduct.

In 2002, largely in response to widespread corporate accounting scandals, Congress passed the Sarbanes–Oxley Act to establish a system of federal oversight of corporate accounting practices. In addition to making fraudulent financial reporting a criminal offense and strengthening penalties for corporate fraud, the law requires corporations to establish codes of ethics for financial reporting and to develop greater transparency in financial reporting to investors and other stakeholders. The Sarbanes–Oxley Act requires corporations to take greater responsibility for their decisions and to provide leadership based on ethical principles. For instance, the law requires top managers to certify that their firms' financial reports are complete and accurate, making CEOs and CFOs personally accountable for the credibility and accuracy of their companies' financial statements. The act establishes an oversight board to oversee the audit of public companies. The oversight board aims to protect the interests of investors and further the public interest in the preparation of informative, accurate, and independent audit reports for companies.

In 2010, largely in response to the widespread misconduct leading to the global recession, the Dodd–Frank Wall Street Reform and Consumer Protection Act was passed. The purpose of the Dodd–Frank Act is to prevent future misconduct in the financial sector, protect consumers from complex financial instruments, oversee market stability, and create transparency in the financial sector. The Act created two financial agencies, the Financial Stability Oversight Council and the Office of Financial Research. It also created the Consumer Financial Protection Bureau to regulate the industry and ensure that consumers are protected against overly complex and/or deceptive financial practices. Whistle-blower protection was extended to include a whistle-blower bounty program whereby whistle-blowers who report corporate misconduct to the SEC may receive 10 percent to 30 percent of settlement money if their reports result in a conviction of more than $1 million in penalties.

Congress passed the Federal Sentencing Guidelines for Organizations (FSGO) in 1991 to create an incentive for organizations to develop and implement programs designed to foster ethical and legal compliance. These guidelines, which were developed by the U.S. Sentencing Commission, apply to all felonies and class A misdemeanors committed by employees in association with their work. As an incentive, organizations that have demonstrated due diligence in developing effective compliance programs that discourage unethical and illegal conduct may be subject to reduced organizational penalties if an employee commits a crime. Overall, the government philosophy is that legal violations can be prevented through organizational values and a commitment to ethical conduct. A 2004 amendment to the FSGO requires that a business's governing authority be well-informed about its ethics program with respect to content, implementation, and effectiveness. This places the responsibility squarely on the shoulders of the firm's leadership, usually the board of directors. The board must ensure that there is a high-ranking manager accountable for the day-to-day operational oversight of the ethics program. The board must provide for adequate authority, resources, and access to the board or an appropriate subcommittee of the board. The board must also ensure that there are confidential mechanisms available so that the organization's employees and agents may report or seek guidance about potential or actual misconduct without fear of retaliation. A 2010 amendment to the FSGO directs chief compliance officers to make their reports to the board rather than to the general counsel.

The FSGO and the Sarbanes–Oxley Act provide incentives for developing core practices that help ensure ethical and legal compliance. Core practices move the emphasis from a focus on the individual's moral capability to a focus on developing structurally sound organizational core practices and structural integrity for both financial performance and nonfinancial performance. The Integrity Institute has developed an integrated model to standardize the measurement of nonfinancial performance. It has developed methodologies to assess communications, compensation, social responsibility, corporate culture, leadership, risk, and stakeholder perceptions, as well as the more subjective aspects of earnings, corporate governance, technology, and other important nonfinancial areas.

Voluntary responsibilities touch on businesses' social responsibility insofar as businesses contribute to the local community and to society as a whole. Voluntary responsibilities provide four major benefits to society: improving the quality of life, reducing government involvement by providing assistance to stakeholders, developing staff leadership skills, and building staff morale. Companies contribute significant amounts of money to education, the arts, environmental causes, and the disadvantaged by supporting local and national charitable organizations. Cause-related marketing ties an organization's product(s) directly to a social concern through a marketing program. Strategic philanthropy involves linking core business competencies to societal and community needs.

IMPORTANT TERMS FOR REVIEW

voluntary practices

philanthropy

core practices

Better Business Bureau

mandated boundaries

civil law

criminal law

procompetitive legislation

consumer protection law

Occupational Safety and Health Administration

sustainability

Environmental Protection Agency

Public Company Accounting Oversight Board

Consumer Financial Protection Bureau

cause-related marketing

strategic philanthropy

RESOLVING ETHICAL BUSINESS CHALLENGES*

Albert Chen was sweating profusely in his Jaguar on the expressway as he thought about his options and the fact that Christmas and the Chinese New Year were at hand. He and his wife, Mary, who were on their way to meet Albert's parents at New York's John F. Kennedy International Airport, seemed to be looking up from an abyss, with no daylight to be seen. Several visits and phone calls from various people had overwhelmed them.

Albert had graduated with honors in finance after marrying Mary in his senior year. They had both obtained prestigious brokerage jobs in the New York area, and both had been working killer hours to develop their accounts. Listening to other brokers, both had learned that there were some added expenses to their professions. For example, they were told that brokers need to "look" and "act" successful. So Albert and Mary bought the appropriate clothes and cars, joined the right clubs, and ate at the right restaurants with the right people. They also took the advice of others, which was to identify the "players" of large corporations at parties and take mental notes. "You'd be surprised at what information you hear with a little alcohol in these people," said one broker. Both started using this strategy, and five months later their clients began to see significant profits in their portfolios.

Their good luck even came from strange places. For example, Albert had an uncle whose work as a janitor gave him access to many law offices that had information on a number of companies, especially those about to file for bankruptcy. Mary and Albert were able to use information provided by this uncle to benefit their clients' portfolios. The uncle even had some of his friends use Albert. To Albert's surprise, his uncle's friends often had nest eggs in excess of $200,000. Because some of these friends were quite elderly, Albert was given permission to buy and sell non-risky stocks at will.

Because both of them were earning good salaries, the Chens soon managed to invest in the market themselves, and their investments included stock in the company for which Mary's father worked. After 18 months, Albert started working for Jarvis, Sunni, Lamar & Morten (JSL&M). JSL&M's reputation was that of a fast mover in the business. "We go up to the line and then measure how wide the line is so that we know how far we can go into it," was a common remark at the brokerage firm.

About six months ago, Mary's father, who was with a major health care company, commented that the management team was running the company into the ground. "If only someone could buy the company and put in a good management team," he mused. After that conversation, Mary investigated the company and discovered that the stock was grossly undervalued. She made a few phone calls and found a company that was interested in doing a hostile takeover. Mary also learned from her father that if a new management were acceptable to the union, the union would do everything in its power to oust the old management—by striking, if necessary—and welcome the new one. As things started to materialize, Mary told several of her best clients, who in turn did very well on the stock. This increased her status in the firm, which kept drawing bigger clients.

Albert soon became a player in initial public stock offerings (IPOs) of new companies. Occasionally when Albert saw a very hot IPO he would talk to some of his best venture-capital friends, who then bought the IPOs and gained some very good returns. This strategy helped attract some larger players in the market. By this point in his young career, Albert had made a great many friends.

One of those friends was Barry, who worked on the stock floor. As they were talking one day, Barry mentioned that if Albert wanted, when placing orders to buy shares, he would occasionally put Albert's or Mary's trade before the client order, as a favor.

The first sign of trouble in their lives came when Mary told Albert about what was happening at her office. "I'm getting e-mail from some of the brokers with off-color jokes and even some nude photos of women and men. I just don't care for it."

"So what are you doing about it?" Albert asked.

"Well, I've just started not even opening my messages if they come from these people," Mary replied.

"What about messages that request that you send them on? What do you do with those?" queried Albert.

"I just e-mail them along without looking at them," was her response.

"This isn't good, Mary. A couple of analysts were just fired for doing that at a big firm last week," said Albert.

Several weeks later the people who were sending Mary the obnoxious messages were fired. Mary was also asked to see the head of her division. When she came to his office, he said, "Please shut the door, Mary. I have some bad news. I know that you weren't involved with what was happening with the e-mail scandal; however, you did forward messages that contained such material. As a result, I have no alternative but to give you your two weeks' notice. I know this is unfair, but I have my orders. Because of this mess, the SEC wants to check all your trades for the last eight months. It seems to be a formality, but it will take time, and as you well know, the chances of going to another firm with that hanging over your head are slim. I'm sorry that it's only two months until the holidays." That night Mary fell into a depression.

To exacerbate the situation, Albert's parents were flying in from the People's Republic of China. They were not happy with Albert's marriage to a non-Chinese woman, but they had consoled themselves that Mary had a good job. They had also said that if things should go badly for Albert and Mary in New York, they could always come to the parents' retirement home in Taiwan. However, the idea of leaving the United States, attempting to learn Mandarin, and raising children in an unfamiliar culture did not appeal to Mary.

Albert was also having some problems. Because their income was cut in half, Albert tried to make up for the loss by trading in some high-risk markets, such as commodities and precious metals. However, many of these investments turned sour, and he found himself buying and selling more and more to pull his own portfolio, as well as those of his clients, into the black. He was getting worried because some of his uncle's friends' portfolios were losing significant value. Other matters, however, were causing him even more anxiety. The previous week Barry had called him, asking for some inside information on several companies that he was working with for an IPO. Albert knew that this could be construed as insider information and had said no.

Today, Barry called again and said, "Look, Al, I've been doing you favors for a while. I need to score big because of the holidays. You probably don't know, but what I've been doing for you could be construed as spinning, which is not looked upon favorably. I'm not asking for the IPO information—I'm demanding it. Is that clear enough for you, Al? E-mail it over by tomorrow morning." Then Barry hung up.

An hour later Albert's supervisor came in and said, "Al, I need a favor from you. I want you to buy some stock for a few friends and me. When it goes to $112, I want you to sell it. We'll pay the taxes and give you a little bonus for Christmas as well. I want you to buy tomorrow as soon as the market opens. Here are the account numbers for the transaction. I must run. See you tomorrow."

QUESTIONS | EXERCISES

1. Identify the ethical and legal issues of which Albert needs to be aware.
2. Discuss the advantages and disadvantages of each decision that Albert could make and has made.
3. Identify the pressures that have brought about these issues.

*This case is strictly hypothetical; any resemblance to real persons, companies, or situations is coincidental.

CHECK YOUR EQ

Check your EQ, or Ethics Quotient, by completing the following. Assess your performance to evaluate your overall understanding of the chapter material.

1. Voluntary practices include documented best practices.   Yes   No

2. The primary method for resolving business ethics disputes is through the criminal court system.   Yes   No

3. The FSGO provides an incentive for organizations to conscientiously develop and implement ethics programs.   Yes   No

4. The Sarbanes–Oxley Act encourages CEOs and CFOs to report their financial statements accurately.   Yes   No

5. Strategic philanthropy represents a new direction in corporate giving that maximizes the benefit to societal or community needs and relates to business objectives.   Yes   No

ANSWERS 1. **No.** Core practices are documented best practices. 2. **No.** Civil litigation is the primary way in which business ethics disputes are resolved. 3. **Yes.** Well-designed ethics and compliance programs can minimize legal liability when organizational misconduct is detected. 4. **No.** The Sarbanes–Oxley Act *requires* CEOs and CFOs to accurately report their financial statements to a federal oversight committee; they must sign the document and are held personally liable for any inaccuracies. 5. **Yes.** Strategic philanthropy helps both society and the organization.

PART 3

© Stanislav Bokrach, Shutterstock

The Decision-Making Process

CHAPTER 5

ETHICAL DECISION MAKING AND ETHICAL LEADERSHIP

CHAPTER OBJECTIVES

- To provide a comprehensive framework for ethical decision making in business
- To examine the intensity of ethical issues as an important element influencing the ethical decision-making process
- To introduce individual factors that may influence ethical decision making in business
- To introduce organizational factors that may influence ethical decision making in business
- To explore the role of opportunity in ethical decision making in business
- To explain how knowledge about the ethical decision-making framework can be used to improve ethical leadership
- To provide leadership styles and habits that promote an ethical culture

AN ETHICAL DILEMMA*

Troy Buchanan was in a bind. As a recent graduate of a prestigious journalism school, he had taken a job in the editorial department of Circa Communications, a fast-growing company in the online publications industry. Circa relocated Troy, his wife, and their two-year-old son from the Southwest to Atlanta, Georgia. On arriving, they bought their first home and

a second car. Troy was told that the company had big plans for him. Therefore, he did not worry about being financially overextended.

Several months into the job, Troy found that he was working late into the night, and even on his days off, to complete his editorial assignments before the deadlines passed. He knew that the company did not want its clients billed for excessive hours and that he needed to become more efficient if he wanted to move up in the company. He asked one of his co-workers, Mary Jo, how she managed to be so efficient in completing her editing duties.

Mary Jo quietly explained: "Troy, there are times when being efficient isn't enough. You need to do what is required to get ahead. The owners just want results—they don't care how you get them."

"I don't understand," said Troy.

"Look," Mary Jo explained, "I had the same problem you have a few years ago, but Mr. Hunt [the supervisor of the editorial department] explained that everyone works 'off the clock' so that the editorial department shows top results and looks good. And when the editorial department looks good, everyone in it looks good. No one cares if a little time gets lost in the shuffle."

Troy realized that "off the clock" meant not reporting all the hours required to complete a project. He also remembered one of Circa's classic catch phrases, "results, results, results." He thanked Mary Jo for her input and went back to work. Troy thought of going over Mr. Hunt's head and asking for advice from the general manager, but he had met her only once and did not know anything about her.

QUESTIONS | EXERCISES

1. What should Troy do?
2. Describe one process through which Troy might attempt to resolve his dilemma.
3. Consider the impact of this company's approach on young editors. How could working long hours be an ethical problem?

*This case is strictly hypothetical; any resemblance to real persons, companies, or situations is coincidental.

To improve ethical decision making in business, one must first understand how individuals make ethical decisions in an organizational environment. Too often it is assumed that individuals in organizations make ethical decisions in the same way that they make ethical decisions at home, in their families, or in their personal lives. Within the context of an organizational work group, however, few individuals have the freedom to decide ethical issues independent of organizational pressures.

This chapter summarizes our current knowledge of ethical decision making in business and provides insights into ethical decision making in organizations. Although it is impossible to describe exactly how any one individual or work group might make ethical decisions, we can offer generalizations about average or typical behavior patterns within organizations. These generalizations are based on many studies and at least six ethical decision models that have been widely accepted by academics and practitioners.[1] Based on these models, we present a framework for understanding ethical decision making in the context of business organizations. In addition to business, this framework integrates concepts from philosophy, psychology, sociology, and organizational behavior. This framework should be helpful in understanding organizational ethics and developing ethical programs.

A FRAMEWORK FOR ETHICAL DECISION MAKING IN BUSINESS

As Figure 5.1 shows, our model of the ethical decision making process in business includes ethical issue intensity, individual factors, and organizational factors such as corporate culture and opportunity. All of these interrelated factors influence the evaluations of and intentions behind the decisions that produce ethical or unethical behavior. This model does not describe how to make ethical decisions, but it does help one to understand the factors and processes related to ethical decision making.

FIGURE 5.1 Framework for Understanding Ethical Decision Making in Business

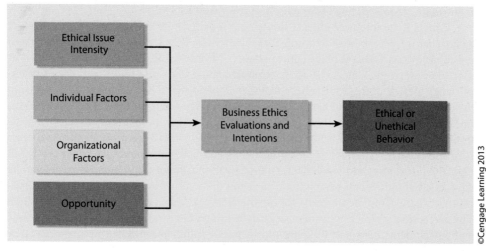

©Cengage Learning 2013

Ethical Issue Intensity

The first step in ethical decision making is to recognize that an ethical issue requires an individual or work group to choose among several actions that various stakeholders inside or outside the firm will ultimately evaluate as right or wrong. The intensity of an ethical issue relates to its perceived importance to the decision maker.[2] **Ethical issue intensity,** then, can be defined as the relevance or importance of an ethical issue in the eyes of the individual, work group, and/or organization. It is personal and temporal in character to accommodate values, beliefs, needs, perceptions, the special characteristics of the situation, and the personal pressures prevailing at a particular place and time.[3] Senior employees and those with administrative authority contribute significantly to intensity because they typically dictate an organization's stance on ethical issues. For instance, insider trading is considered to be a serious ethical issue by the government as the intent is to take advantage of inside information not available to the public. Therefore, it is an ethical issue of high intensity for regulators and government officials. Consider the government's investigation of so-called "expert-network" firms. These firms try to appear as legitimate consultants, but the government believes they might be providing inside information. Technology companies that are on the verge of new products, patents, or other innovations that will affect their market price are especially targeted by these consultants. However, if investigations show these firms to be legitimate, it is possible that the ethical issues they have raised will not turn out to be of high intensity.[4]

Under current law, managers can be held liable for the unethical and illegal actions of subordinates. In the United States, the Federal Sentencing Guidelines for Organizations contain a liability formula that judges use as a guideline regarding illegal activities of corporations. For example, many of the Enron employees and managers who were aware of the firm's use of off-balance-sheet partnerships—which turned out to be the major cause of the energy firm's collapse—were advised that these partnerships were legal, so they did not perceive them as an ethical issue. Although such partnerships were legal at that time, the way that some Enron officials designed them and the methods they used to provide collateral (that is, Enron stock) created a scheme that brought about the collapse of the company.[5] Thus, ethical issue intensity involves individuals' cognitive state of concern about an issue, or whether or not they have knowledge that an issue is unethical, which in turn indicates their involvement in making choices. The identification of ethical issues often requires the understanding of complex business relationships.

Ethical issue intensity reflects the ethical sensitivity of the individual and/or work group that faces the ethical decision-making process. Research suggests that individuals are subject to six "spheres of influence" when confronted with ethical choices—the workplace, family, religion, legal system, community, and profession—and that the level of importance of each of these influences will vary depending on how important the decision maker perceives the issue to be.[6] Additionally, the individual's moral intensity increases his or her perceptiveness of potential ethical problems, which in turn reduces his or her intention to act unethically.[7] **Moral intensity** relates to individuals' perceptions of social pressure and the harm they believe their decisions will have on others.[8] All other factors in Figure 5.1, including individual factors, organizational factors, and intentions, determine why different individuals perceive ethical issues differently. Unless individuals in an organization share common concerns about ethical issues, the stage is set for ethical conflict. The perception of ethical issue intensity can be influenced by management's use of rewards and punishments, corporate policies, and corporate values to sensitize employees. In other words, managers can affect the degree to which employees perceive the importance of an ethical issue through positive and/or negative incentives.[9]

For some employees, ethical issues may not reach the critical awareness level if managers fail to identify and educate employees about specific problem areas. One study found that more than a third of the unethical situations that lower and middle-level managers face come from internal pressures and ambiguity surrounding internal organizational rules. Many employees fail to anticipate these issues before they arise.[10] This lack of preparedness makes it difficult for employees to respond appropriately when they encounter an ethics issue. For example, subprime lenders such as Countrywide Financial failed to educate brokers about the damages of misrepresenting financial data to help individuals secure loans. This contributed to widespread organizational misconduct. Organizations that consist of employees with diverse values and backgrounds must therefore train them in the way the firm wants specific ethical issues handled. Identifying the ethical issues and risks that employees might encounter is a significant step toward developing their ability to make ethical decisions. Many ethical issues are identified by industry groups or through general information available to a firm. Flagging certain issues as high in ethical importance could trigger increases in employees' ethical issue intensity. The perceived importance of an ethical issue has been found to have a strong influence on both employees' ethical judgment and their behavioral intention. In other words, the more likely individuals are to perceive an ethical issue as important, the less likely they are to engage in questionable or unethical behavior.[11] Therefore, ethical issue intensity should be considered a key factor in the ethical decision-making process.

> "Identifying the ethical issues and risks that employees might encounter is a significant step toward developing their ability to make ethical decisions."

Individual Factors

When people need to resolve ethical issues in their daily lives, they often base their decisions on their own values and principles of right or wrong. They generally learn these values and principles through the socialization process with family members, social groups, and religion, and in their formal education. Good personal values have been found to decrease unethical practices and increase positive work behavior. The moral philosophies of individuals, discussed in more detail in Chapter 6, provide principles and rules that people use to decide what is right or wrong. Values of individuals can be derived from moral philosophies to apply to daily decisions. However, values are subjective and vary a great deal across different cultures. For example, one individual might place greater importance on keeping one's promises and commitments than another would. Values could also relate to negative rationalizations, such as "Everyone does it," or "We have to do what it takes to get the business."[12] Research demonstrates that individuals with destructive personalities who violate basic core values can cause a work group to suffer a performance loss of 30 percent to 40 percent compared to groups with no "bad apples."[13] The actions of specific individuals in scandal-plagued financial companies such as AIG and Countrywide Financial often raise questions about those individuals' personal character and integrity. They appear to operate in their own self-interest or in total disregard for the law and the interests of society.

Although an individual's intention to engage in ethical behavior relates to individual values, organizational and social forces also play a vital role. An individual's attitudes as well as social norms will help create behavioral intentions that will shape his or her decision-making process. While an individual may intend to do the right thing, organizational or social forces can alter this intent. For example, an individual may intend to report the misconduct of a coworker, but when faced with the social consequences of doing so, may decide to remain complacent. In this case, social forces have overcome a person's individual values when it comes to taking appropriate action.[14] At the same time, individual values have a strong influence over how people assume ethical responsibilities in the work environment. In turn, individual decisions can be heavily dependent on company policy and the corporate culture.

The way the public perceives individual ethics generally varies according to the profession in question. Telemarketers, car salespersons, advertising practitioners, stockbrokers, and real estate brokers are often perceived as having the lowest ethics. Research regarding individual factors that affect ethical awareness, judgment, intent, and behavior include gender, education, work experience, nationality, age, and locus of control.

Extensive research has been done regarding the link between **gender** and ethical decision making. The research shows that in many aspects there are no differences between men and women, but when differences are found, women are generally more ethical than men.[15] By "more ethical," we mean that women seem to be more sensitive to ethical scenarios and less tolerant of unethical actions. In a study on gender and intentions for fraudulent financial reporting, females reported higher intentions to report them than male participants.[16] As more and more women work in managerial positions, these findings may become increasingly significant.

Education is also a significant factor in the ethical decision-making process. The important thing to remember about education is that it does not reflect experience. Work experience is defined as the number of years in a specific job, occupation, and/or industry. Generally, the more education or work experience that a person has, the better he or she is at ethical decision making. The type of education someone has received has little or no effect on ethics. For example, it doesn't matter if you are a business student or a liberal arts student—you are pretty much the same in terms of ethical decision making. Current research, however, shows that students are less ethical than businesspeople, which is likely because businesspeople have been exposed to more ethically challenging situations than students.[17]

Nationality is the legal relationship between a person and the country in which he or she is born. In the twenty-first century, nationality is being redefined by regional economic integration such as the European Union (EU). When European students are asked their nationality, they are less likely to state where they were born than where they currently live. The same thing is happening in the United States, as someone born in Florida who lives in New York might consider him- or herself to be a New Yorker. Research about nationality and ethics appears to be significant in that it affects ethical decision making; however, just how nationality affects ethics is somewhat hard to interpret.[18] Because of cultural differences, it is impossible to state that ethical decision making in an organizational context will differ significantly among individuals of different nationalities. The reality of today is that multinational companies look for businesspeople who can make decisions regardless of nationality. Perhaps in 20 years, nationality will no longer be an issue in that the multinational individual's culture will replace national status as the most significant factor in ethical decision making.

Age is another individual factor that has been researched within business ethics. Several decades ago, we believed that age was positively correlated with ethical decision making. In other words, the older you are, the more ethical you are. However, recent research suggests that there is probably a more complex relationship between ethics and age.[19] We do believe that older employees with more experience have greater knowledge to deal with complex industry-specific ethical issues. Younger managers are far more influenced by organizational culture than are older managers.[20]

Locus of control relates to individual differences in relation to a generalized belief about how one is affected by internal versus external events or reinforcements. In other words, the concept relates to how people view themselves in relation to power. Those who believe in **external control** (that is, externals) see themselves as going with the flow because that is all they can do. They believe that the events in their lives are due to uncontrollable forces. They consider that what they want to achieve depends on luck, chance, and powerful people in their company. In addition, they believe that the probability of being able to control their lives by their own actions and efforts is low. Conversely, those who believe in **internal control** (that is, internals) believe that they control the events in their lives by their own effort and skill, viewing themselves as masters of their destinies and trusting in their capacity to influence their environment.

Current research suggests that we still can't be sure how significant locus of control is in terms of ethical decision making. One study that found a relationship between locus of control and ethical decision making concluded that internals were positively correlated whereas externals were negatively correlated.[21] In other words, those who believe that their fate is in the hands of others were more ethical than those who believed that they formed their own destiny.

Organizational Factors

Although people can and do make individual ethical choices in business situations, no one operates in a vacuum. Indeed, research has established that in the workplace, the organization's values often have greater influence on decisions than a person's own values.[22] Ethical choices in business are most often made jointly, in work groups and committees, or in conversations and discussions with coworkers. Employees approach ethical issues on the basis of what they have learned not only from their own backgrounds, but also from others in the organization. The outcome of this learning process depends on the strength of each person's personal values, the opportunities he or she has to behave unethically, and the exposure he or she has to others who behave ethically or unethically. An alignment between a person's own values and the values of the organization help to create positive work attitudes and organizational outcomes. Research has further demonstrated that congruence in personal and organizational values is related to commitment, satisfaction, motivation, ethics, work stress, and anxiety.[23] Although people outside the organization, such as family members and friends, also influence decision makers, an organization's culture and structure operate through the relationships of its members to influence their ethical decisions.

A **corporate culture** can be defined as a set of values, norms, and artifacts, including ways of solving problems that members (employees) of an organization share. As time passes, stakeholders come to view the company or organization as a living organism with a mind and will of its own. The Walt Disney Co., for example, requires all new employees to take a course in the traditions and history of Disneyland and Walt Disney, including the ethical dimensions of the company. The corporate culture at American Express stresses that employees help customers out of difficult situations whenever possible. This attitude is reinforced through numerous company legends of employees who have gone above and beyond the call of duty to help customers. This strong tradition of customer loyalty might encourage an American Express employee to take unorthodox steps to help a customer who encounters a problem while traveling overseas. Employees learn that they can take some risks in helping customers. Such strong traditions and values have become a driving force in many companies, including Starbucks, IBM, Procter & Gamble, Southwest Airlines, and Hershey Foods.

An important component of corporate, or organizational, culture is the company's ethical culture. Whereas corporate culture involves values and norms that prescribe a wide range of behavior for organizational members, **ethical culture** reflects whether the firm also has an ethical conscience. Ethical culture is a function of many factors, including corporate policies on ethics, top management's leadership on ethical issues, the influence of coworkers, and the opportunity for unethical behavior. Communication is also important in the creation of an effective ethical culture. There is a positive correlation between effective communication and empowerment and the development of an organizational ethical climate.[24] Within the organization as a whole, subclimates can develop within individual departments or work groups, but they are influenced by the strength of the firm's overall ethical culture, as well as the function of the department and the stakeholders it serves.[25]

The more ethical employees perceive an organization's culture to be, the less likely they are to make unethical decisions. Corporate culture and ethical culture are closely associated with the idea that significant others within the organization help determine ethical decisions within that organization. Research also indicates that the ethical values embodied in an organization's culture are positively correlated to employees' commitment to the firm and their sense that they fit into the company. These findings suggest that companies should develop and promote ethical values to enhance employees' experiences in the workplace.[26]

> "The more ethical employees perceive an organization's culture to be, the less likely they are to make unethical decisions."

Those who have influence in a work group, including peers, managers, coworkers, and subordinates, are referred to as **significant others.** They help workers on a daily basis with unfamiliar tasks and provide advice and information in both formal and informal ways. Coworkers, for instance, can offer help in the comments they make in discussions over lunch or when the boss is away. Likewise, a manager may provide directives about certain types of activities that employees perform on the job. Indeed, an employee's supervisor can play a central role in helping employees develop and fit in socially in the workplace.[27] Numerous studies conducted over the years confirm that significant others within an organization may have more impact on a worker's decisions on a daily basis than any other factor.[28]

Obedience to authority is another aspect of the influence that significant others can exercise. Obedience to authority helps to explain why many employees resolve business ethics issues by simply following the directives of a superior. In organizations that emphasize respect for superiors, for example, employees may feel that they are expected to carry out orders by a supervisor even if those orders are contrary to the employees' sense of right and wrong. Later, if the employee's decision is judged to have been wrong, he or she is likely to say, "I was only carrying out orders," or "My boss told me to do it this way." In addition, the type of industry and the size of the organization have also been researched and found to be relevant factors, with bigger companies more at risk for unethical activities.[29]

Opportunity

Opportunity describes the conditions in an organization that limit or permit ethical or unethical behavior. Opportunity results from conditions that either provide rewards, whether internal or external, or fail to erect barriers against unethical behavior. Examples of internal rewards include feelings of goodness and personal worth generated by performing altruistic acts. External rewards refer to what an individual expects to receive from others in the social environment in terms of social approval, status, and esteem.

An example of a condition that fails to erect barriers against unethical behavior is a company policy that does not punish employees who accept large gifts from clients. The absence of punishment essentially provides an opportunity for unethical behavior because it allows individuals to engage in such behavior without fear of consequences. The prospect of a reward for unethical behavior can also create an opportunity for questionable decisions. For example, a salesperson who is given public recognition and a large bonus for making a valuable sale that he or she obtained through unethical tactics will probably be motivated to use such tactics again, even if such behavior goes against the salesperson's personal value system. If 10 percent of employees report observing others at the workplace abusing drugs or alcohol and there is a failure to report and respond to this conduct, then the opportunity for others to engage in these activities exists.[30]

Opportunity relates to individuals' **immediate job context**—where they work, whom they work with, and the nature of the work. The immediate job context includes the motivational "carrots and sticks" that superiors use to influence employee behavior. Pay raises, bonuses, and public recognition act as carrots, or positive reinforcements, whereas demotions, firings, reprimands, and pay penalties act as sticks, or negative reinforcements. The U.S. Chamber of Commerce reports that 75 percent of employees steal from their workplaces, and most do so repeatedly.[31] As Figure 5.2 shows, many office supplies, particularly smaller ones, tend to "disappear" from the workplace. Pens, pencils, and highlighters appear to be the most commonly pilfered items, with 81 percent of respondents to an Office Max survey reporting that these supplies go missing most often. If there is no policy against this practice, one concern is that employees will not learn where to draw the line and will get into the habit of taking even more expensive items for personal use.

The opportunities that employees have for unethical behavior in an organization can be eliminated through formal codes, policies, and rules that are adequately enforced by management. For instance, the American Economic Association is considering new ethical guidelines to help academic economists become more transparent about their relationships with hedge funds, banks, and financial institutions. These guidelines are a

FIGURE 5.2 Office Supplies Reported Missing Most Often

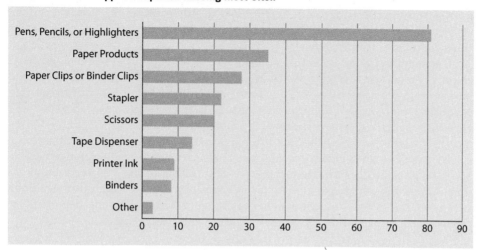

Source: "The Truth behind Disappearing Office Supplies," OfficeMax, May 2010, http://multivu.prnewswire.com/mnr/officemax/44541/docs/44541-Report_OfficeMaxWorkplaceUncoveredSurvey.pdf (accessed January 6, 2011).

response to the criticisms levied against academic economists over the consulting services and derivative risk models that they provided to financial companies such as Lehman Brothers—services that have been partially blamed for the U.S. financial crisis.[32] Financial companies—such as banks, savings and loan associations, and securities companies—have also developed elaborate sets of rules and procedures to avoid creating opportunities for individual employees to manipulate or take advantage of their trusted positions. In banks, one such rule requires most employees to take a vacation and stay out of the bank a certain number of days every year so that they cannot be physically present to cover up embezzlement or other diversions of funds. This rule prevents the opportunity for inappropriate conduct.

Despite the existence of rules, misconduct can still occur without proper oversight. In Kabul, Afghanistan, a major scandal in the country's largest bank nearly led to its ruin. Two top executives were implicated in a massive fraud, and later investigations revealed that the bank had made questionable loans that could cost it hundreds of millions of dollars. Failure of the bank could cause the entire banking system in Afghanistan to collapse. How did the bank manage to get away with such a widespread fraud? Investigators believe the bank may have been paying off certain government officials for years to look the other way. If this is true, the corruption would also include some of the country's top leaders.[33] To avoid similar situations, there must be checks and balances that create transparency.

Opportunity also comes from knowledge. A major type of misconduct observed among employees in the workplace is lying to employees, customers, vendors, or the public or withholding needed information from them.[34] A person who has expertise or information about the competition has the opportunity to exploit this knowledge. An individual can be a source of information because he or she is familiar with the organization. Individuals who have been employed by one organization for many years become "gatekeepers" of its culture and often have the opportunity to make decisions related to unwritten traditions and rules. They help socialize newer employees to abide by the rules and norms of the company's internal and external ways of doing business, as well as understanding when the opportunity exists to cross the line. They may function as mentors or supervise managers in training. Like drill sergeants in the army, these trainers mold the new recruits into what the company wants. Their training can contribute to either ethical or unethical conduct.

The opportunity for unethical behavior cannot be eliminated without aggressive enforcement of codes and rules. A national jewelry store chain president explained to us how he dealt with a jewelry buyer in one of his stores who had taken a bribe from a supplier. There was an explicit company policy against taking incentive payments to deal with a specific supplier. When the president of the firm learned about the accepted bribe, he immediately traveled to the office of the buyer in question and terminated his employment. He then traveled to the supplier (manufacturer) selling jewelry to his stores and terminated his relationship with the firm. The message was clear: Taking a bribe is unacceptable for the store's buyers, and salespeople from supplying companies could cost their firm significant sales by offering bribes. This type of policy enforcement illustrates how the opportunity to commit unethical acts can be eliminated or at least significantly reduced.

Business Ethics Evaluations and Intentions

Ethical dilemmas involve problem-solving situations in which the rules governing decisions are often vague or in conflict. The results of an ethical decision are often uncertain; it is not always immediately clear whether or not we have made the right decision. There are no magic formulas, nor is there computer software that ethical dilemmas can be plugged into to get a solution. Even if they mean well, most businesspeople will make ethical mistakes. Therefore there is no substitute for critical thinking and the ability to take responsibility for our own decisions.

An individual's intentions and the final decision regarding what action he or she will take are the last steps in the ethical decision-making process. When the individual's intentions and behavior are inconsistent with his or her ethical judgment, the person may feel guilty. For example, when an advertising account executive is asked by her client to create an advertisement that she perceives as misleading, she has two alternatives: to comply or to refuse. If she refuses, she stands to lose business from that client and possibly her job. Other factors—such as pressure from the client, the need to keep her job to pay her debts and living expenses, and the possibility of a raise if she develops the advertisement successfully—may influence her resolution of this ethical dilemma. Because of these other factors, she may decide to act unethically and develop the advertisement even though she believes it to be inaccurate. Because her actions are inconsistent with her ethical judgment, she will probably feel guilty about her decision.

Guilt or uneasiness is the first sign that an unethical decision has occurred. The next step is changing one's behavior to reduce such feelings. This change can reflect a person's values shifting to fit the decision or the person changing his or her decision type the next time a similar situation occurs. Finally, one can eliminate some of the problematic situational factors by resigning one's position. For those who begin the value shift, the following are the usual justifications that will reduce and finally eliminate guilt:

1. I need the paycheck and can't afford to quit right now.

2. Those around me are doing it, so why shouldn't I? They believe it's okay.

3. If I don't do this, I might not be able to get a good reference from my boss or company when I leave.

4.   This is not such a big deal, given the potential benefits.

5.   Business is business with a different set of rules.

6.   If not me, someone else would do it and get rewarded.

The road to success depends on how the businessperson defines *success*. The success concept drives intentions and behavior in business either implicitly or explicitly. Money, security, family, power, wealth, and personal or group gratification are all types of success measures that people use. The list described is not comprehensive, and in the next chapter, you will understand more about how success can be defined. Another concept that affects behavior is the probability of rewards and punishments, an issue that will be explained further in Chapter 6.

USING THE ETHICAL DECISION-MAKING FRAMEWORK TO IMPROVE ETHICAL DECISIONS

The ethical decision-making framework presented in this chapter cannot tell you if a business decision is ethical or unethical. It bears repeating that it is impossible to tell you what is right or wrong; instead, we are attempting to prepare you to make informed ethical decisions. Although this chapter does not moralize by telling you what to do in a specific situation, it does provide an overview of typical decision-making processes and factors that influence ethical decisions. The framework is not a guide for how to make decisions, but instead is intended to provide you with insights and knowledge about typical ethical decision-making processes in business organizations.

Because it is impossible to agree on normative judgments about what is ethical, business ethics scholars developing descriptive models have instead focused on regularities in decision making and the various phenomena that interact in a dynamic environment to produce predictable behavioral patterns. Furthermore, it is unlikely that an organization's ethical problems will be solved strictly by having a thorough knowledge about how ethical decisions are made. By its very nature, business ethics involves value judgments and collective agreement about acceptable patterns of behavior.

We propose that gaining an understanding of typical ethical decision making in business organizations will reveal several ways that such decision making could be improved. With more knowledge about how the decision process works, you will be better prepared to analyze critical ethical dilemmas and to provide ethical leadership regardless of your role in the organization. One important conclusion that should be taken from our framework is that ethical decision making within an organization does not rely strictly on the personal values and morals of individuals. Knowledge of moral philosophies or values must be balanced with business knowledge and an understanding of the complexities of the dilemma requiring a decision. For example, a manager who embraces honesty, fairness, and equity has to understand the diverse risks associated with a complex financial instrument such as options or derivatives. Business competence must exist, along with personal accountability, in ethical decisions. Organizations take on a culture of their own, with managers and coworkers exerting a significant influence on ethical decisions. While formal codes, rules, and compliance are essential in organizations, an organization built on informal relationships is more likely to develop a high integrity corporate culture.[35]

THE ROLE OF LEADERSHIP IN A CORPORATE CULTURE

Top managers provide a blueprint for what a firm's corporate culture should be.[36] If these leaders fail to express desired behaviors and goals, a corporate culture will evolve on its own but will still reflect the values and norms of the company. **Leadership,** the ability or authority to guide and direct others toward achievement of a goal, has a significant impact on ethical decision making because leaders have the power to motivate others and enforce the organization's norms and policies as well as their own viewpoints. Leaders are key to influencing an organization's corporate culture and ethical posture. Research suggests that ethical leadership has a positive correlation to follower organizational citizenship and a negative correlation to deviance. In other words, ethical business leaders are more likely to have employees that follow their example and less likely to have deviants that create trouble in the company.[37]

Although we often think of CEOs and other top managers as the most important leaders in an organization, the corporate governance reforms discussed in Chapter 4 make it clear that a firm's board of directors is also an important leadership component. Indeed, directors have a legal obligation to manage companies "for the best interests of the corporation." To determine what is in the best interest of the firm, directors can consider the effects that a decision may have not only on shareholders and employees but also on other important stakeholders.[38] Therefore, when we discuss leadership, we include corporate directors as well as top executives.

In the long run, if stakeholders are not reasonably satisfied with a company's leader, he or she will not retain a leadership position. A leader must not only have his or her followers' respect but must also provide a standard of ethical conduct. The former chairman of the Korean electronics giant Samsung Group, Lee Kun-hee, resigned in disgrace after 20 years on the Samsung board after being accused of evading $128 million in taxes. His son and heir to the company, Lee Jae-yong, also resigned from the board. This was only the last in a long string of corruption charges against Lee. He was also convicted of bribery 12 years ago. Since his resignation, the company has sought to improve its image.[40] Table 5.1 summarizes the steps executives should take to demonstrate that they understand the importance of ethics in doing business.

DEBATE ISSUE TAKE A STAND

Examining Warren Buffett as an Effective Leader

Warren Buffett has been the leader of Berkshire Hathaway, Inc., for more than 40 years. Buffett has been viewed as an ethical leader who emphasizes integrity in his manager choices. His conglomerate is one of the largest companies in the United States. Buffett relies on the character of the CEOs of the various companies in his conglomerate, and in many cases, he may only have a few conversations with the CEO over the course of a year. His trust in his associates was undermined when David Sokol, the leading contender to succeed him, resigned after revelations that he had purchased $10 million in shares of a chemical maker a week before recommending the purchase of the company to Buffett. This broke the company's insider trading rules and duty of candor. While Sokol's trading may fall in a gray area of the law, there are certainly questions about Sokol's disclosures.[39]

1. Warren Buffett is correct in trusting those around him to have high integrity and the ability to make ethical decisions based on their character.
2. Warren Buffett needs to focus more on organizational ethical codes and compliance and less on the character of the manager that he puts in charge of the company.

TABLE 5.1 The Managerial Role in Developing Ethics Program Leadership

1. Obtain organizational commitment from the board of directors and top management

2. Develop organizational resources for ethics initiatives

3. Determine ethical risks and develop contingency plans

4. Develop an effective ethics program to address risks and maintain compliance with ethical standards

5. Provide oversight for implementation and audits of ethical programs

6. Communicate with stakeholders to establish shared commitment and values for ethical conduct

LEADERSHIP STYLES INFLUENCE ETHICAL DECISIONS

Leadership styles influence many aspects of organizational behavior, including employees' acceptance of and adherence to organizational norms and values. Styles that focus on building strong organizational values among employees contribute to shared standards of conduct. They also influence the organization's transmission and monitoring of values, norms, and codes of ethics.[41] In short, the leadership style of an organization influences how its employees act. The challenge for leaders is in gaining the trust and commitment of organizational members, which is essential if organizational leaders are to steer their companies toward success. Those leaders who are recognized as trustworthy are more likely to be perceived as ethical stewards.[42] Studying a firm's leadership styles and attitudes can also help to pinpoint where future ethical issues may arise. Even for actions that may be against the law, employees often look to their organizational leaders to determine how to respond.

Ethical leadership by a CEO requires an understanding of his or her firm's vision and values, as well as of the challenges of responsibility and the risks involved in achieving organizational objectives. Lapses in ethical leadership can occur even in people who possess strong ethical character, especially if they view the organization's ethical culture as being outside the realm of decision making that exists in the home, family, and community. This phenomenon has been observed in countless cases of so-called good community citizens engaging in unethical business activities. For example, Robin Szeliga, former CFO of Qwest, who pleaded guilty for insider trading, was an excellent community leader, even serving on a business college advisory board.

Ethical leaders need both knowledge and experience to make decisions. Strong ethical leaders must have the right kind of moral integrity. Such integrity must be transparent; in other words, they must "do in private as if it were always public." This type of integrity relates to values and is discussed in later chapters. Ethical leaders must be proactive and ready to leave the organization if its corporate governance system makes it impossible to make the right choice. Such right choices are complex by definition. The ethical leader must balance current issues with potential future issues. Such a person must be concerned with shareholders as well as with the lowest-paid employees. Experience shows that no leader can always be right or judged ethical by stakeholders in every case. The acknowledgment of this fact may be perceived as a weakness, but in reality it supports integrity and increases the debate exchange of views on ethics and openness.

Six leadership styles that are based on emotional intelligence—the ability to manage ourselves and our relationships effectively—have been identified by Daniel Goleman.[43]

1. The coercive leader demands instantaneous obedience and focuses on achievement, initiative, and self-control. Although this style can be very effective during times of crisis or during a turnaround, it otherwise creates a negative climate for organizational performance.

2. The authoritative leader—considered to be one of the most effective styles—inspires employees to follow a vision, facilitates change, and creates a strongly positive performance climate.

3. The affiliative leader values people, their emotions, and their needs and relies on friendship and trust to promote flexibility, innovation, and risk taking.

4. The democratic leader relies on participation and teamwork to reach collaborative decisions. This style focuses on communication and creates a positive climate for achieving results.

5. The pacesetting leader can create a negative climate because of the high standards that he or she sets. This style works best for attaining quick results from highly motivated individuals who value achievement and take the initiative.

6. The coaching leader builds a positive climate by developing skills to foster long-term success, delegating responsibility, and skillfully issuing challenging assignments.

The most successful leaders do not rely on one style but alter their techniques based on the characteristics of the situation. Different styles can be effective in developing an ethical culture depending on the leader's assessment of risks and the desire to achieve a positive climate for organizational performance.

Another way to consider leadership styles is to classify them as transactional or transformational. **Transactional leaders** attempt to create employee satisfaction through negotiating, or "bartering," for desired behaviors or levels of performance. **Transformational leaders** strive to raise employees' level of commitment and to foster trust and motivation.[44] Both transformational and transactional leaders can positively influence the corporate culture.

Transformational leaders communicate a sense of mission, stimulate new ways of thinking, and enhance as well as generate new learning experiences. They consider employee needs and aspirations in conjunction with organizational needs. They also build commitment and respect for values that promote effective responses to ethical issues. Thus, transformational leaders strive to promote activities and behavior through a shared vision and common learning experience. As a result, they have a stronger influence on coworker support for ethical decisions and building an ethical culture than do transactional leaders. Transformational ethical leadership is best suited for organizations that have higher levels of ethical commitment among employees and strong stakeholder support for an ethical culture. A number of industry trade associations—including the American Institute of Certified Public Accountants, Defense Industry Initiative on Business Ethics and Conduct, Ethics and Compliance Officer Association, and Mortgage Bankers Association of America—are helping companies provide transformational leadership.[45]

In contrast, transactional leaders focus on ensuring that required conduct and procedures are implemented. Their negotiations to achieve desired outcomes result in a dynamic relationship with subordinates in which reactions, conflict, and crisis influence the relationship more than ethical concerns. Transactional leaders produce employees who achieve a negotiated level of performance, including compliance with ethical and legal standards. As long as employees and leaders both find this exchange mutually rewarding, the relationship is likely to be successful. However, transactional leadership is best suited for rapidly changing situations, including those that require responses to ethical problems or issues. For example, when Eric Pillmore took over as senior vice president of corporate governance at Tyco after a major scandal involving CEO Dennis Kozlowski, the company needed transitional leadership. To turn the company around, many ethics and corporate governance decisions needed to be made quickly. The company also needed cross-functional leadership, improved accountability, and empowered leaders to improve corporate culture. Pillmore helped install a new ethics program that changed leadership policies and allowed him direct communications with the board in order to help implement the leadership transition.[46]

HABITS OF STRONG ETHICAL LEADERS

Archie Carroll, a University of Georgia business professor, crafted "7 Habits of Highly Moral Leaders" based on the idea of Stephen Covey's *The 7 Habits of Highly Effective People*.[47] We have adapted Carroll's "7 Habits of Highly Moral Leaders"[48] to create our own "Seven Habits of Strong Ethical Leaders" (Table 5.2). In particular, we believe that ethical leadership is based on holistic thinking that embraces the complex and challenging issues that companies face on a daily basis. Ethical leaders need both knowledge and experience to make the right decisions. Strong ethical leaders have both the courage and the most complete information to make decisions that will be best in the long run. Strong ethical leaders must stick to their principles and, if necessary, be ready to leave the organization if its corporate governance system is so flawed that it is impossible to make the right choice.

Many corporate founders—such as Sam Walton, Bill Gates, Milton Hershey, Michael Dell, Steve Jobs, and Ben Cohen and Jerry Greenfield—left their ethical stamp on their companies. Their conduct set the tone, making them role models for desired conduct in the early growth of their respective corporations. In the case of Milton Hershey, his legacy endures, and Hershey Foods continues to be a role model for ethical corporate culture. In the case of Sam Walton, Walmart embarked on a course of rapid growth after his death and became involved in numerous conflicts with various stakeholder groups, especially

TABLE 5.2 Seven Habits of Strong Ethical Leaders

1. Ethical leaders have strong personal character.
2. Ethical leaders have a passion to do right.
3. Ethical leaders are proactive.
4. Ethical leaders consider stakeholders' interests.
5. Ethical leaders are role models for the organization's values.
6. Ethical leaders are transparent and actively involved in organizational decision making.
7. Ethical leaders are competent managers who take a holistic view of the firm's ethical culture.

©Cengage Learning 2013

employees, regulators, competitors, and communities. Despite the ethical foundation left by Sam Walton, Walmart, like most large corporations, deals with hundreds of reported ethical lapses every month.[49]

Ethical Leaders Have Strong Personal Character

There is general agreement that ethical leadership is highly unlikely without a strong personal character. The question is how to teach or develop a moral person in a corporate environment. Thomas I. White, a leading authority on character development, believes the focus should be on developing "ethical reasoning" rather than on being a "moral person." According to White, the ability to resolve the complex ethical dilemmas encountered in a corporate culture requires intellectual skills.[50] For example, when Lawrence S. Benjamin took over as president of U.S. Food Service after a major ethical disaster, he initiated an ethics and compliance program to promote transparency and to teach employees how to make difficult ethical choices. A fundamental problem in traditional character development is that specific values and virtues are used to teach a belief or philosophy. This approach may be inappropriate for a business environment where cultural diversity and privacy must be respected. On the other hand, teaching individuals who want to do the right thing regarding corporate values and ethical codes, and equipping these individuals with the intellectual skills to address the complexities of ethical issues, is the correct approach.

Ethical Leaders Have a Passion to Do Right

The passion to do right is the glue that holds ethical concepts together. Some leaders develop this trait early in life, whereas others develop it over time through experience, reason, or spiritual growth. They often cite familiar arguments for doing right—to keep society from disintegrating, to alleviate human suffering, to advance human prosperity, to resolve conflicts of interest fairly and logically, to praise the good and punish the guilty, or just because something "is the right thing to do."[51] Having a passion to do right indicates a personal characteristic of recognizing the importance of ethical behavior and having the willingness to face challenges and make tough choices. Courageous leadership requires making and defending the right decision. Consider the crisis faced by Harry Kraemer, the CEO of Baxter International, after 53 dialysis patients died during treatment. "We have this situation," he said. "The financial people will assess the potential financial impact. The legal people will do the same. But at the end of the day, if we think it's a problem that a Baxter product was involved in the deaths of 53 people, then those other issues become pretty easy. If we don't do the right thing, then we won't be around to address those other issues."[52]

Ethical Leaders Are Proactive

Ethical leaders do not hang around waiting for ethical problems to arise. They anticipate, plan, and act proactively to avoid potential ethical crises.[53] One way to be proactive is to take a leadership role in developing effective programs that provide employees with guidance and support for making more ethical choices, even in the face of considerable pressure to do otherwise. Ethical leaders who are proactive understand social needs and apply or even develop the best practices of ethical leadership that exist in their industry. One of *Fortune* magazine's "Best Companies to Work for" in 2011 was DreamWorks Animation, which takes a proactive stance toward seeking top talent. CEO Jeffrey Katzenberg calls job candidates personally to encourage them to join the company. Additionally, DreamWorks has adopted a culture that supports employee contributions and creativity. Any employee at DreamWorks can pitch a movie idea to the top executives, and the company even sponsors workshops to help employees learn how to do so.[54] Such strong leadership is crucial in maintaining impressive credentials over the long term.

Ethical Leaders Consider Stakeholders' Interests

Ethical leaders consider the interests of and implications for all stakeholders, not just those that have an economic impact on the firm. This level of oversight requires acknowledging and monitoring the concerns of all legitimate stakeholders; actively communicating and cooperating with them; employing processes that are respectful of them; recognizing interdependencies among them; avoiding activities that would harm their human rights: and recognizing the potential conflicts between leaders' "own role as corporate stakeholders and their legal and moral responsibilities for the interests of other stakeholders."[55]

Ethical leaders have a responsibility to balance stakeholder interests to ensure that the organization maximizes its role as a responsible corporate citizen. For instance, while Waste Management is the largest waste management provider in the United States, it is also the nation's largest recycler. Its environmental initiatives have earned it a spot among *Ethisphere*'s 2010 World's Most Ethical Companies. Although Waste Management is known for its green trucks hauling trash to the dump, CEO David Steiner is taking the company in a more ecofriendly direction. With its tagline "Think Green," the company has invested in about 25 businesses to capture and reuse the energy and materials found in waste. Waste Management's LampTracker business is also the largest recycler of compact fluorescent light bulbs in the nation. Although recycling and zero waste practices represent a threat to traditional waste management services, Waste Management is taking a long-term stakeholder perspective with the belief that such practices are the future of the industry.[56]

Ethical Leaders Are Role Models for the Organization's Values

If leaders do not actively serve as role models for the organization's core values, then those values become nothing more than lip service. According to behavioral scientist Brent Smith, as role models, leaders are the primary influence on individual ethical behavior. Leaders whose decisions and actions are contrary to the firm's values send a signal that the firm's values are trivial or irrelevant.[57] Firms such as Countrywide Financial articulated core values that were nothing more than window dressing. On the other hand, when leaders model the firm's core values at every turn, the results can be powerful.

Consider Whole Foods, the world's largest organic and natural grocer. Ever since its conception in Austin, Texas, in 1980, Whole Foods has demonstrated a commitment to social responsibility and strong core values (see Table 5.3). In addition to providing consumers with fresh, healthy foods, Whole Foods cares for its employees by creating a transparent and friendly work environment. The company encourages a sense of teamwork through imposing a salary cap for top executives. The company also works to support growers and the environment through sourcing from sustainable growers and supporting such efforts as recycling and reducing energy whenever possible. Whole Foods donates a minimum of

TABLE 5.3 Whole Food's Core Values

- Selling the highest quality natural and organic products
- Satisfying and delighting our customers
- Supporting team member happiness and excellence
- Creating wealth through profits and growth
- Caring about our communities and our environment
- Creating ongoing win-win partnerships with our suppliers
- Promoting the health of our stakeholders through healthy eating education

Source: "Our Core Values," Whole Foods Markets, www.wholefoodsmarket.com/company/corevalues.php (accessed March 1, 2011).

5 percent of profits to local communities in which it operates. Many people are drawn to Whole Foods because of its high quality standards, educational initiatives, and close relationships with suppliers.[58]

Ethical Leaders Are Transparent and Actively Involved in Organizational Decision Making

Transparency fosters openness, the freedom to express ideas, and the ability to question conduct. It also encourages stakeholders to learn about and comment on what a firm is doing. Transparent leaders will not be effective unless they are personally involved in the key decisions that have ethical ramifications. Transformational leaders are collaborative, which opens the door for transparency through interpersonal exchange. Earlier we noted that transformational leaders instill commitment and respect for values that provide guidance on how to deal with ethical issues. Herb Baum, former CEO of the Dial Corp., says, "In today's business environment, if you're a leader—or want to be—and you aren't contributing to a values-based business culture that encourages your entire organization to operate with integrity, your company is as vulnerable as a baby chick in a pit of rattlesnakes." Baum's three remarkably simple principles of transparency are to (1) tell the whole truth, (2) build a values-based culture, and (3) hire "people people."[59]

Ethical Leaders Are Competent Managers Who Take a Holistic View of the Firm's Ethical Culture

Ethical leaders can see a holistic view of their organization and therefore view ethics as a strategic component of decision making, much like marketing, information systems, production, and so on. For instance, Bill Marriott of Marriott Hotels was selected as one of the 100 Most Influential People in Business Ethics by the Ethisphere Institute in 2010. Marriott has demonstrated a commitment to social responsibility by guiding his company toward more ethical sourcing practices and working toward equal rights worldwide.[60]

As the business environment constantly changes, effective leaders must learn to change their strategies accordingly. Figure 5.3 shows four important trends at companies with strong leadership. Note that many of these trends, such as working from home, have only taken on significant importance in the last few years. Top leadership must have a clear

FIGURE 5.3 Leadership Is More Challenging in Today's Business Environment

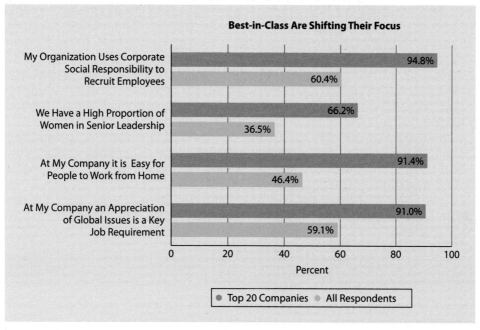

Best-in-Class Are Shifting Their Focus

My Organization Uses Corporate Social Responsibility to Recruit Employees — 94.8% / 60.4%

We Have a High Proportion of Women in Senior Leadership — 66.2% / 36.5%

At My Company it is Easy for People to Work from Home — 91.4% / 46.4%

At My Company an Appreciation of Global Issues is a Key Job Requirement — 91.0% / 59.1%

Percent

● Top 20 Companies ● All Respondents

understanding of key social and global concerns if they hope to lead their companies to success. Leadership continues to be one of the most important drivers of ethical conduct in organizations.

UNDERSTANDING ETHICAL DECISION MAKING AND THE ROLE OF LEADERSHIP

Our ethical decision-making framework demonstrates the many factors that influence ethical decisions. Ethical issue intensity, individual factors, organizational factors, and opportunity result in business ethics evaluations and decisions. An organizational ethical culture is shaped by effective leadership. Without top level support for ethical behavior, the opportunity for employees to engage in their own personal approaches to ethical decision making will evolve. An ethical corporate culture needs shared values along with proper oversight to monitor the complex ethical decisions being made by employees. It requires the establishment of a strong ethics program to educate and develop compliance policies. Consider Kathleen Edmond, the Chief Ethics Officer at Best Buy. Edmond, a continual winner of *Ethisphere*'s Most Influential People in Business Ethics list, has created a culture of transparency at Best Buy. Edmond created a blog that is available to the public that discusses ethics issues, including instances of misconduct at Best Buy. Such transparency keeps the company accountable to its stakeholders. Consequently, Best Buy has also earned a spot as one of *Ethisphere*'s World's Most Ethical Companies.[61]

On the other hand, some companies that have a strong reputation for ethical leadership sometimes fail to maintain their ethical culture. For example, Johnson and Johnson's quick action during the Tylenol murders secured its reputation for putting customer safety first. However, Johnson and Johnson has experienced several quality control issues that have put its reputation as an ethical company into jeopardy. The company underwent 50 product recalls in 15 months due to product contamination or defects. The government has accused it of not acting quickly enough in recalling products. A unit of Johnson and Johnson, DePuy Orthopedics, also recalled two types of replacement hips that had been causing pain in patients, but 93,000 of these devices had already been implanted. This has led to a string of lawsuits as well as increased government scrutiny of Johnson and Johnson plants.[62]

Finally, the more you know about ethical decision making in business, the more likely you will be to make good decisions. There are many challenges in organizations that are beyond the control of any one individual. On the other hand, as you move to higher levels of the organization, there is the opportunity for ethical leadership to become a role model for good ethics. The descriptive framework of ethical decision making in this chapter should provide many insights into the relationships that can contribute to an ethical culture.

SUMMARY

The key components of the ethical decision-making framework include ethical issue intensity, individual factors, organizational factors, and opportunity. These factors are interrelated and influence business ethics evaluations and intentions, which result in ethical or unethical behavior.

The first step in ethical decision making is to recognize that an ethical issue requires an individual or work group to choose among several actions that will ultimately be evaluated as ethical or unethical by various stakeholders. Ethical issue intensity is the perceived relevance or importance of an ethical issue to an individual or work group. It reflects the ethical sensitivity of the individual or work group that triggers the ethical decision-making process. Other factors in our ethical decision-making framework influence this sensitivity, and therefore different individuals often perceive ethical issues differently.

Individual factors such as gender, education, nationality, age, and locus of control can affect the ethical decision-making process, with some factors being more important than others. Organizational factors such as an organization's values often have greater influence on an individual's decisions than that person's own values. In addition, decisions in business are most often made jointly, in work groups and committees, or in conversations and discussions with coworkers. Corporate cultures and structures operate through the ability of individual relationships among the organization's members to influence those members' ethical decisions. A corporate culture can be defined as a set of values, beliefs, goals, norms, and ways of solving problems that members (employees) of an organization share. Corporate culture involves norms that prescribe a wide range of behavior for the organization's members. The ethical culture of an organization indicates whether it has an ethical conscience. Significant others—including peers, managers, coworkers, and subordinates—who influence the work group have more daily impact on an employee's decisions than any other factor in the decision-making framework. Obedience to authority may explain why many business ethics issues are resolved simply by following the directives of a superior.

Ethical opportunity results from conditions that either provide rewards, whether internal or external, or limit barriers to ethical or unethical behavior. Included in opportunity is a person's immediate job context, which includes the motivational techniques superiors use to influence employee behavior. The opportunity employees have for unethical behavior in an organization can be eliminated through formal codes, policies, and rules that are adequately enforced by management.

The ethical decision-making framework is not a guide for making decisions. It is intended to provide insights and knowledge about typical ethical decision-making processes in business organizations. Ethical decision making within organizations does not rely strictly on the personal values and morals of employees. Organizations have cultures of their own, which when combined with corporate governance mechanisms may significantly influence business ethics.

Leadership styles and habits promote an organizational ethical climate. Leadership styles include coercive, authoritative, affiliative, democratic, and coaching elements. Transactional leaders negotiate or barter with employees. Transformational leaders strive for a shared vision and common learning experience. Strong ethical leaders have a strong personal character, have a passion to do the right thing, are proactive, focus on stakeholders' interests, are role models for the organization's values, make transparent decisions, and take a holistic view of the firm's ethical culture.

IMPORTANT TERMS FOR REVIEW

ethical issue intensity	moral intensity	gender
education	nationality	locus of control
external control	internal control	corporate culture
ethical culture	significant other	obedience to authority
opportunity	immediate job context	leadership
transactional leader	transformational leader	

Peter had been a human resource (HR) manager for 18 years and vice president for two more years at Zyedego Corporation, a small company in New Orleans. In the last decade, there have been many changes to what potential/actual employees can be asked and what constitutes fair and equitable treatment. As a result, Peter was having trouble reconciling his individual values with what could be best for the company. Some of the human resource problems that Peter was facing also had legal implications that he would have to consider.

The first issue began with Hurricane Katrina. In its wake, Zyedego employees worked around the clock to get the company up and running again. The company called all employees (if they could locate them) to get them to return to work. Gwyn, one of Peter's HR managers, was planning on asking Dana Gonzales to return to work but found out that Dana was pregnant. Because of the rough condition of the workplace, Gwyn was concerned for Dana's safety. Due to the extreme cutbacks the company was facing after the hurricane, Gwyn felt that the company could not afford to pay Dana for maternity leave or handle any interruptions in productivity that Dana's pregnancy could impose. In addition, Gwyn had some concerns over Dana's citizenship because her passport appeared to be questionable. The flooding had destroyed the original documents, and although Gwyn requested new documents, Dana was slow in providing them. Gwyn asked some difficult questions about Dana's citizenship, and Dana stated that if she did not return to work soon, she would go to a competitor and expected the company to pay severance of two weeks' wages for the time she was out of work during the hurricane.

Another human resource issue involved the hiring of truck drivers. Zyedego hired many truck drivers and routinely requested driving records as part of the preemployment process. Several of the potential new hires had past DWI records. All stated that they would never do it again, had maintained a clean record for at least five years, and understood the consequences of another infraction. Gwyn hired some drivers with infractions to secure the necessary number of drivers needed for the company. However, Gwyn had some concerns over whether she was exposing the company to unnecessary risk because of the increased potential for accidents or repeat DWI violations. Gwyn needed guidance from Peter on the wisdom of continuing these hiring practices.

However, Zyedego had even deeper problems, which was what primarily concerned Peter. The problem really started when Peter was still an HR manager, and involves one family. Guy Martin started working for Zyedego 20 years ago. At the time he was married with two children and had a mortgage. A little over a year ago, Guy separated from his wife, and they eventually divorced, only to remarry six months later. When Guy was hired, Peter had made sure that Guy's son, who has asthma, would be covered by health insurance. Peter also helped out the family several times when money was tight, and provided Guy with overtime work. But tragedy struck the Martins when Guy was killed in the hurricane. Police and rescue workers hunted for his body, but it was never found. Because Martha, Guy's wife, was a stay-at-home mother, their only income had been from Zyedego. The company's death benefits would provide only 50 percent of the deceased's pension for a surviving spouse. Also, because the body had not been found, there was the legal question of death. Usually it takes seven years before one can claim any type of insurance or death-benefit payments, as well as medical insurance, for the family. Even with Social Security benefits, Martha would probably lose the house and could be forced to seek employment.

Zyedego had sustained substantial losses since the hurricane. Insurance companies were extremely slow concerning payments to all the small businesses, arguing about wind versus water damage. Impeding the process of obtaining benefits was the lack of many documents that had been destroyed in the storm.

The trouble really began for Peter when he met with the insurance company about medical reimbursements, death benefits, and pension plans. Darrell Lambert was the chief adjuster for Zyedego's insurance and pension provider.

"Here's another case that we will not cover," said Darrell as he flipped the file to Peter. "We can't help the Martins for a variety of reasons. There is no body, which means no payment until after a judge declares him legally dead. That will take at least a year. While that is being settled, Mrs. Martin and her family will not be eligible for medical coverage unless Zyedego is going to pay their full amount. Finally, and I know this may sound heartless, but Mrs. Martin will only get a maximum of half of Mr. Martin's pension."

"But he was killed on the job!" exclaimed Peter.

"Did you require him to work that day? Did he punch in or out? Is there any record that he was called in from Zyedego to help? The answer is no to all of the above. He helped because he felt obligated to Zyedego. But I am not Zyedego, and I do not have any obligation to the Martins," Darrell said with a smile.

"Peter," continued Darrell, "I know that Zyedego is under intense financial pressure, but we are too. You have approximately 100 families that we will have to pay something to. You and I can spend the next 12 months going over every case, bit by bit, item by item, but if that's what you want, Zyedego will go into bankruptcy. We don't want that to happen. But we also are not going to pay for everything that you claim you are due. Our lawyers will stall the system until you go broke, and your 100 families will get nothing. Well, maybe something in five to seven years. What I am proposing is a way for you to stay in business and for my company to reduce its financial payouts. Remember, we have hundreds of small businesses like you to deal with."

Darrell then calmly said, "My proposal is that you look over these files and reduce your total reimbursements to us by 40 percent. To help you out, I'll start with this case [Martin's]. You decide whether we pay out 40 percent or nothing. Tomorrow at 9:00 A.M., I want you to have 25 cases, including this one, pared down by 40 percent. If not, well, I'm sure my superiors have informed your superiors about this arrangement by now. You should be getting a call within the hour. So, I'll see you here at 9:00," and Darrell walked out the door.

Several hours later, Peter received a phone call from upper management about the deal he was to implement to save the company.

QUESTIONS | EXERCISES

1. What are the legal and ethical risks associated with the decision about hiring truck drivers at Zyedego?
2. What should Peter recommend to Gwyn about Dana's case?
3. Do you think Peter is too emotionally attached to the Martin case to make an objective decision?

*This case is strictly hypothetical; any resemblance to real persons, companies, or situations is coincidental.

CHECK YOUR EQ

Check your EQ, or Ethics Quotient, by completing the following. Assess your performance to evaluate your overall understanding of the chapter material.

1. The first step in ethical decision making is to understand the individual factors that influence the process.   Yes   No

2. "Opportunity" describes the conditions within an organization that limit or permit ethical or unethical behavior.   Yes   No

3. Transactional leaders negotiate compliance and ethics.   Yes   No

4. The most significant influence on ethical behavior in an organization is the opportunity to engage in (un)ethical behavior.   Yes   No

5. Obedience to authority relates to the influence of corporate culture.   Yes   No

ANSWERS **1. No.** The first step is to become more aware that an ethical issue exists and to consider its relevance to the individual or work group. **2. Yes.** Opportunity results from conditions that provide rewards or fail to erect barriers against unethical behavior. **3. Yes.** Transactional leaders barter or negotiate with employees. **4. No.** Significant others have more impact on ethical decisions within an organization. **5. No.** Obedience to authority relates to the influence of significant others and supervisors.

CHAPTER 6

INDIVIDUAL FACTORS:
MORAL PHILOSOPHIES AND VALUES

AN ETHICAL DILEMMA*

One of the problems that Lael Matthews has had to deal with in trying to climb the corporate ladder is the glass ceiling faced by minorities and women. And now, in her current position, she must decide which of three managers to promote, a decision that, as her superior has informed her, could have serious repercussions for her future. The following people are the candidates.

Liz is a 34-year-old African American, divorced with one child, who graduated in the lower half of her college class at Northwest State. She has been with the company for four years and in the industry for eight years, with mediocre performance ratings but a high energy level. She has had some difficulties in managing her staff. Her child has had various medical problems, so higher pay would be helpful. If promoted, Liz would be the first African American female manager at this level. Although Lael has known Liz only a short time, they seem to have hit it off; in fact, Lael once babysat Liz's daughter, Janeen, in an emergency. One downside to promoting Liz might be a perception that Lael is playing favorites.

Roy is a 57-year-old Caucasian, married with three children, who graduated from a private university in the top half of his class. Roy has been with the company for 20 years and in the industry for 30, and he has always been a steady performer, with mostly average ratings. Roy has been passed over for promotions in the past because of his refusal to relocate, but that is no longer a problem. Roy's energy level is average to low; however, he has produced many of the company's top sales performers. This promotion would be his last before retirement, and many in the company feel he has earned it. In fact, one senior manager stopped Lael in the hall and said, "You know, Lael, Roy has been with us for a long time. He has done many good things for the company, sacrificing not only himself but also his family. I really hope that you can see your way to promoting him. It would be a favor to me that I wouldn't forget."

Quang Yeh, a single, 27-year-old Asian American, graduated from State University in the top 3 percent of her class and has been with the company for three years. She is known for putting in 60-hour weeks and for her meticulous management style, which has generated some criticism from her sales staff. The last area that she managed showed record increases, despite the loss of some older accounts who, for some reason, did not like dealing with Quang. Moreover, Quang sued her previous employer for discrimination and won. Lael had heard that Quang was intense and that nothing would stop her from reaching her goals. As Lael was going over some of her notes, another upper-management individual came to her office and said, "You know, Lael, Quang is engaged to my son. I've looked over her personnel files, and she looks very good. She looks like a rising star, which would indicate that she should be promoted as quickly as possible. I realize that you're not in my division, but the way people get transferred, you never know. I would really like to see Quang get this promotion."

As she was considering the choices, Lael's immediate supervisor came to her to talk about Liz. "You know, Lael, Liz is one of a very few people in the company who is both an African American woman and qualified for this position. I've been going over the company's hiring and promotion figures, and it would be very advantageous for me personally and for the company to promote her. I've also spoken to public relations, and they believe that this would be a tremendous boost for the company."

As Lael pondered her decision, she mentally went through each candidate's records and found that each had advantages and disadvantages. While she was considering her problem, the phone rang. It was Liz, sounding frantic. "Lael, I'm sorry to disturb you at this late hour, but I need you to come to the hospital. Janeen has been in an accident, and I don't know who to turn to." When Lael got to the hospital, she found that Janeen's injuries were fairly serious and that Liz would have to miss some work to help with the recuperation process. Lael also realized that this accident would create a financial problem for Liz, which a promotion could help solve.

The next day seemed very long and was punctuated by the announcement that Roy's son was getting married to the vice president's daughter. The wedding would be in June, and it sounded as though it would be a company affair. By 4:30 that afternoon, Lael had gone through four aspirins and two antacids. Her decision was due in two days. What should she do?

QUESTIONS | EXERCISES

1. Discuss the advantages and disadvantages of each candidate.
2. What are the ethical and legal considerations for Lael?
3. Identify the pressures that have made her promotion decision an ethical and legal issue.
4. Discuss the implications of each decision that Lael could make.

*This case is strictly hypothetical; any resemblance to real persons, companies, or situations is coincidental.

Most discussions of business ethics address the role of the individual in ethical decision making, and the model we provided in Chapter 5 identifies individual moral perspectives as a central component of ethical decision making. In this chapter, we provide a detailed description and analysis of how individuals' backgrounds and philosophies influence their decisions. People often use their individual moral philosophies to justify decisions or explain their actions. To understand how people make ethical decisions, it is useful to have a grasp of the major types of moral philosophies. In this chapter, we discuss the stages of cognitive development as they relate to these moral philosophies. We also examine white-collar crime as it relates to moral philosophies and personal values.

MORAL PHILOSOPHY DEFINED

When people talk about philosophy, they are usually referring to the general system of values by which they live. **Moral philosophy,** on the other hand, refers to the specific principles or rules that people use to decide what is right and wrong. It is important to understand the distinction between moral philosophies and business ethics. Moral philosophies are person-specific, while business ethics is based on decisions made by groups or when carrying out tasks to meet business objectives. A moral philosophy is a person's principles and values. In the context of business, ethics refers to what the group, firm, or strategic business unit (SBU) defines as right or wrong actions that pertain to its business operations and the objective of profits, earnings per share, or some other financial measure of success. For example, a production manager may be guided by a general philosophy of management that emphasizes encouraging workers to get to know as much as possible about the product that they are manufacturing. However, the manager's moral philosophy comes into play when he must make decisions such as whether to notify employees in advance of upcoming layoffs. Although workers would prefer advance warning, giving it might adversely affect the quality and quantity of production. Such decisions require a person to evaluate the "rightness," or morality, of choices in terms of his or her own principles and values.

Moral philosophies present guidelines for "determining how conflicts in human interests are to be settled and for optimizing mutual benefit of people living together in groups."[1] They direct businesspeople as they formulate business strategies and resolve specific ethical issues. However, there is no single moral philosophy that everyone accepts. Moral philosophies are often used to defend a particular type of economic system and individuals' behavior within these systems.

Adam Smith is considered the father of free-market capitalism. He was a professor of logic and moral philosophy and wrote the treatise "The Theory of Moral Sentiments" (1759) and the book *Inquiry into the Nature and Causes of the Wealth of Nations* (1776). Smith believed that business was and should be guided by the morals of good people. But in the eighteenth century, Smith could not imagine the complexity of modern markets or the size of multinationals or the fact that four or five companies could gain control of the vast majority of the resources of the world. His ideas did not envision the full force of democracy, or the immense wealth and power some firms could wield within countries.

Under capitalism, some managers view profit as the ultimate goal of an enterprise and therefore may not be concerned about the impact of their firms' decisions on society. The economist Milton Friedman supports this viewpoint, contending that the market will reward or punish companies for unethical conduct without the need for government regulation.[2] The emergence of this Friedman-type capitalism as the dominant and most widely accepted economic system has created market-driven societies around the world. Over the past six decades, the United States has been waging an ideological war over capitalism, first with the Soviet Union, then with Latin America in the 1980s, and finally with China. Even China's communist government has adapted capitalism and free enterprise to help it become a leading economic power. Of the 43 million companies in China, 93 percent are private, and they employ 92 percent of Chinese workers.[3]

The United States has been exporting the idea that the invisible hand of free-market capitalism can solve the troubles of mankind and guide societies toward greater happiness and prosperity as a result of the increased availability of products and services. Marketing helps consumers to understand, compare, and obtain these products and services, thereby increasing the efficiency and effectiveness of the exchange. However, free markets may not solve all problems. For example, excessive consumption has negative effects on the environment and can be psychologically, spiritually, and physically unhealthy.[4] In other words, more is not necessarily best in every situation.

Economic systems not only allocate resources and products within a society but also influence, and are influenced by, the actions and beliefs of individuals and of society as a whole. The success of an economic system depends on both its philosophical framework and on the individuals within the system who maintain moral philosophies that bring people together in a cooperative, efficient, and productive marketplace. There is a long Western tradition going back to Aristotle of questioning whether a market economy and individual moral behavior are compatible. The fact of the matter is that individuals in today's society exist within a framework of social, political, and economic institutions.

> "People who face ethical issues often base their decisions on their own values and principles of right or wrong."

People who face ethical issues often base their decisions on their own values and principles of right or wrong, most of which they have learned through the socialization process with the help of family members, social groups, religions, and formal education. Individual factors that influence decision making include personal moral philosophies. Ethical dilemmas arise in problem-solving situations in which the rules governing decision making are vague or in conflict. In real-life situations, there is no substitute for an individual's own critical thinking and ability to accept responsibility for his or her decisions.

Moral philosophies are ideal moral perspectives that provide individuals with abstract principles for guiding their social existence. For example, a person's decision to recycle waste or to purchase or sell recycled or recyclable products is influenced by moral philosophies and individual attitudes toward recycling.[5] It is often difficult to implement an individual moral philosophy within the complex environment of a business organization. On the other hand, our economic system depends on individuals coming together and sharing philosophies to create the values, trust, and expectations that allow the system to work. Most employees within a business organization do not think about the particular moral philosophy they are using when they are confronted with an ethical issue.

Many theories associated with moral philosophies refer to a value orientation and to concepts such as economics, idealism, and relativism. The concept of the **economic value orientation** is associated with values that can be quantified by monetary means; according to this theory, if an act produces more value for its effort, then it should be accepted as ethical. **Idealism,** on the other hand, is a moral philosophy that places special value on ideas and ideals as products of the mind. The term refers to the efforts required to account for all objects in nature and experience and to assign to thema higher order of existence. Studies have found that there is a positive correlation between idealistic thinking and ethical decision making. **Realism** is the view that an external world exists independent of our perception of it. Realists assume that humankind is not naturally benevolent and kind, but instead inherently self-centered and competitive. According to realists, each person is ultimately guided by his or her own self-interest. Research shows a negative correlation between realistic thinking and ethical decision making. The belief that all actions are ultimately self-motivated seems to lead to a tendency toward unethical decision making.

MORAL PHILOSOPHIES

There are many moral philosophies, but because a detailed study of all of them is beyond the scope of this book, we will limit our discussion to those that are most applicable to the study of business ethics. Our approach focuses on the most basic concepts needed to help you understand the ethical decision-making process in business. We do not prescribe the use of any particular moral philosophy, for there is no one correct way to resolve ethical issues in business.

To help you understand how the moral philosophies discussed in this chapter may be applied in decision making, we use a hypothetical situation as an illustration. Suppose that Sam Colt, a sales representative, is preparing a sales presentation for his firm, Midwest Hardware, which manufactures nuts and bolts. Sam hopes to obtain a large sale from a construction firm that is building a bridge across the Mississippi River near St. Louis, Missouri. The bolts manufactured by Midwest Hardware have a 3 percent defect rate, which, although acceptable in the industry, makes them unsuitable for use in certain types of projects, such as those that may be subject to sudden, severe stress. The new bridge will be located near the New Madrid Fault line, the source of the United States' greatest earthquake in 1811. The epicenter of that earthquake, which caused extensive damage and altered the flow of the Mississippi, is less than 200 miles from the new bridge site. Earthquake experts believe there is a 50 percent chance that an earthquake with a magnitude greater than 7 will occur somewhere along the New Madrid Fault by the year 2030. Bridge construction in the area is not regulated by earthquake codes, however. If Sam wins the sale, he will earn a commission of $25,000 on top of his regular salary. But if he tells the contractor about the defect rate, Midwest may lose the sale to a competitor that markets bolts with a lower defect rate. Sam's ethical issue is whether to point out to the bridge contractor that, in the event of an earthquake, some Midwest bolts could fail, possibly resulting in the collapse of the bridge.

We will come back to this illustration as we discuss particular moral philosophies, asking how Sam Colt might use each philosophy to resolve his ethical issue. We don't judge the quality of Sam's decision, and we do not advocate any one moral philosophy; in fact, this illustration and Sam's decision rationales are necessarily simplistic as well as hypothetical. In reality, the decision maker would probably have many more factors to consider in making his or her choice and thus might reach a different decision. With that note of caution, we introduce the concept of goodness and several types of moral philosophy: teleology, deontology, the relativist perspective, virtue ethics, and justice (see Table 6.1).

Instrumental and Intrinsic Goodness

To appreciate moral philosophy, one must understand the different perspectives on the notion of goodness. Is there a clear and unwavering line between "good" and "bad"? What is the relationship between the ends and the means in generating "good" and "bad" outcomes? Is there some way to determine if the ends can be identified independently as good or bad? Aristotle, for example, argued that happiness is an intrinsically good end—in other words, its goodness is natural and universal, without relativity. On the other hand, the philosopher Immanuel Kant argued that goodwill, seriously applied toward accomplishment, is the only thing good in itself.

TABLE 6.1 A Comparison of the Philosophies Used in Business Decisions

Teleology	Stipulates that acts are morally right or acceptable if they produce some desired result, such as realization of self-interest or utility
Egoism	Defines right or acceptable actions as those that maximize a particular person's self-interest as defined by the individual
Utilitarianism	Defines right or acceptable actions as those that maximize total utility, or the greatest good for the greatest number of people
Deontology	Focuses on the preservation of individual rights and on the intentions associated with a particular behavior rather than on its consequences
Relativist	Evaluates ethicalness subjectively on the basis of individual and group experiences
Virtue ethics	Assumes that what is moral in a given situation is not only what conventional morality requires but also what the mature person with a "good" moral character would deem appropriate
Justice	Evaluates ethicalness on the basis of fairness: distributive, procedural, and interactional

©Cengage Learning 2013

Two basic concepts of goodness are monism and pluralism. **Monists** believe that only one thing is intrinsically good, and pluralists believe that two or more things are intrinsically good. Monists are often characterized by **hedonism**—the idea that pleasure is the ultimate good, or that the best moral end involves the greatest balance of pleasure over pain. Hedonism defines right or acceptable behavior as that which maximizes personal pleasure. Moral philosophers describe those who believe that more pleasure is better as **quantitative hedonists** and those who believe that it is possible to get too much of a good thing (such as pleasure) as **qualitative hedonists.**

Pluralists, often referred to as non-hedonists, take the opposite position that no *one* thing is intrinsically good. For example, a pluralist might view beauty, aesthetic experience, knowledge, and personal affection as ultimate goods. For example, Plato argued that the good life is a mixture of (1) moderation and fitness, (2) proportion and beauty, (3) intelligence and wisdom, (4) sciences and arts, and (5) pure pleasures of the soul.

Although all pluralists are non-hedonists, all monists are not necessarily hedonists. An individual can believe in a single intrinsic good other than pleasure; Machiavelli and Nietzsche held power to be the sole good, for example, and Kant's belief in the single virtue of goodwill classifies him as a monistic non-hedonist.

A more modern view is expressed in the instrumentalist position. Sometimes called pragmatists, **instrumentalists** reject the ideas that (1) ends can be separated from the means that produce them and that (2) ends, purposes, or outcomes are intrinsically good in and of themselves. The philosopher John Dewey argued that the difference between ends and means is merely a matter of the individual's perspective; thus, almost any action can be an end or a mean. Dewey gives the example that people eat to be able to work, and they work to be able to eat. From a practical standpoint, an end is only a remote mean, and the means are but a series of acts viewed from an earlier stage. From this conclusion it follows that there is no such thing as a single, universal end.

A discussion of moral value often revolves around the nature of goodness, but theories of moral obligation change the question to "What makes an action right or obligatory?"

Goodness theories typically focus on the *end result* of actions and the goodness or happiness created by them. **Obligation theories** emphasize the *means* and *motives* by which actions are justified, and are divided into the categories of teleology and deontology.

Teleology

Teleology (from the Greek word for "end" or "purpose") refers to moral philosophies in which an act is considered morally right or acceptable if it produces some desired result, such as pleasure, knowledge, career growth, the realization of self-interest, utility, wealth, or even fame. Teleological philosophies assess the moral worth of a behavior by looking at its consequences, and thus moral philosophers today often refer to these theories as **consequentialism.** Two important teleological philosophies that often guide decision making in individual business decisions are egoism and utilitarianism.

Egoism defines right or acceptable behavior in terms of its consequences for the individual. Egoists believe that they should make decisions that maximize their own self-interest, which is defined differently by each individual. Depending on the egoist, self-interest may be construed as physical well-being, power, pleasure, fame, a satisfying career, a good family life, wealth, or something else. In an ethical decision-making situation, an egoist will probably choose the alternative that contributes most to his or her self-interest. Many believe that egoistic people and companies are inherently unethical, short-term oriented, and willing to take advantage of any opportunity for gain. Some telemarketers demonstrate this egoism in action when they prey on elderly consumers who may be vulnerable because of loneliness or fear of losing their financial independence. Thousands of senior citizens fall victim to fraudulent telemarketers every year, in many cases losing all their savings and sometimes even their homes.

However, there also is **enlightened egoism.** Enlightened egoists take a long-range perspective and allow for the well-being of others although their own self-interest remains paramount. An example of enlightened egoism is a person helping a turtle across a highway because if it were killed the person would feel distressed.[6] Enlightened egoists may abide by professional codes of ethics, control pollution, avoid cheating on taxes, help create jobs, and support community projects. Yet they do so not because these actions benefit others but because they help achieve some ultimate individual goal, such as advancement within their firms. An enlightened egoist might call management's attention to a coworker who is making false accounting reports, but only to safeguard the company's reputation and thus the egoist's own job security. In addition, an enlightened egoist could become a whistle-blower and report misconduct to a regulatory agency to receive a reward for exposing misconduct. When businesses donate money, resources, or time to specific causes and institutions, their motives may not be purely altruistic either. For example, IBM donates or reduces the cost of computers to educational institutions in exchange for tax breaks. In addition, IBM hopes to build future sales by placing its products on campuses. When students enter the workforce, they may request the IBM products with which they have become familiar. Although the company's actions benefit society in general, in the long run they also benefit IBM.

Let's return to the hypothetical case of Sam Colt, who must decide whether to warn the bridge contractor that 3 percent of Midwest Hardware's bolts are likely to be defective. If he is an egoist, he will choose the alternative that maximizes his own self-interest. If he defines his self-interest in terms of personal wealth, his personal moral philosophy may lead him to value a $25,000 commission more than a chance to reduce the risk of a bridge collapse. As a result, an egoist might well resolve this ethical dilemma by keeping quiet about the bolts' defect rate, hoping to win the sale and the $25,000 commission. He may rationalize that there is a slim chance of an earthquake, that bolts would not be a factor in a major earthquake, and that, even if defective bolts were a factor, no one would actually be able to prove that they had caused the bridge to collapse.

> "The utilitarian seeks the greatest good for the greatest number of people."

Like egoism, **utilitarianism** is concerned with consequences, but unlike the egoist, the utilitarian seeks the greatest good for the greatest number of people. Utilitarians believe that they should make decisions that result in the greatest total *utility,* or the greatest benefit for all those affected by a decision. An example of utilitarianism may be President Obama's 2009 economic stimulus package. The administration may have weighed its costs to the American taxpayer against the greater costs of allowing the entire economy to fall into a depression.

Utilitarian decision making relies on a systematic comparison of the costs and benefits to all affected parties. Using such a cost–benefit analysis, a utilitarian decision maker calculates the utility of the consequences of all possible alternatives and then selects the one that results in the greatest benefit. For example, the U.S. Supreme Court has ruled that supervisors are responsible for the sexual misconduct of employees, even if the employers knew nothing about the behavior, a decision that established a strict standard for harassment on the job. One of the justices wrote that the burden on the employer to prevent harassment is "one of the costs of doing business."[7] The Court had decided that the greatest utility to society would result from forcing businesses to prevent harassment.

In evaluating an action's consequences, utilitarians must consider all of the potential costs and benefits for all of the people affected by a decision. For example, Baxter Pharmaceuticals sells an anticoagulant drug called heparin, and for a time Baxter's suppliers in China were deliberately cutting their raw heparin batches with a counterfeit product to reduce costs. The U.S. Food and Drug Administration discovered problems with heparin from China when patients reported difficulty breathing, vomiting, excessive sweating, rapidly falling blood pressure, and even death.[8] If Baxter Pharmaceuticals or its suppliers had done a utilitarian analysis and realized that the costs associated with false heparin could include patient death, they might have chosen to pay more money for the real drug.

Utilitarians use various criteria to evaluate the morality of an action. Some utilitarian philosophers have argued that general rules should be followed to decide which action is best.[9] These **rule utilitarians** determine behavior on the basis of principles or rules designed to promote the greatest utility, rather than on individual examinations of each situation they encounter. One such rule might be "Bribery is wrong." If people felt free to offer bribes whenever they might be useful, the world would become chaotic; therefore, a rule prohibiting bribery would increase utility. A rule utilitarian would not bribe an official, even to preserve workers' jobs, but instead would adhere strictly to the rule. Rule utilitarians do not automatically accept conventional moral rules, however; if they determined that an alternative rule would promote greater utility, they would advocate its use instead.

Other utilitarian philosophers have argued that the rightness of each individual action must be evaluated to determine whether it produces the greatest utility for the greatest number of people.[10] These **act utilitarians** examine specific actions, rather than the general rules governing them, to assess whether they will result in the greatest utility. Rules such as "Bribery is wrong" serve only as general guidelines for act utilitarians. They would likely agree that bribery is generally wrong, not because there is anything inherently wrong with bribery, but because the total amount of utility decreases when one person's interests are placed ahead of those of society. In a particular case, however, an act utilitarian might argue that bribery is acceptable. For example, a sales manager might believe that his or her firm will not win a construction contract unless a local government official gets a bribe, and if the firm does not obtain the contract, it will have to lay off 100 workers. The manager might therefore argue that bribery is justified because saving 100 jobs creates more utility than obeying a law. For example, IBM paid $10 million to settle civil charges of bribery; according to the SEC, hundreds of IBM employees allegedly gave South Korean and Chinese officials cash, computers, travel, and entertainment in exchange for millions of dollars in government contracts.[11] These IBM employees may have decided that winning the contracts generated the most utility for themselves and for the company.

Now suppose that Sam Colt, the bolt salesperson, is a utilitarian. Before making his decision, he would conduct a cost–benefit analysis to assess which alternative would create the greatest utility. On the one hand, building the bridge would improve roadways and allow more people to cross the Mississippi River to reach jobs in St. Louis. The project would create hundreds of jobs, enhance the local economy, and unite communities on both sides of the river. Additionally, it would increase the revenues of Midwest Hardware, allowing the firm to invest more in research to lower the defect rate of the bolts it produces in the future. On the other hand, a bridge collapse could kill or injure as many as 100 people. But the bolts have only a 3 percent defect rate, there is only a 50 percent probability of an earthquake *somewhere* along the fault line, and there might be only a few cars on the bridge at the time of a disaster.

After analyzing the costs and benefits of the situation, Sam might rationalize that building the bridge with his company's bolts would create more utility (jobs, unity, economic growth, and company growth) than would result from telling the bridge contractor that the bolts might fail in an earthquake. If so, a utilitarian would probably not alert the bridge contractor to the defect rate of the bolts.

Deontology

Deontology (from the Greek word for "ethics") refers to moral philosophies that focus on the rights of individuals and on the intentions associated with a particular behavior rather than its consequences. Fundamental to deontological theory is the idea that equal respect must be given to all persons. Unlike utilitarians, deontologists argue that there are some things that we should *not* do, even to maximize utility. For example, deontologists would consider it wrong to kill an innocent person or commit a serious injustice against someone, no matter how much greater social utility might result from doing so, because such an action would infringe on individual rights. The utilitarian, however, might consider an action that resulted in a person's death acceptable if that action lead to some greater benefit. Deontological philosophies regard certain behaviors as inherently right, and the determination of this rightness focuses on the individual actor, not on society. Therefore these perspectives are sometimes referred to as **nonconsequentialism,** a system of ethics based on *respect for persons.*

Contemporary deontology has been greatly influenced by the German philosopher Immanuel Kant, who developed the so-called **categorical imperative:** "Act as if the maxim of thy action were to become by thy will a universal law of nature."[12] Simply put, if you feel comfortable allowing everyone in the world to see you commit an act and if your rationale for acting in a particular manner is suitable to become a universal principle guiding behavior, then committing that act is ethical. A person who borrows money and promises to return it with no intention of keeping that promise cannot "universalize" his or her act. If everyone were to borrow money without the intention of returning it, no one would take such promises seriously, and all lending would cease.[13] The rationale for the action would not be a suitable universal principle, and the act could not be considered ethical.

The term *nature* is crucial for deontologists. In general, deontologists regard the nature of moral principles as permanent and stable, and they believe that compliance with these principles defines ethicalness. Deontologists believe that individuals have certain absolute rights, including freedom of conscience, freedom of consent, freedom of privacy, freedom of speech, and due process.[14]

To decide whether a behavior is ethical, deontologists look for conformity to moral principles. For example, if a manufacturing worker becomes ill or dies as a result of conditions in the workplace, a deontologist might argue that the company must modify its production processes to correct the condition, no matter what the cost—even if it means bankrupting the company and thus causing all workers to lose their jobs. In contrast, a utilitarian would analyze all the costs and benefits of modifying production processes and make a decision on that basis. This example is greatly oversimplified, of course, but it helps to clarify the difference between teleology and deontology. In short, teleological philosophies consider the *ends* associated with an action, whereas deontological philosophies consider the *means*.

> "Teleological philosophies consider the *ends* associated with an action, whereas deontological philosophies consider the *means*."

Returning again to our bolt salesperson, let's consider a deontological Sam Colt. He would probably feel obligated to tell the bridge contractor about the defect rate because of the potential loss of life that might result from an earthquake-caused bridge collapse. Even though constructing the bridge would benefit residents and earn Sam a substantial commission, the failure of the bolts during an earthquake would infringe on the rights of any person crossing the bridge at the time of the collapse. Thus, the deontological Sam would be likely to inform the bridge contractor about the defect rate and point out the earthquake risk, even though he would probably lose the sale as a result.

As with utilitarians, deontologists may be divided into those who focus on moral rules and those who focus on the nature of the acts themselves. **Rule deontologists** believe that conformity to general moral principles based on logic determines ethicalness. Examples include Kant's categorical imperative and the Golden Rule of the Judeo-Christian tradition: "Do unto others as you would have them do unto you." Such rules, or principles, guiding ethical behavior override the imperatives that emerge from a specific context. One could argue that Jeffery Wigand—who exposed the underside of the tobacco industry when he blew the whistle on his employer, Brown & Williamson Tobacco—was such a rule deontologist. Although it cost him financially and socially, Wigand testified to Congress about the realities of marketing cigarettes and their effects on society.[15]

Rule deontology is determined by the relationship between the basic rights of the individual and a set of rules governing conduct. For example, a video store owner accused of distributing obscene materials could argue from a rule deontological perspective that the basic right to freedom of speech overrides the indecent or pornographic aspects of his business. Indeed, the free-speech argument has held up in many U.S. courts. Kant and rule deontologists would support a process of discovery to identify the moral issues relevant to a firm's mission and objectives. Then they would follow a process of justifying that mission or those objectives based on rules.[16] An example of a rule deontologist is JetBlue's former CEO David Neeleman. Because of a severe snowstorm, several JetBlue flights were delayed for as many as nine hours on the runway, and passengers were kept in their seats. After the incident, Neeleman issued a public apology for his company's mismanagement of the situation, introduced a "Customer Bill of Rights,"[17] and offered $40 million in compensation to the affected passengers.

Act deontologists, in contrast, hold that actions are the proper basis on which to judge morality or ethicalness. Act deontology requires that a person use equity, fairness, and impartiality when making and enforcing decisions.[18] For act deontologists, past experiences are more important than rules; rules serve only as guidelines in the decision-making process. In effect, act deontologists suggest that people simply *know* that certain acts are right or wrong, regardless of their consequences. In addition, act deontologists consider that the unique characteristics of a particular act or moment in time take precedence over any rule. For example, many people view data collection by Internet sites as a violation of personal privacy; regardless of any website's stated rules or policies, many Internet users want to be left alone unless they provide permission to be tracked while online. Privacy has become such an issue that the government is considering regulation to protect online users, including the adoption of "do not track" technology.[19] Research suggests that rule and act deontological principles play a larger role in a person's decision than teleological philosophies.[20]

As we have seen, ethical issues can be evaluated from many different perspectives. Each type of philosophy discussed here would provide a clear basis for deciding whether a particular action was right or wrong. Adherents of different personal moral philosophies may disagree in their evaluations of a given action, yet all are behaving ethically *according to their own standards*. The relativist perspective may be helpful in understanding how people make such decisions in practice.

Relativist Perspective

From the **relativist perspective,** definitions of ethical behavior are derived subjectively from the experiences of individuals and groups. Relativists use themselves or the people around them as their basis for defining ethical standards, and the various forms of relativism include descriptive, metaethical, and normative.[21] **Descriptive relativism** relates to observations of other cultures. Different cultures exhibit different norms, customs, and values, but these observations say nothing about the higher questions of ethical justification. At this point metaethical relativism comes into play. **Metaethical relativism** proposes that people naturally see situations from their own perspectives, and that there is no objective way of resolving ethical disputes between different value systems and individuals. Simply put, one culture's moral philosophy cannot logically be preferred to another's because no meaningful basis for comparison exists. Because ethical rules are embedded in a specific culture, the values and behaviors of people in one culture do not generally influence the behaviors of people in another culture.[22] Finally, at the individual level of reasoning, we have **normative relativism**. Normative relativists assume that one person's opinion is as good as another's.[23]

Basic relativism acknowledges that we live in a world in which people have many different views and bases from which to justify decisions as right or wrong. The relativist looks to the interacting groups and tries to determine probable solutions based on group consensus. When formulating business strategies and plans, for example, a relativist would try to anticipate the conflicts that might arise between the different philosophies held by members of the organization, its suppliers, its customers, and the community at large.

The relativist observes the actions of members of an involved group and attempts to determine that group's consensus on a given behavior. A positive consensus signifies that the group considers the action to be ethical. However, such judgments may not remain valid forever. As circumstances evolve or the makeup of the group changes, a formerly accepted behavior may come to be viewed as wrong or unethical, or vice versa. Within the accounting profession, for example, it was traditionally considered unethical to advertise. However, advertising has now gained acceptance among accountants. This shift in ethical views may be the result of the increase in the number of accountants, which has led to greater competition. Moreover, the federal government investigated the restrictions that accounting groups placed on their members and concluded that they inhibited free competition. Consequently, advertising is now acceptable because of the informal consensus that emerged on this issue in the accounting industry.

One problem with relativism is that it emphasizes peoples' differences while ignoring their basic similarities. Similarities across different people and cultures—such as beliefs against incest, murder, and theft, or beliefs that reciprocity and respect for the elderly are good—may be hard to explain from the relativist perspective. Additionally, studies suggest that relativism is negatively correlated to a person's sensitivity to ethical issues. Thus, if someone is a relativist, he or she will be less likely to detect issues that have an ethical component.[24] On the other hand, managers with high relativism may show more commitment to completing a project. This indicates that relativism is associated with dedication to group values and objectives, leading to less independent ethical decision making.[25]

If Midwest Hardware salesperson Sam Colt were a relativist, he would attempt to determine consensus before deciding whether to tell his prospective customer about the bolts' defect rate. The relativist Sam Colt would look at his company's policy and at the general industry standards for disclosure. He might also informally survey his colleagues and superiors as well as consult industry trade journals and codes of ethics. Such investigations would help him determine the group consensus, which should reflect a variety of moral philosophies. If he learns that company policy and industry practice suggest discussing defect rates with those customers for whom faulty bolts may cause serious problems, he may infer that there is a consensus on the matter. As a relativist, he probably would inform the bridge contractor that some of the bolts may fail, perhaps leading to a bridge collapse in the event of an earthquake. Conversely, if he determines that the normal practice in his company and the industry is not to inform customers about defect rates, he would probably not discuss the bolt defect rate with the bridge contractor.

Virtue Ethics

Virtue ethics argues that ethical behavior involves not only adhering to conventional moral standards but also considering what a mature person with a "good" moral character would deem appropriate in a given situation. A moral virtue represents an acquired disposition that is valued as a part of an individual's character. As individuals develop socially, they come to behave in ways that they consider to be moral.[26] For example, a person who has the character trait of honesty will be disposed to tell the truth because it is considered to be the right approach in terms of human communication.

A virtue is considered praiseworthy because it is an achievement that an individual has developed through practice and commitment.[27] Proponents of virtue ethics often list basic goods and virtues, which are presented as positive and useful mental habits or cultivated character traits. Aristotle named loyalty, courage, wit, community, and judgment as "excellences" that society requires. While listing the most important virtues is a popular theoretical task, however, the philosopher John Dewey cautions that virtues should not be looked at separately, and points out that examining interactions between virtues actually provides the best idea of a person's integrity of character.

The virtue ethics approach to business can be summarized as follows:

1. Good corporate ethics programs encourage individual virtue and integrity.
2. By the employee's role in the community (organization), these virtues form a good person.
3. An individual's ultimate purpose is to serve society's demands and the public good and to be rewarded in his or her career.
4. The well-being of the community goes hand in hand with individual excellence.[28]

The difference between deontology, teleology, and virtue ethics is that the first two are applied *deductively* to problems, whereas virtue ethics is applied *inductively*. Virtue ethics assumes that societal moral rules form the foundation of virtue. Our political, social, and economic systems depend upon the presence of certain virtues among citizens in order to function successfully.[29]

Indeed, virtue ethics could be thought of as a dynamic theory of how to conduct business activities. The virtue ethicist believes that a successful market economy depends upon social institutions such as family, school, church, and community, in which virtues can be nurtured. These virtues, including honesty, trust, tolerance, and restraint, create obligations that make cooperation possible. In a market economy based on virtues, individuals have powerful incentives to conform to prevailing standards of behavior. Some philosophers think that social virtues may be eroded by the market, but virtue ethicists believe that economic institutions are in balance with, and support, other social institutions.[30] Some of the virtues that could be seen as driving a market economy are listed in Table 6.2. Although not comprehensive, the list provides examples of the types of virtues that support the conduct of business.

> "In a market economy based on virtues, individuals have powerful incentives to conform to prevailing standards of behavior."

The elements of virtue that are most important to business transactions are trust, self-control, empathy, fairness, and truthfulness. Unvirtuous characteristics include lying, cheating, fraud, and corruption. In their broadest sense, concepts of virtue appear across all cultures. The problem of virtue ethics comes in its implementation within and between cultures. For example, if a company tacitly approves of corruption, the employee who adheres to the virtues of trust and truthfulness would consider it wrong to sell unneeded repair parts despite the organization's approval of such acts. Other employees might view this truthful employee as highly ethical; however, in order to rationalize their own behavior, they may judge his or her ethics as going beyond what is required by the job or society. Critics of virtue ethics argue that true virtue is an unattainable goal, but to virtue ethicists, this relativistic argument is meaningless because they believe in the universality of the elements of virtue.

If bolt salesperson Sam Colt were a virtue ethicist, he would consider the elements of virtue (such as honesty and trust) and then tell the prospective customer about the defect rate and about his concerns regarding the building of the bridge. Sam would not resort to puffery to explain the product or its risks, and might even suggest alternative products or companies that would lower the probability of the bridge collapsing.

Justice

Justice is fair treatment and due reward in accordance with ethical or legal standards, including the disposition to deal with perceived injustices of others. The justice of a situation is based on the perceived rights of individuals and on the intentions of the people involved

TABLE 6.2 Virtues that Support Business Transactions

Trust: The predisposition to place confidence in the behavior of others while taking the risk that the expected behavior will not be performed	Eliminates the need for and associated cost of monitoring compliance with agreements, contracts, and reciprocal agreements, as there is the expectation that a promise or agreement can be relied on
Self-control: The disposition to pass up an immediate advantage or gratification; the ability to avoid exploiting a known opportunity for personal gain	Gives up short-term self-interest for long-term benefits
Empathy: The ability to share the feelings or emotions of others	Promotes civility because success in the market depends on the courteous treatment of people who have the option of going to competitors; the ability to anticipate needs and satisfy customers and employees contributes to a firm's economic success
Fairness: The disposition to deal equitably with the perceived injustices of others	Often relates to doing the right thing with respect to small matters in order to cultivate a long-term business relationship
Truthfulness: The disposition to provide the facts or correct information as known to the individual	Involves avoiding deception and contributes to trust in business relationships
Learning: The disposition to constantly acquire knowledge internal and external to the firm, whether about an industry, corporate culture, or other societies	Gaining knowledge to make better, more informed decisions
Gratitude: A sign of maturity that is the foundation of civility and decency	The recognition that people do not succeed alone
Civility: The disposition or essence of courtesy, politeness, respect, and consideration for others	Relates to the process of doing business in a culturally correct way, thus decreasing communication errors and increasing trust
Moral leadership: Strength of character, peace of mind and heart, leading to happiness in life	A trait of leaders who follow a consistent pattern of behavior based on virtues

Source: Adapted from Ian Maitland, "Virtuous Markets: The Market as School of the Virtues," *Business Ethics Quarterly* (January 1997): 97; and Gordon B. Hinckley, *Standing for Something: 10 Neglected Virtues that Will Heal Our Hearts and Homes* (New York: Three Rivers Press, 2001).

in a business interaction. In other words, justice relates to the issue of what individuals feel they are due based on their rights and performance in the workplace. For this reason, justice is more likely to be based on deontological moral philosophies than on teleological or utilitarian philosophies.

Three types of justice provide a framework for evaluating different situations (see Table 6.3). **Distributive justice** is based on the evaluation of the outcomes or results of a business relationship. If some employees feel that they are paid less than their coworkers for the same work, they have concerns about distributive justice. Distributive justice is difficult to effect when one member of the business exchange intends to take advantage of the relationship. A boss who forces his employees to do more work so that he can take more time off would be unjust because he is taking advantage of his position. Situations such as this cause an imbalance in distributive justice.

TABLE 6.3 Types of Justice

Justice Type	Areas of Emphasis
Distributive justice: Based on the evaluation of *outcomes* or *results* of the business relationship	Benefits derived Equity in rewards
Procedural justice: Based on the *processes* and *activities* that produce the outcome or results	Decision-making process Level of access, openness, and participation
Interactional justice: Based on *relationships* and the *treatment* of others	Accuracy of information Truthfulness, respect, and courtesy in the process

©Cengage Learning 2013

Procedural justice considers the processes and activities that produce a particular outcome. A climate that emphasizes procedural justice positively influences employees' attitudes and behaviors toward work-group cohesion. The visibility of supervisors and the work group's perceptions of its own cohesiveness are products of a climate of procedural justice.[31] When there is strong employee support for decisions, decision makers, organizations, and outcomes, procedural justice is less important to the individual. In contrast, when employees' support for decisions, decision makers, organizations, or outcomes is not very strong, then procedural justice becomes more important.[32] For example, Nugget Markets in Woodland, California, has a corporate culture that focuses on employees, who create policies for each store. Because of the economy and as a result of employee comments, Nugget Markets gives employees cards good for 10 percent discounts on $500 worth of groceries every month, and at one employee-appreciation event, the executive team members washed the cars of all the associates.[33] Thus, Nugget Markets uses methods of procedural justice to establish positive stakeholder relationships by promoting understanding and inclusion in the decision-making process. Evaluations of performance that are not consistently developed and applied can lead to problems with procedural justice. For instance, employees' concerns about unequal compensation relate to their perceptions that the processes of justice in their company are inconsistent.

Interactional justice is based on the relationships between organizational members, including the way employees and management treat one another. Interactional justice is linked to fairness within member interactions. It often involves an individual's relationship with the accuracy of the information a business organization provides. Although interactional justice often refers to how managers treat their subordinates, employees can also be guilty in creating interactional justice disputes. For example, many employees admit that they stay home when they are not really sick if they feel they can get away with it. Such workplace absenteeism costs businesses millions of dollars each year.

All three types of justice—distributive, procedural, and interactional—could be used to measure a single business situation and the fairness of the organization and individuals involved. In general, justice evaluations result in restitution seeking, relationship building, and evaluations of fairness in business relationships. Using the example of Sam Colt, Sam would feel obligated to tell all affected parties about the bolt defect rate and the possible consequences in order to create a fair transaction process.

APPLYING MORAL PHILOSOPHY
TO ETHICAL DECISION MAKING

> "Individuals use different moral philosophies depending on whether they are making a personal decision or a work-related decision."

Individuals use different moral philosophies depending on whether they are making a personal decision or a work-related decision.[34] Two things may explain this behavior. First, in the business arena, some goals and pressures for success differ from the goals and pressures in a person's life outside of work. As a result, an employee might view a specific action as good in the business sector but unacceptable outside the work environment. Some suggest that business managers are morally different from other people. In a way, this is correct, in that business contains one variable that is absent from other situations: the profit motive. The various factors that make up a person's moral philosophy are weighted differently in a business (profit) situation. The comment "It's not personal, it's just business" demonstrates the conflict businesspeople can experience when their personal values do not align with utilitarian or profit-oriented decisions. The reality is that if firms do not make a profit, they will fail. However, this fact should not be a justification for seeking excessive profits or executive pay, issues which are now being questioned by stakeholders.

The second reason people change moral philosophies is the corporate culture in which they work. When children enter school, they learn certain rules, such as raising their hands to speak or asking permission to use the restroom. So it is with a new employee. Rules, personalities, and precedents exert pressure on the employee to conform to the new firm's culture. As this process occurs, the individual's moral philosophy may change to become compatible with the work environment. Many people are acquainted with those who are respected for their goodness at home or in their communities but make unethical decisions in the workplace. Even Bernard Madoff, the perpetrator of the largest Ponzi scheme in history, had a reputation as an upstanding citizen before his fraud was uncovered.

Obviously, the concept of a moral philosophy is inexact. For that reason, moral philosophies must be assessed on a continuum rather than as static entities. Each philosophy states an ideal perspective, and most individuals shift between different moral philosophies as they experience and interpret ethical dilemmas. In other words, implementing moral philosophies from an individual perspective requires individuals to apply their own accepted value systems to real-world situations. Individuals make judgments about what they believe to be right or wrong, but in their business lives they make decisions that also take into consideration how to generate the greatest benefits with the least harm. Such decisions should respect fundamental moral rights as well as perspectives on fairness, justice, and the common good, but these issues become complicated in the real world.

Problems arise when employees encounter ethical situations that they cannot resolve. Sometimes gaining a better understanding of their decision rationale can help employees to choose the right solutions. For instance, to decide whether they should offer bribes to potential customers to secure a large contract, salespeople need to understand their own personal moral philosophies as well as their firm's core values and the relevant laws. If complying with company policy or legal requirements is an important motivation to the individual, he or she is less likely to offer a bribe. On the other hand, if the salesperson's ultimate goal is a successful career and if offering a bribe seems likely to result in a promotion, then bribery might not be inconsistent with that person's moral philosophy of acceptable business behavior. Even though bribery is illegal under U.S. law, the employee may rationalize that bribery is necessary "because everyone else does it."

The virtue approach to business ethics, as discussed earlier, assumes that there are certain ideals and values that everyone should strive for in order to achieve the maximum welfare and happiness of society.[35] Aspects of these ideals and values are expressed through individuals' specific moral philosophies. Every day in the workplace, employees must decide what is right or wrong and act accordingly. At the same time, as a member of a larger organization, an employee cannot simply enforce his or her own personal perspective, especially if he or she adheres narrowly to a single moral philosophy. Because individuals cannot control most of the decisions in their work environment, they rarely have the power (especially in entry-level and middle-management positions) to impose their own personal moral perspectives on others. In fact, although they are always responsible for their own actions, a new employee is not likely to have the freedom to make independent decisions on a variety of job responsibilities.

Sometimes a company makes decisions that could be questionable from the perspective of individual customers' values and moral philosophies. For example, some stakeholders might consider a brewery or a distributor of sexually explicit movies unethical, based on their personal perspectives. A company's core values will determine how it makes decisions in which moral philosophies are in conflict. Most businesses have developed a mission statement, a corporate culture, and a set of core values that express how they want to relate to their stakeholders, including customers, employees, the legal system, and society. It is usually impossible to please all stakeholders at once.

COGNITIVE MORAL DEVELOPMENT

Many people believe that individuals advance through stages of moral development as their knowledge and socialization progress. In this section, we examine a model that describes this cognitive moral development process. Cognitive moral processing is based on a body of literature in psychology that focuses on the study of children and their cognitive development.[36] However, cognitive moral processing is also an element in ethical decision making, and many models attempt to explain, predict, and control individuals' ethical behavior.

Psychologist Lawrence Kohlberg developed a six-stage model of cognitive development. Although not specifically designed for business contexts, this model provides an interesting perspective on the issue of moral philosophy in business. According to **Kohlberg's model of cognitive moral development,** people make different decisions in similar ethical situations because they are in different moral development stages. The six stages identified by Kohlberg are as follows.

1. *The stage of punishment and obedience.* An individual in Kohlberg's first stage defines *right* as literal obedience to rules and authority. A person in this stage will respond to rules and labels of "good" and "bad" in terms of the physical power of those who determine such rules. Right and wrong are not connected with any higher order or philosophy but rather with a person who has power. Stage 1 is usually associated with small children, but signs of stage 1 development are also evident in adult behavior. For example, some companies forbid their buyers to accept gifts from salespeople. A buyer in stage 1 might justify a refusal to accept gifts from salespeople by referring to the company's rule, or the buyer may accept the gift if he or she believes that there is no chance of being caught and punished.

2. *The stage of individual instrumental purpose and exchange.* An individual in stage 2 defines *right* as that which serves his or her own needs. In this stage, the individual no longer makes moral decisions solely on the basis of specific rules or authority figures; he or she now evaluates behavior on the basis of its fairness to him or her. For example, a sales representative in stage 2 doing business for the first time in a foreign country may be expected by custom to give customers gifts. Although gift giving may be against company policy in the United States, the salesperson may decide that certain company rules designed for operating in the United States do not apply overseas. In the cultures of some foreign countries, gifts may be considered part of a person's pay. So, in this instance, not giving a gift might put the salesperson at a disadvantage. Some refer to stage 2 as the stage of reciprocity because, from a practical standpoint, ethical decisions are based on an agreement that "you scratch my back and I'll scratch yours" instead of on principles of loyalty, gratitude, or justice.

3. *The stage of mutual interpersonal expectations, relationships, and conformity.* An individual in stage 3 emphasizes the interests of others rather than simply those of him- or herself, although ethical motivation is still derived from obedience to rules. A production manager in this stage might obey upper management's order to speed up an assembly line if he or she believed that doing so would generate more profit for the company and thus save employee jobs. This manager not only considers his or her own well-being in deciding to follow the order but also tries to put him- or herself in upper management's and fellow employees' shoes. Thus, stage 3 differs from stage 2 in that fairness to others is one of the individual's ethical motives.

4. *The stage of social system and conscience maintenance.* An individual in stage 4 determines what is right by considering his or her duty to society, not just to certain other people. Duty, respect for authority, and the maintenance of the social order become the focal points at this stage. For example, some managers consider it a duty to society to protect privacy and therefore refrain from monitoring employee conversations.

5. *The stage of prior rights, social contract, or utility.* In stage 5, an individual is concerned with upholding the basic rights, values, and legal contracts of society. Individuals in this stage feel a sense of obligation or commitment to other groups—they feel, in other words, that they are part of a social contract—and recognize that in some cases legal and moral points of view may conflict. To reduce such conflict, stage 5 individuals base their decisions on a rational calculation of overall utility. For example, the president of a firm may decide to establish an ethics program because it will provide a buffer against legal problems, and the firm will be perceived as a responsible contributor to society.

6. *The stage of universal ethical principles.* A person in this stage believes that right is determined by universal ethical principles that everyone should follow. Stage 6 individuals believe that certain inalienable rights exist that are universal in nature and consequence. These rights, laws, or social agreements are valid not because of a particular society's laws or customs, but because they rest on the premise of universality. Justice and equality are examples of principles that some individuals and societies deem universal in nature. A person in this stage may be more concerned with social ethical issues and therefore not rely on the business organization for ethical direction. For example, a businessperson at this stage might argue for discontinuing a product that has caused death and injury because the inalienable right to life makes killing wrong, regardless of the reason. Therefore, company profits would not be a justification for the continued sale of the product.[37]

Kohlberg's six stages can be reduced to three levels of ethical concern. At the first level, a person is concerned with his or her own immediate interests and with external rewards and punishments. At the second level, an individual equates *right* with conformity to the expectations of good behavior of the larger society or some other significant reference group. Finally, at the third, or "principled," level, an individual sees beyond the norms, laws, and authority of groups or individuals. Employees at this level make ethical decisions regardless of negative external pressures. However, research has shown that most workers' abilities to identify and resolve moral dilemmas do not reside at this third level and that their motives are often a mixture of selflessness, self-interest, and selfishness.

Kohlberg suggests that people continue to change their decision-making priorities after their formative years, and as a result of time, education, and experience, they may change their values and ethical behavior. In the context of business, an individual's moral development can be influenced by corporate culture, especially ethics training. Ethics training and education have been shown to improve managers' cognitive development scores.[38] Because of corporate reform, most employees in *Fortune* 1000 companies today receive some type of ethics training. Training is also a requirement of the Federal Sentencing Guidelines for Organizations.

Some experts believe that experience in resolving moral conflicts accelerates an individual's progress in moral development. A manager who relies on a specific set of values or rules may eventually come across a situation in which these rules do not apply. For example, suppose Sarah is a manager whose policy is to fire any employee whose productivity declines for four consecutive months. Sarah has an employee, George, whose productivity has suffered because of depression, but George's coworkers tell Sarah that George will recover and soon become a top performer again. Because of the circumstances and the perceived value of the employee, Sarah may bend the rule and keep George. Managers in the highest stages of the moral development process seem to be more democratic than autocratic, and they are more likely than those at lower stages to consider the ethical views of the other people involved in an ethical decision-making situation.

WHITE-COLLAR CRIME

For many people, the terms *crime* and *criminal* tend to evoke thoughts of rape, arson, armed robbery, or murder. These violent crimes are devastating, but they are no less destructive than the crimes perpetrated every year by nonviolent business criminals. So-called **white-collar crime** (WCC) does more damage in monetary and emotional loss in one year than violent crimes do over several years combined.[39]

White-collar criminals tend to be highly educated people who are in positions of power, trust, respectability and responsibility within a business or organization. They commit illegal acts for personal and/or organizational gains by abusing the trust and authority normally associated with their positions. The victims of WCC are often trusting consumers who believe that businesses are legitimate.

At first glance, deciding what constitutes a white-collar crime seems fairly simple. According to the U.S. Department of Justice, a WCC is a "non-violent criminal act involving deceit, concealment, subterfuge and other fraudulent activity." The corporate executive who manipulates the stock market, the tax cheat, or the doctor who falsely bills Medicaid are all obvious white collar criminals. But a government official who accepts illegal

FIGURE 6.1 Top 10 Internet Crime Complaint Categories

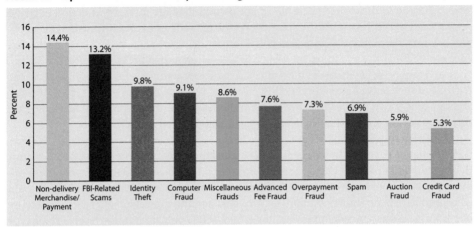

Source: "2010 Internet Crime Report," Internet Crime Complaint Center, http://www.ic3.gov/media/annualreport/2010_IC3Report.pdf.

payments is also a white-collar criminal, and guilty of official corruption. Additionally, a corporate executive who approves the illegal disposal of toxic waste is a white-collar criminal guilty of violating environmental regulations.

Online white-collar crime is a growing problem around the world. Because many companies rely on advanced technology systems, anyone with the ability to hack into a system can access the highly sensitive information necessary to commit WCC. WCCs that previously originated at the top of organizations can now occur at any level of a firm. Common online white-collar crimes include non-delivery of merchandise or payment, FBI-related scams, and identity theft (see Figure 6.1).

White-collar crime is also a major problem in the financial world. One infamous example is Barry Minkow, a white-collar criminal who found ways to manipulate the financial system for his own personal gain. In the 1980s he developed a firm, ZZZZ Best, which turned into a giant stock fraud that fooled experts on Wall Street. After his first term in prison, Minkow became a prominent financial-fraud investigator, even receiving praise from the FBI. However, in 2011 he pled guilty to insider trading after allegedly receiving nonpublic information about Lennar Corp., purchasing stock options on the company, and releasing a video that caused Lennar's stock to plummet.[40] Another example of a white-collar criminal is Bernard Madoff; his case is examined in detail in Part 5.

White-collar crime is increasing steadily (see Table 6.4). Complaints linked to fraud increased 22.3 percent in one year, representing a $559.7 million loss to companies. A few

TABLE 6.4 U.S. Consumer Fraud Complaints

Year	Complaints Received	Dollar Loss
2009	336,655	$559.7 million
2008	275,284	$265 million
2007	206,884	$239.09 million
2006	207,492	$198.44 million

Source: U.S. Census Bureau, "Fraud and Identity Theft—Consumer Complaints by State: 2009," http://www.census.gov/compendia/statab/2011/tables/11s0333.pdf (accessed April 8, 2011).

common white-collar offenses include antitrust violations, computer and Internet fraud, credit card fraud, bankruptcy fraud, health care fraud, tax evasion, violating environmental laws, insider trading, bribery, kickbacks, money laundering, and theft of trade secrets.

In response to the surge in white-collar crime, the U.S. government has stepped up efforts to combat it. The government is concerned about the destabilizing effect that WCC has on U.S. households and on the economy in general. The government can charge individuals and corporations for WCC offenses. The penalties include fines, home detention, paying for the cost of prosecution, forfeitures, and even prison time. However, sanctions often are reduced if the defendant takes responsibility for the crime and assists the authorities in their investigation. Many people do not feel that the government is devoting enough resources to combat WCC.

Why do individuals commit white-collar crimes? Advocates of the organizational deviance perspective argue that a corporation is a living, breathing organism that can collectively become deviant. When companies have lives that are separate and distinct from biological persons, the corporate culture of the company transcends the individuals who occupy these positions. With time, patterns of activities become institutionalized within the organization, and these patterns sometimes encourage unethical behaviors.

Another common cause of WCC is the views and behaviors of an individual's acquaintances within an organization. Employees, at least in part, self-select the people with whom they associate within an organization. For companies with a high number of ethical or unethical employees, people who are undecided about their behavior (about 40 percent of businesspeople) are more likely go along with their coworkers.

DEBATE ISSUE   TAKE A STAND

Why Do People Engage in White-Collar Crime?

White-collar crime occurs when highly trusted and educated individuals commit criminal misconduct. Two examples of white-collar criminals are Bernard Madoff, who developed one of the largest Ponzi schemes ever, and R. Allen Stanford, who developed an $8 billion certificate of deposit program promising unrealistically high interest rates. Different theories exist as to why individuals become white-collar criminals. Research has shown that 1 percent of business executives may be corporate psychopaths with a predisposition to lie, cheat, and take any other measures necessary to come out ahead. This possibility may account for the fact that many white-collar criminals become entrepreneurs, thus putting themselves in a position to control others. This theory might account for rogue individuals such as Bernard Madoff.

Many believe that white-collar crime evolves when corporate cultures do not have effective oversight and controls over individuals' behavior. Such toxic organizational cultures occur when unethical activities are overlooked or even encouraged. For instance, many employees engaged in liar loans at Countrywide Financial because they received rewards for bringing in additional profits. It seems unlikely that they all had psychological maladies.[41]

1. White-collar criminals tend to have psychological disorders that encourage misconduct as a route to success.
2. White-collar crime occurs as a result of organizational cultures that do not effectively control organizational behavior.

©Cengage Learning 2013

Additionally, the incidence of WCCs tends to increase in the years following economic recessions. When companies downsize, the stressful business climate may anger some employees and force others to act out of desperation. Furthermore, as businesses begin to expand and grow, fraudsters find gaps in corporate processes and exploit growth opportunities.[42]

TABLE 6.5 Common Justifications for White-Collar Crime

1. Denial of responsibility. (Everyone can, with varying degrees of plausibility, point the finger at someone else.)

2. Denial of injury. (White-collar criminals often never meet or interact with those who are harmed by their actions.)

3. Denial of the victim. (The offender is playing tit-for-tat and claims to be responding to a prior offense inflicted by the supposed victim.)

4. Condemnation of the condemners. (Executives dispute the legitimacy of the laws under which they are charged, or impugn the motives of the prosecutors who enforce them.)

5. Appeal to a higher authority. ("I did it for my family" remains a popular excuse.)

6. Everyone else is doing it. (Because of the highly competitive marketplace, certain pressures exist to perform that may drive people to break the law.)

7. Entitlement. (Criminals simply deny the authority of the laws they have broken.)

Source: Adapted from Daniel J. Curran and Claire M. Renzetti, *Theories of Crime* (Needham Heights, MA: Allyn & Bacon, 1994).

Finally, as with criminals in the general population, there is the possibility that some businesspeople may have personalities that are inherently criminal.[43] Corporate psychopaths, or managers who are nonviolent, selfish, and remorseless, exist in many large corporations. Employees of corporate psychopaths are less likely to believe that their organization is socially responsible, that the organization shows commitment to employees, or that they receive recognition for their work.[44] Some organizations use personality tests to predict behavior, but such tests presuppose that individual values and philosophies are constant; therefore, they seem to be ineffective in understanding the motivations of white-collar criminals.[45]

The reasons for the increases in WCC are not easy to pinpoint because many variables may cause good people to make bad decisions. Businesspeople must make a profit on revenue to exist, a fact that slants their orientation toward teleology and creates a culture in which white-collar crimes can become normalized. Table 6.5 lists some of the top justifications given by perpetrators of white-collar crimes. The Federal Sentencing Guidelines for Organizations state that all organizations should develop effective ethics and compliance programs as well as internal controls to prevent WCC.

INDIVIDUAL FACTORS IN BUSINESS ETHICS

Of course, not everyone agrees on the roles of collective moral philosophies in ethical decision making within an organization. Unfortunately, many people believe that individual values are the main driver of ethical behavior in business. This belief can be a stumbling block in assessing ethical risk and preventing misconduct in an organizational context. The moral values learned within the family and through religion and education are certainly key factors that influence decision making, but as indicated in the models in Chapter 5, these values are only one factor. Many companies and business schools focus mainly on personal character or moral development in their training programs, reinforcing the notion that employees can control their work environments. Although a personal moral compass is important, it is not sufficient to prevent ethical misconduct in an organizational context. According to ethics consultant David Gebler, "Most unethical behavior is not done for personal gain, it's done to meet performance goals."[46] The rewards for meeting performance goals and the corporate culture in general have been found to be the most important drivers of ethical decision making, especially for coworkers and managers.[47]

The development of strong abilities in ethical reasoning will probably lead to more ethical business decisions in the future than individualized character education for each employee.[48] Equipping employees with intellectual skills that allow them to understand and resolve the complex ethical dilemmas they encounter in complex corporate cultures will help them to make the right decisions. This approach will hopefully keep employees from being negatively influenced by peer pressure and lulled by unethical managers.[49] The West Point model for character development focuses on the fact that competence and character must be developed simultaneously. This model assumes that ethical reasoning has to be approached in the context of a specific profession. The military has been effective in teaching skills and developing principles and values that can be used in most of the situations that a soldier will encounter. In a similar manner, accountants, managers, and marketers need to develop ethical reasoning in the context of their jobs.

SUMMARY

Moral philosophy refers to the set of principles, or rules, that people use to decide what is right or wrong. These principles or rules provide guidelines for resolving conflicts and for optimizing the mutual benefit of people living in groups. Businesspeople are guided by moral philosophies as they formulate business strategies and resolve specific ethical issues, even if they may not realize it.

Teleological, or consequentialist, philosophies stipulate that acts are morally right or acceptable if they produce some desired result, such as the realization of self-interest or utility. Egoism defines right or acceptable behavior in terms of the consequences for the individual. In an ethical decision-making situation, the egoist will choose the alternative that contributes most to his or her own self-interest. Egoism can be further divided into hedonism and enlightened egoism. Utilitarianism is concerned with maximizing total utility, or providing the greatest benefit for the greatest number of people. In making ethical decisions, utilitarians often conduct cost–benefit analyses, which consider the costs and benefits to all affected parties. Rule utilitarians determine behavior on the basis of rules designed to promote the greatest utility rather than by examining particular situations. Act utilitarians examine the action itself, rather than the rules governing the action, to determine whether it will result in the greatest utility.

Deontological, or nonconsequentialist, philosophies focus on the rights of individuals and on the intentions behind an individual's particular behavior rather than on its consequences. In general, deontologists regard the nature of moral principles as permanent and stable, and they believe that compliance with these principles defines ethical behavior. Deontologists believe that individuals have certain absolute rights that must be respected. Rule deontologists believe that conformity to general moral principles determines ethical behavior. Act deontologists hold that actions are the proper basis on which to judge morality or ethicalness and that rules serve only as guidelines.

According to the relativist perspective, definitions of ethical behavior are derived subjectively from the experiences of individuals and groups. The relativist observes behavior within a relevant group and attempts to determine what consensus group members have reached on the issue in question.

Virtue ethics states that what is moral in a given situation is not only what is required by conventional morality or current social definitions, however justified, but also by what a person with a "good" moral character would deem appropriate. Those who profess virtue ethics do not believe that the end justifies the means in any situation.

The concept of justice in business relates to fair treatment and due reward in accordance with ethical or legal standards. Distributive justice is based on the evaluation of the outcome or results of a business relationship. Procedural justice is based on the processes and activities that produce outcomes or results. Interactional justice is based on an evaluation of the communication process in business.

The concept of a moral philosophy is not exact; moral philosophies can only be assessed on a continuum. Individuals use different moral philosophies depending on whether they are making a personal or a workplace decision.

According to Kohlberg's model of cognitive moral development, individuals may make different decisions in similar ethical situations because they are in a different stage of moral development. In Kohlberg's model, people progress through six stages of moral development: (1) punishment and obedience; (2) individual instrumental purpose and exchange; (3) mutual interpersonal expectations, relationships, and conformity; (4) social system and conscience maintenance; (5) prior rights, social contract, or utility; and (6) universal ethical principles. Kohlberg's six stages can be further reduced to three levels of ethical concern: immediate self-interest, social expectations, and general ethical principles. Cognitive moral development may not explain as much as people once believed.

White-collar crime occurs when an individual who is educated and in a position of power, trust, respectability, and responsibility commits an illegal act in relation to his or her employment, and who abuses the trust and authority normally associated with the position for personal and/or organizational gains. White-collar crime is not being heavily researched because this type of behavior does not normally come to mind when people think of crime; the offender (or organization) is in a position of trust and respectability; criminology and criminal justice systems look at white-collar crime differently than average crimes; and many researchers have not moved past the definitional issues. New developments in technology seem to be increasing the opportunity to commit white-collar crime with less risk.

Individual factors such as religion, moral intensity, and a person's professional affiliations can influence an employee's decision-making process. The impacts of ethical awareness, biases, conflict, personality type, and intelligence on ethical behavior remain unclear. One thing we do know is that the interrelationships among moral philosophies, values, and business are extremely complex.

IMPORTANT TERMS FOR REVIEW

moral philosophy

economic value orientation

idealism

realism

monist

hedonism

quantitative hedonist

qualitative hedonist

pluralist

instrumentalist

goodness theory

obligation theory

teleology

consequentialism

egoism

enlightened egoism

utilitarianism

rule utilitarian

act utilitarian

deontology

nonconsequentialism

categorical imperative

rule deontologist

act deontologist

relativist perspective

descriptive relativism

metaethical relativism

normative relativism

virtue ethics

justice

distributive justice

procedural justice

interactional justice

Kohlberg's model of cognitive moral development

white-collar crime

RESOLVING ETHICAL BUSINESS CHALLENGES*

Twenty-eight-year-old Elaine Hunt, who is married and has one child, has been with United Banc Corp. (UBC) for several years. During that time, she has seen the company grow from a relatively small to a medium-sized business with domestic and international customers. Elaine's husband, Dennis, is in the import-export business.

The situation that precipitated their current problem began six months ago. Elaine had just been promoted to senior financial manager, which put her in charge of 10 branch-office loan managers, each of whom had five loan officers reporting to him or her. For the most part, the branch loan officers would review their loan officers' numbers, as well as sign off on loans under $250,000. However, recently this limit had been increased to $500,000. Elaine had to sign off on loans over this amount and up to $40 million. For larger loans, a vice president would have to be involved.

Recently, Graphco, Inc., requested a $10 million loan, which Elaine had been hesitant to approve. Graphco was a subsidiary of a tobacco firm embroiled in litigation concerning the promotion of its products to children. When reviewing the numbers, Elaine could not find any glaring problems, yet she had decided against the loan even when Graphco had offered to pay an additional interest point. Some at UBC applauded her moral stance but others did not, arguing that it was not a good decision for a financial business. The next prospective loan was for a Canadian company that was importing cigars from Cuba. Elaine cited the U.S. policy against Cuba as the reason for not approving that loan. "The Helms-Burton Amendment gives us clear guidance on dealings with Cuba," she said to others in the company, even though the loan was to a Canadian firm. The third loan application she was unwilling to approve came from Electrode International, which sought $50 million. The numbers were marginal, but the sticking point for Elaine was Electrode's unusually high profits during the last two years. During dinner with Dennis, she had learned about a meeting in Zurich during which Electrode and others had allegedly fixed the prices on their products. Because only a handful of companies manufactured these particular products, the price increases were very successful. When Elaine suggested denying the loan on the basis of this information, she was overruled. At the same time, a company in Brazil was asking for an agricultural loan to harvest parts of the rain forest. The Brazilian company was willing to pay almost 2 points over the going rate for a $40 million loan. Because of her stand on environmental issues, Elaine rejected this application as well. The company obtained the loan from one of UBC's competitors.

Recently, Elaine's husband's decision making had fallen short of his superior's expectations. First, there was the problem of an American firm wanting to export nicotine and caffeine patches to Southeast Asia. With new research showing both these drugs to be more problematic than previously thought, the manufacturing firm had decided to attempt a rapid-penetration marketing strategy—that is, to price the products very low or at cost in order to gain market share and then over time slightly increase the margin. With 2 billion potential customers, a one-cent markup could result in millions of dollars in profits. Dennis had rejected the deal, and the firm had gone to another company. One person in Dennis' division had said, "Do you realize that you had the perfect product— one that was low cost and both physically and psychologically addictive? You could have serviced that one account for years and would have had enough for early retirement. You're nuts for turning it down!"

Soon afterward, an area financial bank manager wanted Elaine to sign off on a revolving loan for ABCO. ABCO's debt-to-equity ratio had increased significantly and did not conform to company regulations. However, Elaine was the one who had written the standards for UBC. Some in the company felt that Elaine was not quite with the times. Several very good bank staff members had left in the past year because they found her regulations too provincial for the emerging global marketplace. As Elaine reviewed ABCO's credit report, she found many danger signals; the loan was relatively large, $30 million, and the company had been in a credit sales slump. As she questioned ABCO, Elaine learned that the loan was to develop a new business venture within the People's Republic of China, and rumor had it that the company was also working with the Democratic People's Republic of Korea. The biotech venture was for fetal tissue research and harvesting. Recently, attention had focused on the economic benefits of such tissue in helping a host of ailments. Anticipated global market sales for such products were being estimated at $10 billion for the next decade. ABCO also was willing to go almost 2 points above the standard interest equation for such a revolving loan. Elaine realized that if she signed off on this sale, it would signal an end to her standards. However, if she did not and ABCO went to another company for the loan and paid off the debt, she would have made a gross error, and everyone in the company would know it.

As Elaine was wrestling with this problem, Dennis's commissions began to slip, putting a crimp in their cash-flow projections. If things did not turn around quickly for him, they would lose their new home, fall behind on other payments, and reduce the number of educational options for their child. Elaine also had a frank discussion with senior management about her loan standards as well as her stand on tobacco, which had lost UBC precious income. The response was, "Elaine, we applaud your moral courage, but it's negatively impacting the bottom line. We can't have that all the time."

QUESTIONS | EXERCISES

1. Discuss the advantages and disadvantages of each decision that Elaine has made.
2. What are the ethical and legal considerations facing Elaine, Dennis, and UBC?
3. Discuss the moral philosophies that may be relevant to this situation.
4. Discuss the implications of each decision that Elaine could make.

*This case is strictly hypothetical; any resemblance to real persons, companies, or situations is coincidental.

CHECK YOUR EQ

1. Teleology defines right or acceptable behavior in terms of its consequences for the individual.	Yes	No
2. A relativist looks at an ethical situation and considers the individuals and groups involved.	Yes	No
3. A utilitarian is most concerned with bottom-line benefits.	Yes	No
4. Act deontology requires that a person use equity, fairness, and impartiality in making decisions and evaluating actions.	Yes	No
5. Virtues that support business transactions include trust, fairness, truthfulness, competitiveness, and focus.	Yes	No

ANSWERS 1. No. That's egoism. 2. Yes. Relativists look at themselves and those around them to determine ethical standards. 3. Yes. Utilitarians look for the greatest good for the greatest number of people and use a cost–benefit approach. 4. Yes. The rules serve only as guidelines, and past experience weighs more heavily than the rules. 5. No. The characteristics include trust, self-control, empathy, fairness, and truthfulness—not competitiveness and focus.

CHAPTER 7

ORGANIZATIONAL FACTORS: THE ROLE OF ETHICAL CULTURE AND RELATIONSHIPS

CHAPTER OBJECTIVES

- To understand the concept of corporate culture
- To examine the influence of corporate culture on business ethics
- To determine how leadership, power, and motivation relate to ethical decision making in organizations
- To assess organizational structure and its relationship to business ethics
- To explore how the work group influences ethical decisions
- To discuss the relationship between individual and group ethical decision making

AN ETHICAL DILEMMA*

Dawn Prarie had been with PCA Health Care Hospitals for three years and had been promoted to marketing director in the Miami area. She had a staff of 10 and a fairly healthy budget. Dawn's job was to attract more patients to the HMO while helping keep costs down. At a meeting with Dawn, Nancy, the vice president, had explained the ramifications of the Balanced Budget Act and how it was affecting all HMOs. "Being here in Miami does not help our division," she told Dawn. "Because of this Balanced Budget Act, we have been losing money on many of our elderly patients. For example, we used to receive $600 or more a month, per patient, from Medicare, but now our minimum reimbursement is just $367 a month!

I need solutions, and that's where you come in. By the end of the month, I want a list of things that will help us show a profit. Anything less than a positive balance sheet will be unacceptable."

It was obvious that Nancy was serious about cutting costs and increasing revenues within the elderly market. That's why Dawn had been promoted to marketing director. The first thing Dawn did after the meeting with Nancy was to fire four key people. She then gave their duties to six others who were at lower salaries, and put the hospital staff on notice that changes would be occurring at the hospital over the next several months. Three weeks later, Dawn presented Nancy with an extensive list of ideas. The list included these suggestions:

1. Trimming some prescription drug benefits
2. Reducing redundant tests for terminal patients
3. Hiring physician assistants to see patients but billing patients at the physician rate
4. Allowing physicians to buy shares in PCA, thus providing an incentive for bringing in more patients
5. Sterilizing and reusing cardiac catheters
6. Instituting a one-vendor policy on hospital products to gain quantity discounts
7. Prescreening "insurance" patients for probability of payment

Dawn's assistants felt that some of the hospital staff could be more aggressive in the marketing area. They urged using more promotional materials, offering incentives for physicians who suggested PCA or required their patients to be hospitalized, and prescreening potential clients into categories. "You see," said Ron, one of Dawn's staff, "we feel that there are four types of elderly patients. There are the healthy elderly, whose life expectancies are 10 or more years. There are the fragile elderly, with life expectancies of two to seven years. Then there are the demented and dying elderly, who usually have one to three years. Finally, we have the high-cost or uninsured elderly. Patients who are designated healthy would get the most care, including mammograms, prostate-cancer screening, and cholesterol checks. Patients in the other categories would get less."

As she implemented some of the recommendations on Dawn's list, Nancy also launched an aggressive plan to destabilize the nurses' union. As a result, many nurses began a work slowdown and were filing internal petitions to upper management. Headquarters told Nancy to give the nurses and other hospital staff as much overtime as they wanted but not to hire anyone new. One floor manager suggested splitting up the staff into work teams, with built-in incentives for those who worked smarter and/or faster. Nancy approved the plan, and in three months productivity had jumped 50 percent, with many of the hospital workers making more money. The downside for Nancy was an increase in worker-related accidents.

When Dawn toured the hospital around this time, she found that some of the most productive workers were using substandard procedures and poorly made products. One nurse said, "Yes, the surgical gloves are somewhat of a problem, but we were told that the quality met the minimum requirements and so we have to use them." Dawn brought this to Nancy's attention, whereupon Nancy drafted the following memo:

Attention Hospital Staff

It has come to management's attention that minor injuries to staff and patients are on the rise. Please review the Occupational Safety and Health Administration guidelines, as well as the standard procedures handbook, to make sure you are in compliance. I also want to thank all those teams that have been keeping costs down. We have finally gone into the plus side as far as profitability. Hang on, and we'll be able to stabilize the hospital to make it a better place to care for patients and to work.

At Nancy's latest meeting with Dawn, she told Dawn, "We've decided to use your staff's segmentation strategy for the elderly market. We want you to develop a questionnaire to prescreen incoming HMO patients, as well as existing clients, into one of the four categories so that we can tag their charts and alert the HMO physicians to the new protocols. Also, because the recommendations that we've put into practice have worked so well, we've decided to use the rest of your suggestions. The implementation phase will start next month. I want you, Dawn, to be the lead person in developing a long-term strategy to break the unions in the hospital. Do whatever it takes. We just need to do more with less. I'm firm on this—so you're either on board or you're not. Which is it going to be?"

QUESTIONS | EXERCISES

1. Discuss PCA Health Care Hospitals' corporate culture and its ethical implications.

2. What factors influence Dawn's options?
3. Discuss the issue of for-profit versus nonprofit healthcare facilities.
4. If you were Dawn, what information would you like to have to help you make your decisions?

*This case is strictly hypothetical; any resemblance to real persons, companies, or situations is coincidental.

Companies are much more than structures in which we work. Although they are not alive, we attribute human characteristics to them. When times are good, we say the company is "well"; when times are not so good, we may try to "save" the company. Understandably, people have strong feelings about the place that provides them with income and benefits, challenges, satisfaction, self-esteem, and often lifelong friendships. In fact, excluding time spent sleeping, we spend almost 50 percent of our lives in this second "home" with our second "family." It is important, then, to examine how the culture and structure of these organizations influence the ethical decisions made within them.

In the ethical decision-making framework described in Chapter 5, we introduced the concept that organizational factors and interpersonal relationships influence the ethical decision-making process. In this chapter, we take a closer look at corporate culture and the ways a company's values and traditions can affect employees' ethical behavior. We also discuss the role of leadership in influencing ethical behavior within a company. Next we describe two organizational structures and examine how they may influence ethical decisions. We discuss new organizational structures that have been created to address the organization's corporate responsibility to employees and other stakeholders. Then we consider the impact of groups within organizations. Finally, we examine the implications of organizational relationships for ethical decision making.

DEFINING CORPORATE CULTURE

Culture is a word that people generally use in relation to genealogy, country of origin, language and the way people speak, the types of food they eat, and other customs. Many define culture as nationality or citizenship. Values, norms, artifacts, and rituals all play a role in culture. Chapter 5 defined corporate culture as a set of values, norms, and artifacts, including ways of solving problems that members (employees) of an organization share.

Corporate culture is also "the shared beliefs top managers in a company have about how they should manage themselves and other employees, and how they should conduct their business(es)."[1] Mutual of Omaha incorporates the concept of corporate culture into its mission statement. Its intent is "to build a corporate culture that respects and values the unique strengths and cultural differences of our associates, customers and community."[2] Its executives believe that the company's corporate culture provides the foundation for its work and objectives, so much so that the organization has adopted a set of core values called "Values for Success." Mutual of Omaha feels that these values form the foundation for a corporate culture that will help the organization realize its vision and achieve its goals. Corporate culture is exhibited through the behavioral patterns, concepts, documents such as codes of ethics, and rituals that emerge in an organization.[3] It gives the members of the organization a sense of meaning and purpose and familiarizes them with the organization's internal rules of behavior.[4]

Southwest Airlines has a very strong and friendly, fun-loving organizational culture that dates all the way back to the days of its key founder Herb Kelleher. Kelleher became legendary for appearing in a dress and feather boa and joining baggage handlers on Southwest flights.

> "All organizations, not just corporations, have some sort of culture."

He organized an awards ceremony for employees that many felt rivaled the Academy Awards. He treated his employees like family. Today, Southwest continues that legacy. For instance, pilots willingly and enthusiastically support the "Adopt a Pilot" program, in which students in classrooms around the country adopt a Southwest pilot for a four-week educational and mentoring program. The pilots volunteer in the students' classrooms and send e-mails and postcards to a variety of destinations. Southwest's culture allows it to attract some of the best talent in the industry.[5] Values, beliefs, customs, rules, and ceremonies that are accepted, shared, and circulated throughout an organization represent its culture. All organizations, not just corporations, have some sort of culture, and therefore we use the terms *organizational culture* and *corporate culture* interchangeably.

A company's history and unwritten rules are a part of its culture. For many years, IBM salespeople adhered to a series of unwritten standards for dealing with clients. The history or stories passed down from generation to generation within an organization are like the traditions that are perpetuated within society at large. Henry Ford, the founder of Ford Motor Co., left a legacy that emphasized the importance of the individual employee. Henry Ford pioneered the then-unheard-of high wage of $5 a day in the early years of the twentieth century, and current company chairman William Clay Ford, Jr., continues to affirm that positive employee relationships create a sustainable competitive advantage for the company.[6] William Ford has maintained his grandfather's legacy by taking a leadership role in improving vehicle fuel efficiency while reducing emissions. Ford is trying to become an industry leader in sustainability through initiatives such as its Go Green Dealership Program. This voluntary program offers dealers the chance to receive energy assessments from Ford's sustainability experts with the intent of increasing their energy efficiency. For dealers that choose to make changes, Ford experts provide guidance on sustainable product selections and state and federal tax incentives.[7]

Leaders are responsible for the actions of their subordinates, and corporations should have ethical corporate cultures. For this reason, the definition and measurement of a corporate culture is very important. It is defined in the Sarbanes–Oxley Act, which was enacted after the Enron, Tyco International, Adelphia, Peregrine Systems, and WorldCom scandals. The characteristics of an ethical corporate culture were codified within the **Sarbanes–Oxley 404** compliance section. This section includes a requirement that management assess the effectiveness of the organization's internal controls and commission an audit of these controls by an external auditor in conjunction with the audit of its financial statements. Section 404 forces firms to adopt a set of values that must form a portion of the company's culture. The evaluation of corporate culture it mandates is meant to provide insight into the character of an organization, its ethics, and its level of openness.

Compliance with Sarbanes–Oxley 404 requires not merely changes in accounting but a change in corporate culture. The intent is to expose mismanagement, fraud, theft, abuse, and to sustain a corporate culture that does not allow these conditions and actions to exist. Many consulting companies that have filled the need of companies wanting to comply have not understood what "culture" means in this case. They have sought to provide direction and criteria for improving an organization's ability to manage risk, not its ethics. In many firms, an ethical corporate culture is measured in the following ways:

- Management and the board demonstrate their commitment to strong controls through their communications and actions.

- Every employee is encouraged and required to have hands-on involvement in the internal control system.

- Every employee is encouraged and empowered to report policy exceptions.

- Employees are expected to be in the communication loop through resolutions and corrective actions.

- Employees have the ability to report policy exceptions anonymously to any member of the organization, including the CEO, other members of management, and the board of directors.[8]

The problem with these standards of measurement is that they evaluate merely risk and compliance. They are not a complete measure of the aspects of a company that make up its ethical culture. Yet many assume that the four afore mentioned items define an ethical corporate culture. Since values, norms, and artifacts are the three major components of culture, all of these elements are important in measuring an ethical culture.

In the past 50 years, scholars have developed at least 164 distinct definitions of culture. More recent reviews indicate that the number of definitions has only been increasing.[9] While these definitions of culture vary greatly, they share three common elements: (1) "culture is shared among individuals belonging to a group or society," (2) "culture is formed over a relatively long period of time," and (3) "culture is relatively stable."[10]

Different models of culture, and consequently different instruments for measuring it, focus on various levels (national, organizational, individual) and aspects (values, practices, observable artifacts and rituals, underlying implicit assumptions). Geert Hofstede, who researched IBM's corporate culture, described it as an onion with many layers, representing different levels within the corporation.[11] Today, IBM describes its culture as a culture of trust. The company has adopted IBM Business Conduct Guidelines, which describe ethics and compliance issues in-depth and provide direction for employees on how to deal with observed misconduct. The company also created an online reporting system that allows employees worldwide to raise issues and report concerns. These measures serve to advance IBM's goal of ensuring that its relationships with stakeholders "are truly built on trust."[12] Many in business define ethics as what society considers right or wrong and develop measures that manage the risk of misconduct. Managing risk is not the same as understanding what makes up a firm's culture, however. We know for certain that culture has a significant effect on the ethical decision-making process of those in business. Ethical audits, ethical compliance, and risk culture surveys may be good tools, but in and of themselves they are not useful in helping to define organizational culture or in explaining what makes a particular organizational culture more ethical or unethical.

THE ROLE OF CORPORATE CULTURE IN ETHICAL DECISION MAKING

Corporate culture has been associated with a company's success or failure. Some cultures are so strong that to outsiders they come to represent the character of the entire organization. For example, Levi Strauss, Ben & Jerry's Homemade Ice Cream, and Hershey Foods are widely perceived as casual organizations with strong ethical cultures, whereas Lockheed Martin, Procter & Gamble, and Texas Instruments are perceived as having more formal ethical cultures. The culture of an organization may be explicitly articulated or left unspoken.

Explicit statements of values, beliefs, and customs usually come from upper management. Memos, written codes of conduct, handbooks, manuals, forms, and ceremonies are all formal expressions of an organization's culture. Many of these statements can be found on company websites, like that of Wells Fargo (Table 7.1).

Corporate culture is often expressed informally, for example through statements, both direct and indirect, that communicate the wishes of management. In some companies, shared values are expressed through instituting informal dress codes, working late, and participating in extracurricular activities. Corporate culture can even be expressed through gestures, looks, labels, promotions, programs, and legends (or the lack thereof). Phil Knight, Nike co-founder and sports icon, has created a strong and appealing organizational culture. Knight seeks out new employees on one of their first few days on the job to "borrow $20 for lunch." The unsuspecting new employees are astounded that Knight spoke to them. Knight uses that tactic as a subtle way to let new employees know that they are on his radar. Interestingly, Knight has never paid back any of the employees. This ritual becomes a source of camaraderie among employees. It has contributed to building trust and commitment, and differentiates Nike's organizational culture from that of its competitors.

The "tone at the top" is a determining factor in the creation of a high-integrity organization. When leaders are perceived as trustworthy, employee trust increases; leaders are seen as ethical and as honoring a higher level of duties.[13] In a KPMG Forensic Integrity Survey (Figure 7.1), employees were asked whether their CEO and other senior executives

TABLE 7.1 Wells Fargo's Ethics Values

We behave ethically when we:
• Value and reward open, honest, two-way communication.
• Be accountable for, and proud of, our conduct and our decisions.
• Only make promises we intend to keep—do what we say we'll do. If things change, let people know.
• Share information with our colleagues that they need, and let them know if things change.
• Avoid any actual or perceived conflict of interest.
• Comply with the letter and the spirit of the law.
• Acknowledge and apologize for our mistakes, and learn from our errors so we don't make them again.

Source: "Our values: What we stand for," Wells Fargo, https://www.wellsfargo.com/invest_relations/vision_values/6 (accessed March 8, 2011).

FIGURE 7.1 Perceived Tone and Culture, Tone at the Top, and Perceptions of the CEO and Other Senior Executives

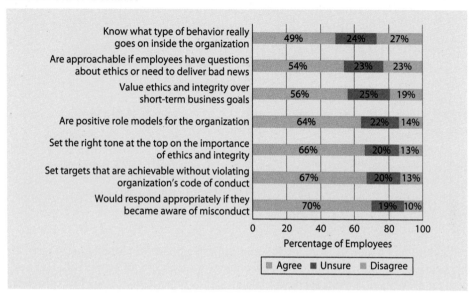

Source: "Forensic Integrity Survey 2008–2009," KPMG, http://www.kpmg.com/SiteCollectionDocuments/Integrity-Survey-2008-2009.pdf (accessed August 19, 2009).

exhibited characteristics attributable to personal integrity and ethical leadership. Nearly two-thirds of employees believed that their leaders served as positive role models for their organizations. However, roughly half exhibited a lack of confidence (based on "unsure" and "disagree" responses) that their CEOs knew about behaviors further down in the organization. Overall, nearly two-thirds of employees agreed that their leaders set the right tone at the top, leaving one-third unsure or in disagreement.

Ethical Frameworks and Evaluations of Corporate Culture

Corporate culture has been conceptualized in many ways. For example, N. K. Sethia and Mary Ann Von Glinow have proposed two basic dimensions to describe an organization's culture: (1) concern for people—the organization's efforts to care for its employees' well-being, and (2) concern for performance—the organization's efforts to focus on output and employee productivity.[14] Figure 7.2 provides examples of companies that display elements of these four organizational cultures.

As Figure 7.2 shows, the four organizational cultures can be classified as apathetic, caring, exacting, and integrative. An **apathetic culture** shows minimal concern for either people or performance. In this culture, individuals focus on their own self-interest. Apathetic tendencies can occur in almost any organization. Steel companies and airlines were among the first to freeze employee pensions to keep their businesses operating. Sweeping changes in corporate America are affecting employee compensation and retirement plans. Simple gestures of appreciation, such as anniversary watches, rings, dinners, or birthday cards for family members, are being dropped. Many companies view long-serving employees as dead wood and do not take into account past performance. This attitude demonstrates the companies' apathetic culture.

A **caring culture** exhibits high concern for people but minimal concern for performance issues. From an ethical standpoint, the caring culture seems very appealing. However, it is

FIGURE 7.2 Company Examples of the Four Organizational Cultures

Ben & Jerry's—A Caring Culture Ben & Jerry's embraces community causes, treats its employees fairly, and expends numerous resources to enhance the well-being of its customers.	*Starbucks—An Integrative Culture* Starbucks is always looking for ways to expand and improve performance. It also exhibits a high concern for people through community causes, sustainability, and employee health care.
Countrywide Financial—An Apathetic Culture Countrywide seemed to show little concern for employees and customers. The company's culture appeared to encourage unethical conduct in exchange for profits.	*United Parcel Systems—An Exacting Culture* Employees are held to high standards to ensure maximum performance, consistency of delivery, and efficiency.

difficult to find nationally recognizable companies that maintain little or no concern for performance. In contrast, an **exacting culture** shows little concern for people but a high concern for performance; it focuses on the interests of the organization. United Parcel Service (UPS) has always been very exacting. With over 8.5 million daily customers in over 200 countries, UPS knows just how many employees it needs to move its 15.6 million pieces per day worldwide.[15] To combat the uncaring, unsympathetic attitude of many of its managers, UPS has developed a community service program for its employees. Global Volunteer Week gives UPS employees around the world the opportunity to help paint schools, renovate shelters, and assist with many other needed projects within their communities. An early innovator, UPS tested ways to use alternate fuels in the 1930s. Now the company operates one of the largest private alternative fleets in the transportation industry with over 1,900 compressed natural gas, liquefied natural gas, hybrid-electric, electric, and propane-powered vehicles.[16]

An **integrative culture** combines a high concern for people with one for performance. An organization becomes integrative when superiors recognize that employees are more than interchangeable parts—that employees have an ineffable quality that helps the firm meet its performance criteria. Many companies, such as the Boston Consulting Group (BCG), have such a culture. The Boston Consulting Group rated second among *Fortune*'s "Best Companies to Work for." BCG is a financially successful global consulting firm with a strong reputation that specializes in business strategy. The company values its employees and creates significant mentorship opportunities and extensive training that allow employees to develop rapidly. In addition, the company provides high pay and refused to lay off employees during the downturn. BCG also has a strong commitment for people outside its immediate circle. The company removed some of its staff from projects so that they could help in the aftermath of the 2010 Haitian earthquake.[17]

Companies can classify their corporate culture and identify its specific values, norms, beliefs, and customs by conducting a cultural audit. A **cultural audit** is an assessment of an organization's values. It is usually conducted by outside consultants but may be performed internally as well. Communication about ethical expectations and support from top management help to identify a corporate culture that either encourages ethical conduct or leads to ethical conflict.[18]

Ethics as a Component of Corporate Culture

As indicated in the framework presented in Chapter 5, ethical culture, the ethical component of corporate culture, is a significant factor in ethical decision making. If a firm's culture encourages or rewards unethical behavior, its employees may well act unethically. If the culture dictates hiring people who have specific, similar values and if those values are perceived as unethical by society, society will view the organization and its members as unethical. Such a pattern often occurs in certain areas of marketing. For instance, salespeople may be seen as unethical because they sometimes use aggressive selling tactics to get customers to buy things they do not need or want. If a company's primary objective is to make as much profit as possible through whatever means, its culture may foster behavior that conflicts with stakeholders' ethical values. After the *Deepwater Horizon* disaster in 2010, the culture of BP, with its emphasis on financial performance, became the focus of criticism. BP has had a history of accidents, explosions, and other events over the last six years. Even in 2011, BP was accused of criminal negligence regarding previous oil spills in Alaska. These events lead to questions about how the BP culture views the prevention of accidents and environmental damage.[19]

On the other hand, if an organization values ethical behaviors, it will reward them. It is important to handle recognition and awards for appropriate behavior in a consistent and balanced manner. All employees should be eligible for recognition, the behaviors or actions being acknowledged should be noted, anyone performing at the threshold level should be acknowledged, and praise or rewards should be given as close to the performance as possible.[20] FedEx's Bravo Zulu award is one example of company recognition. The award is given to employees who demonstrate exceptional performance above and beyond job expectations. Rewards for recipients can include cash bonuses, theater tickets, gift certificates, and more. By rewarding employees who go above their normal duties, FedEx provides motivation for other workers to strive for excellent work conduct.[21]

Management's sense of an organization's culture may not be in line with the values and ethical beliefs that are actually guiding a firm's employees. Table 7.2 provides an example of a corporate culture ethics audit. Companies interested in assessing their culture can use this tool and benchmark against previous years' results to measure organizational improvements. Ethical issues may arise because of conflicts between the cultural values perceived by management and those actually at work in the organization. For example, managers may believe that their firm's organizational culture encourages respect for peers and subordinates. On the basis of the rewards or sanctions associated with various behaviors, however, the firm's employees may believe that the company encourages competition among organizational members. A competitive orientation may result in a less ethical corporate culture. This was the case at Enron when the employees in the lowest 20 percent for performance were fired. On the other hand, employees appreciate working in an environment that is designed to enhance workplace experiences through goals that encompass more than just maximizing profits.[22] Therefore it is very important for top managers to determine their organization's culture and to monitor its values, traditions, and beliefs to ensure that they represent the desired culture. It is also important to note that if corporate communication to improve social responsibility and ethics is reactive or focused on avoiding negative consequences, it may not make a significant contribution to creating an ethical culture. Reactive communication without commitment could therefore fail to improve business ethics.[23] The rewards and punishments imposed by an organization must also reflect the culture that those at the top wish to create. As two business ethics experts

TABLE 7.2 Corporate Culture Ethics Audit

		Answer Yes or No to each of the following questions*
Yes	No	Has the founder or top management of the company left an ethical legacy to the organization?
Yes	No	Does the company have methods for detecting ethical concerns both within the organization and outside it?
Yes	No	Is there a shared value system and understanding of what constitutes appropriate behavior within the organization?
Yes	No	Are stories and myths embedded in daily conversations about appropriate ethical conduct?
Yes	No	Are codes of ethics or ethical policies communicated to employees?
Yes	No	Are there ethical rules or procedures in training manuals or other company publications?
Yes	No	Are penalties for ethical transgressions publicly discussed?
Yes	No	Are there rewards for good ethical decisions even if they don't always result in a profit?
Yes	No	Does the company recognize the importance of creating a culture that is concerned about people and their investment in the business?
Yes	No	Does the company have a value system of fair play and honesty toward customers?
Yes	No	Do employees treat each other with respect, honesty, and fairness?
Yes	No	Do employees spend their time working in a cohesive way on what is valued by the organization?
Yes	No	Are there ethically based beliefs and values about how to succeed in the company?
Yes	No	Are there heroes or stars in the organization who communicate a common understanding about which positive ethical values are important?
Yes	No	Are there day-to-day rituals or behavior patterns that create direction and prevent confusion or mixed signals on ethics matters?
Yes	No	Is the firm more focused on the long run than on the short run?
Yes	No	Are employees satisfied or happy, and is employee turnover low?
Yes	No	Do the dress, speech, and physical aspects of the work setting contribute to a sense of consistency about what is right?
Yes	No	Are emotional outbursts about role conflict and ambiguity rare?
Yes	No	Has discrimination and/or sexual harassment been eliminated?
Yes	No	Is there an absence of open hostility and severe conflict?
Yes	No	Do people act on the job in a way that is consistent with what they say is ethical?
Yes	No	Is the firm more externally focused on customers, the environment, and the welfare of society than on its own profits?
Yes	No	Is there open communication between superiors and subordinates about ethical dilemmas?
Yes	No	Have employees ever received advice on how to improve ethical behavior or been disciplined for committing unethical acts?

©Cengage Learning 2013

*Add up the number of "Yes" answers. The greater the number of "Yes" answers, the less likely ethical conflict is in your organization.

have observed, "Employees will value and use as guidelines those activities for which they will be rewarded. When a behavior that is rewarded comes into conflict with an unstated and unmonitored ethical value, usually the rewarded behavior wins out."[24]

Compliance versus Value-based Ethical Cultures

During the latter part of the twentieth century a distinction evolved between types of corporate cultures. The traditional ethics-based culture focused on compliance. The accounting professional model of rules created a **compliance culture** organized around risk. Compliance-based cultures use a legalistic approach to ethics. They use laws and regulatory rules to create codes and requirements. Codes of conduct are established with compliance as their focus, with rules and policies enforced by management. Instead of revolving around an ethical culture, the company revolves around risk management. The compliance approach is good in the short term because it helps management, stakeholders, and legal agencies to ensure that laws, rules, and the intent of compliance are fulfilled. A problem with the compliance approach, however, is its lack of long-term focus on values and integrity. In addition, it does not teach employees to navigate ethical gray areas.

Within the last 10 years there has been a shift from an approach focused on compliance to a values-based approach. A **values-based ethics culture** approach to ethical corporate cultures relies upon an explicit mission statement that defines the core values of the firm and how customers and employees should be treated. The board of directors as well as upper management might add to the general value statements by formulating more specific value statements for its strategic business units (SBU), which can be organized by product, geography, or function within the firm's management structure. Certain areas may have rules that are associated with stated values, enabling employees to understand the relationship between the two. The focus of this type of corporate culture is on values such as trust, transparency, and respect to help employees identify and deal with ethical issues. It is important when using a values-based approach to explain why rules exist, what the penalties are if rules are violated, and how employees can help improve the ethics of the company. The crux of any ethical culture is top-down integrity with shared values, norms that provide guides for behavior, and visible artifacts such as codes of ethics that provide a standard of conduct. In developing a values-based ethical culture, a compliance element is also necessary because every organization has employees who will try to take advantage if the risk of being caught is low.

IKEA represents a values-based culture, with a mission "to create a better everyday life for the many." The company maintains a strong commitment to best business practices, ethical behavior, and environmental initiatives. Not only does IKEA sell ecofriendly products and use alternative energy to power its stores, it also supports numerous causes such as Save the Children and American Forests. IKEA's dedication to ethics and social responsibility has earned it a spot on *Ethisphere*'s 2010 list of the World's Most Ethical Companies.[25]

Differential Association

Differential association refers to the idea that people learn ethical or unethical behavior while interacting with others who are part of their role-sets or who belong to other intimate personal groups.[26] The learning process is more likely to result in unethical behavior

> "The learning process is more likely to result in unethical behavior if the individual associates primarily with persons who behave unethically."

if the individual associates primarily with persons who behave unethically. Associating with others who are unethical, combined with the opportunity to act unethically, is a major influence on ethical decision making, as described in the decision-making framework in Chapter 5.[27]

Consider a company in which salespeople incur travel expenses each week. When a new salesperson is hired, the other salespeople encourage the new employee to pad his or her expense accounts because there are some expenses that cannot be charged to the company. The new employee is shown how to pad the expense account and is told that failure to engage in this conduct will make others' expense reports look too high. In other words, the new employee is pressured to engage in misconduct.

A variety of studies have supported the notion that such differential association influences ethical decision making, and superiors in particular have a strong influence on the ethics of their subordinates. The actions of Mark Hernandez, who worked at NASA's Michoud Assembly Facility applying insulating foam to the space shuttles' external fuel tanks, provide an example of how coworker influence can produce tragic results. Within a few weeks on the job, coworkers taught him to repair scratches in the insulation without reporting the repairs. Supervisors encouraged the workers not to fill out the required paperwork on the repairs so that they could meet the space shuttle program's tight production schedules. After the shuttle *Columbia* broke up on reentry, killing all seven astronauts on board, investigators found that a piece of foam falling off a fuel tank during liftoff had irreparably damaged the shuttle.[28]

Several research studies have found that employees, especially young managers, tend to go along with their superiors' moral judgments to demonstrate loyalty. In one study, an experiment was conducted to determine how a hypothetical board of directors would respond to the marketing of one of its company's most profitable drugs, which resulted in 14 to 22 unnecessary deaths a year. When the imaginary board of directors learned that a competitor's drug was coming into the market with no side effects, more than 80 percent supported continuing to market the drug and taking legal and political action to prevent a ban. When asked their personal view on this situation, 97 percent believed that continuing to market the drug was irresponsible.[29] We have made it clear that *how* people typically make ethical decisions is not necessarily the way they *should* make ethical decisions. But we believe that you will be able to improve your own ethical decision making once you understand the potential influence of your interactions with others in your intimate work groups.

Whistle-Blowing

Interpersonal conflict occurs when employees think they know the right course of action in a situation, yet their work group or company promotes or requires a different, unethical decision. In such cases, employees may choose to follow their own values and refuse to participate in the unethical or illegal conduct. If they conclude that they cannot discuss what they are doing or what should be done with their coworkers or immediate supervisors, and if there is no method or protection for anonymous reporting, these employees may go outside the organization to publicize and correct the unethical situation, becoming whistle-blowers. A number of laws exist to protect whistle-blowers.

Whistle-blowing means exposing an employer's wrongdoing to outsiders such as the media or government regulatory agencies. The term *whistle-blowing* is sometimes used to refer to internal reporting of misconduct to management, especially through anonymous reporting mechanisms, often called hotlines. Legal protection for whistle-blowers exists to encourage reporting of misconduct. Whistle-blower laws have provisions against retaliation and are enforced by a number of government agencies. For example, under the Sarbanes–Oxley Act, the U.S. Department of Labor (DOL) directly protects whistle-blowers who report violations of the law and refuse to engage in any action made unlawful. The Corporate and Criminal Fraud Accountability (CCFA) Act protects employees of publicly traded firms from retaliation if they report violations of any rule or regulation of the Securities and Exchange Commission, or any provision of federal law relating to fraud against shareholders. It also requires attorneys to become internal whistle-blowers as well.

The 2010 passage of the Dodd–Frank Act proposed additional incentives for whistle-blowers. Under the new rules, whistle-blowers who provide information that aids in the recovery of over $1 million could receive 10 to 30 percent of that amount. The belief is that monetary incentives will prompt observers of corporate misconduct to come forward, which could prevent future scandals like those leading up to the 2008–2009 financial crisis. One major concern with this new provision, however, is that it may cause whistle-blowers to go external with the information rather than internal. In other words, because of the potential for monetary rewards, whistle-blowers might be tempted to go straight to the Securities and Exchange Commission with their reports rather than first reporting the misconduct to the company's internal compliance officers.[30]

The Sarbanes–Oxley Act and the Federal Sentencing Guidelines for Organizations (FSGO) have institutionalized internal whistle-blowing to encourage discovery of organizational misconduct. For example, billionaire R. Allen Stanford's worst enemies may be former employees turned whistle-blowers who once worked for his company Stanford Financial Group. One lawsuit alleges that an employee hired to edit the firm's corporate magazine objected to and raised concerns about firm practices that he believed violated federal and state laws. He was later fired. Others who filed industry arbitration claims alleged that they were

DEBATE ISSUE   TAKE A STAND

Is Government Support for External Whistle-Blowing Effective?

A number of laws have been enacted to encourage members of organizations to report misconduct. While most firms support internal reporting of misconduct through anonymous hotlines, many organizations are concerned about employees going public or reporting misconduct to the government. Whistle-blowers are protected through the Sarbanes–Oxley Act and a number of other government agencies that deal with fraud, stock trading, and corrupt practices. In 2010 the Dodd–Frank Act gave additional incentives for whistle-blowers. Whistle-blowers are even encouraged to turn themselves in if they were part of a team or group that engaged in misconduct. Doing so could result in monetary rewards. Despite these incentives, whistle-blowers in general do not get good treatment and often have trouble finding employment after they have reported misconduct. It has also been found that companies with good internal reporting systems have fewer whistle-blowers that go external in an attempt to obtain rewards. This could be because employees feel that their concerns will be taken seriously and misconduct will be halted before it becomes a major problem.

1. Government support through financial incentives for reporting misconduct in organizations is effective and benefits society.

2. Government support of whistle-blowing should be redirected toward stronger incentives for internal reporting of misconduct, not external whistle-blowing that could be harmful to the individual.

©Cengage Learning 2013

forced out of the fast-growing firm after questioning the ability of Stanford International Bank to justify high CD rates. In the Stanford case, whistle-blowers provided pivotal evidence documenting corporate malfeasance at a number of companies.[31] Yet historically, the fortunes of external whistle-blowers have not been positive; most were labeled traitors, and many lost their jobs. Even Sherron Watkins was a potential candidate for firing as the Enron investigation unfolded, with law firms assessing the implications of terminating her in light of her ethical and legal concerns about Enron.[32]

A study of 300 whistle-blowers by researchers at the University of Pennsylvania found that 69 percent lost their jobs or were forced to retire after exposing their companies' misdeeds.[33] For example, the whistle-blower who exposed Walmart chairman Thomas Coughlin for defrauding the company was terminated about a week after Coughlin resigned. Jared Bowen, a former vice president for Walmart Stores, Inc., claims that he was terminated for his exposure of Coughlin, in violation of a provision of the Sarbanes–Oxley Act protecting whistle-blowers.[34] If an employee provides information to the government about a company's wrongdoing, under the Federal False Claims Act the whistle-blower is known as a *qui tam relator*. Upon investigation of the matter by the U.S. Department of Justice, the whistle-blower can receive between 15 and 25 percent of the recovered funds, depending upon how instrumental his or her claims were in holding the firm accountable for its wrongdoing.[35] Although most whistle-blowers do not receive positive recognition for pointing out corporate misconduct, some have turned to the courts and obtained substantial settlements. However, whistle-blowers have traditionally had a difficult time winning their cases. During the Clinton and Bush administrations, less than 5 percent of whistle blowers won settlements.[36]

To be truly effective, whistle-blowing requires that the individual have adequate knowledge of wrongdoing that could damage society. It is important to minimize risk to the whistle-blower while dealing with ethical issues.[37] Table 7.3 provides a checklist of questions an employee should ask before blowing the whistle externally. Figure 7.3 shows the types of retaliation whistle-blowers may face should they report misconduct. Although 15 percent of respondents to the National Business Ethics Survey indicated that they had experienced some form of retaliation after reporting misconduct, whistle-blowing had increased 5 percent from two years before.[38]

If whistle-blowers present an accurate picture of organizational misconduct, they should not fear for their jobs. Indeed, Sarbanes–Oxley and Dodd–Frank make it illegal

TABLE 7.3 Questions to Ask before Engaging in External Whistle-Blowing

1. Have I exhausted internal anonymous reporting opportunities within the organization?

2. Have I examined company policies and codes that outline acceptable behavior and violations of standards?

3. Is this a personal issue that should be resolved through other means?

4. Can I manage the stress that may result from exposing potential wrongdoing in the organization?

5. Can I deal with the consequences of resolving an ethical or legal conflict within the organization?

FIGURE 7.3 Forms of Retaliation Experienced as a Result of Reported Misconduct

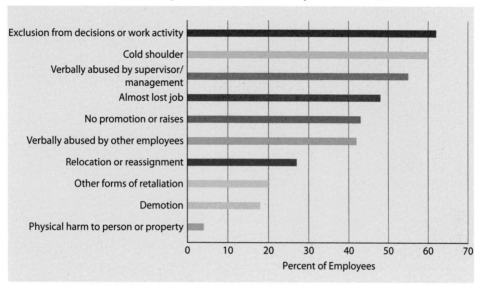

Source: Ethics Resource Center, 2009 National Business Ethics Survey, p. 36.

to "discharge, demote, suspend, threaten, harass, or in any manner discriminate against" a whistle-blower and set penalties of up to 10 years in jail for executives who retaliate against whistle-blowers. The law also requires publicly traded companies to implement an anonymous reporting mechanism that allows employees to question actions that they believe may indicate fraud or other misconduct.[39] Additionally, the FSGO provides rewards for companies that systematically detect and address unethical or illegal activities. Within the federal stimulus funds, new whistle-blower protection was supported for state and local government employees and contractors, subcontractors, and grantees. The new law provides specific protections including the right to seek investigation and review by federal Inspectors General for "adverse actions" such as termination or demotions.[40]

Most public companies are setting up computer systems that encourage internal whistle-blowing. With over 5,500 employees, Marvin Windows (one of the world's largest custom manufacturers of wood windows and doors) wants employees to feel comfortable reporting violations of safety conditions, bad management, fraud, or theft. The system is anonymous and allows for reporting in employees' native languages. This system is used to alert management to potential problems in the organization and to facilitate investigations.[41]

Even before the passage of the Sarbanes–Oxley Act, an increasing number of companies were setting up anonymous reporting services, often through toll-free numbers, through which employees could report suspected violations or seek input on how to proceed when encountering ambiguous situations. These internal reporting services are perceived to be most effective when they are managed by an outside organization that specializes in maintaining ethics hotlines.

Figure 7.4 reveals that the majority of employees report misconduct to their immediate supervisors. However, the presence of hotlines and other mechanisms helps employees

FIGURE 7.4 To Whom Do You Report Misconduct?

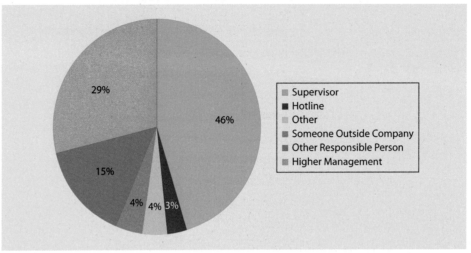

Source: Ethics Resource Center, Research Brief from the 2009 NBES, p. 15.

who feel uncomfortable reporting to their superiors. The results of a study show that three internal actions—confrontation, reporting to management, and calling the company ethics hotline—were positively correlated to several dimensions of an ethical culture. Conversely, inaction and external whistle-blowing were negatively correlated to several dimensions of an ethical culture. External whistle-blowing generally reflects a weakness in the ethical culture.[42] The extent to which employees feel that there will be no corrective action or that there will be retaliation as a result of their actions is a leading factor influencing their decisions not to report observed misconduct.

LEADERS INFLUENCE CORPORATE CULTURE

Organizational leaders can shape and influence corporate culture, resulting in ethical or unethical leadership. Leaders need to be both effective and ethical. An effective leader is one who does well for the stakeholders of the corporation. Effective leaders are good at getting followers to their common goals or objectives in the most effective and efficient way. Ken Lay and Jeffery Skilling were effective in that they transformed Enron from a small oil and gas pipeline firm into one of the largest entities in its industry. They were inspirational, imaginative, creative, and they motivated their personnel to achieve. But because their ethics were flawed they were not good for the company in the long term. According to Alan Yuspeh, Senior Vice President and Chief Ethics and Compliance Officer of Hospital Corporation of America (HCA), ethical companies and leadership should possess "aspirations that are higher than observing the law." The CEO of HCA and its board of directors have empowered Yuspeh to provide such leadership and supporting values to help employees appropriately respond to difficult ethical situations.[43] Consistency is also important for successful leaders.

Power Shapes Corporate Culture

Power refers to the influence that leaders and managers have over the behavior and decisions of subordinates. An individual has power over others when his or her presence causes them to behave differently. Exerting power is one way to influence the ethical decision-making framework described in Chapter 5.

The status and power of leaders is directly correlated to the amount of pressure that they can exert on employees to get them to conform to their expectations. A superior can put strong pressure on employees, even when employees' personal ethical values conflict with the superior's wishes. For example, a manager might say to a subordinate, "I want the confidential information about our competitor's sales on my desk by Monday morning, and I don't care how you get it." A subordinate who values his or her job or who does not realize the ethical questions involved may feel pressure to do something unethical to obtain the data.

There are five power bases from which one person may influence another: (1) reward power, (2) coercive power, (3) legitimate power, (4) expert power, and (5) referent power.[44] These five bases of power can be used to motivate individuals either ethically or unethically.

REWARD POWER   **Reward power** refers to a person's ability to influence the behavior of others by offering them something desirable. Typical rewards might be money, status, or promotion. Consider, for example, an auto salesperson who has two cars (a Toyota and a Kia) for sale. Let's assume that the Toyota is rated as higher quality than the Kia but is priced about the same. In the absence of any form of reward power, the salesperson would logically attempt to sell the Toyota. However, if the Kia had a higher commission, he would probably focus his efforts on selling the Kia. Such "carrot dangling" and incentives have been shown to be very effective in getting people to change their behavior in the long run. Therefore, rewards could encourage individuals to act in their own self-interest, not necessarily in the interest of stakeholders. In the short run, reward power is not as effective as coercive power.

COERCIVE POWER   **Coercive power** is essentially the opposite of reward power. Instead of rewarding a person for doing something, coercive power penalizes actions or behavior. As an example, suppose a valuable client asks an industrial salesperson for a bribe and insinuates that he will take his business elsewhere if his demands are not met. Although the salesperson believes bribery is unethical, her boss has told her that she must keep the client happy or lose her chance at promotion. The boss is imposing a negative sanction if certain actions are not performed. Many companies have used a system whereby they systematically fire the lowest performing employees in their organization on an annual basis. Enron called it "rank and yank" and annually fired the lowest 20 percent. Motorola, Dow Chemical, and Microsoft have used similar systems for firing employees. Coercive power relies on fear to change behavior. For this reason, it has been found to be more effective in changing behavior in the short run than in the long run. Coercion is often employed in situations where there is an extreme imbalance of power. However, people who are continually subjected to coercion may seek a counterbalance by aligning themselves with other, more powerful persons or by simply leaving the organization. In firms that use coercive power, relationships usually break down in the long run. Power is an ethical issue not only for individuals but also for work groups that establish policy for large corporations.

LEGITIMATE POWER   **Legitimate power** stems from the belief that a certain person has the right to exert influence and that certain others have an obligation to accept it. The titles and positions of authority that organizations bestow on individuals appeal to this traditional view of power. Many people readily acquiesce to those who wield legitimate power, sometimes committing acts that are contrary to their beliefs and values. Betty Vinson, an accountant at WorldCom, objected to her supervisor's requests to produce improper accounting entries in an effort to conceal WorldCom's deteriorating financial condition. She finally gave in, however, accepting that this was the only way to save the company. She and other WorldCom accountants eventually pled guilty to conspiracy and fraud. She was sentenced to five months in prison and five months of house arrest.[45]

Such loyalty to authority figures can also be seen in corporations that have strong charismatic leaders and centralized structures. In business, if a superior tells an employee to increase sales "no matter what it takes" and that employee has a strong affiliation to legitimate power, the employee may try anything to fulfill that order. Dysfunctional leaders that are abusive and treat employees with contempt and disrespect can use legitimate power to pressure subordinates into unethical conduct. In these situations, employees may not voice their concerns or may use anonymous reporting systems to deal with the dysfunctional leader.[46]

EXPERT POWER   **Expert power** is derived from a person's knowledge (or a perception that a person possesses knowledge). Expert power usually stems from a superior's credibility with subordinates. Credibility, and thus expert power, is positively correlated to the number of years that a person has worked in a firm or industry, the person's education, and the honors that he or she has received for performance. The perception that a person is an expert on a specific topic can also confer expert power on him or her. A relatively low-level secretary may have expert power because he or she knows specific details about how the business operates and can even make suggestions on how to inflate revenue through expense reimbursements.

Expert power may cause ethical problems when it is used to manipulate others or to gain an unfair advantage. Physicians, lawyers, and consultants can take unfair advantage of unknowing clients, for example. Accounting firms may gain extra income by ignoring concerns about the accuracy of financial data that they examine in an audit.

REFERENT POWER   **Referent power** may exist when one person perceives that his or her goals or objectives are similar to another's. The second person may attempt to influence the first to take actions that will allow both to achieve their objectives. Because they share the same goals, the first person will perceive the other's use of referent power as beneficial. For this power relationship to be effective, however, some sort of empathy must exist between the individuals. Identification with others helps boost the decision maker's confidence, thus increasing his or her referent power.

Consider the following situation: Lisa Jones, a manager in the accounting department of a manufacturing firm, is being pressured to increase the rate at which sales are processed. She has asked Michael Wong, a salesperson, to speed up the delivery of sales contracts, and, if possible, to encourage advanced sales with delayed delivery. Michael protests that he does not want to push customers for future sales. Lisa therefore makes use of referent power. She invites Michael to lunch, and they discuss some of their work concerns, including the problem of increasing sales for accounting purposes. They agree that if document processing can be done through advanced sales, both will benefit. Lisa then suggests that

Michael start sending sales contracts for the *next* quarter. He agrees to give it a try, and within several weeks the contracts are moving faster, and sales are increasing for the next quarter. Lisa's job is made easier, and Michael gets his commission checks a little sooner. On the other hand, this may be the beginning of what is called channel stuffing, or inflating the sales and income in the current quarter.

The five bases of power are not mutually exclusive. People typically use several power bases to effect change in others. Although power in itself is neither ethical nor unethical, its use can raise ethical issues. Sometimes a leader uses power to manipulate a situation or a person's values in a way that creates a conflict with the person's value structure. For example, a manager who forces an employee to choose between staying home with his sick child and keeping his job is using coercive power and creating a direct conflict with the employee's values. In business, titles and salary signify power, but power and wealth often breed arrogance and are easily abused.

MOTIVATING ETHICAL BEHAVIOR

A leader's ability to motivate subordinates plays a key role in maintaining an ethical organization. **Motivation** is a force within the individual that focuses his or her behavior toward achieving a goal. **Job performance** is considered to be a function of ability and motivation that can be represented by the equation (job performance = ability × motivation). This equation shows that employees can be motivated to accomplish things, but that resources and know-how are also needed to get a job done. To create motivation, an organization offers incentives that will encourage employees to work toward organizational objectives. Understanding motivation is important to effective management, and it also helps explain employees' ethical behavior. For example, a person who aspires to higher positions in an organization may sabotage a coworker's project to make that person look bad. This unethical behavior is directly related to the first employee's ambition (motivation) to rise in the organization. Employees want to feel that they are a good fit with their organization, have a clear understanding of job expectations, are supported in their role, and are valued and inspired to perform well. If an organization has shared values and an ethical culture, employees should be highly engaged and motivated because of their trust in others.

As businesspeople move into middle management and beyond, higher-order needs (social connections, esteem, and recognition) tend to become more important than lower-order needs (salary, safety, and job security). Research has shown that an individual's career stage, age, organization size, and geographic location affect the relative priority that he or she gives to satisfying respect, self-esteem, and basic physiological needs. An individual's hierarchy of needs may influence his or her motivation and ethical behavior. After basic needs such as food, working conditions (existence needs), and survival are satisfied, relatedness needs and growth needs become important. **Relatedness needs** are satisfied by social and interpersonal relationships, and **growth needs** are satisfied by creative or productive activities.[47]

From an ethics perspective, needs or goals may change as a person progresses through the ranks of the company. This shift may cause or help to solve problems depending on the person's current ethical status relative to the company or society. For example, junior executives might inflate purchase or sales orders, overbill time worked on projects, or accept cash gratuities if they are worried about providing for their families' basic physical necessities. As they continue up the ladder and are able to fulfill these needs, such concerns may become less important. Consequently, these managers may go back to obeying company policy or conforming to organizational culture and be more concerned with internal recognition and achievement than their families' physical needs. Younger employees tend to rely on organizational culture for guidance, but older employees have been found to improve ethical performance.

Examining the role that motivation plays in ethics offers a way to relate business ethics to the broader social context in which workers live and the deeper moral assumptions on which society depends. Workers are individuals, and they will be motivated by a variety of personal interests. Although we keep emphasizing that managers are positioned to exert pressure and force individuals' compliance on ethically related issues, we also acknowledge that an individual's personal ethics and needs will significantly affect his or her ethical decisions.

ORGANIZATIONAL STRUCTURE AND BUSINESS ETHICS

An organization's structure is important to the study of business ethics because the various roles and job descriptions that comprise that structure may create opportunities for unethical behavior. The structure of organizations can be described in many ways. For simplicity's sake, we will discuss two broad categories of organizational structures—centralized and decentralized. Note that these are not mutually exclusive structures; in the real world, organizational structures exist on a continuum. Table 7.4 compares some strengths and weaknesses of centralized and decentralized structures.

In a **centralized organization**, decision-making authority is concentrated in the hands of top-level managers, and little authority is delegated to lower levels. Responsibility, both internal and external, rests with top-level managers. This structure is especially suited to organizations that make high-risk decisions and whose lower-level managers are not highly skilled in decision making. It is also suitable for organizations in which production processes are routine and efficiency is of primary importance. These organizations are usually extremely bureaucratic, and the division of labor is typically very well defined. Each worker knows his or her job and what is specifically expected, and each has a clear understanding of how to carry out assigned tasks. Centralized organizations stress formal rules, policies, and procedures, which are backed up with elaborate control systems. Their codes of ethics may specify the techniques to be used for decision making. General Motors, the Internal Revenue Service, and the U.S. Army are examples of centralized organizations.

Because of their top-down approach and the distance between managers and the decision maker, centralized organizational structures can lead to unethical acts. If formal rules and policies are unfairly executed, they lose their validity or efficacy. To some extent, rules can be deactivated even if they are formally still in force.[48] If the centralized organization is very bureaucratic, some employees may behave according to the letter of the law rather than the spirit. For example, a centralized organization can have a policy about bribes that does not include wording about donating to a client's favorite charity before or after a sale. Such donations or gifts can, in some cases, be construed as a tacit bribe because the employee buyer could be swayed by the donation, or gift, to act in a less than favorable way or not to act in the best interests of his or her firm.

TABLE 7.4 Structural Comparison of Organizational Types

	Emphasis	
Characteristic	**Centralized**	**Decentralized**
Hierarchy of authority	Centralized	Decentralized
Flexibility	Low	High
Adaptability	Low	High
Problem recognition	Low	High
Implementation	High	Low
Dealing with changes	Poor environmental complexity	Good
Rules and procedures	Many and formal	Few and informal
Division of labor	Clearcut	Ambiguous
Span of control	Many employees	Few employees
Use of managerial techniques	Extensive	Minimal
Coordination and control	Formal and impersonal	Informal and personal

©Cengage Learning 2013

Other ethical concerns may arise in centralized structures because they typically have very little upward communication. Top-level managers may not be aware of problems and unethical activity. Some companies' use of sweatshop labor may be one manifestation of this lack of upward communication. Sweatshops produce products such as garments by employing laborers, sometimes through forced immigrant labor, who often work 12- to 16-hour shifts for little or no pay. The UN International Labor Office says that forced labor costs approximately $21 billion a year in the form of children enslaved in sweatshops, migrant laborers working on farms and building homes, illegal immigrants subservient to their smugglers, and other forms of coercion. Asia is home to nearly three-quarters of all forced workers in the world. Industries that benefit the most from the cheap labor they provide include electronics, automobiles, textiles, construction, fishing, and agriculture.[49] Another ethical issue that may arise in centralized organizations is blame shifting, or scapegoating. People may try to transfer blame for their actions to others who are not responsible. The specialization and rigid division of labor in centralized organizations can also create ethical problems. Employees may not understand how their actions can affect the overall organization because they work with only one piece of a much larger puzzle. This lack of connectedness can lead employees to engage in unethical behavior because they fail to understand the overall ramifications of their behavior.

In a **decentralized organization,** decision-making authority is delegated as far down the chain of command as possible. Such organizations have relatively few formal rules, and coordination and control are usually informal and personal. They focus instead on increasing the flow of information. As a result, one of the main strengths of decentralized organizations is their adaptability and early recognition of external change. With greater flexibility, managers can react quickly to changes in their ethical environment. Google is known for being decentralized and for empowering its employees. A parallel weakness of

TABLE 7.5 Examples of Centralized and Decentralized Corporate Cultures

Company	Organizational Culture	Characterized by
Nike	Decentralized	Creativity, freedom, informality
Southwest Airlines	Decentralized	Fun, teamwork orientation, loyalty
General Motors	Centralized	Unions, adherence to task assignments, structured
Microsoft	Decentralized	Creative, investigative, fast paced
Procter & Gamble	Centralized	Experienced, dependable, a rich history and tradition of products, powerful

©Cengage Learning 2013

decentralized organizations is the difficulty they have in responding quickly to changes in policy and procedures established by top management. In addition, independent profit centers within a decentralized organization may deviate from organizational objectives. Decentralized firms may have fewer internal controls and use shared values for their ethical standards. If a firm depends on abstract values without specific rules of conduct, there may be more variation in behavior. Also, it may be harder to control rogue employees who engage in misconduct. Table 7.5 gives examples of centralized versus decentralized organizations and describes their different corporate cultures.

Due to the strict formalization and implementation of ethics policies and procedures in centralized organizations, they tend to be more ethical in their practices than decentralized organizations. Centralized organizations may also exert more influence on their employees because they have a central core of policies and codes of ethical conduct. Decentralized organizations give employees extensive decision-making autonomy because management empowers the employees. Ambiguity in the letter versus the spirit of rules can create ethical challenges, especially for newer managers.[50] However, it is also true that decentralized organizations may be able to avoid ethical dilemmas through the use of effective codes of conduct and ethics. If widely shared values and effective ethics programs are in place in decentralized organizations, there may be less need for excessive compliance systems. However, different units in the company may evolve with diverse value systems and approaches to ethical decision making. For example, a high-tech defense firm like Lockheed Martin, which employs more than 200,000 people, might have to cope with many different decisions on the same ethical issue if it did not have a centralized ethics program. Boeing has become more centralized since the entrance of CEO W. James McNerney, Jr., and the exit of previous CEO Harry Stonecipher, who carried on a relationship with a female vice president of the company. Before McNerney stepped in, Boeing had gone through several years of ethics and legal difficulties, including the jailing of the former CFO for illegal job negotiations with Pentagon officials, indictment of a manager for stealing 25,000 pages of proprietary documents, abuse of attorney-client privilege to cover up internal studies showing pay inequities, and other scandals.[51]

Unethical behavior is possible in either centralized or decentralized structures when specific corporate cultures permit or encourage workers to deviate from accepted standards or ignore corporate legal and ethical responsibilities. Centralized firms may have a more difficult time uprooting unethical activity than decentralized organizations as the latter has a more fluid structure in which changes may affect only a small portion of the company. Often, when a centralized firm uncovers unethical activity and it appears to be pervasive, the leadership is removed so that the old unethical culture can be uprooted and replaced with a more ethical one. For example, Mitsubishi Motors suggested significant management changes after it was discovered that a cover-up of auto defects had been going on for more than two decades.

GROUP DIMENSIONS OF CORPORATE STRUCTURE AND CULTURE

When discussing corporate culture, we tend to focus on the organization as a whole. But corporate values, beliefs, patterns, and rules are often expressed through smaller groups within the organization. Moreover, individual groups within organizations often adopt their own rules and values.

Types of Groups

Two main categories of groups affect ethical behavior in business. A **formal group** is defined as an assembly of individuals with an organized structure that is explicitly accepted by the group. An **informal group** is defined as two or more individuals with a common interest but without an explicit organizational structure.

FORMAL GROUPS   Formal groups can be divided into committees, work groups, and teams.

Committees, Work Groups, and Teams   A *committee* is a formal group of individuals assigned to a specific task. Often a single manager could not complete the task, or management may believe that a committee can better represent different constituencies and improve the coordination and implementation of decisions. Committees may meet regularly to review performance, develop plans, or make decisions. Most formal committees in organizations operate on an ongoing basis, but their membership may change over time. A committee is an excellent example of a situation in which coworkers and significant others within the organization can influence ethical decisions. Committee decisions are legitimized in part by agreement or majority rule. In this respect, minority views on issues such as ethics can be pushed aside through the majority's authority. Committees bring diverse personal moral values to the ethical decision-making process, which may expand the number of alternatives considered. Also inherent in the committee structure is a lack of individual responsibility. Because of the diverse composition of the group, members may not be committed or willing to assume responsibility for the group decision. Groupthink may emerge, enabling the majority to explain ethical considerations away.

Although many organizations have financial, diversity, personnel, or social responsibility committees, only a very few organizations have committees that are devoted exclusively to ethics. An ethics committee might raise ethical concerns, resolve ethical dilemmas in the organization, and create or update the company's code of ethics. Motorola, for example, maintains a Business Ethics Compliance Committee that interprets, classifies, communicates, and enforces the company's code and ethics initiatives. An ethics committee can gather information on functional areas of the business and examine manufacturing practices, personnel policies, dealings with suppliers, financial reporting, and sales techniques to find out whether the company's practices are ethical. Though much of a corporation's culture operates informally, an ethics committee is an example of a highly formalized approach for dealing with ethical issues.

Work groups are used to subdivide duties within specific functional areas of a company. For example, on an automotive assembly line, one work group might install the seats and interior design elements of the vehicle while another group installs all the dashboard instruments. This enables production supervisors to specialize in a specific area and provide expert advice to work groups.

While work groups operate within a single functional area, *teams* bring together the expertise of employees from several different areas of the organization—for example, finance, marketing, and production—on a single project, such as developing a new product. Many manufacturing firms, including General Motors, Westinghouse, and Procter & Gamble, are using the team concept to improve participative management. Ethical conflicts may arise because team members come from different functional areas. Each member of the team has a particular role to play and has probably had limited interaction with other members of the team. Conflicts often occur when members of different organizational groups must interact. However, airing viewpoints representative of all the functional areas helps provide more options from which to choose.

Work groups and teams provide the organizational structure for group decision making. One of the reasons why individuals cannot implement only their own personal ethical beliefs in organizations is that work groups collectively reach so many decisions. However, those who have legitimate power are in a position to influence ethics-related activities. The work group and team often sanction certain activities as ethical or define others as unethical.

INFORMAL GROUPS   In addition to the groups that businesses formally organize and recognize—such as committees, work groups, and teams—most organizations contain a number of informal groups. These groups are usually composed of individuals, often from the same department, who have similar interests and band together for companionship or for purposes that may or may not be relevant to the goals of the organization. For example, four or five people who have similar tastes in outdoor activities and music may discuss their interests while working, and they may meet outside work for dinner, concerts, sports events, or other activities. Other informal groups may evolve to form a union, improve working conditions or benefits, get a manager fired, or protest work practices that they view as unfair. Informal groups may generate disagreement and conflict, or they may enhance morale and job satisfaction.

"Informal groups help develop informal channels of communication, sometimes called the "grapevine," which are important in every organization."

Informal groups help develop informal channels of communication, sometimes called the grapevine, which are important in every organization. Informal communication flows up, down, diagonally, and horizontally, not necessarily following the communication lines on a company's organizational chart. Information passed along the grapevine may relate to the job, the organization, or an ethical issue, or it may simply be gossip and rumors. The grapevine can act as an early warning system for employees. If employees learn informally that their company may be sold or that a particular action will be condemned as unethical by top management or the community, they have time to think about how they will respond. Because gossip is not uncommon in an organization, the information passed along the grapevine is not always accurate, but managers who understand how the grapevine works can use it to reinforce acceptable values and beliefs.

The grapevine is also an important source of information for individuals to assess ethical behavior within their organization. One way an employee can determine acceptable behavior is to ask friends and peers in informal groups about the consequences of certain actions such as lying to a customer about a product-safety issue. The corporate culture may provide employees with a general understanding of the patterns and rules that govern behavior, but informal groups make this culture come alive and provide direction for employees' daily choices. For example, if a new employee learns anecdotally through the grapevine that the organization does not punish ethical violations, he or she may seize the next opportunity for unethical behavior if it accomplishes the organization's objectives. There is a general tendency to discipline top sales performers more leniently than poor sales performers for engaging in identical forms of unethical selling behavior. A superior sales record appears to induce more lenient forms of discipline, despite organizational policies that state otherwise.[52] In this case, the grapevine has clearly communicated that the organization rewards those who break the ethical rules to achieve desirable objectives.

Group Norms

Group norms are standards of behavior that groups expect of their members. Just as corporate culture establishes behavior guidelines for an organization's members, group norms help define acceptable and unacceptable behavior within a group. In particular, group norms define the limit allowed on deviations from group expectations.

Most work organizations, for example, develop norms that govern groups' rates of production and communication with management as well as provide a general understanding of behavior considered right or wrong, ethical or unethical, within the group. For example, other group members may punish an employee who reports to a supervisor that a coworker has covered up a serious production error. Other members of the group may glare at the informant, who has violated a group norm, and refuse to talk to or sit next to him or her.

Norms have the power to enforce a strong degree of conformity among group members. At the same time, norms define the different roles for various positions within the organization. For example, a low-ranking member of a group may be expected to carry out an unpleasant task such as accepting responsibility for someone else's ethical mistake. Abusive behavior toward new or lower-ranking employees could be a norm in an informal group.

Sometimes group norms conflict with the values and rules prescribed by the organization's culture. For example, the organization may have policies prohibiting the use of personal social networking sites during work hours and may use rewards and punishments to encourage this culture. In a particular informal group, however, norms may encourage using personal social networking sites during work hours and avoiding management's attention. Issues of equity may arise in this situation if other groups believe they are unfairly forced to follow policies that are not enforced. These other employees may complain to management or to the offending group. If they believe management is not taking corrective action they, too, may begin to use social networking for personal use, thus hurting the whole organization's productivity. For this reason, management must carefully monitor not only the corporate culture but also the norms of all the various groups within the organization. Sanctions may be necessary to bring in line a group whose norms deviate sharply from the overall culture.

VARIATION IN EMPLOYEE CONDUCT

Although a corporation is required to take responsibility for conducting its business ethically, a substantial amount of research indicates that significant differences exist in individual employees' values and philosophies and therefore in how they deal with ethical issues.[53] In other words, because people are culturally diverse and have different values, they interpret situations differently and the ethical decisions they make on the same ethical issue will vary.

Table 7.6 shows that approximately 10 percent of employees take advantage of situations to further their own personal interests. These individuals are more likely to manipulate, cheat, or act in a self-serving manner when the benefits to be gained from doing so are greater than the penalties for the misconduct. Such employees may choose to take office supplies from work for personal use if the only penalty they will suffer if caught is having to pay for the supplies. The lower the risk of being caught is, the higher the likelihood that the 10 percent most likely to take advantage of the company will be involved in unethical activities.

Another 40 percent of workers go along with the work group on most matters. These employees are most concerned about the social implications of their actions and want to fit into the organization. Although they have their own personal opinions, they are easily influenced by what the people around them are doing. These individuals may know that using office supplies for personal use is improper, yet they view it as acceptable because their coworkers do so. These employees rationalize their actions by saying that the use of office supplies is one of the benefits of working at their particular company, and it must be acceptable because the company does not enforce a policy prohibiting the behavior. Coupled with this philosophy is the belief that no one will get into trouble for doing what everybody else is doing.

About 40 percent of a company's employees, as shown in Table 7.6, always try to follow company policies and rules. These workers not only have a strong grasp of their corporate culture's definition of acceptable behavior, but also attempt to comply with codes of ethics, ethics training, and other communications about appropriate conduct. If the company has a policy prohibiting taking office supplies from work, these employees probably will observe it. However, they are not likely to speak out about the 40 percent who choose to go along with the work group, for these employees prefer to focus on their jobs and steer clear of any organizational misconduct. If the company fails to communicate standards of appropriate behavior, members of this group will devise their own.

The final 10 percent of employees try to maintain formal ethical standards that focus on rights, duties, and rules. They embrace values that assert certain inalienable rights

TABLE 7.6 Variation in Employee Conduct*

10%	40%	40%	10%
Follow their own values and beliefs; believe that their values are superior to those of others in the company	Always try to follow company policies	Go along with the work group	Take advantage of situations if the penalty is less than the benefit and the risk of being caught is low

*With kind permission from Springer Science+Business Media: Journal of the Academy of Marketing Science, "Cognitive Consistency of Marketing Managers in Ethical Situations," 20(3), January 1, 1992, pp. 243–252, John Fraedrich and O.C. Ferrell.

and actions, which they perceive to be always ethically correct. In general, members of this group believe that their values are right and superior to the values of others in the company, or even to the company's value system, when an ethical conflict arises. These individuals have a tendency to report the misconduct of others or to speak out when they view activities within the company as unethical. Consequently, members of this group will probably report colleagues who take office supplies.

The significance of this variation in the way individuals behave ethically is simply the fact that employees use different approaches when making ethical decisions. Because of the probability that a large percentage of any work group will either take advantage of a situation or at least go along with the work group, it is vital that companies provide communication and control mechanisms to maintain an ethical culture. Companies that fail to monitor activities and to enforce ethics policies provide a low-risk environment for those employees who are inclined to take advantage of situations to accomplish their personal, and sometimes unethical, objectives.

Good business practices and concern for the law require organizations to recognize this variation in employees' desire to be ethical. The percentages cited in Table 7.6 are only estimates, and the actual percentages of each type of employee may vary widely across organizations based on individuals and corporate culture. The specific percentages are less important than the fact that our research has identified these variations as existing within most organizations. Organizations should focus particular attention on managers who oversee the day-to-day operations of employees within the company. They should also provide training and communication to ensure that the business operates ethically, that it does not become the victim of fraud or theft, and that employees, customers, and other stakeholders are not abused through the misconduct of people who have a pattern of unethical behavior.

As we have seen throughout this book, many examples can be cited of employees and managers who have no concern for ethical conduct but who are nonetheless hired and placed in positions of trust. Some corporations continue to support executives who ignore environmental concerns, poor working conditions, or defective products, or who engage in accounting fraud. Executives who can get results, meaning profits, regardless of the consequences, are often admired and lauded, especially in the business press. When their unethical or even illegal actions become public knowledge, however, they risk more than the loss of their positions. Table 7.7 summarizes the penalties that corporate executives have experienced over the past several years.

CAN PEOPLE CONTROL THEIR OWN ACTIONS WITHIN A CORPORATE CULTURE?

Many people find it hard to believe that an organization's culture can exert so strong an influence on individuals' behavior within the organization. In our society, we want to believe that individuals control their own destinies. A popular way of viewing business ethics is therefore to see it as a reflection of the alternative moral philosophies that individuals use to resolve their personal moral dilemmas. As this chapter has shown, however, ethical decisions within organizations are often made by committees and formal and informal groups, not by individuals. Decisions related to financial reporting, advertising, product design, sales practices, and pollution-control issues are often beyond the influence of

TABLE 7.7 Penalties for Convictions of Organizational Wrongdoing

Executive/Company	Trial Outcome
Franklin Brown, former general counsel, Rite Aid	Convicted and sentenced to 10 years in prison
Bernard Ebbers, former chairman and CEO, WorldCom	Convicted and sentenced to 25 years to life in prison
Dennis Kozlowski, former CEO, Tyco	Mistrial in first trial; in second, convicted and sentenced to 8 1/3 to 25 years in prison
Jeffery Skilling, former president of Enron	Convicted of multiple felony charges and currently serving a 24-year, 4-month prison sentence
Joseph P. Nacchio, former CEO of Qwest Communications International	Convicted of insider trading, $19 million fine, forfeit of $52 million, and 6 years in prison
Xujia Wang, vice president of finance, Morgan Stanley Company	Convicted of securities fraud and conspiracy to commit securities fraud, 18 months in prison and $611,248 fine
Attorney Raymond Joseph Costanzo, Jr.	Provided false qualifying information and falsified down payments, 3 years, 5 months in prison to be followed by 4 years of supervised release and ordered to pay $7,843,184 in restitution
Gandhi Ben Morka, real estate appraiser	Convicted of mortgage fraud, 60 months in prison, and ordered to pay more than $2.3 million in restitution
Bernard Madoff, stockbroker and founder of Bernard L. Madoff Investment Securities LLC	Convicted of operating $65 billion Ponzi scheme, sentenced to 150 years in prison

Source: From *The Wall Street Journal* online, "White-Collar Defendants: Take the Stand, or Not?," April 2, 2006; FBI Report, http://www.fbi.gov/publications/financial/fcs_report2007/financial_crime_2007.htm (accessed August 19, 2009); "Bernard L. Madoff," *The New York Times,* http://topics.nytimes.com/top/reference/timestopics/people/m/bernard_l_madoff/index.html (accessed March 8, 2011).

individuals alone. In addition, these decisions are frequently based on business rather than personal goals.

Most new employees in highly bureaucratic organizations have limited input into the basic operating rules and procedures for getting things done. Along with learning sales tactics and accounting procedures, employees may be taught to ignore a design flaw in a product that could be dangerous to users. Although many personal ethics issues may seem straightforward and easy to resolve, individuals entering business will usually need several years of experience within a specific industry to understand how to resolve ethical close calls. Both individual ethics and organizational ethics have an impact on an employee's ethical intention. If there is congruence between individual ethics and the organizational ethical culture, there is an increase in the potential for making ethical choices in organizational decision-making. Younger managers may need more support and guidance from the organization because of their limited experience in dealing with complex issues.[54] Research has also indicated that congruence between individual and organizational values is greater in the private sector. On the other hand, age and organizational type aside, personal values appear to be a strong factor in decreasing unethical practices and increasing appropriate work behavior as compared to congruence in personal and organizational values.[55]

It is not our purpose to suggest that you ought to go along with management or the group on business ethics issues. Honesty and open discussions of ethical issues are important to successful ethical decision making. We believe that most companies and business-people try to make ethical decisions. However, because there is so much difference among individuals, ethical conflict is inevitable. If you manage and supervise others, it will be necessary to maintain ethical policies for your organization and report misconduct that occurs. Ethics is not just a personal matter.

Regardless of how a person or organization views the acceptability of a particular activity, if society judges it to be wrong or unethical, then this larger view directly affects the organization's ability to achieve its goals. Not all activities deemed unethical by society are illegal. But if public opinion decries or consumers protest against a particular activity, the result may be legislation that restricts or bans a specific business practice. For instance, concern about promoting unhealthy products to children has prompted some governments to take action. Santa Clara County in California and the San Francisco, California, Board of Supervisors banned toys in fast food offerings such as Happy Meals that do not meet certain nutritional standards. Restaurants were given until the end of 2011 to ensure that their food offerings contained fewer than 600 calories if they still want to offer toys with the meals. Proponents see this as a step in the right direction, as they believe that the toys basically sell the meals—in other words, children convince their parents to buy unhealthy meals simply to obtain the toy. Opponents argue that the city is taking it upon itself to discourage children from wanting to eat at McDonald's—thereby trying to protect them from obesity—when in fact that duty belongs to the parents. McDonald's restaurants affected by the ban feel they are being unfairly targeted because of their size and fear that the ban could harm business.[56] Sometimes businesses themselves will take action in order to prevent future government regulation that could limit their activities. For instance, Coca-Cola, Cadbury Schweppes, and PepsiCo all voluntarily agreed to stop selling soda in schools.[57]

If a person believes that his or her personal ethics severely conflict with the ethics of the work group and those of superiors in an organization, that person's only alternative may be to leave the organization. In the highly competitive employment market of the twenty-first century, quitting a job because of an ethical conflict requires courage and, possibly, the ability to survive without a job. Obviously, there are no easy answers for resolving ethical conflicts between the organization and the individual. Our goal is not to tell you what you should do. But we do believe that the more you know about how ethical decision making occurs within organizations, the more opportunity you will have to influence decisions positively and help resolve ethical conflicts more effectively.

SUMMARY

Corporate culture refers to the set of values, beliefs, goals, norms, and ways of solving problems that the members (employees) of an organization share. These shared values may be formally expressed or unspoken. Corporate cultures can be classified in several ways, and a cultural audit can identify an organization's culture. If an organization's culture rewards unethical behavior, people within the company are more likely to act unethically. A company's failure to monitor or manage its culture may foster questionable behavior.

Leadership—the ability or authority to guide others toward achieving goals—has a significant impact on the ethical decision-making process because leaders have the power to motivate others and enforce both the organization's rules and policies and their own viewpoints. A leader must not only gain the respect of his or her followers but must also provide a standard of ethical conduct. Leaders exert power to influence the behaviors and decisions of subordinates. There are five power bases from which a leader may influence ethical behavior: reward power, coercive power, legitimate power, expert power, and referent power. Leaders also attempt to motivate subordinates; motivation is an internal force that focuses an individual's behavior toward achieving a goal. It can be created by the incentives that an organization offers employees.

The structure of an organization may create opportunities to engage in unethical behavior. In a centralized organization, decision-making authority is concentrated in the hands of top managers, and little authority is delegated to lower levels. In a decentralized organization, decision-making authority is delegated as far down the chain of command as possible. Centralized organizations tend to be more ethical than decentralized ones because they enforce more rigid controls, such as codes of ethics and corporate policies, on ethical practices. However, unethical conduct can occur in both types of structures.

In addition to the values and customs that represent the culture of an organization, individual groups within the organization often adopt their own rules and values and even create subcultures. The main types of groups are formal groups—which include committees, work groups, and teams—and informal groups. Informal groups often feed an informal channel of communication called the grapevine. Group norms are standards of behavior that groups expect of their members. They help define acceptable and unacceptable behavior within a group and especially define the limits on deviating from group expectations. Sometimes group norms conflict with the values and rules prescribed by the organization's culture.

Sometimes an employee's own personal ethical standards conflict with what is expected of him or her as a member of an organization and its corporate culture. This is especially true given that an organization's ethical decisions are often resolved by committees, formal groups, and informal groups rather than by individuals. When such ethical conflict is severe, the individual may have to decide whether to leave the organization.

IMPORTANT TERMS FOR REVIEW

Sarbanes–Oxley 404	whistle-blowing	relatedness needs
apathetic culture	*qui tam relator*	growth needs
caring culture	reward power	centralized organization
exacting culture	coercive power	decentralized organization
integrative culture	legitimate power	formal group
cultural audit	expert power	informal group
compliance culture	referent power	group norm
values-based ethics culture	motivation	
differential association	job performance	

RESOLVING ETHICAL BUSINESS CHALLENGES*

As Gerard sat down in his expensive new chair, he felt worried. What had he gotten himself into? How could things have gone so wrong so fast? It was as if he'd been walking along and a truck had blindsided him. Gerard had been with Trawlers Accounting, a medium-sized firm, for several years. His wife, Vicky, had a job in the pharmaceutical industry, and their first child was due any day now. The doctor had told her that she would need to stop work early because hers was a high-risk pregnancy. So three months before her due date, she asked for and received a four-month leave of absence. This was great, but the leave was without pay. Luckily, Gerard had received a promotion and now headed a department.

Some interesting changes were occurring in the accounting industry. For example, Gerard's superior had decided that all CPAs would take exams to become registered investment advisers. The rationale for such a new development was simple. The firm could use its relationships with clients to increase investment revenues. Because of the long-term nature of these relationships with many firms and individuals as well as the implicit sense of honesty that CPAs must bring to their jobs, clients understood that a violation of so high a trust was unlikely—or so Gerard's boss argued. Many of the people in Gerard's department didn't like this new policy; however, some who had passed the exams had increased their pay by 15 percent. During lunch, one of Gerard's financial friends engaged him heatedly.

"What you're doing, Gerard, is called unfair competition," the friend accused him. "Your CPAs have exclusive access to confidential client taxpayer information, which could give you insight into people's financial needs. Besides, you could easily direct clients to mutual funds that you already own in order to keep your own personal investments afloat. Also, if your people start chasing commissions and fees on mutual funds that go bad, your credibility will become suspect, and no one will trust you again. Plus, your people will now have to keep abreast of financial, tax, and accounting changes."

When Gerard got to his office, he found that some of his people had been recommending a group of mutual funds that Trawlers had been auditing. Then someone from another of his company's accounting clients, CENA Mutual Funds, telephoned.

"What's the idea of having your people suggest PPI Mutual Funds when they are in direct competition with us?" the caller yelled. "We pay you a lot to do our accounting procedures, and that's how you reward us? I want to know by the end of the day if you are going to continue to push our competitor's product. I don't have to tell you that this will directly affect your department and you. Also, things like this get around the business circles, if you know what I mean."

With these words, the caller hung up on Gerard.

QUESTIONS | EXERCISES

1. Identify the ethical and legal issues of which Gerard needs to be aware.
2. Discuss the advantages and disadvantages of each decision Gerard has made and could make.
3. Discuss the issue of accounting firms going into the financial services market.
4. Discuss the types of groups that are influencing Gerard.

*This case is strictly hypothetical; any resemblance to real persons, companies, or situations is coincidental.

CHECK YOUR EQ

Check your EQ, or Ethics Quotient, by completing the following. Assess your performance to evaluate your overall understanding of the chapter material.

1. Decentralized organizations tend to put the blame for unethical behavior on lower-level personnel.   Yes   No

2. Decentralized organizations give employees extensive decision-making autonomy.   Yes   No

3. Corporate culture provides rules that govern behavior within the organization.   Yes   No

4. An integrative culture shows high concern for performance and little concern for people.   Yes   No

5. Coercive power works in the same manner as reward power.   Yes   No

ANSWERS 1. **No.** This is more likely to occur in centralized organizations. 2. **Yes.** This is known as empowerment. 3. **Yes.** Values, beliefs, customs, and ceremonies represent what is acceptable and unacceptable in the organization. 4. **No.** This describes an exacting culture. An integrative culture combines a high concern for people with a high concern for production. 5. **No.** Coercive power is the opposite of reward power. One offers rewards and the other responds with punishment to encourage appropriate behavior.

©Paul Aniszewski, Shutterstock

PART 4

Implementing Business Ethics in a Global Economy

CHAPTER 8

DEVELOPING AN EFFECTIVE ETHICS PROGRAM

©Paul Aniszewski, Shutterstock

AN ETHICAL DILEMMA*

Victoria was starting to wonder about her company's strategy as well as about the implications of her own actions. She had begun working for Koke International (KI) after graduating from Pacific West University with degrees in both finance and marketing. KI was the leader in franchised home repair outlets in the United States. In 25 years, KI had grown from several stores in the Pacific Northwest to 250 stores located across the United States and Canada. Koke International came to dominate the markets that it entered by undercutting local competitors on price and quality. The lower prices were easy to charge because KI received large quantity discounts from its vendors. The franchise concept also helped create another barrier to entry for KI's competitors. By expanding rapidly, KI was able to spread the costs of marketing to many more stores, giving it still another differential advantage. This active nourishment of its brand image coupled with some technological advances such as just-in-time inventory and electronic scanners had sent KI's stock soaring. As a result, it had a 50 percent share of the market. Koke International had done such an excellent job of positioning itself in its field that articles in major business newspapers were calling it "the Microsoft of home improvements." The view was that "KI is going to continue to be a very profitable enterprise, with less expected direct competition in a slow-growth, high-margin market for the future."

Wendy, Victoria's boss, had brought her in on KI's next potential conquest: the New England states of Maine, Vermont, New Hampshire, Connecticut, and Massachusetts.

"This is the last big potential market," Wendy said at a planning session with her senior staff. "I want you to realize that when we launch into these states we're going to have to be ruthless. I'd like your suggestions as to how we're going to eliminate the competition."

One person spoke up: "We first need to recognize that there are only five major players (multiple-store chains), with Home Designs being the largest."

"The top corporate people want us to attack Maine, New Hampshire, and Vermont first and then make a secondary attack on the other two states," interjected Victoria.

"Our buildings are four months from completion," Wendy pointed out, "and the media blitz is due to start one month prior to the 20-store grand opening. With that much exposed capital from our franchises, we need to make sure everything goes well. Vicky, have you completed your price analysis of all of the surrounding home repair stores?"

"Yes, and you're not going to like the news," Victoria replied. "Many of the stores are going to be extremely competitive relative to our normal pricing. In a few cases, they seem to have an edge."

Wendy turned to Ed. "Ed, how much cash reserves have you been able to calculate from the five players?"

"Well, Wendy, it looks like if we slash our prices for about six months to a year, we could drive all but Home Designs into near bankruptcy, providing that our promotional campaign doesn't have a misstep."

"What about personnel, Frank?" Wendy cut in. "Have you done the usual research to see about hiring away the five players' key personnel?"

"Yes, but many won't go unless they get a 50 percent raise, which is way out of line with our other stores."

At this point, Wendy slammed her fist on the table and shouted, "I'm tired of hearing negative reports! It's our job to drive out the competition, and I want solutions!"

There was a long silence in the room. Wendy was noted for her quick temper and her quick firings when things didn't go as planned. She had been the first woman to make it this high in the company, and it wasn't the result of being overly pleasant.

"So this is what we're going to do," Wendy said softly. "Frank, you're going to hire those key people at a 50 percent increase. You're going to keep the unions away from the rest of the people. In 18 months, when these overpriced employees have trained the others, we'll find some way of getting rid of them. Ed, you're going to lean on the players' bankers. See if we do business with them as well. See what other information you can squeeze out of them. Victoria, since you're the newest, I'm putting you in charge of breaking the pricing problem. I want you to come up with a unique pricing strategy for each of the 20 stores that will consistently undercut the competition for the next 18 months, even if we have to lose money on everything in the stores! The franchisees will go with this once we explain the payout."

One of the newer staff members asked, "If we're successful, doesn't that make us a monopoly in the area? Don't we have to worry about antitrust issues?"

Wendy raised her eyebrow a little and said, "We don't mention the word *monopoly* around here as if it were a dirty word. It took the Feds decades to break up AT&T. Microsoft was next on their list, and now it's MasterCard. We're in retail. No one has ever had problems with the Feds in this industry. By the time they get around to dealing with what we're doing, we will all be retired."

QUESTIONS | EXERCISES

1. Identify the issues of which Victoria needs to be aware.
2. Discuss the implications of each decision that Wendy made.
3. Discuss why the federal government has determined that monopolies are not in the public's best interest.

*This case is strictly hypothetical; any resemblance to real persons, companies, or situations is coincidental.

P rograms that are designed to foster ethical decision making in business are controversial today because much unethical and illegal business conduct has continued to occur even in organizations that have adopted such programs. Many companies that had codes of ethics were ruined by unethical activities and corporate scandals. Enron, AIG, and Merrill Lynch are all examples of organizations with codes of ethics that nonetheless experienced ethical disasters. Many business leaders believe that ethics initiatives should arise naturally from a company's corporate culture and that simply hiring good employees will limit unethical conduct. Moreover, many business executives and board members often do not understand how organizational ethics can be systematically implemented. In business, many ethical issues are very complex and require that organizations reach a consensus on appropriate action. Top executives and boards of directors must provide the leadership and a system with which to resolve these issues. Legislation and regulatory rules require leadership to create and implement effective ethics programs. These requirements come into play when misconduct is investigated by the government. We believe that customized ethics and compliance programs will help businesses provide guidance such that employees from diverse backgrounds will understand what behaviors are acceptable (and unacceptable) within the organization.

Business ethics programs have the potential to help top managers establish an ethical culture and eliminate the opportunity for unethical conduct. This chapter therefore provides a framework for developing an ethics program that is consistent with research, best practices, and the decision-making process described in Chapter 5, as well as with the Federal Sentencing Guidelines for Organizations (FSGO), the Sarbanes–Oxley Act, and the Dodd–Frank Act described in Chapter 4. These legislative reforms require both executives and boards of directors to assume responsibility and ensure that ethical standards are properly implemented on a daily basis.

In this chapter, we first examine the corporation as a social entity, and then provide an overview of why businesses need to develop organizational ethics programs. Next, we consider the factors that must be part of such a program: a code of conduct, an ethics officer and the appropriate delegation of authority, an effective ethics-training program, a system for monitoring and supporting ethical compliance, and continual efforts to improve the ethics program. Finally, we consider common mistakes in designing and implementing ethics programs.

THE RESPONSIBILITY OF THE CORPORATION AS A MORAL AGENT

Increasingly, corporations are viewed not merely as profit-making entities but also as moral agents that are accountable for their conduct to their stakeholders, including employees, investors, suppliers, government, and customers. Companies are more than the sum of their parts or participants. Because corporations are chartered as citizens of a state and/or nation, they generally have the same rights and responsibilities as individuals. Through legislation and court precedents, society holds companies accountable for the conduct of their employees as well as for their decisions and the consequences of those decisions. Coverage in the news media of specific issues such as employee benefits, executive compensation, defective products, competitive practices, and financial reporting contributes to a firm's reputation as a moral agent.

As moral agents, companies are required to obey the laws and regulations that define acceptable business conduct. However, it is important to acknowledge that they are not human beings who can think through moral issues. Because companies are not human, laws and regulations are necessary to provide formal structural restraints and guidance on ethical issues. Employees have a moral obligation to responsibly think through complex

FIGURE 8.1 Root Causes of Misconduct

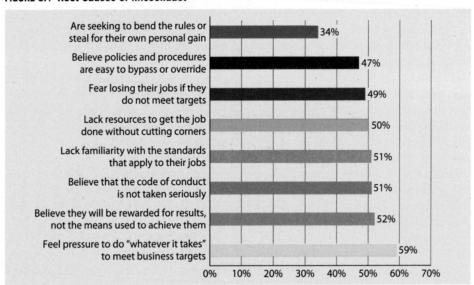

Source: KPMG Forensic Integrity Survey: 2008–2009, http://www.kpmg.com/SiteCollectionDocuments/Integrity-Survey-2008-2009.pdf, p. 6 (accessed August 20, 2009).

ethical issues to contribute to the ethical conduct of the corporation as a whole.[1] Figure 8.1 illustrates the basic causes of individual misconduct. The key reason why people seem to engage in misconduct is because they feel pressured to do "whatever it takes to meet business targets."

Though obviously not a person, a corporation can be considered a moral agent in society, one that has been created to perform specific social functions and is therefore responsible to society for its actions. Because corporations have the characteristics of agents, responsibility for ethical behavior is assigned to them as legal entities, as well as to individuals or work groups they employ. As Figure 8.1 indicates, a corporate culture without values and appropriate communication about ethics can facilitate individual misconduct. Some corporate outcomes cannot be tied to one individual or even a group, and misconduct can be the result of a collective pattern of decisions supported by a corporate culture. Therefore, corporations can be held accountable when they are found to be operating in a manner inconsistent with major legal requirements. Some organizations receive such large fines and negative publicity that they have to go out of business. On the other hand, companies that have been selected as top corporate citizens, including Google, Salesforce.com, IKEA, and AstraZeneca, receive awards and recognition for being responsible moral agents in society.[2]

In many cases, a coherent ethical corporate culture does not evolve through independent individual and interpersonal relationships. Because ethics is often viewed as an individual matter, many reason that the best way to develop an ethical corporate culture is to provide character education to employees or to hire individuals with good character and sensitize them to ethical issues. This theory assumes that ethical conduct will develop through company-wide agreement and consensus. Although these assumptions are laudable and contain some truth, companies that are responsible for most of the economic activity in the world employ thousands of culturally diverse individuals who will never reach agreement on all ethical issues. Many ethical business issues are complex close calls, and the only way to ensure consistent decisions that represent the interests of all stakeholders is to require ethical policies. This chapter provides support for the idea that implementing a centralized corporate ethics program can provide a cohesive, internally consistent set of statements and policies representing the corporation as a moral agent.

THE NEED FOR ORGANIZATIONAL ETHICS PROGRAMS

To understand why companies need to develop ethics programs, judge whether each of the following actions is unethical versus illegal.

- You want to skip work to go to a baseball game, but you need a doctor's excuse, so you make up some symptoms so that your insurance company pays for the doctor's visit. (unethical, illegal)

- While having a latte at a local café, you run into an acquaintance who works as a salesperson for a competing firm. You wind up chatting about future product prices. When you get back to your office, you tell your supervisor what you heard. (unethical, illegal)

- You are fired from your company, but before leaving for a position with another company, you copy a confidential list of client names and telephone numbers that you compiled for your former employer. (unethical, illegal)

- You receive a loan from your parents to make the down payment on your first home, but when describing the source of the down payment on the mortgage application, you characterize it as a gift. (unethical, illegal)

- Your manager asks you to book some sales revenue from the next quarter into this quarter's sales report to help the firm reach target sales figures. You agree to do so. (unethical, illegal)

You probably labeled one or more of these five scenarios as unethical rather than illegal. The reality is that all of them have the potential to be illegal. You may have chosen incorrectly because it is nearly impossible to know every detail of the highly complex laws relevant to these situations. Consider that there are 10,000 laws and regulations associated with the processing and selling of a single hamburger. Unless you are a lawyer who specializes in a particular area, it is difficult to know every law associated with your job. However, you can become more sensitized to what might be unethical or, in these cases, illegal. One reason why ethics programs are required in one form or another is to help sensitize employees to the potential legal and ethical issues within their work environments.

As we have mentioned throughout this book, ethics scandals in U.S. businesses have destroyed employees' trust in top management and significantly lowered the public's trust of business. And government agencies are not immune from this growing distrust. After it was revealed that the former legal counsel for the Securities and Exchange Commission had inherited money generated through investments with Bernard Madoff, the public was outraged that he had not recused himself from decisions related to the Madoff fraud. Since he had profited—albeit indirectly—from the Madoff fraud, many thought that his participation represented a serious conflict of interest. This occurrence led the SEC to announce a review of the agency's ethics program, particularly its conflict-of-interest policies.[3]

Pepsi CEO Indra Nooyi believes that all businesses are challenged to help restore consumer confidence and trust. She stated that rebuilding trust will require "all companies to think again about what they do to build trust, and to think again about how they make, give, and add value. And most of all, it will require all companies to ensure that they embrace not just the commercial idea of value, but the ethical ideal of values too."[4] Understanding the factors that influence the ethical decision-making process, as discussed in Chapter 5, can help companies encourage ethical behavior and discourage undesirable conduct. Fostering ethical decision making within an organization requires terminating unethical employees and improving the firm's ethical standards. Consider the "bad apple–bad barrel" analogy. Some people are simply "bad apples" who will always do things in their own self-interest regardless of their organization's goals or accepted standards of conduct.[5] For example, Raj Rajaratnam, co-founder of the hedge fund Galleon Group, allegedly used a "corrupt network" of consultants to make illegal profits. According to prosecutors, Rajaratnam and employees at Galleon Group engaged in insider trading on over 35 stocks, generating $45 million in profits. The corporate culture at Galleon Group appears to have promoted illegal behavior simply as a way of doing business.[6] Eliminating such bad apples through screening techniques and enforcement of a firm's ethical standards can help improve the firm's overall behavior.[7]

Organizations can also become "bad barrels," not because the individuals within them are bad, but because the pressures to succeed create opportunities that reward unethical decisions. In the case of such bad barrels, firms must redesign their image and culture to conform to industry and social standards of acceptable behavior.[8] Most companies attempt to improve ethical decision making by establishing and implementing a strategic approach to improving their organizations' ethics. Companies as diverse as Texas Instruments, Starbucks, Ford Motor Co., and Whole Foods have adopted a strategic approach to organizational ethics. They continuously monitor their programs and make adjustments when problems occur.

To promote legal and ethical conduct, an organization should develop an organizational ethics program by establishing, communicating, and monitoring the ethical values and legal requirements that characterize its history, culture, industry, and operating environment. Without such programs, uniform standards, and policies of conduct, it is difficult for employees to determine what behaviors are acceptable within a company. As discussed in Chapters 6 and 7, in the absence of such programs and standards, employees will generally make decisions based on their own observations of how their coworkers and superiors behave. A strong ethics program includes a written code of conduct; an ethics officer to oversee the program; careful delegation of authority; formal ethics training; and rigorous auditing, monitoring, enforcement, and revision of program standards. Without a strong program, problems are likely to occur. For example, despite laws protecting intellectual property in China, weak compliance programs have created piracy problems for businesses. One business that has been accused of Internet piracy is Baidu, the most popular search engine in China. Music companies have accused Baidu's MP3 service of allowing users to download songs without paying the copyright owners. Baidu, on the other hand, claims that it is acting legitimately and simply linking users to music websites. After a lawsuit was filed, the Chinese government ruled in favor of Baidu.[9]

Although there are no universal standards that can be applied to organizational ethics programs, most companies develop codes, values, or policies to provide guidance on business conduct. However, it would be naïve to think that simply having a code of ethics will solve all the ethical dilemmas that a company might face.[10] Indeed, most of the companies that have experienced ethical and legal difficulties in recent years have had formal ethics codes and programs. The problem is that top managers have not integrated these codes, values, and standards into their firms' corporate cultures where they can provide effective guidance for daily decision making. High-status officials like top managers may be more inclined to engage in unethical organizational conduct because of social isolation that creates insensitivity and a lower motivation to regulate ethical decision making.[11] Top managers tend to focus on financial performance because their jobs and personal identities are often intimately connected to their firms' quarterly returns. A culture of short-term performance as a company's highest priority can diminish ethical decision making. On the other hand, corporations owned by Warren Buffett's Berkshire Hathaway, such as Burlington Northern Santa Fe and GEICO, are not subject to Wall Street's quarterly returns and can focus on an unusual commitment to long-run performance and responsible conduct.[12]

> "A culture of short-term performance as a company's highest priority can diminish ethical decision making."

If a company's leadership fails to provide the vision and support needed for ethical conduct, then an ethics program will not be effective. Ethics is not something to be delegated to lower-level employees. To satisfy the public's escalating demands for ethical decision making, companies need to develop plans and structures for addressing ethical considerations. Some directions for improving ethics have been mandated through regulations, but companies must be willing to put in place a system for implementing values and ethics that exceeds the minimum requirements.

AN EFFECTIVE ETHICS PROGRAM

Throughout this book, we have emphasized that ethical issues are at the forefront of organizational concerns as managers and employees face increasingly complex decisions. These decisions are often made in a group environment composed of different value systems, competitive pressures, and political concerns that contribute to the opportunity for misconduct. The more misconduct occurs at a company, the less trust employees feel toward the organization—and the greater the turnover will likely be. A Deloitte LLP Ethics & Workplace survey indicated that 48 percent of employee respondents who were looking for a new job cited a loss of workplace trust as the primary reason for their departure. About 40 percent indicated unethical treatment as the reason.[13] When opportunities to engage in unethical conduct abound, companies are vulnerable to both ethical problems and legal violations if their employees do not know how to make the right decisions.

A company must have an effective ethics program to ensure that all employees understand its values and comply with the policies and codes of conduct that create its ethical culture. If the culture encourages unethical conduct, then misconduct is likely to occur even if the company has ethical guidelines in place. Consider that a French court sentenced a Société Générale trader to three years in prison for his role in one of the world's biggest trading scandals. The trader and his lawyers claimed that the company ignored red flags because the trader was making the company so much money. Even the bank admitted that it shared some of the responsibility for the misconduct.[14]

Because we come from diverse business, educational, and family backgrounds, it cannot be assumed that we know how to behave appropriately when we enter a new organization or job. The pharmaceutical company Merck requires all employees to be responsible for supporting its Code of Business Conduct, which is available in 27 languages. Employees take classes in ethics to help them understand how to resolve ethical dilemmas in the workplace, as well as receiving online training to raise their awareness of ethical issues and assist them in maintaining an ethical organizational culture.[15] According to a fraud survey, 66 percent of executives feel that inadequate ethics and compliance programs are the reason for much of the unchecked misconduct in business.[16] It would therefore appear that the creation of effective ethics programs like Merck's Code of Business Conduct are important deterrents to organizational misconduct.

An Ethics Program Can Help Avoid Legal Problems

As mentioned in Chapter 7, some corporate cultures provide opportunities for or reward unethical conduct because their management is not sufficiently concerned about ethics or because the company has failed to comply with the minimum requirements of the FSGO (Table 8.1). Companies may face penalties and the loss of public confidence if one of their employees breaks the law. The FSGO encourages companies to assess their key risk areas and to customize a compliance program that will address these risks and satisfy key effectiveness criteria. The guidelines also hold companies responsible for the misconduct of their employees. Indeed, an Ernst & Young global survey of over 1,400 CFOs and heads of internal audit, legal, and compliance divisions in major corporations revealed that while instances of fraud are rising in some regions, reported fraud in the United States. has been decreasing. Figure 8.2 shows the percentage of boards within Latin America, the Middle East, Africa, Europe, Australia, and North America that are concerned about key risk areas related to corporate bribery, fraud, and corruption. Note that although 72 percent of boards in North America have such concerns, the survey indicates that U.S. boards are beginning to ask more questions in an attempt to root out bribery and fraud within their companies.[17] Ethics programs that provide guidelines outlining board responsibilities encourage compliance at the highest levels of the organization.

At the heart of the FSGO is a "carrot-and-stick" philosophy. Companies that act to prevent misconduct by establishing and enforcing ethical and legal compliance programs may receive a "carrot" and avoid penalties should a violation occur. The ultimate "stick" is the possibility of being fined or put on probation if convicted of a crime. Organizational probation involves using on-site consultants to observe and monitor a company's legal compliance efforts as well as to report the company's progress toward avoiding misconduct to the

TABLE 8.1 Minimum Requirements for Ethics and Compliance Programs

1. Standards and procedures, such as codes of ethics, that are reasonably capable of detecting and preventing misconduct

2. High-level personnel who are responsible for an ethics and compliance program

3. No substantial discretionary authority given to individuals with a propensity for misconduct

4. Standards and procedures communicated effectively via ethics training programs

5. Systems to monitor, audit, and report misconduct

6. Consistent enforcement of standards, codes, and punishment

7. Continuous improvement of the ethics and compliance program

Source: Adapted from U.S. Sentencing Commission, *Federal Sentencing Guidelines Manual*, effective November 1, 2004 (St. Paul, MN: West, 2008).

FIGURE 8.2 Percentage of Boards in Different Countries that are Concerned About Their Personal Liability for Corporate Fraud, Bribery, and Corruption

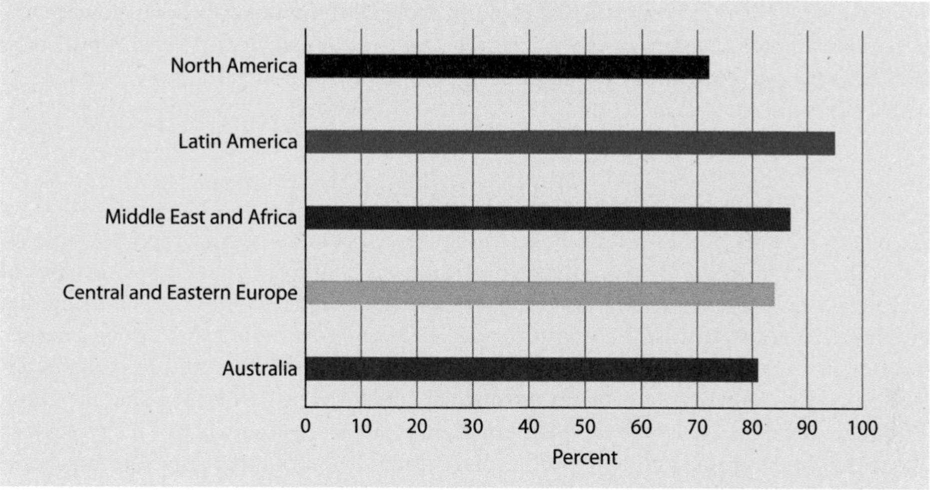

Source: "Global Survey Shows Business Fraud Up," *Corporate Compliance Insights*, May 19, 2010, http://www.corporatecomplianceinsights.com/2010/global-survey-shows-business-fraud-up-boards-have-increased-concern-about-liability/?pfstyle=wp (accessed March 15, 2011).

U.S. Sentencing Commission. Table 8.2 shows the fines that the Securities and Exchange Commission has levied against well-known firms for corporate misconduct.

The FSGO encourages federal judges to increase fines for organizations that continually tolerate misconduct and to reduce or eliminate fines for firms with extensive compliance programs that are making due diligence attempts to abide by legal and ethical standards. Until the guidelines were formulated, courts were inconsistent in holding corporations responsible for employee misconduct. There was no incentive to build effective programs to encourage employees to make ethical and legal decisions. Now companies earn credit for creating ethics programs that meet a rigorous standard. The effectiveness of a program is determined by its design and implementation. In other words, it must deal effectively with the risks associated with a particular business, and it must become part of the corporate culture.

An ethics program can help a firm avoid civil liability, but the company still bears the burden of proving that it has an effective program. A program developed in the absence of misconduct will be much more effective than one imposed as a reaction to scandal or

TABLE 8.2 Penalties for Corporate Misconduct

Company	Penalty	Reason
WorldCom	$750 million	Accounting fraud
Goldman Sachs	$550 million	Misleading investors
Fannie Mae	$400 million	Accounting fraud
Time Warner	$300 million	Accounting fraud
Qwest	$250 million	Accounting fraud

Source: Matt Phillips, "SEC's Greatest Hits: Biggest. Penalties. Ever." *The Wall Street Journal*, July 16, 2010, http://blogs.wsj.com/marketbeat/2010/07/16/secs-greatest-hits-some-of-the-other-biggest-penalties/ (accessed March 13, 2011).

prosecution. A legal test of a company's ethics program may occur when an individual employee is charged with misconduct. The court system or the U.S. Sentencing Commission evaluates the organization's responsibility for the individual's behavior during the process of an investigation. If the courts find that the company contributed to the misconduct or failed to show due diligence in preventing misconduct, then the firm may be convicted and sentenced.

Values versus Compliance Programs

No matter what their goals, ethics programs are developed as organizational control systems, the aim of which is to create predictability in employee behavior. Two types of control systems can be created. A **compliance orientation** creates order by requiring that employees identify with and commit to specific required conduct. It uses legal terms, statutes, and contracts that teach employees the rules and penalties for noncompliance. The other type of system is a **values orientation,** which strives to develop shared values. Although penalties are attached, the focus is more on an abstract core of ideals such as accountability and commitment. Studies have found that when personal and organizational values are compatible with one another, it tends to positively influence workplace ethics.[18]

The advantage of a values orientation is that it gives employees a clearly defined basis on which to make decisions, one in which fairness, compassion, respect, and transparency are paramount. At the same time, diversity in employees' experience and personal values requires explicit communication and training on subject matter areas such as financial reporting, use of company resources, and intellectual property. Establishing compliance standards helps employees understand rules of conduct when there are identified risks. For example, rules on the recruiting and hiring of new employees will help enforce company policy and prevent legal violations. When there are new, unexpected, or ambiguous issues with no compliance requirements, values may help the employee navigate through the ethical issues at hand.

Research into compliance- and values-based approaches reveals that both types of programs can interact or work toward the same end but that a values orientation has the added benefit of sparking ethical reasoning among employees. Values-based programs increase employees' awareness of ethics at work, their integrity, their willingness to deliver information to supervisors, their use of reporting mechanisms, and their perception that better ethical decisions are being made. Compliance-based programs are linked to employees' awareness of ethical risks at work and to a clear understanding of rules and expectations that facilitates decision making. In the final analysis, both orientations can be used to help employees and managers; however, a values-based program is the foundation of an organizational ethical culture.

CODES OF CONDUCT

As the perception of business accountability has changed over the years, expectations for organizational codes of ethics have grown. Today, society expects to see employees adhere to ethical principles and standards specified through company ethics programs.[19] Most companies begin the process of establishing organizational ethics programs by developing

codes of conduct, which are formal statements that describe what an organization expects of its employees. Such statements may take three different forms: a code of ethics, a code of conduct, and a statement of values. A **code of ethics** is the most comprehensive and consists of general statements, sometimes altruistic or inspirational, that serve as principles and as the basis for rules of conduct. A code of ethics generally specifies methods for reporting violations, disciplinary action for violations, and a structure of due process. Table 8.3 describes some benefits of having a comprehensive code of conduct. A code of conduct is a written document that may contain some inspirational statements but that mainly specifies acceptable and unacceptable types of behavior. A code of conduct is more akin to a regulatory set of rules and, as such, tends to elicit less debate about specific actions. Some of the key reasons that codes of ethics fail are that (1) the code is not promoted and employees do not read it; (2) the code is not easily accessible; (3) the code is written too legalistically and therefore is not understandable by average employees; (4) the code is written too vaguely, providing no accurate direction; and (5) top management never refers to the code in body or spirit.[20]

The final type of ethical statement is a **statement of values,** which serves the general public and also addresses distinct groups such as stakeholders. Values statements are conceived by management and are fully developed with input from all stakeholders. Despite the distinction made in this book between a code of ethics and a values statement, it is important to recognize that these terms are often used interchangeably.

Regardless of its degree of comprehensiveness, a code of ethics should reflect upper managers' desires for compliance with the values, rules, and policies that support an ethical culture. The development of a code of ethics should involve the president, board of directors, and chief executive officers who will be implementing the code. Legal staff should also be called on to ensure that the code has correctly assessed key areas of risk and that it provides buffers for potential legal problems. A code of ethics that does not address specific high-risk activities within the scope of daily operations is inadequate for maintaining standards that can prevent misconduct. Table 8.4 shows factors to consider when developing and implementing a code of ethics.

Codes of ethics may address a variety of situations, from internal operations to sales presentations and financial disclosure practices. Research has found that corporate

---

DEBATE ISSUE   TAKE A STAND

Examining Banking and Insurance Companies' Codes of Conduct

The financial industry was blamed for significant misconduct that contributed to the last major recession. Codes of conduct, sometimes referred to as codes of ethics, should provide behavioral expectations that an organization maintains for its managers, employees, and agents. The Ethisphere Institute has developed a grade methodology for evaluating codes of conduct, using the criteria of public availability, tone from the top, readability and tone, non-retaliation and reporting, values and commitments, risk topics, comprehension aids, and presentation and style. Of the 25 companies evaluated in the banking industry, only two banks received a relatively high ranking. In the insurance industry, only two companies received above a C rating. It is interesting that in the banking industry, 19 of the 25 companies received an F for tone at the top, indicating a lack of communication from the CEO or Chairman of the Board. This seems to suggest that misconduct tends to occur more frequently in organizations with badly written codes of conduct.[21]

1. The Ethisphere Institute's analysis of banking and insurance codes of conduct explains why widespread misconduct has been so prevalent in the financial industry.

2. Written codes of conduct are only a small part of the ethical culture of a company and cannot by themselves explain why misconduct has been so widespread in the financial industry.

©Cengage Learning 2013

TABLE 8.3 Benefits of Having an Ethics Code

A Comprehensive Code of Conduct Can...
1. Guide employees in situations where the ethical course of action is not immediately obvious.
2. Help the company reinforce—and acquaint new employees with—its culture and values. A code can help create a climate of integrity and excellence.
3. Help the company communicate its expectations for its staff to suppliers, vendors, and customers.
4. Minimize subjective and inconsistent management standards.
5. Help a company remain in compliance with complex government regulations.
6. Build public trust and enhance business reputations.
7. Offer protection in preempting or defending against lawsuits.
8. Enhance morale, employee pride, loyalty, and the recruitment of outstanding employees.
9. Help promote constructive social change by raising awareness of the community's needs and encouraging employees and other stakeholders to help.
10. Promote market efficiency, especially in areas where laws are weak or inefficient, by rewarding the best and most ethical producers of goods and services.

Source: "Ten Benefits of Having an Ethics Code," Josephson Institute Center for Business Ethics, http://josephsoninstitute.org/business/blog/2010/11/ten-benefits-of-having-an-ethics-code/ (accessed March 14, 2010). Originally adapted from *Good Ideas for Creating a More Ethical and Effective Workplace.*

TABLE 8.4 Developing and Implementing a Code of Ethics

1. Consider areas of risk and state the values as well as conduct necessary to comply with laws and regulations. Values are an important buffer in preventing serious misconduct.
2. Identify values that specifically address current ethical issues.
3. Consider values that link the organization to a stakeholder orientation. Attempt to find overlaps in organizational and stakeholder values.
4. Make the code understandable by providing examples that reflect values.
5. Communicate the code frequently and in language that employees can understand.
6. Revise the code every year with input from organizational members and stakeholders.

©Cengage Learning 2013

codes of ethics often contain about six core values or principles in addition to more detailed descriptions and examples of appropriate conduct.[22] The six values that have been suggested as being desirable for codes of ethics are (1) trustworthiness, (2) respect, (3) responsibility, (4) fairness, (5) caring, and (6) citizenship.[23] These values will not be effective without distribution, training, and the support of top management in making these values a part of the corporate culture. Employees need specific examples of how these values can be implemented.

Research has demonstrated that employees at organizations with effective ethical codes of conduct tend to be less tolerant of unethical behavior toward stakeholders than those at companies without ethical codes.[24] Codes of conduct will not resolve every ethical issue encountered in daily operations, but they help employees and managers deal with ethical dilemmas by prescribing or limiting specific activities. Many companies have a code of ethics, but it is not communicated effectively. A code that is placed on a website or in a training manual is useless if it is not reinforced every day. By communicating to employees both what is expected of them and what punishments they face if they violate the rules, codes of conduct curtail opportunities for unethical behavior and thereby improve ethical decision making. For example, the American Society for Civil Engineers' code of ethics specifies that engineers must act with zero tolerance toward bribery, fraud, and corruption in all engineering and construction projects in which they are engaged.[25] Codes of conduct do not have to be so detailed that they take into account every situation, but they should provide guidelines and principles that are capable of helping employees achieve organizational ethical objectives and address risks in an accepted way.

In Japan, Kao Corporation has gained recognition for its leading ethics programs. The company has won numerous ethics awards as well as the Environmental Technology Award from the Japan Chemical Industry Association. It is also the only Japanese company to be included on *Ethisphere*'s World's Most Ethical Companies list for four consecutive years. Kao is extremely focused on ethics and integrity. The company ensures that its employees are provided with training in ethics and in the characteristics and cultures of other countries. Kao has also created new ecofriendly products that will save resources and that are well-suited to areas like China, where water is scarce.[26] Ethics programs are essential in large corporations such as Kao Corporation. However, it is not only large companies that need to develop an ethics and compliance program; small companies need to do so as well.

ETHICS OFFICERS

Organizational ethics programs must have oversight by high-ranking persons known to respect legal and ethical standards. These individuals—often referred to as **ethics officers**—are responsible for managing their organizations' ethics and legal compliance programs. They are usually responsible for (1) assessing the needs and risks that an organization-wide ethics program must address, (2) developing and distributing a code of conduct or ethics, (3) conducting training programs for employees, (4) establishing and maintaining a confidential service to answer employees' questions about ethical issues, (5) making sure that the company is in compliance with government regulation, (6) monitoring and auditing ethical conduct, (7) taking action on possible violations of the company's code, and (8) reviewing and updating the code. Ethics officers are also responsible for knowing thousands of pages of relevant regulations as well as communicating and reinforcing values that build an ethical corporate culture. The Ethics Resource Center reports that having a comprehensive ethics program in place, one that includes an ethics officer, helps companies reduce incidences of misconduct by as much as 75 percent. However, only 9 percent of corporations included in the survey have an ethics program deemed comprehensive by the ERC.[27] Corporate wrongdoings and scandal-grabbing headlines have a profound negative impact on public trust. To ensure compliance with state and federal regulations, many corporations are now appointing chief compliance officers and ethics and business conduct professionals to develop and oversee corporate compliance programs.[28]

The Ethics and Compliance Officer Association (ECOA) has over 1,200 members who are frontline managers of ethics programs in over 30 countries.[29] Ethics officers often move into their position from other jobs in their companies. Ethics and compliance officers have backgrounds in law, finance, and human resource management. Sarbanes–Oxley and the amendments to the FSGO have increased the responsibility that ethics officers and boards of directors have for oversight of financial reporting. Ethics officers' positions are still relatively new and somewhat ill-defined. Although tough economic times call all expenditures into question, economic uncertainty brings about the greatest need for an investment in and formalization of the ethics and compliance roles within an organization. Times of economic distress tend to generate significant organizational and individual wrongdoing.[30]

Although recommended as best practice, it is not common for ethics officers to report directly to the board of directors. Ethics officers often report directly to the chief executive officer and may have some access to the board. In a survey of chief financial officers, more than 30 percent indicated that their operations had been impacted or disrupted by unexpected circumstances in the past year. Oversight, monitoring, and review of operating procedures and outcomes by the ethics and compliance function can prevent such surprises.[31]

ETHICS TRAINING AND COMMUNICATION

A major step in developing an effective ethics program is implementing a training program and communication system to educate employees about the firm's ethical standards. The National Business Ethics Survey looked at 18 dimensions of ethical culture and formal programs and found that companies with strong ethical cultures and formal ethics programs were 36 percentage points less likely to observe misconduct than employees in organizations with weak cultures and ethics programs.[32] A significant number of employees report that they frequently find such training useful. Training can educate employees about the firm's policies and expectations, relevant laws and regulations, and general social standards. Training programs can also make employees aware of available resources, support systems, and designated personnel who can assist them with ethical and legal advice. They can empower employees to ask tough questions and make ethical decisions. Many organizations are now incorporating ethics training into their employee and management development training efforts. For instance, the National Science Foundation (NSF) adopted new ethics rules that require researchers who receive grants to undergo ethics training. Starting in 2010, NSF grant recipients must participate in a formal training program to educate them on ethical research techniques and oversight.[33] Sometimes governments mandate ethics training for officials. In Russia, President Vladimir Putin ordered drivers with blue lights on their vehicles to undergo professional ethics training after other drivers complained of unruly behavior. Blue lights are used by Russian police officers, government and emergency vehicles, and many middle-ranking state officials (they can also be obtained illegally for bribes). Several owners of these blue lights have harassed or even injured others who would or could not get out of their way on the roads. This unethical behavior prompted Putin to order mandatory ethics training in the hopes of preventing future misconduct.[34]

As we emphasized in Chapters 5 and 7, ethical decision making is influenced by corporate culture, by coworkers and supervisors, and by the opportunities available to engage in unethical behavior. Ethics training can impact all three types of influence. Full awareness of a company's philosophy of management, rules, and procedures can strengthen both the corporate culture and the ethical stance of peers and supervisors. Such awareness, too, arms employees against opportunities for unethical behavior and lessens the likelihood of misconduct. Thus, the existence and enforcement of company rules and procedures limit unethical practices in the organization. If adequately and thoughtfully designed, ethics training can make employees aware of ethical issues, increase the importance of ethics training to employees, and increase employees' confidence that they can make the correct decision when faced with an ethical dilemma.[35] If ethics training is to be effective, it must start with a theoretical foundation, a code of ethics, a procedure for airing ethical concerns, line and staff involvements, and clear executive priorities on ethics, all of which must be communicated to employees. Managers from every department must be involved in the development of an ethics training program. Training and communication initiatives should reflect the unique characteristics of an organization: its size, culture, values, management style, and employee base. To be successful, business ethics programs should educate employees about formal ethical frameworks and models for analyzing business ethics issues. Then employees can base ethical decisions on their knowledge of choices rather than on emotions.

> "The existence and enforcement of company rules and procedures limit unethical practices in the organization."

A key component of managing an effective and efficient ethics and compliance program is a firm grasp of techniques that clearly communicate the company's culture, policies, and procedures for dealing with ethical issues to employees. Many feel that "hands on" training in which employees are forced to confront actual or hypothetical ethical dilemmas helps them to understand how their organization would like them to deal with potential problems. Lockheed Martin, for example, has developed training games that include dilemmas that can be resolved in teams. Each team member can offer his or her perspective, thereby helping other team members fully understand the ramifications of a decision for coworkers and the organization.

Another training device is the behavioral simulation, which gives participants a short, hypothetical ethical issue situation to review. Each participant is assigned a role within a hypothetical organization and is provided with varying levels of information about the scenario. Participants must then interact to develop recommended courses of action representing short-term, mid-term, and long-term considerations. Such simulations recreate the complexities of organizational relationships as well as the realities of having to address difficult situations with incomplete information. They help participants gain awareness of the ethical, legal, and social dimensions of business decision making; develop analytical skills for resolving ethical issues; and gain exposure to the complexity of ethical decision making in organizations. Research indicates that "the simulation not only instructs on the importance of ethics but on the processes for managing ethical concerns and conflict."[36]

Top executives must communicate with managers at the operations level (in production, sales, and finance, for instance) and enforce overall ethical standards within the organization. Table 8.5 lists the goals for successful ethics training. Making employees aware of the key risk areas for their occupation or profession is of a major importance in any

TABLE 8.5 Key Goals of Successful Ethics Training Programs

1. Identify key risk areas that employees will face.

2. Provide experience in dealing with hypothetical or disguised ethical issues within the industry through mini-cases, online challenges, CD-ROMs, or other experiential learning opportunities.

3. Let employees know that wrongdoing will never be supported in the organization and that employee evaluations will take their conduct in this area into consideration.

4. Let employees know that they are individually accountable for their behavior.

5. Align employee conduct with organizational reputation and branding.

6. Provide ongoing feedback to employees about how they are handling ethical issues.

7. Allow a mechanism for employees to voice their concerns that is anonymous, but that provides answers to key questions (24-hour hotlines).

8. Provide a hierarchy of leadership for employees to contact when they are faced with an ethical dilemma that they do not know how to resolve.

©Cengage Learning 2013

ethics training program. In addition, employees need to know whom to contact for guidance when they encounter gray areas in which the organization's values, rules, policies, and training do not provide adequate direction.

Although training and communication should reinforce values and provide employees with opportunities to learn about rules, they represent just one aspect of an effective ethics program. Moreover, ethics training will be ineffective if conducted solely because it is required or because it is something that competing firms are doing. For example, Enron had an ethics program in place. However, unethical executives knew they had the support of Arthur Andersen, the firm's auditing and accounting consulting partner, as well as that of law firms, investment analysts, and in some cases, government regulators. Enron's top managers therefore probably believed that their efforts to hide debt in off-balance-sheet partnerships would not be exposed.

When measuring the effectiveness of an ethics program, it is important to get input from employees. Employee surveys and the incorporation of ethics measurements in performance appraisal systems are two ways to help determine the effectiveness of a firm's ethics training. If ethical performance is not a part of regular performance appraisals, employees will get the message that ethics is not an important component of decision making in their company. For ethics training to make a difference, employees must understand why it is conducted, how it fits into the organization, and what their own role in implementing it is.

SYSTEMS TO MONITOR AND ENFORCE ETHICAL STANDARDS

An effective ethics program employs a variety of resources to monitor ethical conduct and measure the program's effectiveness. Observing employees, conducting internal audits and investigations, circulating surveys, and instituting reporting systems are ways that a company can assess compliance with its ethical code and standards. An external audit and review of company activities may sometimes be helpful in developing benchmarks of compliance. (We examine the process of ethical auditing in Chapter 9.)

To determine whether a person is performing his or her job adequately and ethically, observers might focus on how the employee handles an ethically charged situation. Many businesses employ role-playing exercises when they train salespeople and managers. Ethical issues can be introduced into the discussion, and the results can be videotaped so that both participants and their superiors can evaluate the outcome of the ethics dilemma.

Questionnaires can serve as benchmarks in an ongoing assessment of ethical performance by measuring employees' ethical perceptions of their company, their superiors, their coworkers, and themselves, as well as by serving as a means of developing ratings of ethical or unethical practices within their firm and industry. Then, if unethical conduct appears to be increasing, management will have a better understanding of what types of unethical practices may be occurring and why. A change in the company's ethics training may then be necessary.

The existence of an internal system by which employees can report misconduct is especially useful for monitoring and evaluating ethical performance. Many companies set up ethics assistance lines, also known as hotlines, to provide support and give employees the opportunity to ask questions or report concerns. The most effective ethics hotlines operate on an anonymous basis and are supported 24 hours a day, 365 days a year. Approximately 50 percent of hotline calls occur at night or on the weekends. Many times troubling ethical issues can cause people to lose sleep and can occupy their thoughts during their free time.[37] Although there is always some concern that employees may misreport a situation or abuse a hotline to retaliate against a coworker, hotlines have become widespread, and employees do use them. An easy-to-use hotline or help desk can serve as a safety net that increases the chance of detecting and responding to unethical conduct in a timely manner. Hotlines serve as a central contact point where critical comments, dilemmas, and advice can be assigned to the person most appropriate for handling a specific case.[38] Employees often prefer to deal with ethical issues through their supervisors or managers or try to resolve the matter directly before using an anonymous reporting system such as a hotline.[39]

Companies are increasingly using firms that provide professional case-management services and software. Software is becoming popular because it provides reports of employee concerns, complaints, or observations of misconduct that can then be tracked and managed. Thus the company can track investigations, analysis, resolutions, and documentation of misconduct reports. This system helps prevent lawsuits and can help a company learn about and analyze ethical lapses. However, it is important for companies to choose the right software for their needs. Although only 10 to 15 percent of companies currently use some type of compliance management tool, many companies are moving toward the automated process that technology and software provide.

If a company is not making progress toward creating and maintaining an ethical culture, it needs to determine why and take corrective action, either by enforcing current standards more strictly or by setting higher standards. Corrective action may involve rewarding employees who comply with company policies and standards and punishing those who do not. When employees abide by organizational standards, their efforts should be acknowledged through public recognition, bonuses, raises, or some other means. On the other hand, when employees violate organizational standards, they must be reprimanded, transferred, docked, suspended, or even fired. If a firm fails to take corrective action against unethical or illegal behavior, the inappropriate behavior is likely to continue. In the Ethics Resource Center Survey, the biggest reason employees gave for not reporting observed misconduct was that they were skeptical that their report would make a difference. The second most common reason was fear of retaliation.[40] However, new laws and court rulings are making it more difficult for businesses to engage in retaliation. The Supreme Court has ruled that an employee can even sue if a close associate or relative is fired by an employer in retaliation for reporting misconduct such as discrimination.[41]

Consistent enforcement and necessary disciplinary action are essential to a functional ethics or compliance program. The ethics officer is usually responsible for implementing all disciplinary actions for violations of the firm's ethical standards. Many companies are including ethical compliance in employee performance evaluations. During performance evaluations, employees may be asked to sign an acknowledgment that they have read the company's current ethics guidelines. The company must also promptly investigate any known or suspected misconduct. The appropriate company official, usually the ethics officer, needs to make a recommendation to senior management on how to deal with a particular ethical infraction. In some cases, a company may be required to report substantiated misconduct to a designated government or regulatory agency so as to receive credit. Under the FSGO, such credit for having an effective compliance program can reduce fines.[42]

Efforts to deter unethical behavior are important to companies' long-term relationships with their employees, customers, and community. If the code of ethics is aggressively enforced and becomes part of the corporate culture, it can effectively improve ethical behavior within an organization. If a code is not properly enforced, however, it becomes mere window dressing and will accomplish little toward improving ethical behavior and decision making.

Continuous Improvement of an Ethics Program

Improving a system that encourages employees to make more ethical decisions differs little from implementing any other type of business strategy. Implementation requires designing activities to achieve organizational objectives using available resources and given existing constraints. Implementation translates a plan for action into operational terms and establishes a means by which an organization's ethical performance will be monitored, controlled, and improved. Figure 8.3 indicates that organizations are more likely to have comprehensive ethics and compliance programs as they grow larger. This fact is in part due to increased resources, but also undoubtedly to increased stakeholder responsibilities and liabilities.

A firm's ability to plan and implement ethical business standards depends in part on how it structures resources and activities to achieve its ethical objectives. People's attitudes and behavior must be guided by a shared commitment to the business rather than by mere obedience to traditional managerial authority. Encouraging diversity of perspectives, disagreement, and the empowerment of people helps align the company's leadership with its employees.

If a company determines that its ethical performance has been less than satisfactory, executives may want to change how certain kinds of decisions are made. For example,

FIGURE 8.3 Percentage of Employees Recognizing Own Companies as Having Comprehensive Ethics Programs Increases with Company Size

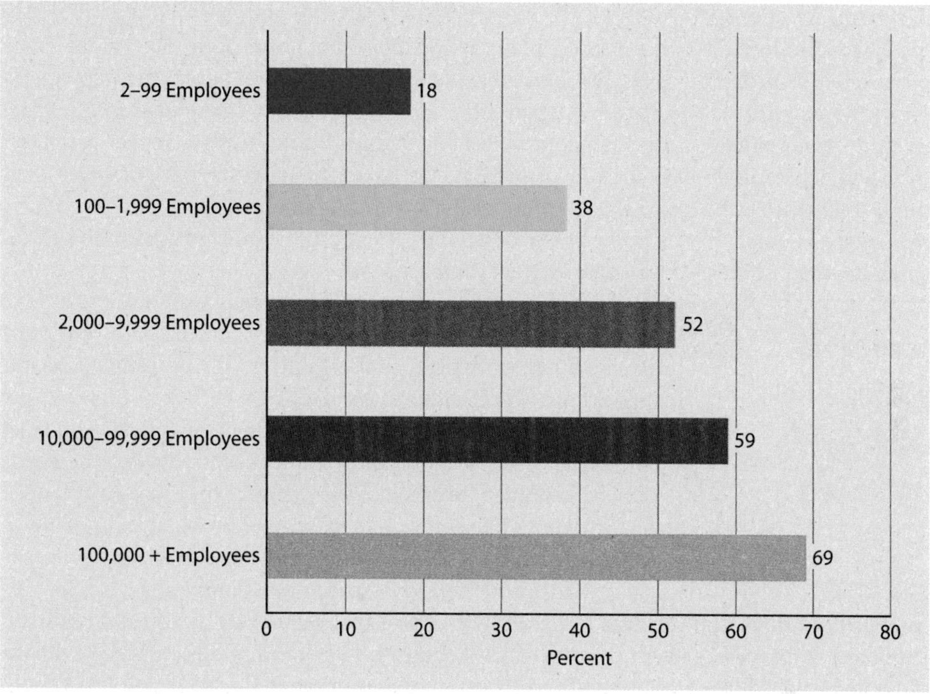

Source: *National Business Ethics Survey 2007* (Arlington, VA: Ethics Resource Center, 2007), 35.

a decentralized organization may need to centralize key decisions, at least for a time, so that upper managers can ensure that these decisions are made in an ethical manner. Centralization may reduce the opportunities that lower-level managers and employees have to make unethical decisions. Executives can then focus on initiatives for improving the corporate culture and infusing more ethical values throughout the firm by rewarding positive behavior and sanctioning negative behavior. In other companies, decentralizing important decisions may be a better way to attack ethical problems so that lower-level managers who are familiar with the local business environment and local culture and values can make more decisions. Whether the ethics function is centralized or decentralized, the key need is to delegate authority in such a way that the organization can achieve ethical performance.

Common Mistakes in Designing and Implementing an Ethics Program

Many business leaders recognize that they need to have an ethics program, but few take the time to answer fundamental questions about the goals of such a program. As we mentioned previously, some of the most common program objectives are to deter and detect unethical behavior as well as violations of the law; to gain competitive advantages through improved relationships with customers, suppliers, and employees; and, especially for multinational corporations, to link employees through a unifying and shared corporate culture. Failure to understand and appreciate these goals is the first mistake that many firms make when designing ethics programs.

A second mistake is not setting realistic and measurable program objectives. Once a consensus on objectives is reached, companies should solicit input through interviews, focus groups, and survey instruments. Finding out how employees might react in a particular situation can help companies better understand how to correct unethical or illegal behavior either reactively or proactively. Research suggests that employees and senior managers often know that they are doing something unethical but rationalize their behavior as being "for the good of the company." As a result, ethics program objectives should contain some elements that are measurable.[43]

> "Maintaining an ethical culture may be impossible if CEOs and other top officers do not support an ethical culture."

The third mistake is senior management's failure to take ownership of the ethics program. Maintaining an ethical culture may be impossible if CEOs and other top officers do not support an ethical culture. As discussed earlier in this chapter, upper-level managers, including chief financial officers and chief marketing officers, may have greater insensitivity to the needs of all stakeholders because of the pressure they feel for financial performance. These top managers may be more vulnerable to pressures placed on them to push employees to engage in unethical activities and thereby become more competitive. It is for this reason that recent amendments to the FSGO suggest that ethics officers should report to the board of directors rather than the general counsel. The board of directors should have ultimate responsibility and oversight to create an organizational ethical culture.

The fourth mistake is developing program materials that do not address the needs of the average employee. Many compliance programs are designed by lawyers to ensure that the company is legally protected. These programs usually yield complex "legalese" that few within the organization can understand. To avoid this problem, ethics programs—including codes of conduct and training materials—should include feedback from employees from across the firm, not just the legal department. Including a question-and-answer section in the program; referencing additional resources for guidance on key ethical issues; and using checklists, illustrations, and even cartoons can help make program materials more user-friendly.

The fifth common mistake made in implementing ethics programs is transferring an "American" program to a firm's international operations. In multinational firms, executives should involve overseas personnel as early as possible in the process in order to help foster an understanding of the company's values and to minimize potential for misconduct stemming from misunderstandings. These aims can be accomplished by developing an inventory of common global management practices and processes and examining the corporation's standards of conduct in light of these international standards.

A final common mistake is designing an ethics program that is little more than a series of lectures. In such cases, participants typically recall less than 15 percent the day after the training. A more practical solution is to allow employees to practice the skills they learn through case studies or small-group exercises.

A firm cannot succeed solely by taking a legalistic compliance approach to ethics. Top managers must seek to develop high ethical standards that serve as barriers to illegal conduct. Although an ethics program should help reduce the possibility of penalties and negative public reaction to misconduct, a company must want to be a good corporate citizen and must recognize the importance of ethics to success in business.

SUMMARY

Ethics programs help sensitize employees to potential legal and ethical issues within their work environments. To promote ethical and legal conduct, organizations should develop ethics programs, establishing, communicating, and monitoring ethical values and legal requirements that characterize the firms' history, culture, industry, and operating environment. Without such programs and uniform standards and policies of conduct, it is difficult for employees to determine what behaviors a company deems acceptable.

A company must have an effective ethics program to ensure that employees understand its values and comply with its policies and codes of conduct. An ethics program should help reduce the possibility of legally enforced penalties and negative public reaction to misconduct. The main objective of the Federal Sentencing Guidelines for Organizations is to encourage companies to assess risk and then self-monitor and aggressively work to deter unethical acts and punish unethical employees. Ethics programs are organizational control systems that create predictability in employee behavior. These control systems may have a compliance orientation, which uses legal terms, statutes, and contracts that teach employees the rules and the penalties for noncompliance, or a values orientation, which consists of developing shared values.

Most companies begin the process of establishing organizational ethics programs by developing codes of conduct, which are formal statements that describe what an organization expects of its employees. Codes of conduct include a company's code of ethics and/or its statement of values. A code of ethics must be developed as part of senior management's desire to ensure that the company complies with values, rules, and policies that support an ethical culture. Without uniform policies and standards, employees will have difficulty determining what qualifies as acceptable behavior in the company.

Having a high-level manager or committee responsible for an ethical compliance program can significantly enhance its administration and oversight. Such ethics officers are usually responsible for assessing the needs and risks to be addressed in an organization-wide ethics program, developing and distributing a code of conduct or ethics, conducting training programs for employees, establishing and maintaining a confidential service to answer questions about ethical issues, making sure the company is complying with government regulations, monitoring and auditing ethical conduct, taking action on possible violations of the company's code, and reviewing and updating the code.

Successful ethics training is important in helping employees identify ethical issues and in providing them with the means to address and resolve such issues. Training can educate employees about the firm's policies and expectations, available resources, support systems, and designated ethics personnel, as well as about relevant laws and regulations and general social standards. Top executives must communicate with managers at the operations level and enforce overall ethical standards within the organization.

An effective ethics program employs a variety of resources to monitor ethical conduct and measure the program's effectiveness. Compliance with the company's ethical code and standards can be assessed through observing employees, performing internal audits and surveys, instituting reporting systems, and conducting investigations, as well as through external audits and review, as needed. Corrective action involves rewarding employees who comply with company policies and standards and punishing those who do not. Consistent enforcement and disciplinary action are necessary for a functioning ethical compliance program.

Ethical compliance can be ensured by designing activities that achieve organizational objectives using available resources and given existing constraints. A firm's ability to plan and implement ethical business standards depends in part on its ability to structure resources and activities to achieve its objectives effectively and efficiently.

In implementing ethics and compliance programs many firms make some common mistakes, including failing to answer fundamental questions about the goals of such programs, not setting realistic and measurable program objectives, failing to have senior management take ownership of the ethics program, developing program materials that do not address the needs of the average employee, transferring an "American" program to a firm's international operations, and designing an ethics program that is little more than a series of lectures. Although an ethics program should help reduce the possibility of penalties and negative public reaction to misconduct, a company must want to be a good corporate citizen and recognize the importance of ethics to successful business activities.

IMPORTANT TERMS FOR REVIEW

compliance orientation	values orientation	code of conduct
code of ethics	statement of values	ethics officers

RESOLVING ETHICAL BUSINESS CHALLENGES*

Jim, now in his fourth year with Cinco Corporation, was made a plant manager three months ago after completing the company's management-training program. Cinco owns pulp-processing plants that produce various grades of paper from fast-growing, genetically altered trees. Jim's plant, Cinco's smallest and oldest, is located in upstate New York near a small town. It employs between 100 and 175 workers, mostly from the nearby town. In fact, the plant boasts about employees whose fathers and grandfathers have also worked there. Every year Cinco holds a Fourth of July picnic for the entire town.

Cinco's policy is to give each manager a free hand in dealing with employees, the community, and the plant itself. Its main measure of performance is the bottom line, and employees are keenly aware of this fact.

Like all pulp-processing plants, Cinco is located near a river. Because of the plant's age, much of its equipment is outdated. Consequently, it takes more time and money to produce paper at Jim's plant than at Cinco's newer plants. Cinco has a long-standing policy of breaking in new managers at this plant to see if they can manage a work force and a mill efficiently and effectively. The tradition is that a manager who does well with the upstate New York plant will be transferred to a larger, more modern one. As a result, the plant's workers have had to deal with many managers and have become hardened and insensitive to change. In addition, most of the workers are older and more experienced than their managers, including Jim.

In his brief tenure as plant manager, Jim had learned much about the business from his workers. Jim's secretary, Ramona, made sure that reports were prepared correctly, that bills were paid, and that Jim learned how to perform his tasks. Ramona has been with the plant for so long that she has become a permanent fixture. Jim's three foremen are all in their late 40s and keep things running smoothly. Jim's wife, Elaine, is having a difficult time adjusting to life in upstate New York. Speaking with other managers' wives, she learned that the "prison sentence," as she called it, typically lasted no longer than two years. She had a large calendar in the kitchen and crossed off each day they were there.

One morning as Jim came into the office, Ramona didn't seem her usual stoic self.

"What's up?" Jim asked her.

"You need to call the EPA," she replied. "It's not really important. Ralph Hoad from the EPA said he wanted you to call him."

When Jim made the call, Ralph told him the mill's waste disposal into the river exceeded Environmental Protection Agency (EPA) guidelines, and he would stop by next week to discuss the situation. Jim hung up the phone and asked Ramona for the water sample results for the last six months from upstream, from downstream, and at the plant. After inspecting the data and comparing them with EPA standards, he found no violations of any kind. He then ordered more tests to verify the original data. The next day Jim compared the previous day's tests with the last six months' worth of data and still found no significant differences and no EPA violations. As he continued to look at the data, however, something stood out on the printouts that he hadn't noticed before. All the tests had been done on the first or second shifts. Jim called the foremen of the two shifts to his office and asked if they knew what was going on. Both men were extremely evasive in their answers and referred him to the third-shift foreman. When Jim phoned him, he, too, was evasive and said not to worry—that Ralph would explain it to him.

That night Jim decided to make a spot inspection of the mill and test the wastewater. When he arrived at the river, he knew by the smell that something was very wrong. Jim immediately went back to the mill and demanded to know what was happening. Chuck, the third-shift foreman, took Jim down to the lowest level of the plant. In one of the many rooms stood four large storage tanks. Chuck explained to Jim that when the pressure gauge reached a certain level, a third-shift worker opened the valve and allowed the waste to mix with everything else.

"You see," Chuck told Jim, "the mill was never modernized to meet EPA standards, so we have to divert the bad waste here; twice a week it goes into the river."

"Who knows about this?" asked Jim.

"Everyone who needs to," answered Chuck.

When Jim got home, he told Elaine about the situation. Elaine's reaction was, "Does this mean we're stuck here? Because if we are, I don't know what I'll do!" Jim knew that all the managers before him must have had the same problem. He also knew that there would be no budget for installing EPA-approved equipment for at least another two years. The next morning Jim checked the EPA reports and was puzzled to find that the mill had always been in compliance. There should have been warning notices and fines affixed, but he found nothing.

That afternoon Ralph Hoad stopped by. Ralph talked about the weather, hunting, fishing, and then he said, "Jim, I realize you're new. I apologize for not coming sooner, but I saw no reason to because your predecessor has taken care of me until this month."

"What do you mean?" Jim asked.

"Ramona will fill you in. There's nothing to worry about. I know no one in town wants to see the mill close down, and I don't want it to either. There are lots of memories in this old place. I'll stop by to see you in another couple of months." With that, Ralph left.

Jim asked Ramona about what Ralph had said. She showed him a miscellaneous expense of $100 a month in the ledgers. "We do this every month," she told him.

"How long has this been going on?" asked Jim.

"Since the new EPA rules," Ramona replied. She went on to clarify Jim's alternatives. Either he could continue paying Ralph, which didn't amount to much, or he could refuse to pay, which would mean paying EPA fines and a potential shutdown of the plant. As Ramona put it, "Headquarters only cares about the bottom line. Now, unless you want to live here the rest of your life, the first alternative is the best for your career. The last manager who bucked the system lost his job. The rule in this industry is that if you can't manage Cinco's upstate New York plant, you can't manage. That's the way it is."

QUESTIONS | EXERCISES

1. Identify the ethical and legal issues of which Jim needs to be aware.
2. Discuss the advantages and disadvantages of each decision that Jim could make.
3. Identify the pressures that have brought about the ethical and legal issues at hand.
4. What is Jim's place in the power structure at the plant?

*This case is strictly hypothetical; any resemblance to real persons, companies, or situations is coincidental.

CHECK YOUR EQ

Check your EQ, or Ethics Quotient, by completing the following. Assess your performance to evaluate your overall understanding of the chapter material.

1. A compliance program should be deemed effective if it addresses the seven minimum requirements for ethical compliance programs.   Yes   No

2. The accountability and responsibility for appropriate business conduct rests with top management.   Yes   No

3. Ethical compliance can be measured by observing employees as well as through investigating and reporting mechanisms.   Yes   No

4. The key goal of ethics training is to help employees identify ethical issues.   Yes   No

5. An ethical compliance audit is designed to determine the effectiveness of ethics initiatives.   Yes   No

ANSWERS 1. No. An effective compliance program has the seven elements of a compliance program in place and goes beyond those minimum requirements to determine what will work in a particular organization. 2. Yes. Executives in an organization determine the culture and initiatives that support ethical behavior. 3. Yes. Sometimes external monitoring is necessary, but internal monitoring and evaluation are the norm. 4. No. It is much more than that—it involves not only recognition but also an understanding of the values, culture, and rules in an organization as well as the impact of ethical decisions on the company. 5. Yes. It helps in establishing the code and in making program improvements.

CHAPTER 9

MANAGING AND CONTROLLING
ETHICS PROGRAMS

AN ETHICAL DILEMMA*

Chantal had been with Butterfly Industries for 13 years. She started out as an assistant buyer and was later promoted to buyer. She threw herself into her work, and within a few years she had moved into the corporate offices.

During Chantal's tenure, Butterfly Industries grew from fewer than 500 employees to more than 35,000. The company had expanded all over the world and opened offices on every continent; it had nearly exclusive arrangements with suppliers from six different countries. Such rapid growth eroded the freedoms of a small firm. So many employees, with different cultures, languages, and time zones, from so many countries, each with its own political realities, made corporate life much more complicated.

To Chantal, it seemed that the firm had grown at a whirlwind pace, and sometimes she thought that whirlwind had become an ugly black cloud. She heard, for example, that some of Butterfly's suppliers in Puerto Rico mistreated their workers. In other foreign locations, Butterfly's products were bringing changes to the environment, as well as to local culture and gender roles. Because Butterfly's workers tended to be women, children were being left to fend for themselves. In some Latin American countries, husbands were angry because their wives earned more than they did. Then there were the rumors that retailers in some countries were selling Butterfly products without adequate service—or worse, diluting the products and selling them as "full strength."

After Butterfly went public, Chantal's sense of foreboding grew. Employees at headquarters scrambled to satisfy shareholders' demands for specific information about products, projected earnings, employee benefit policies, and equal employment opportunity records. Chantal was also troubled that so many of the corporate people were men; only she and one other woman were directly involved in the inner workings of the increasingly complex firm.

Six months ago, Chantal began hearing that some plant employees were suffering pay cuts while others weren't. In some cases, employees who had been working for Butterfly for 15 years were been cut to 36-hour workweeks, losing their full-time benefits. She began to notice political alliances being formed among marketing, finance, manufacturing, and corporate headquarters. Because each plant operated as an independent profit-making entity, each was guarded in its communication with other plants, knowing that if it could increase its profits it could also increase overall pay.

Chantal was not the only one to recognize that Butterfly needed guidance in a variety of areas, but no one had stepped forward. Then Butterfly's president, Jermaine, asked Chantal to lunch. This was not unusual, but the conversation soon took a significant twist that Chantal was unprepared for.

"Chantal, you've been with the company for 13 years now, right?" asked Jermaine.

"Yes, that's right," Chantal answered.

"You know as well as anyone that I haven't kept pace with the growth," Jermaine continued with a mixture of sadness and determination. "When I founded this company, I could tell a few staffers to check out an idea, and several weeks later we'd talk about whether it would work. There was a time when I knew every employee, and even their families, but not anymore. Chantal, I think Butterfly has outgrown my style of management. What this company needs is a comprehensive set of rules and guidelines for every part of the company. I need to delegate more. That's why I wanted to talk to you."

Chantal asked, "Jermaine, what are you saying to me?"

"Chantal, I've always been impressed with your work ethic and your sense of values. You know this company and its culture so well. I know you've heard some of the same rumors, so we both know that all is not well at Butterfly. What I'd like is for you to become the head of Butterfly's ethics committee. Of course, we don't yet have an ethics committee, so that's where you come in."

"Me?" Chantal asked with surprise.

"Yes, you. If you're willing, I want you to create this entity and run it so that we all can be proud of Butterfly again. So that people inside and outside the company will know that we stand for what is right. You will be promoted to vice president, your salary will be doubled, and you can select your own team. Chantal, this is your chance to make a huge difference. What's your answer?" asked Jermaine.

Chantal hesitated for a moment and then said, "Yes."

"Great! I knew I could count on you. The first thing I need is a proposed outline of the responsibilities of the new ethics committee, enforcement procedures—the works—and I want it in two weeks along with a list of people for the committee."

That night, Chantal began to plan.

QUESTIONS | EXERCISES

1. Prioritize the issues that Butterfly needs to deal with. How can an ethics program address these issues?
2. Develop an outline of who should be on the new ethics committee and describe what the committee's first steps should be toward implementing an effective ethics program.
3. Should the new ethics committee commission an ethics audit? If yes, when should the audit be conducted? If no, why not?

*This case is strictly hypothetical; any resemblance to real persons, companies, or situations is coincidental.

I n Chapter 8, we introduced the idea of ethics programs as a way for organizations to improve ethical decision making and conduct in business. To properly implement these programs and ensure their effectiveness, companies need to measure their impact. Increasingly, companies are applying the principles of auditing to ascertain whether their ethics codes, policies, and corporate values are having a positive impact on the firm's ethical conduct. These audits can help companies identify risks and areas of non-compliance with laws and company policies as well as other areas that need improvement. An audit should provide a systematic and objective survey of the firm's ethical culture and values.

We begin this chapter by examining some of the requirements of a successful ethics program. We then discuss the concept of an ethics audit as a way to execute such a program. We define the term *ethics audit* and explore its relationship to a social audit. Next, we examine the benefits and limitations of this implementation tool, especially with regard to avoiding a management crisis. We consider the challenges of measuring nonfinancial ethical performance, and review evolving standards from AA1000 and the Open Compliance Ethics Group. We then describe our framework for the steps of an ethics audit, including securing the commitment of directors and top managers; establishing a committee to oversee the audit; defining the scope of the audit process; reviewing the firm's mission, values, goals, and policies and defining ethical priorities; collecting and analyzing relevant information; and verifying and reporting the results. Finally, we consider the strategic importance of ethics auditing.

IMPLEMENTING ETHICS PROGRAMS

Developing an effective business ethics program requires organizations to cope with the realities of implementing such a program. Implementation requires executing specific actions that will ensure the achievement of business ethics objectives. The organization must have ways of managing, evaluating, and controlling business ethics programs. Five items in particular can have a significant impact on whether an ethics program is successful: (1) the content of the company's code of ethics, (2) the frequency of communication regarding the ethical code and program, (3) the quality of communication, (4) senior management's ability to successfully incorporate ethics into the organization, (5) and local management's ability to do the same.[1] If an organization has a culture that is more focused on planning than on implementation, employees may come to view unethical conduct as acceptable behavior. Without proper controls in place, lying to customers, manipulating prices, abusive behavior, and misuse of organizational resources can become a part of some employees' conduct.

Viewing a business ethics program as a part of strategic planning and management activities is critical to the success of any firm. Some companies still do not understand that ethics is a critical aspect of business strategy in action. This misunderstanding stems from a belief that the ethics of employees is primarily an individual matter, and not the responsibility of managers. The nature of ethics programs in corporate America is to determine risks, develop policies and codes of conduct, and require specific standards of conduct. However, in order to do the right thing and know when to say no or ask for assistance in gray areas, employees must have a strong sense of personal ethics.

Shared values among employees are the glue of successful management as well as of business ethics programs. When business ethics programs help to align and direct employees' activities toward an ethical culture, employees will feel a commitment to the long-term ethical progress of the firm. Green Mountain Coffee Roasters, Inc., is a firm that has been recognized for its emphasis on socially responsible business activities. It has consistently earned a place in *Business Ethics/CR Magazine*'s "100 Best Corporate Citizens" and was honored by the Society for Human Resource Management for its ethical practices.[2] The firm focuses on ethical management and implementation with open communication. It uses a process called the "after-action review" that asks four questions: What did we set out to do? What happened? Why did it happen? What are we going to do about it?

Formal controls for business ethics include input controls such as the proper selection of employees, effective ethics training and strong structural systems (including communication systems). In Chapter 8 we discussed internal control systems whereby employees can report misconduct. Ethics assistance lines, sometimes called hotlines, provide support and give employees the opportunity to get assistance, ask questions, or report concerns. Another internal control system that can improve ethical assistance is an ethics help desk. An ethics help desk is a point of contact within an organization where employees and managers can bring their concerns and receive assistance from the most appropriate person in the firm to handle the situation. For this model to be successful, the help desk must be supportive of employees, be easily accessible, and have simple procedures for employees to follow when they express concerns.[3]

Process controls include management's commitment to the ethics program and to the methods or system for ethics evaluation. These methods might involve daily coaching for managers and employee reminders regarding appropriate ethical conduct. The best way to provide leadership on ethics is to set a good example, and there are many examples of effective corporate leaders who promote ethics from the top. For example, Jeffrey Swartz, the CEO of Timberland, has won recognition as a strong and ethical corporate leader. Swartz has expanded Timberline's Green Index—a measurement that shows the product's environmental impact based on climate impact, chemicals used, and resource consumption—to include its entire footwear collection. He has also announced his company's commitment to plant 5 million trees in a five-year period. Swartz exhibits good leadership qualities in the care he shows his employees and in his willingness to take responsibility for past mistakes.[4]

Output controls involve comparing standards with actual behavior. One of the most popular methods of evaluating ethical performance is an ethics audit. The primary purpose of an ethics audit is to identify the risks and problems in outgoing activities and plan the necessary steps to adjust, correct, or eliminate these ethical concerns. Regardless of the complexity of a firm's ethics program, an ethics audit is critical to the program's success; therefore, a major part of this chapter focuses on how such audits should be conducted. The Federal Sentencing Guidelines for Organizations' recent amendment suggests that the results of an ethics audit be reported directly to the board of directors. Such direct reporting would prevent the CEO or another top officer from covering up misconduct.

This chapter will help complete your understanding of how organizational ethics is managed and controlled to create an effective ethics program. Although you may never be in charge of such a program, as a manager or employee you will be part of it. The greater your understanding of the role and function of the various parts of the program, the more effective you will be in engaging and guiding others to make ethical decisions. Business ethics in an organization is not simply a personal matter that is based on your individual values. You will be responsible, both ethically and legally, for engaging in ethical conduct and reporting the unethical conduct of others in your organization.

THE ETHICS AUDIT

An **ethics audit** is a systematic evaluation of an organization's ethics program and performance to determine whether it is effective. A major component of the ethics program described in Chapter 8, the ethics audit includes "regular, complete, and documented measurements of compliance with the company's published policies and procedures."[5] As such, the audit provides an opportunity to measure conformity to the firm's desired ethical standards. An audit can even be a precursor to setting up an ethics program, as it identifies the firm's ethical standards as well as its existing policies and risk areas. Recent legislation and FSGO amendments encourage greater ethics auditing as companies attempt to demonstrate to various stakeholders that they are abiding by the law and have established programs to improve ethical decision making. While companies are not required to report the results of their audits to the public, some firms, such as New Belgium Brewing, do report the results of audits in areas such as employment practices, sustainability efforts, and community outreach.

The concept of ethics auditing emerged from the movement to evaluate and report on companies' broader social responsibility initiatives, particularly with regard to sustainability. An increasing number of companies are auditing their social responsibility programs and reporting the results so as to document their efforts to be more responsible to various interested stakeholder groups. A **social audit** is the process of assessing and reporting on a business's performance in fulfilling the economic, legal, ethical, and philanthropic responsibilities expected of it by its stakeholders.[6] Social reports often discuss issues related to a firm's performance in the four dimensions of social responsibility as well as specific social responsibility and ethical issues such as employment issues, community economic development, volunteerism, and environmental impact.[7] In contrast, ethics audits focus more narrowly on a firm's ethical and legal conduct. However, an ethics audit can be a component of a social audit; indeed, many companies include ethical issues in their social audits. Walmart, for example, includes ethical performance in its Sustainability Report.[8]

Regardless of the breadth of the audit, ethics auditing is a tool that companies can employ to identify and measure their ethical commitment to stakeholders. Employees, customers, investors, suppliers, community members, activists, the media, and regulators are increasingly demanding that companies be ethical and accountable for their conduct. In response, businesses are working to incorporate accountability into their actions, from long-term planning, everyday decision making, and rethinking processes for corporate governance and financial reporting to hiring, retaining, and promoting employees and building relationships with customers. The ethics audit provides an objective method for demonstrating a company's commitment to improving strategic planning, including its compliance with legal and ethical standards and standards of social responsibility. The auditing process is important to business because it can improve a firm's performance and effectiveness, increase its attractiveness to investors, improve its relationships with stakeholders, identify potential risks, and decrease the risk of misconduct and adverse publicity that could harm its reputation.[9] As we discussed in Chapter 1, the "World's Most Ethical Companies" have shown better financial performance than the firms in the general stock indexes.

> "Ethics auditing is a tool that companies can employ to identify and measure their ethical commitment to stakeholders."

Ethics auditing employs procedures and processes similar to those found in financial auditing to create an objective report of a company's performance. As in an accounting audit, someone with expertise from outside the organization may be chosen to conduct an ethics audit. Although the standards used in financial auditing can be adapted to provide an objective foundation for ethics reporting, there are significant differences between the two types of audits. Whereas financial auditing focuses on all systems related to money flow and on financial assessments of value for tax purposes and managerial accountability, ethics auditing deals with the internal and broad external impact of an organization's ethical performance. Another significant difference is that ethics auditing is not usually associated with regulatory requirements, while financial audits are required of public companies that issue securities. Because ethics and social audits are voluntary, there are fewer standards that a company can apply with regard to reporting frequency, disclosure requirements, and remedial actions that it should take in response to results. This may change as more companies develop ethics programs in the current regulatory environment, in which regulatory agencies support requiring boards of directors to oversee corporate ethics. If boards are to track the effectiveness of ethics programs, audits will be required. In addition, nonfinancial auditing standards are developing, with data available for benchmarking and comparing a firm's nonfinancial ethical performance with its own past performance and with the performance of other firms.

BENEFITS OF ETHICS AUDITING

There are many reasons why companies choose to analyze, report on, and improve their ethical conduct. Assessment of an organization's ethical culture is necessary to improve ethical performance and to document in legal proceedings that a firm has an effective ethics program. Companies can use ethical audits to detect ethical misconduct before it becomes a major problem, and audits provide evidence of a firm's attempts to identify and deal with major ethical risks. ATM manufacturer Diebold, Inc., was charged by the Securities and Exchange Commission with manipulating earnings from 2002 to 2007 to meet its financial forecasts. This manipulation is estimated to have inflated Diebold's reported earnings by $127 million. Diebold agreed to settle with the SEC for $25 million, and the company's former chief executive agreed to pay back $470,000.[10] Such accounting scandals and legal and ethical transgressions have encouraged companies to better account for their actions in a wide range of areas, including corporate governance, ethics programs, customer relationships, employee relations, environmental policies, and community involvement.

One company may want to achieve the most ethical performance possible, whereas another may use an ethics audit merely to project a good image to hide its corrupt culture. Top managers might use an ethics audit to identify ethical problems in their companies, but identification alone does not mean that they will take steps to correct these lapses through punishments or sanctions.[11] Without appropriate action on the part of management, an ethics audit can be mere lip service intended to enhance the firm's reputation without actually improving its ethical conduct. Other firms might conduct ethics audits in an attempt to comply with the Federal Sentencing Guidelines for Organizations, (FSGO) requirements that the board of directors oversee the discovery of ethical risk, design and implement an ethics program, and evaluate performance. Some companies view the auditing process as tied to continuous improvement, which is closely related to improved financial performance. Companies' reasons for supporting the FSGO are complex and diverse. For example, it is common for firms to conduct audits of business practices with legal ramifications such as employee safety, environmental impact, and financial reporting. Although these practices are important to a firm's ethics and social responsibility, they are also legally required and therefore constitute the minimum level of commitment. However, because stakeholders are demanding increased transparency and taking a more active role through external organizations that represent their interests, government regulators are calling on companies to improve their ethical conduct and make more decisions based on principles rather than on laws alone.

Measuring the ethical work climate of an organization is one way to learn about its ethical culture. While most measurements of ethical climate are conducted by academic researchers, some firms are becoming proactive in working with consultants to measure their ethical climate. Some measures of ethical climate include collective ethical sensitivity (empathetic concern and awareness), collective character, collective judgment (focus on others and focus on self), and collective moral motivation.[12] These measures can be used to help evaluate changes in a firm's ethical culture after the development of ethics programs.

The auditing process can highlight trends, improve organizational learning, and facilitate communication and working relationships.[13] Auditing can also help companies assess the effectiveness of their programs and policies, which often improves their operating efficiencies and reduces costs. Information from audits and reports can allow a company to ensure that it is achieving the greatest possible impact with available resources.[14] The process of ethics auditing can also help an organization identify potential risks and liabilities and improve its compliance with the law. Furthermore, the audit report may help document a firm's compliance with legal requirements as well as demonstrate its progress in areas where it previously failed to comply, for example by describing the systems it is implementing to reduce the likelihood of a recurrence of misconduct.[15]

For organizations, one of the greatest benefits of the auditing process is improved relationships with stakeholders who desire greater transparency. Many stakeholders have become wary of corporate public relations campaigns. Verbal assurances by corporate management are no longer sufficient to gain stakeholders' trust. An ethics audit could have saved Countrywide Financial if liar loans and the manipulation of borrowers' financial data had been identified earlier. When companies and their employees, suppliers, and investors trust each other, the costs of monitoring and managing these relationships are lower. Companies experience less conflict with these stakeholders, which results in a heightened capacity for innovation and collaboration.

Because of these benefits shareholders and investors have welcomed the increased disclosure that comes with corporate accountability. Table 9.1 indicates the top challenges that CEOs will be facing in the future. Keeping pace with regulation, protecting against risks, and reputation management are three of the top 10 challenges. These issues can be considered major risks associated with managing and controlling ethics programs. Therefore, they represent key areas that could be important in an ethics audit. A growing number of investors are considering nonfinancial measures—such as the existence of ethics programs, legal compliance, board diversity and independence, and other corporate governance issues like CEO compensation—when they analyze the quality of current and potential investments. Research suggests that investors may be willing to pay higher prices for the stock of companies that deem to be accountable,[16] such as stock from *Fortune's* "World's Most Admired Companies," including Adobe Systems, Whirlpool, Berkshire Hathaway, Google, Marriott International, Procter & Gamble, 3M, Deere, UPS, and BMW, who have generally avoided major ethical disasters.[17]

TABLE 9.1 Top Challenges for CEOs

1. Managing growth

2. Employee turnover

3. Customer relationships

4. Social media

5. Regulatory issues

6. Risk management

7. Globalization

8. Reputation

9. Technology competence

10. Competitive advantage

Source: Adapted from Sheryl Nance-Nash, "Top Challenges for CEOs in 2011," *Daily Finance*, December 15, 2010, http://www.dailyfinance.com/story/top-10-challenges-for-corporate-ceos-in-2011/19760107/ (accessed March 23, 2011).

However, even companies that have experienced legal issues or have had their ethics questioned can make a comeback. Walmart CEO Mike Duke has been recognized for his leadership in the arena of business ethics as a result of his investment in sustainable supply chain practices. Under his leadership, Walmart has set forth an ambitious initiative to "green" its supply chain. The company is asking its suppliers to examine the carbon life-cycle of its products and make meaningful changes in sourcing, manufacturing, packaging, and transporting products. Walmart also plans to reduce greenhouse gas emissions from its supply chain by 20 million metric tons by 2015. Duke agreed that the company would invest $1 billion over the next five years to create a more sustainable supply chain. The company has strived to learn from its mistakes, settling more than 60 wage and hour abuse lawsuits. Walmart consistently ranks near the top of *Fortune*'s Most Admired Companies in spite of past ethical and legal concerns.[18]

Regular audits permit shareholders and investors to judge whether a firm is achieving the goals it has established, and whether it abides by the values that it has specified as important. Moreover, it permits stakeholders to influence the organization's behavior.[19] Increasingly, a broad range of stakeholder groups are seeking specific, often quantifiable, information from companies. These stakeholders expect companies to take a deeper look at the nature of their operations and to publicly disclose their progress and problems in addressing these issues. Some investors are using their rights as stockholders to encourage companies to modify their plans and policies to address specific ethical issues. On a broader scale, the Obama administration sought to impose limits on executive compensation of those firms seeking government financial support. The 2010 passage of the Dodd–Frank Wall Street Reform and Consumer Protection Act implemented new regulations for executive compensation. Under these new provisions, shareholders of public companies can cast advisory votes on whether they approve of the compensation awarded to top executives. Additionally, top executives must provide more disclosure on how their compensation aligns with the company's financial performance.[20]

Ethical Crisis Management and Recovery

A significant benefit of ethics auditing is that it may help prevent crises resulting from ethical or legal misconduct, crises that can potentially be more devastating than natural disasters or technological disruptions. Just as companies develop crisis management plans to respond to and recover from natural disasters, they should also prepare for ethical disasters, which can not only result in substantial legal and financial costs but which can also disrupt routine operations, paralyze employees, reduce productivity, destroy organizational reputation, and erode stakeholder confidence. Ethical and legal crises have resulted in the demise or acquisition of a number of well-known companies including Lehman Brothers, Merrill Lynch, and Washington Mutual. Many other companies—HealthSouth, Firestone, Waste Management, Rite Aid, U.S. Foodservice, Qwest, Kmart, Mitsubishi Motors, and Archer Daniels Midland, for example—have survived ethical and legal crises but paid a high price both financially and in terms of compromised reputation and diminished stakeholder trust. In recent years, companies have spent up to $7 million a month on outside legal counsel to defend against alleged organizational wrongdoing. One study found that publicity about unethical corporate behavior lowers stock prices for at least six months.[21] For example, bribery allegations and an internal bribery probe at Avon Products, Inc., temporarily lowered its share prices because of fears that a scandal could harm operations.[22]

Organizational members who engage in questionable or even illegal conduct are guilty of ethical misconduct, and these employees can threaten the overall integrity of the organization. Top leaders in particular can magnify ethical misconduct to disastrous proportions. The misconduct of Raj Rajaratnam at the Galleon Group, Andrew Fastow at Enron, Dennis Kozlowski at Tyco, and Bernie Ebbers at WorldCom, among others, has caused financial disasters on both organizational and global levels.[23] An ethics audit can uncover rogue employees who are violating the firm's ethical standards and policies or laws and regulations.

Ethical disasters follow recognizable phases of escalation, from ethical issue recognition and the decision to act unethically to the organization's discovery of and response to the act. Appropriate anticipation of and intervention during these situations can stave off major problems. Such contingency planning assesses risks, plans for eventualities, and provides ready tools for responding to ethical crises. The process of ethical disaster-recovery planning involves assessing an organization's values, developing an ethics program, performing an ethics audit, and developing contingency plans for potential ethical disasters. The ethics audit itself provides the key to preventing ethical disasters.

Formal mechanisms should be in place to discover risk as a part of evaluating compliance and the effectiveness of ethics programs. The greatest fear of most corporate leaders is discovering misconduct or illegal activity that could be reported by the mass media, used by competitors, or prosecuted by the government. Yet this process is extremely important to the long-term well-being of an organization. While risks such as earthquakes, fires, hurricanes, and other natural disasters cannot always be determined, companies can plan for these types

> "The greatest fear of most corporate leaders is discovering misconduct or illegal activity."

of disasters. Unfortunately, ethical risks are often given the lowest priority. Table 9.2 lists the wide range of approaches that companies use to manage risks. Only about one-fourth of the companies surveyed by the Open Compliance Ethics Group had a risk management committee that was separate from the audit committee as part of its board of directors. As Table 9.2 indicates, 14 percent of the firms report having no risks team at all.

TABLE 9.2 How Do Corporations Manage Risk?

Incorporation of risk management into business management strategies	28%
Teams that combine business management and internal audits	25%
Independent risk management teams	26%
Risk management as part of internal audit	7%
No formal risk team or committee	14%

Source: Survey of 250 respondents conducted by the Open Compliance Ethics Group, April 2010, http://www.oceg.org/resource/oceg-one-minute-poll-how-do-you-manage-risk (accessed March 23, 2011).

Measuring Nonfinancial Ethical Performance

Although much of the regulation of corporate ethics and compliance is focused on financial measures, to truly have integrity, an organization also has to focus on nonfinancial areas of performance. The word *integrity* in this context implies a balanced organization that not only makes ethical financial decisions but also is ethical in the more subjective aspects of its corporate culture. The Sarbanes–Oxley Act has focused on questionable accounting and the metrics that destroy shareholder value, but other models have been developed—such as Six Sigma, the Balanced Scorecard, and the triple bottom Line—to capture structural and behavioral organizational ethical performance. Six Sigma is a methodology designed to manage process variations that cause defects, defined as unacceptable deviations from the mean or target, and to systematically work toward managing variation to eliminate those defects. The objective of Six Sigma is to deliver world-class performance, reliability, and value to the end customer. The Balanced Scorecard is a management system that focuses on all the elements that contribute to organizational performance and success, including financial, customer, market, and internal processes. Its goal is to develop a broader perspective on performance factors and to foster a culture of learning and growth that improves all organizational communication. The triple bottom line provides a perspective that takes into account the social, environmental, and financial impacts of decisions made within an organization. When making an increased commitment to social responsibility, sustainability, or ethics, companies consider implementing triple bottom line reporting as a way to confirm that their investments and initiatives are supporting their organization's values and overall success. Table 9.3 provides additional detail on these three measurement tools. The purpose of a variety of measures of performance and goal achievement is to determine the quality and effectiveness of environmental, social, and ethics initiatives. Many believe that an inherent gain is realized by companies with strong ethical cultures and environmental commitments, paid in customer commitment and in avoiding the negative publicity and costs associated with wrongdoing.

The Global Reporting Initiative (GRI) has become a prominent framework that companies have adopted to report their social and sustainability progress.[24] The GRI advances sustainability reporting, which incorporates the triple bottom line factors of economic, social, and environmental indicators. The primary goal of the GRI is "the mainstreaming of disclosure on environmental, social, and governance performance."[25] Businesses can use the GRI to come up with a more standardized method of reporting nonfinancial results in a way that users of the reports can understand. Companies benefit because the GRI

TABLE 9.3 Description of Measurement Tools

Measurement Systems	Description
Balanced Scorecard	Developed by Drs. Robert Kaplan and David Norton, the Balanced Scorecard incorporates nonfinancial performance indicators into the evaluation system to provide a more "balanced" view of organizational performance. The system uses four metrics—financial, internal business processes, learning and growth, and customer—to measure the overall performance of the firm.
Six Sigma	Six Sigma focuses on improving existing processes that do not meet quality specifications or that need to be improved as well as developing new processes that meet Six Sigma standards. To meet Six Sigma specifications, the process must not produce more than 3.4 defects per million opportunities.
Triple Bottom Line	This approach to measuring social, financial, and environmental factors (or people, places, and planet) recognizes that business has a responsibility to positively influence a variety of stakeholders, including customers, employees, shareholders, community, and the natural environment. The challenge is how to evaluate a business's social and environmental impacts, since there are no universally standard forms of measuring these criteria.

Source: "Balanced Scorecard Basics," Balanced Scorecard Institute, http://www.balancedscorecard.org/BSCResources/AbouttheBalancedScorecard/tabid/55/Default.aspx (accessed March 23, 2011); "What is Six Sigma," iSix Sigma, http://www.isixsigma.com/index.php?option=com_k2&view=item&id=1463:what-is-six-sigma?&Itemid=155 (accessed March 23, 2011); "Triple bottom line," *The Economist*, November 17, 2009, http://www.economist.com/node/14301663?story_id=14301663 (accessed March 23, 2011).

provides tools for improving their implementation of the triple bottom line, as well as assisting with the disclosure of their progress in this area and giving them the ability to compare their sustainability efforts with those of other companies and the chance to enhance their reputation in the eyes of stakeholders. Users benefit because this standardized sustainability reporting gives them a point of comparison with other companies' sustainability initiatives.[26] GRI continually revises its framework to ensure that it remains relevant and encourages multiple stakeholders from global business, civil society, labor, and academic sectors to participate in the process.[27]

AccountAbility is an international membership organization committed to enhancing the performance of organizations and to developing the competencies of individuals in social and ethical accountability and sustainable development. Figure 9.1 illustrates the AccountAbility AA1000 framework for ethics and social responsibility. The AA1000 process standards link the definition and embedding of an organization's values to the development of performance targets and to the assessment and communication of organizational performance. Through this process, focused around the organization's engagement with stakeholders, AA1000 ties social and ethical issues into the organization's strategic management and operations. AA1000 recognizes these different traditions. It combines the terms *social* and *ethical* to refer to the systems and individual behavior within an organization, as well as to the *direct* and *indirect* impact of an organization's activities on stakeholders. *Social* and *ethical issues* (relating to systems, behavior, and impacts) are defined by an organization's values and aims, as shaped by the influence of the interests and expectations of its stakeholders and by societal norms and expectations. *Assessment* means measuring

FIGURE 9.1 AA1000 Framework for Ethics and Social Accountability

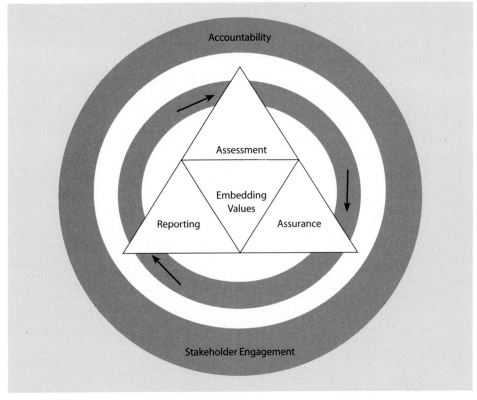

Source: Adapted from AccountAbility AA1000 Series of Standards, http://www.accountability21.net/aa1000series (accessed March 12, 2009). Reprinted with permission of The Institute of Social and Ethical Accountability.

organizational responsiveness or the extent to which an organization takes action on the basis of stakeholder engagement. This is followed by *assurance,* including control mechanisms, and then reporting to document the process. The *embedding* of an organization's values to assure performance is a continuous process.

Figure 9.2 shows the Open Compliance Ethics Group's functions of governance, risk, and compliance framework. The Open Compliance Ethics Group (OCEG) (http://www.oceg.org) has worked with more than 100 companies to create a universal framework for compliance and ethics management. The OCEG focuses on nonfinancial compliance and the more qualitative elements of internal controls. The OCEG framework deals with complex issues of compliance and solutions to address the development of organizational ethics. By establishing guidelines rather than standards, OCEG provides a tool for each company to use as it sees fit, given its size, scope, structure, industry, and other factors that create individualized needs. The OCEG guidelines and benchmarking studies can be very valuable to a firm conducting an ethics audit. Most significant is the opportunity to compare an organization's activities to those of other organizations. To this end, the OCEG has created tools and certification procedures to help businesses, such as the Burgundy Book, which assists in assessing "the design and operation of government, risk management, and compliance processes."[28] Additionally, the organization awards certification to companies

FIGURE 9.2 Roles and Functions of Risk, Management, and Compliance

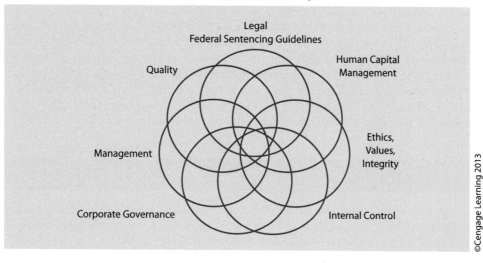

Legal
Federal Sentencing Guidelines

Human Capital
Management

Quality

Ethics,
Values,
Integrity

Management

Corporate Governance

Internal Control

©Cengage Learning 2013

and individuals that demonstrate to stakeholders that they operate at the highest standards regarding governance, risk management, and compliance.[29]

Risks and Requirements in Ethics Auditing

Although ethics audits provide many benefits for individual companies and their stakeholders, they do have the potential to create risks. For example, a firm may uncover a serious ethical problem that it would prefer not to disclose until it has remedied the situation. It may find that one or more of its stakeholders' criticisms cannot be easily addressed. Occasionally, the process of conducting an ethics audit may foster stakeholder dissatisfaction rather than stifle it. Moreover, the auditing process imposes burdens (especially with regard to record keeping) and costs for firms that undertake it. Auditing, although a prudent measure, provides no assurance that ethical risks and challenges can be avoided. Another challenge is in assessing risk and identifying standards of comparison. How can a company sufficiently analyze and manage its risks, and what goals for improvement should it develop? Some initiatives to benchmark risk assessment and best practices have begun to emerge, but this process is in its early stages.

Many companies suspected of misconduct respond to public scrutiny of their practices by conducting an ethics audit to show their concern and respond appropriately to weaknesses in their ethics programs. Companies in the public eye as a result of questionable conduct or legal violations, such as AIG, Fannie Mae, Freddie Mac, and Merrill Lynch, should conduct ethics audits to demonstrate their visible commitment to improving decision making and business conduct.

Research suggests that generating ethics and corporate social responsibility auditing procedures can be tricky because of a lack of standardization and widely accepted measures.[30] Although ethics and social responsibility are defined and perceived differently by various stakeholders, a core of minimum standards for ethical performance is evolving.

These standards represent a fundamental step in the development of minimum ethics requirements that are specific, measurable, achievable, and meaningful to a business's impact on communities, employees, consumers, the environment, and economic systems. They help companies set measurable and achievable targets for improvement, and they form an objective foundation for reporting the firm's efforts to all direct stakeholders. Disagreements may still arise over key issues, but overall these standards should enable companies to make progress in meeting their goals. The FSGO's seven steps for effective ethical compliance, discussed in Chapters 3 and 8, as well as the Sarbanes–Oxley Act and the Dodd–Frank Act, provide standards that organizations can use in ethics auditing.

THE AUDITING PROCESS[31]

There are many questions to address when conducting an audit, such as how broad the audit should be, what standards of performance should be applied, how often the audit should be conducted, whether—and how—the audit's results should be reported to stakeholders, and what actions should be taken in response to audit results. Therefore, corporate approaches to ethics audits are as varied as their approaches to ethics programs and their responses to improving social responsibility.

It is our belief that an ethics audit should be unique to each company, reflecting its size, industry, corporate culture, and identified risks as well as the regulatory environment in which it operates. Thus, an ethics audit for a bank will differ from one for an automobile manufacturer or a food processor. Each company has different regulatory concerns and unique risks stemming from the nature of its business. For this reason, we have mapped out a framework (see Table 9.4) that is somewhat generic and that most companies can expand on when conducting their own ethics audits. The steps in our framework can also be applied to broader social audits that include specific ethical issues as well as other economic, legal, and philanthropic concerns of interest to various stakeholders. As with any new initiative, companies may choose to begin their effort with smaller, less formal audits and work up to more

TABLE 9.4 Framework for an Ethics Audit

- Secure the commitment of top managers and board of directors

- Establish a committee to oversee the ethics audit

- Define the scope of the audit process, including subject matter areas important to the ethics audit

- Review the organization's mission, policies, goals, and objectives and define its ethical priorities

- Collect and analyze relevant information in each designated subject matter area

- Have the results verified by an independent agent

- Report the findings to the audit committee and, if approved, to managers and stakeholders

Sources: These steps are compatible with the social auditing methods prescribed by Warren Dow and Roy Crowe in *What Social Auditing Can Do for Voluntary Organizations* (Vancouver: Volunteer Vancouver, July 1999), and Sandra Waddock and Neil Smith in "Corporate Responsibility Audits: Doing Well by Doing Good," *Sloan Management Review* 41 (2000): 79.

comprehensive social audits. For example, a firm may choose to focus on primary stakeholders in its initial audit year and then expand to secondary groups in subsequent audits.

Our framework encompasses a wide range of business responsibilities and relationships. The audit entails an individualized process and outcomes for a particular firm, as it requires a careful consideration of the unique issues that face a particular organization. For example, the auditing process at Coca-Cola must consider several factors specific to that company. To ensure an effective internal audit, Coca-Cola's board of directors appoints a special audit committee whose responsibilities include a review of the company's financial statements as well as an assessment of its risk management, internal and disclosure controls, complaints procedures, and compliance programs (including the Company's Code of Business Conduct). The committee's statement of purpose is as follows:

> The Committee will represent and assist the Board in fulfilling its oversight responsibility to the shareowners and others relating to the integrity of the Company's financial statements and the financial reporting process, the systems of internal accounting and financial controls, the internal audit function, the annual independent audit of the Company's financial statements, the Company's compliance with legal and regulatory requirements, and its ethics programs as established by management and the Board, including the Company's Code of Business Conduct. The Committee shall also oversee the independent auditors' qualifications and independence. The Committee will evaluate the performance of the Company's internal audit function (responsibilities, budget and staffing) and the Company's independent auditors, including a review and evaluation of the engagement partner and coordinating partner. In so doing, it is the responsibility of the Committee to maintain free and open communication between the Committee, independent auditors, the internal auditors and management of the Company. The Committee is also responsible for producing an annual report for inclusion in the Company's proxy statement.[32]

Figure 9.3 provides a fictional example of how a corporate social responsibility structure might be organized within a well-known company. Notice that the 2010 amendments to the Federal Sentencing Guidelines for Organizations recommend that chief ethics and compliance officers report directly to the board of directors. Although this chapter presents a structure and recommendations for both general social and ethics-specific audits, there is no generic approach that will satisfy every firm's circumstances. Nevertheless, the benefits and limitations that companies derive from auditing are relatively consistent.

Secure Commitment of Top Managers and Board of Directors

The first step in conducting any audit is securing the commitment of the firm's top management and, if it is a public corporation, its board of directors. Indeed, the push for an ethics audit may come directly from the board itself in response to specific stakeholder concerns or corporate governance reforms related to the Sarbanes–Oxley Act, which suggests that boards of directors should provide oversight for *all* auditing activities. In addition, court decisions related to the FSGO hold board members responsible for the ethical and legal compliance programs of the firms they oversee. Rules and regulations associated with the Sarbanes–Oxley Act require that boards include members who are knowledgeable and qualified to oversee accounting and other types of audits to ensure that these reports are accurate and include all material information. Although a board's financial audit

FIGURE 9.3 Model Corporate Social Responsibility Structure

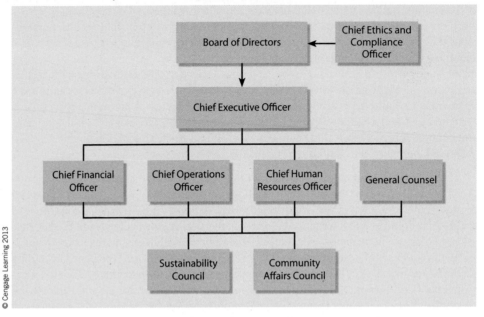

© Cengage Learning 2013

committee will examine ethical standards throughout the organization as they relate to financial matters, it will also deal with the implementation of codes of ethics for top financial officers. Many of those issues relate to such corporate governance issues as compensation, stock options, and conflicts of interest. An ethics audit can demonstrate that a firm has taken steps to prevent misconduct, which can be useful in cases where civil lawsuits blame the firm and its directors for the actions of a rogue employee.

Pressure for an audit can also come from top managers who are looking for ways to track and improve ethical performance and perhaps give their firm an advantage over competitors that are facing questions about their ethical conduct. Additionally, under the Sarbanes–Oxley Act, CEOs and CFOs may be criminally prosecuted if they knowingly certify misleading financial statements. They may request an ethics audit as a tool to help improve their confidence in their firm's reporting processes. Some companies have established a high-level ethics office in conjunction with an ethics program, and the ethics officer may campaign for an ethics audit as a way to measure the effectiveness of the firm's ethics program. Regardless of where the impetus for an audit comes from, its success hinges on the full support of top management, particularly the CEO and the board of directors. Without this support, an ethics audit will not improve the firm's ethics program or the corporate culture.

Establish a Committee to Oversee the Ethics Audit

The next step in our framework is to establish a committee or team to oversee the audit process. Ideally, the board of directors' financial audit committee would oversee the ethics audit, but this does not happen in most companies. In most firms, managers or ethics officers, who do not always report to the board of directors, conduct social and ethics auditing. In any case, this team should include employees who are knowledgeable about the nature and role of ethics audits, and those people should come from various departments within the firm. The team may recruit individuals from within the firm or hire outside consultants to coordinate the audit and report the results directly to the board of directors. The Ethics Resource Center, a nonprofit organization engaged in supporting ethical conduct in the public and private sector, assists companies with assessments and audits of their ethics programs.[33] As with a financial audit, an external auditor should not have other consulting or conflict-of-interest relationships with top managers or board members. Based on the best practices of corporate governance, audits should also be monitored by an independent board of directors' committee, as recommended by the Sarbanes–Oxley Act.

> "An external auditor should not have other consulting or conflict-of-interest relationships with top managers or board members."

Define the Scope of the Audit Process

The ethics audit committee should establish the scope of the audit and monitor its progress to ensure that it stays on track. The scope of an audit depends on the type of business, the risks it faces, and the opportunities it has available to manage ethics. This step includes defining the key subject matter or risk areas that are important to the ethics audit (for example, sustainability, discrimination, product liability, employee rights, privacy, fraud, financial reporting, and/or legal compliance) as well as the bases on which these areas should be assessed. Assessments can be made on the basis of direct consultation, observation, surveys, or focus groups.[34] Table 9.5 lists some sample subject matter areas and the audit items for each.

Review Organizational Mission, Values, Goals, and Policies and Define Ethical Priorities

Because ethics audits generally involve comparing an organization's ethical performance to its goals, values, and policies, the audit process should include a review of the current mission statement and strategic objectives. A company's overall mission may incorporate ethics objectives, but these may also be found in separate documents, including those that focus on social responsibility. For example, a firm's ethics statement or statement of values may offer guidance for managing transactions and human relationships that support the firm's reputation, thereby fostering the confidence of the firm's external stakeholders.[35] Franklin Energy, for example, specifies the five core values it uses in managing its business, and which contribute to its success: ingenuity, results orientation, frugality, integrity, and environmental stewardship.[36]

This review step should include an examination of all formal documents that make explicit commitments to ethical, legal, or social responsibility, as well as less formal documents including marketing materials, workplace policies, ethics policies, and standards for suppliers or vendors. This review may reveal a need to create additional statements to fill the identified gaps or to create a new comprehensive mission statement or ethical policy that addresses any deficiencies.[37]

TABLE 9.5 The Ethics Audit

		Organizational Issues*
Yes	No	1. Does the company have a code of ethics that is reasonably capable of preventing misconduct?
Yes	No	2. Does the board of directors participate in the development and evaluation of the ethics program?
Yes	No	3. Is there a person with high managerial authority responsible for the ethics program?
Yes	No	4. Are there mechanisms in place to prevent the delegation of authority to individuals with a propensity for misconduct?
Yes	No	5. Does the organization effectively communicate standards and procedures to its employees via ethics training programs?
Yes	No	6. Does the organization communicate its ethical standards to suppliers, customers, and significant others that have a relationship with the organization?
Yes	No	7. Do the company's manuals and written documents guiding operations contain messages about appropriate behavior?
Yes	No	8. Is there formal or informal communication within the organization about procedures and activities that are considered acceptable ethical behavior?
Yes	No	9. Does top management have a mechanism in place to detect ethical issues relating to employees, customers, the community, and society?
Yes	No	10. Is there a system in place for employees to report unethical behavior?
Yes	No	11. Is there consistent enforcement of standards and punishments in the organization?
Yes	No	12. Is there a committee, department, team, or group that deals with ethical issues in the organization?
Yes	No	13. Does the organization make a continuous effort to improve its ethical compliance program?
Yes	No	14. Does the firm perform an ethics audit?

Examples of Specific Issues That Could Be Monitored in an Ethics Audit†

Yes	No	1. Are there any systems or operational procedures in place to safeguard individual employees' ethical behavior?
Yes	No	2. Is it necessary for employees to break the company's ethical rules to get the job done?
Yes	No	3. Is there an environment of deception, repression, and cover-ups concerning events that would embarrass the company?
Yes	No	4. Are there any participatory management practices that allow ethical issues to be discussed?
Yes	No	5. Are compensation systems totally dependent on performance?
Yes	No	6. Does sexual harassment occur?

Yes	No	7. Does any form of discrimination—race, sex, or age—occur in hiring, promotion, or compensation?
Yes	No	8. Are the only standards about environmental impact those that are legally required?
Yes	No	9. Do the firm's activities show any concern for the ethical value systems of the community?
Yes	No	10. Are there deceptive and misleading messages in promotion?
Yes	No	11. Are products described in misleading or negative ways or without communicating their limitations to customers?
Yes	No	12. Are the documents and copyrighted materials of other companies used in unauthorized ways?
Yes	No	13. Are expense accounts inflated?
Yes	No	14. Are customers overcharged?
Yes	No	15. Does unauthorized copying of computer software occur?

*A high number of "Yes" answers indicates that ethical control mechanisms and procedures are in place within the organization.
†The number of "Yes" answers indicates the number of possible ethical issues to address.

It is also important to examine all of the firm's policies and practices with respect to the specific areas covered by the audit. For example, in an audit that scrutinizes discrimination issues, this review step would consider the company's goals and objectives as well as its policies related to discrimination. It would consider the means available for communicating the firm's policies and assess their effectiveness. Such an evaluation should also look at whether and how managers are rewarded for meeting their goals and the systems employees have through which to give and receive feedback. An effective ethics audit will review all these systems and assess their strengths and weaknesses.[38]

Concurrent with this step in the auditing process, the firm should define its ethical priorities. Determining these priorities is a balancing act because identifying the needs and assessing the priorities of each stakeholder can be difficult. Because there may be no legal requirements for ethical priorities, it is up to management's strategic planning processes to determine risks, designate appropriate standards, and outline processes of communication with stakeholders. It is very important at this stage to articulate the firm's ethical priorities and values as a set of parameters or performance indicators that can be objectively and quantitatively assessed. Because the ethics audit is a structured report that offers quantitative and descriptive assessments, actions should be measurable by quantitative indicators. However, it is sometimes not possible to go beyond description.[39]

At some point, a firm must demonstrate action-oriented responsiveness to those ethics issues to which it has given top priority. For example, Niagara Mohawk Power Co. has a long history of working to minimize damage to the environment. The firm has adopted the international standard for environmental management systems, ISO 14001, and the guidelines specified by ISO 14001 require external auditing by a certified auditor. Additionally, Niagara Mohawk has a global Corporate Responsibility Summary Report on its corporate website.[40]

Collect and Analyze Relevant Information

The next step in the ethical audit framework is to identify the tools or methods for measuring a firm's progress in improving employees' ethical decisions and conduct. In this step, the firm should collect relevant information for each designated subject matter area. To understand employee issues, for example, the auditing committee should work with the firm's human resources department to gather employee survey information and other statistics and feedback. A thorough ethics audit will review all relevant reports, including external documents sent to government agencies and others. Attempts to measure a firm's sustainability strategy will often depend upon a company's own reports and secondary data.[41] The information collected in this measurement step should help determine baseline levels of compliance as well as the internal and external expectations of the company. This step will also identify where the company has, or has not, met its commitments, including those dictated by its mission statement and other policy documents. The documents reviewed in this process will vary from company to company, depending on the firm's size and the nature of its business, as well as the scope of the audit process.[42] At Green Mountain Coffee, the audit committee of the board of directors is responsible for providing oversight of reporting procedures and audits. Green Mountain's code of ethics, described in Table 9.6, provides a framework for the principles that are the backbone of the ethics audit.[43]

Some techniques for collecting evidence might involve examining both internal and external documents, observing the data-collection process (for example by consulting with stakeholders), and confirming information in the organization's accounting records. Auditors may also employ ratio analysis of relevant indicators to identify any inconsistencies or unexpected patterns. Objective measurement is the key consideration of the ethics auditor.[44]

Stakeholder involvement is another important component in the successful implementation of an ethics audit, as stakeholders can yield significant insights. In one study

TABLE 9.6 Green Mountain Coffee's Code of Ethics

- Respect the rights and the property of others
- Maintain accurate records and report unethical behavior
- Comply with all laws, rules, and regulatory requirements
- Avoid conflicts of interest and any appearance of impropriety
- Be responsible stewards in the use, protection, and management of GMCR's assets and resources
- Understand antitrust laws and uphold fair competitive practices
- Share GMCR's story while following the Media Relations guidelines on consistent communications
- Act with integrity while maintaining the confidentiality of GMCR information
- Support GMCR's Purpose, Principles, Policies, and Procedures and encourage GMCR's business partners to do so as well

Source: Adapted from GMC's Code of Ethics, http://files.shareholder.com/downloads/GMCR/1200861996x0x383775/36dbb352-934f-4e7b-9001-9d0c581a6410/GMCR_WebDoc_7206.pdf (accessed March 23, 2011).

examining reporting channels, employees were asked to whom they would "feel comfortable" reporting misconduct if they suspected or became aware of it. Supervisors and local managers received the most favorable responses, suggesting the need for organizations to ensure that front-line managers are equipped to respond appropriately to allegations. It is worth noting that those functions primarily charged with taking action in response to alleged misconduct (legal, internal audit, and board or audit committee functions) were cited among the less likely channels that employees would feel comfortable using to report allegations. A company's ethical culture also determines whether those who report misconduct experience retaliation—and could also determine how often employees feel comfortable enough to report misconduct. Figure 9.4 shows that retaliation occurs more often in weaker ethical cultures. This makes it essential for management to create a strong ethical culture in which employees are encouraged to report observed misconduct.

Because integrating stakeholder feedback in the ethics audit process is so crucial, these stakeholders must first be defined and then interviewed during the data-collection stage. For most companies, stakeholders include employees, customers, investors, suppliers, community groups, regulators, nongovernment organizations, and the media. Both social and ethics audits typically interview and conduct focus groups with these stakeholders to gain an understanding of how they perceive the company. For example, the Chris Hani Baragwanath Hospital (CHBH) in Johannesburg, South Africa, conducted an ethics audit that included focus groups with the hospital's management, doctors, nurses, related health professionals, support staff, and patients. Using the trends uncovered in these focus groups, CHBH then developed an ethics survey questionnaire that it administered to a larger group of individual stakeholders.[45] The more stakeholders that auditors include in this measurement stage, the more time and resources the audit will consume. However, a larger sample of stakeholders may yield a more useful variety of opinions

FIGURE 9.4 Correlation between Retaliation and Corporate Culture

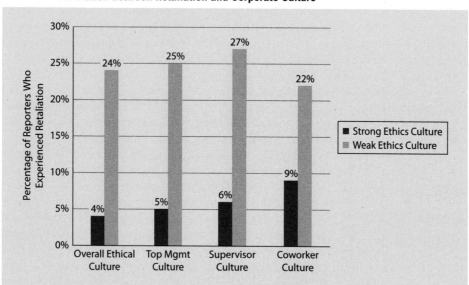

Source: Retaliation: The Cost to Your Company and Its Employees, (Arlington, VA: Ethics Resource Center, 2010), p. 10.

about the company. Multinational corporations must also make decisions about whether to include in the audit only the main office or headquarters region or all of its facilities around the globe.[46]

Because employees carry out a business's operations, including its ethics initiatives, understanding employee issues is vital to a successful audit. Useful indicators for assessing employee issues include staff turnover and employee satisfaction. High turnover rates could indicate poor working conditions, an unethical culture, inadequate compensation, or general employee dissatisfaction. Companies can analyze these factors to determine key areas for improvement.[47] Questionnaires that survey employees' perceptions of the ethics of their company, their superiors, their coworkers, and themselves, as well as ratings of ethical or unethical practices within the firm and industry, can serve as benchmarks in an ongoing assessment of ethical performance. Then, if unethical behavior increases, management will better understand what types of unethical practices may be occurring and why. For example, the CHBH ethics survey asked employees about many issues, including corporate culture and values, their work space, human resources issues, misconduct, standards of patient care, and problems and sources of stress.[48] Most organizations recognize that employees will behave in ways that lead to recognition and rewards and avoid behavior that results in punishment. Therefore, companies can design and implement human resources policies and procedures for recruiting, hiring, promoting, compensating, and rewarding employees that encourage ethical behavior.[49]

Customers are another primary stakeholder group because their patronage and loyalty determines a company's financial success. Providing meaningful feedback is critical to creating and maintaining customer satisfaction. Through surveys and customer-initiated communication systems such as response cards, online social networks, e-mail, and toll-free numbers, organizations can monitor and respond to customer issues and its perceived social performance. Procter & Gamble uses online social networking sites such as Facebook to determine which social issues consumers are passionate about, as well as to gain insights into consumers' product needs and reactions to products.

A growing number of investors are seeking to include in their investment portfolios the stocks of companies that conduct ethics and social audits. They are becoming more aware of the financial benefits that can stem from socially responsible management systems—as well as the negative consequences of a lack of responsibility. President Obama praised City National Bancshares CEO Leonard Abess after he distributed his entire $60 million bonus to employees. On the other hand, Martin Sullivan, former CEO of AIG, approved $165 million and $121 million in bonuses to the Financial Products Group and executives and other employees, respectively. Sullivan was ousted before the company took $200 billion in government bailout money, which was funded by U.S. taxpayers.[50]

> "Even the hint of wrong doing can affect a company's relations with investors."

Even the hint of wrongdoing can affect a company's relations with investors. Moreover, many investors simply do not want to invest in companies that engage in certain business practices, such as the use of sweatshops or child labor, which fail to provide employees with adequate working conditions. It is therefore critical that companies understand the issues of this very important group of stakeholders and what they expect from corporations in which they have invested, both financially and socially.

Organizations can obtain feedback from stakeholders through standardized surveys, interviews, and focus groups. Companies can also encourage stakeholder exchanges by inviting specific groups together for discussions. Such meetings also may include an office or facility tour or a field trip by company representatives to sites in the community. Regardless of how companies collect information about stakeholders' views, the primary objective is to generate a variety of opinions about how the company is perceived and whether it is fulfilling stakeholders' expectations.[51]

Once this information has been collected, the firm should compare its internal perceptions to those discovered during the stakeholder assessment stage and summarize its findings. During this phase, the audit committee should draw some conclusions about the information it obtained in the previous stages. These conclusions may involve descriptive assessments of the findings, such as the costs and benefits of the company's ethics program, the strengths and weaknesses of the firm's policies and practices, the nature of feedback from stakeholders, and issues that should be addressed in future audits. In some cases, it may be appropriate to see how the findings fit with standards identified earlier, both quantitatively and qualitatively.[52]

Data analysis should also include an examination of how other organizations in the industry are performing in the designated subject areas. For example, the audit committee can investigate the successes of some other benchmark firm that is considered the best in a particular area and compare the auditing company's performance to it. Some common examples of the benchmark information available from most corporate ethics audits are employee or customer satisfaction, how community groups perceive the company, and the impact of the company's philanthropy. For example, the Ethics and Compliance Officer Association (ECOA) conducts research on legal and ethical issues in the workplace. These studies allow ECOA members to compare their responses to the aggregate results obtained through the study.[53] Such comparisons can help the audit committee identify best practices for a particular industry or establish a baseline for minimum ethics requirements. It is important to note that a wide variety of standards are emerging that apply to ethics accountability. The aim of these standards is to create a tool for benchmarking and a framework for businesses to follow.

Verify the Results

The next step is to have an independent party—such as a social/ethics audit consultant, a financial accounting firm that offers social auditing services (such as KPMG), or a nonprofit special interest group with auditing experience (for example, the New Economics Foundation)—verify the results of the data analysis. Business for Social Responsibility, a nonprofit organization supporting social responsibility initiatives and reporting, has defined *verification* as an independent assessment of the quality, accuracy, and completeness of a company's social report. Independent verification offers a company, its stakeholders, and the general public a measure of assurance that the company has reported its ethical performance fairly and honestly, as well as providing an assessment of the company's social and environmental reporting systems.[54] It also lends an audit report credibility and objectivity.[55] Siemens AG in Munich, for example, had its sustainability report verified by the accounting firm PricewaterhouseCoopers.[56] However, a survey conducted by one of the Big Four accounting firms found that only a few social reports contained any form of external verification.

This lack of third-party assurance may have contributed to the criticism that social and ethics auditing and reporting have more to do with public relations than genuine change. But though the independent validation of ethics audits is not required, the number of independently verified reports is increasing.[57] Many public policy experts believe that an independent, objective audit can be provided only if the auditor has played no role in the reporting process—in other words, consulting and auditing should be distinctly separate roles. The Sarbanes–Oxley Act essentially legalized this belief.

Verification of the results of an audit should involve standard procedures that control the reliability and validity of the information. As with a financial audit, auditors can apply substantive tests to detect material misstatements in the audit data and analysis. The tests commonly used in financial audits—confirmation, observation, tracing, vouching, analytical procedures, inquiry, and recomputing—can be used in ethics and social audits as well. For example, positive confirmations can be requested from the participants of a stakeholder focus group to verify that the reported results are consistent with the results the focus group believed it found. Likewise, an ethics auditor can observe a company's procedures for handling ethical disputes to verify statements made in the report. And just as a financial auditor follows supporting documents to financial statements to test their completeness, an ethics auditor or verifier may examine employee complaints about an ethics issue to check whether the reporting of such complaints was complete. An auditor can also employ analytical procedures by examining plausible relationships such as the prior year's employee turnover ratio or the average turnover rate commonly reported within the industry. With the reporting firm's permission, an auditor can contact the company's legal counsel to inquire about pending litigation that may shed light on ethical and legal issues currently facing the firm.[58]

Additionally, a financial auditor may be asked to provide a letter to the company's board of directors and senior managers to highlight inconsistencies in the reporting process. The auditor may request that management reply to particular points in the letter to indicate the actions it intends to take to address problems or weaknesses. The financial auditor is required to report to the board of directors' financial audit committee (or equivalent) any significant adjustments or difficulties encountered during the audit as well as any disagreements with management. Therefore, ethics auditors should be required to report to the board of directors' audit committee the same issues that a financial auditor would report.[59] Green Mountain Coffee uses this method.

Report the Findings

The final step in our framework is issuing the ethics audit report. This involves reporting the audit findings through a formal report to the relevant internal parties, namely, the board of directors and top executives, and, if approved, to external stakeholders. Although some companies prefer not to release the results of their audits to the public, more companies are choosing to make their reports available to a broad group of stakeholders. Some companies, including the U.K.-based Co-operative Bank and the British newspaper *The Guardian,* integrate the results of their social audits with their annual financial reports and other important information. Many other companies, including Johnson and Johnson, Shell, and Green Mountain Coffee, also make their audit reports available on their corporate websites.[60]

Based on the guidelines established by the Global Reporting Initiative and Accountability, the report should spell out the purpose and scope of the audit, the methods used in the audit process (evidence gathering and evaluation), the role of the (preferably independent) auditor, any auditing guidelines followed by the auditor, and any reporting guidelines followed by the company.[61] The ethics audit of Johannesburg's Chris Hani Baragwanath Hospital followed these guidelines.[62] The report is more meaningful if it is integrated with other organizational information available, such as financial reports, employee surveys, regulatory filings, and customer feedback. The firm might also want to include in its ethics audit a section on best industry practices and how the firm compares to other companies in its field. Such a comparison can help a firm to identify its weaknesses and develop suggestions for improvement. The use of information such as the OCEG Benchmarking Study pinpoints key elements of corporate and ethics programs that could help assess best practices across the industry.[63]

As mentioned earlier, ethics audits may resemble financial audits, but they take quite different forms. In a financial audit, the Statement of Auditing Standards dictates literally every word found in a financial audit report in terms of content and placement. Based on the auditor's findings, the report issued can take one of the following four forms, among other variations. An *unqualified opinion* states that the financial statements are fairly stated. A *qualified opinion* asserts that although the auditor believes the financial statements are fairly stated, an unqualified opinion is not possible either because of limitations placed on the auditor or because of minor issues involving disclosure or accounting principles. An *adverse opinion* states that the financial statements are not fairly stated. Finally, a *disclaimer of opinion* states that the auditor did not have full access to records or discovered a conflict of interest. These different opinions each have enormous consequences for companies.

DEBATE ISSUE   TAKE A STAND

Which Ethics Audit Process Works Better for Smaller Companies?

ABC Specialty Marketing, Inc., is considering a formal ethics audit. The company has about 200 employees, including 50 salespeople that sell promotional printing products. Recent ethical issues have raised concerns within the company, causing the last board of directors to think about implementing a formal ethics audit. During the meeting, one of the board members who had examined the auditing process represented in Table 9.5 indicated that for a small company, this approach looked too formal. He felt that the Better Business Bureau Torch Award Criteria for ethical companies was a more practical approach to auditing ethical risks and conduct. Another member pointed out that the BBB criteria were more for judging than for understanding the risk areas and ethics program implementation concerns. This led to a discussion about how to implement an ethics audit in such a small company with a fairly limited ethics program. The meeting ended without a clear decision on which approach to use.

1. The Better Business Bureau Torch Award Criteria is the best method for conducting a formal ethics audit in a smaller company.

2. The auditing process represented in Table 9.5 offers a better way to understand a small company's ethical risks and conduct.

THE STRATEGIC IMPORTANCE OF ETHICS AUDITING

Although the concept of auditing implies an official examination of ethical performance, many organizations audit their performance informally. Any attempt to verify outcomes and compare them with standards can be considered an auditing activity. Many smaller firms probably would not use the word *audit,* but they do perform auditing activities. Organizations such as the Better Business Bureau (BBB) provide awards and assessment tools to help any organization evaluate its ethical performance. Companies with fewer resources may wish to use the judging criteria from the BBB's Torch Award Criteria for Ethical Companies (Table 9.7) as

TABLE 9.7 Better Business Bureau's Torch Award Criteria for Ethical Companies

A business should demonstrate its superior commitment to exceptional standards that benefit its customers, employees, suppliers, shareholders and surrounding communities. The business must provide supporting documentation in four areas for consideration in the Marketplace Excellence category. While examples from all four areas must be provided, the bullet points below are only suggestions and not all bullet points are required to be addressed in order for a business to compete in this category.

Management Practices
Note: Owners of companies with no employees must explain how a personal commitment to exceptional standards is applied in business practices.

- Pertinent sections from an employee handbook, business manual or training program (formal or informal) showing how the business's commitment to exceptional standards are communicated to and implemented by employees

- A vision, mission or core values statement describing the business's commitment to exceptional standards that benefit its customers, employees, suppliers, shareholders and surrounding communities

- Formal training and/or procedures used to address concerns an employee may have in dealing with ethical issues

- Management practices and policies that foster positive employee relations

- Employee benefits and/or workplace practices contributing to the quality of family life

- Actions taken to assess and mitigate risks, and prevent workplace injury

- Examples of sound environmental practices

- Examples of operational practices focused on security and privacy issues—on and offline

- Illustrations of your business's commitment to standards that build trust in the marketplace (i.e., customer service program, employee relation policy or practice, vendor/supplier relationship, etc.)

Community/Investor/Stakeholder Relations

- Examples of the business's vision, mission and/or core values statement in action—describing how the business's beliefs have been leveraged for the benefit of consumers, employees, suppliers, shareholders, and surrounding communities

- Business policies and practices that demonstrate accountability and responsibility to communities, investors and other stakeholder audiences

- Corporate governance practices address accountability and responsibility to shareholders

- Complimentary feedback from customers, vendors, suppliers and/or community leaders

- Actions taken by the business demonstrating service "beyond the call of duty"

- Brief case study examples of circumstances in which the business made tough decisions that had negative short-term consequences, but created long-term value and benefits

- Examples of, and results produced by, pro bono work

- Examples of the business working closely within the community and making a positive social impact—and any recognition for charitable and/or community service projects.

Communications and Marketing Practices

- Descriptions of methods the business uses to ensure all sales, promotional materials and advertisements are truthful and accurate

- Sales training policies and/or codes of ethics used by sales personnel that ensure all transactions are made in a transparent, honest manner

- Crisis communications efforts and associated marketing actions that educated audiences, prevented negative outcomes and restored trust and confidence in the business, its products and services

- Examples of internal communications practices benefiting employees and contributing to overall business effectiveness and efficiency

Industry Reputation

- Media coverage reflecting the business's industry and community reputation as a trustworthy business

- Awards, recognition and/or complimentary letters from within the business's industry, trade group or community

Source: "International Torch Award Judging Criteria," Better Business Bureau, http://www.bbb.org/international-torch-awards/critera.html (accessed March 23, 2011).

benchmarks for their informal self-audits. Recent winners of this award included Amazon. com, Verizon, and Villa Springfield Health & Rehabilitation Center.[64] The award criteria even provide a category for companies with less than 10 employees.

An ethics audit, like a financial audit, should be conducted regularly rather than in response to problems or questions about a firm's priorities and conduct. In other words, the ethics audit is not a control process to be used during a crisis, although it can pinpoint potential problem areas and generate solutions in a crisis situation. As mentioned earlier, an audit may be comprehensive and encompass all the ethics and social responsibility areas of a business, or it can be specific and focus on one or two areas. One specialized audit could be an environmental impact audit in which specific environmental issues, such as proper waste disposal, are analyzed. According to the KPMG International Survey of Corporate Responsibility Reporting, 80 percent of the 2,200 companies in 22 countries surveyed include CSR in their reporting, up from 50 percent in 2005.[65] Examples of other specialized audits include diversity, employee benefits, and conflicts of interest. Ethics audits can present several problems. They can be expensive and time consuming, and selecting the auditors may be difficult if objective, qualified personnel are not available. Employees sometimes fear comprehensive evaluations, especially by outsiders, and in such cases ethics audits can be extremely disruptive.

Despite these problems, however, auditing ethical performance can generate many benefits, as we have seen throughout this chapter. The ethics audit provides an assessment of a company's overall ethical performance as compared to its core values, ethics policy, internal operating practices, management systems, and most importantly, key stakeholder expectations.[66] As such, ethics and social audit reports are a useful management tool for helping companies identify and define their impacts and facilitate important improvements.[67] This assessment can be used to reallocate resources and activities as well as to focus on new opportunities. The audit process can also help companies fulfill their mission statements in ways that boost profits and reduce risks.[68] More specifically, a company may seek continual improvement in its employment practices, its customer and community relations, and the ethical soundness of its general business practices.[69] An audit can pinpoint areas where improving operating practices can improve bottom-line profits and stakeholder relationships.[70]

Most managers view profitability and ethics and social responsibility as a trade-off. This "either/or" mindset prevents them from taking a more proactive "both/and" approach.[71] But the auditing process can demonstrate the positive impact of ethical conduct and social responsibility initiatives on the firm's bottom line, convincing managers—and other primary stakeholders—of the value of adopting more ethical and socially responsible business practices.[72]

SUMMARY

Viewing a business ethics program as a part of strategic planning and management activities is critical to the success of any firm. However, for such programs to be successful, firms must put controls and systems in place to ensure that they are being executed effectively. Controls include input, output, and process controls. Input controls are concerned with providing necessary tools and resources to the organization, such as good employees and effective ethics training and structural systems. Process controls include managerial commitment to an ethics program and to the methods or system for the evaluation of ethics. Output controls involve comparing standards with actual behavior. One of the most popular methods of evaluating ethical performance is an ethics audit.

An ethics audit is a systematic evaluation of an organization's ethics program and/or its ethical performance. Such audits provide an opportunity to measure conformity with the firm's desired ethical standards. The concept of ethics auditing has emerged from the movement toward auditing and reporting on companies' broader social responsibility initiatives. Social auditing is the process of assessing and reporting a business's performance in fulfilling the economic, legal, ethical, and philanthropic social responsibilities expected of it by its stakeholders. An ethics audit may be conducted as a component of a social audit. Auditing is a tool that companies can use to identify and measure their ethical commitment to stakeholders and to demonstrate their commitment to improving strategic planning, including their compliance with legal, ethical, and social responsibility standards.

The auditing process can highlight trends, improve organizational learning, and facilitate communication and working relationships. It can help companies assess the effectiveness of their programs and policies, identify potential risks and liabilities, improve compliance with the law, and demonstrate progress in areas of previous noncompliance. One of the greatest benefits of these audits for businesses is improved relationships with stakeholders. Ethics auditing may help prevent public relations crises associated with ethical or legal misconduct. Although ethics audits provide many benefits for companies and their stakeholders, they do have the potential to expose risks; the process of auditing cannot guarantee that a firm will not face challenges. Additionally, there are few common standards for judging disclosure and effectiveness or for making comparisons within an industry.

An ethics audit should be unique to each company based on its size, industry, corporate culture and identified risks, and the regulatory environment in which it operates. This chapter has offered a framework for conducting an ethics audit that can also be used for a broader social audit.

The first step in conducting an audit is securing the commitment of the firm's top management and/or its board of directors. The push for an ethics audit may come directly from the board of directors in response to specific stakeholder concerns or corporate governance reforms, or from top managers looking for ways to track and improve ethical performance. Whatever the source of the audit, its success hinges on the full support of top management.

The second step is establishing a committee or team to oversee the audit process. Ideally the board of directors' financial audit committee would oversee the ethics audit, but in most firms, managers or ethics officers conduct auditing. This committee recruits an individual from within the firm or hires an outside consultant to coordinate the audit and report the results.

The third step is establishing the scope of the audit, which depends on the type of business, the risks faced by the firm, and available opportunities to manage ethics. This step includes defining the key subject matter or risk areas that are important to the ethics audit.

The fourth step is a review of the firm's mission, values, goals, and policies. This step should include an examination of formal documents that make explicit commitments with regard to ethical, legal, or social responsibility, and less formal documents including marketing materials, workplace policies, and ethics policies and standards for suppliers or vendors. During this step, the firm should define its ethical priorities and articulate them as a set of parameters or performance indicators that can be objectively and quantitatively assessed.

The fifth step is identifying the tools or methods that can be used to measure the firm's progress, and then collecting and analyzing the relevant information. Some evidence-collection techniques include examining internal and external documents, observing the data-collection process (such as discussions with stakeholders), and confirming the information in the organization's accounting records. During this step, a company's stakeholders need to be defined and then interviewed to understand how they perceive the company, for example through standardized surveys, interviews, and focus groups. Once this information has been collected, it should be analyzed and summarized. Analysis should include an examination of how other organizations in the industry are performing in the designated subject matter areas.

The sixth step is having an independent party—such as a social/ethics audit consultant, a financial accounting firm that offers social auditing services, or a nonprofit special interest group with auditing experience—verify the results of the data analysis. Verification is an independent assessment of the quality, accuracy, and completeness of a company's audit process. Such verification gives stakeholders confidence in a company's ethics audit and lends the audit report credibility and objectivity. The verification of the results of an audit should involve standard procedures that control the reliability and validity of the information.

The final step in the audit process is reporting the audit findings to the board of directors and top executives and, if approved, to external stakeholders. The report should spell out the purpose and scope of the audit, the methods used in the audit process (evidence gathering and evaluation), the role of the (preferably independent) auditor, any auditing guidelines followed by the auditor, and any reporting guidelines followed by the company.

Although the concept of auditing implies an official examination of ethical performance, many organizations audit informally. Ethics audits should be conducted regularly. Although social auditing may present problems, it can also generate many benefits. Through the auditing process, a firm can demonstrate the positive impact of ethical conduct and social responsibility initiatives on its bottom line, which may convince stakeholders of the value of adopting more ethical and socially responsible business practices.

IMPORTANT TERMS FOR REVIEW

ethics audit   social audit

RESOLVING ETHICAL BUSINESS CHALLENGES*

As Jerry looked around at the other members of the board, he wondered if it was too late to resign. How could he have been stupid enough to get dragged into this ethics audit quagmire? It had started innocently enough. With the passing of the Sarbanes–Oxley Act, everyone was aware of the consequences of accounting problems and their potential negative impact on a company, its board members, and its employees. So when Jerry's friend John Jacobs, the president of Soumey Corp., asked him to be on the company's board of directors, Jerry had checked out the company. It wasn't that he didn't trust John; he just felt that he should never take unnecessary chances. But when Jerry's investigation of Soumey uncovered nothing unusual, he accepted the board position.

Besides Jerry and John, Soumey's board of directors included Alan Kerns, a retired Soumey executive; Alice Finkelstein, a retired executive from a similar company; and Latisha Timme, a consultant within the industry. After Jerry joined the board, one of its first tasks was to conduct an ethics audit. The directors decided to contract the task to Teico, Inron, and Wurrel (TIW), an accounting firm highly recommended by Latisha. A few months later, TIW filed its final report of the audit with the board. The report indicated that, with a few exceptions, Soumey was doing a good job of monitoring ethical issues. Among the recommendations that the report offered were that the company should appoint a person with high managerial authority to be responsible for its ethical compliance program, that it establish a confidential hotline for employees who had ethical or legal concerns, and that it create an ethics committee to address ethical issues in the organization.

At the next board meeting, John suggested that Alan be the ethics compliance officer because he lived close to the main offices and had time to do it. Alan quickly agreed, provided there was substantial remuneration for his time, which John affirmed. Jerry asked a few questions, such as whether Alan had sufficient managerial authority.

Alice responded, "Jerry, this industry is rather small. There are only a few large players, Soumey being one of them. Trust me when I say that Alan, as a retired president of the company, will definitely have the respect of the employees."

Jerry had no more questions, and Alan became Soumey's new compliance officer. The confidential hotline was quickly installed, and announcements about its existence were widely distributed around the various offices and plant buildings to ensure that it reached each of the firm's several thousand employees. The board also discussed TIW's final suggestion for an ethics committee, and all but Jerry agreed that the board could handle that task as well.

Jerry pointed out, "I don't think this is wise, John. This is a conflict of interest for you, isn't it?"

After a moment of hesitation, John replied, "You're right, Jerry, it is a conflict of interest for me to serve on the ethics committee." After another bit of silence, John suggested, "Wouldn't you agree that I should not be on the committee, Alan, Alice, and Latisha?" They all discussed the matter and agreed that Jerry's suggestion made perfect sense.

Time passed, and the board held its quarterly meetings. Nothing unusual was brought up, just the same old issues that any publicly held company must deal with relative to shareholders, lawyers, regulators, and the public. Alan had suggested that the ethics compliance committee meet twice a year so that he could fill everyone in on what was happening. At these meetings, Alan would usually report the number of calls to the hotline, the status of complaints, and whether there were any serious allegations such as sexual harassment or any reported forms of race, sex, or age discrimination in hiring personnel.

After two years of quarterly board meetings and semiannual ethics meetings, Jerry suggested to Alan that they conduct another ethics audit.

"Why would we want to do that, Jerry? Things are going smoothly with the approach we're taking. Why have another outside audit? Do you think that we're doing a bad job?"

Jerry hedged. "I'm not saying that, Alan. What I'm saying is that we may need to have an outside audit just to make sure everything looks good to the public. Why don't we discuss this with Latisha and Alice this week?"

Alan agreed, but when the ethics committee met that week it was obvious to Jerry that Alan had spoken to Alice and Latisha about his and Jerry's meeting. He wasn't surprised when the committee decided that another audit would diminish confidence in Alan's performance as ethics compliance officer. Several weeks later, John sent all the board members a letter announcing an increase in their pay as board directors as well as doubling their pay as ethics committee members. The letter stated, "Soumey Corp. has decided that your service to the company has been exemplary, both as board members and as an ethics committee."

In Jerry's third year on the board of directors, he was finally able to attend Soumey's annual company picnic with his wife and children. They arrived late, after all of the introductions, and everyone was already in the buffet line. As a result, no one really knew who he was. The children were having fun, and Jerry and his wife, Rosa, were too. However, after a while Jerry began to overhear some interesting comments. In one conversation, a production worker spoke about a toxic spill that had occurred because of the lack of safeguards. He told his companion, "Yeah, I know it was pretty messy, but only a few of my crew were hurt."

His friend asked, "Did they or you report it to management?"

He exclaimed, "Are you kidding? My guys don't want to lose their bonuses. Remember what happened to Bob's crew when the same thing happened and some of his guys complained? They had them filling out paperwork for a whole day, and the next week they were assigned a project

with no incentives. They lost 40 percent of what they'd been making with all the overtime and performance-based stuff. The guys and I agreed not to report it for those reasons."

Jerry couldn't help interrupting, "So why didn't the company fix the problem after it happened the first time?"

One of the men asked, "Are you new here?"

"Yeah, been here only a few weeks," Jerry lied.

The production worker answered, "You want to boost your pay, right? So you cut a few corners to get by."

Later that evening, after Jerry and his family had returned home, Rosa told him about a conversation she had overheard. "These women were talking about how unfair it is that most of the incentive-based pay seems to go to men with families. One woman said that she heard of a man over 55 who should have gotten a promotion, but who was turned down because his supervisor was told not to give it to him. Rumor was that this guy had bucked the last president of Soumey, and that was his payback. Jerry, you should have heard what they say about Alan—that he's like Santa Claus and the Grinch. You never see him—and if you do, it's not a pleasant experience. One woman told me that when she was working for him, he used to be a little too friendly. She said that's why no one really uses the ethics hotline for certain issues. They know that the fox is guarding the hen house."

A little later, one of Jerry's sons bounced into the room and asked him a question about the picnic. "Dad, how come all the Spanish-speaking workers are on the night shift? It really makes it hard for a couple of my friends to get their parents to drop them off for soccer."

The picnic opened Jerry's eyes to an uglier side of Soumey. At the next board meeting, he indirectly addressed some of the problems he had noticed. But John responded, "We're going into a recession, and we have to cut a few corners to keep our dividends up to the market's expectations. Latisha has been watching and consulting me on the best way to keep ahead of the pack on this."

Latisha and Alice both commented, "Thank goodness we have a large Hispanic workforce to offset some price increases. They're hard workers and don't complain."

"You're absolutely right," said Alan. "We don't have the EPA, OSHA, or other agencies on our backs because these people know how to work and keep quiet. If some federal agencies do start to poke around, I have some contingency plans to prevent any type of ethical disaster."

That evening Jerry and Rosa were talking about the situation. He told Rosa, "I think Soumey has some potentially ethical issues that need to be addressed—but what can I do?"

"Well," sighed Rosa, "We've lived in this town for a long time. We know the families that are on the board. They're good people. However, there's one thing you didn't hear at that picnic because of your lack of Spanish. I've told you that it's important to learn it, even if it's just for my family. A few of the people I overheard were talking about how the hotline isn't really anonymous. That's just not right, Jerry. You need to do something even if it

does mean losing the extra income." Rosa's points struck a nerve because Jerry knew they were a little overextended financially.

"I'll see what I can do," he told her.

Still, she warned him, "That's good, honey, but remember I don't want you to make too many waves. We still have to live here, and you know we can't swing a dead cat and not hit one of the people at Soumey."

QUESTIONS | EXERCISES

1. What areas of its ethics audit should Soumey change?
2. Does Jerry have a duty to report any of the items that he has heard to an outside authority?
3. Is Jerry responsible for the problems associated with Soumey over the last three years? Explain why or why not.

*This case is strictly hypothetical; any resemblance to real persons, companies, or situations is coincidental.

CHECK YOUR EQ

CHAPTER 10

GLOBALIZATION OF ETHICAL DECISION-MAKING

CHAPTER OBJECTIVES

- To discuss global values, goals, and business practices within ethics

- To understand the role of capitalism and economics as factors in business ethics

- To assess the role of multinational corporations in business ethics

- To assess the role of the International Monetary Fund in business ethics

- To assess the role of the United Nations Global Compact in business ethics

- To assess the role of the World Trade Organization in business ethics

- To explore and discuss common global business practices

- To gain awareness of global ethical issues

AN ETHICAL DILEMMA*

At the Dun and Ready (D&R) Company, Sid was responsible for monitoring the Japanese stock market to determine patterns and identify stocks that could become active. One of 10 company representatives in Japan, Sid, who was of Japanese descent and fluent in the language, had been assigned to Tokyo. Being relatively new to the firm, he was told to gather information for his boss, Glenna. Glenna had been with D&R for 10 years, but because of the cultural barriers, she was not enthusiastic about her Tokyo assignment. Glenna encouraged Sid to get to know the Japanese brokers, traders, and other key people in the business. Thanks to his background, he found that he blended easily into the culture.

In Japan, ceremony and giving favors is a way of life. Sid learned that, by observing Japanese customs and perfecting his Japanese, he became not only an information resource on the Japanese stock market and its players for his company but also a resource for the Japanese who wanted to invest in the U.S. market. He found that the locals would talk to him about important investments rather than coming into the office to see Glenna.

Sid's duties included taking key customers to bars, restaurants, and vacation spots for entertainment. One day a government official in the group that Sid was entertaining hinted that he and the others would like to play golf on some famous U.S. courses. Sid understood what the government official wanted and relayed the request to Glenna, who told him that granting a favor of this kind would normally be against policy, but because such favors seemed to be the custom in Japan, they could do some "creative bookkeeping." "When in Rome, right, Sid?" was Glenna's response to the whole situation. By pulling some strings, Glenna managed to enable these officials to play at 10 of the most exclusive U.S. golf courses. Later, several officials passed the word to people in Japan's elite financial circle about Sid's helpfulness.

Six months later, Glenna was transferred back to the States. Rumor had it that expenses were too high and revenue too low. Her replacement, Ron, didn't like being sent to Japan either. In his first week on the job, he told the staff that he would shorten his tour in Tokyo by slashing expenses and increasing productivity. Ron was a "by-the-book" person. Unfortunately, company rules had not caught up with the realities of cultural differences. After two months with Ron, seven of the original 10 company representatives had quit or been fired.

Sid was barely surviving. Then one of his contacts in the government repaid a favor by recommending several stocks to buy and sell. The information paid off, and Sid gained some breathing room from Ron. Around the same time, some of Sid's Japanese clients lost a considerable amount of money in the U.S. markets and wanted a "discount"—the term used for the practice in some large Japanese brokerage houses of informally paying off part of their best clients' losses. When Glenna was still in Tokyo, she had dipped into the company's assets several times to fund such discounts. Because everything required Ron's approval, Sid and his colleagues believed that this practice would not be tolerated. However, late one

afternoon Sid and a few others provided the proper forms, and Ron signed them without realizing what he had done.

Several months passed, and the three survivors resorted to lowering their expenses by using their own funds. This in turn led to Sid "churning" some of his accounts; that is, he bought and sold stocks for the express purpose of increasing his own revenues. Churning was tolerated in Japan, along with other practices that would be deemed questionable in the United States. Ron was oblivious to what Sid was doing because his focus was on reducing expenses.

The previous month, a group of important D&R clients had thrown a party for a few of their favorite brokers at one of their local haunts. After the customary toasts and small talk, it was suggested to Sid that a Japanese cartel might be interested in D&R. Sid was cautious and nothing else was mentioned. Several weeks later at another party, Sid and the two remaining D&R people were told that a takeover was imminent. But to make the takeover painless, the cartel needed certain sensitive information. Sid's reward for providing it would be a high position in the new, reorganized company and a "wink/nod" agreement that he could go anywhere in the world for his next assignment.

That week Ron announced that headquarters was pleased with the productivity of the Tokyo group. "It's only a matter of time before I get transferred, and I want out of Tokyo," he told them. The office knew that if Ron succeeded, his next position would be that of vice president. Ron also informed the group that corporate representatives would be coming to Tokyo the following week.

"It seems they've heard rumors of a possible hostile takeover attempt on D&R from someone in Japan, and they want us to check it out," Ron said, with a tight smile. "There will be some changes next week."

Sid suspected that this meant there would be even fewer people working even harder. It might also mean, however, that someone knew that Sid and the other two representatives had been talking to the wrong people. Or maybe one of the three had sold out the other two. If Sid was to gather the information sought by the cartel, he would have to act quickly.

QUESTIONS | EXERCISES

1. What are the ethical issues in this situation?
2. Identify the pressures that have caused the ethical issues to develop.

3. Discuss the advantages and disadvantages of each decision that Sid could make.

*This case is strictly hypothetical; any resemblance to real persons, companies, or situations is coincidental.

Advances in communication, technology, and transportation have minimized the world's borders, creating a new global economy in which more and more countries are industrializing and competing internationally. These transactions across national boundaries define **global business,** a practice that brings together people from countries that have different cultures, values, laws, and ethical standards. Therefore, the international businessperson must not only understand the values, culture, and ethical standards of his or her own country, but must also be sensitive to those of other countries.

In this chapter, we explore the ethical complexities and challenges facing businesses that operate internationally. We try to help you understand how global business ethics has more complexity than business in a domestic context. The global business environment, if not understood, can destroy the trust companies need to be successful. To transition from one well-understood culture or country to the global arena requires additional knowledge. Our goal in this chapter is to help you avoid, or at least become aware of, the many ethical quagmires that lurk in this domain. To help you become more ethically sensitive to the global environment of business ethics, we start with the basics, discussing global values and cultural dimensions that can be used by companies to help modify their business practices to different countries. Next, we examine the economic foundations of business ethics. In addition, we help you understand that there are global entities that do not necessarily conform to your country's view of the world or the way to do business. In this chapter we also examine multinational corporations and the ethical problems they face. We move on to discuss the International Monetary Fund, the United Nations Global Compact, and the World Trade Organization. We conclude with an analysis of current and future ethical problems facing global businesses, including global ethical risks, bribery, antitrust activity, Internet security and privacy, human rights, health care, labor and right to work issues, compensation, and consumerism. Our goal is to help you understand how international business activities can create ethical conflicts and help you improve your ethical decision-making ability.

GLOBAL CULTURE, VALUES, AND PRACTICES

Country cultural values are subjective, are based on the social environment, and are used to develop norms that are socially and legally enforced. These values can be specific to countries, regions, sects, or groups. **National culture** is a much broader concept than organizational culture. It includes everything in our surroundings that are made by people—both tangible items, such as artifacts, and intangible entities, such as concepts and values. Language, law, politics, technology, education, social organizations, general values, and ethical standards are all included within this definition. Each nation contains unique cultures and, consequently, distinctive beliefs about what business activities are acceptable or unethical. Subcultures can also be found within many nations, ethnic groups, and religious groups. Therefore, when transacting international business, individuals encounter values, beliefs, and ideas that may diverge from their own because of cultural differences. When someone from another culture mentions "integrity" or "democracy," most Americans might feel reassured that these are familiar concepts. However, these concepts mean different things to different people, depending on their culture. Moreover, you must keep in mind that organizational culture is different from national culture, though often organizational cultures are derived from—and influenced by—national cultures.

Most cultures need auditors, directors, or other entities associated with corporate governance to provide independent oversight of the operations of an organization. In the Japanese banking system, the concept of "independent oversight" has been blurred by the fact that retired Japanese bureaucrats often become auditors and directors. They are trusted simply because of their status. When those providing oversight also have relationships within and/or a vested interest in the success of the company, a truly independent relationship does not exist and there could be conflicts of interest or corporate governance oversight failure.

Different cultural values and how they affect business have intrigued management experts for years. Many have developed frameworks for classifying cultural behavior patterns that can help businesspeople who work in different countries. One of the most well-known frameworks was proposed by Dutch management professor Geert Hofstede. Hofstede identified four cultural dimensions that can have a profound impact on the business environment: individualism/collectivism, power distance, uncertainty avoidance, and masculinity/femininity.[1] We will discuss the first three in the following paragraphs.

The individualism/collectivism dimension of culture refers to how self-oriented members of a culture are in their behavior. Individualist cultures place a high value on individual achievement and self-interest. The United States is an example of an individualistic culture. Collectivist cultures value working toward collective goals and group harmony. Mexico and several countries in Asia adhere to more collectivistic principles. Collectivist cultures tend to avoid public confrontations and disagreements.[2] In Thailand, for instance, negatives such as "no" tend to be avoided in business settings. By understanding this cultural dimension, you will be more likely to maneuver correctly within different cultural business settings.

The power distance dimension refers to the power inequality between superiors and subordinates. The United States has some elements of both a higher and a lower power distance culture. Over the years, the U.S. business environment has adopted forms of management, such as participative management, that place supervisors and subordinates on a more equal footing. In some businesses, employees address their superiors by their first names and have the power to make decisions that are normally reserved for management. Arab countries score higher on the power distance dimension. Cultures with high power distance tend to be more hierarchal, and respect for (or fear of) supervisors may be so great that managerial misconduct could become hard to pinpoint.[3]

Uncertainty avoidance refers to how members of a society respond to uncertainty or ambiguity. Cultures that score high on the uncertainty avoidance dimension, such as Great Britain, tend to want to avoid risk-taking. Organizations within these cultures may have more rules in place to ensure that employees do not deviate from accepted standards. Cultures with less uncertainty avoidance, such as Canada, believe that risk-taking and innovation are important in achieving successful outcomes.[4] Businesses from either culture will need to be aware of how a particular culture views uncertainty avoidance. For instance, if a businessperson from the United States is giving a sales presentation to a business in Uruguay—a culture with higher uncertainty avoidance—the American businessperson might try to reassure the Uruguayan company by attempting to mitigate the risks involved.

As Hofstede's dimensions suggest, businesspeople who travel to other countries quickly perceive that other business cultures have different modes of operation. The perception exists that American companies are different from those in other countries, and some people perceive U.S. companies as being superior to their foreign counterparts. This implied perspective of ethical superiority—"us" versus "them"—is also common in other countries. Figure 10.1 indicates the countries that businesspeople, risk analysts, and the general public have perceived as the most and least corrupt.

In business, the idea that "we" differ from "them" is called the self-reference criterion (SRC). The SRC is the unconscious reference to one's own cultural values, experiences, and knowledge. When confronted with a situation, we react on the basis of knowledge we have accumulated over a lifetime, which usually is grounded in our culture of origin. Our reactions are based on meanings, values, and symbols that relate in a certain way to our culture but may not have the same relevance to people of other cultures.

Walmart's foray into Germany is one example of how the SRC can cause problems. A German labor court ruled that parts of the ethics code of Walmart Stores, Inc., including a ban on relationships between employees, violate German law. The same court also ruled against a proposed hotline for employees to report on colleagues' violations of the code of conduct. Labor representatives from the 91 German Walmart stores sued the retail giant over the code after it was introduced without their prior approval. Under German law, employee–management councils must sign off on a wide range of workplace conditions.[5] These, as well as other cultural differences, led Walmart to close its German stores. Walmart

FIGURE 10.1 Transparency International's Corruption Index Rankings by Country.

The 2010 Corruption Perceptions Index measures the perceived levels of public-sector corruption in 178 countries around the world.

Very Clean

	9.0 – 10
	8.0 – 8.9
	7.0 – 7.9
	6.0 – 6.9
	5.0 – 5.9
	4.0 – 4.9
	3.0 – 3.9
	2.0 – 2.9
	1.0 – 1.9
	0 – 0.9
	No Data

Highly Corrupt

Source: Reprinted from Corruption Perceptions Index 2010. Copyright 2010 Transparency International: the global coalition against corruption. Used with permission. For more information, visit http://www.transparency.org.

learned that its ethical controls, which it had assumed would be accepted without complaint, were not acceptable under German law and in the context of German cultural values.

One of the critical ethical business issues linked to cultural differences is the question of whose values and ethical standards take precedence during international negotiations and business transactions. When conducting business outside their home country, should businesspeople impose their own values, ethical standards, and laws on members of other cultures? Or should they adapt to the values, ethical standards, and laws of the countries in which they are doing business? As with many ethical issues, there are no easy answers to these questions.

"When in Rome, do as the Romans do," or "you must adapt to the cultural practices of the country in which you are operating" are rationalizations that businesspeople sometimes offer for straying from their own ethical values when doing business abroad. By defending the payment of bribes or "greasing the wheels of business" and other questionable practices in this fashion, they are resorting to **cultural relativism,** the concept that morality varies from one culture to another and that "right" and "wrong" are therefore defined differently.

Despite the various differences in values between countries, there are also certain values that are broadly accepted worldwide. These **global common values** are shared across most cultures. Most laws are directly or indirectly the result of values derived from the major religions of Hinduism, Buddhism, Confucianism, Judaism, Islam, and Christianity. Although most of these religions have similar core virtues, the importance placed on these virtues may vary. For instance, cultures that are predominately Hindu tend to value nonviolence, mind and sense control, and austerity;[6] traditional Chinese cultures value respect, righteousness, and loyalty; Islamic cultures value wisdom, tolerance, self-restraint, and mercy;[7] Judaism values the virtues of kindness, peace, and hospitality; predominately Christian cultures tend to value forgiveness, mercy, and faith;[8] and Buddhist cultures place high importance on the "four immeasurables" of equanimity, joy, loving-kindness, and generosity.[9] By understanding what a particular culture values, global businesses will have a better chance of forming relationships with individuals and organizations in that culture. They may also be able to avoid conduct that is offensive to citizens of certain countries (e.g., shaking with the left hand in Islamic nations). It is beyond our scope to explain all such nuances, but there does appear to be a consensus on the following desirable and undesirable common values.[10]

- Desirable common values: Integrity, family and community unity, equality, honesty, fidelity, sharing, and unselfishness
- Undesirable common values: Ignorance, pride and egoism, selfish desires, lust, greed, adultery, theft, deceit, lying, murder, hypocrisy, slander, and addiction

ECONOMIC FOUNDATIONS OF BUSINESS ETHICS

Economic and political events as well as natural disasters can reflect and affect the environment for global ethical decision making. We first examine how recent developments have influenced global systems that structure the business world.

The last economic recession highlighted the fact that firms were taking extreme risks, bending rules, and engaging in unethical activity. A major part of the problem was the excessive focus on rewards and the bottom line that pervaded the global financial industry. The global financial market is a highly interconnected system that can exhibit a lack of transparency in decision making, accountability, and accounting methods. This system, combined with rampant leveraging and the widespread use of highly complex financial computer models that many experts did not even fully understand, resulted in a global financial meltdown.

Our financial system is very complex, and this complexity can provide ample opportunity to take excessive risks and manipulate various stakeholders. Many who should have known about such risks were ignorant because of risk compartmentalization. **Risk compartmentalization** occurs when various profit centers within corporations become unaware of the overall consequences of their actions on the firm as a whole. As a result, no one person, company, or agency should be blamed—the problems were systemic. Before the financial meltdown, most companies tried to remain in compliance with legal systems, while many simultaneously looked for legal loopholes and unregulated means of maximizing profits and financial rewards. Many companies tried to do what was ethical. Yet the complex nature of the global economy prevented them from seeing the impending disaster, as everyone was too focused on their own bottom lines.

As the world continues to recover from the recession, conflicts and disasters have intensified the risks and challenges that global businesses will encounter. For instance, widespread changes are occurring in the Middle East. While democracy is becoming more of a possibility, instability within these regions has led to an exodus of foreign businesspeople.[11] The instability of Middle Eastern governments and their views toward global commerce could strain business relations. New technologies are also affecting regimes. For example, Egyptians used social media during a national uprising to communicate with one another and the world about political and social issues.[12] In many ways, the Egyptian protests were reflections of the widespread dissent felt throughout the region. Although it is possible that the protests will lead to positive long-term change, the economies of these countries may take some time to stabilize. Economic stability is affected by the supply and commodity price fluctuations caused by such political events. Changes in governments result in the necessity for new social and legal processes, processes that will support ethical and legal systems that fit into the global economy.

National disasters can also destabilize economies and affect the economic system. For example, the devastating 2011 earthquake and tsunami in Japan resulted in a destabilization of the economic and social institutions within that country. Japan also faced the challenge of a nuclear meltdown after the tsunami breached the seawall around the Fukushima Daiichi complex and damaged the reactors. The combined crises caused the Tokyo Stock Exchange to lose $700 billion within a three-day period.[13] The year before, massive earthquakes in Haiti and Chile had severely damaged those countries' economies.

Many ethical issues emerge in coping with crises. The disruption of necessities and global supply chains creates opportunities for individuals and organizations to engage in exploitation. For instance, an unethical organization might charge exorbitant prices during a time of crisis because the people are dependent upon its products for survival. Conversely, the global community is expected to engage in aid and philanthropic efforts to help countries recover from disasters. Corporations, particularly multinationals, are often expected to help in recovery efforts since many have profited from doing business within the affected countries.

Finally, the world is still coping with the aftereffects of the last global recession, which caused massive public distrust of the stability of governmental institutions as well as of those charged with managing the money of individuals, corporations, and countries. Some countries, such as Iceland, Zimbabwe, Hungary, Ukraine, and Serbia, even declared

> "Today people are discussing, and even revising, some of the fundamental concepts and assumptions of capitalism."

a form of bankruptcy as a result of the recession.[14] As a lack of trust, honesty, and fairness has caused major investors to question the competence of regulatory institutions, which in turn has caused instability and public mistrust in the entire financial system, many have questioned the foundations of capitalism and the policies needed to make it function. Today people are discussing, and even revising, some of the fundamental concepts and assumptions of capitalism. Because you will enter this new reality, we will briefly explain the global economic debate.

Economic Systems

To understand capitalism—and the types of businesses that operate in different types of economies—you must understand basic economic systems. These systems have a significant impact on business ethics, as they can determine the role of governments in business, the types of laws that regulate businesses, and the amount of freedom companies have in their activities. The main forms of capitalism and socialism are derived from the works of Adam Smith, John Maynard Keynes, and Milton Friedman.

Adam Smith was a professor of logic and moral philosophy during the late eighteenth century, as we noted earlier in this text, and he developed critical economic ideas that are still considered important today. Smith observed the supply and demand, contractual efficiency, and division of labor of various companies within England and wrote about what he saw. His idea of **laissez-faire**, or the "invisible hand," is critical to capitalism in that it assumes that the market, through its own inherent mechanisms, will keep commerce in equilibrium.

The second form of capitalism gained support at the beginning of the Great Depression. During the 1930s **John Maynard Keynes** argued that the state could stimulate economic growth and improve stability in the private sector—through, for example, controlling interest rates, taxation and public projects.[15] Keynes argued that government policies could be used to increase aggregate demand, thus increasing economic activity and reducing unemployment and deflation. He believed that the solution was to stimulate the economy through some combination of a reduction in interest rates and government investment in infrastructure. President Franklin D. Roosevelt employed Keynesian economic theories during his time in office when he was seeking to pull the United States out of the Great Depression.

The third and most recent form of capitalism is associated with **Milton Friedman,** and it represents a swing to the right of the political spectrum. Friedman had lived through the Great Depression but rejected the Keynesian conclusion that markets sometimes need intervention to function efficiently. Instead, he believed that deregulation could reach equilibrium without government intervention.[16] Friedman's ideas were the guiding principles for government policy making in the United States, and increasingly throughout the world, starting in the second half of the twentieth century.

Both Keynes and Friedman agreed that "(1) People have rational preferences among outcomes that can be identified and associated with a value; (2) Individuals maximize utility and firms maximize profits; (3) People act independently on the basis of full and relevant information."[17] Today, however, these assumptions are being questioned.

Socialism refers to economic theories advocating the creation of a society in which wealth and power are shared and distributed evenly based on the amount of work expended in production. Modern socialism originated in the late nineteenth century and was a working-class political movement that criticized the effects of industrialization and private ownership. Karl Marx was one of socialism's most famous and strongest advocates. Marxism was Marx's own interpretation of socialism, and it was transformed into communism in countries such as the Soviet Union and Cuba. History has shown that communism, strictly interpreted, causes economies to fail. For example, Cuba has traditionally held an antagonistic view toward capitalism and private enterprise. As a result, most of the population was employed in the public sector. However, during the most recent recession, the Cuban government realized it could not support so many workers. In an attempt to save its struggling economy, the government took the unprecedented step of laying off half a million state workers to make room for private sector jobs.[18] In the 1940s forms of **social democracy** emerged. Social democracy allows for the private ownership of property and also features a large government equipped to offer such services as education and health care to its citizens. Social democracies take on such problems as disease, ignorance, squalor, and idleness, and advocate governmental intervention. Scandinavian countries such as Denmark, Sweden, and Finland are examples of social democracies. Studies indicate that the populations of these small European democratic nations are some of the happiest in the world.[19]

Past economists could not have imagined the multinational corporation, or that the world's energy resources would be concentrated under the control of a handful of corporations. Our world has grown increasingly bimodal in wealth distribution. **Bimodal wealth distribution** occurs when the middle class shrinks, resulting in highly concentrated wealth amongst the rich and large numbers of poor people with very few resources. This is not a desirable scenario and can result in instability. The size and power of today's multinational corporations are immense. For instance, companies can pit one government against another for strategic advantages. One can see the same strategy by country group in trade blocs such as NAFTA (North American Free Trade Agreement), the EU (European Union), and ASEAN (Association of Southeast Nations). These trade blocs give economic leverage to country groups and use the same economic principles as multinationals. To understand the future global perspective, we next discuss the difference between rational and behavioral economics.

Rational economics is based upon the assumption that people are predictable and will maximize the utility of their choices relative to their needs and wants. For example, if you are hungry and have $10 to spend, rational economics suggests that you will spend the money on food that satisfies your hunger needs and wants (it tastes good). However, people are not always rational. For example, no one wants to go to jail. Even those who have stolen millions admit that the reward was probably not worth the punishment. Yet this does not stop individuals from engaging in crimes to secure short-term gains. For instance, as mentioned in Chapter 6, so-called fraud investigator Barry Minkow pleaded guilty to securities fraud as a result of trying to manipulate the stock of Lennar Corp. Minkow had already served seven years in prison after being convicted in 1988 of operating a Ponzi scheme through his business.[20] Minkow clearly did not act in a rational manner when he decided to commit another instance of securities fraud.

The second assumption is that people act independently on the basis of full and relevant information. Normally, we might assume that a criminal did not have full or relevant information concerning his/her actions. However, Minkow had already experienced prison time and, as a fraud investigator, likely knew the penalties he would face should he get caught. His example illustrates that some individuals will act irrationally even when they have a clear idea of the consequences of their actions. There are many individuals and organizations that are willing to take risks and act in an irrational manner to achieve their objectives. This high-risk approach often results in manipulation and misconduct.

Behavioral economics assumes that humans may not act rationally because of genetics, emotions, learned behavior, and heuristics, or rules of thumb. Heuristics are based upon past experiences and do not always yield the most rational response. In other words, behavioral economics assumes that economic decisions are influenced by human behavior. Figure 10.2 depicts where countries may be in the process of developing economic philosophies, and helps to understand where they may want to go. For example, China, Sweden, and the former Soviet Union are in the lower left quadrant, representing socialism as a society with behavioral economics as the vehicle to happiness. As we mentioned, each of these country's definitions of happiness is derived from social democratic goals. They are behavioral in that they believe very little in laissez-faire. The dates on the points are important, because they show that countries can change their positions over time. In the upper right quadrant, Figure 10.2 shows how certain countries' economies have defined happiness and government's role. Finally, in the upper left quadrant are the United States and (again) Sweden, representing Sweden's shift to capitalism and more laissez-faire economics and the United States' shift to a less laissez-faire economy.

The conflict between capitalism and socialism stems partly from the Cold War. Many in the United States perceive socialism as Marxism; it is not. Outside the United States, socialism is often perceived as group-oriented, as it relates to social problems. Socialism argues for the good of the community, with government helping people through manipulation of the economy. The American form of capitalism is grounded

FIGURE 10.2 The Economic Capitalism Country Differential

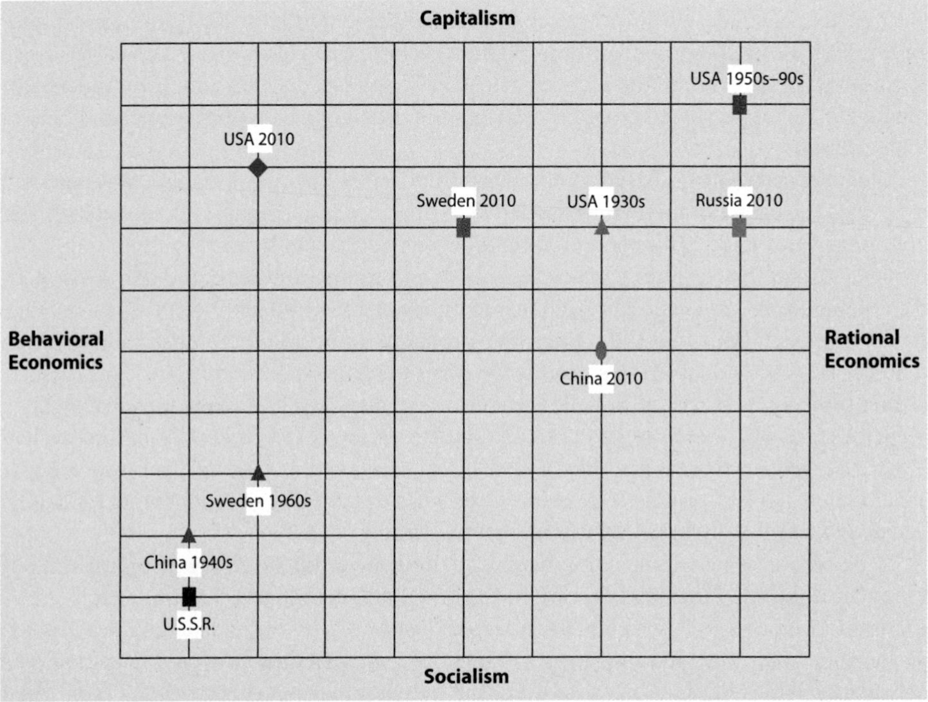

©Cengage Learning 2013

in individualism, where government is perceived as more of a hindrance in the pursuit of happiness.

Today, capitalism is one of the United States' many cultural exports. But while the United States practices one kind of capitalism, there are many other forms. The success of the U.S. model of capitalism during the 1990s and 2000s led many businesses and countries to champion it as the premier economic model. However, the last recession, combined with the collapse of some of the world's largest financial firms, has dampened global enthusiasm for this model. It is likely that in the future, more attention will be paid to other forms of capitalism.[21]

Sweden was one of the poorest countries in Western Europe in the 1880s. During the 1890s, it became more worker friendly. From 1918 to 1970, Sweden's standard of living rose faster than most countries'.[22] After 1970 the country changed some of its worker policies to become more corporate friendly and has continued to enjoy one of the highest standards of living in the world.

India and China have introduced the free market into their systems, although their models are very different. China has a very large communist government that blurs the lines between organizations, businesses, and government because organizations must comply with government mandates. India, on the other hand, is democratic and has a lively civil society that often is empowered to stand up against the government and capitalism. These two countries represent about one-third of the world's population and are considered rising powers—yet their forms of capitalism are radically dissimilar. China's government involvement in business, combined with the rapid growth of its economy, may cause us to question the notion that large governments stand in the way of business success—in fact, in China government often seems to be the premier entrepreneur.[23] In 2010 China superseded Japan to become the world's second largest economy.[24]

Is capitalism with minimal government interaction and the free flow of goods and services across national boundaries best? Or should governments be more protectionist to give local businesses the upper hand? Economists are still searching for the answer. On the one hand, corporations can create competitive barriers via government legislation or by collusion to form oligopolies for managed competition. The argument is that without government intervention, local businesses could decline. On the other hand, certain forms of capitalism argue that the corporation should pay shareholders as much as possible and that other stakeholders are of secondary importance.

Despite these differing viewpoints, there is a general consensus amongst experts, academics, and businesspeople that corporations that operate with social responsibility in mind must take into account the norms and mores of the societies in which they operate. Corporations may take varying views of corporate social responsibility (CSR).[25] A broad view would include thinking about the consequences of their actions on a wide range of stakeholders and using the corporation as a tool for public policy, while a very narrow view would involve only looking at the number of jobs created, for example. These are some of the ethical questions that businesses and governments need to address as they operate on a globalized scale. There is no agreement that one form of free-market system is more ethical than others. Ethical business systems are not restricted to capitalist models, either; socialist countries also develop ethical businesses. Countries, institutions, social systems, technology, and other cultural factors can have a major effect on organizational ethics. To better understand global ethics, we start by examining some of the ethical dimensions surrounding multinational firms.

MULTINATIONAL CORPORATION

Multinational corporations (MNCs) are public companies that operate on a global scale without significant ties to any one nation or region. MNCs represent the highest level of international business commitment and are characterized by a global strategy of focusing on opportunities throughout the world. Examples of U.S.–based multinational corporations include Nike, Monsanto, and Cisco Systems. Some of these firms have grown so large that they generate higher revenues than the gross domestic product (GDP)—the sum of all the goods and services produced in a country during one year—of some of the countries in which they do business, as shown in Table 10.1.

Based on revenues versus GDP, Wal-Mart Stores, Inc., is greater in size than the economies of Greece and Denmark, and both Wal-Mart and Royal Dutch Shell are larger than the economy of Denmark. Because of their size and financial power, MNCs have been the subject of much ethical debate, and their impact on the countries in which they do business has been controversial. Both American and European labor unions argue that it is unfair for MNCs to transfer jobs overseas to countries where wage rates are lower. Other critics have charged that multinationals use labor-saving devices that increase unemployment in the countries where they manufacture. MNCs have been accused of increasing the gap between rich and poor nations and of misusing and misallocating scarce resources. Their size and financial clout enable them to control money, supplies, employment, and even the economic well-being of less-developed countries. In some instances, MNCs have controlled entire cultures and countries. For example, a Los Angeles judge determined that former petroleum exporter Unocal may be liable for the conduct of the Myanmar government

TABLE 10.1 A Comparison Between Countries and Corporations Based on Gross Domestic Products and Revenues

Country	GDP (millions $ U.S.)*	Company	Revenues (millions $ U.S.)
United States	14,720,000	Wal-Mart Stores	421,849.0
China	9,872,000	Royal Dutch Shell	378,152
Japan	4,338,000	Exxon Mobil	354,674
India	4,046,000	BP	308,928
Germany	2,960,000	Sinopec Group	221,760
Iran	863,500	China National Petroleum	203,958
Taiwan	823,600	State Grid	273,422
Argentina	596,000	Toyota Motor	226,294
Greece	321,700	Japan Post Holdings	196,337
Denmark	201,400	Chevron	240,192

*2010 estimates

Source: Adapted from "Global 500: Fortune's Annual Ranking of the World's Largest Corporations," *CNNMoney*, http://money.cnn.com/magazines/fortune/global500/2011/index.html (accessed July 7, 2011). CIA *World Fact Book*, https://www.cia.gov/library/publications/the-world-factbook/rankorder/rankorderguide.html (accessed March 25, 2011).

after documents presented in court suggested that forced labor was used in Myanmar to build Unocal projects. According to documents, workers who refused to work were imprisoned and/or executed by the Myanmar army. Unocal's financial size and willingness to complete certain projects at any cost prompted the Myanmar government to sanction the use of forced labor.[26] Years later, Unocal announced that it had reached a final settlement with the parties.[27]

Critics believe that the size and power of MNCs create ethical issues involving the exploitation of both natural and human resources. One question is whether MNCs should be able to pay a low price for the right to remove minerals, timber, oil, and other natural resources, and then sell products made from those resources for a much higher price. In many instances, only a small fraction of the ultimate sale price of such resources comes back to benefit the country of origin. This complaint led many oil-producing countries to form the Organization of Petroleum Exporting Countries (OPEC) in the 1960s to gain control over the revenues from oil produced in those lands.

> "Critics believe that the size and power of MNCs create ethical issues involving the exploitation of both natural and human resources."

Critics also accuse MNCs of exploiting the labor markets of host countries. As noted earlier, MNCs have been accused of paying inadequate wages. Sometimes MNCs pay higher wages than local employers can afford to match; then local businesses complain that the most productive and skilled workers go to work for multinationals. Measures have been taken to curtail such practices. For example, host governments have levied import taxes that increase the prices that MNCs charge for their products and reduce their profits. Import taxes are meant to favor local industry as sources of supply for an MNC manufacturing in the host country. If such a tax raises the MNC's costs, it might lead the MNC to charge higher prices or accept lower profits, but such effects are not the fundamental goal of the law. Host governments also have imposed export taxes on MNCs to force them to share more of their profits.

The activities of MNCs also raise issues of unfair competition. Because of their diversified nature, MNCs can borrow money from local capital markets in much higher volume than smaller local firms. MNCs also have been accused of failing to carry an appropriate share of the cost of social development. They frequently apply advanced, high-productivity technologies that local companies cannot afford or cannot implement because they lack qualified workers. The MNCs thus become more productive and can afford to pay higher wages to workers. Because of their technology, however, they require fewer employees than the local firms would hire to produce the same product. Additionally, given their economies of scale, MNCs also can negotiate lower tax rates. By manipulating transfer payments among their affiliates, they pay fewer taxes. All these special advantages explain why some claim that MNCs compete unfairly.

Sometimes countries refuse outright to allow MNCs into their countries. For example, heavy-equipment companies from industrialized nations argue that their equipment will make it possible to complete infrastructure projects sooner, which could help boost the economies of less-developed countries. However, countries such as India believe that it is better in the long run to hire laborers to do construction work since this practice provides much-needed employment and keeps currency within the local economy. Therefore, they often choose to use local laborers instead of purchasing equipment from foreign countries.

Although it is usually MNCs' unethical or illegal conduct that grabs world headlines, some MNCs also strive to be good global citizens with strong ethical values. Texas Instruments (TI), for example, has adopted a three-tiered global approach to ethical integrity that asks: "(1) Are we complying with all legal requirements on a local level? (2) Are there business practices or requirements at the local level that affect how we interact with co-workers in other parts of the world? (3) Do some of our practices need to be adapted based on the local laws and customs of a specific locale? On what basis do we define the universal standards that apply to TI employees everywhere?"[28] One of the ways Texas Instruments puts this approach into practice is by specifying rules on excessive gift giving. Since what is considered to be "excessive" tends to vary depending on country, Texas Instruments has adopted an approach that forbids gift-giving "in a way that exerts undue pressure to win business or implies a quid-pro-quo [sic]."[29]

Many companies, including Coca-Cola, DuPont, Hewlett-Packard, Levi Strauss & Co., Texaco, and Walmart, endorse following responsible business practices abroad. These companies support a globally based resource system called **Business for Social Responsibility** (BSR). BSR tracks emerging issues and trends, provides information on corporate leadership and best practices, conducts educational workshops and training, and assists organizations in developing practical business ethics tools. It addresses such issues as community investment, corporate social responsibility, the environment, governance, and accountability. BSR also has established formal partnerships with other organizations that focus on corporate responsibility in Brazil, Israel, the United Kingdom, Chile, and Panama.[30]

Although MNCs are not inherently unethical, their size and power often seem threatening to people and businesses in less-developed countries. The ethical problems that MNCs face arise from the opposing viewpoints inherent in multicultural situations. Differences in cultural perspectives may be as important as differences in economic interests. Because of their size and power, MNCs must therefore take extra care to make ethical decisions that not only achieve their own objectives, but also benefit the countries where they manufacture or market their products. Even the most respected MNCs sometimes find themselves in ethical conflict and face liability as a result.

The U.S. model of the MNC is fading as developing countries such as China, India, Brazil, and South Korea form MNCs as alliances, joint ventures, and wholly owned subsidiaries.[31] The turn away from the American model does not mean less concern for ethics and social responsibility. As corporations expand internationally, ethics and social responsibility are important firm-specific capabilities that can be a resource and lend a company an advantage for growth and profit. The development of trust and corporate citizenship is a necessary capability, much like technology or marketing. A number of Chinese businesses, for example, have learned that long-term success cannot be achieved by selling products that are unsafe or of inferior quality. Ethical and responsible business conduct is a requirement for long-term success in global business. As a result, several global organizations have been formed to support global cooperation and responsible business practices.

GLOBAL COOPERATION TO SUPPORT RESPONSIBLE BUSINESS

International Monetary Fund

The **International Monetary Fund** (IMF) originated from the Bretton Woods agreement of July 1944, in which a group of international leaders decided that the primary responsibility for the regulation of monetary relationships among national economies should rest in an extranational body, the IMF. The IMF makes short-term loans to member countries that have deficits and provides foreign currencies for its members. The IMF also provides information about countries that might not be able to repay their debts. Member states provide resources to fund the IMF through a system of quotas that are proportional to the size of their respective economies. Member states also receive IMF voting power relative to these quota contributions. Under this rule, the United States has just under one-fifth of the votes. The IMF has become the international coordinator of regulatory policy for the world.

Although the IMF's main function is to regulate monetary relationships between national economies, the organization also has taken steps to promote responsible global business conduct. For instance, the IMF has suggested that governments adopt a "binding code of conduct across nations" to determine the conditions necessary for interceding in troubled firms and how to share losses from financial institutions operating across multiple borders. The IMF has also recommended new regulations for large firms that pose the biggest "systemic risk."[32] The concept of risk and IMF bailouts took on significant importance during the last global recession. Because of a massive amount of debt, the European countries of Greece, Ireland, and Portugal required major bailout packages from the IMF. These bailouts had a negative economic impact that was felt throughout the European Union.[33]

United Nations Global Compact

The United Nations (UN) was founded in 1945 by 51 nations. Its goals are to promote worldwide peace, establish beneficial relationships between countries, and support the creation of better standards and human rights on a global scale. Today, the UN includes 192 member states from across the world. Although the United Nations is generally thought of as a peacekeeping organization, this coalition of diverse countries also focuses extensively on sustainable development, human rights and gender equality, global environmental issues, and more.[34] Another major concern for the UN is business development. Recognizing that business is "a primary driver in globalization," the UN views business as a way to increase the economic outlook of countries, help create equality with fair labor practices, combat corruption, and promote environmental sustainability.[35] Conversely, unethical businesses that go global just to take advantage of favorable factors such as cheap labor could have the opposite effect.

To support business as a driver for positive change, the UN created the **United Nations Global Compact,** a set of 10 principles that promote human rights, sustainability, and the eradication of corruption. Table 10.2 gives a brief description of these principles. Above all, the UN hopes that the Global Compact will create a collaborative arrangement among businesses, governments, nongovernmental organizations, societies, and the United Nations to overcome challenges and advocate for positive economic, social, and political change. The Global Compact is voluntary for organizations. However, those that join are held accountable, and are required to annually post the organization's progress toward Global Compact goals and show commitment to UN guiding principles. Global members are also expected to cooperate with the UN on social projects within developing nations in which they do business. More than 8,700 entities participate in the UN Global Compact.[36]

While global business ethics is essential knowledge for companies, it is also critical knowledge for business students. The Association to Advance Collegiate Schools of Business (AACSB) International, an international organization that represents about 1,200 business schools, joined with groups such as the UN Global Compact to inspire a set of six principles for business schools. These principles are encapsulated under the title "Principles for

TABLE 10.2 Ten Principles of the UN Global Compact for Businesses

- Support and respect the protection of internationally proclaimed human rights
- Ensure that businesses are not complicit in human rights abuses
- Uphold the freedom of association and the right to collective bargaining
- Work toward the elimination of forced and compulsory labor
- Work toward the abolition of child labor
- Eliminate discrimination in employment and occupation
- Support a precautionary approach to environmental challenges
- Undertake initiatives toward greater environmental responsibility
- Work toward the development and diffusion of environmentally friendly technologies
- Resist corruption of all forms, including extortion and bribery

Source: "The Ten Principles," United Nations Global Compact, http://www.unglobalcompact.org/AboutTheGC/TheTenPrinciples/index.html (accessed March 25, 2011).

Responsible Management Education."[37] The first principle encourages students to become future leaders in creating sustainable value for business, society, and the global economy. Other principles include incorporating global social responsibility into curricula; creating educational materials that cultivate responsible leaders; and encouraging dialogue among educators, students, businesses, and other stakeholders to address social responsibility and sustainability issues. The Principles for Responsible Management Education are powerfully influenced by the idea of sustainable development and corporate social responsibility.[38]

World Trade Organization (WTO)

The **World Trade Organization** (WTO) was established in 1995 at the Uruguay round of negotiations of the General Agreement on Tariffs and Trade (GATT). Today, the WTO has 153 member and observer nations. On behalf of its membership, the WTO administers its own trade agreements, facilitates trade negotiations, settles trade disputes, and monitors the trade policies of member nations. The WTO addresses economic and social issues involving agriculture, textiles and clothing, banking, telecommunications, government purchases, industrial standards, food sanitation regulations, services, and intellectual property. It also provides legally binding ground rules for international commerce and trade policy. The organization attempts to reduce barriers to trade between and within nations and to settle trade disputes. For instance, the WTO ruled in favor of China in a trade dispute against the European Union. The EU believed that China was dumping its Chinese-manufactured steel fasteners into the EU market. **Dumping** is the practice of charging high prices for products in domestic markets while selling the same products in foreign markets at low prices, often at below cost. It places local firms at a disadvantage and is therefore illegal in many countries. In response, the EU instituted a tariff of 63 to 87 percent on Chinese-manufactured steel fasteners. The dispute was brought to the WTO, which ruled that the extremely high tariffs were unfair and discriminatory against Chinese manufacturers.[39]

Not all countries have agreed with the WTO's particular stance on free trade. In the past few years, import tariffs have been increased on Asian plastic bags in Europe; oil in

South Korea; Chinese steel pipes in the United States; and all imports in Ukraine. According to the WTO, shoes, cars, and steel are among the goods most vulnerable to protectionism, or trade restrictions among countries.[40] During global downturns, such as the last global recession, countries tend to restrict trading. However, many firms find ways to get around tariffs. For example, if a company wants instant free trade access to the United States, it can manufacture in Israel. If the company wants free trade access for low-tech products to the EU, the company can manufacture in the African country of Senegal because of its free trade agreement with France. Companies with the right knowledge can find a number of bypasses around tariffs, particularly as trading blocs such as the EU continue to grow.[41]

GLOBAL ETHICS ISSUES

In this section we focus on issues that have a dramatic impact upon global business, including risks, bribery, antitrust activities, and Internet security and privacy. We also discuss fundamental rights such as human rights, health care, labor, and compensation, as well as the issue of consumerism. Bribery and antitrust issues are among the most targeted areas of concern for governments worldwide. However, human and labor rights are some of the more commonly abused in global business environments.

Global Ethical Risks

Although globalization has many benefits, it is not without risks. Risk creates ethical issues for global companies to manage. The organization known as the Eurasia Group has identified 10 key areas of international risk. According to the Carnegie Council, four of these risks require organizations to make "fundamental ethical choices" when doing business globally. These risks are described as follows.

- The "G-Zero" risk refers to the idea that countries are increasingly opting to advance their own interests through nationalistic policies instead of adopting more globalized forms of leadership. We see this reflected in businesses with an "us versus them" point of view. If this trend continues, it could affect trade and business with increases in tariffs and taxes.

- Internet security and privacy are becoming key issues for governments and businesses alike. While some cyberattacks are state or government sponsored, cyberattacks from smaller entities such as WikiLeaks are also becoming a threat. The WikiLeaks scandal has taken on great importance because it brings up the question of security versus freedom of speech.

- Relations with China are becoming increasingly strained, and the Chinese government's reluctance to make quick policy changes and its regulations limiting foreign companies could place additional burdens on businesses.

- Emerging markets offer many opportunities for investors but are not without significant risks. Political unrest, imbalances in power, nationalism, and faltering economies represent major risks for global businesses hoping to invest in these areas of the world.[42]

TABLE 10.3 Global Business Ethics and Legal Issues

U.S. Ranking	European Ranking	Important Issues
1	1	Code of Conduct
2	5	U.S. Antitrust
3	3	Mutual Respect
4	7	U.S. Foreign Corrupt Practices Act (FCPA)
5	4	Conflicts of Interest and Gifts
6	9	Proper Use of Computers
7		Insider Trading
8	6	Financial Integrity
9		Confidentiality
10		Records Management
11		Labor and Employment Law
12	8	Intellectual Property
	2	Global Competition Law
	10	Global Antibribery Requirements
	11	Ethics and Values
	12	Export Controls

Source: Adapted from Integrity Interactive Corporation, "Top Compliance Concerns of Global Companies," http://www.i2c.com (accessed March 20, 2011).

Corporations worldwide have become more global in their compliance actions. Table 10.3 represents a compilation of important compliance issues of global companies based in the United States and in the European Union. Global competition laws, antibribery requirements, ethics and values, and export controls are considered to be more relevant by the EU than confidentiality, records management, and labor and employment laws. These differences give us clues as to what types of laws governments will be formulating in the future.

Bribery

Bribery is a difficult topic because its acceptance varies from country to country. While bribery between businesses is illegal in countries such as the United States, it is an accepted way of doing business in other countries. Today, most developed countries recognize that bribery is not a responsible or fair way of conducting business. It has the potential to damage consumers and competition. But companies must determine what constitutes a bribe. In Japan it is considered courteous to present a small gift before doing business. Are such gifts bribes or merely acts of gratitude? Without clear guidelines, the topic of bribery remains ambiguous enough for misconduct to occur. For this reason, both the United States and the United Kingdom have passed regulations defining bribery and set legal precedents for businesses that encounter these situations.

U.S. FOREIGN CORRUPT PRACTICES ACT (FCPA)

U.S. FOREIGN CORRUPT PRACTICES ACT (FCPA) The U.S. Foreign Corrupt Practices Act (FCPA) prohibits American companies from making payments to foreign officials for the purpose of obtaining or retaining business. In 1988 Congress became concerned that American companies were operating at a disadvantage compared to foreign companies whose governments do not forbid bribes. In 1998 the United States and 33 other countries signed an agreement intended to combat the practice of bribing of foreign public officials in international business transactions, with an exception for payments made to facilitate or expedite routine governmental actions (known as facilitation or "grease" payments). Prosecution of bribery has increased, with the U.S. Justice Department making violations of the FCPA a top priority.

Bribery has become a problem for some major corporations. IBM, Daimler AG, and Monsanto were all charged with violating the FCPA and paid heavy fines. Although sometimes bribery is done with the full compliance of top management, larger companies with multiple branches, global operations, and many employees have a harder time detecting misconduct such as bribery. The FCPA was modified recently and now provides a "best practices" guide for companies. The change was prompted by two major cases. In one case, RAE Systems Chinese joint ventures paid about $400,000 to Chinese officials in exchange for contracts worth $3 million. The company's sales force used cash advances to fund the bribes. The SEC claimed that RAE lacked solid internal controls and that it failed to respond to red flags. The other case related to the company Panalpina and also involved bribery. [43] The resulting settlements led to the creation of guidelines that can be used by the U.S. Department of Justice and the Securities and Exchange Commission in assessing FCPA compliance. The guidelines can also be helpful for businesses to ensure that they are complying with the Foreign Corrupt Practices Act. These guidelines are outlined in Table 10.4.

TABLE 10.4 FCPA "Best Practices" for Compliance Guidelines

The development of clear policies against FCPA violations
Support by senior management for the company's compliance policy
The development of standards and policies relating to the acceptance of gifts, hospitality, entertainment, expenses, customer travel, political contributions, charitable donations and sponsorships, facilitation payments, solicitation, and extortion
The development of compliance procedures that include risk assessment and internal controls
Annual reviews of compliance procedures and updates when needed
The development of appropriate financial and accounting procedures
The implementation of policies to properly communicate procedures to directors, officers, employees, and other appropriate stakeholders
The establishment of a system that provides legal guidance to appropriate stakeholders
Disciplinary procedures for violations of anticorruption rules
The exercise of due diligence to ensure compliance with anticorruption policies
The inclusion of anticorruption provisions in agreements and contracts with suppliers, agents, and other partners
Periodic reviews of codes and procedures to ensure they measure up to FCPA regulations
Prompt reporting of violations to the SEC

Source: Adapted from "U.S. Securities and Exchange Commission and Department of Justice Clarify 'Best Practices' for FCPA Compliance," *Mayer Brown*, January 11, 2011.

Violations of the act can result in individual fines of $100,000 and jail time. Penalties for companies can reach into the millions.[44] Some FCPA violations are easier to detect than others. For example, some of the riskiest practices include payment for airline tickets, hotel and meal expenses of traveling foreign officials, the wiring of payments to accounts in offshore tax havens, and the hiring of agents recommended by government officials to perform "consulting" services.[45] Current enforcement agencies are targeting these third-party bribery payments.

U.K. ANTIBRIBERY ACT   Many nations, including China and European nations, are taking a tougher stance against bribery. However, the United Kingdom has instituted perhaps the most sweeping antibribery legislation to date.[46] The U.K.'s new Antibribery Act will likely cause companies doing business in the U.K. to dramatically change their compliance reports. While the act overlaps with the U.S. Foreign Corrupt Practices Act, it takes further steps to curb bribery. For example, under the law British residents and businesses, as well as foreign companies with operations in the U.K., can all be held liable for bribery, no matter where the offense is committed or who in the company commits the act, even if the bribe itself has no connection with the U.K. Unlike under the FCPA, companies are not required to have explicit knowledge of a bribe to be held criminally liable.[47] Additionally, the Antibribery Act classifies bribes between private businesspeople as illegal and does not make provisions similar to those in the FCPA allowing for "grease payments"—small payments used to speed up services that otherwise would be delayed. Another part of the law requires corporations to find out whether their subsidiaries or joint-venture partners are involved in bribery at any level.[48] The act has increased the maximum jail time for bribery from seven to 10 years.[49]

> "Many nations, including China and European nations, are taking a tougher stance against bribery."

Such encompassing provisions against bribery have created concern for businesses that operate in the United Kingdom. Some fear that something as simple as taking a business client out to dinner will be considered a bribe under U.K. law. However, U.K. officials and legal experts have stated that acts of hospitality will not be considered illegal. Additionally, businesses can protect themselves from heavy penalties by instituting an effective compliance program that management supports. In other words, managers should set the correct tone at the top along with implementing proper reporting procedures, periodic reviews of the company's code of conduct and compliance programs, risk assessments, and other policies discussed in this book and outlined in the U.S. Federal Sentencing Guidelines.[50] Some legal experts question whether the Serious Fraud Office in the U.K. will choose to prosecute cases that deal with small "grease" payments or prosecute cases that occur outside the United Kingdom.[51]

Antitrust Activity

Fair competition is viewed favorably in many countries, with the belief that competition yields the best products and services at the best prices. This basic concept of capitalism has begun to change, however. During the nineteenth and early twentieth centuries, U.S. corporations began using what today would be considered anticompetitive practices, creating high barriers of entry for competitors in an attempt to dominate markets. These practices led to higher prices and fewer options for consumers. In 1890 the United States passed the Sherman Antitrust Act to prevent such anticompetitive behavior. Other countries have similar laws. However, issues of competition become more complicated when companies do business in different countries with differing laws. For instance, the EU has stricter antitrust laws than does the United States, which makes it harder for some MNCs to compete in Europe. EU antitrust probes have been launched against Google, Microsoft, and IBM, among other companies.

Because large MNCs create economies of scale and barriers to entry, they tend to reduce overall competition and can put smaller companies out of business. If these firms continue to remain unregulated, they could engage in a vertical systems approach to become monopolies. A **vertical system** is where a channel member (manufacturer, wholesaler, distributor, or retailer) has control of the entire business system, via ownership or contract, or through its purchasing ability. Vertical systems create inertia, which causes channel members to stay with their various retailers and distributors even though competitors may have better products and prices. Sometimes MNCs use their size to coerce other companies to do business exclusively with them. For instance, the EU charged Intel $1.45 billion for anticompetitive behavior. Intel had allegedly provided rebates to retailers if they bought only their computer chips, as well as paying manufacturers for delaying or restricting the distribution of products from their main rival, Advanced Micro Devices (AMD).[52]

Internet Security and Privacy

Earlier, we mentioned Internet security as one of the top 10 global risks. Today's computer hackers can use tools like the Internet and computer viruses to commit corporate espionage, launch cyberattacks against government infrastructures, and steal confidential information.[53] Until recently, Internet security has not been a significant part of business ethics. However, serious Internet crimes have brought this issue to the public's attention. Computer hackers have become particularly problematic in the United States and China. For example, in China two computer hackers created a hacking device known as the "Panda Burns Incense" worm, which they used to steal information that they sold to other hackers in their network. The worm showed up in people's emails posing as a harmless message that fooled recipients into opening it. Once a computer was infected, every desktop icon would become a picture of a panda holding three incense sticks. If the user clicked on the panda, the worm would collect passwords and financial information and relay it back to the senders. Although the two original perpetrators were finally caught, copycat versions and more advanced viruses have since been launched.[54]

Hacking, Trojan horses (devices that look desirable but that steal information once installed), and worms are not necessarily illegal in some countries. However, the global community has begun to classify many such practices as unethical, arguing they should become illegal. Although companies are developing software to track down viruses and malware and keep them from infecting computers, hackers are constantly creating new ways to bypass these systems. In addition, many companies themselves use questionable Internet practices that may not be illegal but could be construed as unethical. For instance, many websites that users visit install cookies, or small identifying strings of text, onto their computers. This allows the website to identify the user's computer when he or she revisits the site. These companies use cookies as a way to tailor their offerings to specific users. For example, Amazon.com uses cookies to make product recommendations to users when they return to their website. Despite the consumer convenience and competitive advantages of cookies, being able to identify users without their consent or direct knowledge may create an ethical issue: privacy.

While some Internet privacy violations, such as breaking into users' accounts and stealing their financial information, are clearly unethical, many other situations present more challenging ethical dilemmas. For instance, WikiLeaks is a nonprofit organization that publishes information provided by whistle-blowers, leaks, and news sources. Although it has been praised for revealing injustice and creating a more transparent news environment, the site has come under scrutiny for leaking confidential U.S. documents. U.S. government officials launched a criminal investigation into WikiLeaks and claimed that the confidential information it revealed on subjects such as the war in Afghanistan could put soldiers at risk. However, legal experts suggest that the First Amendment right to freedom of speech likely will prevail as long as WikiLeaks does not pay for or collect the information itself.[55] Such conflicts between freedom of speech and revealing confidential information that could threaten national security are significant ethical issues that require greater scrutiny by lawmakers.

Another ethical dilemma regarding privacy is the use of personal information by companies. Facebook, the most popular social networking site worldwide, has been criticized for lax privacy policies and for making member information too public. Privacy has become such a concern that governments have begun considering new legislation to regulate information collection on the Internet. For instance, the United States government is debating on whether to create a "Do Not Track" bill for the Internet to limit what types of information websites are allowed to track.[56] This pending legislation is prompting advertising firms to engage in self-regulation for digital advertising, and both Google and Facebook have spent money to lobby against government intervention.[57]

In countries such as Saudi Arabia and China, Internet privacy is not just a corporate issue. Rather, governments take an active role in censoring citizens' use of the Internet. For instance, Saudi Arabia nearly banned BlackBerry smartphones because Blackberrys use overseas routing. Overseas routing gives the government less control, and Saudi Arabia feared that it would allow third parties outside the country to gain access to encrypted messages. The Saudi government also censors websites and provides users with online messages telling them that they have been denied access to a particular site.[58] The Chinese government routinely uses an Internet-filtering system called the "Great Firewall" to censor Internet sites. It often does not tell its citizens when it is censoring materials. Instead, the filtering looks like a technical glitch. Some networks, such as YouTube and Facebook, are blocked completely. This has made it difficult for foreign businesses such as Google, which adheres to a "Don't Be Evil" policy, to justify doing business with China. Google has experienced repeated clashes with the Chinese government over censorship, including accusations that the government disrupted the company's email services among its Chinese users.[59] These scenarios demonstrate some of the types of ethical issues that companies encounter when conducting business globally.

Human Rights

The meaning of the term **human rights** has been codified in a UN document, in which it is defined as an inherent dignity with equal and inalienable rights and the foundation of freedom, justice, and peace in the world. The concept of human rights is not new in business. It was established decades ago, but few companies took it into consideration until recently. Table 10.5 presents three articles from the UN Human Rights Declaration. Their implementation in the world of business can have serious ethical ramifications. For example, Article 18 concerns freedom of religion. From a Western perspective this appears to be straightforward. However, how should firms respond to employees from countries where it is acceptable to have multiple wives? Should they all be granted health insurance?

TABLE 10.5 Selected Articles from the UN Human Rights Declaration

Article 18. Freedom of religion … either alone or in community … in public or private …

Article 23. The right to work … to just and favorable conditions of work and to protection against unemployment … equal pay for equal work … ensuring for himself and his family an existence worthy of human dignity … right to form and to join trade unions …

Article 25. Right to a standard of living adequate for the health and well-being … Motherhood and childhood are entitled to special care and assistance.

Source: United Nations Human Rights Declaration, http://www.un.org/en/rights/ (accessed June 22, 2009).

In response to such challenges, Ford Motor Co. started the Ford Interfaith Network to educate employees about different religions and foster respect for the beliefs of its diverse employees across the world.[60] However, for a worker in Saudi Arabia, such an interfaith group does not exist. The Saudi government prohibits the public practice of non-Muslim religions. In general, it recognizes the right of non-Muslims to worship in private; however, this right is not extended to the public domain. Within Saudi Arabia, freedom of religion is not legally defined.

Health Care

Another ethical issue that is gaining in importance is health care. Globally, a billion people lack access to health care systems, and about 11 million children under the age of five die from malnutrition and preventable diseases each year.[61] As a result, global concern about the priorities of pharmaceutical companies is on the rise. This ethical dilemma involves profits versus health care. Those who believe pharmaceutical companies are inherently unethical suggest that the quest for profits has led these companies to research drugs aimed at markets that can afford luxuries, such as cures for baldness or impotence, rather than focusing on cures for widespread deadly diseases such as malaria, HIV, and AIDS. Patents are another challenging issue. Since patents give pharmaceutical companies exclusive rights to their products for a certain period, the companies can charge higher prices—prices that those in emerging economies cannot often afford. A documentary released by True Vision, an international documentary film company, featured a child in Honduras who ultimately died from the ravages of AIDS. Pfizer produces one of the drugs he needed, but it cost $29 per tablet. The family only earned $19 a week. The generic version of the drug was cheaper in neighboring Guatemala, but the maker of that form of the drug had no license to produce or sell in Honduras.[62]

On the other hand, pharmaceutical companies argue that high prices are needed to recoup the costs of creating the drugs, and without profits their companies would not be able to function. Another argument is that since other firms are allowed to patent their products, pharmaceutical companies should be allowed the same privileges. Yet when the issue is one of life or death, businesses must find ways to balance profitability with human need.

A related issue affecting both developing and developed countries is the affordability of health care. Rising health care costs continue to pose a critical challenge, particularly in the United States, where millions of people remain uninsured. Studies have revealed that the United States spends more per capita on health care than other industrialized countries—but without better results to show for it. Prices of health care products and procedures can vary greatly within the country.[63] When health care becomes too costly, businesses tend to either

DEBATE ISSUE   TAKE A STAND

Is Health Care a Right or a Privilege?

The Universal Declaration of Human Rights, adopted by the United Nations in 1948, proclaims that "everyone has the right to a standard of living adequate for the health and well-being of oneself and one's family, including food, clothing, housing, and medical care." Hard work and healthy living does not assure being healthy. With the high costs of health care, many consumers cannot afford health insurance. The U.S. government plans to follow other industrialized nations in adopting universal health care.

However, critics argue that it is the individual's responsibility, not the government's, to ensure personal health. Many health problems, such as obesity and diabetes, can often be prevented by individuals choosing to live healthier lifestyles. Another concern involves the cost of health care. Critics believe universal health insurance will increase costs because more people will depend upon the government for health care. This in turn might cause costs to be passed onto the consumers and prompt the government to limit certain types of care. Guaranteeing health care for all may lead people to make riskier decisions because they know that if they get hurt, they are guaranteed health care coverage.

1. Because health care protects life, it is a fundamental right and should therefore be ensured by the federal government.

2. Health care is a privilege and should not be provided by the government because of the high costs involved.

drop health care packages offered to employees or downgrade to less expensive—and less inclusive—packages. For instance, some unions, companies, and insurers have begun dropping mental health care plans due to a law that states mental health care, if offered, must be as "robust" as the rest of the medical benefits. Rather than offer the more costly mental health benefits, companies are choosing to drop them entirely.[64]

Global health care fraud is a serious ethics issue, costing businesses and governments millions and depriving individuals of funds needed for critical care. One estimate places the losses from global health care fraud at $260 billion annually.[65] Fraud can include providing less medicine in packages for the same price, filing false Medicare claims, and providing kickbacks for referrals, and it can be committed by individuals, companies, doctors, and pharmacists. Insurance companies are not immune, either. The Justice Department filed charges against Blue Cross Blue Shield of Michigan for allegedly creating illegal agreements with state hospitals. According to these agreements, hospitals would charge patients insured by Blue Cross's rivals equal or higher prices for the same procedures. This would make Blue Cross look less expensive and therefore more attractive to patients.[66]

The fundamental issue leading some businesses into ethical and legal trouble around the world is the question of whether health care is a right or a privilege. For example, many people in the United States see health care as a privilege, not a right; thus, it is the responsibility of individuals to provide for themselves. People in other countries, such as Germany, consider it a right. German employees have been guaranteed access to high-quality, comprehensive health care since 1883.[67] Many countries believe health care is important because it increases productivity; therefore, governments ought to provide it. As health care costs continue to increase, the burden for providing it falls on companies, countries, employees, or all three.

Labor and the Right to Work

Another global issue that businesses encounter is labor. Today, many people live and work in a country other than their homeland. In the European Union, workers can carry benefits across countries within the EU without any reductions or changes. Many are therefore asking the question, "Am I a multinational employee first and then a citizen of a country, or am I a citizen first and an employee second?" Because businesses must make a profit, there are increasing occasions when nationality no longer is a deciding factor. In business, we are becoming global citizens. As a result, firms need to understand that certain employee issues, once country-specific, have become global.

One example of a global labor issue involves gender pay inequality. This debate has spread throughout the globe, in both developing and industrialized countries. For instance, a report from the United Nations Development Programme found that female computer programmers in Singapore earn 80 percent of what male workers earn in comparable jobs. Similarly, female computer programmers in Korea earn 90 percent of what male computer programmers earn.[68] Such statistics are not just limited to the East. In 2010 the European Commission reported that women within the EU were earning 82 percent of what their male counterparts were earning.[69] Despite these disparities, equal pay is recognized as a fundamental right by the UN Human Rights Declaration, and gender pay inequality is illegal in many countries. Businesses, particularly multinationals, must consider this issue carefully. Failure to do so could lead to lawsuits or reputational damages. Walmart spent years fighting a class-action lawsuit from hundreds of female employees who claimed they were discriminated against in pay and promotions. Companies that work to eliminate gender pay inequalities within their organizations will not only be acting ethically, but will be protecting themselves legally as well.

In addition to equal pay, Article 23 of the UN Human Rights Declaration discusses the right to work and join trade unions. Within the European Union, trade unions are accepted, but in many other countries, including Burma, North Korea, Cuba, and Iran, trade unionists risk imprisonment. China, Laos, and Vietnam only allow one trade union.[70] European companies with employees in these countries will face many ethically charged decisions. Trade unions are an ethically charged issue in the United States, too. For example, McDonald's and Walmart have discouraged attempts to unionize in the United States, but they acquiesced to their workers in China and allowed them to unionize. Both companies have unions in all of their Chinese facilities, yet they continue to fight against unions in their home countries.[71]

Article 25 of the UN Human Rights Declaration mentions a standard of living and special rights related to pregnancy. The United States lags behind other industrialized nations in its treatment of pregnant women and new mothers. While other countries allow female employees a certain amount of paid maternity leave, the United States guarantees only 12 weeks of unpaid leave.[72] Some countries have been arguing for allowing men to take off the same amount of leave (either paid or unpaid). This debate would never happen in Sweden because Swedish parents get 480 paid days off that can be split between parents at 100 percent pay.[73]

Compensation

The last global recession set off a spark that prompted employees worldwide to question their compensation relative to those of others. Employees, particularly those in places without strong employee protections, have begun questioning why high-level executives get so many benefits while their own real incomes have stayed the same or fallen. These questions highlight two wage issues that are having a profound effect on business: the living wage and executive compensation.

A LIVING WAGE   A living wage refers to the minimum wage that workers require to meet basic needs. Many countries have passed minimum wage laws to try and provide employees with a living wage (whether the "minimum wage" is actually enough to meet a worker's

> "The problem that multinationals face is trying to find a solution that balances the interests of the company as a whole with those of its employees and other interested stakeholders."

basic needs is highly debatable). These laws vary from country to country. For instance, while the United States has a federal minimum wage law of $7.25 per hour, Australia's minimum wage equals about $15.37 per hour, while the United Kingdom's minimum wage equals about $9.53 per hour for workers 21 or older.[74] Some regions within these countries may adopt higher regional minimum wage laws to account for higher costs of living. The issue of a living wage is a controversial topic for MNCs. Because laws of industrialized countries dictate that employers must pay a minimum wage, some MNCs choose to outsource their labor to other countries where no minimum wage exists. While not necessarily unethical in and of itself, this practice becomes a significant ethical dilemma when the public perceives the organization as paying foreign laborers unfair wages. The problem that multinationals face is trying to find a solution that balances the interests of the company as a whole with those of its employees and other interested stakeholders. For instance, Nike continues to be criticized for the wages it pays its factory workers in other countries. While Nike claims that it pays its workers in these countries higher than the mandated minimum wage laws of the country, critics point out that the amount is not suitable enough to cover living expenses of workers or their families. Nike in turn contends that a "fair" wage is hard to determine when dealing with other countries, a statement with which many multinationals would likely agree.[75] However, the concept of a living wage is a challenge that companies must acknowledge if they hope to successfully do business in the global environment.

EXECUTIVE COMPENSATION   The issue of executive pay came to the forefront during the last global recession. In the United States, for instance, the government felt it necessary to bail out firms that would go bankrupt otherwise. However, when companies that received taxpayer money such as American International Group and Merrill Lynch subsequently paid their executives millions in compensation, the public was outraged. These types of incidents have led to a global demand for a better alignment between managerial performance and compensation.

Some companies have begun to heed this demand. The Swiss financial institution UBS, for example, cut its bonus pool by 10 percent.[76] Meanwhile, the Chinese government ruled that the disparity between the country's executives and its workers was too great. It therefore cut the salaries of top executives at state-owned banks and insurers.[77] The gap between executive and worker compensation will likely remain a major business ethics issue until stakeholders are satisfied that executives are earning their additional compensation.

Consumerism

Consumerism is the belief that the interests of consumers, rather than those of producers, should dictate the economic structure of a society. It refers to the theory that the consumption of goods at an ever-increasing rate is economically desirable, and it equates personal happiness with the purchase and consumption of material possessions. However, over the past 50 years consumption has placed significant strains on the environment. Many scientists argue that human factors (such as the increase in fossil fuel emissions from industrialization and development and deforestation), have caused global warming. Many countries contend that consumer choices are moral choices, that choosing a high rate of consumption will affect vulnerable groups such as the poor, and that the world will be increasingly less habitable if people refuse to change their behaviors.[78]

As nations increase their wealth, consumers increase their quality of living with luxury items and technological innovations that improve the comfort, convenience, and efficiency of their lives. Such consumption beyond basic needs is not necessarily a bad thing in and of itself; however, as more people engage in this type of behavior, waste and pollution increase. Some important issues must be addressed in relation to consumerism. For example:

- What are the impacts of production on the environment, on society, and on individuals?
- What are the impacts of certain forms of consumption on the environment, on society, and on individuals?
- Who influences consumption, and how and why are goods and services produced?
- What goods are necessities, and what are luxuries?
- How much of what we consume is influenced by corporations rather than by our needs?
- What is the impact on poorer nations of the consumption patterns of wealthier nations?[79]

China's rise to dominance in manufacturing and world trade has caused it to outpace the United States as a consumer. It now leads the United States in consumption of basic goods such as grain, meat, coal, and steel. China has also surpassed the United States in greenhouse gas emissions. Some fear that China's newfound consumerism will drive up global prices for goods, as well as speed up global warming, even as other nations take measures to stop it. Consumption patterns are being created by businesses in China that will cause large resource requirements. Chinese consumers are pushing for more cars, appliances, and technology like never before. With 1.3 billion consumers, this will cause a major strain on the environment. China has taken steps to curb its negative environmental impact, such as becoming the largest investor in wind turbines in the world. Unfortunately, most of China's energy needs are still produced by fossil fuels, which are causing its carbon dioxide emissions to worsen.[80]

India, with its 1.1 billion people, is following China and the West on the consumerist path. India has the world's fastest-growing information technology market, creating skilled, high-wage jobs for software engineers, business process experts, and call-center workers. The country is well-situated to weather global recessions because much of the country's demand for goods is domestic. India has the second-largest domestic market for goods in the world.[81] While this demand has helped fuel growth, it also has led to an enormous increase in greenhouse gas emissions. One government study revealed that greenhouse gas emissions within India increased 58 percent between 1994 and 2007.[82]

The ethics of these consumerism issues for business are many. These large emerging economies are the profit-making centers of the future. Most in business understand that it is in the best interests of the firm that consumer needs and desires are never completely or permanently fulfilled, so that consumers can repeat the consumption process and buy more products. For example, **made-to-break,** or planned obsolescence, products are better for business in that they keep consumers returning to buy more. It also is profitable to make products part of a continuously changing fashion market. Thus, items that are still in good condition and could last for many years are deemed in need of constant replacement to keep up with fashion trends. In this way, steady profits are assured—as well as waste. The top 20 percent of consumers in the highest-income countries comprise 86 percent of global consumption expenditures, whereas the poorest 20 percent comprise 1.3 percent of consumption expenditures. The richest 20 percent also consume 58 percent of the total energy used on the planet.[83]

One ethical question that is being asked by more people and countries is, "Does consumerism lead to happiness?" Consumer detractors are gaining ground globally, and the United States is their example of nonsustainable consumption. They note that while the United States comprises 4.6 percent of the world's population, it consumes 33 percent of the world's resources. The world's poorest 2.3 billion people consume 3 percent of the world's resources. The average American generates twice as much waste per person per year as the average European.[84]

These consumption statistics point to a very different lifestyle for the future, and global business will drive it. The moral conflict between countries, especially between the United States and the developing world, will increase, with corresponding ethical challenges for business. The future may be one filled with international violence, to which business must respond, or it may be characterized by a lifestyle that global business creates and markets to avoid civil and global war. It will be up to you and others to decide.

THE IMPORTANCE OF ETHICAL DECISION MAKING IN GLOBAL BUSINESS

Ethical decision making is essential if a company is to operate successfully within a global business context. Without a clear understanding of the complexities of global ethics, companies will face a variety of legal and political snares that could result in disaster. It is important to realize that many of the same issues we discussed in this chapter can be applied to domestic markets as well. Internet security, for instance, can be just as much of an ethical issue domestically as it is in companies operating internationally. As such, businesses should incorporate both global and domestic ethical issues into their risk management strategies.

For companies looking to expand globally, the multitude of ethical issues to consider seems daunting. Many companies choose to adopt global business codes of ethics to provide guidelines for their international operations. To this end, several organizations have created ethics and social responsibility frameworks that businesses can adopt in formulating their own global ethics codes. As discussed in Chapter 2, the International Organization for Standardization has developed ISO 26000 and ISO 14000, among other guidelines, to address issues such as ethics and social responsibility. Another set of global principles were developed by Reverend Leon Sullivan as a way to rise above the discrimination and struggles in postapartheid South Africa. Reverend Sullivan worked with the UN Secretary General to revise the principles to meet global needs. Since that time period, both large and small companies have agreed to abide by the Global Sullivan Principles, which encourage social responsibility throughout the world. The Global Sullivan Principles, the UN Global Compact, the UN Human Rights Declaration, as well as others promote foundational principles of conduct for global businesses. Table 10.6 provides a synthesis of typical foundational statements.

For multinational corporations, risk management and global ethics are so integral to the stability of their overseas operations that they have created special officers or committees to oversee global compliance issues. Walmart created a global ethics office to communicate company values and encourage ethical decision making throughout its global stores.[85] General Motors' Board Audit Committee created the Global Ethics and

TABLE 10.6 Global Principles for Ethical Business Conduct

Global principles are integrity statements about foundational beliefs that should remain constant and not change as businesses operate globally. These principles address issues such as accountability, transparency, trust, natural environment, safety, treatment of employees, human rights, importance of property rights, and adhering to all legal requirements. The principles are designed to focus on areas which may present challenges to the ethical conduct of global business.

1. **Require accountability and transparency in all relationships.** Accountability requires accurate reporting to stakeholders, and transparency requires openness and truthfulness in all transactions and operations.

2. **Comply with the spirit and intent of all laws.** Laws, standards, and regulations must be respected in all countries as well as global conventions and agreements developed among nations.

3. **Build trust in all stakeholder relationships through a commitment to ethical conduct.** Trust is required to build the foundation for high integrity relationships. This requires organizational members to avoid major international risks such as bribery and conflicts of interest. Laws supporting this principle include the U.S. Foreign Corrupt Practices Act, the U.K. Anti-bribery Act, OECD Convention, and UN Convention Against Corruption.

4. **Be mindful and responsible in relating to communities where there are operations.** The communities in which businesses operate should be supported and improved as much as possible to benefit employees, suppliers, customers, and the community overall.

5. **Engage in sustainable practices to protect the natural environment.** This requires the protection of the long-term well-being of the natural environment including all biological entities as well as the interaction among nature, individuals, organizations, and business strategies.

6. **Provide equal opportunity, safety, and fair compensation for employees.** Employees should be treated fairly, not exploited or taken advantage of, especially in developing countries. Laws supporting this principle include equal opportunity legislation throughout the world.

7. **Provide safe products and create value for customers.** Product safety is a global issue as various governments and legal systems sometimes provide opportunities for firms to cut corners on safety. All products should provide their represented value and performance.

8. **Respect human rights as defined in the UN Global Compact.** Human rights is a major concern of the UN Global Compact and most other respected principles statements of international business.

9. **Support the economic viability of all stakeholders.** Economic viability supports all participants in business operations. Concerns such as fair trade and payment of a living wage are embedded in this principle.

10. **Respect the property of others.** Respect for property and those who own it is a broad concept that is an ethical foundation for the operation of economic systems. Property includes physical assets as well as the protection of intellectual property.

Source: *O.C. Ferrell and Linda Ferrell, Anderson School of Management, University of New Mexico, Copyright © 2011.*

Compliance Department after revisions were implemented to the U.S. Federal Sentencing Guidelines. GM not only wanted to comply with these guidelines, it also wanted to create a centralized system of compliance that would be used at all GM locations worldwide.[86]

The successful implementation of a global ethics program requires more than just a global ethics committee, however. It also requires extensive training for employees. As this chapter has demonstrated, various differences exist between cultures and businesses from different countries. Employees of global companies should be trained to understand and respect these differences, particularly those employees who will be directly involved in global operations. Ford Motor Co. has an online global ethics training program for employees that is available in 13 languages. The company also offers hotlines for employees in 24 countries and trains its Office of the General Counsel on how to handle global complaints.[87] Codes of global ethical conduct, global ethics training, and global channels for employees to communicate misconduct are important mechanisms in creating a culture of globalized ethical decision making.

A global firm cannot succeed simply by applying its domestic ethical programs to other global environments. Although ethical issues such as honesty and integrity are common to most countries, differences in laws, political systems, and cultures require a more targeted approach to ethical decision making. Global ethics is not a "one size fits all" concept. With that said, it is important for companies to act with integrity even if they are doing business in a country with lax laws on certain ethical subjects. Those companies who incorporate globalized ethical decision making throughout their international operations will not only enhance their reputations, but will also demonstrate a respect for their employees and their cultures—as well as avoid the costly litigation that often accompanies misconduct.

SUMMARY

In this chapter we have tried to sensitize you to the important topic of ethical decision making in an international context. We began by looking at values and culture. A country's values are influenced by ethnic groups, social organizations, and other cultural aspects. Hofstede identified four cultural dimensions that can have a profound impact on the business environment: individualism/collectivism, power distance, uncertainty avoidance, and masculinity/femininity. The self-reference criterion is the unconscious reference to one's own cultural values, experiences, and knowledge and is a common stumbling block for organizations. Another approach organizations tend to take is that of cultural relativism, or the idea that morality varies from one culture to another and that business practices are therefore defined as right or wrong differently.

Risk compartmentalization is an important ethical issue, and it occurs when various profit centers within corporations become unaware of the overall consequences of their actions on the firm as a whole. The last financial meltdown was in part the result of risk compartmentalization. Understanding rational economics and systems is an important foundation for understanding business ethics. Rational economics assumes that people will make decisions rationally based upon utility, value, profit maximization, and relevant information. Capitalism bases its models on these assumptions. Behavioral economics, by contrast, argues that humans may not act in a rational way as a result of genetics, learned behavior, emotions, framing, and heuristics, or rules of thumb. Social democracy, a form of socialism, allows for private ownership of property and also features a large government equipped to offer services such as education and health care to its citizens. Sweden, Denmark, and Finland are social democracies.

Multinational corporations are public companies that operate on a global scale without significant ties to any one nation or region. MNCs have contributed to the growth of global economies but are by no means immune to criticism. The International Monetary

Fund makes short-term loans to member countries that have deficits and provides foreign currencies for its members. The UN Global Compact is a set of 10 principles that promote human rights, sustainability, and the eradication of corruption, while the World Trade Organization administers its own trade agreements, facilitates trade negotiations, settles trade disputes, and monitors the trade policies of member nations.

There are several critical ethics issues of which global businesses should be aware. Global risks create ethical issues for global companies to manage. Bribery is becoming a major ethical issue, prompting legislation such as the U.S. Foreign Corrupt Practices Act and the U.K. Antibribery Act. Antitrust activities are illegal in most industrialized countries and are pursued even more ardently in the European Union than in the United States. Internet security is an important ethical issue, as hacking and privacy violations are on the rise. The United Nations has codified human rights as a function of inherent human dignity, and including equal and inalienable rights such as the foundation of freedom, justice, and peace in the world. Health care and labor issues are important ethical issues but tend to vary by country. Wage issues such as a living wage and executive compensation are controversial topics that affect a variety of global stakeholders. Consumerism is the belief that the interests of consumers should dictate the economic structure of a society, rather than the interests of producers; it refers to the theory that an increasing consumption of goods is economically desirable, and equates personal happiness with the purchase and consumption of material possessions.

TERMS FOR REVIEW

global business	consumerism	made-to-break
self-reference criterion	country cultural values	national culture
risk compartmentalization	cultural relativism	global common values
John Maynard Keynes	Adam Smith	laissez-faire
social democracy	Milton Friedman	socialism
behavioral economics	bimodal wealth distribution	rational economics
Business for Social Responsibility	International Monetary Fund	multinational corporation
dumping	United Nations Global Compact	World Trade Organization
vertical system	human rights	

RESOLVING ETHICAL BUSINESS CHALLENGES*

George Wilson, the operations manager of the CornCo plant in Phoenix, Arizona, has a problem. He is in charge of buying corn and producing chips marketed by CornCo in the United States and elsewhere. Several months ago, George's supervisor, CornCo's vice president, Jake Lamont, called to tell him that corn futures were on the rise, which would ultimately increase the overall costs of production. In addition, a new company called Abco Snack Foods had begun marketing corn chips at competitive prices in CornCo's market area. Abco already had shown signs of eroding CornCo's market share. Jake was concerned that George's production costs would not be competitive with Abco's—hence, profitability would decline. Jake had already asked George to find ways to cut costs. If he couldn't, Jake said, layoffs would begin soon.

George scoured the Midwest looking for cheap corn and finally found some. But when the railcars started coming in, one of the company's testers reported the presence of aflatoxin—a naturally occurring carcinogen that induces liver cancer in lab animals. Once corn has been ground into corn meal, however, aflatoxin is virtually impossible to detect. George knew that by blending the contaminated corn with uncontaminated corn he could reduce the aflatoxin concentrations in the final product—a technique, he had heard, other managers sometimes used. According to U.S. law, corn contaminated with aflatoxin cannot be used for edible products sold in the United States, and fines are to be imposed for such use. So far, however, no one has been convicted. And no U.S. law prohibits shipping the contaminated corn to other countries.

George knew that, because of his competitors' prices, if he didn't sell the contaminated corn his production costs would be too high. When he spoke to Jake, Jake's response was, "So how much of the corn coming in is contaminated?"

"It's about 10 percent," George answered. "They probably knew that the corn was contaminated. That's why we're getting such a good deal on it."

Jake thought for a moment and said, "George, call the grain elevators, complain to them, and demand a 50 percent discount. If they agree, buy all they have."

"But if we do, the blends will just increase in contamination!" George exclaimed.

"That's OK," Jake answered. "When the blends start getting high, we'll stop shipping into the U.S. market and go foreign. Remember, there are no fines for contaminated corn going to Mexico."

George learned that one other person, Lee Garcia, an operations manager for the breakfast cereals division, had sold contaminated corn once.

"Yeah, so what about it?" Lee said. "I've got a family to support and house payments. For me there was no alternative. I had to do it or face getting laid off."

As George thought about the problem, word spread about his alternatives. The following notes appeared in the plant suggestion box:

"Use the corn or we all get laid off!"

"Process it and ship it off to Mexico!"

"It's just wrong to use this corn!"

When George balked at Jake's proposed solution, Jake said, "George, I understand your situation. I was there once—just like you. But you've got to look at the bigger picture. Hundreds of workers would be out of a job. Sure, the FDA says that aflatoxin is bad, but we're talking about rats eating their weight in this stuff. What if it does get detected—so what? The company gets a fine, the FDA tester gets reprimanded for screwing up, and it's back to business as usual."

"Is that all that will happen?" George asked.

"Of course. Don't worry," Jake replied.

But George's signature, not Jake's, was on the receipts for the contaminated railcars.

"So if I do this, at what aflatoxin percentage do I stop, and will you sign off on this?" George asked.

"Look," said Jake, "that's up to you. Remember that the more corn chips that are produced for the U.S. market, the more profit the company gets, and the higher your bonus will be. As for me signing off on this, I'm shocked that you would even suggest something like that. George, you're the operations manager. You're the one who's responsible for what happens at the plant. It just isn't done that way at CornCo. But whatever you do, you had better do it in the next several hours. Because, as I see it, the contaminated corn has to be blended with something, and the longer you wait, the higher the percentages will get."

QUESTIONS | EXERCISES

1. Discuss the corporate ethical issue of providing questionable products to other markets.
2. Discuss the suggestions submitted in the suggestion box in light of the decision that George must make. Should the suggestions have an influence?
3. Identify the pressures that have caused the ethical and legal issues in this scenario to arise.

*This case is strictly hypothetical; any resemblance to real persons, companies, or situations is coincidental.

CHECK YOUR EQ

Check your EQ, or Ethics Quotient, by completing the following. Assess your performance to evaluate your overall understanding of the chapter material.

1. Most countries have a strong orientation toward ethical and legal compliance. **Yes**   **No**

2. The self-reference criterion is an unconscious reference to one's own cultural values, experience, and knowledge. **Yes**   **No**

3. One of the critical ethical business issues linked to cultural differences is the question of whose values and ethical standards take precedence during international negotiations and business transactions. **Yes**   **No**

4. Multinational corporations have identifiable home countries but operate globally. **Yes**   **No**

5. Certain facilitating payments are acceptable under the Foreign Corrupt Practices Act. **Yes**   **No**

ANSWERS 1. No. That's an ethnocentric perspective; in other countries laws may be viewed more situationally. 2. Yes. We react based on what we have experienced over our lifetimes. 3. Yes. Ethical standards and values differ from culture to culture, and this can be a critical point in effective business negotiations. Some people believe in cultural relativism, which means that the standards of the host country hold sway. However, many MNCs are legally bound to adhere to the standards of the host country. 4. No. Multinational corporations have no significant ties to any nation or region. 5. Yes. A violation of the FCPA occurs when the payments are excessive or are used to persuade the recipients to perform other than normal duties.

PART 5

Cases

CASE 1

Monsanto Attempts to Balance Stakeholder Interests*

Think Monsanto, and the phrase *genetically modified* likely comes to mind. The Monsanto Company is the world's largest seed company, with sales of over $10.5 billion. It specializes in biotechnology, or the genetic manipulation of organisms. Monsanto scientists have spent the last few decades modifying crops, often by inserting new genes or adapting existing genes within plant seeds, to better meet certain aims, such as higher yield or insect resistance. Monsanto produces plants that can survive weeks of drought, ward off weeds, and kill invasive insects. Monsanto's genetically modified (GM) seeds have increased the quantity and availability of crops, helping farmers worldwide increase food production and revenues.

Today, 90 percent of the world's GM seeds are sold by Monsanto or by companies that use Monsanto genes. Monsanto also holds a 70 to 100 percent market share on certain crops. Yet Monsanto has met with its share of criticism from sources as diverse as governments, farmers, activists, and advocacy groups. Monsanto supporters say it is creating solutions to world hunger by generating higher crop yields and hardier plants. Critics accuse the multinational giant of trying to take over the world's food supply and destroying biodiversity. Since biotechnology is relatively new, critics also express concerns about the possibility of negative health and environmental effects from biotech food. However, such criticisms have not kept Monsanto from becoming one of the world's most successful companies.

The following analysis first looks at the history of Monsanto as it progressed from a chemical company to an organization focused on biotechnology, and then examines Monsanto's current focus on developing genetically modified seeds, including stakeholder concerns regarding the safety and environmental effects of these seeds. Next, we discuss some ethical concerns, including organizational misconduct and patent issues. We also look at some of Monsanto's corporate responsibility initiatives. We conclude by examining the challenges and opportunities that Monsanto may face in the future.

HISTORY: FROM CHEMICALS TO FOOD

Monsanto was founded by John F. Queeny in 1901 in St. Louis, Missouri. He named it after his wife, Olga Monsanto Queeny. The company's first product was the artificial sweetener saccharine, which it sold to Coca-Cola. Monsanto also sold Coca-Cola caffeine extract and vanillin, an artificial vanilla flavoring. At the start of World War I, company leaders realized the growth opportunities in the industrial chemicals industry and renamed the

---

*This case was prepared by Jennifer Sawayda for and under the direction of O. C. Ferrell and Linda Ferrell. It was prepared for classroom discussion rather than to illustrate either effective or ineffective handling of an administrative, ethical, or legal decision by management. All sources used for this case were obtained through publicly available material.

company The Monsanto Chemical Company. The company began specializing in plastics, its own agricultural chemicals, and synthetic rubbers.

Due to its expanding product lines, the company's name was changed back to the Monsanto Company in 1964. By this time, Monsanto was producing such diverse products as petroleum, fibers, and packaging. A couple of years later, Monsanto created its first Roundup herbicide, a successful product that would propel the company even more into the public consciousness.

However, during the 1970s, Monsanto encountered a major legal obstacle. The company had produced a chemical known as Agent Orange, which was used during the Vietnam War to quickly deforest the thick Vietnamese jungles. Agent Orange contained dioxin, a chemical that caused a legal nightmare for Monsanto. Dioxin was found to be extremely carcinogenic, and in 1979, a lawsuit was filed against Monsanto on behalf of hundreds of veterans who claimed they had been harmed by the chemical. Monsanto and several other manufacturers agreed to settle for $180 million, but the repercussions of dioxin would continue to plague the company for decades.

In 1981 Monsanto leaders determined that biotechnology would be the company's new strategic focus. The quest for biotechnology was on, and in 1994 Monsanto introduced the first biotechnology product to win regulatory approval. Soon the company was selling soybean, cotton, and canola seeds that were engineered to be tolerant to Monsanto's Roundup Ready herbicide. Many other herbicides killed the good plants as well as the bad ones. Roundup Ready seeds allowed farmers to use the herbicide to eliminate weeds while sparing the crop.

In 1997 Monsanto spun off its chemical business as Solutia, and in 2000 the company entered into a merger and changed its name to the Pharmacia Corporation. Two years later, a new Monsanto, focused entirely on agriculture, broke off from Pharmacia, and the companies became two legally separate entities. The company before 2000 is often referred to as "old Monsanto," while today's company is known as "new Monsanto."

The emergence of new Monsanto was tainted by some disturbing news about the company's conduct. It was revealed that Monsanto had been covering up decades of environmental pollution. For nearly forty years, the Monsanto Company had released toxic waste into a creek in the Alabama town of Anniston. It had also disposed of polychlorinated biphenyls (PCBs), a highly toxic chemical, in open-pit landfills in the area. The results were catastrophic. Fish from the creek were deformed, and the population had elevated PCB levels that astounded environmental health experts. A paper trail showed that Monsanto leaders had known about the pollution since the 1960s, but had not stopped the dumping. Once the cover-up was discovered, thousands of plaintiffs from the city filed a lawsuit against the company. In 2003 Monsanto and Solutia agreed to pay a settlement of $700 million to more than 20,000 Anniston residents.

When current CEO Hugh Grant took over in 2003, scandals and stakeholder uncertainty over Monsanto's GM products had tarnished the company's reputation. The price of Monsanto's stock had fallen by almost 50 percent, down to $8 a share. The company had lost $1.7 billion the previous year. Grant knew the company was fragile; yet through a strategic focus on GM foods, the company has recovered and is now prospering.

In spite of their controversial nature, GM foods have become popular both in developed and developing countries. Monsanto became so successful with its GM seeds that it acquired Seminis, Inc., a leader in the fruit and vegetable seed industry. The acquisition transformed Monsanto into a global leader in the seed industry. Today, Monsanto employs over 21,000 people in 160 countries. It has been recognized as a top employer in Brazil, India, and Canada.

MONSANTO'S EMPHASIS ON BIOTECHNOLOGY

While the original Monsanto had made a name for itself through the manufacturing of chemicals, the new Monsanto took quite a different turn. It switched its emphasis from chemicals to food. Today's Monsanto owes its $10.5 billion in sales to biotechnology, specifically to its sales of genetically modified (GM) plant seeds. These seeds have revolutionized the agriculture industry.

Throughout history, weeds, insects, and drought have been the bane of the farmer's existence. In the twentieth century, synthetic chemical herbicides and pesticides were invented to ward off pests. Yet applying these chemicals to an entire crop was both costly and time consuming. Then Monsanto scientists, through their work in biotechnology, were able to implant seeds with genes that make the plants themselves kill bugs. They also created seeds containing the herbicide Roundup Ready, an herbicide that kills weeds but spares the crops.

Since then Monsanto has used technology to create many more innovative products, such as drought-tolerant seeds for dry areas like Africa. The company also utilizes its technological prowess to gain the support of stakeholders. For example, Monsanto has a laboratory in St. Louis that gives tours to farmers. One of the technologies that the company shows visiting farmers is a machine known as the corn chipper, which picks up seeds and takes genetic material from them. That material is then analyzed to see how well the seed will do if planted. The "best" seeds are the ones Monsanto sells for planting. Impressing farmers with its technology and the promise of better yields is one way that Monsanto attracts potential customers.

However, genetically modified crops are not without their critics. Opponents believe that influencing the gene pools of the plants we eat could result in negative health consequences. Others are worried about the health effects on beneficial insects and plants, fearing that pollinating GM plants could affect nearby insects and non-GM plants. CEO Hugh Grant decided to curtail the tide of criticism by focusing biotechnology on products that would not be directly placed on the dinner plate, but instead on seeds that produce goods like animal feed and corn syrup. In this way, Grant was able to reduce some of the opposition. The company invests largely in four crops: corn, cotton, soybeans, and canola. Monsanto owes approximately 60 percent of its revenue to its work on GM seeds, and today more than half of U.S. crops, including most soybeans and 70 percent of corn, are genetically modified.

> "Farmers who purchase GM seeds can now grow more crops on less land and with less left to chance."

Farmers who purchase GM seeds can now grow more crops on less land and with less left to chance. GM crops have saved farmers billions by preventing loss and increasing crop yields. For example, in 1970 the average corn harvest yielded approximately 70 bushels an acre. With the introduction of biotech crops, the average corn harvest has increased to roughly 150 bushels an acre. Monsanto predicts even higher yields in the future, possibly up to 300 bushels an acre by 2030. "As agricultural productivity increases, farmers are able to produce more food, feed, fuel, and fiber on the same amount of land, helping to ensure that agriculture can meet humanity's needs in the future," said Monsanto CEO Hugh Grant about the benefits of Monsanto technology.

As a result of higher yields, the revenues of farmers in developing countries have increased. According to company statistics, the cotton yield of Indian farmers rose by

50 percent, doubling their income in one year. Additionally, the company claims that its insect-protected corn has raised the income level in the Philippines to above poverty level. Critics argue that these numbers are inflated; they say the cost of GM seeds is dramatically higher than that of traditional seeds, and therefore they actually reduce farmers' take-home profits.

Monsanto's GM seeds have not been accepted everywhere. Attempts to introduce them into Europe have been met with extreme consumer backlash. The European Union has banned most Monsanto crops except for one variety of corn. Consumers have gone so far as to destroy fields of GM crops and arrange sit-ins. Greenpeace has fought Monsanto for years, especially in the company's efforts to promote GM crops in developing countries. This animosity toward Monsanto's products is generated by two main concerns: worries about the safety of GM food and concerns about the environmental effects of genetic modification.

Concerns About the Safety of GM Food

Of great concern to many stakeholders are the moral and safety implications of GM food. Many skeptics see biotech crops as unnatural, with the Monsanto scientist essentially "playing God" by controlling what goes into the seed. Also, because GM crops are relatively new, critics maintain that the health implications of biotech food may not be known for years to come. They also contend that effective standards have not been created to determine the safety of biotech crops. Some geneticists believe the splicing of these genes into seeds could create small changes that might negatively impact the health of humans and animals that eat them. Also, even though the FDA has declared biotech crops safe, critics say they have not been around long enough to gauge their long-term effects.

One concern is toxicity, particularly considering that many Monsanto seeds are equipped with a gene to allow them to produce their own Roundup Ready herbicide. Could ingesting this herbicide, even in small amounts, cause detrimental effects on consumers? Some stakeholders say yes, and point to statistics on glyphosate, Roundup's chief ingredient, for support. According to an ecology center fact sheet, glyphosate exposure is the third most commonly reported illness among California agriculture workers, and glyphosate residues can last for a year. Yet the Environmental Protection Agency (EPA) lists glyphosate as having a low skin and oral toxicity, and a study from the New York Medical College states that Roundup does not create a health risk for humans.

Despite consumer concerns, the FDA has proclaimed that GM food is safe to consume. As a result, it also has determined that Americans do not need to know when they are consuming GM products. Therefore, this information is not placed on labels in the United States, although other countries, notably those in the European Union, do require GM food products to state this fact in their labeling.

Concerns About Environmental Effects of Monsanto Products

Some studies have supported the premise that Roundup herbicide, which is used in conjunction with the GM seeds called "Roundup Ready," can be harmful to birds, insects, and particularly amphibians. Such studies have revealed that small concentrations of Roundup may be deadly to tadpoles, which is a major concern, as frog and toad species are rapidly disappearing around the globe. Other studies suggest that Roundup might have a detrimental effect on human cells, especially embryonic, umbilical, and placental cells. Monsanto has countered these claims by questioning the methodology used in the studies, and the Environmental Protection Agency maintains that glyphosate is not dangerous at recommended doses.

> "Some scientists fear that GM seeds that are spread to native plants may cause those plants to adopt the GM trait."

Another concern with GM seeds in general is the threat of environmental contamination. Bees and other insects and wind can carry a crop's seeds to other areas, sometimes to fields containing non-GM crops. These seeds and pollens might then mix in with the farmer's crops. In the past, organic farmers have complained that genetically modified seeds from nearby farms have "contaminated" their crops. This environmental contamination could pose a serious threat. Some scientists fear that GM seeds that are spread to native plants may cause those plants to adopt the GM trait, thus creating new genetic variations of those plants that could negatively influence (through genetic advantages) the surrounding ecosystem. The topic has taken on particular significance in Mexico. For eleven years, Mexico had a moratorium on genetically modified corn. It lifted the moratorium in 2005, enabling Monsanto to begin testing its genetically modified corn in northern Mexico a few years later. Monsanto is seeking authorization to begin the pre-commercial stage in Mexico, in which it would be able to expand its growing area to approximately 500 acres. However, consumers are putting up a fight. Believing that GM corn could contaminate their over 60 maize varieties, Mexicans have staged protests and formed groups to try and keep GM corn out of the country.

Monsanto has not been silent on these issues and has acted to address some of these concerns. The company maintains that the environmental impact of everything it creates has been studied by the EPA and approved. Monsanto officials claim that glyphosate in Roundup Ready does not usually end up in ground water, and claims that when it does contaminate ground water, it is soluble and will not have much effect on aquatic species. Stakeholders are left to make their own decisions regarding genetically modified crops

Crop Resistance to Pesticides and Herbicides

Another environmental problem that has emerged is the possibility of weed and insect resistance to the herbicides and pesticides on Monsanto crops. Critics fear that continual use of the chemicals could result in "super weeds" and "super bugs," much as overuse of antibiotics in humans has resulted in drug-resistant bacteria. The company's Roundup Ready line, in particular, has come under attack. Genetically modified plants labeled Roundup Ready are genetically engineered to withstand large doses of the herbicide Roundup, and as Roundup is being used more frequently and exclusively because of the Roundup Ready plants' tolerance, now even weeds have started developing a resistance to this popular herbicide. As early as 2003, significant numbers of Roundup resistant weeds had been found in the United States and Australia.

To combat "super bugs," the government requires farmers using Monsanto's GM products to create "refuges," in which they plant 20 percent of their fields with a non-genetically modified crop. The theory is that this allows nonresistant bugs to mate with those that are resistant, preventing a new race of super bugs. To prevent resistance to the Roundup herbicide, farmers are required to vary herbicide use and practice crop rotations. However, since Roundup is so easy to use, particularly in conjunction with Roundup Ready seeds, some farmers may not take the time to institute these preventative measures. When they do rotate their crops, some will rotate one Roundup Ready crop with another type of Roundup Ready crop, which does little to solve the problem. This is of particular concern in Latin America, Africa, and Asia, where farmers may not be as informed of the risks of herbicide and pesticide overuse.

DEALING WITH ORGANIZATIONAL ETHICAL ISSUES

In addition to concerns over the safety of GM seeds and environmental issues, Monsanto has had to deal with concerns about organizational conduct. Organizations face significant risks from strategies and also from employees striving for high performance standards. Such pressure sometimes encourages employees to engage in illegal or unethical conduct. All firms have these concerns, and in the case of Monsanto, bribes and patents have resulted in legal, ethical, and reputational consequences.

Bribery Issues

Bribery presents a dilemma to multinational corporations because different countries have different perspectives on it. While it is illegal in the United States, other countries allow it. Monsanto faced such a problem in Indonesia, and its actions resulted in the company being fined a large sum.

In 2002 a Monsanto manager instructed an Indonesian consulting firm to pay a bribe of $50,000 to an official in the country's environment ministry. The official accepted the bribe in exchange for bypassing an environmental study. It was later revealed that such bribery was not an isolated event; the company had paid off many officials between 1997 and 2002. Monsanto headquarters became aware of the problem after discovering irregularities at its Indonesian subsidiary in 2001. As a result, the company launched an internal investigation and reported the bribery to the U.S. Department of Justice (DOJ) and the Securities and Exchange Commission (SEC). Monsanto accepted full responsibility for its employees' behavior and agreed to pay $1 million to the Department of Justice and $500,000 to the SEC. It also agreed to three years of close monitoring of its activities by American authorities.

Patent Issues

Like most businesses, Monsanto wants to patent its products. A problem arises, however, when it comes to patenting seeds. As bioengineered creations of the Monsanto Company, Monsanto's seeds are protected under patent law. Under the terms of the patent, farmers using Monsanto seeds are not allowed to harvest seeds from the plants for use in upcoming seasons. Instead, they must purchase new Monsanto seeds each season. By issuing new seeds each year, Monsanto ensures it will secure a profit as well as maintain control over its property.

However, this is a new concept for most farmers. Throughout agricultural history, farmers have collected and saved seeds

"Farmers using Monsanto seeds are not allowed to harvest seeds from the plants for use in upcoming seasons."

from previous harvests to plant the following year's crops. Critics argue that requiring farmers to suddenly purchase new seeds year after year puts an undue financial burden on them and gives Monsanto too much power. However, the law protects Monsanto's right to have exclusive control over its creations, and farmers must abide by these laws. When they are found guilty of using Monsanto seeds from previous seasons, either deliberately or out of ignorance, they are often fined.

Since it is fairly easy for farmers to violate the patent, Monsanto has found it necessary in the past to employ investigators from law firms to investigate suspected violations. The resulting investigations are a source of contention between Monsanto and accused farmers. According to Monsanto, investigators deal with farmers in a respectful manner. They approach the farmers suspected of patent infringement and ask them some questions. The company claims that investigators practice transparency with the farmers and tell them why they are there and who they represent. If, after the initial interview is completed, suspicions still exist, the investigators may pull the farmer's records. They may bring in a sampling team, with the farmer's permission, to test the farmer's fields. If found guilty, the farmer often has to pay Monsanto. But some farmers tell a different story about Monsanto and its seed investigators. They claim that Monsanto investigators have used unethical practices to get them to cooperate. They call the investigators the "seed police" and say they behave like a "Gestapo" or "mafia."

Monsanto is not limiting its investigations to farmers. It also filed a lawsuit against DuPont, the world's second-largest seed maker, for combining DuPont technology with Roundup Ready. Monsanto won the lawsuit, but was countersued by DuPont for anticompetitive practices. These accusations of anticompetitive practices have garnered the attention of federal antitrust lawyers. With increased pressure coming from different areas, Monsanto agreed to allow patents to expire on its seeds starting in 2014. This will allow other companies to create less expensive versions of Monsanto seeds. However, Monsanto announced that it would continue to strictly enforce patents for new versions of its products, such as Roundup Ready 2 soybeans.

In order to prevent patent infringement, some have suggested that Monsanto make use of GURT, or gene use restriction technology. This technology would let Monsanto create "sterile" seeds. These so-called "Terminator seeds" have spurred much controversy among the public, including a concern that these sterile seeds might cross-pollinate with other plants, which could create sterile plants that would reduce genetic diversity. In 1999 Monsanto pledged not to commercialize sterile seed technology in food crops. The company has promised that it will only do so in the future after consulting with experts, stakeholders, and relevant NGOs.

Legal Issues

Many major companies have government and legal forces to deal with, and Monsanto is no exception. Recently, the government has begun to more closely examine Monsanto's practices. In 1980 the Supreme Court for the first time allowed living organisms to be patented, giving Monsanto the ability to patent its seeds; but Monsanto has now come to the attention of the American Antitrust Institute for alleged anticompetitive activities. The institute wrote a paper suggesting that Monsanto is hindering competition, exerting too much power over the transgenic seed industry, and limiting seed innovation. When Monsanto acquired DeKalb and Delta Land and Pine, it had to get the approval of antitrust authorities, and gained that approval only after agreeing to certain concessions. However, Monsanto may be walking a fine line with the Department of Justice (DOJ) and could soon become a target for antitrust litigation. Monsanto's competitor DuPont even complained to the DOJ about Monsanto's alleged anticompetitive practices. DuPont has filed a lawsuit claiming that Monsanto is using its power and licenses to block DuPont products. As a result of complaints, the DOJ has begun a civil investigation into Monsanto's practices. If the DOJ agrees that Monsanto's practices are anticompetitive, resulting decisions could affect how Monsanto does business.

CORPORATE RESPONSIBILITY AT MONSANTO

Today the public generally expects multinational corporations to help advance the interests and well-being of the people in the countries in which they do business. Monsanto has given millions of dollars in programs to help improve communities in developing countries. In fact, *Corporate Responsibility Magazine* ranked Monsanto number 31 on its 100 Best Corporate Citizens list of 2010, a jump from number 88 the previous year.

In addition, as an agricultural company, Monsanto must address the grim reality that the world's population is fast increasing, and the amount of land and water available for agriculture is decreasing. Some experts believe that our planet will have to produce more food in the next 50 years to feed the world's population than it has grown in the past 10,000 years, requiring us to double our food output. As a multinational corporation dedicated to agriculture, Monsanto is expected to address these problems. The company has developed a three-tiered commitment policy: (1) produce more yield in crops, (2) conserve more resources, and (3) improve the lives of farmers. The company hopes to achieve these goals by taking some initiatives in sustainable agriculture.

Sustainable Agriculture

Monsanto CEO Hugh Grant has said, "Agriculture intersects the toughest challenges we all face on the planet. Together, we must meet the needs for increased food, fiber, and energy while protecting the environment. In short, the world needs to produce more and conserve smarter." Monsanto is quick to point out that its biotech products added more than 100 million tons to worldwide agricultural production in a ten-year period, which the company estimates has increased farmers' incomes by $33.8 billion. Monsanto has also created partnerships between nonprofit organizations across the world to enrich the lives of farmers in developing countries. Two regions on which Monsanto is now focusing are India and Africa.

The need for better agriculture is apparent in India, where the population is estimated to hit 1.3 billion by 2017. Biotech crops have helped to improve the size of yields in India, allowing some biotech farmers to increase their yields by 50 percent. Monsanto estimates that cotton farmers in India using biotech crops earn approximately $176 more in revenues per acre than their non-biotech contemporaries. In 2009 Monsanto launched Project SHARE, a sustainable yield initiative created in conjunction with the nonprofit Indian Society of Agribusiness, to try and improve the lives of 10,000 cotton farmers in 1,100 villages.

In Africa, Monsanto has partnered with the African Agricultural Technology Foundation, scientists, and philanthropists to embark on the Water Efficient Maize for Africa (WEMA) initiative. During this five-year project, Monsanto will help to develop drought-tolerant maize seeds; small-scale African farmers will not have to pay Monsanto royalties for their use. As CEO Hugh Grant writes, "This initiative isn't simply altruistic; we see it as a unique business proposition that rewards farmers and shareowners." But not all view Monsanto's presence in Africa as an outreach in corporate responsibility. Some see it as another way for Monsanto to improve its bottom line. Critics see the company as trying to take control of African agriculture and destroy African agricultural practices that have lasted for thousands of years.

Charitable Giving

In 1964 the Monsanto Company established the Monsanto Fund. This fund contributed $30.2 million to projects across the world between 2008 and 2009. One recipient of the Monsanto Fund was Africare, which received a $400,000 grant from Monsanto to fund a two-year food security project to study the availability of food and the access people have to food.

The Monsanto Company also supports youth programs. In the first decade of the twenty-first century, the company donated nearly $1.5 million in scholarships to students wanting to pursue agriculture-related degrees. The company supports 4-H programs and the program Farm Safety 4 Just Kids, a program that helps teach rural children about safety while working on farms. Additionally, Monsanto donated $4 million dollars' worth of seeds to Haiti after the massive 2010 earthquake.

THE FUTURE OF MONSANTO

Monsanto faces some challenges that it must address, including lingering concerns over the safety and the environmental impact of its products. The company needs to enforce its code of ethics effectively to avoid organizational misconduct (such as bribery) in the future. Monsanto is also facing increased competition from other companies. The seed company Pioneer Hi-Bred International, Inc., has been using pricing strategies and seed sampling to attract price-conscious customers. Chinese companies are becoming formidable rivals for Monsanto as their weed killers began eating up some of Monsanto's Roundup profits. As a result, Monsanto was forced to lower the prices of Roundup and announced plans to restructure the Roundup area of the business.

Yet despite the onslaught of criticism from Monsanto detractors and the challenge of increased competition from other companies, Monsanto has numerous opportunities to thrive in the future. The company is currently working on new innovations that could increase its competitive edge as well as benefit farmers worldwide, and after a plunge in Roundup sales, Monsanto's profits are bouncing back once more. The company is also preparing several biotech products for commercialization. Additionally, Monsanto sees major opportunities for expansion into places like China. The company has been discussing a possible deal with chemicals conglomerate Sinochem Corp., which has been tasked with ensuring food security for China's large population. If Monsanto can enter into the largely untapped Chinese market for genetically-modified foods, perhaps through a joint venture or by acquiring a stake in a Chinese company, it might be able to gain access to an additional 1.34 billion consumers.

Although Monsanto has made ethical errors in the past, it is trying to portray itself as a socially responsible company dedicated to improving agriculture. As noted, the company still has some problems. The predictions from Monsanto critics about biotech food have not yet come true, but that has not eradicated the fears of stakeholders. Faced with the increasing popularity of organic food and staunch criticism from opponents, Monsanto will need to continue working with stakeholders to promote its technological innovations and to eliminate fears concerning its industry.

QUESTIONS

1. Does Monsanto maintain an ethical culture that can effectively respond to various stakeholders?

2. Compare the benefits of growing GM seeds for crops with the potential negative consequences of using them.

3. How should Monsanto manage the potential harm to plant and animal life from using products such as Roundup?

SOURCES

Barlett, Donald L., and James B. Steele. "Monsanto's Harvest of Fear." *Vanity Fair,* May 5, 2008, http://www.vanityfair.com/politics/features/2008/05/monsanto200805 (accessed August 25, 2009); Berman, Dennis K., Gina Chon, and Scott Kilman. "Monsanto Pushes Deeper Into China." *The Wall Street Journal,* July 11, 2011, B1-B2; Berry, Ian. "Monsanto's Seeds Sow a Profit." *The Wall Street Journal,* January 7, 2011, B3; "CR's 100 Best Corporate Citizens 2010," *CRO,* http://www.thecro.com/files/CR100Best.pdf (accessed February 14, 2011); EPA. "R.E.D. Facts." EPA, September 1993, http://www.epa.gov/oppsrrd1/REDs/factsheets/0178fact.pdf (accessed April 1, 2009); Hindo, Brian. "Monsanto: Winning the Ground War." *Business Week,* 35–41; "Even Small Doses of Popular Weed Killer Fatal to Frogs, Scientist Finds." *ScienceDaily,* August 5, 2005, http://www.sciencedaily.com/releases/2005/08/050804053212.htm (accessed March 24, 2009); Gammon, Crystal and Environmental Health News. "Weed-Whacking Herbicide Proves Deadly to Human Cells." *Scientific American,* June 23, 2009, http://www.scientificamerican.com/article.cfm?id=weed-whacking-herbicide-p&page=3 (accessed February 14, 2011); Gibson, Ellen. "Monsanto." *Business Week,* December 22, 2008, 51; "GMOs under a Microscope." Science and Technology in Congress, October 1999, http://www.aaas.org/spp/cstc/pne/pubs/stc/bulletin/articles/10-99/GMOs.htm (accessed March 25, 2009); Grunwald, Michael. "Monsanto Hid Decades of Pollution." *The Washington Post,* January 1, 2002, A1; Guerrero, Jean. "Altered Corn Advances Slowly in Mexico." *The Wall Street Journal,* December 9, 2010, B8; Kaskey, Jack. "Monsanto Sets a Soybean Free." *Bloomberg Businessweek,* February 1 & 8, 2010, 19; Kaskey, Jack. "Monsanto 'Warrior' Grant Fights Antitrust Accusations, Critics." *Bloomberg Businessweek,* March 4, 2010, http://www.businessweek.com/news/2010-03-04/monsanto-warrior-grant-fights-antitrust-accusations-critics.html (accessed February 14, 2011); Kilman, Scott. "Monsanto's Net Profit Declines by 45%." *The Wall Street Journal,* July 1, 2010, B7; Miller, John W. "Monsanto Loses Case in Europe over Seeds." *The Wall Street Journal,* July 7, 2010, B1; Monsanto. "2008–2009 Global Contributions Report." http://www.monsantofund.org/pdf/mon_fund_08-09_report.pdf (accessed February 14, 2011); Monsanto. "Agriculture Scholarships." http://www.monsanto.com/responsibility/youth/scholarship.asp (accessed April 1, 2009); Monsanto. "Backgrounder: Glyphosate and Environmental Fate Studies." http://www.monsanto.com/monsanto/content/products/productivity/roundup/gly_efate_bkg.pdf (accessed April 1, 2009); Monsanto. "Biotech Cotton Improving Lives of Farmers, Villages in India." http://www.monsanto.com/responsibility/sustainable-ag/biotech_cotton_india.asp (accessed March 31, 2009); Monsanto. "Corporate Profile." http://www.monsanto.com/investors/corporate_profile.asp (accessed March 15, 2009); Monsanto. "Monsanto Donates Corn and Vegetable Seeds to Haiti." http://www.monsanto.com/ourcommitments/Pages/haiti-seed-donation.aspx (accessed February 14, 2011); Monsanto. "Drought-Tolerant Corn Promises to Aid Sub-Sahara African Farmers." Monsanto, http://www.monsanto.com/ourcommitments/Pages/water-efficient-maize-for-africa.aspx (accessed February 14, 2011); Monsanto. "Farm Safety 4 Just Kids." http://www.monsanto.com/responsibility/youth/fs4jk.asp (accessed April 1, 2009); Monsanto. "Great Place to Work." http://www.monsanto.com/careers/culture/great_place.asp (accessed April 2009); Monsanto. "Is Monsanto Going to Develop or Sell 'Terminator' Seeds?" http://www.monsanto.com/monsanto_today/for_the_record/monsanto_terminator_seeds.asp (accessed March 28, 2009); Monsanto. "Monsanto & NGO ISAP Launch Project Share—Sustainable Yield Initiative to Improve Farmer Lives." http://monsanto.mediaroom.com/index.php?s=43&item=693 (accessed March 31, 2009); Monsanto. "Produce More." http://www.monsanto.com/responsibility/sustainable-ag/produce_more.asp (accessed April 1, 2009); Monsanto. "Seed Police?" http://www.monsanto.com/seedpatentprotection/monsanto_seed_police.asp (accessed March 30, 2009); "Monsanto Company—Company Profile, Information, Business Description, History, Background Information on Monsanto Company." http://www.referenceforbusiness.com/history2/92/Monsanto-Company.html (accessed March 20, 2009); "Monsanto Fined $1.5M for Bribery." *BBC News,* January 7, 2005, http://news.bbc.co.uk/2/hi/business/4153635.stm (accessed March 15, 2009); "Monsanto Mania: The Seed of Profits." *iStockAnalyst,* http://www.istockanalyst.com/article/viewarticle.aspx?articleid=1235584&zoneid=Home (accessed April 12, 2009); Oxborrow, Claire, Becky Price, and Peter Riley. "Breaking Free." *Ecologist* 38, no. 9 (November 2008): 35–36; Pollack, Andrew. "So What's the Problem with Roundup?" Ecology Center, January 14, 2003, http://www.ecologycenter.org/factsheets/roundup.html (accessed March 25, 2009); Pollack, Andrew. "Widely Used Crop Herbicide Is Losing Weed Resistance." *The New York Times,* January 14, 2003, http://www.nytimes.com/2003/01/14/business/widely-used-crop-herbicide-is-losing-weed-resistance.html (accessed August 25, 2009); Pollan, Michael. "Playing God in the Garden." *The New York Times Magazine,* October 25, 1998, http://www.michaelpollan.com/article.php?id=73 (accessed July 11, 2011); Scientific Committee on Animal Health and Animal Welfare. "Report on Animal Welfare Aspects of the Use of Bovine Sematotrophin." March 10, 1999, http://ec.europa.eu/food/fs/sc/scah/out21_en.pdf (accessed August 25, 2009); "$700 Million Settlement in Alabama PCB Lawsuit." *The New York Times,* August 21, 2001, http://www.nytimes.com/2003/08/21/business/700-million-settlement-in-alabama-pcb-lawsuit.html (accessed March 15, 2009); Weintraub, Arlene. "The Outcry over 'Terminator' Genes in Food." *BusinessWeek,* July 14, 2003, http://www.businessweek.com/magazine/content/03_28/b3841091.htm (accessed March 25, 2009; Williams, G. M., R. Kroes, and I. C. Monro. "Safety Evaluation and Risk Assessment of the Herbicide Roundup and Its Active Ingredient, Glyphosate, for Humans." NCBI, April 2000, http://www.ncbi.nlm.nih.gov/pubmed/10854122 (accessed April 1, 2009); World Health Organization. "Food Security." http://www.who.int/trade/glossary/story028/en/ (accessed July 11, 2011); "The parable of the sower." *The Economist,* November 21, 2009, 71–73; Yahoo Finance! "Monsanto Co. (MON)." http://finance.yahoo.com/q/is?s=MON+Income+Statement&annual (accessed February 14, 2011).

CASE 2

Starbucks' Mission: Social Responsibility and Brand Strength*

Starbucks was founded in 1971 by three partners in Seattle's renowned open-air Pike Place Market and was named after the first mate in Herman Melville's *Moby Dick*. Howard Schultz joined Starbucks in 1982 as director of retail operations and marketing. Returning from a trip to Milan, Italy, with its 1,500 coffee bars, Schultz recognized an opportunity to develop a similar retail coffee-bar culture in Seattle.

In 1985 the company tested the first downtown Seattle coffeehouse, served the first Starbucks café latté, and introduced its Christmas Blend. Since then, Starbucks has been expanding across the United States and around the world, now operating nearly 17,000 stores in 55 countries. Historically, Starbucks has grown at a rate of about three stores a day, although the company has cut back on expansion in recent years. The company nevertheless serves millions of customers a week and has net revenues of approximately $11 billion a year. It has become the third largest chain restaurant in the United States.

Starbucks locates its retail stores in high-traffic, high-visibility locations. The stores are designed to provide an inviting coffee-bar environment that is an important part of the Starbucks product and experience. It was the intention of Howard Schulz to make Starbucks into "the third place" for consumers to frequent, after home and work. Because the company is flexible regarding size and format, it can locate stores in or near a variety of settings, including office buildings, bookstores, and university campuses. It can also situate retail stores in select rural and off-highway locations to serve a broader array of customers outside major metropolitan markets and to further expand brand awareness. To provide a greater degree of access and convenience for non-pedestrian customers, the company has increased development of stores with drive-through lanes.

In addition to selling its products through retail outlets, Starbucks sells coffee and tea products and licenses its trademark through other channels and some of its partners. For instance, its Frappuccino coffee drinks, Starbucks Doubleshot espresso drinks, super-premium ice creams, and VIA coffees can be purchased in grocery stores and through retailers like Walmart and Target. Starbucks is also partnering with Courtesy Products to create single-cup Starbucks packets that will be marketed for hotel rooms. With Starbucks intending to expand its offerings of food and complementary products, consumers will likely see many more Starbucks-related items in grocery stores, hotels, and restaurants.

*This case was prepared by Jennifer Sawayda, Ben Siltman, and Melanie Drever for and under the direction of Linda Ferrell, O. C. Ferrell, and Jennifer Jackson. It was prepared for classroom discussion rather than to illustrate either effective or ineffective handling of an administrative, ethical, or legal decision by management. All sources used for this case were obtained through publicly available material and the Starbucks website.

A common criticism of Starbucks has to do with the company's strategy for location and expansion. Its "clustering" strategy, placing a Starbucks literally on every corner in some cases, has forced many smaller coffee shops out of business. This strategy was so dominant for most of the 1990s and 2000s that Starbucks became the butt of jokes. Many people began to wonder whether we really needed two Starbucks directly across the street from each other. The recent global recession brought a change in policy, however. Starbucks pulled back on expansion, closed hundreds of stores around the United States, and began focusing more on international markets.

NEW PRODUCT OFFERINGS

Starbucks has introduced a number of new products over the years to remain competitive. In 2008 Starbucks decided to go back to its essentials with the introduction of its Pike Place Blend, which the company hoped would bring it back to its roots of distinctive, expertly blended coffee. In order to get the flavor perfect, Starbucks enlisted the input of 1,000 customers over 1,500 hours. To kick off the new choice, Starbucks held the largest nationwide coffee tasting in history. To make the brew even more appealing, Starbucks joined forces with Conservation International to ensure that the beans were sustainably harvested.

The global recession also caused Starbucks to respond with new product offerings. For instance, the company began offering a value meal called Breakfast Pairings that enabled customers to order oatmeal or coffee cake and a latte or a breakfast sandwich and a drip coffee for $3.95. Oatmeal has become one of the most popular food offerings at Starbucks.

Starbucks is also seeking to ride another recession-spawned trend. As people cut back on their expenditures, many began choosing to brew their own coffee rather than purchase more expensive coffee shop concoctions. To gain a foothold in the potentially lucrative instant coffee market, Starbucks introduced VIA instant coffee. VIA is aiming for a more premium market, as it retails for around $1 per serving. Starbucks VIA coffee has achieved $200 million in annual revenue and has become the official brew aboard select JetBlue flights in the United Kingdom and Spain.

Starbucks executives believe that the experience customers have in their stores should be consistent. Therefore, Starbucks has begun to refocus on the customer experience as one of the key competitive advantages of the Starbucks brand. To enhance the European coffee shop experience for which Starbucks is known, shops are replacing their old espresso machines with new high-tech ones, and some Starbucks are switching over to Clover Brand single-cup brewing machines so that each customer receives a freshly brewed cup of coffee made to his or her specifications. To keep the drink-making operation running efficiently, Starbucks mandated that baristas can make no more than two drinks at the same time. The company hopes that this will reduce errors and increase product quality.

Additionally, Starbucks tries to foster brand loyalty by increasing repeat business. One of the ways it has done this is through the Starbucks Card, a reloadable card that was introduced in 2001. By the end of 2011 consumers will also be able to use their cards to get rewards for Starbucks products purchased in grocery stores. For the more tech-savvy visitor, Starbucks introduced a Starbucks Card mobile app that can be used to pay for purchases at approximately 6,800 company-owned Starbucks stores, along with Starbucks Card eGifts that can be sent to friends through the Internet.

STARBUCKS CULTURE

In 1990 Starbucks' senior executive team created a mission statement that laid out the guiding principles for the company. They hoped that the principles included in the mission statement would help their partners determine the appropriateness of later decisions and actions. After drafting the mission statement, the executive team asked all Starbucks partners to review and comment on the document. Based on their feedback, the final statement put "people first and profits last." In fact, the number one guiding principle in Starbucks' mission statement was to "provide a great work environment and treat each other with respect and dignity."

Starbucks has done three things to keep the mission and guiding principles alive over the decades. First, it distributes the mission statement and comment cards for feedback during orientation to all new partners. Second, Starbucks continually relates decisions back to the guiding principle or principles that it supports. And finally, the company has formed a "Mission Review" system so partners can comment on a decision or action relative to its consistency with one of the six principles. These guiding principles and values have become the cornerstone of a strong ethical culture of predominately young and educated workers.

> "Starbucks continually relates decisions back to the guiding principle or principles that it supports."

Starbucks founder and chair Howard Schultz has long been a public advocate for increased awareness of ethics in business. In a 2007 speech at Notre Dame, he spoke to an audience of students about the importance of balancing "profitability and social consciousness." Schultz is a true believer that ethical companies do better in the long run, something that has been borne out by research. Schultz maintains that, while it can be difficult to do the right thing at all times, it is better for a company to take some short-term losses than to lose sight of its core values in the long term.

Due to its strong corporate culture, Starbucks has been ranked one of *Fortune*'s "100 Best Companies to Work for" for nearly a decade. However, the company has slipped in recent years due to cutbacks and store closings. In 2011 the company ranked 98th out of 100 companies. Despite these challenges, Starbucks has been praised for not cutting back on employee health care costs. The care the company shows its employees is a large part of what sets it apart. Starbucks offers all employees who work more than 20 hours per week a comprehensive benefits package that includes stock options as well as medical, dental, and vision benefits. Starbucks has also been recognized for its ethical practices in other countries. In 2010 it was voted "Most Ethical Company" in the European Coffee Industry by Allegra Strategies for the second consecutive year.

Another key part of the Starbucks image involves its commitment to ethics and sustainability. To address concerns related to these issues, Starbucks launched the Shared Planet website. Shared Planet has three main goals: to achieve ethical sourcing, environmental stewardship, and greater community involvement. The website is a means of keeping customers up to date on initiatives within the company. It describes how well Starbucks is faring on achieving its social responsibility goals, and it even provides a means for customers to learn about things like the nutrition data of Starbucks' offerings and other concerns related to Starbucks products.

Starbucks also actively partners with nonprofits around the globe. In one year Starbucks increased its total purchases of Fair Trade Certified coffee from 19 million pounds to

39 million pounds. Starbucks joined with Bono's Product RED in an effort to raise money for HIV and AIDs research. Additionally, Starbucks makes $14.5 million in loans to poor farmers around the world and plans to increase that number to $20 million by 2015. Conservation International joined with Starbucks in 1998 to promote sustainable agricultural practices, namely shade-grown coffee, and to help prevent deforestation in endangered regions around the globe. The results of the partnership proved to be positive for both the environment and farmers. For example, in Chiapas, Mexico, shade-grown coffee acreage (which reduces the need to cut down trees for coffee plantations) has increased well over 220 percent, while farmers receive a price premium above the market price. Starbucks also tried to increase awareness of its company while simultaneously building goodwill through its "Check In for Charity" initiative. For every Starbucks check-in on Facebook Places, Starbucks would donate $1 to Conservation International up to $75,000.

Starbucks works with many other organizations as well, including the African Wildlife Foundation and Business for Social Responsibility. The company's efforts at transparency, the treatment of its workers, and its dozens of philanthropic commitments demonstrate how genuine Starbucks is in its mission to be an ethical and socially responsible company.

CORPORATE SOCIAL MISSION

Although Starbucks has supported responsible business practices virtually since its inception, as the company has grown, so has the importance of defending its image. At the end of 1999 Starbucks created a Corporate Social Responsibility department, now known as the Global Responsibility Department. Global Responsibility releases an annual report in order to allow shareholders to keep track of its performance, which can be accessed through the Shared Planet website. Starbucks is concerned about the environment, its employees, suppliers, customers, and its communities.

Environment

In 1992, long before it became trendy to be "green," Starbucks developed an environmental mission statement to more clearly articulate the company's environmental priorities and goals. This initiative created the Environmental Starbucks Coffee Company Affairs team, the purpose of which was to develop environmentally responsible policies and minimize the company's "footprint." As part of this effort, Starbucks began using environmental purchasing guidelines and set out to reduce waste through recycling and energy conservation and educate partners through the company's "Green Team" initiatives. Concerned stakeholders can now track the company's progress through its Shared Planet website, which clearly outlines Starbucks' environmental goals and how the company is faring in living up to those goals.

Employees

Growing up poor with a father whose life was nearly ruined by an unsympathetic employer that did not offer health benefits, Howard Schultz has always considered the creation of a good work environment a top priority. "I watched what would happen to the plight of working class families when society and companies turned their back on the worker," Schultz said. "I wanted to build the kind of company my father never got to work for." The result is one of the best health care programs in the coffee shop industry. Schultz's key to maintaining a strong business is "creating an environment where everyone believes they're part of something larger than themselves but believes they also have a voice." Understanding how vital employees are, Shultz is the first to admit that his company centers on personal interactions: "We are not in the coffee business serving people, but in the people business serving coffee."

However, being a great employer does take its toll on the company. In 2005 Starbucks spent more on health insurance for its employees than on the raw materials required to brew its coffee. The company has faced double-digit increases in insurance costs for multiple years running. Nonetheless, Starbucks' benefits package is a key reason why it has remarkably low employee turnover and high productivity.

> "Starbucks' benefits package is a key reason why it has remarkably low employee turnover and high productivity."

Suppliers

Even though it is one of the largest coffee brands in the world, Starbucks maintains a good reputation for social responsibility and business ethics throughout the international community of coffee growers. It attempts to build positive relationships with small coffee suppliers while also working with governments and nonprofits wherever it operates. Starbucks practices conservation as well as Starbucks Coffee and Farmer Equity Practices (C.A.F.E.), which is a set of socially responsible coffee buying guidelines that ensure preferential buying status for participants who receive high scores in best practices. Starbucks pays coffee farmers premium prices to help them make profits and support their families. Over 80 percent of total coffee purchases are C.A.F.E. verified.

The company is also involved in social development programs, investing in programs to build schools and health clinics, as well as other projects that benefit coffee-growing communities. Starbucks collaborates directly with some of its growers through Farmer Support Centers, located in Costa Rica and Rwanda, with another center planned for China. Farmer Support Centers provide technical support and training to ensure high-quality coffee into the future. It also is a major purchaser of Fair Trade Certified, shade-grown, and certified organic beans, which further supports environmental and economic efforts.

In 1991 Starbucks began contributing to CARE, a worldwide relief and development foundation, as a way to give back to coffee-origin countries. By 1995 Starbucks was CARE's largest corporate donor. Starbucks' donations help with projects like clean water systems, health and sanitation training, and literacy efforts. Starbucks continues its long-term relationship with CARE, making Pike Place Blend its first CARE-certified brew.

Customers

Strengthening its brand and customer satisfaction is more important than ever as Starbucks seeks to regroup after the global economic crisis forced the company to rethink its strategy. In addition to shutting down stores, Starbucks refocused the brand by upgrading its coffee-brewing machines, introducing new food and drink items for budget-conscious consumers, and refocusing on its core product. While Starbucks had for years been looking for ways to branch out into music, movies, and other merchandise, economic troubles forced Starbucks to start thinking smaller. The company started to focus more on the quality of the coffee, the atmosphere of the coffee shops, and the overall Starbucks experience, rather than on continuing its rapid expansion of stores and products. Enhancing the customer experience in its stores also became a high priority. As a way to encourage people to relax and spend time there, Starbucks offers free wireless Internet access in all its U.S. stores.

Communities

Starbucks coffee shops have long sought to become the "instant gathering spot" wherever they locate, a "place that draws people together." To enhance the local, community-oriented feel of Starbucks shops, store managers are encouraged to donate to local causes. For example, one Seattle store donated more than $500,000 to Zion Preparatory Academy, an African American school for inner-city youth. Howard Schultz believes that literacy has the power to improve lives and to give hope to underprivileged children. Schultz even used the advance and ongoing royalties from his book, *Pour Your Heart into It,* to create the Starbucks Foundation, which provides "opportunity grants" to nonprofit literacy groups, sponsors young writers' programs, and partners with Jumpstart, an organization helping children to prepare developmentally for school.

Starbucks also encourages community involvement with the creation of websites such as mystarbucks.com. This website asks users to submit ideas for making Starbucks a better place. Users can submit their ideas for new products, a better Starbucks experience, or ways that Starbucks can engage in the community. Starbucks used the site as a forum to ask consumers what the company could do to bring them back into their stores. The number one response was the Starbucks loyalty program, so Starbucks instituted a Starbucks reward program for frequent patrons.

BRAND EVOLUTION

Although Starbucks has achieved massive success in the last 40 years, the company realizes that it must modify its brand to appeal to changing consumer tastes. All established companies, no matter how successful, must learn to adapt their products and image to appeal to the shifting demands of their target markets. Starbucks is no exception. The company is mostly associated with premium coffee beverages, an association that has served it well over the years. However, as competition in specialty coffee drinks increases, Starbucks has recognized the need to expand its brand in the eyes of consumers.

One way it is doing this is by adopting more products. In addition to coffee, Starbucks stores now sell coffee accessories, teas, muffins, CDs, water, grab-and-go products, its new line of Starbuck Petites, and more. Food sales make up 20 percent of Starbucks' revenue. With coffee prices projected to increase in the near future, an expansion into consumer packaged goods will help protect Starbucks against the risks of relying solely on coffee. To symbolize this shift into the consumer packaged goods business, Starbucks is giving its logo a new look. Until recently, the company's circular logo featured a mermaid with the words "Starbucks Coffee" encircling it. In 2011 Starbucks announced it was removing the words and enlarging the mermaid to signal to consumers that Starbucks is more than just the average coffee retailer.

Starbucks is also looking to capture some of the "night life." As the majority of Starbucks' business currently comes before 2 p.m., Starbucks is experimenting with a new type of store to appeal to the evening crowd. This store serves regional wine, beer, and cheeses during the evening. Starbucks incorporated customer suggestions into the design of its trial store in Seattle. As a result, its experimental store boasts an indoor–outdoor deck and a barista bar running through the center of the retail outlet. If Starbucks can succeed in creating a hip location for adults in the evening, it could experience a major influx in revenue. Such a move does not come without potential costs, however. Redesigning Starbucks stores will be expensive, and Starbucks risks eroding its established brand with too many changes. Perhaps for this reason, CEO Howard Schultz announced that these experimental stores will not be released on a broad-based scale. Instead, it is a way for the company to try new product offerings without overhauling the brand.

Starbucks is also partnering with Green Mountain Coffee Roasters to introduce Starbucks-branded coffee and tea pods to the market. These pods are targeted toward consumers who own Keurig single-cup brewing machines. Although the two businesses would normally be rivals, this partnership will prove mutually beneficial for both Green Mountain and Starbucks. Since Green Mountain owns Keurig's single-serve machines, the partnership enables Starbucks to access this technology to market a new product. Green Mountain benefits because the partnership will generate new users of Keurig single-cup brewing machines who are attracted to the Starbucks name. It also keeps Starbucks from becoming a key rival in this area. The deal represents a first step in Starbucks' quest to break into the single-serve market.

SUCCESS AND CHALLENGES

For decades, Starbucks has been revolutionizing our leisure time. Starbucks is not only the most prominent brand of high-end coffee in the world, it is also one of the defining brands of our time. In most large cities, it is impossible to go more than a few blocks without seeing the familiar mermaid logo.

For nearly two decades, Starbucks achieved amazing levels of growth, creating financial success for shareholders. Starbucks' reputation is built on product quality, stakeholder concern, and a balanced approach to all of its business activities. Of course, Starbucks does receive criticism for putting other coffee shops out of business and creating a uniform retail culture in many cities. Yet Starbucks excels in its relationship with its employees and is a role model for the fast-food industry in employee benefits. In addition, in an age of shifts in supply chain power, Starbucks is as concerned about its suppliers and meeting their needs as it is about any other primary stakeholder.

> "Starbucks' reputation is built on product quality, stakeholder concern, and a balanced approach to all of its business activities."

In spite of Starbucks' efforts to support sustainability and maintain high ethical standards, in the past the company has garnered harsh criticism on issues such as a lack of fair trade coffee, hormone-added milk, Howard Shultz's alleged financial links to the Israeli government, and the fact that the company's relentless growth has forced locally run coffee shops out of business. In an attempt to counter these criticisms, in 2002 Starbucks began offering Fair Trade Certified coffee, a menu item that was quickly made permanent. In Ireland and the U.K., all Starbucks Espresso is now 100 percent Fair Trade certified, although this is not yet true for the United States.

Starting in late 2008, Starbucks had something new to worry about. A global recession caused the market to bottom out for expensive coffee drinks. The company responded by slowing its global growth plans after years of expanding at a nonstop pace and instead refocused on strengthening its brand, satisfying customers, and building consumer loyalty. After Starbucks stock started to plummet, Howard Schultz returned as CEO to try to return the company to its former glory.

Schultz was successful, and Starbucks was able to rebound from the effects of the recession. The company is once again looking toward possibilities in international markets.

This represents both new opportunities and challenges. When attempting to break into the U.K. market, for instance, Starbucks met with serious resistance. Realizing that the homogenization of its stores did not work as well in the United Kingdom, Starbucks began to refit its stores so that they would take on a more local feel. Starbucks is also looking toward China for expansion. The company currently operates 700 stores in China, with plans to open hundreds more. Effectively tapping into the Chinese market will no doubt require Starbucks to overcome unexpected obstacles and adapt its strategy to attract Chinese consumers. Despite these potential challenges, however, Starbucks has announced that it intends for China to become its biggest market.

Another challenge that Starbuck must address is the fact that, despite the company's emphasis on sustainability, an estimated 3 billion disposable Starbucks cups are thrown into landfills each year. Only 5 percent of its stores recycle the cups. Although Starbucks has taken initiatives to make its cups more ecofriendly, such as switching from polyethylene No. 1 to the more ecofriendly polypropylene No. 5, the cup represents a serious waste problem for Starbucks. Starbucks is encouraging consumers to bring in reusables (such as the Starbucks tumblers it sells) for a 10-cent rebate, yet these account for less than 2 percent of drinks served. The company remains determined to tackle this issue, with the goal of achieving 100-percent recyclability by 2015. In 2010 Starbucks held a two-day "Cup Summit," inviting outside participants to brainstorm on how to create a more sustainable cup. It remains to be seen whether Starbucks will achieve its goal of total recyclability in the short term.

Despite the setbacks it experienced during the recession, the future looks bright for Starbucks. The challenges that the company has experienced, and will continue to experience in the future, have convinced it to focus on its strengths and embrace the opportunity to emphasize community involvement, outreach work, and its overall image and offerings. The company must continue to apply the balanced stakeholder orientation that has been so crucial to its success.

QUESTIONS

1. Why do you think Starbucks has been so concerned with social responsibility in its overall corporate strategy?

2. Is Starbucks unique in being able to provide a high level of benefits to its employees?

3. Do you think that Starbucks has grown rapidly because of its ethical and socially responsible activities or because it provides products and an environment that customers want?

SOURCES

Burkitt, Laurie. "Starbuck Menu Expands in China." *The Wall Street Journal,* March 9, 2011, B7; Eartheasy.com. "Shade Grown Coffee." http://www.eartheasy.com/eat_shadegrown_coffee.htm (accessed May 7, 2009); *Fortune.* "100 Best Companies to Work for." http://money.cnn.com/magazines/fortune/bestcompanies/2010/snapshots/93.html (accessed February 10, 2011); Gossage, Bobbie. "Howard Schultz, on Getting a Second Shot." *Inc.,* April 2011, 52–54; Horovitz, Bruce. "Starbucks Aims beyond Lattes to Extend Brand to Films, Music and Books." *USA Today,* May 19, 2006, A1, A2; Horovitz, Bruce. "Starbucks remakes its future." *USA Today,* October 18, 2010, 1B–2B; Horovitz, Bruce. "Starbucks sales pass BK, Wendy's." *USA Today,* April 27, 2011, 1A; Horovitz, Bruce. "Starbucks Unveils Menu Deal to Halt Slide." *USA Today,* February 8, 2009, www.usatoday.com/money/industries/food2009-02-08-value-menu-starbucks_N.htm (accessed May 5, 2009); Horovitz, Bruce, and Howard Schultz. "Starbucks Hits 40 Feeling Perky." *USA Today,* March 7, 2011, 1B, 3B; Jannarone, John. "Green Mountain Eclipses Starbucks." *The Wall Street Journal,* March 9, 2011, C14; Jannarone, John. "Grounds for Concern at Starbucks." *The Wall Street Journal,* May 3, 2011, C10; Jargon, Julie. "At Starbucks, Baristas Told No More than Two Drinks." *The Wall Street Journal,* October 13, 2010, http://online.wsj.com/article/SB10001424052748704164004575548403514060736.html (accessed February 10, 2011); Jargon, Julie. "Coffee Talk: Starbucks Chief on Prices, McDonald's Rivalry." *The Wall Street Journal,* March 7, 2011, B6; Jargon, Julie. "Starbucks Logo Loses 'Coffee,' Expands Mermaid as Firm Moves to Build Packaged-Goods Business." *The Wall Street Journal,* January 6, 2011, B4; Jargon, Julie. "Starbucks in Pod Pact." *The Wall Street Journal,* March 11, 2011, B4; Kamenetz, Anya. "'What are you going to do about this damn cup?'" *Fast Company,* November 2010, www.fastcompany.com/magazine/150/a-story-of-starbucks-and-the-limits-of-corporate-sustainability.html (accessed December 20, 2010); La Monica, Paul R. "Starbucks at 40: No mid-life crisis for stock." *CNNMoney,* March 8, 2011, http://money.cnn.com/2011/03/08/news/companies/thebuzz/index.htm (accessed March 10, 2011); McClelland, Kate. "Starbucks Founder Speaks on Ethics." *Notre Dame Observer,* March 30, 2007, http://media.www.ndsmcobserver.com/media/storage/paper660/news/2007/ 03/30/News/Starbucks.Founder.Speaks.On.Ethics-2814792.shtml (accessed September 1, 2009); MSNBC.com. "Health Care Takes Its Toll on Starbucks." http://www.msnbc.msn.com/id/9344634/, September 14, 2005 (accessed May 5, 2009); Sanchanta, Mariko. "Starbucks Plans Big Expansion in China." *The Wall Street Journal,* April 14, 2010, B10; Schorn, Daniel. "Howard Schultz: The Star of Starbucks." 60 Minutes, http://www.cbsnews.com/stories/2006/04/21/60minutes/main1532246.shtml (accessed February 10, 2011); Schultz, E. J. "How VIA Steamed up the Instant Coffee Category." *AdvertisingAge,* January 24, 2011, http://adage.com/article?article_id=148403 (accessed February 10, 2011); Starbucks. "2008 Annual Report." http://media.corporate-ir.net/media_files/irol/99/99518/AR2008.pdf (accessed April 1, 2009); Starbucks. "C.A.F.E. Practices (Coffee and Farmer Equity Practices)." http://www.starbucks.ca/ en-ca/_Social+Responsibility/C.A.F.E.+Practices.htm (accessed May 7, 2009); Starbucks. "Check in at Starbucks." http://blogs.starbucks.com/blogs/customer/archive/2010/11/04/check-in-at-starbucks.aspx, November 1, 2010 (accessed February 10, 2011); Starbucks. "Coffee Purchasing." http://www.starbucks.com/responsibility/learn-more/goals-and-progress/coffee-purchasing (accessed February 10, 2011); Starbucks. "Introducing Starbucks Card eGifts." http://www.starbucks.com/blog/introducing-starbucks-card-egifts, January 25, 2011 (accessed March 10, 2011); Starbucks. "Farmer Loans." http://www.starbucks.com/responsibility/learn-more/goals-and-progress/farmer-loans (accessed February 10, 2011); Starbucks. "Mobile Applications." http://www.starbucks.com/coffeehouse/mobile-apps (accessed February 10, 2011); Starbucks. "The Proof Is in the Cup: Starbucks Launched Historic New Pike Place Roast™." http://news.starbucks.com/article_display.cfm?article_id=51, April 7, 2008 (accessed May 4, 2009); Starbucks. "Responsibly Grown Coffee." http://www.starbucks.com/responsibility/sourcing/coffee (accessed February 10, 2011); Starbucks. "Starbucks Company Profile." http://assets.starbucks.com/assets/aboutuscompanyprofileq12011final13111.pdf (accessed February 10, 2011); Starbucks. "Starbucks Company Fact Sheet." http://www.starbucks.com/aboutus/Company_Factsheet.pdf (accessed May 5, 2009); Starbucks. "Starbucks Honored with 'Most Ethical Company in Europe' Award for the Second Year Running and 'Best Branded Coffee Shop Chain in Europe' Award." http://news.starbucks.com/news/starbucks+honored+with+most+ethical+company+in+europe+award+for+second+year.htm, November 9, 2010 (accessed February 10, 2011); Starbucks. "Starbucks VIA Ready Brew Launches on EasyJet Airline across Selected Routes in United Kingdom and Spain." http://news.starbucks.com/article_display.cfm?article_id=209, April 21, 2009 (accessed May 4, 2009); Starbucks. "When you care about what you do, it shows." http://www.starbuckscoffee.co.uk/when-you-care-about-what-you-do-it-shows/, February 10, 2010 (accessed February 10, 2011); "Starbucks to Enter China's Tea Drinks Market." *China Retail News,* March 11, 2010, www.chinaretailnews.com/2010/03/11/3423-starbucks-to-enter-chinas-tea-drinks-market (accessed June 14, 2010); "Starbucks unveils minimalist new logo." *USA Today,* January 6, 2011, 11B; Teather, David. "Starbucks legend delivers recovery by thinking smaller." *The Guardian,* January 21, 2010, www.guardian.co.uk/business/2010/jan/21/starbucks-howard-schultz (accessed June 12, 2010); Welch, Dan. "Fairtrade beans do not mean a cup of coffee is entirely ethical." guardian.co.uk, February 28, 2011, http://www.guardian.co.uk/environment/green-living-blog/2011/feb/28/coffee-chains-ethical (accessed July 11, 2011); Wire reports. "Coffee deal has stocks soaring," *USA Today,* March 11, 2011, 5B.

CASE 3

Walmart: The Future Is Sustainability*

Walmart Stores, Inc., is an icon of American business. From small-town business to multinational corporation, from a hugely controversial company to a leader in renewable energy, Walmart has long been a lightning rod for news and criticism. With 2010 sales of more than $408 billion and more than 2 million employees, the world's largest public corporation must carefully manage many different stakeholder relationships. It is a challenge that has sparked significant debate.

Although Walmart reportedly can save the average family $3,100 annually, the company has received plenty of criticism regarding its treatment of employees, suppliers, and economic impacts on communities. According to its estimates, Walmart saves consumers more than $287 billion annually, equating to about $950 per person. At the same time, however, research shows that communities can be negatively affected by Walmart's arrival in their areas. Moreover, feminists, activists, and labor union leaders have all voiced their belief that Walmart has engaged in misconduct. However, Walmart has been turning over a new leaf. New emphases on diversity, charitable giving, and sustainability have contributed to Walmart's revitalized image.

This analysis begins by briefly examining the growth of Walmart; next, it discusses the company's various relationships with its stakeholders, including competitors, suppliers, and employees. The ethical issues concerning these stakeholders include accusations of discrimination, illegal immigration issues, and leadership misconduct, as demonstrated by Walmart former vice chair Thomas Coughlin. We also examine Walmart's sustainability plans and ethical initiatives. The analysis concludes by examining what Walmart is currently doing to increase its competitive advantage, both domestically and globally.

HISTORY: THE GROWTH OF WALMART

The story of Walmart begins in 1962, when founder Sam Walton opened the first Walmart Discount Store in Rogers, Arkansas. Although it got off to a slow start caused by a lack of funds, over the next 40 years the company grew from a small chain to more than 8,000 facilities in 15 countries. The company now serves more than 200 million customers weekly. Much of the success that Walmart has experienced can be attributed to its founder. A shrewd businessman, Walton believed in customer satisfaction and hard work. He convinced many of his associates to abide by the "10-foot rule," whereby employees pledged that whenever they got within 10 feet of a customer, they would look the customer in the

---

*This case was prepared by O.C. Ferrell, Jennifer Sawayda, and Jennifer Jackson. Melanie Drever, Rob Boostrum, Lisa Heldt, and Tabitha Peyton made significant contributions to previous editions of this case. It was prepared for classroom discussion rather than to illustrate either effective or ineffective handling of an administrative, ethical, or legal decision by management. All sources used for this case were obtained through publicly available material and the Walmart website.

eye, greet him or her, and ask if he or she needed help with anything. Walton's famous mantra, known as the "sundown rule," was: "Why put off until tomorrow what you can do today?" Due to this staunch work ethic and dedication to customer care, Walmart claimed early on that a formal ethics program was unnecessary because the company had Mr. Sam's ethics to follow.

In 2002 Walmart officially became the largest grocery chain, topping the *Fortune* 500 (a position it held eight times between 2002 and 2010). The company has also become known for its efforts toward sustainable growth. Former CEO Lee Scott was ranked seventh in the Ethisphere Institute's list of 100 top contributors to business ethics based on his support of sustainability. Additionally, *Fortune* named Walmart the "most admired company in America" in 2003 and 2004. Although it has slipped since then, it remains high on the list. In 2010 Fortune ranked Walmart as the ninth most admired company in the world.

Effects on Competitive Stakeholders

Possibly the greatest complaint against Walmart is that it puts other companies out of business. With its low prices, Walmart makes it harder for local stores to compete. Walmart is often accused of being responsible for the downward pressure on wages and benefits in towns in which the company is located. Some businesses have filed lawsuits against Walmart, claiming that the company uses predatory pricing to put competing stores out of business, with mixed success. Walmart has countered by defending its pricing, asserting that its purpose is to provide quality, low-cost products to the average consumer. Yet although Walmart has saved consumers millions of dollars and is a popular shopping spot for many, there is no denying that many competing stores do go out of business once Walmart comes to town.

In order to compete against the retail giant, other stores must reduce wages. Studies have shown that overall payroll wages, including Walmart wages, are reduced by 5 percent after Walmart enters a new market. As a result, some activist groups and citizens have refused to allow Walmart to take up residence in their areas.

Relationships with Supplier Stakeholders

Walmart achieves its "everyday low prices" (EDLPs) by streamlining the company. Well-known for operational excellence in its ability to handle, move, and track merchandise, Walmart expects its suppliers to continually improve their systems as well. Walmart typically works with suppliers to reduce costs of packaging and shipping, which lessens costs for consumers. The company also launched a plan to reduce packaging by 5 percent by 2013, an initiative reflecting Walmart's desire to improve sustainability.

In 2008 Walmart introduced its "Global Responsible Sourcing Initiative." The following list provides details of the policies and requirements included in new supplier agreements.

- "Manufacturers' facilities must certify compliance with laws and regulations where they operate, as well as rigorous social and environmental standards set by government agencies, beginning with suppliers in China in January 2009 and for all other Walmart suppliers in 2011."

- "By 2012, suppliers must work with Walmart to make a 20 percent improvement in the energy efficiency inside the top 200 factories in China that Walmart directly sources from." Currently, 119 of these factories have improved their energy efficiency by five percent or higher.

- "Suppliers must create a plan to eliminate, by 2012, defective merchandise reaching the Walmart supply chain." One year later, Walmart's customer returns of defective merchandise had decreased to 1.97 percent.

- "[B]y 2012, all suppliers Walmart buys from must source 95 percent of their production from factories that receive the highest ratings on environmental and social practices." By 2010, 93 percent of Walmart's direct sourcing products came from factories with high ratings.

If fully achieved, these goals will increase the sustainability of Walmart suppliers significantly. Some critics, however, believe that pressures to achieve these standards will shift more of a cost burden onto suppliers. Since Walmart is specifically targeting its largest supplier network in China, many believe these goals will be hard to implement in the allotted time period and will be hard to enforce and track due to the intricate maze of suppliers in China and other countries. When suppliers do not meet its demands, Walmart ceases to carry the supplier's product or, often, will find another supplier for the product at the desired price.

Walmart's power centers around its size and the volume of products it requires. Many companies depend on Walmart for much of their business. This type of relationship allows Walmart to influence terms with its vendors, and indeed, there are benefits to being a Walmart supplier; as suppliers become more efficient and streamlined for Walmart, they help their other customers as well. Numerous companies believe that supplying Walmart has been the best thing for their businesses.

However, many others have found the amount of power that Walmart wields to be disconcerting. The constant drive by Walmart for lower prices can have a negative effect on suppliers. Many have been forced to move production from the United States to less expensive locations in Asia. Walmart imports more than $18 billion in products from China and encourages its suppliers to move production there in order to lower costs. It is estimated that Walmart ranks as China's seventh-largest trading partner. Companies such as Master Lock, Fruit of the Loom, and Levi's, as well as many other Walmart suppliers, have moved production overseas at the expense of U.S. jobs.

This was not founder Sam Walton's original intention. In the 1980s, after learning that his stores were putting other American companies out of business, Walton started his "Buy American" campaign. However, the quest to maintain low prices has pushed many Walmart suppliers overseas, and some experts now estimate that as much as 80 percent of Walmart's global suppliers are stationed in China.

Ethical Issues Involving Employee Stakeholders

EMPLOYEE BENEFITS   Much of the Walmart controversy over the years has focused on the way the company treats its employees, or "associates" as Walmart refers to them. Although Walmart is the largest retail employer in the world, it also has been roundly criticized for its low wages and benefits. Walmart has been accused of failing to provide health insurance for more than 60 percent of its employees. Many part-time employees are not eligible. In a memo sent to the board of directors by Susan Chambers, Walmart's executive vice-president for benefits, she encouraged the hiring of more part-time workers while also encouraging the hiring of "healthier, more productive employees." After this bad publicity, between 2000 and 2005 Walmart's stock decreased 27 percent.

As a result of the deluge of bad press, Walmart has taken action to improve relations with its employee stakeholders. In 2006 Walmart raised pay tied to performance in about one-third of its stores. The company also improved its health benefits package by offering lower deductibles and implementing a generic prescription plan estimated to save employees $25 million. Walmart estimates that over three-fourths of its employees have insurance (though not always through Walmart). Walmart is quick to point out that the company offers health care benefits that are competitive in the retail industry. However, Walmart has also verbally expressed the need for reform in the health care industry. In 2009 the company sent a letter to President Obama to express support for health care reform with an emphasis on controlling costs and increasing efficiency.

WALMART'S STANCE ON UNIONS

Some critics believe that workers' benefits could be improved if workers could become unionized. Unions have been discouraged since Walmart's foundation; Sam Walton believed that they were a divisive force and might render the company uncompetitive. Walmart maintains that it is not against unions in general, but that it sees no need for unions to come between workers and managers. The company says that it supports an "open-door policy" in which associates can bring problems to managers without having to resort to third parties. Walmart associates have voted against unions in the past.

Although the company officially states that it is not opposed to unions, Walmart often seems to fight against them. Critics claim that when the word "union" surfaces at a Walmart location, the top dogs in Bentonville are called in. In 2000 seven of ten Walmart butchers in Jacksonville, Texas, voted to join the United Food Workers Union. Walmart responded by announcing it would only sell precut meat in its Supercenters, getting rid of its meat-cutting department entirely. Although Walmart offers justifications for actions such as this, many see the company as aggressively working to prevent unionization in its stores.

However, Walmart's stance against unions has not always held up in foreign countries. In China, Walmart faced a similar decision regarding unions. To grow in China, it appeared necessary to accept a union. Poor working conditions and low wages were generating social unrest, and the government was attempting to craft a new set of labor laws giving employees greater protection and giving the All-China Federation of Trade Unions (ACFTU) more power. In 2004 the Chinese Labor Federation pushed Walmart to allow the formation of unions. As a result, Walmart technically allowed this, but critics claimed that Walmart made it increasingly difficult for the workers to join a union. In 2006 a district union announced the first formation of a Walmart union at a store in China, and within a week, four more branches had announced their formations of unions. Walmart initially reacted to these announcements by stating it would not renew the contracts of unionized workers. However, the pressure mounted, and later that year Walmart signed a memorandum with the ACFTU allowing unions in stores.

> "Walmart's stance against unions has not always held up in foreign countries."

WORKPLACE CONDITIONS AND DISCRIMINATION

Despite accusations of low employee benefits and a strong stance against unions, Walmart remains the largest nongovernment employer in the United States, Mexico, and Canada. It provides jobs to millions of people and has been a mainstay of *Fortune*'s "Most Admired Companies" list since the start of the twenty-first century. However, in December 2005, Walmart was ordered to pay $172 million to more than 100,000 California employees in a class-action lawsuit claiming that Walmart routinely denied meal breaks. The California employees also alleged that they were denied rest breaks and that Walmart managers deliberately altered time cards to prevent overtime. Similar accusations began to pop up in other states as well. Walmart denied the allegations and filed an appeal in 2007. In 2008 Walmart agreed to pay up to $640 million to settle sixty-three such lawsuits.

Walmart has also been accused of discrimination by employees. Although women account for more than two-thirds of all Walmart employees, they make up less than 10 percent of store management. Walmart insists that it trains and promotes women fairly, but in 2001 an internal study showed that the company paid female store managers less than males in the same positions. In 2004 a federal judge in San Francisco granted class-action status to a sex-discrimination lawsuit against Walmart involving 1.6 million current and former female Walmart employees. The plaintiffs claimed that Walmart discriminated against them in regard to promotions, pay, training, and job assignments. Walmart argued against the class-action suit, claiming that promotions were made on an individual basis by each store. Walmart took the case to the Supreme Court, claiming that the suit violates the company's right of due process. The Supreme Court determined that the women in the lawsuit do not have enough in common to classify for class-action status. Although the women can still sue Walmart individually, the impact on the company will likely be far less than if a class-action lawsuit had been allowed to proceed.

In 2009 Walmart paid $17.5 million to settle a class action lawsuit accusing the company of discrimination in its hiring of truck drivers. The U.S. Equal Employment Opportunity Commission also sued the company, alleging that Hispanic workers at a California Sam's Club subsidiary were subjected to a hostile work environment. A year later Walmart experienced another discriminatory incident, this time perpetrated by a customer. A 16-year-old boy used one of Walmart's courtesy phones to announce "Attention, Walmart customers: All black people, leave the store now." Although a Walmart employee reacted quickly to apologize, many customers complained. Walmart worked with investigators to find the culprit (he was later arrested) and promised to update their intercom system so as to prevent future incidents. The National Association for the Advancement of Colored People (NAACP) in Gloucester County, New Jersey, expressed concerns over the incident. However, at the same time the organization also commended Walmart for its recent efforts in embracing diversity.

Indeed, in spite of these incidents, Walmart has received recognition for its good treatment of female workers. Between 2007 and 2010 the National Association for Female Executives recognized the company four years in a row as a "Top Company for Executive Women." This commendation makes one wonder if Walmart truly is trying to turn over a new leaf in how it treats its employees.

ILLEGAL IMMIGRANTS   In October 2003 a series of raids by U.S. Immigration and Customs Enforcement officials revealed that 250 illegal immigrants were working on cleaning crews at 61 Walmart stores in 21 states. Several Walmart contractors had hired the undocumented workers from Mexico, Eastern Europe, and other countries. In March 2005 this investigation ended in a landmark $11 million civil settlement. According to a *Wall Street Journal* article, three top Walmart executives knew the company's cleaning contractors used illegal immigrants yet did nothing to stop the practice. Walmart denied these allegations. The immigrants worked as many as seven days a week for less than minimum wage. The immigrants filed a class-action racketeering lawsuit against Walmart accusing the retailer of failing to pay their wages and keeping them in involuntary servitude. A New Jersey judge dismissed the civil racketeering class-action lawsuit after claiming that the immigrants did not have sufficient evidence to support their claims.

Ethical Leadership Issues

Aside from Sam Walton, other distinguished people have been associated with Walmart. One of them is Hillary Clinton, who served on Walmart's board for six years before her husband assumed the presidency. However, the company has not been immune from scandal at the top. In March 2005, board vice chair Thomas Coughlin was forced to resign because he had stolen as much as $500,000 from Walmart in the form of bogus expenses, reimbursements, and the unauthorized use of gift cards. Coughlin, a protégé and hunting buddy of Sam Walton, was a legend at Walmart. He often spent time on the road with Walton expanding the Sam's Club aspect of the business. At one time, he was the second highest-ranking Walmart executive and a candidate for CEO.

In January 2006 Coughlin agreed to plead guilty to federal wire-fraud and tax-evasion charges. Although he took home millions of dollars in compensation, Coughlin had secretly been using Walmart funds to pay for a range of personal expenses, including hunting vacations, a $2,590 dog enclosure at his home, and a pair of handmade alligator boots. Coughlin's deceit was discovered when he asked a subordinate to approve $2,000 in expense payments without receipts. Walmart rescinded Coughlin's retirement agreement, worth more than $10 million. For his crimes, he was sentenced to 27 months of home confinement, $440,000 in fines, and 1,500 hours of community service.

Problems with Environmental Stakeholders

Like many large corporations, Walmart has been targeted as a violator of safe environmental practices. In 2005 Walmart received a grand jury subpoena from the U.S. Attorney's Office in Los Angeles, California, seeking documents and information relating to the company's receipt, transportation, handling, identification, recycling, treatment, storage, and disposal of certain merchandise constituting hazardous material or hazardous waste.

However, probably the greatest environmental concern associated with Walmart has been urban sprawl. The construction of a Walmart can stress a city's infrastructure of roads, parking, and traffic flow. There have been concerns about the number of acres of city green space devoured by Walmart construction (Walmart Supercenters occupy about twenty to thirty acres of land). Another issue is the number of abandoned stores, deserted when the company outgrows locations. Currently, over 26 million square feet of empty Walmart space exists—enough to fill 534 football fields. Walmart allegedly goes out of its way to prevent other retail companies from buying its abandoned stores.

> "Probably the greatest environmental concern associated with Walmart has been urban sprawl."

Walmart's large stores have also put it at a disadvantage when trying to expand into urban areas. In places like New York City where space is a significant issue, there is less room for Walmart stores. Walmart plans to launch hundreds of smaller stores consisting of about 15,000 square feet in urban and rural areas within the next few years. This strategy of smaller stores is already showing promise, with Chicago's zoning committee finally approving a Walmart on its south side. Walmart also announced plans to open two dozen of these smaller stores in San Francisco by 2012. However, not all these big cities are eager to embrace Walmart. Walmart experienced a verbal backlash from officials and citizens of New York City at the mere suggestion of Walmart entering the city. To break into urban areas, the company will need to work on changing how Walmart is perceived among these stakeholders.

Sustainability 360

Walmart has attempted to address the concerns of its environmental stakeholders by becoming a "greener" company. Some of the company's goals include the following:

- Reducing greenhouse gases at stores, clubs, and distribution centers worldwide by 20 percent of its 2005 levels by 2012 (by 2010 Walmart had decreased its greenhouse gas emissions at its facilities by approximately 5 percent);

- Designing prototypes to be 25 to 30 percent more efficient than its 2005 levels by 2009 (Walmart successfully accomplished this goal in all of its international markets);

- Developing and installing innovative energy-efficient technology into stores.

Currently Walmart is working on four main green areas: waste improvement and recycling, natural resources, energy, and social/community impact. Walmart's long-term goals are to be supplied 100 percent by renewable energy, create zero waste, and carry products that sustain the environment and its resources.

Sustainability Leadership

Walmart has already taken strides to achieve its sustainability objectives. In 2010 the company installed the largest retail wind turbine installation to date at a Sam's Club in Palmdale, California. The seventeen turbines provide 5 percent of the store's energy needs. In Lancaster, California, another Walmart store gets half its energy needs from fuel-cell technology. The company also announced plans to double the number of its facilities that have solar technology. Walmart hopes these "greener" stores will provide examples of the ways building owners, scientists, engineers, architects, contractors, and landscape designers can work together to create facilities designed to save energy, conserve natural resources, and reduce pollution. Walmart estimates that its solar facilities have already saved it $1 million in energy costs since 2008.

To reduce energy consumption, Walmart facilities are conserving energy in two major ways. First, most new stores include a "daylighting" feature enabling stores to dim or turn off lights as daylight increases and enters through skylights, thereby reducing the demand for electricity during peak hours. Second, Walmart manages energy consumption by centrally controlling the heating and cooling of U.S. Walmart stores. Walmart is also attempting to reduce fossil fuel use and to sell more "green" products. For instance, the retailer has begun selling more toys made from sustainable or recycled materials and has started a program to sell more local produce (produce grown and sold in the same state). By 2015 Walmart wants 9 percent of the produce it sells in the United States to be from local sources. It is aiming for 30 percent of the produce sold in its Canadian stores to be locally grown. Walmart is also investing in medium and smaller-sized farms, particularly in emerging economies. To measure the sustainability of its products and suppliers, Walmart has launched its Sustainability Index. This index consists of three parts, each with its own goal. The first goal is to create a more transparent supply chain in terms of sustainability. As part of the first step toward achieving this goal, Walmart surveyed its suppliers about their companies' sustainability. The second step will involve forming a consortium of universities, suppliers, NGOs, government officials, and retailers to create a database on product life cycles, enabling Walmart and other companies to understand more about the sustainability of their products. The third step will involve conveying this information to consumers to help them make informed decisions.

One way in which Walmart might achieve this last step is through "green labels." In 2009 the company announced it would begin a green labeling program for certain products. These products would be provided with ratings to inform consumers about how "green" the products really are.

Although Walmart's environmental overhaul seems to be a step in the right direction, some are skeptical as to whether it can accomplish its goals. Suppliers are worried that products receiving higher "sustainability" rankings might be given preferential treatment over their own. Also, the concept of "being green" can be subjective, as not everyone agrees on how it should be defined or even whether one environmentally friendly practice is more beneficial than another. Walmart will have to overcome many obstacles as it works to make its goals a reality.

Walmart is also partnering with other large companies to promote green jobs. For instance, the company contributed $5.7 million in grants to the U.S. Conference of Mayors and Veterans Green Jobs to support the creation of green jobs in the United States. Walmart expects the money to be used to train the workforce in the growing sector of the green industry. The company believes it is making a profitable investment, as 10 percent of job growth in the United States is expected to be in the "green-collar" sector by 2032. With this investment, Walmart hopes to encourage mayors to promote jobs in their cities' green industries and provide veterans with training in green skills. It is clear that Walmart is trying to improve its relationship with environmental activists and stakeholders. Although the company might lag behind the competition in areas such as compensation, many experts agree that Walmart is ahead of its rivals in sustainability.

Walmart's Sustainability Goals and Achievements

Walmart Long-Term Sustainability Goals:

Become packaging neutral
Use 100% renewable energy
Achieve zero-waste levels in operations

Walmart's Short- to Mid-term Sustainability Goals:

Double the number of facilities that have fuel-cell technology
Launch green labeling program
Increase locally grown produce sold in U.S. stores by 9%
Invest in additional wind technology
Sell more products made from sustainable materials
Double fuel-efficiency in heavy-duty trucks

Current Sustainability Initiatives:

Launching sustainability index to help suppliers create a more sustainable supply chain
Selling organic produce in stores
Selling more toys made from sustainable products

Achievements:

Installed largest retail wind turbine installation at Sam's Club in Palmdale, CA
Installed fuel cell technology at store in Lancaster, CA
Designed international prototype stores to be 25% to 30% more efficient
Increased fuel efficiency by 60% of 2005 levels
Partnered with Samsung, Gazelle, and ecoNEW in recycling and trade-in programs

Source: "Sustainability," Walmart Corporate, http://walmartstores.com/Sustainability/ (accessed September 30, 2011).

Savings: Is Going Green Cost-Effective?

Walmart's green initiatives have secured it the goodwill of many environmentally conscious consumers, but does going green save the company costs in other ways? So far, Walmart's initiatives have racked up $25 million a year in savings from auxiliary power systems on trucks to run the air conditioning when trucks are stopped. The company announced plans to double the fuel efficiency of its new heavy-duty trucks by 2015, and has made significant progress toward this goal, as it has been able to achieve a 60 percent increase in the efficiency of its trucks to date. The company has also saved $7 million a year as a result of replacing all incandescent bulbs in store display ceiling fans with compact fluorescent bulbs.

WHAT IS WALMART DOING TO IMPROVE ETHICS AND SOCIAL RESPONSIBILITY?

Although it has received much criticism, Walmart has been working to improve its ethical reputation along with its reputation for sustainability and corporate governance. In 2004 Walmart formed its Global Ethics Office and released a revised Global Statement of Ethics. The intent of the Global Ethics Office is to spread an ethical corporate culture among its global stakeholders. The Global Ethics Office provides guidance on ethical decision making based on the Global Statement of Ethics and an ethics helpline. The helpline is an anonymous and confidential way for associates to contact the company regarding ethical issues. Additionally, Walmart has an Ethical Standards Team to monitor the compliance of supplier factories with the company's "Standards for Suppliers" and local laws.

Walmart also has contributed significantly to disaster management projects. The company donated over $1.5 million in relief aid for the victims of the Haiti earthquake, including money, in-kind donations, and goods. The company held fundraising campaigns that contributed an additional $3 million. It attempts to help its associates who are caught in disasters, allocating $2 million in grants for associates whose homes have been damaged and creating a toll-free number for associates who need help.

The company's reputation for low prices helped Walmart to remain a healthy business even during the 2008–2009 recession. Walmart claims to have made a commitment to improving the standard of living for customers worldwide, and has backed that claim with large charitable donations provided through the Walmart Foundation, including recent contributions of $10 million to the veteran community over five years and a $2 billion commitment to fight hunger in America. Its key retailing strategy is offering a broad assortment of merchandise and services at everyday low prices (EDLP) while fostering a culture claiming to reward and embrace mutual respect, integrity, and diversity. Walmart has always targeted lower-income customers, a strategy that paid dividends during the 2008–2009 recession. While many companies struggled to re-brand themselves as affordable, Walmart had an early advantage. Walmart is known for excellent market orientation—focusing on consumers, defeating competitors, and increasing shareholder value.

The company has also recently embarked on a health initiative to address the growing problem of obesity in America. In January 2011 Walmart U.S. President Bill Simon met with First Lady Michelle Obama to discuss the issue. Walmart announced that it would lower the prices of its fruits and vegetables and reduce the amounts of fats, sugars, and salts in the foods it sells. Specifically, the company formulated goals that include cutting sodium by 25 percent and sugars by 10 percent in food under its Great Value brand over a five-year period. By putting its weight behind solving the obesity epidemic, the world's largest retailer might be able to create significant change toward healthier eating habits.

Walmart Today

Walmart remains the preferred shopping destination of many consumers, particularly after the financial meltdown of 2008–2009. Of course, its influx of daily shoppers has created problems as well. Walmart was forced to create better crowd-control measures in its New York stores after an employee was trampled to death and others were injured on Black Friday 2008 by a mob of shoppers. Although refusing to admit any wrongdoing in the incident, Walmart agreed to have its crowd-control measures approved by safety consultants (in addition to providing $400,000 to victims of the incident).

> "Walmart remains the preferred shopping destination of many consumers."

In addition to creating better safety measures, Walmart has launched new initiatives targeting families facing financial dilemmas. For example, the company formed the Walmart MoneyCard, a reloadable Visa debit card to help lower-income consumers who do not use traditional checking accounts. During the economic crisis, Walmart decreased the fees for this card; consumers can now purchase it for $3, rather than the $9 it cost originally. The card has no overdraft fees, and the fees for maintenance and reloading are low. With this move, Walmart hopes to save consumers $500 million in money service fees each year. Walmart will also cash government, payroll, and tax refund checks for $3 maximum for checks up to $1,000 and $6 for checks over $1000.

Although Walmart prospered during the recession while other retailers suffered, the company's U.S. sales have begun to decline. Walmart itself has acknowledged that it has strayed from Sam Walton's original vision of everyday low prices in order to court higher-income customers. Several initiatives, such as Walmart's adoptions of organic food and trendy clothes, did not achieve much success with discount shoppers. Walmart also underwent a renovation effort that cut certain products, such as fishing tackle, from its stores. These actions alienated Walmart's original customer base. Households earning less than $70,000 annually began defecting to discounters like Dollar Tree and Family Dollar. Analysts believe that Walmart's mistake was in trying to be everything to everyone, along with trying to copy its more "chic" rivals like Target. Because of these blunders, Walmart's domestic sales are experiencing their worst slump ever. As a result, Walmart is returning to Sam Walton's original vision and returning to its "everyday low prices" mantra. The company has unleashed a new campaign, "It's Back," to signal the return of the merchandise it had removed. Walmart executives are encouraging store managers to compare prices with competitors to ensure that Walmart is offering the lowest prices. Walmart has also announced plans to expand its micro-stores in urban and rural areas.

In spite of these problems at its domestic stores, Walmart's revenues are on the rise thanks to its international stores. While the company works to reboot domestic sales, it continues to expand internationally to make up for lower growth in the home market. This strategy will require Walmart to adapt to different social, cultural, regulatory, economic, and political factors. Walmart is known for its ability to adapt quickly to different environments, but even this large-scale retailer has experienced trouble. For instance, it was forced to close its stores in Germany and South Korea after failing to take off with the local population. Walmart was finally able to open stores in India after years of protests, but only after forming a joint venture with Bharti Enterprises. Because Indian law forbids foreign retailers from competing directly with Indian retailers, India's Walmarts operate as wholesale and cash-and-carry stores under the name Best Price Modern Wholesale. The more Walmart expands internationally, the more the company must decide what concessions it is willing to make in order to enter certain markets.

Despite the difficulties of operating globally, Walmart has achieved a number of successes. After years of struggling in the Japanese market, for example, Walmart began turning a profit in 2008 through its acquisition of Japanese retailer Seiyu Ltd. Walmart is investing half a billion dollars in its Canadian operations, with plans to open 40 supercenter stores in a single year. Walmart is also turning its sights to Africa. South Africa's Massmart, the country's largest retailer, has approved the sale of 51 percent of the company to Walmart. However, Walmart is likely to experience serious opposition from South Africa's unions, which have threatened to boycott the company. But though the company will likely experience several bumps in the road, its international markets appear to offer strong growth potential.

The Future of Walmart

Walmart can be viewed through two very different lenses. Some think that the company represents all that is wrong with America, while others love it. In response to criticism, and in an attempt to initiate goodwill with consumers, the company has continued to improve stakeholder relationships and has made efforts to demonstrate that it is an ethically responsible company. Although it has faced controversy regarding competition, suppliers, employees, and workplace discrimination, it has increasingly demonstrated concern for its stakeholders, with sustainability initiatives and efforts to be more socially responsible. Its goals of decreasing its waste and carbon emissions extend to all facets of its operations, including suppliers. These efforts demonstrate Walmart's desire (whether through genuine concern for the environment or for its own bottom-line profits) to become a more sustainable company.

Similarly, Walmart's creation of an ethics and compliance program shows that it has come a long way since its beginning, when formal ethics programs were deemed unnecessary. Likewise, its initiatives to help families during the recession have helped to reinforce its image as a caring company. Both critics and supporters of Walmart alike are waiting to see whether Walmart's efforts will position the company as a large retail company dedicated to social responsibility.

QUESTIONS

1. Do you think Walmart is doing enough to become more sustainable?
2. What are the problems that Walmart has faced, and what has the company done to address them?
3. Why has Walmart tended to improve performance while other retail outlets have been suffering financially?

SOURCES

"Arrest Made in N.J. Wal-Mart 'All Black People' Case." Fox News, March 20, 2010, http://www.foxnews.com/us/2010/03/20/arrest-nj-walmart-black-people-case/ (accessed February 6, 2011); Associated Press. "Affidavit says Wal-Mart execs knew of illegal workers." *USA Today*, November 8, 2005, http://www.usatoday.com/news/nation/2005-11-08-walmart-illegal_x.htm?csp=34 (accessed July 11, 2011); Associated Press. "Ex-Wal-Mart Vice Chairman Pleads Guilty in Fraud Case." *The Wall Street Journal*, January 31, 2006; The Associated Press. "Wal-Mart at-a-glance." *The Wall Street Journal*, February 5, 2011, http://online.wsj.com/article/AP34bbe45fa23c495983e16f1a72669698.html (accessed February 6, 2011); Bandler, James. "Former No. 2 at Wal-Mart Set to Plead Guilty." *The Wall Street Journal*, January 7, 2006, A1; Bandler, James, and Ann Zimmerman. "A Wal-Mart Legend's Trail of Deceit." *The Wall Street Journal*, April 8, 2005, A10; Barbaro, Michael. "Image Effort by Wal-Mart Takes a Turn." *The New York Times*, May 12, 2006, C1, C4; Barbaro, Michael. "Return to Low-Price Basics Pays Off Well for Wal-Mart." WalmartStores.com, January 12, 2009, http://www6.lexisnexis.com/publisher/EndUser?Action=UserDisplayFullDocument&orgId=2708&topicId=100019774&docId=l:7 28129992 (accessed February 20, 2009); BBC News. "South African retailer Massmart backs sale to Wal-Mart." January 17, 2011, http://www.bbc.co.uk/news/business-12205922 (accessed February 8, 2011); Bellman, Eric. "Wal-Mart Exports Big-Box Concept to India." *The Wall Street Journal*, May 28, 2009, http://online.wsj.com/article/SB124346697277260377.html?mg=com-wsj (accessed February 8, 2011); Burritt, Chris. "Wal-Mart Overseas Expansion to Accelerate, CEO Says (Update5)." *Bloomberg Businessweek*, June 2, 2010, http://www.businessweek.com/news/2010-06-02/wal-mart-overseas-expansion-to-accelerate-ceo-says-update5-.html (accessed February 8, 2011); Bustillo, Miguel, and Timothy W. Martin. "Beyond the Big Box: Wal-Mart Thinks Smaller." *The Wall Street Journal*, April 28, 2010, B1; Bustillo, Miguel. "Wal-Mart Pledges to Promote Healthier Foods." *The Wall Street Journal*, January 20, 2011, http://online.wsj.com/article/SB10001424052748704881304576093872178374258.html, accessed January 25, 2011; Bustillo, Miguel. "Wal-Mart to Assign New 'Green Ratings.'" *The Wall Street Journal*, July 16, 2009, http://online.wsj.com/article/SB124766892562645475.html (accessed July 30, 2009); Bustillo, Miguel. "Wal-Mart to Expand Express Stores." *The Wall Street Journal*, March 11, 2011, B1; Bustillo, Miguel. "Wal-Mart Merchandise Goes Back to Basics." *The Wall Street Journal*, April 11, 2011, B3; Bustillo, Miguel. "Wal-Mart Tries to Recapture Mr. Sam's Winning Formula." *The Wall Street Journal*, February 22, 2011, A1, A11; Bustillo, Miguel. "With Sales Flabby, Wal-Mart Turns to Its Core." *The Wall Street Journal*, March 21, 2011, B1, B8; "Buy Blue: Wal-Mart." http://www.buyblue.org/node/2137/view/summary (accessed January 10, 2006); Center for American Progress. "Health Care Reform Letter to President Obama." June 30, 2009; Chan, Anita. "Made in China: Wal-Mart Unions." *Yale Global Online*, October 12, 2006, http://yaleglobal.yale.edu/display.article?id=8283 (accessed February 21, 2009); Clifford, Stephanie. "Wal-Mart Gains in Its Wooing of Chicago." June 24, 2010, *The New York Times*, www.nytimes.com/2010/06/25/business/25walmart.html (accessed July 30, 2010); Clifford, Stephanie. "Wal-Mart to Buy More Local Produce." *The New York Times*, October 14, 2010, http://www.nytimes.com/2010/10/15/business/15walmart.html (accessed February 7, 2011); Clark, Andrew. "Wal-Mart, the U.S. retailer, taking over the world by stealth." guardian.co.uk, http://www.guardian.co.uk/business/2010/jan/12/walmart-companies-to-shape-the-decade (accessed February 6, 2011); CNN Money. "The World's Most Admired Companies 2010." http://money.cnn.com/magazines/fortune/mostadmired/2010/index.html (accessed February 6, 2010); Coleman-Lochner, Lauren. "Independent Look at Wal-Mart Shows Both Good and Bad: With Savings and Jobs Come Falling Wages and Rising Medicaid Costs." *The San Antonio Express-News*, November 5, 2005, 4D; Connolly, Ceci. "At Wal-Mart, a Health Care Turnaround." *The Washington Post*, February 13, 2009, http://www.washingtonpost.com/wp-dyn/content/article/2009/02/12/AR2009021204096_pf.html (accessed February 21, 2009); Deprez, Esmé D. "Wal-Mart Spurs Sustainable Toy Animals into $1 Billion Market." *Bloomberg Businessweek*, March 26, 2010, http://www.businessweek.com/news/2010-03-26/wal-mart-spurs-sustainable-toy-animals-into-1-billion-market.html (accessed February 7, 2011); *Ethisphere*. "100 Most Influential People in Business Ethics 2008," December 31, 2009, http://ethisphere.com/100-most-influential-people-in-business-ethics-2008/#6 (accessed February 20, 2009);

Etter, Lauren. "Gauging the Wal-Mart Effect." *The Wall Street Journal,* December 3–4, 2005, A9; Fishman, Charles. "The Wal-Mart You Don't Know: Why Low Prices Have a High Cost." *Fast Company,* December 2003, 68–80; Fisk, Margaret Cronin. "Civil racketeering claims against Wal-Mart dropped." *Seattle Pi,* August 28, 2006, http://www.seattlepi.com/default/article/Civil-racketeering-claims-against-Wal-Mart-dropped-1212883.php (accessed July 11, 2011); Fong, Mei, and Ann Zimmerman. "China's Union Push Leaves Wal-Mart with Hard Choice." *TheWall Street Journal,* May 13–14, 2006, A1, A6; Global Insight. "Global Insight Releases New Study on the Impact of Wal-Mart on the U.S. Economy." http://www.globalinsight.com/MultiClientStudy/MultiClientStudyDetail2438.htm (accessed January 23, 2005); Gold, Russell, and Ann Zimmerman. "Papers Suggest Wal-Mart Knew of Illegal Workers." *The Wall Street Journal,* November 5, 2005, A3; Grant, Lorrie. "Wal-Mart Faces a New Class Action." *USA Today,* September 14, 2005, 63; Jannarone, John. "Wal-Mart's Tough Work Experience." *The Wall Street Journal,* February 23, 2011, C14; Kabel, Marcus. "Wal-Mart at War: Retailer Faces Bruised Image, Makes Fixes." *Marketing News,* January 15, 2006, 25; McGinn, Daniel. "Wal-Mart Hits the Wall." *Newsweek,* November 14, 2005, 44–46; Morrison, Kimberly. "Coughlin's Sentence Will Stand: U.S. Attorney Will Not Appeal." NWA Online, March 28, 2008, http://www.nwaonline.net/articles/2008/03/29/news/032908wzcoughlinappeal.txt, (accessed February 21, 2009); Much, Marilyn. "Wal-Mart Holds up in Sharp Recession, Beating EPS Views; Rare Winner: Shares Up 4%; Middle Class Now Willing to Shop at Discount King for Low Prices on Basics." WalmartStores.com, http://www6.lexisnexis.com/publisher/EndUser?Action=UserDisplayFullDocument&orgId=2708&topicId=100019774&docId=l:928281151 (accessed February 20, 2009); National Association for Female Executives. "NAFE 2010 Top 50 Companies for Executive Women." http://www.nafe.com/web?service=direct/1/ViewArticlePage/dlinkFullTopArticle1&sp=3059&sp=5117 (accessed February 6, 2011); *Newser.* "Wal-Mart Will Pay $640M to Settle Wage Lawsuits," http://www.newser.com/story/46142/wal-mart-will-pay-640m-to-settle-wage-lawsuits.html?utm_source=ssp&utm_medium=cpc&utm_campaign=story, December 23, 2008 (accessed May 12, 2009); Norman, Al. "The Case against Wal-Mart." Raphel Marketing, 2004; Olsson, Karen. "Up against Wal-Mart." www.MotherJones.com, March/April 2003, http://www.motherjones.com/news/feature/2003/03/ma_276_01.html (accessed January 10, 2006); PR Newswire. "Wal-Mart Foundation Donates $5.7 Million to Support the Creation of Green Jobs in U.S." CNBC, http://www.cnbc.com/id/28993728/site/14081545 (accessed February 20, 2009); Reuters. "Ex-Wal-Mart Exec Pleads Guilty to Fraud Case, Tax Evasion." *Fox News,* January 31, 2006, http://www.foxnews.com/story/0,2933,183341,00.html (accessed July 11, 2011); Rhodes, Margaret. "Mini-(Wal)mart vs. Micro-Target: Inside the Battle for the Next Frontier of Big-Box Retail." *Fast Company,* January 12, 2011, 32; Quinn, Steve. "Wal-Mart Green with Energy." *The Fort Collins Coloradoan,* July 24, 2005, E1–E2; Rockwood, Kate. "Will Wal-Mart's 'Sustainability Index' Actually Work?" *Fast Company,* February 1, 2010, http://www.fastcompany.com/magazine/142/attention-walmart-shoppers-clean-up-in-aisle-nine.html (accessed February 7, 2011); Sanchanta, Mariko. "Wal-Mart Bargain Shops for Japanese Stores to Buy." *The Wall Street Journal,* November 14, 2010, http://online.wsj.com/article/SB10001424052748704327704575613861567263350.html, (accessed February 8, 2011); Schmit, Julie. "Going greener: Wal-Mart plans new solar power initiative." *USA Today,* September 20, 2010, http://www.usatoday.com/money/industries/environment/2010-09-20-walmartenergy20_ST_N.htm (accessed February 7, 2011); Smith, Robert. "New York City Officials to Wal-Mart: Keep Out." *NPR,* February 4, 2011, http://www.npr.org/2011/02/04/133483848/new-york-city-officials-to-walmart-keep-out (accessed February 7, 2011); Stohr, Greg. "Wal-Mart vs. a Million Angry Women." *Bloomberg Businessweek,* November 22–28, 2010, 39–40; United States Security and Exchange Commission. "Wal-Mart Stores, Inc." http://msnmoney.brand.edgar-online.com/EFX_dll/EDGARpro.dll?FetchFilingHTML1?ID=5835838&SessionID=5RgcWZDBP11rCl9, January 31, 2008 (accessed February 21, 2009); Wailgum, Thomas. "Wal-Mart's Green Strategy: Supply Chain Makeover Targets Chinese Manufacturers." *CIO,* http://www.cio.com/article/456625/Wal_Mart_s_Green_Strategy_Supply_Chain_Makeover_Targets_Chinese_Manufacturers?page=1 (accessed May 13, 2009); Wal-Mart. "2009 Global Sustainability Report." http://walmartstores.com/sites/sustainabilityreport/2009/ (accessed July 11, 2011); Wal-Mart. "Annual Report 2008." http://walmartstores.com/sites/AnnualReport/2008/ (accessed February 21, 2009); Wal-Mart. "Convenient In-Store Check Cashing." http://www.walmart.com/cp/Check-Cashing/632047 (accessed February 7, 2011); Wal-Mart. "Ethical Sourcing." http://walmartstores.com/

Sustainability/7785.aspx (accessed May 12, 2009); Wal-Mart. "Global Ethics Office." https://www.walmartethics. com/ (accessed December 13, 2008); Wal-Mart. "Global Sustainability Report 2010 Progress Update." http:// walmartstores.com/sites/sustainabilityreport/2010/commitments_energy.aspx (accessed February 6, 2011); Wal-Mart. "Haiti Earthquake Relief." http://walmartstores.com/CommunityGiving/9596.aspx (accessed February 6, 2011); Wal-Mart. "Sustainability Index."http://walmartstores.com/Sustainability/9292.aspx (accessed February 7, 2011); Wal-Mart. "Wal-Mart Americas Aim to Reduce Detergent Phosphates 70%." http://walmartstores.com/ FactsNews/NewsRoom/8938.aspx, January 26, 2009 (accessed February 20, 2009); Wal-Mart. "Wal-Mart Commits $10 Million to the Veteran Community." http://walmartstores.com/pressroom/news/10468.aspx (accessed February 7, 2011); Wal-Mart. "The Wal-Mart Foundation." http://walmartstores.com/CommunityGiving/203.aspx (accessed February 7, 2011); Wal-Mart. "Wal-Mart Foundation Teams Up with United Way and One Economy to Provide Free Tax Preparation and Filing Services." http://walmartstores.com/FactsNews/NewsRoom/8962.aspx, February 10, 2009 (accessed February 20, 2009); Wal-Mart. "Wal-Mart's Healthcare Benefits Are Competitive in the Retail Sector." February 8, 2011, http://walmartstores.com/pressroom/news/5575.aspx (accessed July 11, 2011); Wal-Mart. "Wal-Mart Steps up Efforts to Help Americans Manage Their Finances with $3 Rollback Price on Key Money Service." http://walmartstores.com/FactsNews/NewsRoom/8982.aspx, February 8, 2009 (accessed February 20, 2009); Wal-Mart. "Wal-Mart Stores, Inc., Recognized as Top Company for Executive Women by the National Association for Female Executives." http://walmartstores.com/FactsNews/NewsRoom/6374.aspx, April 3, 2007 (accessed May 12, 2009); "Wal-Mart Concedes China Can Make Unions." *China Daily,* November 23, 2004, http://www.chinadaily.com.cn/english/doc/2004-11/23/content_394129.htm (accessed February 21, 2009); Wal-Mart Watch. "Event Highlights the Wal-Mart Health Care Crisis: New Study Declares Wal-Mart in Critical Condition." http://Walmartwatch.com, November 16, 2005 (accessed January 18, 2006); Wal-Mart Watch. "Is Wal-Mart Really a 'Green' Company?" http://walmartwatch.com/img/blog/environmental_fact_sheet.pdf (accessed December 13, 2008); Weinberg, Stuart, and Phred Dvorak. "Wal-Mart's New Hot Spot: Canada." *The Wall Street Journal,* January 27, 2010, B3; Zimmerman, Anne. "Federal Officials Asked to Probe Wal-Mart Firing." Wake Up Wal-Mart, April 28, 2005, http://www.wakeupwalmart.com/news/20050428-wsj.html (accessed February 21, 2009); Zimmerman, Anne. "Labor Pains: After Huge Raid on Illegals, Wal-Mart Fires Back at U.S." *The Wall Street Journal,* December 19, 2003, A1.

CASE 4

BP Struggles to Resolve Sustainability Disaster*

BP, formerly British Petroleum and the Anglo-Persian Oil Company, has experienced a lot of ups and downs over its hundred-year history. It nearly bankrupted its founder William D'Arcy but went on to become one of the world's largest energy companies. BP has also experienced its fair share of controversies regarding problematic business practices, environmental damage, hazards to workers, and the emission of greenhouse gases. For some time, BP has been attempting to position itself as an environmentally friendly organization through investments in renewable energy and ethics initiatives. It became the first oil company to recognize the presence of global warming and to launch initiatives focusing on cleaner forms of energy. British Petroleum changed its name to BP and then tried to rebrand itself as Beyond Petroleum. This rebranding was a signal to stakeholders that it was focused on sustainability and the need to move beyond nonrenewable energy sources. But when a company tries to reposition itself as socially responsible and sustainable, it has an obligation to attempt to live up to its promises. BP's failures to do so became tragically clear when on April 20, 2010, the *Deepwater Horizon* oil rig, operated under the oversight of BP, exploded in the Gulf of Mexico, creating one of the greatest offshore oil disasters in history.

This case is separated into two parts. The first half describes BP's investments in sustainability and its rebranding efforts. We start by providing a background of BP's origins as British Petroleum. We then detail some questionable conduct that tarnished the company's image, prompting it to take the initiative to reposition itself as a socially responsible company. The next three sections describe BP's sustainability investments, stakeholder engagement, and extensive code of conduct. The second half of this case examines the BP oil spill crisis. After providing details concerning the oil spill, we touch upon the repercussions of the spill on BP and the industry as a whole, as well as the many steps BP must take to begin repairing its reputation.

THE 100-YEAR HISTORY OF BP

BP was founded more than a century ago by William D'Arcy, a wealthy Englishman who had invested all his savings in the quest for oil in the Middle East. While experts and scientists had encouraged D'Arcy to pursue the venture, after more than six years of drilling, both his patience and finances were running low. Finally, in 1908, the drillers had reached almost 1,200 feet when a fountain of oil spewed out. After long years of disappointment,

---

*This case was prepared by Jennifer Sawayda and Jennifer Jackson for and under the direction of O. C. Ferrell and Linda Ferrell. It was prepared for classroom discussion rather than to illustrate either effective or ineffective handling of an administrative, ethical, or legal decision by management. All sources used for this case were obtained through publicly available material.

the Anglo-Persian Oil Company was born. The company quickly went public and D'Arcy, who had lost nearly his entire net worth, became rich.

A naptha field in Iran, located around 130 miles from the mouth of the Persian Gulf, was the first place the Anglo-Persian Oil Company established a refinery. (Naptha refers to any sort of petroleum product; in this case, the Anglo-Persian Oil Company was pumping crude oil.) George Reynolds, D'Arcy's head manager, quickly discovered that navigating this rugged land could take months. To facilitate transportation of the oil, BP started building a pipeline through the area. Many of the necessary supplies had to be shipped from the United States. The pipeline project took over two years to complete, and the huge scope of the undertaking drew workers from across the world.

By 1914 BP was about to go bankrupt again. The company had a lot of oil, but demand for that oil was low. The automobile had not yet become a mass-market product, and companies in the New World and Europe had first-mover advantages in the industrial oils market. An even worse problem was the strong smell of Persian oil, which kept it from being sold for heating and lighting.

However, Winston Churchill, who was at the time Britain's First Lord of the Admiralty, felt that the British navy needed a reliable and dedicated source of oil. Oil executives had been courting the navy for some years, but until Churchill, commanders had been reluctant to abandon coal. Churchill was adamant about using Anglo-Persian, because it was a British-owned company. Parliament overwhelmingly agreed and soon became a major shareholder in the oil company. Thus began the debate over the repercussions of involving politics in the oil industry, a debate that only grew louder throughout World War II, the Persian Gulf War, and the Iraq War.

The twentieth century saw enormous growth in the oil industry, along with massive power shifts in the Middle East. In 1969 Muammar al-Gaddafi led a coup in Libya and promptly demanded a tax increase on all oil exports. Gaddafi eventually nationalized BP's share of an oil operation in Libya. This move eventually led other oil-rich countries in the Middle East, including Iran, Saudi Arabia, Abu Dhabi, and Qatar, to nationalize. The effect on BP was massive: between 1975 and 1983, oil production in the Middle East fell from 140 million to 500,000 barrels.

In order to survive, BP had to find new places to dig for oil. The Forties Field off the coast of Scotland, capable of producing 400,000 barrels of crude oil a day, and Prudhoe Bay in Alaska, where BP tapped its largest oil field yet in 1969, were the two great hopes for BP's future at this time. However, transportation of the oil was a problem. The Forties Field pipeline would eventually become the largest deepwater pipeline ever constructed, a project that required special attention due to the harsh weather. The Trans-Alaska pipeline system would become the largest civil engineering project in North America, measuring nearly 746 miles. The company tried to assure concerned stakeholders that it took environmental concerns seriously. However, BP's actions have not always coincided with its words. BP has engaged in numerous instances of questionable behavior including fraud, environmental crimes, negligence leading to worker deaths, and endangering habitats.

QUESTIONS ABOUT BP'S ETHICAL CONDUCT

In March 2005, a huge explosion occurred at a BP-owned oil refinery in Texas that killed 15 employees and injured another 170 people. The company was found guilty by the Southern District of Texas of violating the Clean Air Act and was ordered to pay $50 million in criminal fines. The explosion was the result of a leak of hydrocarbon liquid and vapor, which then ignited. BP admitted that it had ignored several procedures required by the Clean Air Act for ensuring mechanical integrity and a safe startup between 1999 until the explosion in 2005. The BP case was the first to be prosecuted under a section of the Clean Air Act created to help prevent injury and death from such accidental leaks of explosive substances.

The company was also charged with violating the Clean Water Act when Alaskan oil pipelines leaked 200,000 gallons of crude oil onto the fragile tundra and a nearby frozen lake, the largest spill to ever occur on the North Slope in March and August of 2006. The fines resulting from this infraction included $12 million in criminal fines, $4 million in payments to the National Fish and Wildlife Foundation, and $4 million in criminal restitution to the state of Alaska. BP would later pay an additional $25 million for violating clean water and clean air laws. The leaks occurred after BP had failed to respond to numerous red flags. One of these flags was a dangerous corrosion in its pipes that had gone on unchecked for more than a decade. A contract worker discovered the first pipeline leak in March of 2006. A second 1,000-gallon leak occurred shortly after the first, in August of 2006. Although it was small, the second leak led to the shutdown of oil production in the east side of Prudhoe Bay until BP could guarantee that the pipelines were fit for use.

Regular routine cleaning of the pipes is simple and would have prevented the 2006 oil leaks in Alaska. Nevertheless, in October 2007, BP recorded yet another spill near Prudhoe Bay, this time of 2,000 gallons of toxic methanol, a deicing agent that spilled onto the tundra and killed many plants and animals.

In 2007 BP was charged with conspiring to violate the Commodity Exchange Act and also to commit mail fraud and wire fraud. The fraud, which had taken place in 2004, involved purchasing more than the available supply of TET propane, and then selling it to other market participants at a price inflated well above market value. BP was forced to pay $100 million in criminal penalties, $25 million to the U.S. Postal Inspection Consumer Fraud Fund, and restitution of $53 million. Additionally, BP had to pay a civil penalty of $125 million to the Commodity Futures Trading Commission. Four former employees were indicted for conspiring to manipulate the propane market at an artificially high price. The estimated loss to consumers who paid over market value exceeded $53 million dollars. The violation resulted in a 20-count indictment by a federal grand jury in Chicago.

BP's legal, environmental, and ethical transgressions clearly demonstrate that the company has a history of disregarding the well-being of stakeholders. It has claimed to be an ethical company, concerned with stakeholder well-being, but its many violations tell a different story.

BP TRIES TO REPAIR ITS IMAGE

After its violations in the mid-2000s, BP attempted to repair its tattered image. The twenty-first century found stakeholders more wary of companies, especially after decades of repeated violations and misconduct on the part of the oil industry. Oil leaks, toxic emissions, rising gas prices, pollution, and dwindling supplies have combined to paint a very ugly picture of the oil industry as a whole. A central topic in the debate over the future of the world's energy supply focuses on global warming and greenhouse gas emissions.

BP responded to these concerns in part by changing its name from British Petroleum to simply BP and increasing alternative energy offerings in its product mix. John Browne, former BP chief executive, proclaimed that "we are all citizens of one world, and we must take shared responsibility for its future and for its sustainable development." BP was the first global energy firm to publicly recognize the problem of climate change. While its primary product is still petroleum, BP accepts that global warming is human-made, and the company has begun to seek alternative revenue streams in wind farms and other lower-emissions energy sources. The company has invested $4 billion in alternative energy and plans to double that amount by 2015.

> "BP was the first global energy firm to publicly recognize the problem of climate change."

BP WORKS TO IMPROVE SUSTAINABILITY

To adapt to a changing world, BP launched its Alternative Energy business in 2005. While still a small part of its overall company, BP sees "going green" as an increasingly important part of its business which it will expand as it becomes more profitable to do so.

Wind

BP has invested significantly in wind energy through the creation of wind farms across the nation. In the United States, BP-operated wind farms have a total capacity of 1,200 MW. In 2010 BP Wind Energy, in partnership with Ridgeline Energy LLC, launched the Goshen North Wind Farm in Idaho, the state's largest wind farm to date. The farm can generate up to 124.5 MW of wind energy, enough to power 37,000 American homes. Other BP wind farms include the Cedar Creek Farm in Colorado, the Edom Hill Wind Farm in California, and the Fowler Ridge Wind Farm in Indiana.

Solar

In order to affordably expand its solar capacity, BP signed agreements with numerous solar panel producers in Asia. BP has installed 4 MW of solar panels at Walmart stores and has reached an agreement to construct a 32 MW solar installation on eastern Long Island, enough to power approximately 5,000 homes. BP has also developed two of the largest solar power plants in the world in Spain, projects that will supply energy to up to a million homes.

As BP has continued its worldwide efforts to reduce greenhouse gas emissions, it is leading a consortium in Australia to create one of five "solar cities"—cities in which a large percentage of houses and businesses will have solar power installations. It has also partnered with Verve Energy to create the largest grid-connected solar facility in Australia. With projects underway in the United States, Australia, the Middle East, China, and other countries, BP is seeking to enlarge its solar energy investments on a global scale.

Biofuels

BP became the single largest foreign stockholder in a Brazilian bioethanol company when it purchased a 50 percent stake in Tropical Energia S.A. The company's facility in Goiás

State, Brazil, has a capacity of 115 million gallons of sugarcane bioethanol. In 2011 BP acquired an 83 percent stake in the Brazilian ethanol producer Companhia Nacional de Açúcar e Álcool. This move increased BP's ethanol production capacity to 1.4 billion liters a year. The company sees these acquisitions as a crucial step toward becoming a leader in Brazil's ethanol market. BP has also been working with Dupont to develop biobutanol, a biofuel with a higher energy content than bioethanol.

BP's push in the alternative energy sector also prompted it to create a special purpose entity (SPE) with Verenium Corporation, a leader in the development of cellulosic ethanol, a fuel that is still in its infancy but that many hope will be the future of biofuels. Cellulosic ethanol is a renewable fuel produced from grasses and nonedible plant parts, such as sugarcane waste, rice straw, switchgrass, and wood chips. Although at this point it is much more difficult and energy-intensive to produce than corn or sugarcane ethanol, many believe that, as the technology improves, cellulosic ethanol will provide such benefits as greater per-acre yields and lower environmental impact. Another potential benefit is that cellulosic ethanol will not affect commodity or food prices, since it uses only waste products. If all goes as planned, BP's investment will help stimulate the development and production of cellulosic ethanol.

In 2010, following the *Deepwater Horizon* spill, BP bought Verenium Corp.'s cellulosic biofuels business for $98.3 million. According to the CEO of BP Biofuels, BP remains dedicated to becoming a leader in the cellulosic biofuel industry.

Carbon Sequestration and Storage

Carbon sequestration and storage (CCS) involves capturing greenhouse gas emissions from smokestacks and other sources and pumping the gases deep underground to empty oil or gas fields or aquifers. BP has been researching CCS since 2000 and opened the Salah Gas Field in Algeria for experimentation in 2004. BP captures and stores up to 1 million tons of carbon dioxide per year at Salah, which is equivalent to removing 250,000 cars from the road. BP hopes to do the same thing at Hydrogen Energy, its joint venture with Rio Tinto (an Australian-British mining company), developing low-emissions power plants for Abu Dhabi and California. While questions remain about the long-term effectiveness of CCS (no one knows for sure if the CO_2 stays underground), BP sees it as a promising technology.

Other Energy-Saving Measures

Beyond alternative energy sources, BP is also looking to save energy through better planning and implementation at its many operations around the world. The BP Zhuhai (BPZ) PTA plant is setting an example by using more efficient forms of energy. This development of more efficient, cleaner energy and the reduction of CO_2 emissions is an increasing priority in China. Many companies in China still use heavy oil and coal for fuel. BPZ is working to set new standards and make a greater contribution in this area. A sequence of heat recovery projects has allowed the plant to optimize the use of steam as a way to reduce liquefied petroleum gas (LPG) consumption significantly. This process has saved energy and reduced emissions. The annual production capacity of the BPZ plant is 350,000 tons. Additionally, by reducing fuel consumption, BPZ also has reduced the road safety and operational risks associated with delivery and unloading of LPG. BPZ is recognized locally and regionally in China for its promotion of environmental values. These green measures have also been cost-efficient, achieving millions in net savings for BP.

BP REACHES STAKEHOLDERS WITH ITS SUSTAINABILITY PROGRAMS

In addition to its Alternative Energy program, BP also has implemented environmental awareness programs in Britain to help stakeholders understand the impacts of global warming and the importance of sustainability issues. BP Educational Service (BPES) initiated the distribution of the Carbon Footprint Toolkit, an award-winning program designed to help high school students understand the effects of climate change and their own carbon footprint. Developed in conjunction with teachers and BP experts, the toolkit enables students to examine their school's carbon footprint and to help develop carbon reduction plans for their schools. The Carbon Footprint Toolkit was originally developed as a response to teachers' requests arising out of a series of "green" workshops that BP held. Available free of charge to all British high school students and their teachers, the Carbon Footprint Toolkit has been a successful initiative for BP. The toolkit received a prestigious award for e-learning at the International Visual Communications Association (IVCA) awards in 2007.

THE CODE OF CONDUCT

To help deal with BP's growing reputation for ethical misconduct at the beginning of the twenty-first century, BP's Ethics and Compliance team organized the creation, publication, and distribution of a company code of conduct in 2005 entitled "Our Commitment to Integrity." The code was distributed to BP employees around the globe and is also publicly available online at the BP website. Given the multinational nature of the BP business, the code seeks to unite its diverse employees behind a set of universal standards of behavior. The cross-functional team that drafted the code of conduct faced many major challenges, such as how to agree upon and communicate consistent standards for all BP employees regardless of location, culture, and language. The code of conduct was the largest mass communications exercise ever attempted at BP. The company holds awareness meetings to help employees understand its contents. The code put in writing, for the first time, BP's ethical and legal expectations. It gives employees clear guidelines in five key areas: health, safety, security, and the environment; employees; business partners; government and communities; and company assets and financial integrity.

> "The code of conduct was the largest mass communications exercise ever attempted at BP."

It is now clear that BP's code of conduct was not sufficient to prevent a man-made environmental disaster on an unprecedented scale. Regardless of the degree of comprehensiveness, ethical codes should always reflect upper management's desire for compliance with values, rules, and policies. Legal staff must be called upon to ensure that the code correctly assesses key areas of risk. Apparently BP's code did not effectively address specific high-risk activities within the scope of daily operations. The BP code of conduct was not designed to resolve every legal and ethical issue that employees might encounter in daily operations, but it should have helped employees and managers deal with ethical dilemmas in high-risk areas by prescribing or limiting specific activities. It would seem that BP did not adequately reinforce its code of conduct throughout the organization.

THE WORST OIL SPILL IN U.S. HISTORY

> **"BP's history of safety violations culminated with the explosion of the *Deepwater* Horizon oil rig."**

In the face of BP's public relations campaigns, safety violations continued at its facilities. In early 2010 U.S. regulators fined the company $3 million for safety problems at an Ohio factory. The Occupational Safety and Health Administration (OSHA) found that workers might be exposed to injury or death should explosive or flammable chemicals be released at the factory. And this violation was not an isolated event. Just four months earlier, OSHA had fined BP a record $87 million for not correcting safety problems that were identified after the 2005 explosion at its Texas refinery. BP's history of safety violations culminated with the explosion of the *Deepwater Horizon* oil rig.

The Explosion

It all started with an opportunity to tap into a new, highly profitable oil reservoir. The reservoir was dubbed "Macondo," after the doomed town in Gabriel García Márquez's novel *One Hundred Years of Solitude*. To tap the reservoir, BP hired an oil rig from Transocean, Ltd. By April the project was behind schedule, but BP was convinced it would lead to success. Then on April 20, 2010, an explosion rocked the rig, killing 11 employees. The burning rig sank two days later.

The situation quickly worsened. The oil well that was being drilled, located nearly a mile below the surface, was damaged in the explosion. Thousands of gallons of crude oil were gushing into the Gulf of Mexico, quickly creating an environmental catastrophe. BP sent submarine robots down onto the seabed in an attempt to activate the switch-off valve on the well. BP began sending out conflicting messages and the entire process soon became a public relations nightmare for the company. One official informed Fox News that BP had successfully activated part of a failed blowout preventer, which was slowing the oil flow. The announcement turned out to be false. BP's underwater robot did in fact trigger a device, but the device did not stop the flow of oil.

BP immediately started drilling other holes in the hopes that they would relieve pressure on the damaged well, but these and other efforts were unsuccessful. Soon as much as 2.5 million gallons of oil was pouring into the Gulf of Mexico daily. Oil washed up on the coasts of Louisiana, Texas, Alabama, Mississippi, and Florida, wreaking havoc on the livelihoods of fishermen and others who depended on the Gulf for income.

Failure to Manage Risks

The main question on everyone's mind after the disaster was how BP could have overlooked such a risk. Indeed, the ocean rig did have safety systems in place, but these systems were not as safe as they could have been. For instance, the rig did not have a remote-control shut-off switch, which could have been used as a last resort in a major spill. At the same time, it must be noted that neither Transocean (the rig's owner) nor BP were breaking any laws by not having one; the Minerals Management Service (MMS), a federal agency charged with oversight of the nation's offshore oil-and-gas industry, did not require such a device as long as the rig had a backup control system that could shut off the well in case of an emergency.

However, this one failure cannot explain other lapses in BP's risk management strategy. Some suggest that BP cut corners in risk management to save time and money. For example, records reveal that nearly three of every four incidents that caused federal investigations into safety on deep-sea drilling rigs in the Gulf of Mexico were on rigs owned by Transocean. (Although it must be noted that Transocean is the largest deep-sea oil driller, and not all of these incidents were determined to be safety violations.) As Transocean's biggest client in the Gulf of Mexico, BP had a responsibility to ensure that appropriate precautions were taken to prevent a disaster. Lawsuits are also pending against Transocean for alleged safety failures.

Even more disturbing, one of the technicians on the *Deepwater Horizon* oil rig has accused BP of willful negligence. He claims that BP had knowledge that the rig's blow-out preventer was leaking weeks before the explosion, but did not halt production. If true, this statement would contradict the one released by Transocean after the explosion claiming that engineers had detected no leaks hours before the explosion occurred. Regardless, it is apparent that the backup systems in place were not sufficient to handle such an emergency.

Later investigations have also revealed that BP's contingency plan in case of disaster was inadequate. The plan contained several important inaccuracies. For instance, one of the wildlife experts listed as an emergency responder had been dead since 2005. The contingency plan also estimated that should a spill occur, the company would be able to recover about 500,000 barrels of oil per day. In reality, it took BP months to contain the leak, at a spill rate of much less than that listed in the contingency plan. The inaccuracies in BP's contingency plan highlight how unprepared the company was for a disaster like the *Deepwater Horizon* spill.

What Caused the Explosion?

The primary event that caused the explosion is unknown. However, investigations have suggested that actions on BP's part made the well more vulnerable. One investigation implies that BP cut short procedures and quality testing of the pipe—tests that are meant to detect gas in the well. Some experts hypothesize that one of the final steps in installing the pipe, which involved cementing the steel pipe in place, could have been the catalyst for the explosion. In addition, BP decided to use a less costly well design that some Congressional investigators have deemed "risky." Installation of this design is easier and costs are lower. However, it also provides a better path for gas to rise outside of the pipe. While this did not cause the explosion, investigators believe it may have contributed to the well's vulnerability. Although BP did not break any laws by using such a design, it ignored safer alternatives that might have prevented, or at least hindered, the accident.

Repercussions of the Disaster

The BP oil spill will have wide-ranging repercussions for both BP and the entire industry. The financial toll on BP alone will be extensive. The Obama administration made BP liable for cleanup costs and damages. Under the Oil Pollution Act of 1990, BP is only liable for $75 million in economic damages. However, the company has chosen to pay more than what is required by law. Estimates place the costs of clean-up at $40 billion. BP has taken a pre-tax charge of $40.9 billion regarding the spill.

The Justice Department has launched a civil lawsuit against BP and eight other companies, claiming the companies were negligent regarding the operation of the well. To successfully prosecute, the government must show that the disaster resulted from a deliberate flouting of the law or from negligence. If nothing else, BP may be charged with violating the federal Clean Water Act (constituting a civil, not criminal, charge). If found guilty, BP could pay up to $4,300 per barrel of oil released in the spill.

Nor does the disaster bode well for other oil companies. Drilling contractors and oil service companies suffered massive losses in their businesses due to plummeting stock values. BP share prices plunged over 50 percent after the accident. The Obama administration also issued a six-month moratorium on deepwater and oil gas drilling in the Gulf of Mexico, which shut down 33 deepwater rigs. With one-third of America's oil coming from the Gulf, the repercussions stemming from the spill will likely be felt for years to come.

One of the most immediate consequences of the disaster was the resignation of BP CEO Tony Hayward. Despite an impressive track record, including a net profit of $6.08 billion in the first quarter of 2010 and a seemingly dedicated attempt to "turn things around" at BP, Hayward became the face of the worst oil spill in U.S. history. Although it is extremely difficult for CEOs to maintain their positions after disasters of such magnitude, experts believe that it was Hayward's verbal blunders and his lack of visible empathy that triggered his downfall. They ascribe his resignation to a failure of effective crisis management. His comments about how he wanted "his life back" and his attendance at a yacht race made him appear callous in the face of the unfolding crisis.

THE LONG ROAD TO RECOVERY

It took nearly three months to contain the oil leaking into the Gulf. In the interim, thousands of marine animals died in the oily waters, oil soaked beaches black, and hundreds of people that depended upon the Gulf of Mexico lost part or all of their income. By the time the leak was finally sealed in August 2010, over 640 miles of shoreline across several states were "tarred" with oil. Fortunately, the oil began biodegrading quicker than expected due to bacteria, which fed on the methane in the crude. But the Gulf had suffered a massive loss of wildlife, and was left with a tremendous amount of oil lurking beneath the water's surface. Scientists are finding evidence that oil has settled across several thousand square miles of seafloor, posing a potential threat to coral reefs and other marine life. Louisiana was forced to divert water from the river into the ocean to keep the oil at bay. The fresh water wiped out Louisiana's oyster beds, which will take at least two years to recover. Dolphins, red snapper, and blue crabs also appear to be at risk.

In an attempt to compensate stakeholders that depend on the Gulf, BP set aside $20 billion in an escrow fund, and a government-appointed administrator is overseeing the claims. As always, though, compensating the right people for the right amounts is tricky. For example, how far from the coast should a claimant be in order to have an effective claim? What about the many workers without sufficient documentation to prove they worked in the Gulf? The company will also have to deal with rooting out fraudulent claims. Although the escrow fund will serve to compensate some individuals for their losses, others will likely receive little or no compensation.

Another issue that concerns the public is safety. Many are worried about the safety of consuming seafood along the Gulf coast. It is largely unknown whether the oil and chemicals will have long-term effects on the quality of seafood. As a result, BP has agreed to contribute $20 million for marketing and seafood inspections in Florida. The case of BP demonstrates that it is often not enough for global companies involved in an ethical crisis to pay only for immediate costs like compensation; often they must also pay for testing, additional safeguards, and environmental degradation in both the short and long term.

BP has embarked on several initiatives to meet stakeholder demands. However, the challenge for BP goes beyond immediate costs. With its role in the disaster along with its public relations blunders, the company's reputation has sustained a severe blow. It will take significant long-term effort if BP is to recover.

Yet such efforts are already underway. After the ousting of CEO Tony Hayward, Bob Dudley took over operations. Several analysts believe that by choosing an American chief executive to lead the company, BP is signaling its commitment to the United States and its government. While BP originally appeared to try to downplay the catastrophe, Dudley freely admitted that the incident was a "catastrophe" and that the company was committed to the cleanup. BP hired former Federal Emergency Management Agency chief James Lee Witt and his public safety and crisis management consulting firm to help manage the incident and establish plans for long-term recovery. BP also created a safety organization that has been given authority to stop operations whenever danger is detected.

After performing an internal investigation of the incident, BP admitted fault but placed much of the blame on its contractors Transocean and Halliburton. A report by the National Commission came to a different conclusion, however. While it places some of the responsibility on Transocean and Halliburton, the panel found that lapses in management and oversight on BP's part contributed to the disaster. The commission also placed some blame on the government, stating that the administration was too slow to respond and then overreacted. The panel's findings have led some to call for massive overhauls in oil industry regulation.

> "After performing an internal investigation of the incident, BP admitted fault but placed much of the blame on its contractors Transocean and Halliburton."

Another investigation sheds additional light on why the oil spill became such a large-scale environmental disaster. Engineers discovered that the blowout preventer was indeed faulty. Instead of sealing the pipe completely, the blowout preventer blades got stuck in the pipe, leaving enough space for oil to leak out. BP has filed lawsuits against the manufacturer of the blowout preventer, Cameron International Corp. It has also filed a $40 billion lawsuit against Transocean for negligence in creating an unsafe drilling rig.

Although BP faces a massive clean-up bill, a slew of negative publicity, and a 2010 loss of $4.9 billion, the company is striving to rebuild its reputation. In addition to a new safety division at BP, CEO Dudley has appointed a board member with knowledge of process safety. The company is committed to continued growth and will pay smaller dividends in order to spend more on oil exploration. Dudley has also promised to make BP into the safest offshore energy operator in the business. Unfortunately, a day after this announcement, it was revealed that BP had been reprimanded by a U.K. safety regulator regarding safety issues on three of its North Sea rigs.

CONCLUSION

BP went from near bankruptcy to being one of the largest energy companies worldwide. After experiencing a range of ethical problems, the company worked to overcome its negative image through launching sustainability initiatives and social responsibility. However, BP's claims of environmental responsibility were undermined by the *Deepwater Horizon* disaster.

Developing an ethical organizational culture requires an examination of the risks to various stakeholders. In the case of BP, the company failed to put in the safeguards necessary to protect employees, local communities, suppliers, and the viability of many industries including fishing, tourism, and the sustainability of the offshore drilling industry. After the *Exxon-Valdez* disaster, there should have been a heightened awareness of the risks of offshore drilling and a mandate to implement every safeguard necessary to protect the environment. BP's outsourcing of its offshore drilling did not eliminate its responsibility for the outcome of any drilling accident. As a global corporation, BP now has the responsibility to engage in the complete recovery and restoration of the environmental damage it wrought as well as repairing the economic damage done to various stakeholders. This process is going to take a very long time, and the ramifications of the damage may not be completely clear for years to come. In the future, there will be no room for BP to take shortcuts or try to cut costs in its production operations. BP has a new responsibility to provide leadership in safety and sustainability. The future survival of BP is dependent upon its ability to commit to a socially responsible approach and stakeholder engagement.

QUESTIONS

1. What aspects of BP's ethical culture could have contributed to the Gulf Coast oil spill disaster?
2. Did BP engage in purposeful avoidance of risk management? Why or why not?
3. What should BP do in the future to rebuild its reputation and manage the risks associated with offshore drilling activities?

SOURCES

Ash, James. "BP to fund Fla. seafood inspections." *USA Today,* October 26, 2010, 3A; Ball, Jeffrey. "BP Spill's Next Major Phase: Wrangling over Toll on Gulf." *The Wall Street Journal,* April 13, 2011, http://online.wsj.com/article/ SB10001424052748704013604576248531530234442.html (accessed May 11, 2011); Ball, Jeffrey. "Strong Evidence Emerges of BP Oil on Seafloor." *The Wall Street Journal,* December 9, 2010, A20; Ball, Jeffrey, Stephen Power, and Russell Gold. "Oil Agency Draws Fire." *The Wall Street Journal,* May 4, 2010, A1; Joel K. Bourne, Jr. "The Deep Dilemma." *National Geographic,* October 2010, pp. 40-53; BP. "Alternative Energy Brochure." http://www. bp.com/liveassets/bp_internet/alternative_energy/alternative_energy_english_new/STAGING/local_assets/ downloads_pdfs/AE_Brochure_2010A4.pdf (accessed February 17, 2011); BP. "History of BP." http://www. bp.com/multipleimagesection.do?categoryId=2010123&contentId=7059226 (accessed May 11, 2011); BP. "BP

Solar Energised by Utility Scale Verve Project." http://www.bp.com/genericarticle.do?categoryId=9024973&contentId=7065138, September 21, 2010 (accessed February 17, 2011); BP. "Ridgeline Energy and BP Wind Energy announce commercial operation of largest wind farm in Idaho." http://www.bp.com/genericarticle.do?categoryId=9024973&contentId=7065987, November 4, 2010 (accessed May 11, 2011); BP. "Sustainability Review 2008." http://www.bp.com/liveassets/bp_internet/globalbp/STAGING/global_assets/e_s_assets/e_s_assets_2008/downloads/bp_sustainability_review_2008.pdf (accessed May 11, 2011); BP. "Zhuhai, China." http://www.bp.com/sectiongenericarticle.do?categoryId=9003705&contentId=7006828 (accessed May 11, 2011); Browne, John. "Breaking Ranks." *Stanford Business,* 1997, http://www.gsb.stanford.edu/community/bmag/sbsm0997/feature_ranks.html (accessed May 11, 2011); Casselman, Ben. "Rig Owner Had Rising Tally of Accidents." *The Wall Street Journal,* May 10, 2010, http://online.wsj.com/article/NA_WSJ_PUB:SB10001424052748704307804575234471807539054.html (accessed May 11, 2011); Casselman, Ben, and Russell Gold. "BP Decisions Set Stage for Disaster." *The Wall Street Journal,* May 27, 2010, http://online.wsj.com/article/SB10001424052748704026204575266560930780190.html (accessed May 11, 2011); CBS News. "BP's Spill Contingency Plans Vastly Inadequate." http://www.cbsnews.com/stories/2010/06/09/national/main6563631.shtml, June 9, 2010 (accessed January 12, 2011); Chazan, Guy. "BP Comeback Is Sidetracked in Arctic." *The Wall Street Journal,* April 19, 2011, B5; Chazan, Guy. "BP Dividend Takes Back Seat to Growth." *The Wall Street Journal,* November 3, 2010, B1–B2; Chazan, Guy. "BP Faces Fine over Safety at Ohio Refinery." *The Wall Street Journal,* March 9, 2010, A4; Chazan, Guy. "BP Struts Deal-Making Ability." *The Wall Street Journal,* January 18, 2011, B3; Chazan, Guy. "BP's Worsening Spill Crisis Undermines CEO's Reforms." *The Wall Street Journal,* May 3, 2010, A1; CNN. "Day 64: Latest oil disaster developments." http://news.blogs.cnn.com/2010/06/22/day-64-latest-oil-disaster-developments/?iref=allsearch, June 22, 2010 (accessed May 11, 2011); Elkind, Peter, David Whitford, and Doris Burke. "'An Accident Waiting to Happen.'" *Fortune,* February 7, 2011, 107–132; Fick, Jeff, and Alexis Flynn. "BP Expands Biofuels Business in Brazil." *The Wall Street Journal,* March 14, 2011, http://online.wsj.com/article/SB10001424052748703597804576194820019691968.html?KEYWORDS=BP+Expands+Biofuels+Business (accessed March 16, 2011); Frey, Darcey. "How Green Is BP?" *The New York Times,* December 8, 2002, http://www.nytimes.com/2002/12/08/magazine/08BP.html?scp=3&sq=how%20green%20is%20BP&st=cse (accessed May 11, 2011); Gold, Russell. "BP Jumps into Next-Generation Biofuels with Plans to Build Florida Refinery." *The Wall Street Journal,* February 19, 2009, B1; Gold, Russell and Tom McGinty. "BP Relied on Cheaper Wells." *The Wall Street Journal,* June 19, 2010, http://online.wsj.com/article/NA_WSJ_PUB:SB10001424052748704289504575313010283981200.html (accessed May 11, 2011); Gold, Russell. "BP Sues Maker of Blowout Preventer." *The Wall Street Journal,* April 21, 2011, B1; Gonzalez, Angel, and Brian Baskin. "'Static Kill' Begins, Raising New Hopes." *The Wall Street Journal,* August 4, 2010, http://online.wsj.com/article/NA_WSJ_PUB:SB10001424052748703545604575407251664344386.html (accessed May 11, 2011); Herron, James. "BP Rapped over North Sea Rig Safety." *The Wall Street Journal,* February 2, 2011, http://online.wsj.com/article/SB10001424052748703960804576119631110061702.html (accessed February 17, 2011); Hughes, Siobhan. "BP Deposits $3 Billion in Spill Fund." *The Wall Street Journal,* August 9, 2010, http://online.wsj.com/article/SB1000142405274870438850457541928162043677.html (accessed May 11, 2011); King, Neil, Jr. "BP Claims Chief Faces Knotty Task." *The Wall Street Journal,* July 17–18, 2010, A5; Jervis, Rick. "New hurdles await survivors of drilling moratorium." *USA Today,* January 18, 2011, 3A; Johnson, Kevin, and Rick Jervis, "Justice Dept. sues BP, others." *USA Today,* December 16, 2010, 3A; Judd, Amy. "British Petroleum Ordered to Pay $180 Million in Settlement Case." NowPublic, February 19, 2009, http://www.nowpublic.com/environment/british-petroleum-ordered-pay-180-million-settlement-case (accessed May 11, 2011); Langley, Monica. "U.S. Drills Deep into BP as Spill Drama Drags on." *The Wall Street Journal,* July 21, 2010, A1, A14; Leonhardt, David. "Spillonomics: Underestimating Risk." *The New York Times,* May 31, 2010, http://www.nytimes.com/2010/06/06/magazine/06fob-wwln-t.html (accessed May 11, 2011); Mackey, Robert. "Rig Worker Says BP Was Told of Leak in Emergency System before Explosion." June 21, 2010, *The New York Times,* http://thelede.blogs.nytimes.com/2010/06/21/rig-worker-claims-bp-knew-of-leak-in-emergency-system-before-explosion/?scp=5&sq=BP&st=cse (accessed May 11, 2011); Orwall, Bruce, Monica Langley, and James Herron. "Embattled BP Chief to Exit." *The Wall Street Journal,* July 26, 2010, A1, A6; Palast, Greg. "British Petroleum's 'Smart Pig.'" Greg Palast: Journalism and Film, August 9, 2006, http://www.gregpalast.com/britishpetroleums-smart-pig/ (accessed May 11, 2011); Polson, Jim. "BP Oil Is Biodegrading, Easing Threat to East Coast." *BusinessWeek,* July 28, 2010, http://www.businessweek.com/news/2010-07-28/bp-oil-is-biodegrading-easing-threat-to-east-coast.html (accessed May 11, 2011); Power, Stephen, and Ben Casselman. "White House Probe Blames BP, Industry in Gulf Blast." *The Wall Street Journal,* January 6, 2011, A2; Power, Stephen, and Tennille Tracy. "Spill Panel Finds U.S. Was Slow to React." *The Wall Street Journal,* October 7, 2011, A6; PR Newswire. "British Petroleum to Pay More than $370 Million in Environmental Crimes, Fraud Cases." http://www.prnewswire.com/cgi-bin/stories.pl?ACCT=104&STORY=/www/story/10-25-2007/0004690834&EDATE= (accessed May 11, 2011); Sonne, Paul. "Hayward Fell Short of Modern CEO Demands." *The Wall Street Journal,* July 26, 2010, A7; Stempel, Jonathon and Paritosh Bansal. "BP sues Transocean for $40 billion over oil spill." *Reuters,* April 21, 2011, http://www.reuters.com/article/2011/04/21/us-bp-cameron-lawsuit-idUSTRE73J7NR20110421 (accessed July 11, 2011); Sweet, Cassandra. "BP Will Pay Fine in Spills." *The Wall Street Journal,* May 4, 2011, B3; Swint, Brian, and Alex Morales. "BP Plc Buys Verenium Corp.'s Cellulosic Biofuels Unit for $98.3 Million." *Bloomberg,* July 15, 2010, http://www.bloomberg.com/news/2010-07-15/bp-plc-buys-verenium-corp-s-cellulosic-biofuels-unit-for-98-3-million.html (accessed May 11, 2011); Walt, Vivienne. "Can BP Ever Rebuild Its Reputation?" *Time,* July 19, 2010, http://www.time.com/time/business/article/0,8599,2004701-2,00.html (accessed May 11, 2011); Weber, Harry R., and Greg Bluestein. "Dudley: Time for 'Scaleback' in BP Cleanup." *Time,* July 30, 2010, http://www.time.com/time/business/article/0,8599,2007638,00.html (accessed August 9, 2010).

CASE 5

New Belgium Brewing: Ethical and Environmental Responsibility*

Although most of the companies frequently cited as examples of ethical and socially responsible firms are large corporations, it is the social responsibility initiatives of small businesses that often have the greatest impact on local communities. These businesses create jobs and provide goods and services for customers in smaller markets that larger corporations often are not interested in serving. Moreover, they also contribute money and other resources and volunteer time to local causes. Their owners often serve as community leaders, and many choose to apply their skills and resources to tackling local problems and issues to the benefit of the whole community. Managers and employees become role models for ethical and socially responsible actions. One such small business is the New Belgium Brewing Company, Inc., based in Fort Collins, Colorado.

HISTORY OF THE NEW BELGIUM BREWING COMPANY

The idea for the New Belgium Brewing Company began with a bicycling trip through Belgium. Belgium is arguably the home of some of the world's finest ales, some of which have been brewed for centuries in that country's monasteries. As Jeff Lebesch, an American electrical engineer, cruised around that country on his mountain bike, he wondered if he could produce such high-quality beers back home in Colorado. After acquiring the special strain of yeast used to brew Belgian-style ales, Lebesch returned home and began to experiment in his Colorado basement. When his beers earned thumbs up from friends, Lebesch decided to market them.

The New Belgium Brewing Company (NBB) opened for business in 1991 as a tiny basement operation in Lebesch's home in Fort Collins. Lebesch's wife, Kim Jordan, became the firm's marketing director. They named their first brew "Fat Tire Amber Ale" in honor of Lebesch's bike ride through Belgium. New Belgium beers quickly developed a small but devoted customer base, first in Fort Collins and then throughout Colorado. The brewery soon outgrew the couple's basement and moved into an old railroad depot before settling into its present custom-built facility in 1995. The brewery includes an automated brew house and

*This case was prepared by Jennifer Sawayda and Jennifer Jackson for and under the direction of O. C. Ferrell and Linda Ferrell. Nikole Haiar and Melanie Drever provided editorial assistance. We appreciate the input and assistance of Greg Owsley, New Belgium Brewing, in developing this case. This case was prepared for classroom discussion rather than to illustrate either effective or ineffective handling of an administrative, ethical, or legal decision by management. All sources used for this case were obtained through publicly available materials.

two quality assurance labs. The company has created numerous technological innovations that have led it to be nationally recognized as a "paradigm of environmental efficiencies."

Today, New Belgium Brewing Company offers a variety of permanent and seasonal ales and pilsners. The company's standard line includes Sunshine Wheat, Blue Paddle, Abbey, Mothership Wit, 1554, Trippel, Ranger IPA, and the original Fat Tire Amber Ale, still the firm's best-seller. The brewery also markets five types of specialty beers on a seasonal basis. Seasonal ales include Frambozen, released at Thanksgiving, Skinny Dip, released during the summer, 2° for winter, Mighty Arrow for spring, and Hoptober, released during the months of August through October. Small batch brews like La Folie, Bière de Mars, and Abbey Grand Cru are created for internal celebrations or landmark events. In addition, New Belgium is working in collaboration with Elysian Brewing Company; each company will be able to use the other's brewhouses though they will remain independent businesses. Through this effort, the two companies hope to become more efficient and innovative.

Until 2005 NBB's most effective form of advertising was word of mouth. Indeed, before New Belgium beers were widely distributed throughout Colorado, one liquor store owner in Telluride is purported to have offered people gas money if they would stop by and pick up New Belgium beer on their way through Fort Collins. Today New Belgium beer is available in 26 states and the company has plans to expand into Virginia, Maryland, and Washington, DC, in 2011 (see Figure 1). The company also plans to open up a brewery on the East Coast. When NBB began distribution in Minnesota, it was so instantly popular that a liquor store had to open early and make other accommodations for the large number of eager customers; the store sold 400 cases of Fat Tire in the first hour it was open. The brewery receives numerous e-mails and phone calls every day inquiring when its beers will be available elsewhere.

Although still a small brewery when compared to companies like its in-state rival Coors, NBB has consistently experienced strong growth and has become the third-largest

FIGURE 1

NEW BELGIUM TERRITORIES

Source: "Frequently Asked Questions," New Belgium, http://www.newbelgium.com/culture/faq.aspx (accessed March 4, 2011).

"craft" brewery in the nation, with sales of over $100 million. New Belgium now has its own blog, Twitter, and Facebook pages. The plant is currently capable of producing 700 bottles of beer a minute, and the company is developing a capacity of 50 to 60 canned beers per minute. Its growth has been driven by connoisseurs who appreciate the high quality of NBB's products as well as the values the company stands for. The brewery is now the seventh largest of any kind in the country.

With expanding distribution, however, the brewery recognized a need to increase opportunities for reaching its far-flung customers. It consulted with Dr. Douglas Holt, an Oxford professor and cultural branding expert. After studying the young company, Holt, together with Marketing Director Greg Owsley, drafted a 70-page "manifesto" describing the brand's attributes, character, cultural relevancy, and promise. In particular, Holt identified in New Belgium an ethos of pursuing creative activities simply for the joy of doing them well and in harmony with the natural environment.

With the brand thus defined, New Belgium has invested in a variety of media, including print, point-of-sale, video, and online ads. In 2010 NBB unleashed its Beer Ranger sales force to promote its newest product, Ranger IPA ale. With the campaign theme "To Protect. To Pour. To Partake," the advertising featured the NBB sales force dressed in tan-and-olive ranger uniforms. The main difference was that the beer rangers substituted bicycles for horses to link the campaign to the New Belgium brand. The campaign took out advertisements in magazines such as *Wired* and *Rolling Stone,* but perhaps the most memorable advertising was the microsite that New Belgium launched for the occasion. It included a short video of the Rangers performing a hip-hop number. The microsite also offers visitors a chance to join NBB on Facebook and includes a "Ranger Yourself?" function that allows visitors to place their headshots on a Ranger's body and upload them to their walls. According to NBB director of public relations Bryan Simpson, the intent is to create a hip identity for the product and brand as a whole. Indeed, the ads have helped position the growing brand as offbeat, whimsical, and thoughtful.

In 2011 NBB began to incorporate new technology into the marketing mix to further promote its Ranger brand. The company adopted quick response (QR) code technology, which are black-and-white squares that have begun to appear in magazines, on posters, and in the case of New Belgium, on cans of Ranger IPA beers. QR codes contain hidden marketing messages that consumers can only access through a free QR app on their smartphones. New Belgium has placed QR codes in two spots on its Ranger IPA 12-pack beers and in national full-page advertisements. NBB's QR codes allow fans to "follow" their favorite ranger by learning more about him or her as well as about upcoming NBB events. As smartphones become increasingly common, New Belgium hopes its use of QR codes will provide a unique and fun way for consumers to learn about the company.

NEW BELGIUM ETHICAL CULTURE

According to Greg Owsley, director of marketing for New Belgium Brewing, the company places great importance on the ethical culture of the brand. The company is aware that if it embraces citizenship in the communities it serves, it can forge enduring bonds with customers. More than ever before what a brand says and what a company does must be synchronized. NBB believes that as the mandate for corporate social responsibility gains momentum, business managers must realize that business ethics are not so much about the installation of compliance codes and standards as they are about the spirit in which such codes and standards are integrated. The modern-day brand steward—usually the most externally focused member of the business management team—must prepare to be the internal champion of the bottom-line necessity for ethical, values-driven company behavior.

At New Belgium, a synergy of brand and values occurred naturally because the firm's ethical culture (in the form of core values and beliefs) was in place long before NBB had a marketing department. Back in early 1991, when New Belgium was just a home-brewed business plan of Lebesch and Jordan, a social worker, the two took a hike into Rocky Mountain National Park armed with a pen and a notebook. There they took their first stab at what the fledgling company's core purpose would be. If they were going forward with this venture, what were their aspirations beyond profitability? What was the real root cause of their dream? What they wrote down that spring day, give or take, are the core values and beliefs that you can read on the NBB website today.

From the very first NBB opted to adopt a triple bottom line (TBL) approach to business. Whereas the traditional bottom line approach for measuring business success is economic, TBL incorporates economic, social, and environmental factors. In other words, rather than just looking at financial data to evaluate company success, NBB looks at its impact upon profits, people, and the planet. One way that it is advancing the TBL approach is through the creation of a high-involvement corporate culture. All employees at NBB are expected to contribute to the company vision, and accountability is spread throughout the organization. Just about any New Belgium worker can list many, if not all, of these shared values. For NBB, branding strategies are rooted in its company values.

NEW BELGIUM'S PURPOSE AND CORE BELIEFS

New Belgium's dedication to quality, the environment, its employees, and its customers is expressed in its mission statement: "To operate a profitable brewery which makes our love and talent manifest." The company's stated core values and beliefs about its role as an environmentally concerned and socially responsible brewer include the following:

- Remembering that we are incredibly lucky to create something fine that enhances people's lives while surpassing our consumers' expectations
- Producing world-class beers
- Promoting beer culture and the responsible enjoyment of beer
- Kindling social, environmental, and cultural change as a business role model
- Environmental stewardship: minimizing resource consumption, maximizing energy efficiency, and recycling
- Cultivating potential through learning, participative management, and the pursuit of opportunities
- Balancing the myriad needs of the company, staff, and their families
- Trusting each other and committing ourselves to authentic relationships, communications, and promises
- Continuous, innovative quality and efficiency improvements
- Having fun

Employees believe that these statements help communicate to customers and other stakeholders what New Belgium as a company is about. These simple values developed twenty years ago are just as meaningful to the company today as they were then.

EMPLOYEE CONCERNS

Recognizing employees' roles in the company's success, New Belgium provides many generous benefits for its employees. In addition to the usual paid health and dental insurance and retirement plans, employees get a free catered lunch every month to celebrate employees' birthdays as well as a free massage once a year. Employees who stay with the company for five years earn an all-expenses-paid trip to Belgium to "study beer culture." Employees are also reimbursed for one hour of paid time for every two hours of volunteer work that they perform. Perhaps most importantly, employees can also earn stock in the privately held corporation, which grants them a vote in company decisions. Employees currently own about 43 percent of the company. Additionally, open-book management allows employees to see the financial costs and performance of the company.

New Belgium also wishes to get its employees involved not only in the company, but in sustainability efforts as well. To help their own sustainability efforts, employees are given a cruiser bike after one year's employment so that they can ride to work instead of drive. A recycling center on-site is provided for employees. Other company perks include inexpensive yoga classes, free beer at quitting time, and a climbing wall. To ensure that workers' voices are heard, NBB has a democratically elected group of coworkers called POSSE. POSSE acts as a liaison between the board, managers, and employees.

SUSTAINABILITY CONCERNS

New Belgium's marketing strategy involves linking the quality of its products, as well as its brand, with the company's ecological philosophy. From leading-edge environmental gadgets and high-tech industry advancements to employee-ownership programs and a strong belief in giving back to the community, New Belgium demonstrates its desire to create a living, learning community.

NBB strives for cost-efficient, energy-saving alternatives for conducting its business and reducing its impact on the environment. In staying true to the company's core values and beliefs, the brewery's employee–owners unanimously agreed to invest in a wind turbine, making New Belgium the first fully wind-powered brewery in the United States. NBB has also invested in the following energy-saving technologies:

- A smart grid installation that allows NBB to communicate with its electricity provider to conserve energy, for example, by alerting NBB to non-essential operational functions, allowing the company to turn them off and save power;

- The installation of a photovoltaic array on top of the packaging hall that produces three percent of the company's electricity;

- A brew kettle, the second of its kind installed in the nation, that heats wort sheets instead of the whole kettle at once, a method that conserves more energy than standard kettles do;

- Sun tubes, which provide natural daytime lighting throughout the brew house all year long;

- A system to capture its waste water and extract methane from it, which can contribute up to 15 percent of the brewery's power needs while reducing the strain on the local municipal water treatment facility.

New Belgium takes pride in reducing waste through recycling and creative reuse strategies. The company strives to recycle as many supplies as possible, including cardboard boxes, keg caps, office materials, and the amber glass used in bottling. The brewery stores spent barley and hop grains in an on-premise silo and invites local farmers to pick up the grains, free of charge, to feed their pigs. Going further down the road to producing products for the food chain, NBB is working with partners to take the same bacteria that create methane from NBB waste water and convert them into a harvestable, high-protein fish food.

New Belgium has been a long-time participant in green building techniques. With each expansion of the facility, it has incorporated new technologies. In 2002 NBB agreed to participate in the U.S. Green Building Council's Leadership in Energy and Environment Design for Existing Buildings (LEED-EB) pilot program. NBB continues to search for new ways to close loops and conserve resources.

Reduce, Reuse, Recycle—the three Rs of environmental stewardship—are taken seriously at NBB. The company's reuse program includes heat for the brewing process, cleaning chemicals and water, and much more. Recycling at New Belgium takes on many forms, from turning "waste" products into something new and useful (like spent grain to animal feed) to supporting the recycling market in creative ways (like turning their keg caps into table surfaces). The company also buys recycled products whenever possible, from paper to office furniture. The graph in Figure 2 depicts New Belgium's recycling efforts.

To measure its efforts in the area of the first "R," reduction, New Belgium has created its own Lifecycle Assessment, which helps the company account for the energy flows of its products' lifecycles in order to see how much energy has been reduced. Its numerous reduction efforts, which include everything from motion sensors on the lights throughout the building to induction fans that pull in cool winter air to chill the beer, offset New Belgium's energy needs. In 2009 the company also implemented the Corporate Greenhouse Gas Accounting Initiative to measure energy flow for its overall operations. Finally, NBB has included an organic beer in its product line. This beer is really a microcosm of the company—it is a wit (white) beer, a traditional Belgian style of unfiltered wheat beer flavored with orange and coriander.

New Belgium has made significant achievements in the area of sustainability, particularly compared to other companies in the industry. For one, New Belgium uses only 3.9 gallons of water to make 1 gallon of beer, which is 20 percent less than most other companies in the industry. The company is attempting to create a closed-loop system for its wastewater with its own Process Water Treatment Plant, which uses microbes. New Belgium recycles over 95 percent of its waste, and today 100 percent of its electricity comes from renewables. Despite these achievements, New Belgium has no intention of halting its sustainability efforts. It hopes to reduce the amount of water used to make its beer by 10 percent through better production processes and to decrease the carbon footprint of its Fat Tire Beer by 25 percent per barrel by 2015. To encourage

FIGURE 2

New Belgium Brewing Co.
2009 Waste Diversion
(sans Spent Grain & Sludge) = 95.6%

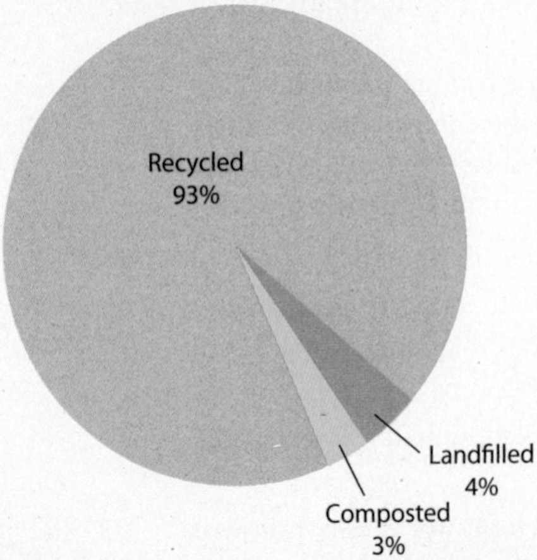

Recycled
93%

Landfilled
4%

Composted
3%

"Corporate Sustainability Report," New Belgium Brewing, http://www.newbelgium.com/culture/alternatively_empowered/sustainable-business-story/planet/waste.aspx (accessed March 4, 2011).

sustainability throughout its supply chain, NBB has adopted Sustainable Purchasing Guidelines. These guidelines allow the company to pinpoint ecofriendly suppliers and work closely with them to create sustainability throughout the entire value chain.

SOCIAL CONCERNS

Beyond its use of environmentally friendly technologies and innovations, New Belgium Brewing Company strives to improve communities and enhance people's lives through corporate giving, event sponsorship, and philanthropic involvement.

Since its inception, NBB has donated more than $2.5 million to philanthropic causes. For every barrel of beer sold the prior year, NBB donates $1 to philanthropic causes within its distribution territory. The donations are divided between states in proportion to their percentage of overall sales. This is the company's way of giving back to the communities that support and purchase NBB products. NBB also announced that it would donate $650,000 in funds for philanthropic programs. Moreover, it participates in One Percent for the Planet, a philanthropic network to which NBB donates 1 percent of its profits.

Funding decisions are made by New Belgium's philanthropy committee, which is comprised of employees from throughout the brewery, including owners, employee–owners, area leaders, and production workers. New Belgium looks for nonprofit organizations that demonstrate creativity, diversity, and an innovative approach to their mission and objectives. The philanthropy committee also looks for groups that involve their communities to reach their goals. Organizations can even apply for grants through the New Belgium Brewing Company website, which has a link designated for this purpose. The company donates to causes with a particular emphasis on water conservation, sensible transportation and bike advocacy, sustainable agriculture, and youth environmental education, among other areas. Additionally, NBB maintains a community bulletin board in its facility where it posts an array of activities and proposals.

NBB also sponsors a number of events, with a special focus on those that involve "human-powered" sports that cause minimal damage to the natural environment. Through events such as the Tour de Fat "traveling bike festival," as the company's website describes it, NBB supports various environmental, social, and cycling nonprofit organizations. During the Tour de Fat, some participants agree to participate in the Car-for-Bike Trade program, in which participants hand over their car keys and vehicle titles in exchange for an NBB commuter bike and trailer. The participants are then filmed for the world to see as they promote sustainable transportation over driving. New Belgium also partners with nonprofit organizations to support Skinny Dip for a Cause, a campaign in which skinny dipping is used to raise awareness of water issues and conservation. In the course of one year, New Belgium can be found at anywhere from 150 to 200 festivals and events across fifteen western states.

ORGANIZATIONAL SUCCESS

New Belgium Brewing Company's efforts to live up to its own high standards have paid off with numerous awards and a very loyal following. It was one of three winners of *Business Ethics* magazine's awards for its "dedication to environmental excellence in every part of its innovative brewing process." Kim Jordan and Jeff Lebesch were the recipients of the Rocky Mountain Region Entrepreneur of the Year Award for manufacturing in 1999, and NBB was listed as one of *The Wall Street Journal's* fifteen best small workplaces in 2008. The company has also won the award for best mid-sized brewing company of the year and best mid-sized brewmaster at the Great American Beer Festival in 2000 and 2001.

According to David Edgar, former director of the Institute for Brewing Studies at the Brewers Association in Boulder, Colorado, "They've created a very positive image for their company in the beer-consuming public with smart decision-making." New Belgium Brewing Company also promotes the responsible appreciation of beer through its participation in and support of the culinary arts.

According to Greg Owsley, the company continually reexamines its ethical, social, and environmental responsibilities. In 2004 New Belgium received the Environmental Protection Agency's regional Environmental Achievement Award. It was both an honor and a motivator for the company to continue its socially responsible goals. After all, there are still many ways for NBB to improve as a corporate citizen. For example, although all its electric power comes from renewable sources, the plant is still heated in part using natural gas. Additionally, there will always be a need for more public dialogue on avoiding alcohol abuse. NBB must acknowledge that as its annual sales increase, the challenges that the brand faces in its efforts to remain true to its vision will increase too. How to boldly grow the brand while maintaining its humble feel has always been a challenge. Moreover, reducing waste to an even greater extent will take lots of work on behalf of both managers and employees.

Every six-pack of New Belgium Beer displays the phrase, "In this box is our labor of love. We feel incredibly lucky to be creating something fine that enhances people's lives." The founders of New Belgium hope this statement captures the spirit of the company. According to employee Dave Kemp, NBB's environmental concern and social responsibility give it a competitive advantage because consumers want to believe in and feel good about the products they purchase. NBB's most important asset is its image—a corporate brand that stands for quality, responsibility, and concern for society. Defining itself as more than just a beer company, the brewer also sees itself as a caring organization that is concerned with all stakeholders, including the community, sustainability, and employees.

QUESTIONS

1. What environmental issues does the New Belgium Brewing Company work to address? How has NBB taken a strategic approach to addressing these issues? Why do you think the company has chosen to focus on environmental issues?

2. Are New Belgium's social initiatives indicative of strategic philanthropy? Why or why not?

3. Some segments of society vigorously contend that companies that sell alcoholic beverages and tobacco products cannot be socially responsible organizations. Do you believe that New Belgium Brewing Company's actions and initiatives are indicative of an ethical and socially responsible corporation? Why or why not?

SOURCES

Asmus, Peter. "Goodbye Coal, Hello Wind." *Business Ethics* 13 (July/August 1999): 10–11; Baun, Robert, "What's in a Name? Ask the Makers of Fat Tire." *The Fort Collins Coloradoan*, October 8, 2000, E1, E3; Better Business Bureau. "Four Businesses Honored with Prestigious International Award for Outstanding Marketplace Ethics."

http://www.bbb.org/us/article/four-businesseshonored-with-prestigious-international-award-for-outstanding-marketplace-ethics-193, September 23, 2002 (accessed March 4, 2011); Brew Public. "Tour de New Belgium." November 23, 2010, http://brewpublic.com/places-to-drink-beer/tour-de-new-belgium/ (accessed March 4, 2011); Dedrick, Jay. "Recession-Proof Brewing." *Colorado Biz,* September 2009, 62–64.; Deter, Stevi. "Fat Tire Amber Ale." The Net Net, www.thenetnet.com/reviews/fat.html (accessed September 8, 2009); Dwyer, Robert F., and John F. Tanner, Jr. *Business Marketing.* Boston: Irwin McGraw-Hill, 1999, 104; Gordon, Julie. "Lebesch Balances Interests in Business, Community." *The Fort Collins Coloradoan,* February 26, 2003; Haiar, Nikole. "New Belgium Brewing Company Tour." November 20, 2000; Haiar, Nikole. "David Kemp, 'Tour Connoisseur.' Personal interview, November 21, 2000; Hawkins, Del I., Roger J. Best, and Kenneth A. Coney. *Consumer Behavior: Building Marketing Strategy,* 8th ed. Boston: Irwin McGraw-Hill, 2001; Koudsi, Suzanne. "Kimberly Jordan, CEO, New Belgium Brewing Co., Fort Collins, Colo. To create award-winning beer, start with environmental passion, then add ideas to clean up the brewing process." *CNN Money,* June 1, 2003, http://money.cnn.com/magazines/fsb/fsb_archive/2003/06/01/346429/index.htm (accessed July 11, 2011); Kreck, Dick. "Strange Brewing standing out." *The Denver Post,* June 2, 2010, http://www.denverpost.com/lifestyles/ci_15198853 (accessed March 4, 2011); LiveGreen blog. "A Tour of the New Belgium Brewery—Act One." http://www.livegreensd.com/2007/04/tour-of-new-belgium-brewery-act-one.html, April 9, 2007 (accessed March 4, 2011); Lukovitz, Karlene. "New Belgium Brewing Gets 'Hopped Up.'" *Media Post News,* http://www.mediapost.com/publications/?fa=Articles.showArticle&art_aid=121806 (accessed March 4, 2011); Nason, Adam. "New Belgium brewing becomes largest craft brewery to use QR code technology." *beernews.org,* April 5, 2011, http://beernews.org/2011/04/new-belgium-brewing-becomes-largest-craft-brewery-to-use-qr-code-technology/ (accessed July 11, 2011); New Belgium Brewery. "2010 Total Donations." http://www.newbelgium.com/Files/NBB-2010-Total-Donations%20.pdf (accessed March 4, 2010); New Belgium Brewery. "Collabeeration." http://www.newbelgium.com/beerline/collabeeration (accessed September 8, 2009); New Belgium Brewery. "Corporate Sustainability Report." http://www.newbelgium.com/culture/alternatively_empowered/sustainable-business-story.aspx (accessed March 4, 2011); New Belgium Brewery. "Employee Perks." http://www.newbelgium.com/Files/nbb_employee_perks.pdf (accessed March 4, 2011); New Belgium Brewery. "Lips of Faith." http://www.newbelgium.com/beerline/lips-of-faith (accessed September 8, 2009); New Belgium Brewery. "Local Grants." http://www.newbelgium.com/Community/local-grants.aspx (accessed March 4, 2011); New Belgium Brewery. "New Belgium Brewing Blog." http://www.newbelgium.com/Community/Blog.aspx (accessed March 4, 2011); New Belgium Brewery. "Sponsorship." http://www.newbelgium.com/sponsorship (accessed March 4, 2011); New Belgium Brewery. "Trade Your Car for a Bike." http://www.newbelgium.com/trade (accessed September 8, 2009); "New Belgium Brewing Company, Inc.," *Businessweek,* http://investing.businessweek.com/research/stocks/private/snapshot.asp?privcapId=919332 (accessed March 4, 2011); "New Belgium Brewing to Cut CO2 Emissions by 25% Per Barrel." *Environmental Leader,* January 20, 2009, http://www.environmentalleader.com/2009/01/20/ new-belgium-brewing-to-cut- co2-emissions-by-25-per-barrel/ (accessed March 4, 2011); "New Belgium Brewing Wins Ethics Award." *Denver Business Journal,* January 2, 2003, http://www.bizjournals.com/denver/stories/2002/12/30/daily21.html (accessed September 8, 2009); Owsley, Greg. "The Necessity for Aligning Brand with Corporate Ethics." In *Fulfilling Our Obligation: Perspectives on Teaching Business Ethics,* Sheb L. True, Linda Ferrell, and O. C. Ferrell, eds. (Kennesaw, GA: Kennesaw State University Press, 2005), 128–132; Raabe, Steve. "New Belgium Brewing Turns to Cans." Denverpost.com, May 15, 2008, http://www.denverpost.com/ci_9262005 (accessed March 4, 2011); Reelbear.com. "GABF 2000 Awards." http://www.realbeer.com/edu/gabf/gabf2000.php (accessed March 4, 2010); Simpson, Bryan. *New Belgium Brewing: Brand Building through Advertising and Public Relations.* http://e-businessethics.com/NewBelgiumCases/newbelgiumbrewing.pdf (accessed March 4, 2011); Spors, Kelly K. "Top Small Workplaces 2008." *The Wall Street Journal,* February 22, 2009, http://online.wsj.com/article/SB122347733961315417.html (accessed March 4, 2011).

CASE 6

Coping with Financial and Ethical Risks at American International Group (AIG)*

When American International Group (AIG) collapsed in September 2008 and was subsequently saved by a government bailout, it became one of the most controversial players in the 2008–2009 financial crisis. The corporate culture at AIG had been involved in a high-stakes risk-taking scheme supported by managers and employees that appeared entirely focused on short-term financial gain. Out of a firm of 116,000 employees, one unit with around 500 employees, AIG Financial Products, was chiefly to blame for bringing down the company, and current CEO Ed Liddy, who was summoned by former Treasury Secretary Hank Paulson, estimates that of that number only twenty to thirty people were directly involved.

The AIG Financial Products unit specialized in derivatives and other complex financial contracts that were tied to subprime mortgages or commodities. While its dealings were risky, the unit generated billions of dollars in profits for AIG. Even so, during his long tenure as CEO of AIG, Maurice "Hank" Greenberg had been open about his suspicions of the AIG Financial Products unit. After Greenberg resigned as chief executive of AIG in 2005, the Financial Products unit became even more speculative in its activities.

Immediately before its collapse, AIG had exposure to $64 billion in potential subprime mortgage losses. The perfect storm formed with the subprime mortgage crisis and a sudden sharp downturn in the value of residential real estate in 2008. Since much of the speculation in the Financial Products unit was tied to derivatives, even small movements in the value of financial measurements could result in catastrophic losses.

In this case, we trace the history of AIG as it evolved into one of the largest and most respected insurance companies in the world, and explore the more recent events that led to its demise. AIG had a market value of close to $200 billion in 2007, but by 2009 this amount had fallen to a mere $3.5 billion. Only a government rescue of what has amounted to $180 billion in loans, investments, guarantees, and financial injections prevented AIG from facing total bankruptcy in late 2008. The government rescued the company not to keep it from bankruptcy, however, but to prevent the bankruptcies of many other global financial institutions that depended on AIG as counterparty on collateralized debt obligations. If AIG had been allowed to fail, it is possible that the financial meltdown that occurred in 2008–2009 would have been worse.

This case first examines the events leading up to the 2008 meltdown, including the philosophy of top management and the corporate culture that set the stage for AIG's downfall. Next, we review the events that occurred in 2008, including ethical issues related to transparency and failed internal controls. Finally, we look at the role of the government and its decision to bail out AIG.

*This case was prepared by O. C. Ferrell, John Fraedrich, and Jennifer Sawayda. Jennifer Jackson assisted in the previous edition of this case. It was prepared for classroom discussion rather than to illustrate either effective or ineffective handling of an administrative, ethical, or legal decision by management. All sources used for this case were obtained through publicly available material.

AIG'S HISTORY

The saga of American International Group (AIG) began in 1919 with the American businessman Cornelius Vander Starr, who founded a company in Shanghai representing American insurance companies selling fire and marine coverage in Asia. Starr's success in Shanghai quickly led to expansion across Asia; Starr opened a branch of the company in the United States in 1926. While AIG began as a representative of American insurance companies abroad, in the United States it provided insurance risk coverage to insurance companies as a way to disperse liabilities. Reinsurers such as AIG were created to remove some of the risk associated with large disasters. Because of AIG and others, insurance companies could grow faster than ever before.

Insurance companies are educated risk takers. When insurance companies feel they have too much risk, they go to their reinsurance companies, such as AIG, to take out insurance so that if something catastrophic happens, they can still pay their clients. AIG utilizes models to determine how much insurance it can sell to insurers and still pay out. To put it simply, AIG charges insurance companies a premium in order to allow them to spread their risk so that they can sell insurance policies and grow more rapidly.

In 1968 Maurice "Hank" Greenberg, a native New Yorker and experienced insurance executive who had been with AIG for many years, took over as CEO. AIG grew exponentially during his tenure. By the end of the 1980s the company had become the largest underwriter of commercial and industrial coverage in the United States and the leading international insurance organization.

AIG continued to expand throughout the 1990s, led by its return to China as the first foreign insurance organization granted a license by the Chinese authorities to operate a wholly owned insurance business in Shanghai. (While many foreign organizations are required to have Chinese investors, wholly owned foreign businesses do not have this requirement.) AIG later expanded to Guangzhou, Shenzhen, and Beijing, as well as Vietnam. In 2001 AIG established two joint ventures in general insurance and life insurance in India with the Tata Group, the leading Indian industrial conglomerate. New AIG subsidiary companies followed the fall of the Soviet Union into Eastern Europe, with general and life insurance companies forming in Russia, Poland, Hungary, and the Czech Republic, among other emerging markets.

In 2001 AIG purchased American General Corporation, a top U.S. life insurer. This acquisition made AIG a leader in the U.S. life insurance industry and consumer lending. Today, the four principal business areas of AIG are General Insurance, Life Insurance and Retirement Services, Financial Services, and Asset Management. For the individual consumer, business, financial professional, or insurance professional, AIG provides accident and health insurance, auto insurance, life insurance, banking and loans, retirement services, travel insurance, additional services, and annuities. Immediately before its 2008 collapse, AIG had revenues exceeding $110 billion, total assets of over $1 trillion, and 116,000 employees around the world.

AIG'S CULTURE

Maurice "Hank" Greenberg was the CEO of AIG for 38 years, and was therefore a key player in shaping the modern face and corporate culture of the company. Many considered Greenberg a genius in the insurance business, and arguably he was one of the most successful and influential executives in the business. But critics called him autocratic in his drive to expand the company into an international powerhouse.

During his career, Greenberg championed innovative products that insure almost any type of risk, including Internet identity theft and hijacking. At least four U.S. presidents sought his advice on international affairs and financial markets. Greenberg was always known for utilizing his contacts and influence to help advance the company. Over the years, Greenberg aggressively lobbied for laws and rulings favorable to AIG. He was very involved with international politics and helped the U.S. government to secure information and develop back-door channels for classified dealings. In return, AIG was given the benefit of the doubt when regulatory agencies came questioning the company's doings. When billions or trillions of dollars are involved, global corporations have powers equal to or greater than those of governments and regulatory agencies.

In spite of Greenberg's active networking, the early 2000s found AIG under investigation by the Securities and Exchange Commission for its "finite insurance" deals—contracts that covered specific amounts of losses rather than unexpected losses of indeterminate size—and what appeared to be loans (since premiums were structured to match policy payouts and eliminate risk) rather than genuine risk allocation vehicles. A federal inquiry later found information that Greenberg might have been personally involved in creating a bogus reinsurance transaction with the General Re Corporation to fraudulently boost AIG's reserves. New York Attorney General Eliot Spitzer subpoenaed Greenberg, who treated the summons far more lightly than he should have. As rumors swirled, AIG's stock began to plummet, and the AIG board started to become concerned.

In 2005 Greenberg was forced out as CEO. Next Martin Sullivan held the CEO position for three years, followed by Robert Willumstad for three months. Willumstad was forced to step down in 2008 in the wake of the corporation's meltdown. He was replaced by Edward Liddy, former CEO of The Allstate Corporation. The SEC leveled charges of fraud against Greenberg resulting from the circumstances surrounding his departure. In order to settle the charges that AIG manipulated financial statements in 2005, the company paid the SEC $1.6 billion in 2006, and Greenberg agreed to pay an additional $15 million in 2009.

WHAT HAPPENED AT AIG TO CAUSE ITS DEMISE?

The heart of AIG's troubles leading up to the 2008 bailout was a kind of derivative called credit default swaps (CDSs). Credit default swaps are financial products that transfer the credit exposure (risk) of fixed-income products (bonds) between parties. The buyer of a credit swap receives credit protection, as the seller of the swap guarantees the creditworthiness of the product. The risk of default is thereby transferred from the holder of the fixed-income security to the seller of the swap. One single credit default swap can be valued at hundreds of millions of dollars.

> "AIG did not have a large enough safety net to weather the subprime mortgage collapse."

As a reinsurer, AIG used CDSs as a kind of insurance policy on complex collateralized debt obligations (CDOs). The company issued the swaps and promised to pay these institutions, AIG's counterparties, if the debt securities defaulted. However, AIG did not have a large enough safety net to weather the subprime mortgage collapse. These insurance contracts became essentially worthless because many people could not pay back their subprime mortgages and AIG did not have the creditworthiness for the big collateral call.

The government took the drastic step of bailing out the company, providing the funds to purchase the CDOs that were being held by banks, hedge funds, and other financial institutions, and in the process ended up with 79.9 percent ownership of AIG. The U.S. government is now the senior partner in a special-purpose entity that will receive interest and share liability in the ownership of these tainted investment instruments. The government had feared that if AIG were allowed to go bankrupt, many banks throughout the world would have gone bankrupt as well.

As we have noted, one unit of the company, AIG Financial Products, was the source of many of the company's woes. Founded in 1987 by Howard Sosin to trade over-the-counter derivatives, its creation was timed perfectly to ride the derivatives market boom. By and large, Financial Products was run like a hedge fund out of Wilton, Connecticut, and London. Hedge funds are a special type of fund available to a select range of investors. They seek to utilize a wide variety of investment tools to mitigate, or *hedge*, risk. Often the term refers to funds that use short selling as a means of increasing investment returns. Short selling is betting that the stock price of a company will change during a specified period of time. When the stocks move the expected direction, the investor makes money.

AIG Financial Products specialized in derivatives that generated billions of dollars in profits over the years. Derivatives are financial contracts or instruments whose value is derived from something else such as commodities (corn, wheat, soybeans, etc.), stocks, bonds, and even home mortgages. Gains or losses from derivatives come from betting on the movement of these values. The unit also dealt in mortgage securities, a sector that turned rancid with the collapse of the housing bubble. Former New York Attorney General Eliot Spitzer, a champion of financial sector reform, claimed that AIG Financial Products was "the black hole of AIG."

When Howard Sosin joined AIG he was given an unusual deal—a 20 percent stake in the unit and 20 percent of its profits. While AIG can be described as a conservative global conglomerate selling insurance policies to businesses and individuals, the Financial Products unit was staffed by quantitative specialists with doctorates in finance and math. Employees of the unit conducted themselves like investment bankers.

In the late 1990s, under the leadership of Joseph Cassano, AIG Financial Products ramped up its business of selling credit default swaps, which were at the heart of the 2008–2009 financial meltdown. AIG Financial Products expanded into writing swaps to cover debt that was backed by mortgages. The unit sold swaps to large institutional investors. These collateralized debt obligations were backed by mortgages, and the swaps issued by AIG backed some $440 billion worth of obligations. To put this in perspective, the entire market worth of AIG was around $200 billion at the time. AIG made millions selling collateralized debt obligations (CDOs) and was able to post modest margin requirements, which is the amount the company keeps as a deposit to protect against the risk of loan defaults or nonpayments. For example, to buy stock on margin, you must have at least 50 percent of the purchase price in your account. AIG was able to make these CDO deals with a very small fraction of actual money on hand. Unfortunately, some of these CDOs were attached to home mortgages.

In spite of the risk, the company involved itself in bad mortgage lending by financial institutions that did not have sufficient capital to cover the loans, which in turn had bought this type of insurance from AIG that created an unstable financial environment. The loans and the CDOs were often sold to people who could not repay their debt. CEO Greenberg became concerned about this unit's derivative dealings and asked a group to shadow its trades. Greenberg was uncomfortable with the results and thought the unit was taking too many risks. However, Greenberg left the company in 2005 because of regulators investigating AIG over its accounting practices.

AIG sold credit protection on CDOs by simply writing pieces of paper that stated that AIG would cover the losses in case these obligations went bad. AIG agreed to either take over the obligations or cover the losses on CDOs. While AIG made billions of dollars in profits and managers received millions of dollars in compensation for selling these so-called insurance policies, it turned out to be a high-risk house of cards. The tools, CDOs, and CDSs were used recklessly and failed to assess systemic risk of counterparties not measuring their own exposures and not paying their obligations. The Financial Products unit was under investigation around the world, including by the United Kingdom's Serious Fraud Office. However, its probe against AIG's Financial Products unit was eventually dropped.

Although they have since gained notoriety, before 2008, derivatives were not widely understood by the public, mass media, regulators, and even many of the executives who were overseeing their use. AIG could have taken another approach, buying mortgages or CDOs and then having some other party package them into a credit default swap as insurance, but since AIG was an insurer it simply wrote policies on CDOs, increasing revenues with the hope that only a few would default.

AIG Lacked Transparency

There were suggestions that AIG knew of potential problems in valuing derivative contracts before the financial meltdown occurred. Outside auditors raised concerns about being excluded from conversations that concerned the evaluation of derivatives. As AIG's auditor, PricewaterhouseCoopers (PwC) had a right to know about the models and about market indicators that indicated that the value of AIG swaps should be lowered. During this period, however, AIG executives Cassano and Sullivan continued to reassure investors and auditors that AIG had accurately identified all areas of exposure to the U.S. residential housing market and stated their confidence in their evaluation methods. The Justice Department launched a probe of AIG executives, including Joseph Cassano, to investigate whether they had misled investors, but eventually decided not to bring criminal charges against them.

The market indicators in question came in the form of demands for collateral by AIG trading partners. At a congressional hearing, Sullivan stated that he believed the evaluations to be accurate based on the information he possessed at the time. This situation is similar to executives at Enron claiming they did not know that Enron had utilized the derivatives and off-the-book balance sheet partnerships that caused its demise. Many Enron executives ended up being found guilty of crimes.

> "The AIG culture was focused on a reward system that placed little responsibility on executives who made very poor decisions."

AIG Provided Incentives to Take Risks

What were the factors within the corporate culture of AIG that promoted speculative risk-taking? Part of the problem may have been AIG's incentives. The AIG culture was focused on a reward system that placed little responsibility on executives who made very poor decisions. Although they produced nearly $40 billion in losses in 2008, a number of managers were selected to receive large bonuses. AIG offered cash awards and other perks to 38 executives and a retention program with payments from $92,500 to $4 million for employees earning salaries between $160,000 and $1 million.

After receiving more than $152 billion in federal rescue funds, AIG publicly claimed that it would eliminate some of these bonuses for senior executives while all the time planning to hand out cash awards that doubled or tripled the salaries of some. AIG asserted that these types of payments were necessary to keep top employees at AIG, even as control of the company was being handed over to the government. The fact of rewards doled out in the face of excessive risk-taking and possible misconduct has met with outrage among most stakeholders. The main reason that AIG was bailed out at all was that the government was seeking to prevent the failure of some of the world's largest banks, thereby potentially causing a global financial catastrophe. AIG's actions reflect an ethical culture that neglects its most important stakeholders.

The demise of AIG's Financial Products unit resulted in part from excessive risk-taking by economists and other financial experts using computer models that failed to take into account real-world market risks. For example, AIG paid Gary Gorton, a finance professor at the Yale School of Management whose work had been cited in speeches by Federal Reserve Chairman Ben Bernanke, large consulting fees for developing computer models to gauge risk for more than $400 billion in complicated credit default swaps. Remember that a single swap can be valued at hundreds of millions of dollars. AIG relied on Gorton's models to determine which swap deals were low risk. Unfortunately, these models did not anticipate how market forces and contract terms could turn swaps into huge financial liabilities. AIG did not assign Gorton to assess those threats, and therefore his models did not consider them.

Like other major firms, AIG entered a very lucrative but perilous new market without truly understanding the sheer complexity of the financial products it was selling. What the company learned too late was that computers and academic experts cannot determine all of the variables, forces, and weights that cause a high- or low-risk investment to go bad. The blame lies with business placing too much trust in models that turn out to contain faulty assumptions. Models cannot predict with absolute certainty what humans will do because humans are not always rational. Warren Buffett, chief executive of Berkshire Hathaway and a billionaire many times over, has said, ". . . beware of geeks . . . bearing formulas."

AIG'S CRISIS AND BAILOUT

AIG's problems came to a boil in September 2008. Due to the many issues outlined earlier, AIG's stock was downgraded by the rating companies, which caused the stock to drop, causing a run on the reinsurer's liquid assets (cash on hand) that revealed its lack of liquidity. Simply put, AIG did not have the capital to repay investors asking for their money back.

AIG ultimately owed Wall Street's biggest firms about $100 billion for speculative trades turned bad; $64 billion of that was tied to losses on subprime mortgages. The company allegedly placed billions of dollars at risk through speculation on the movements of various mortgage pools, and there were no actual securities backing these speculative positions on which AIG was losing money. The losses stemmed from market wagers that were essentially bets on the performance of bundles of derivatives linked to subprime residential mortgages.

The government rescue of AIG protected many of its policyholders and counterparties from immediate losses on traditional insurance contracts, but these speculative trades were not a part of the government risk rescue. Over the course of a month, the government doled out over $152 billion in taxpayer money, creating a line of credit for the company and buying up AIG stock. This was a highly controversial move, particularly since the government had not done the same thing for the other struggling financial giant, Lehman Brothers. In March 2009, the government made the controversial decision to dole out another $30 billion in capital to AIG. The decision was made even more contentious when it was revealed that $165 million of the bailout money had gone to bonuses of employees of the failed Financial Products unit. The company stated that the bonuses were part of the employees' contracts and could not be revoked.

Both consumers and government officials were outraged. Pressure on AIG became so great that CEO Edward Liddy asked executives who were making over $100,000 a year to return the bonuses. The House of Representatives voted to implement a 90 percent tax on bonuses at companies that received over $5 billion in bonus funds. However, due to the high level of pressure against the company, most of the executives in question returned the money. In 2010 AIG announced that it was revamping its bonus system. While previous bonuses were largely based on length of time employed with the company, AIG vowed to better align future bonuses with performance. To prevent such an occurrence from happening in the future, the government also resolved to increase its oversight of new bailout funds.

When questioned about the decision to repeatedly bail out AIG, Federal Reserve Chair Ben Bernanke told U.S. lawmakers, "AIG exploited a huge gap in the regulatory system. There was no oversight of the financial products division. This was a hedge fund, basically, that was attached to a large and stable insurance company." He stated that AIG was the single case out of the entire 2008–2009 financial crisis that made him the angriest. However, Bernanke went on to say, "We had no choice but to try to stabilize the system because of the implications that the failure would have had for the broad economic system."

Although the bailouts were massive, they did not cover all that AIG owed, and the company has had to sell off numerous assets. Two-thirds of the company needed to be sold in a tough market for sellers, resulting in auctions of dozens of the company's units around the world. Many of these sales resulted in disappointing prices for AIG. For example, Munich Re, the world's biggest reinsurer, agreed to buy AIG's Hartford unit for $742 million, about a third less than AIG had paid for it eight years before. The company also has given more than 2,000 employees cash incentives to stop them from quitting, saying that the payments are necessary. "Anybody who wants to start an insurance company or beef up their position, they will come to our organization and pick people off," said then-CEO Edward Liddy in an interview. "If that happens, we can't maintain the businesses we want to keep and we won't be able to sell them for the kinds of values that we need."

Former CEO Greenberg insists that the company's upper management was the root cause of the collapse after he left. "AIG had a unique culture when I was its CEO, particularly in comparison with the way many large public companies operate today," he said. "Neither I nor other members of my senior management team had employment contracts. I received no severance package in connection with my retirement, and I never sold a single share of AIG stock during the more than 35 years that I served as CEO." In a 2008 interview, Greenberg explained what he sees as the real cause of the financial collapse. He blames low interest rates and excessively easy credit for the reckless risk-taking and poor decisions made within the financial industry. He also cites excessive leveraging and mark-to-market accounting practices as contributing to the meltdown. "Mark-to-market" means assigning a value to a position held in a financial instrument based on the current market price for the instrument. For example, the final value of a financial contract (say, grain futures) that expires in nine months will not be known until it expires. If it is marked to market, for accounting purposes it is assigned the value that it would have at the end of each day. Greenberg believes that all these factors grew out of control to the point where the entire system had nowhere to go but toward failure.

The controversies regarding AIG have not ended with government ownership. In fact, the problems that critics had identified regarding the company's culture and reckless spending were on full display a mere two months after it had received its bailout money. Top AIG executives were spotted holding a lavish conference at a posh Point Hilton Squaw Peak Resort in Phoenix for 150 financial planners and top AIG executives. The three-day event reportedly cost over $343,000. Representatives of the corporation defend the conference, stating that most of the costs were underwritten by sponsors; however, such an episode mere weeks after receiving a government bailout funded by taxpayers did not sit well with stakeholders. Many believe it demonstrated how little remorse AIG has for the decisions leading up to the failure, and how little has changed since the company received government money.

CHANGES AT AIG

AIG has a tough road ahead of it, not only in repaying tax-payers but also in restoring its damaged reputation. The best way for AIG to restore its credibility will be by increasing its transparency and accountability. This requires a more realistic assessment of its risks and liabilities. In 2011 AIG decided to increase its claims estimates for insurance policies that it had sold in the past, particularly those associated with its property and casualty insurance business Chartis. AIG will increase loss reserves for these insurance policies by $4.1 billion, a move that will eliminate much of its operating profit for 2010 but serve to clean up its balance sheet.

> "The best way for AIG to restore its credibility will be by increasing its transparency and accountability."

AIG is also selling off some of its businesses to generate the proceeds needed to repay taxpayers. The company sold its American Life Insurance Division to MetLife for $15.5 billion, its Asia-based life insurer AIA Group to Great Britain's Prudential PLC for $35.5 billion, and its ownership in the third largest insurance company in Taiwan for $2.2 billion. Additionally, AIG has reached an agreement with the U.S. government, which plans to end its involvement with AIG within the next two years. In early 2011 the government announced plans to begin selling off its 92.1 percent stake in AIG through stock offerings. Together the AIG and the Treasury released $8.89 billion in stock. AIG has been able to repay $40 billion to the Federal Reserve and Treasury. However, the success of AIG's stock will largely be based upon how well investors believe AIG will perform in the future. AIG will need to implement strategies to reestablish investor trust if it hopes to repay its debts and return to profitability.

CONCLUSION

The question remains: Was a bailout really necessary? Some, such as Greenberg himself, say yes. "You have to have a bailout," Greenberg argued. "But I would call it something else rather than a bailout. That implies the wrong thing. It is really also helping Main Street, not just Wall Street, because if the economy doesn't grow, jobs are going to be lost and we're going to go into a depression rather than a recession. The taxpayer is not going to take a hit long-term because the money involved will be repaid over a period of time."

Others are not so certain. Critics of the AIG and auto industry bailouts, for example, cite a lack of accountability in how the funds are to be used. Many also oppose this level of government intervention in corporations because it seems to be rewarding companies that have blatantly ignored the needs and desires of their stakeholders in favor of enriching themselves in the short term. Even months after the bailout, AIG continued to lose massive amounts of money. Although the company is beginning to show signs of recovery, the damage to its reputation over this matter has been massive, and some critics wonder if it will ever recover.

The company has also had a difficult time selling off its assets in order to repay its debts, as many of its potential buyers also have been working to recover from the 2008–2009 recession. Without a doubt, the failure of AIG was massive and, bailout or not, its effects have rippled across the globe.

QUESTIONS

1. Discuss the role that AIG's corporate culture played in its downfall.

2. Discuss the ethical conduct of AIG executives and how a stronger ethics program might help the company to strengthen the ethics of its corporate culture.

3. What could AIG have done differently to prevent its failure and subsequent bailout?

SOURCES

"American International Group, Inc." *The New York Times,* December 9, 2010, http://topics.nytimes.com/top/news/business/companies/american_international_group/index.html (accessed February 16, 2011); Anderson, Jenny. "AIG Profit Is Reduced by $4 Billion." *The New York Times,* June 1, 2005, http://www.nytimes.com/2005/06/01/business/01insure.html (accessed February 21, 2011); Anderson, Jenny. "Greenberg Fires Back at Directors." *The New York Times,* August 5, 2005, http://query.nytimes.com/gst/fullpage.html?res=9A02E7DE163EF936A3575BC0A9639C8B63 (accessed February 21, 2011); Behan, Beverly. "Memo to the Board of AIG." *BusinessWeek,* November 16, 2008, http://www.businessweek.com/managing/content/nov2008/ca20081118_408443.htm (accessed February 21, 2011); Browning, Lynnley. "A.I.G.'s House of Cards." *Portfolio,* September 29, 2008, http://www.portfolio.com/news-markets/top-5/2008/09/28/AIGs-Derivatives-Run-Amok/ (accessed February 21, 2011); Byrnes, Nanette. "The Unraveling of AIG." *BusinessWeek*, September 16, 2008, http://www.businessweek.com/bwdaily/dnflash/content/sep2008/db20080915_552271_page_2.htm (accessed February 21, 2011); Desmond, Mauma. "AIG. CDOs. CDS. It's a Mess." Forbes.com, November 15, 2008, http://www.forbes.com/2008/11/15/aig-credit-default-markets-equity-cx_md_1110markets24.html (accessed February 21, 2011); Drucker, Jesse. "AIG's Tax Dispute with U.S. Has Twist of Irony." *The Wall Street Journal,* November 14, 2008, C2; Eichenwald, Kurt, and Jenny Anderson. "How a Titan of Insurance Ran Afoul of the Government." *The New York Times,* April 4, 2005, http://www.nytimes.com/2005/04/04/business/04aig.html (accessed February 21, 2011); Gogoi, Pallavi. "AIG plans on 'completely repaying' taxpayers." *USA Today,* January 16, 2011, http://www.usatoday.com/money/industries/insurance/2011-01-14-aig-repay_N.htm (accessed February 18, 2011); Goldman, David. "AIG overhauls bonus system." CNN Money, February 10, 2010, http://money.cnn.com/2010/02/10/news/companies/aig_bonuses/index.htm (accessed February 16, 2011); "The Great Untangling." *The Economist,* November 8, 2008, 85–86; Henry, David,

Matthew Goldstein, and Carol Matlack. "How AIG's Credit Loophole Squeezed Europe's Banks." *BusinessWeek*, October 16, 2008, http://www.businessweek.com/magazine/content/08_43/b4105032835044.htm (accessed February 21, 2011); Krisher, Tom. "AIG Executives Won't Face Criminal Charges, Lawyers Say." *The Huffington Post*, May 22, 2010, http://www.huffingtonpost.com/2010/05/22/aig-executives-no-criminal-charges_n_586203.html (accessed February 18, 2011); Kroft, Steve. "Why AIG Stumbled, and Taxpayers Now Own It." CBS News, March 17, 2009, http://www.cbsnews.com/stories/2009/05/15/60minutes/main5016760.shtml (accessed February 21, 2011); Loomis, Carol J. "AIG: The Company That Came to Dinner." *Fortune*, January 19, 2009, 70–78; Mason, Rowena. "Serious Fraud Office Drops UK Probe." *The Telegraph*, May 26, 2010, http://www.telegraph.co.uk/finance/newsbysector/banksandfinance/7768815/Serious-Fraud-Office-drops-UK-probe-into-AIG.html (accessed July 7, 2011); Mollenkamp, Carrick, Serena Ng, Liam Pleven, and Randall Smith. "Behind AIG's Fall, Risk Models Failed to Pass Real-World Test." *The Wall Street Journal*, November 3, 2008, A1, A16; Morgenson, Gretchen. "AIG: Whiter Shade of Enron." *The New York Times*, April 3, 2005, http://www.nytimes.com/2005/04/03/business/yourmoney/03gret.html?_r=1&scp=1&sq=%22whiter%20shade%20of%20enron%22&st=cse (accessed February 21, 2011); Morgenson, Gretchen. "Feds end probe of AIG chief with no charges." SFGate.com, May 24, 2010, http://articles.sfgate.com/2010-05-24/business/20911444_1_financial-products-unit-aig-executive-joseph-cassano (accessed July 7, 2011); Ng, Serena, Carrick Mollenkamp, and Michael Siconolfi. "AIG Faces $10 Billion in Losses on Trades." *The Wall Street Journal*, December 10, 2008, A1–A2; Ng, Serena, and Erik Holm. "AIG to Book Charge Tied to Chartis." *The Wall Street Journal*, February 10, 2011, C1–C2; Ng, Serena, and Liam Pleven. "Revised AIG Rescue Is Bank Boon." *The Wall Street Journal*, November 12, 2008, C1, C5; O'Brian, Timothy L. "Guilty Plea Is Expected in AIG-Related Case." *The New York Times*, June 10, 2005, http://query.nytimes.com/gst/fullpage.html?res=9801E3DC1138F933A25755C0A9639C8B63&sec=&spon=&pagewanted=2 (accessed December February 21, 2011); Pleven, Liam and Amir Efrati. "Documents Show AIG Knew of Problems with Valuations." *The Wall Street Journal*, October 11–12, 2008, B1–B2; Rosenthal, Justine A. "Maurice Greenberg on What's Next for Wall Street." *National Interest Online*, October 2, 2008, http://nationalinterest.org/article/maurice-greenberg-on-whats-next-for-wall-street-2876 (accessed February 21, 2011); Scherer, Ron. "A Top Insurance Company as the New Enron? An Accounting Probe at AIG Worries Wall Street, and Involves Some of America's Richest Men." *The Christian Science Monitor*, April 1, 2005, http://www.csmonitor.com/2005/0401/p03s01-usju.html (accessed February 21, 2011); Son, Hugh. "AIG Plans to Repay U.S. in 2009, Liddy Tells CNBC." *Bloomberg*, December 22, 2008, http://www.bloomberg.com/apps/news?pid=20601087&sid=aDXR6Ayuezx4&refer=home (accessed February 21, 2011); Son, Hugh. "AIG Says More Managers Get Retention Payouts Topping $4 Million." *Bloomberg*, December 9, 2008, http://www.bloomberg.com/apps/news?pid=newsarchive&sid=aKIvmgvNl6zA (accessed February 21, 2011); Stephen, Bernard. "AIG, after taxpayer bailout, returns to profitability." *USA Today*, May 7, 2010, http://www.usatoday.com/money/companies/earnings/2010-05-07-aig_N.htm (accessed February 18, 2011); Stout, David, and Brian Knowlton. "Fed chief says insurance giant acted irresponsibly." *The New York Times*, http://www.nytimes.com/2009/03/03/business/worldbusiness/03iht-03webecon.20567563.html (accessed February 21, 2011); Walsh, Mary Williams. "AIG Cuts Losses Sharply to $4.35 Billion in First Quarter." *The New York Times*, May 8, 2009, B5; Walsh, Mary Williams. "Bigger Holes to Fill." *The Wall Street Journal*, November 11, 2008, B1, B5; Weisman, Jonathan, Sudeep Reddy, and Liam Pleven. "Political Heat Sears AIG." *The Wall Street Journal*, March 17, 2009, http://online.wsj.com/article/SB123721970101743003.html (accessed February 21, 2011); Smith, Randall, Deborah Soloman, and Joann S. Lublin. "AIG Offering Near Low End of Range." *The Wall Street Journal*, May 11, 2011, http://online.wsj.com/article/SB10001424052748704681904576316002595361180.html?KEYWORDS=AIG+stock+offering (accessed May 11, 2011).

CASE 7

Microsoft Manages Legal and Ethical Issues*

When Bill Gates and Paul Allen founded Microsoft in 1975, they had no idea that their company would become the world's leading supplier of software for personal computers. With annual revenues of more than $66 billion, Microsoft Corporation is a leader in the technology industry. Its business is based on developing, manufacturing, and licensing software and electronics, including operating systems, gaming devices, productivity software, and Internet software and services. In addition, the company's extensive social responsibility efforts focus on information technology and underserved communities around the world. Microsoft has faced legal and ethical issues that have tested its reputation; however, the company has survived the threat of a breakup, changes in its leadership, and multiple legal battles, including antitrust charges in the United States and the European Union. Today, Microsoft is still not only the world's leading distributor of computer software but is also a leader in corporate social responsibility (CSR) and philanthropy.

ETHICS AND SOCIAL RESPONSIBILITY AT MICROSOFT

Microsoft has a positive reputation based on its brand image, product quality, history of innovation, and numerous philanthropic and educational programs. The company has consistently topped the Cision Corporate Media Reputation Index, which ranks companies based on positive coverage in the media. Microsoft has created several charitable and socially responsible programs that help the company and its employees to achieve their corporate mission, "[T]o enable people and businesses throughout the world to realize their full potential."

Microsoft's Corporate Citizenship strategy focuses on "increasing opportunities and helping solve societal challenges in communities around the world." The company emphasizes issues that Microsoft and its shareholders believe are most important for the company's global business, including strengthening economies, addressing societal challenges, promoting a healthy online ecosystem, and operating responsibly.

Microsoft's community initiatives include workforce development, disaster and humanitarian responses, and improving nonprofits' access to technology. In addition, when

---

*This case was prepared by Harper Baird and Renee Wright for and under the direction of O. C. Ferrell and Linda Ferrell. It was prepared for classroom discussion rather than to illustrate either effective or ineffective handling of an administrative, ethical, or legal decision by management. All sources used for this case were obtained through publicly available material.

Microsoft employees donate to the annual giving campaign, the company matches their contributions up to $12,000. In 2010 Microsoft and its employees donated $84 million as well as thousands of volunteer hours to nonprofit organizations including low-income housing developments, the YMCA, Easter Seals, Boys and Girls Clubs of America, museums, and schools.

One of the key community programs at Microsoft is Unlimited Potential (UP). UP strives to bring the benefits of information and communications technology to underserved communities around the world by transforming education, fostering local innovation, and creating jobs and opportunities. Another important program is Libraries Online, through which Microsoft provides computers, cash, and software to help link libraries to the Internet. The goal is to enable people who may not have access to computers to learn about PCs, explore the latest software, and experience the Internet. Microsoft has extended this program to include nonprofit organizations that provide veterans and their spouses with the support they need to successfully transition to civilian careers.

Microsoft also contributes to global economic growth, job creation, and innovation. The company has almost 90,000 full-time employees globally, including 35,000 international employees. In addition, Microsoft relies on a network of partners that are valuable to their own communities to generate further innovation, growth, and opportunity. It also runs programs to support start-up software companies. Microsoft estimates that these business partnerships create nearly 15 million information technology jobs globally.

Microsoft has stated that it is committed to responsible and sustainable business practices that consider the social and environmental consequences of its actions. In addition to several recycling and carbon reduction programs, the company also strives to make its products efficient. Additionally, Microsoft works with businesses, governments, and law enforcement agencies to combat cybercrime and find joint solutions to keep people safer online. To achieve the long-term interests of the company's shareholders, Microsoft takes into account the needs of other stakeholders, including employees, customers, partners, suppliers, and the many communities around the world where it does business.

> "Microsoft has stated that it is committed to responsible and sustainable business practices that consider the social and environmental consequences of its actions."

Even though he stepped down from his daily role at the company several years ago, the brand name and reputation of Microsoft seems inseparable from Bill Gates, and Microsoft has benefitted from the positive public associations related to the philanthropic efforts of the Bill & Melinda Gates Foundation. The Gates started the foundation in 1994 to improve philanthropic endeavors that address global health and community needs. Warren Buffet joined Bill and Melinda Gates as a director in 2006 after donating $31 billion in stock to the foundation. In 2010 the Bill & Melinda Gates Foundation granted $2.6 billion to improving global health, development, and education. With a $37.1 billion endowment, the Bill & Melinda Gates Foundation is currently the world's largest philanthropic organization.

Microsoft also prides itself on its ethical standards. The company says, "We aim to be open about our business operations, transparent in our dealings with stakeholders, and compliant with the laws and regulations that apply to our business. We strive to exceed legal requirements by conducting our business ethically, responsibly, and with integrity." All Microsoft employees must follow the Microsoft Standards of Business Conduct and receive training in ethics and compliance. Microsoft's vendors are also subject to ethical standards under the Vendor Code of Conduct, which exists in over 35 languages. The company has several programs dedicated to antitrust compliance and responsible competition due to a decade of legal issues surrounding its dominance of the software market.

LEGAL ISSUES IMPACTING MICROSOFT

Microsoft is in a highly competitive and constantly evolving industry. Software firms try to protect their competitive advantage through constant innovation, and conflicts have developed between Microsoft and its competitors related to anticompetitive activities and intellectual property disputes.

Antitrust Issues

In 1990 the Federal Trade Commission (FTC) began investigating Microsoft for possible violations of the Sherman and Clayton Antitrust Acts, which limit monopolies and anti-competitive activities. By August 1993 the FTC was deadlocked on a decision regarding possible violations and handed the case over to the U.S. Department of Justice. Microsoft eventually agreed to settle the charges without admitting any wrongdoing. Part of the settlement provided the Department of Justice with complete access to Microsoft's documents for use in subsequent investigations.

Another important part of that settlement was a provision to end Microsoft's practice of selling Windows to original equipment manufacturers (OEMs) at a 60 percent discount. OEMs received the discount only if they agreed to pay Microsoft for every computer they sold (a "per processor" agreement) as opposed to paying Microsoft for every computer they sold with Windows preinstalled (a "per copy" agreement). If an OEM wished to install a different operating system on some of its computers, the manufacturer would, in effect, be paying for both the Microsoft and the other operating system—that is, paying "double royalties." Critics argued that this practice was unfair to both consumers, who effectively paid Microsoft even when they bought a rival operating system, and manufacturers, because it made it uneconomical to give up the 60 percent discount in favor of installing a less popular operating system on some of its computers. It appears that Microsoft was using its large share of the market to squeeze out smaller companies.

> "Competitors claimed that Microsoft's business practices were monopolistic."

Competitors claimed that Microsoft's business practices were monopolistic. A monopoly power, as defined by the Supreme Court, has the "power to control prices or exclude competition." A monopoly may engage in practices that any company, regardless of size, could legally employ; however, it cannot use its market power to prevent competition. Competitors and government regulators believed that Microsoft was acting as a monopoly power and engaging in unfair competition.

The next legal battle for Microsoft was against Apple Computer, which accused Microsoft's CEO, Bill Gates, of threatening to stop making Macintosh-compatible products if Apple did not stop developing a competing software product. Because Microsoft was the largest producer of Macintosh-compatible programs, Apple argued that it was being forced to choose between a bad deal and extinction. Apple also alleged that Microsoft would not send copies of Windows 95 until Apple dropped Microsoft's name from a lawsuit. The two companies eventually worked out their differences, and in 1998, Microsoft bought

$150 million of non-voting stock in Apple and paid $100 million for access to Apple's patents. Once again, Microsoft seemed to be using its market power to force a competitor to play by Microsoft's rules.

Another legal issue for Microsoft was Sun Microsystems' trademark and breach-of-contract case against the company, accusing Microsoft of deliberately trying to sabotage Sun's Java "write once, run anywhere" promise by making Windows implementations incompatible with those that run on other platforms. Specifically, the suit alleged that Microsoft's Java-compatible products omitted features that help developers write Java code. Sun acknowledged that Microsoft had fixed some of the earlier problems but added two new alleged incompatibilities to its list.

In 1998 Sun requested an injunction that would require Microsoft either to make the Java features compatible with its tests or include Sun's version of Java with every copy of Windows sold. In 2000 the Ninth District Court of Appeals ruled that it was software developers and consumers, not Sun, who would decide the value of Microsoft's language extensions. The court ruled that the compatibility test was a contractual issue, not a copyright issue. Furthermore, Sun's motion to reinstate the injunction on the basis of copyright infringement was denied. Microsoft was allowed to support its development tools with its own Java enhancements.

After various companies, particularly Netscape Communications, continued to complain about Microsoft's anticompetitive practices, the federal government took an aggressive stand, charging Microsoft with creating a monopolistic environment that substantially reduced competition in the industry. Microsoft settled the charges in 1995 and consented to stop imposing anticompetitive licensing terms on PC manufacturers by tying its software to its operating systems.

In October 1997 the Justice Department asked a federal court to hold Microsoft in civil contempt for violating the terms of the 1995 consent decree and to impose a $1 million-per-day fine. This time the issue was over Microsoft's "bundling" of its Internet Explorer web browser into the Windows 95 operating system. Microsoft argued that Internet Explorer was an integral, inseparable part of Windows 95 and that it had not bundled the browser technology solely to disadvantage rivals such as Netscape. A U.S. District Court judge disagreed and issued an injunction prohibiting the company from requiring Windows 95 licensees to bundle Internet Explorer with the operating system. Microsoft filed an appeal; meanwhile, it supplied PC makers with a version of Windows 95 that did not have Internet Explorer files. However, the product would not boot, a problem that Microsoft later admitted it knew about it beforehand. Consequently, the Justice Department asked the district court to hold Microsoft in contempt. Microsoft's stock price began to drop. Possibly fearing larger stock devaluation, Microsoft agreed to provide computer vendors with the most up-to-date version of Windows 95 without the Internet Explorer desktop icon.

At the same time, Microsoft denied all of the essential allegations, arguing that it had planned to integrate Internet Explorer into the Windows operating system long before rival Netscape even existed. Microsoft argued that its Internet Explorer was gaining popularity with consumers for the simple reason that it offered superior technology. In addition, Microsoft rejected allegations that the company had tried to "illegally divide the browser market" with rival Netscape and denied that it had entered into exclusionary contracts with Internet service providers or Internet content providers. Finally, Microsoft argued that it did not illegally restrict the ability of computer manufacturers to alter the Windows desktop screen that users see when they turn on their computers for the first time.

Like other software products, Microsoft products are protected by the Federal Copyright Act of 1976, which states that copyright owners have the right to license their products to third parties in an unaltered form. Microsoft asserted a counterclaim against the state attorneys general alleging that the officials were inappropriately trying to use state antitrust laws to infringe on Microsoft's federal rights.

MICROSOFT ON TRIAL

In 1998 the federal government, along with 20 states, charged Microsoft with monopolistic practices in the computer software business. The three primary issues raised in the lawsuit were (1) bundling the Internet Explorer Web browser with the Windows 98 operating system to damage competition, particularly Netscape Communications, Inc., (2) using cross-promotional deals with Internet providers to extend its monopoly, and (3) illegally preventing PC makers from customizing the opening screen showing Microsoft.

In August 1998, the deposition of Microsoft management began in Redmond, Washington. CEO Bill Gates was placed under oath and before a camera for 30 hours. During the deposition, Gates refused to answer most questions on his own, and it seemed that Gates was not concerned about the forthcoming trial.

The trial began on October 19, 1998, with the government accusing Microsoft and Gates of illegal bullying, coercion, and predatory pricing to undermine Netscape. Gates denied being concerned about Netscape's increasing browser market, but memorandums and email messages presented in court suggested otherwise. Moreover, Netscape's CEO, James Barksdale, told the court that Microsoft and Netscape executives had met in June 1995 to discuss "ways to work together." Barksdale testified that Microsoft's proposal at the time involved illegally dividing the market. When Netscape rejected the proposal, Microsoft supposedly used predatory pricing, along with other tactics, to "crush" the company.

By the time Microsoft began its defense in January 1999, the company's credibility had been severely damaged. The most damaging testimony came from Jim Allchin, a Microsoft employee and computer expert often referred to as "Microsoft's Lord of Windows." Allchin's testimony was supposed to demonstrate that Internet Explorer could not be separated from Windows without detrimental effects. His videotaped demonstration proved otherwise, however, when a reappearing Explorer icon made it apparent that the tape had been doctored.

This led to an effort by Microsoft to settle the case, but the two sides could not agree to the terms of a settlement. The government wanted to place government-appointed people as active members on Microsoft's board of directors, which Microsoft viewed as an attempt to take control of the company. In November 1999 Judge Thomas Penfield Jackson released his findings, a document consisting of 412 paragraphs, only four of which were favorable toward Microsoft. Jackson also named Allchin as the mastermind behind the bundling of Internet Explorer and the operating system in an attempt to destroy Netscape.

On June 7, 2000, Judge Jackson ordered Microsoft to split into two independent companies—one company to sell Windows and the other to sell everything else. Jackson offered several grounds for his dramatic decision, the first being simply that Microsoft would not admit to any wrongdoing. He also stated that the intent of his decision was to prevent Microsoft from insulting the government by refusing to comply with antitrust laws. Jackson said he found Microsoft to be "untrustworthy" as a result of its past behavior, including sending defective Windows software when ordered to unbundle the Internet browser from the operating system. Jackson further indicated that he was trying to prevent Microsoft from bullying its competitors. First, the split was intended to reignite competition in the industry. Second, dividing Microsoft into two companies could potentially spur some innovation that had been stifled by the size and force of the software giant. Third, the split might rejuvenate some of the "dead zones" in the industry, such as word processing, spreadsheets, databases, and email. Fourth, and perhaps most importantly, reducing Microsoft's power in the industry would hopefully renew creativity among software engineers.

Gates and other Microsoft executives viewed the idea of splitting the company into two as the equivalent of a "corporate death sentence." They countered that rather than spur innovation, the split would stifle it by making software development more complex; it would be more difficult to effectively integrate two or more programs across two businesses. They further argued that separate marketing of software would drive up prices for consumers. Finally, Microsoft saw the split as causing a delay in product completion and introduction. Gates began appearing in national television ads and meeting with President Clinton and members of Congress. Microsoft also took out full-page advertisements in newspapers across the country, publicly defending its record and touting its success. Regardless, by April 28, 2000, the company's stock had reached a 52-week low.

Microsoft appealed Judge Jackson's decision, thereby suspending the implementation of the ruling. Although the Department of Justice had wanted the Supreme Court to review the case, bypassing the District of Columbia Circuit Court of Appeals, the Supreme Court declined the case. In June 2001 a federal appeals panel agreed with Jackson's ruling that Microsoft had violated antitrust laws, but reversed his breakup order and returned the case to the lower court for a new remedy. In November 2001 the U.S. government and nine states reached an agreement with Microsoft on a tentative settlement, although nine other states continued to hold out for stricter remedies and stronger enforcement.

Finally, on November 1, 2002, U.S. District Judge Colleen Kollar-Kotelly approved most of the provisions of the settlement, thus barring Microsoft from retaliating against computer manufacturers, permitting customers to delete desktop icons for some Microsoft features, and requiring the company to disclose specific technical data to software developers. Kollar-Kotelly included a provision in the settlement that made independent Microsoft board members responsible for its compliance efforts instead of the technical committee that Microsoft had sought to oversee compliance. Although the company's stock rose on the news of the final settlement, some critics expressed concern that the decision failed to eliminate Microsoft's virtual monopoly over some aspects of the computer industry.

Thus, in lieu of a breakup into two different businesses, Microsoft was ordered to change its business practices. To ensure Microsoft's compliance with the original judgment in the antitrust case, reviews of Microsoft were regularly conducted for a period of five years from the original judgment decided in 2002. Although some portions of the original judgment expired in 2007, others did not expire or were extended until 2011 in order to open the browser market.

> "In lieu of a breakup into two different businesses, Microsoft was ordered to change its business practices."

MICROSOFT'S LEGAL ISSUES CONTINUE

Microsoft has continued to have legal problems stemming from antitrust issues as well as several patent infringement cases since 2002. In addition to the antitrust case in the United States, Microsoft paid record fines to the European Union (EU) related to antitrust rules because it bundled its software with its Microsoft Windows operating system. Microsoft had been under scrutiny by the EU since 1998, when the two battled over the bundling of Windows Media Player with its Windows operating system. Microsoft's lawyers argued that the simple act of bundling applications in one product is not an abuse of market dominance, especially since most users use more than one type of media player. From 2004 to 2007, however, the EU forced Microsoft to pay $2.4 billion for abusing its dominant market position against rival software makers, including RealNetwork, developers of the Real Audio player. In 2008 the EU fined Microsoft an additional $1.4 billion for failing to comply with the 2004 antitrust ruling. Additionally, the EU began another antitrust investigation but dropped the case after Microsoft agreed to offer consumers a choice of rival web browsers and also agreed to make its products compatible with other products of the software industry.

Microsoft's battle with Sun Microsystems also continued beyond the original antitrust case. However, in 2004, the two companies agreed to work together to improve interoperability of their products while still remaining competitors in the industry. The ten-year agreement also resolved previous litigation, with Microsoft paying Sun $700 million to resolve pending antitrust issues and $900 million to resolve patent infringement issues. In addition, each company agreed to pay royalties to the other for each other's technology.

In 2004 software maker Novell filed a private antitrust lawsuit against Microsoft, accusing the company of withholding technical information about Windows that would help its WordPerfect and Quattro Pro Programs work with Microsoft's operating systems. The company said that Microsoft's anticompetitive behavior harmed its business in the 1990s. The case was dismissed in 2010, but Novell appealed and later won the right to sue Microsoft on one antitrust claim.

In 2007 Google, Inc., considered reopening state and federal government antitrust action against Microsoft after Microsoft released its new Windows Vista operating system. Google claimed that Vista would put other software companies at a disadvantage since the indexing system on Vista makes it difficult to use other indexing software. Microsoft disputed Google's charges and claimed that it worked closely with federal officials to ensure compliance. Since users can still run alternative software in addition to Microsoft's software, U.S. antitrust officials refused to consider reopening the antitrust case.

Additionally, from 2007 to 2011, Canadian software company i4i accused Microsoft of patent infringement, resulting in a $290 million penalty for Microsoft. The decision, the largest ever American patent infringement verdict, barred Microsoft from selling Microsoft Word 2003 and 2007. Microsoft filed a series of appeals, arguing that the standard in patent infringement should be lowered so that patents become more vulnerable to legal challenges, which could increase innovation and competition. The case reached the Supreme Court in 2011.

CONCLUSIONS

Industry experts believe that the software market is much more competitive today than in 2001. Part of this change undoubtedly stems from the shift in Microsoft's behavior, but the real difference may have been new developments in technology, as downloading alternative browsers has become much more quick, simple, and popular. Microsoft also became more cautious in its business practices, which led to less aggressive innovation and expansion in the software market. Although Microsoft continues to lead the software industry, its dominance is no longer unchallenged.

As Microsoft competes with other companies such as Apple and Google, it must continuously devise new ways to remain competitive. One problem it must overcome is slower sales of its two staple software products, the Windows operating system and Office suite, as new PC sales drop. To guarantee growth outside of its software distribution, Microsoft continues to improve the capacity of its own search engine, Bing, and has modernized Microsoft Office by making a free online version. It also continues to find ways to deliver technology to the younger generation of consumers. In 2010 new product lines included Windows Phone 7, a wireless cellular telephone; Internet Explorer 9; cloud computing, a new way to deliver Internet Technology (IT) services via the Internet; and Kinect, a motion-based gaming system for Xbox 360.

By realizing its own potential not only in developing new technology but also in corporate citizenship, Microsoft can grow while remaining a trustworthy company in the eyes of consumers and the software industry. Improving the way the company handles relationships with customers and competitors will allow Microsoft to move forward in its mission to enable people and businesses throughout the world to realize their full potential.

QUESTIONS

1. What unique aspects of the software industry created the opportunity for Microsoft's monopoly and anticompetitive practices?

2. Discuss the role of Microsoft's leadership and corporate culture in generating a large volume of ethical and legal issues.

3. How do Microsoft's social responsibility and philanthropic efforts relate to its reputation and ability to overcome its legal problems?

SOURCES

Allen, Roy. *A History of the Personal Computer: the people and the technology.* Allan Publishing, 2001; Barr, Christopher. "The Justice Department's Lawsuit against Microsoft." CNET, www.cnet.com/content/voices/Barr/012698/ss01.html (accessed July 13, 1998); Bridis, Ted. "More Accusations Hit Microsoft." *Denver Post,* Oct. 23, 1998, sec. B; Brill, Steven. "Making Bill Gates." *Content Magazine,* September 1998, 106, 108; Bill and Melinda Gates Foundation. "Foundation Fact Sheet." May 2011, http://www.gatesfoundation.org/about/Pages/foundation-fact-sheet.aspx (accessed May 25, 2011); Boston College Center for Corporate Citizenship (BCCCC). 2010 CSR Index. http://www.bcccc.net/pdf/CSRIReport2010.pdf (accessed December 15, 2010); Buckman, Rebecca. "Go Figure: In Valuing a Split Microsoft, Analysts Offer a Wide Range of Numbers." *The Wall Street Journal,* May 2, 2000, C1, C3; Buckman, Rebecca. "Looking through Microsoft's Window: On the Firm's Sprawling Campus, It's Almost Business as Usual as Talk of Breakup Brews." *The Wall Street Journal,* May 1, 2000, B1, B10; CBS News. "Microsoft Chronology." http://www.cbsnews.com/elements/2006/06/16/In_depth_business/timeline1720211.shtml (accessed December 21, 2010); Chan, Sharon. "Antitrust saga ends for Microsoft." *The Seattle Times,* May 12, 2011, http://seattletimes.nwsource.com/html/microsoftprio/2015034116_antitrust_saga_ends_for_microsoft.html (accessed May 25, 2011); Chan, Sharon. "Microsoft Office hits market for business clients, tries to adjust in shifting market." *The Chicago Tribune,* May 12, 2010, http://www.chicagotribune.com/2010-05-12/business/sc-biz-0513-microsoft--20100512_1_microsoft-office-microsoft-business-division-google-docs (accessed February 15, 2011); Check, Dan. "The Case against Microsoft." http://ourworld.compuserve.com/homepages/spazz/mspaper.htm (accessed Spring 1996); Cision Index. "Microsoft maintains its media reputation lead among 100 largest U.S. companies for fifth straight year." http://us.cision.com/news_room/press_releases/2009/2009-2-20 cision_index. asp, February 20, 2009 (accessed December 15, 2010); Clark, Don, and Ted Bridis. "Creating Two Behemoths? Company Bets Appeals Court Will Overturn Jackson, Making Any Remedy Moot." *The Wall Street Journal,* April 28, 2000, B1, B4; Clark, Tim. "Go Away." Cnet News, http://ne2.news.com/News/Item/0,4,2076,00.html (accessed August 7, 1996); "COMPANY NEWS: Microsoft buys software unit." *The New York Times,* http://www.nytimes. com/1987/07/31/business/company-news-microsoft-buys-software-unit.html, July 31, 1987 (accessed Jan. 5, 2011); Resnikoff, Don Allen. "Section 2 Enforcement: A State-Enforcement View of the DOJ Section 2 Report." The Antitrust Source, October 2008, http://www.americanbar.org/content/dam/aba/publishing/antitrust_source/ Oct08_Resnikoff10_24f.authcheckdam.pdf (accessed July 8, 2011); CourtTV. "Microsoft Antitrust Ruling." www. courttv.com/legaldocs/cyberlaw/mseruling.html (accessed July 13, 1998); Davidson, Paul. "Expert's View May Influence Ruling." *USA Today,* February 2, 2000, B1; Davidson, Paul. "Microsoft Awaits a New Hand: Executives Expect Appeals Judges to Be More Amenable." *USA Today,* June 8, 2000, B1, B2; Davidson, Paul. "Microsoft Responds to Judge's Findings." *USA Today,* January 19, 2000, B1; Davidson, Paul. "Microsoft Split Ordered: Appeal Could Go Directly to Supreme Court." *USA Today,* June 8, 2000, A1; Deutschman, Alan. "Bill Gates' Next Challenge. His aim: to lead the information revolution of the 1990s that will land Microsoft, already the envy of its rivals, in a vast new competitive free-for-all." *Fortune,* December 28, 1992; Dyer, Dafydd Neal. "Under the Hood: Part 8." *Computer Source,* November 4, 2004, http://web.archive.org/web/20060207035559/www. computersourcemag.com; Egan, Timothy. "Microsoft's Unlikely Millionaires." *The New York Times,* June 28, 1992; Elmer-DeWitt, Philip. "Microsoft in the Steve Ballmer Era." *Fortune,* May 27, 2010 (accessed Jan. 14, 2011); "Feud Heats Up." Cnet News, http://ne2.news.com/SpecialFeature...d/0,6,2216_2,00.html'st.ne.ni.prev (accessed July 13, 1998); Foley, Mary Jo. "Microsoft's $300 million makeover." *ZDNet,* May 20, 2008, http://www.zdnet.com/blog/ microsoft/microsofts-300-million-makeover/1408; Foley, Mary Jo. "Supreme Court agrees to hear Microsoft patent infringement appeal." *The Wall Street Journal,* November 29, 2010; Gardner, Dana. "Java Is an Unleashed Force of Nature, Says JavaOne Panel." *InfoWorld Electric,* March 26, 1998; Gates, Bill, and Steve Ballmer. "To Our Customers, Partners and Shareholders." *USA Today,* April 5, 2000, B7; Gomes, Lee, and Rebecca Buckman. "Creating Two Behemoths? Microsoft Split Might Not Be Much Help for Competitors and Could Harm Consumers." *The Wall Street Journal,* April 28, 2000, B1; Goodin, Dan. "New Microsoft Java Flaws Alleged." www. news.com/News/Item/Textonly/0,25,24007,00.html?st.ne.ni.pfv (accessed August 3, 1998); Goodin, Dan. "New Microsoft Java Flaws Alleged." www.microsoft.com/ BillGates/billgates_1/speeches/6-25win98launch.htm#bill (accessed July 9, 1998); Graves, Jacqueline. "Most Innovative Companies." *Fortune,* December 13, 1993; Greene, Jay, Steve Ham, and Jim Kerstetter. "Ballmer's Microsoft." *BusinessWeek,* June 17, 2002 (accessed February 18, 2011); Gross, Grant. "DOJ details opposition to judgment extension." *PCWorld,* November 10, 2007; Harwood, John, and David Bank. "CyberSpectacle: Senate Meets Electronic Elite." *The Wall Street Journal,* March 4, 1998, B1, B13; Hackman, Mark. "Microsoft, i4i Argue Patent Rights at Supreme Court." *PC Magazine,* April 18, 2011, http://www. pcmag.com/article2/0,2817,2383769,00.asp (accessed April 25, 2011); Helft, Miguel. "Why don't you Bing it?" *The New York Times,* May 29, 2009, http://www.nytimes.com/2009/05/29/technology/internet/29bing.html?_ r=2&ref=media; Hof, Rob. "Antitrust suit filed against Google." *Business Week,* February 17, 2009 (accessed December 5, 2010); Iwata, Edward and John Swartz. "Bill Gates Won't Be Dethroned So Easily: Software King— and His Myth—to Survive on Iron Will, Talent." *USA Today,* June 8, 2000, B3; Jacobs, Margaret A. "Injunction Looms as Showdown for Microsoft." *The Wall Street Journal,* May 20, 1998, B1, B6; Johnston, Stuart J. "Office for Windows bundles popular Microsoft applications." *InfoWorld,* October 1, 1990, 16 (accessed February 15, 2011); Keizer, Greg. "Ballmer's CEO ranking plummets, Steve Jobs' climbs." *Computer World,* December 20, 2010, http:// www.computerworld.com/s/article/9201801/Ballmer_s_CEO_ranking_plummets_Steve_Jobs_climbs (accessed July 8, 2011); Kim, Eun-Kyung. "Microsoft Court Gets Lesson on Monopolies." *The Fort Collins Coloradoan,*

November 20, 1998, B2; Kolakowski, Nicholas. "Windows 95 marks 15th anniversary." *eWeek Microsoft Watch,* August 25, 2010, http://www.microsoft-watch.com/content/windows_7/windows_95_marks_15th_anniversary. html (accessed January 4, 2011); Lasar, Matthew. "The eternal antitrust case: Microsoft versus the world." *Ars Technica,* September 2010, http://arstechnica.com/tech-policy/news/2010/09/the-eternal-antitrust-case-microsoft-versus-the-world.ars/ (accessed December 5, 2010); Lohr, Steve. "U.S. VS. MICROSOFT: NEWS ANALYSIS; For Microsoft, Ruling Will Sting But Not Really Hurt." *The New York Times,* http://www.nytimes. com/2002/11/02/business/us-vs-microsoft-analysis-for-microsoft-ruling-will-sting-but-not-really-hurt.html (accessed July 8, 2011); "Lotus Net up, Microsoft Rises." *The New York Times,* April 17, 1986, D4; Lyons, Daniel. "Microsoft running out of excuses." *Newsweek,* May 27, 2010, http://www.newsweek.com/blogs/techtonic-shifts/2010/05/27/microsoft-running-out-of-excuses.html# (accessed February 7, 2011); Maclachlan, Malcolm. "New Lawsuit Is over Java, Sun Says." *TechWeb News,* May 12, 1998, www.techweb.com/wire/story/ TWB19980512S0012; Maclachlan, Malcolm. "Sun Attacks an Embattled Microsoft." *TechWeb News,* May 14, 1998, www.techweb.com/wire/story/msftdoj/TWB19980514S0002; Maclachlan, Malcolm. "Sun Targets Microsoft: Software Maker Says Windows 98 Must Be Java Compatible." *Tech Web News,* www.techweb.com/news/story/ TWB19980512S0012 (accessed May 12, 1998); Maney, Kevin. "Microsoft's Uncertain Future Rattles Investors: Justice Must Make Recommendation: Breakup Possible." *USA Today,* April 25, 2000, B1; Markoff, John. "IBM going on offensive to promote key software." *The New York Times,* April 15, 1991; Martinez, Michael J. "Microsoft Buys Time to Retool." *The Fort Collins Coloradoan,* September 27, 2000, A1, A2; McKenzie, Richard B. *Trust on Trial: How the Microsoft Case Is Reframing the Rules of Competition.* Cambridge, MA: Perseus Publishing, 2000; McMahon, Patrick. "Stoic Staffers Shake Heads, Return to Work." *USA Today,* June 8, 2000, B3; McWilliams, Brian. "Microsoft plans sneak PR Campaign." *PCWorld,* April 13, 1998 (accessed Jan. 10, 2011); Menn, Joseph, and Jube Shiver. "The Microsoft Decision." *The Los Angeles Times,* November 2, 2002, A1; "Microsoft Corporation." *The New York Times,* August 2, 2010, http://topics.nytimes.com/top/news/business/companies/microsoft_ corporation/index.html?scp=3&sq=Microsoft%20ANd%20ethics&st=cse (accessed February 15, 2010); Moeller, Michael. "Amended Complaint: Microsoft Wants Access to 'Highly Confidential' Documents." *PC Week Online,* August 4, 1998; Montalbano, Elizabeth. "Burden of proof on Google in Vista antitrust claim." *PCWorld,* June 11, 2007 (accessed December 14, 2010); Microsoft. "2010 Citizen Report." http://www.microsoft.com/citizenship (accessed April 25, 2011); Microsoft. "About Microsoft." www.microsoft.com/presspass/inside_ms.asp (accessed April 23, 2003); Microsoft. "Corporate Citizenship at Microsoft." http://www.microsoft.com/about/ corporatecitizenship/en-us/our-commitments/reporting/citizenship-approach (accessed November 30, 2010); Microsoft. "International Design for Office 2000." www.microsoft.com/Office/ORK/2000Journ/LangPack.htm (accessed September 8, 2000); Microsoft. "Java Contract Lawsuit Update." http://msdn.microsoft.com/visualj/ lawsuitruling.asp (accessed September 8, 2000); Microsoft. "Microsoft Corporate Information: What We Do." www.microsoft.com/mscorp/ (accessed August 3, 1998); Microsoft. "Key Events in Microsoft History." 2004, download.microsoft.com/download/7/e/a/7ea5ca8c-4c72-49e9-a694-87ae755e1f58/keyevents.doc (accessed December 30, 2010); Microsoft. "Microsoft signs consent decree with U.S. Government to settle antitrust case." http://www.microsoft.com/presspass/press/2001/nov01/11-02settlementpr.mspx, November 2, 2001 (accessed December 1, 2010); Microsoft. "Microsoft and Sun Microsystems Enter Broad Cooperation Agreement; Settle Outstanding Litigation." Microsoft News Center, April 2, 2004, http://www.microsoft.com/presspass/press/2004/ apr04/04-02SunAgreementPR.mspx (accessed January 4, 2011); Microsoft. "Notice Regarding Java Lawsuit Ruling: Notice to Customers." http://msdn.microsoft.com/visualj/statement.asp (accessed September 8, 2000); Microsoft. "Statement by Microsoft Corporation to U.S. Justice Department and State Attorneys General." www. microsoft.com/presspass.doj.7-28formalresponse.htm (accessed August 3, 1998); Microsoft. "Technology for Jobs, Workforce Development & Innovation." http://www.microsoft.com/about/corporatecitizenship/en-us/reporting/ extending-technology/technology-for-workforce-development-and-innovation (accessed April 25, 2011); Microsoft. "Microsoft Corporate Citizenship." http://www.microsoft.com/about/corporatecitizenship/en-us/our-actions (accessed December 3, 2010); *Reuters.* "Novell wins appeal in Microsoft antitrust lawsuit." May 3, 2011, http://www.reuters.com/article/2011/05/04/us-microsoft-novell-idUSTRE74301O20110504 (accessed May 25, 2011);

O'Brien, Kevin. "Europe drops Microsoft antitrust case." *The New York Times,* December 17, 2009 http://www. nytimes.com/2009/12/17/business/global/17msft.html?_r=1&scp=1&sq=Microsoft%20EU%20drops%20 case&st=cse (accessed December 17, 2010); O'Brien, Robert. "Kodak, Lexmark Lead Decline as Profit Warnings Hurt Stocks." *The Wall Street Journal,* September 27, 2000, C2; Oreskovic, Alexei, and David Lawsky. "Google joins EU antitrust case against Microsoft." *Wired,* February 25, 09, http://www.wired.com/techbiz/media/ news/2009/02/reuters_us_google_microsoft (accessed January 31, 2011); Picarille, Lisa. "Microsoft, Sun Postpone Java Hearing." *Computer Reseller News,* http://headlines.yahoo.com/Full_Coverage/Tech/Sun_Microsoft_Lawsuit/ (accessed July 7, 1998); Pollack, Andrew. "Microsoft and I.B.M. join forces." *The New York Times,* August 22, 1985 (accessed January 4, 2011); Reimer, Jeremy. "Total share: 30 years of personal computer market share figures." *Ars Technica,* December 14, 2005 (accessed December 30, 2010); Sandberg, Jared. "Bring on the Chopping Block." *Newsweek,* May 8, 2000, 34–35; Sandberg, Jared. "Microsoft's Six Fatal Errors." *Newsweek,* June 19, 2000, 23–27; Schmit, Julie. "Tech Industry's Direction Hangs in Balance." *USA Today,* October 16, 1998, 3B; Singel, Ryan. "Google vs. Microsoft: What you need to know." *Wired,* July 13, 2009, http://www.wired.comp/epicenter/2009/07/ google-vs-microsoft-what-you-need-to-know (accessed January 31, 2011); Swartz, Jon. "Microsoft Split Ordered: Will Breakup Help or Hurt Consumers?" *USA Today,* June 8, 2000, A1, A2; Thibodeau, Patrick. "For Bill Gates, antitrust fight was a personal crucible." *Computer World,* June 26, 2008, http://www.computerworld.com/s/ article/9103578/For_Bill_Gates_antitrust_fight_was_a_personal_crucible?taxonomyId=125&pageNumber=3 (accessed January 11, 2011); Trott, Bob, and David Pendery. "Allchin E-Mail Adds to Microsoft's Legal Woes." InfoWorld, December 1, 1997, http://www.highbeam.com/Library/Search.asp?fn=ss&q=Bob+Trott+and+David+ Pendery%20publication:[InfoWorld] (accessed July 28, 2006); Tucker, Geri Coleman, and Will Rodger. "Facing Breakup, Gates to Take Case to People; Microsoft Says Don't Punish Success." *USA Today,* May 1, 2000, B1, B2; Tynan, Dan. "The 15 biggest tech disappointments in 2007." *PC World,* December 17, 2007, http://www.pcworld. com/article/140583/the_15_biggest_tech_disappointments_of_2007.html, (accessed February 7, 2011); "U.S. vs. Microsoft Timeline." *Wired,* November 4, 2002 (accessed December 21, 2010); Vicini, James. "Top court hears Microsoft appeal on i4i patent." *Reuters,* April 18, 2011, http://www.reuters.com/article/2011/04/18/us-microsoft-i4i-idUSTRE73H59Z20110418 (accessed May 25, 2011); Wilke, John R., and David Bank. "Microsoft's Chief Concedes Hardball Tactics." *The Wall Street Journal,* March 4, 1998, B1, B13; Wingfield, Nick. "Net Assault." Cnet News, http://ne2.news.com/News/Item/0,4,1940,00.html (accessed July 25, 1996); Wingfield, Nick, and Tim Clark. "Dirty." Cnet News, http://ne2.news.com/News/Item/0,4,2072,00.html (accessed August 7, 1996); Yahoo News. "Microsoft Asks Court to Limit Gates Deposition." http://dailynews.yahoo.com/headlines/politics/story.html/ s=z/reuters/980805/politics/stories/microsoft_1.html; Zitner, Aaron. "Feds Assail Gates." *The Denver Post,* October 30, 1998, sec. C.

CASE 8

Countrywide Financial:
The Subprime Meltdown*

Not long ago, Countrywide Financial seemed to have everything going for it. Cofounded by Angelo Mozilo in 1969, by the early 2000s it had become the largest provider of home loans in the United States. At that time one in six U.S. loans originated with Countrywide. In 1993 its loan transactions reached the $1 trillion mark. Additionally, it was the primary provider of home loans to minorities in the United States and had lowered the barriers of homeownership for lower-income individuals. Countrywide also offered loan closing, capital market, insurance, and banking services to its clients. In the 1970s Countrywide had diversified into the securities market as well.

In 1992 Countrywide created a program called "House America" that enabled more consumers to qualify for home loans, as well as to make smaller down payments. In 2003 the company proposed the "We House America" program with the goal of providing $1 trillion in home loans to low-income and minority borrowers by 2010.

At the beginning of the twenty-first century, Countrywide's reputation in the industry was stellar. *Fortune* magazine called it the "23,000% stock" because between 1982 and 2003, Countrywide had delivered investors a 23,000 percent return, exceeding the returns of Washington Mutual, Walmart, and Warren Buffett's Berkshire Hathaway. In 1999 the company serviced $216.5 billion in loans. By 2000 the company's continued increase in revenues was connected in part to home equity and subprime loans. The annual report for that year states, "Fiscal 2000 shows a higher margin for home equity and sub-prime loans (which, due in part to their higher cost structure charge a higher price per dollar loaned)." Subprime loans were a key factor in Countrywide's immense success and rapid growth. However, the company's reliance on a lending practice that was originally intended to aid low-income individuals also ended up contributing to its downfall.

UNDERSTANDING SUBPRIME LOANS

To understand Countrywide's failure, one must first understand the concept of subprime lending. Simply put, subprime lending means lending to borrowers, generally people who would not qualify for traditional loans, at a rate higher than the prime rate (market rate), although just how far above depends on factors like credit score, down payment, debt-to-income ratio,

*This case was prepared by John Fraedrich, O. C. Ferrell, Jennifer Jackson, and Jennifer Sawayda. It was prepared for classroom discussion rather than to illustrate either effective or ineffective handling of an administrative, ethical, or legal decision by management. All sources used for this case were obtained through publicly available material.

and payment delinquencies. Subprime lending is risky because clients are less likely to be able to pay back their loans.

Although subprime loans can be made for a variety of purposes, mortgages have gained the most news coverage. Subprime mortgages fall into three categories. First is the interest-only mortgage, in which borrowers pay only the loan's interest for a set period of time. The second type allows borrowers to pay monthly, but these borrowers often opt to pay an amount smaller than that needed to reduce the amount owed on the loan. Third, borrowers can find themselves with mortgages featuring a fixed interest rate that converts to variable rates after a set period.

Typically, subprime loans are offered to high-risk clients who do not qualify for conventional loans. The average borrower has a credit score of below 620 and is generally in the low-income bracket. However, a 2007 *Wall Street Journal* study revealed that from 2004 to 2006, the rate of middle- and upper-income subprime loan borrowers rose dramatically. During the early to mid 2000s, when real estate prices were booming and consumer confidence levels were high, even clients who could have qualified for regular loans chose to take out subprime loans to finance their real estate speculations. As real estate prices peaked, more well-to-do investors turned to subprime mortgages to finance their expensive homes.

Although they have caused an immense amount of damage in the financial sector, subprime loans comprise a relatively small part of the loan market as a whole. In 2008 more than 6 million U.S. homeowners had subprime loans with a combined value of over $600 billion. In comparison, all other U.S. loans amounted to over $10 trillion. However, although these loans make up only a small chunk of the overall loan market, many consider subprime loans to be a key contributor to the 2008–2009 financial crisis.

One of the tools of the subprime loan is the adjustable rate mortgage (ARM), which allows borrowers to pay low introductory payments for three to five years, payments that will then be adjusted annually as the prime interest rate increases or decreases. Another type of ARM involves paying interest for a set number of years with balloon payments, meaning that people make interest payments only for the life of the loan, and then are expected to pay the entire principal at once upon maturity of the loan. These tools worked as long as the housing market remained on an upward trajectory, but when housing prices fell or interest rates increased, people discovered that they were unable to pay.

Many financial experts contributed to the problem by telling clients that in the future they would certainly have more income because of the increases in their property value. They assured homebuyers that even if their monthly payments increased, they would be able to afford them because the value of their homes would have increased accordingly. Even consumers with good credit looking to refinance were attracted to the attractive interest rates of these mortgages without fully recognizing the possible consequences.

THE SUBPRIME CRISIS

When first popularized, the financial tool of subprime loans was praised for lowering barriers to home ownership. The U.S. Department of Housing and Urban Development stated that subprime loans were helping many minorities afford homes and were therefore a good tool.

Although subprime lending became a major news topic only in the early part of the twenty-first century, the subprime concept began in the 1970s in Orange County, California.

At this time, rural farmland was being converted into suburbs, and subprime loans were a way for people to buy homes even if their credit was poor. The typical subprime recipient would not have met normal lending standards. At that time, the subprime loans made sense as a means to fuel southern California's growth. Homes were appreciating rapidly, so if a family decided to buy a house and live there for three to five years, they could reasonably expect that home to sell for over 50 percent more than what they had paid for it. In addition, Congress passed the Equal Credit Opportunity Act in 1974 to help ensure that all consumers had an equal chance to receive a loan. Potential homeowners, in theory, would no longer be rejected based on sex, race, national origin, or any other factor considered discriminatory.

Contractors also wanted a part of the action. They began to build houses and "flip" them. Flipping occurs when a contractor builds homes without buyers on credit, and then takes the sale of the homes to the lending institution as collateral to obtain more credit to build more homes. Speculators also flipped existing homes by buying them on credit with no intention of keeping them, waiting until the value had increased, and selling them at a profit.

Industries that supplied homebuilders were profiting as well, and costs of materials increased with the high demand. Realtors were motivated to push sales through because of the commissions they would earn (on average 6 percent of the sales price). Commissions were a significant part of many mortgage officers' compensation. Even real estate appraisers began to inflate the value of homes to ensure that loans would go through. One of the chief accusations against Countrywide during the financial crisis was that it had engaged in this practice.

But then something happened that no one had considered. The U.S. economy began to slow. People started working more and earning less money. Jobs started moving abroad, health insurance became more expensive, gas prices increased, and the baby boomers began to sell their homes to fund their retirement. In spite of this, builders kept on building, and the financial industry continued to lend to increasingly risky buyers. Homeowners found that they had less and less disposable income to make housing payments.

The result was a surplus of housing that homeowners could no longer afford. Banks began to foreclose on houses when the owners could not meet their mortgage payments. As the demand for housing decreased, banks lost significant amounts of money. Many other industries, like the automobile industry and insurance companies, were also negatively affected as struggling citizens tried to cope with the economic downturn. With plummeting stock prices, the United States began experiencing a financial crisis that had a rippling effect across the world.

Late 2007 marked the tipping point for the burgeoning mortgage crisis. Foreclosure rates skyrocketed, and borrowers and investors began to feel the full ramifications of taking the subprime risk. Mortgage defaults played a part in triggering a string of serious bank and financial institution failures as well. Investors began to abandon their mortgage-backed securities, causing huge institutions such as Morgan Stanley, Merrill Lynch, and Citigroup to lose large sums of money. Morgan Stanley, for example, lost over $265 billion internationally. Bear Stearns required government intervention to stay afloat. Analysts have attributed the banks' failings to poor intrabank communication and a lack of effective risk management.

> "Mortgage defaults played a part in triggering a string of serious bank and financial institution failures."

Although the chief financial officer (CFO) is supposed to be in charge of risk management, it appears that many institutions viewed the role as merely advisory. It was highly risky for these firms to downplay the importance of the CFO. Not only did many of these banks fail at risk management, but they also were in violation of the Sarbanes–Oxley Act, which requires that a company verify its ability to internally control its financial reporting. A CFO not directly in charge of a company's finances is signing off on something that he or she actually knows little about. The extent of the 2008–2009 financial crisis has made it clear to many that a massive overhaul of the financial industry's regulatory system is needed.

COUNTRYWIDE'S INVOLVEMENT IN THE SUBPRIME CRISIS

During the early 2000s, Countrywide reaped the benefits of subprime lending. In 2001 mortgages contributed to 28 percent of Countrywide's earnings, with subprime loans up to $280 million (the year before, subprime loans represented $86.9 million). In 2002 Countrywide's loan portfolio to minorities and low- to moderate-income borrower tracts had dramatically and rapidly increased. Countrywide had also increased its commissioned sales force by nearly 60 percent by 2003, with the goal of increasing overall market share.

Some critics have argued that salespeople were given incentives to undertake riskier transactions in order to continue to grow the company at a rapid rate. One allegation against Countrywide is that, in order to increase its profit, it would even offer subprime loans to people who qualified for regular loans. Leading the day-to-day operations of the Consumer Markets Division was David Sambol, whom the Securities and Exchange Commission would later charge with securities fraud.

After years of fast growth and upbeat projections, Countrywide's 2007 annual report had a somber tone. The financial crisis had begun and the company was feeling its effects. A significant amount of the report focused on the details of accounting for its mortgage portfolio and default rates. In one year Countrywide depreciated over $20 billion and absorbed over $1 billion in losses. By 2008 the company had accrued over $8 billion in subprime loans with a 7 percent delinquency rate. The industry average was 4.67 percent delinquency. That year foreclosures doubled, and the firm laid off 10 to 20 percent of its employees, or 10,000 to 20,000 people.

The company attempted to ease loan terms on more than 81,000 homeowners with a program called the Countrywide Comprehensive Home Preservation Program. The program allowed consumers to refinance or modify loans with an adjustable rate mortgage for a lower interest rate, or switch to a fixed-rate mortgage. President and chief operating officer David Sambol stated, "Countrywide believes that none of our subprime borrowers that have demonstrated the ability to make payments should lose their home to foreclosure solely as a result of a rate [increase]. This is yet another step in our continuing effort to identify and improve existing programs that assist our customers."

Countrywide also created special divisions to help borrowers and actively informed its customers about their options. The company offered phone counseling teams, personalized resource mailings, and counselors within communities who could meet face to face. Countrywide appeared to be genuine in its attempts to help homeowners, but it was too little too late.

In 2008 Alphonso Jackson, Secretary of Housing and Urban Development (HUD), reported that more than 500,000 Countrywide consumers were in danger of facing foreclosure. The blame for this development was placed primarily on subprime lending and adjustable rate mortgages. Countrywide Financial countered that there were other reasons for delinquencies and foreclosures. It maintained that the main causes of delinquencies and foreclosures were issues like medical problems, divorce, and unemployment—not adjustable rate mortgages. It further claimed that less than 1 percent of its consumers had defaulted on account of adjustable rate mortgages. Still, consumers and government officials began to question whether Countrywide's risky lending played a role in the larger financial crisis.

ISSUES RELATED TO THE BANK OF AMERICA ACQUISITION

In 2008 Bank of America, one of the United States' top financial institutions with $2,264.9 billion in total assets, offered to buy Countrywide Financial for $4 billion. The price tag was a substantial discount on what the company was actually worth. Bank of America paid approximately $8/share, when shares had been valued at $20/share earlier in the year. Kenneth D. Lewis, chair, president, and CEO of Bank of America, said at the time, "We are aware of the issues within the housing and mortgage industries. The transaction reflects those challenges. Mortgages will continue to be an important relationship product, and we now will have an opportunity to better serve our customers and to enhance future profitability."

At the time Bank of America held $1.5 trillion in assets, which better equipped the company to deal with the crisis. "Their balance sheet can take a shock much better than Countrywide," said CreditSights senior analyst David Hendler. "When you take the shocks at Countrywide, they have a big, busting consequence that's negative." Bart Narter, senior analyst at Celent, a Boston-based financial research and consulting firm, said, "There's still plenty of risk involved. He's brave to do it. But I think that it's very likely down the road to be profitable, maybe not immediately, but long-term."

However, there may have been other reasons why Countrywide allowed Bank of America to acquire it. It may be that Countrywide thought Bank of America was better able to handle the ethical investigations concerning Countrywide that the government had initiated. Among other issues, Countrywide was coming under increased scrutiny for giving out so-called liar loans. Liar loans are mortgages that require no proof of the borrower's income or assets. These loans allowed consumers to purchase homes while having few or no assets. With the additional burden of the financial crisis, many homeowners with liar loans could not pay their mortgages, nor were they able to refinance their homes because housing prices plummeted. Some were forced into foreclosure, generating substantial losses for mortgage companies and the economy.

Countrywide Financial was one of the top providers of liar loans. These loans allowed the industry to profit, at least for a little while, because people with liar loans were riskier clients, and therefore had to pay higher fees and interest rates to the mortgage company. Many accuse Countrywide of negligence, of giving out highly risky loans to people who could not afford them for the sake of quick profits. Others accuse the company of even more unethical dealings. Some homeowners who are now struggling under liar loans are accusing Countrywide of predatory lending, saying the company misled them.

> "Countrywide Financial was one of the top providers of liar loans."

Although some homeowners may have been truly misled into liar loans, an estimated 90 percent of liar loan applicants knowingly overstated their income, with three out of five overstating it by at least 50 percent. This rampant dishonesty, critics charge, could not have occurred without the mortgage company's awareness. It has sparked new investigations into whether Countrywide aided borrowers in falsifying information. Hence, some attest that Countrywide's buyout by Bank of America may have been more than just an economic choice. Instead, it could have been a way to prepare for the onslaught of criticism that would arise against Countrywide.

In March 2008 Bank of America decided to retain David Sambol in the position of Executive Managing Director of Business Segment Operations at Countrywide, as well as to pay him a hefty compensation package. Sambol had received a bachelor's degree in Business Administration and Accounting from California State University–Northridge in 1982. Prior to joining Countrywide in 1985, Sambol had served as a certified public accountant with the accounting firm of Ernst & Whinney. His unit at Countrywide led all revenue-generating functions of the company. He was instrumental in expanding Countrywide's mortgage division to become the most comprehensive in the industry.

In March 2008 Bank of America agreed to set up a $20 million retention account for Sambol, payable in equal installments on the first and second anniversaries of the merger, plus $8 million in restricted stock. Sambol's retention package also included the use of a company car or car allowance, country club dues, and financial consulting services through the end of 2009. He was also to continue to have access to a company plane for business and personal travel.

Much of the public was outraged that Sambol had received such generous compensation after his role in Countrywide's questionable business dealings. The outcry over the events at Countrywide and other companies that had participated in the subprime mortgage market was so great that in 2008 the U.S. Congress held a series of hearings to investigate dealings in the subprime market. Senator Charles E. Schumer, D–NY, chair of Congress' Joint Economic Committee, asked Bank of America to reconsider the decision to put Sambol in charge of home lending. "There seem to be two economic realities operating in our country today," said Representative Henry A. Waxman, D–CA, the committee chair. "Most Americans live in a world where economic security is precarious and there are real economic consequences for failure. But our nation's top executives seem to live by a different set of rules. The question before the committee was: when companies fail to perform, should they still give millions of dollars to their senior executives?" After the hearings, Bank of America announced that Barbara Desoer, Bank of America's chief technology and operations officer, would replace Sambol.

THE ROLE OF COUNTRYWIDE'S CEO ANGELO MOZILO

Angelo Mozilo is being investigated by the SEC for potential fraud, although he maintains his innocence. The SEC is particularly concerned about the sale of company stock options that netted Mozilo over $400 million between 2002 and 2008. In a 2007 *Businessweek* interview, Mozilo was asked about allegations that he had made over $100 million on stock sales in the previous year. Mozilo asserted, "I have not sold any stock, to my recollection, in 10 years. Everything I've sold was options. The selling is because [when the options] expire, I no longer have the benefit of what I have built and what this team has built for the last 40 years. Up until this debacle, I created $25 billion in value for shareholders. There have been very few—only about 11 stocks—that have performed better over the last 25 years than Countrywide. I could have sold all of those shares at 40 bucks a share and didn't because I want to be aligned with the shareholders."

The public did not seem to believe Mozilo's defense, especially after he received a $100 million severance package when Countrywide was sold to Bank of America. Mozilo was named as a defendant in many subsequent lawsuits. The plaintiffs included:

- Arkansas Teacher Retirement System
- Fire & Police Pension Association of Colorado
- Public Employees' Retirement System of Mississippi
- New York City Employees' Retirement System
- New York Life Insurance Co., TIAA-CREF Life Insurance Co., Dexia Holdings, Inc.
- The State of California, which settled for $6.5 million paid by Countrywide
- Allstate, which filed a lawsuit against Countrywide and Mozilo for over $700 million in mortgage-backed securities.

One lawsuit alleged misconduct and disregard of fiduciary duties, including a lack of good faith and lack of oversight of Countrywide's lending practices. The lawsuit also accused Countrywide of improper financial reporting and lack of internal controls, alleging that Mozilo was paid $10 million more than was disclosed. Additionally, the company claimed that Countrywide's officers and directors unlawfully sold over $848 million of stock between 2004 and 2008 at inflated prices using insider information. In 2010 Countrywide agreed to pay $600 million to settle class-action lawsuits filed against the company.

> "Countrywide agreed to pay $600 million to settle class-action lawsuits filed against the company."

Mozilo's pay also drew heavy scrutiny from members of Congress. Federal securities regulators and congressional investigators found that easy bonus targets and other underhanded methods helped him inflate his pay. In the hearings about executive pay, Congressman Elijah E. Cummings of Maryland said, "We've got golden parachutes drifting off to the golf course and have people I see every day who are losing their homes and wondering where their kids will do their homework." He then asked Mozilo about an e-mail message he had sent demanding that the taxes due on his wife's travel on the corporate jet be covered by the company. "It sounds out of whack today because it is out of whack, but in 2006 the company was going great," said Mozilo. "In today's world I would never write that memo." He also apologized for another e-mail message in which he had complained about his compensation. "It was an emotional time," he said. In the same hearings, however, Mozilo also reminded the audience that Countrywide's stock price had appreciated over 23,000 percent from 1982 to 2007. Shareholders did approve Mozilo's performance-based bonuses, and he exercised the options as he prepared for retirement. "In short, as our company did well, I did well," he said.

In June 2009 the SEC charged Mozilo, David Sambol, and former financial chief Sieracki with securities fraud, accusing the men of misleading the market and not providing adequate disclosure about Countrywide's risks. The SEC pointed to seemingly incriminating emails that Mozilo had sent, including one in which he described their loans as a "toxic product." In another email, Mozilo expressed concern over adjustable rate mortgages, stating that he had "personally observed a serious lack of compliance within our origination system as it relates to documentation and generally a deterioration in the quality of loans originated." Mozilo, who was also charged with insider trading, agreed to pay $67.5 million to settle with the SEC and has been permanently barred from serving on a board or as an officer of any company. Sambol settled for $5.52 million and has been barred from serving in a public company for three years, while Sieracki settled for $130,000. Mozilo's penalty was the largest filed against a senior executive to date.

BANK OF AMERICA PLANS A RECOVERY

In July 2008 Bank of America bought Countrywide without Sambol or Mozilo. Since 2001 Bank of America has been focused on profit, not growth, and it might be a while before the company profits from the acquisition. According to the Securities and Exchange Commission, Bank of America took on $16.6 billion in Countrywide's debts. Exiting the subprime lending market is part of Bank of America's long-term plan. The company liquidated $26.3 billion of its subprime real estate portfolio in 2008–2009 and has managed its existing $9.7 billion portfolio over its remaining term.

Bank of America clearly understood that in buying Countrywide, it had inherited a volatile earning stream that had become unattractive from a risk-reward standpoint. Kenneth Lewis, CEO of Bank of America, said at the time, "We are committed to achieving consistent, above-average shareholder returns and these actions are aimed at achieving that mission."

In addition to managing Countrywide's debt, Bank of America must also handle the stream of lawsuits being filed against the company. Many of these lawsuits claim that the company duped homeowners with predatory loan practices. Bank of America's Barbara Doeser, who replaced David Sambol, said the company is committed to helping homeowners and is cutting interest rates to as low as 2.5 percent. Bank of America also created a unit called Legacy Asset Servicing to manage over a million troubled mortgages, many of which are subprime loans.

Countrywide is facing additional investigations for other alleged cases of misconduct. In March 2008 the FBI started an investigation to find out whether Countrywide misrepresented its financial information. Additionally, the FBI is investigating Countrywide's VIP program that, according to an insider, provided special mortgage deals to certain high-up officials, known as "Friends of Angelo's." These deals included discount rates and fees not offered to ordinary Countrywide customers. Those implicated in these dealings include Democratic senators Chris Dodd and Kent Conrad, two former cabinet members, and two CEOs from Fannie Mae. These officials have denied that they knew they were getting special discounts. Prosecutors are looking into whether these discounts constituted improper gifts.

CONCLUSION

Countrywide was not the only cause of the financial crisis. Numerous other Wall Street companies are being investigated for unethical practices related to this scandal. (The list includes Bank of America, which has been investigated for potential breaches of fiduciary duty concerning employee retirement funds.) However, Countrywide's unethical behavior was a key contributor to the problems in the economy during 2008–2009. Many consider it to be one of the central villains in this crisis. They allege that Countrywide knowingly engaged in risky loans and offered subprime loans even to those who qualified for regular loans in order to profit from the higher rates. In the process, it may have helped to falsify lender information, allowing those with no assets to obtain loans. The consequence was a surplus of housing, plummeting housing prices, and a slew of foreclosures, all of which placed the economy in a precarious state. The United States has lost global credibility as an economic leader of the free world.

The Countrywide scandal has brought up other issues, including that of executive compensation. Should executives receive hefty compensation packages and severance pay when their companies flounder? Should they be called into account for not exercising due care? Many people think so, as evidenced by the enormous public outrage facing those like David Sambol and Angelo Mozilo. It is clear that Countrywide has failed the majority of its stakeholders. Ethical misconduct and high-risk business practices helped to create the disaster at Countrywide, and it remains to be seen whether Bank of America will be able to salvage the reputation and to save the business that was once Countrywide Financial.

QUESTIONS

1. Are subprime loans an unethical financial instrument, or are they ethical tools that were misused?

2. Discuss the ethical issues that caused the downfall of Countrywide Financial.

3. How should Bank of America deal with potential ethical and legal misconduct discovered at Countrywide?

SOURCES

Associated Press. "Investors allege massive fraud by Countrywide." *The Wall Street Journal*, January 25, 2011, http://online.wsj.com/article/AP0cb3b6db114a4a93b2ff62d19a9bd363.html (accessed February 15, 2011); "Bank of America Assumes $16.6B in Countrywide Debt." *Dayton Business Journal*, November 10, 2008, http://www.bizjournals.com/dayton/stories/2008/11/10/daily7.html (accessed November 14, 2008); "BANK OF AMERICA CORP (BAC: New York)." *Bloomberg Businessweek*, http://investing.businessweek.com/businessweek/research/stocks/financials/financials.asp?ticker=BAC:US&dataset=balanceSheet&period=A&currency=native (accessed February 14, 2011); Bartiromo, Maria. "Countrywide Feels the Heat." *BusinessWeek*, August 29, 2007, http://www.businessweek.com/bwdaily/dnflash/content/aug2007/db20070829_117563.htm?chan=search (accessed March 16, 2008); Benoit, David. "Allstate Sues Countrywide." *The Wall Street Journal*, December 29, 2010, C2; Caputo, Angela. "Countrywide Accord Paves Way for More Loan Remodifications." *Progress Illinois*, November 12, 2008, http://progressillinois.com/2008/11/12/loan-modification-plan (accessed July 7, 2011); Countrywide Financial. http://about.countrywide.com (accessed September 1, 2009). "Countrywide Moves to Ease Mortgage Misery." *BusinessWeek*, October 23, 2007, www.businessweek.com/investor/content/oct2007/pi20071023_454573.htm (accessed March 16, 2008); Colvin, Geoff. "Signs of Life from the Mortgage Frontline." *Forbes*, November 13, 2008, http://money.cnn.com/2008/11/12/magazines/fortune/colvin_desoer.fortune/?postversion=2008111311 (accessed November 14, 2008); Emshwiller, John. "Countrywide: Case of Full Disclosure." *The Wall Street Journal*, September 3, 2010, C1; Faber, David. "SEC Charges Ex-Countrywide CEO with Insider Trading." CNBC, June 4, 2009, http://www.cnbc.com/id/31108460 (accessed February 14, 2011); Farzad, Roben. "In Search of a Subprime Villain." *BusinessWeek*, January 24, 2008, http://www.businessweek.com/magazine/content/08_05/b4069077193810.htm?chan=search (accessed March 16, 2008); Federal Trade Commission. "Equal Credit Opportunity Act." http://www.ftc.gov/bcp/edu/pubs/consumer/credit/cre15.shtm (accessed September 1, 2009); Gimein, Mark. "Inside the

Liar's Loan: How the Mortgage Industry Nurtured Deceit." *Slate,* April 24, 2008, http://www.slate.com/id/2189576/ (accessed November 14, 2008); Greenspan, Alan. "We Will Never Have a Perfect Model of Risk." *Financial Times,* March 16, 2008, http://www.ft.com/cms/s/edbdbcf6-f360-11dc-b6bc-0000779fd2ac,Authorised=false. html?_i_location=http%3A%2F%2Fwww.ft.com%2Fcms%2Fs%2F0%2Fedbdbcf6-f360-11dc-b6bc-0000779fd2ac. html%3Fnclick_check%3D1&_i_referer=http%3A%2F%2Fsearch.yahoo.com%2Fsearch%3Fp%3Dthe%2Bm ost%2Bwrenching%2Bsince%2Bthe%2Bend%2Bof%2Bthe%2Bsecond%2Bworld%2Bwar%252C%2BAlan%2B Greenspan%26fr%3Dyfp-t-501%26toggle%3D1%26cop%3Dmss%26ei%3DUTF-8&nclick_check=1 (accessed November 15, 2008); Gutierrez, Carl. "Countrywide's New Bad News." *Forbes,* March 10, 2008, http://www.forbes. com/markets/2008/03/10/countrywide-fbi-mortgage-markets-equity-cx_cg_0310markets26.html (accessed September 1, 2009); Staff infoZine,"Kansas, 11 Other States Reach Agreement with Countrywide Financial Corporation." *Kansas City infoZine,* November 14, 2008, http://www.infozine.com/news/stories/op/storiesView/ sid/31858/ (accessed September 1, 2009); LenderRATEMATCH. "Mortgage Industry Statistics." freeratesearch. com/en/newsroom/mortgage_statistics/ (accessed April 1, 2008); Marco, Meg. "Subprime Meltdown: Inside the Countrywide Subprime Lending Frenzy." *The Consumerist,* August 27, 2008, http://consumerist.com/consumer/ subprime-meltdown/inside-the-countrywide-subprime-lending-frenzy-293902.php (accessed November 13, 2008); Morgenson, Gretchen. "Judge Says Countrywide Officers Must Face Suit by Shareholders." *The New York Times,* May 15, 2008,http://www.nytimes.com/2008/05/15/business/15countrywide.html (accessed July 7, 2011); Morgenson, Gretchen. "Lending Magnate Settles Fraud Case." *The New York Times,* October 15, 2010, http://www. nytimes.com/2010/10/16/business/16countrywide.html (accessed February 14, 2011); Moyer, Liz. "A Subprime Solution." *Forbes,* December 6, 2007, http://www.forbes.com/wallstreet/2007/12/05/subprime-paulson-bush-biz-wall-cx_lm_1206subprime.html (accessed March 25, 2008); MSNBC. "'Liar Loans' Threaten to Prolong Mortgage Mess." August 18, 2008, http://www.msnbc.msn.com/id/26270434/ (accessed November 14, 2008); Myers, Lisa, and Amna Nawaz. "Feds Probe Countrywide's 'VIP' Program." NBC News, October 30, 2008, http:// deepbackground.msnbc.msn.com/archive/2008/10/30/1613877.aspx (accessed November 14, 2008); Reckard, Scott. "Countrywide Head Ousted by Bank of America." *The Los Angeles Times,* May 29, 2008, http://www2. tbo.com/content/2008/may/29/bz-countrywide-head-ousted-by-bank-of-america/?news-money. (accessed June 2008); Rosenblatt, Joel. "Angelo Mozilo Settles Lending Suit for $6.5 Million." *Bloomberg Businessweek,* February 2, 2011, http://www.businessweek.com/news/2011-02-02/angelo-mozilo-settles-lending-suit-for-6-5-million.html (accessed February 14, 2011); Schwartz, Nelson D. "Bank of America to Create Troubled Loans Unit." *The New York Times,* February 4, 2011, http://www.nytimes.com/2011/02/05/business/05bank.html (accessed February 14, 2011); United States Department of Housing and Urban Development. "Subprime Lending." http://www.hud.gov/ offices/fheo/lending/subprime.cfm (accessed March 16, 2008); Wartzman, Rick. "The Countrywide Conundrum." *BusinessWeek,* November 9, 2007, http://www.businessweek.com/managing/content/nov2007/ca2007119_693870. htm?chan=search (accessed March 16, 2008); U.S. Securities and Exchange Commission. "Former Countrywide CEO Angelo Mozilo to Pay SEC's Largest-Ever Financial Penalty against a Public Company's Senior Executive." October 15, 2010, http://www.sec.gov/news/press/2010/2010-197.htm (accessed February 14, 2011); U.S. Securities and Exchange Commission. "SEC Charges Former Countrywide Executives with Fraud." June 4, 2009, http://www. sec.gov/news/press/2009/2009-129.htm (accessed February 14, 2011); Zibel, Alan. "Countrywide Settlement: $600 Million to Settle Lawsuits over Subprime Loans." *The Huffington Post,* August 3, 2010, http://www.huffingtonpost. com/2010/08/03/countrywide-settlement_n_668429.html (accessed February 14, 2011).

CASE 9

Enron: Questionable Accounting Leads to Collapse*

Once upon a time, there was a gleaming office tower in Houston, Texas. In front of that gleaming tower was a giant "E," slowly revolving, flashing in the hot Texas sun. But in 2001 the Enron Corporation, which once ranked among the top *Fortune* 500 companies, would collapse under a mountain of debt that had been concealed through a complex scheme of off-balance-sheet partnerships. Forced to declare bankruptcy, the energy firm laid off 4,000 employees; thousands more lost their retirement savings, which had been invested in Enron stock. The company's shareholders lost tens of billions of dollars after the stock price plummeted. The scandal surrounding Enron's demise engendered a global loss of confidence in corporate integrity that continues to plague markets today, and eventually it triggered tough new scrutiny of financial reporting practices. In an attempt to understand what went wrong, this case will examine the history, culture, and major players in the Enron scandal.

ENRON'S HISTORY

The Enron Corporation was created out of the merger of two major gas pipeline companies in 1985. Through its subsidiaries and numerous affiliates, the company provided products and services related to natural gas, electricity, and communications for its wholesale and retail customers. Enron transported natural gas through pipelines to customers all over the United States. It generated, transmitted, and distributed electricity to the northwestern United States, and marketed natural gas, electricity, and other commodities globally. It was also involved in the development, construction, and operation of power plants, pipelines, and other energy-related projects all over the world, including the delivery and management of energy to retail customers in both the industrial and commercial business sectors.

Throughout the 1990s, Chairman Ken Lay, CEO Jeffrey Skilling, and CFO Andrew Fastow transformed Enron from an old-style electricity and gas company into a $150 billion energy company and Wall Street favorite that traded power contracts in the investment markets. From 1998 to 2000 alone, Enron's revenues grew from about $31 billion to more than $100 billion, making it the seventh-largest company in the *Fortune* 500. Enron's wholesale energy income represented about 93 percent of 2000 revenues, with another 4 percent derived from natural gas and electricity. The remaining 3 percent came from

*This case was prepared by Harper Baird, Jennifer Jackson, and Neil Herndon for and under the direction of O. C. Ferrell and Linda Ferrell. It was prepared for classroom discussion rather than to illustrate either effective or ineffective handling of an administrative, ethical, or legal decision by management. All sources used for this case were obtained through publicly available material.

broadband services and exploration. However, a bankruptcy examiner later reported that although Enron had claimed a net income of $979 million in that year, it had really earned just $42 million. Moreover, the examiner found that despite Enron's claim of $3 billion in cash flow in 2000, the company actually had a cash flow of negative $154 million.

ENRON'S CORPORATE CULTURE

When describing the corporate culture of Enron, people like to use the word "arrogant," perhaps justifiably. A large banner in the lobby at corporate headquarters proclaimed Enron "The World's Leading Company," and Enron executives believed that competitors had no chance against it. Jeffrey Skilling even went so far as to tell utility executives at a conference that he was going to "eat their lunch." This overwhelming aura of pride was based on a deep-seated belief that Enron's employees could handle increased risk without danger. Enron's corporate culture reportedly encouraged flouting the rules in pursuit of profit. And Enron's executive compensation plans seemed less concerned with generating profits for shareholders than with enriching officer wealth.

> "Enron's corporate culture reportedly encouraged flouting the rules in pursuit of profit."

Skilling appears to be the executive who created the system whereby Enron's employees were rated every six months, with those ranked in the bottom 20 percent forced out. This "rank and yank" system helped create a fierce environment in which employees competed against rivals not only outside the company but also at the next desk. Delivering bad news could result in the "death" of the messenger, so problems in the trading operation, for example, were covered up rather than being communicated to management.

Ken Lay once said that he felt that one of the great successes at Enron was the creation of a corporate culture in which people could reach their full potential. He said that he wanted it to be a highly moral and ethical culture and that he tried to ensure that people honored the values of respect, integrity, and excellence. On his desk was an Enron paperweight with the slogan "Vision and Values." Despite such good intentions, however, ethical behavior was not put into practice. Instead, integrity was pushed aside at Enron, particularly by top managers. Some employees at the company believed that nearly anything could be turned into a financial product and, with the aid of complex statistical modeling, traded for profit. Short on assets and heavily reliant on intellectual capital, Enron's corporate culture rewarded innovation and punished employees deemed weak.

ENRON'S ACCOUNTING PROBLEMS

Enron's bankruptcy in 2001 was the largest in U.S. corporate history at the time. The bankruptcy filing came after a series of revelations that the giant energy trader had been using partnerships, called "special-purpose entities" or SPEs, to conceal losses. In a meeting with Enron's lawyers in August 2001, the company's then-CFO Fastow stated that Enron had established the SPEs to move assets and debt off its balance sheet and to increase cash flow by showing that funds were flowing through its books when it sold assets. Although these practices produced a very favorable financial picture, outside observers believed they constituted fraudulent financial reporting because they did not accurately represent the company's true financial condition. Most of the SPEs were entities in name only, and

Enron funded them with its own stock and maintained control over them. When one of these partnerships was unable to meet its obligations, Enron covered the debt with its own stock. This arrangement worked as long as Enron's stock price was high, but when the stock price fell, cash was needed to meet the shortfall.

After Enron restated its financial statements for fiscal year 2000 and the first nine months of 2001, its cash flow from operations went from a positive $127 million in 2000 to a negative $753 million in 2001. With its stock price falling, Enron faced a critical cash shortage. In October 2001, after it was forced to cover some large shortfalls for its partnerships, Enron's stockholder equity fell by $1.2 billion. Already shaken by questions about lack of disclosure in Enron's financial statements and by reports that executives had profited personally from the partnership deals, investor confidence collapsed, taking Enron's stock price with it.

For a time, it appeared that Dynegy might save the day by providing $1.5 billion in cash, secured by Enron's premier pipeline Northern Natural Gas, and then purchasing Enron for about $10 billion. However, when Standard & Poor's downgraded Enron's debt to below investment grade on November 28, 2001, some $4 billion in off-balance-sheet debt came due, and Enron didn't have the resources to pay. Dynegy terminated the deal. On December 2, 2001, Enron filed for bankruptcy. Enron now faced 22,000 claims totaling about $400 billion.

The Whistle-Blower

Assigned to work directly with Andrew Fastow in June 2001, Enron vice president Sherron Watkins, an eight-year Enron veteran, was given the task of finding some assets to sell off. With the high-tech bubble bursting and Enron's stock price slipping, Watkins was troubled to find unclear, off-the-books arrangements backed only by Enron's deflating stock. No one seemed to be able to explain to her what was going on. Knowing she faced difficult consequences if she confronted then-CEO Jeffrey Skilling, she began looking for another job, planning to confront Skilling just as she left for a new position. Skilling, however, suddenly quit on August 14, saying he wanted to spend more time with his family. Chair Ken Lay stepped back in as CEO and began inviting employees to express their concerns and put them into a box for later collection. Watkins prepared an anonymous memo and placed it into the box. When Lay held a companywide meeting shortly thereafter and did not mention her memo, however, she arranged a personal meeting with him.

On August 22, 2001, Watkins handed Lay a seven-page letter she had prepared outlining her concerns. She told him that Enron would "implode in a wave of accounting scandals" if nothing was done. Lay arranged to have Enron's law firm, Vinson & Elkins, look into the questionable deals, although Watkins advised against having a party investigate that might be compromised by its own involvement in Enron's scam. Near the end of September, Lay sold some $1.5 million of personal stock options, while telling Enron employees that the company had never been stronger. By the middle of October, Enron was reporting a third-quarter loss of $618 million and a $1.2 billion write-off tied to the partnerships about which Watkins had warned Lay.

For her trouble, Watkins had her computer hard drive confiscated and was moved from her plush executive office suite on the top floor of the Houston headquarters tower to a sparse office on a lower level. Her new metal desk was no longer filled with the high-level projects that had once taken her all over the world on Enron business. Instead, now a vice president in name only, she faced meaningless "make work" projects. In February 2002 she testified before Congress about Enron's partnerships and resigned from Enron in November of that year.

The Chief Financial Officer

In 2002 the U.S. Justice Department indicted CFO Andrew Fastow on 98 counts for his alleged efforts to inflate Enron's profits. The charges included fraud, money laundering, conspiracy, and one count of obstruction of justice. Fastow faced up to 140 years in jail and millions of dollars in fines if convicted on all counts. Federal officials attempted to recover all of the money Fastow had earned illegally, and seized some $37 million.

> "Federal prosecutors argued that Enron's case was not about exotic accounting practices but about fraud and theft."

Federal prosecutors argued that Enron's case was not about exotic accounting practices but about fraud and theft. They contended that Fastow was the brain behind the partnerships used to conceal some $1 billion in Enron debt and that this debt led directly to Enron's bankruptcy. The federal complaints alleged that Fastow had defrauded Enron and its shareholders through off-balance-sheet partnerships that made Enron appear to be more profitable than it actually was. They also alleged that Fastow made about $30 million both by using these partnerships to get kickbacks that were disguised as gifts from family members, and by taking income himself that should have gone to other entities.

Fastow initially denied any wrongdoing and maintained that he was hired to arrange the off-balance-sheet financing and that Enron's board of directors, chair, and CEO had directed and praised his work. He also claimed that both lawyers and accountants had reviewed his work and approved what was being done, and that "at no time did he do anything he believed was a crime." Skilling, COO from 1997 to 2000 before becoming CEO, had reportedly championed Fastow's rise at Enron and supported his efforts to keep up Enron's stock prices.

Fastow eventually pleaded guilty to two counts of conspiracy, admitting to orchestrating myriad schemes to hide Enron debt and inflate profits while enriching himself with millions. He surrendered nearly $30 million in cash and property, and agreed to serve up to 10 years in prison once prosecutors no longer needed his cooperation. He was a key government witness against Lay and Skilling. His wife Lea Fastow, former assistant treasurer, quit Enron in 1997 and pleaded guilty to a felony tax crime, admitting to helping hide ill-gotten gains from her husband's schemes from the government. She later withdrew her plea, and then pleaded guilty to a newly filed misdemeanor tax crime. In 2005 she was released from a year-long prison sentence, and then had a year of supervised release.

In the end, Fastow received a lighter sentence than he otherwise might have because of his willingness to cooperate with investigators. In 2006 Fastow gave an eight-and-a-half-day deposition in his role as government witness. He helped to illuminate how Enron had managed to get away with what it did, including detailing how many major banks were complicit in helping Enron manipulate its financials to help it look better to investors. In exchange for his deposition, Fastow's sentence was lowered to six years from 10.

The case against Fastow had been largely based on information provided by Michael Kopper, the company's managing director and a key player in the establishment and operation of several of the off-balance-sheet partnerships and the first Enron executive to plead guilty to a crime. Kopper, a chief aide to Fastow, pleaded guilty to money laundering and wire fraud. He faced up to 15 years in prison and agreed to surrender $12 million earned from illegal dealings with the partnerships. However, Kopper only had to serve three years and one month of jail time because of the crucial role he played in providing prosecutors with information. After his high-powered days at Enron, Kopper's next job was as a salaried grant writer for Legacy, a Houston-based clinic that provides services to HIV-positive and other chronically ill patients.

Others charged in the Enron affair included Timothy Belden, Enron's former top energy trader, who pleaded guilty to one count of conspiring to commit wire fraud. He was sentenced to two years of court-supervised release and required to pay $2.1 million. Three British bankers, David Bermingham, Giles Darby, and Gary Mulgrew, were indicted in Houston on wire-fraud charges related to a deal at Enron. According to the U.S. Justice Department, they had used secret investments to take $7.3 million in income that belonged to their employer. The three men, employees of the finance group Greenwich National Westminster Bank, were arrested in 2004 and extradited to America to face sentencing. They were sentenced to thirty-seven months in prison but were eventually sent back to Britain to serve out the remainder of their time.

The Chief Executive Officer

Former CEO Jeffrey Skilling, generally perceived as Enron's mastermind, was the most difficult to prosecute. At the time of the trial, he was so confident that he waived his right to avoid self-incrimination and testified before Congress, saying, "I was not aware of any inappropriate financial arrangements." However, Jeffrey McMahon, who took over as Enron's president and COO in February 2002, told a congressional subcommittee that he had informed Skilling about the company's off-balance-sheet partnerships in 2000, when he was Enron's treasurer. McMahon said that Skilling had told him that "he would remedy the situation."

Calling the Enron collapse a "run on the bank" and a "liquidity crisis," Skilling said that he did not understand how Enron had gone bankrupt so quickly. He also said that the off-balance-sheet partnerships were Fastow's creation. However, the judge dealt a blow to Lay and Skilling when he instructed the jury that it could find the defendants guilty of consciously avoiding knowing about wrongdoing at the company.

Many former Enron employees refused to testify because they were not guaranteed that their testimony would not be used against them in future trials, and therefore questions about the company's accounting fraud remain. Skilling was found guilty of honest services fraud and sentenced to 24 years in prison, which he has been serving in Colorado. He maintains his innocence and has appealed his conviction. In 2008 a panel of judges from the Fifth Circuit Court of Appeals in New Orleans rejected his request to overturn the convictions of fraud, conspiracy, misrepresentation, and insider trading. However, the judges did grant Skilling one concession. The three-judge panel determined that the original judge had applied flawed sentencing guidelines in determining Skilling's sentence. The Court ordered that Skilling be resentenced. The matter was taken to the Supreme Court.

In June 2010 the United States Supreme Court ruled that the honest services law could not be used to convict Skilling because the honest services law applies to bribes and kickbacks, not to conduct that is ambiguous or vague. The Supreme Court decision did not suggest that there had been no misconduct, only that Skilling's conduct was not in violation of a criminal fraud law. The court's decision did not overturn the conviction and sent the case back to a lower court for evaluation.

The Chair

Ken Lay became chair and CEO of the company that was to become Enron in 1986. A decade later, Lay promoted Jeffrey Skilling to president and chief operating officer, and then, as expected, Lay stepped down as CEO in 2001 to make way for Skilling. Lay remained as chair of the board. When Skilling resigned later that year, Lay resumed the role of CEO.

> "Lay said he believed the transactions were legal because attorneys and accountants had approved them."

Lay, who held a doctorate in economics from the University of Houston, contended that he knew little of what was going on, even though he had participated in the board meetings that allowed the off-balance-sheet partnerships to be created. Lay said he believed the transactions were legal because attorneys and accountants had approved them. Only months before the bankruptcy in 2001, he reassured employees and investors that all was well at Enron, based on strong wholesale sales and physical volume delivered through the marketing channel. He had already been informed that there were problems with some of the investments that could eventually cost Enron hundreds of millions of dollars. In 2002, on the advice of his attorney, Lay invoked his Fifth Amendment right not to answer questions that could be incriminating.

Lay was expected to be charged with insider trading, and prosecutors investigated why he had begun selling about $80 million of his own stock beginning in late 2000, even as he encouraged employees to buy more shares of the company. It appears that Lay drew down his $4 million Enron credit line repeatedly and then repaid the company with Enron shares. These transactions, unlike usual stock sales, do not have to be reported to investors. Lay says that he sold the stock because of margin calls on loans he had secured with Enron stock and that he had no other source of liquidity. According to Lay, he was largely unaware of the ethical situation within the firm. He had relied on lawyers, accountants, and senior executives to inform him of issues such as misconduct. He felt that he had been protected from certain knowledge that would have been beneficial and would have enabled him to engage in early correction of the misconduct. Lay claims that all decisions he made related to financial transactions were approved by the company's lawyers, and the Enron board of directors. Lynn Brewer, a former Enron executive, states that Lay was not informed about alleged misconduct in her division. Additionally, Mike Ramsey, the lead attorney for Lay's defense, claimed that he was not aware of most of the items in the indictment. In the end Lay was convicted on 19 counts of fraud, conspiracy, and insider trading. However, the verdict was thrown out in 2005 after he died of heart failure at his home in Colorado. The ruling protected some $43.5 million of Lay's estate that the prosecution had claimed Lay stole from Enron.

The Lawyers

Enron was Houston law firm Vinson & Elkins' top client, accounting for about 7 percent of its $450 million revenue. Enron's general counsel and a number of members of Enron's legal department came from Vinson & Elkins. Vinson & Elkins seems to have dismissed Sherron Watkins's allegations of accounting fraud after making some inquiries, but this does not appear to leave the firm open to civil or criminal liability. Of greater concern are allegations that Vinson & Elkins helped structure some of Enron's special-purpose partnerships. In her letter to Lay, Watkins had indicated that the firm had written opinion letters supporting the legality of the deals. In fact, Enron could not have done many of the transactions without such opinion letters. The firm did not admit liability, but agreed to pay $30 million to Enron to settle claims that Vinson & Elkins had contributed to the firm's collapse.

Merrill Lynch

The brokerage and investment-banking firm Merrill Lynch also faced scrutiny by federal prosecutors and the SEC for its role in Enron's 1999 sale of Nigerian barges. The sale allowed Enron to improperly record about $12 million in earnings and thereby meet its earnings goals at the end of 1999. Merrill Lynch allegedly bought the barges for $28 million, of which Enron financed $21 million. Fastow gave his word that Enron would buy Merrill Lynch's investment out in six months with a 15 percent guaranteed rate of return. Merrill Lynch went ahead with the deal despite an internal document that suggested that the transaction might be construed as aiding and abetting Enron's fraudulent manipulation of its income statement. Merrill Lynch denies that the transaction was a sham and said that it never knowingly helped Enron to falsify its financial reports.

There are also allegations that Merrill Lynch replaced a research analyst after his coverage of Enron displeased Enron executives. Enron reportedly threatened to exclude Merrill Lynch from an upcoming $750 million stock offering in retaliation. The replacement analyst is reported to have then upgraded his report on Enron's stock rating. Merrill Lynch maintains that it did nothing improper in its dealings with Enron. However, the firm agreed to pay $80 million to settle SEC charges related to the questionable Nigerian barge deal.

Merrill Lynch continued to use risky investment practices, which contributed to severe financial losses for the company as the economy entered a recession in 2008. In 2008 Bank of America agreed to purchase the company for $50 billion, possibly after pressure from the federal government.

ARTHUR ANDERSEN LLP

In its role as Enron's auditor, Arthur Andersen was responsible for ensuring the accuracy of Enron's financial statements and internal bookkeeping. Investors used Andersen's reports to judge Enron's financial soundness and future potential, and expected that Andersen's certifications of accuracy and application of proper accounting procedures would be independent and free of any conflict of interest.

However, Andersen's independence was called into question. The accounting firm was one of Enron's major business partners, with more than one hundred employees dedicated to its account, and it sold about $50 million a year in consulting services to Enron. Some Andersen executives even accepted jobs with the energy trader. In March 2002 Andersen was found guilty of obstruction of justice for destroying relevant auditing documents during an SEC investigation of Enron. As a result, Andersen was barred from performing audits. The damage to the firm was such that the company no longer operates, although it has not been dissolved formally.

It is still not clear why Andersen auditors failed to ask Enron to better explain its complex partnerships before certifying Enron's financial statements. Some observers believe that the large consulting fees Enron paid Andersen unduly influenced the company's decisions. An Andersen spokesperson said that the firm looked hard at all available information from Enron at the time. However, shortly after speaking to Lay Vice President Sherron Watkins took her concerns to an Andersen audit partner who reportedly conveyed her questions to senior Andersen management responsible for the Enron account. It is not clear what action, if any, Andersen took.

THE FALLOUT

Although Enron executives obviously engaged in misconduct, some people have questioned the tactics that federal investigators used against Enron. Many former Enron employees feel that it was almost impossible to obtain a fair trial for Lay and Skilling. The defense was informed that 130 of Enron's top managers, who could have served as witnesses for the defense, were considered unindicted co-conspirators with Lay and Skilling. Therefore, the defense could not obtain witnesses from Enron's top management teams under fear that the prosecution would indict the witnesses.

Enron's demise caused tens of billions of dollars of investor losses, triggered a collapse of electricity-trading markets, and ushered in an era of accounting scandals that precipitated a global loss of confidence in corporate integrity. Today companies must defend legitimate but complicated financing arrangements. Legislation like Sarbanes–Oxley, passed in the wake of Enron, has placed more restrictions on companies. Four thousand former Enron employees struggled to find jobs, and many retirees lost their entire retirement portfolios. One senior Enron executive committed suicide.

In 2003 Enron announced its intention to restructure and pay off its creditors. It was estimated that most creditors would receive between 14.4 cents and 18.3 cents for each dollar they were owed—more than most had expected. Under the plan, creditors would receive about two-thirds of the amount in cash and the rest in equity in three new companies, none of which would carry the tainted Enron name. The three companies were CrossCountry Energy Corporation, Prisma Energy International, Inc., and Portland General Electric.

CrossCountry Energy Corporation would retain Enron's interests in three North American natural gas pipelines. In 2004 Enron announced an agreement to sell Cross-Country Energy to CCE Holdings LLC for $2.45 billion. The money was to be used for debt repayment, and represented a substantial increase over a previous offer. Similarly, Prisma Energy International, Inc., which took over Enron's nineteen international power and pipeline holdings, was sold to Ashmore Energy International Ltd. The proceeds from the sale were given out to creditors through cash distributions. The third company, Portland General Electric (PGE), Oregon's largest utility, emerged from bankruptcy as an independent company through a private stock offering to Enron creditors.

All remaining assets not related to CrossCountry, Prisma, or Portland General were liquidated. Although Enron emerged from Chapter 11 bankruptcy protection in 2004, the company was wound down once the recovery plan had been carried out. That year all of Enron's outstanding common stock and preferred stocks were cancelled. Each record holder of Enron Corporation stock on the day it was cancelled was allocated an uncertified, nontransferable interest in one of two trusts that held new shares of the Enron Corporation.

The Enron Creditors Recovery Corporation was formed to help Enron creditors. It states that its mission is "to reorganize and liquidate the remaining operations and assets of Enron following one of the largest and most complex bankruptcies in U.S. history." In the very unlikely event that the value of Enron's assets would exceed the amount of its allowed claims, distributions were to be made to the holders of these trust interests in the same order of priority of the stock they previously held. According to the Enron Creditors Recovery Corporation, over $128 million was distributed to creditors, which brings the total amount of recovery to $21.549 billion.

In addition to trying to repay its shareholders, Enron also had to pay California for fraudulent activities it committed against the state's citizens. The company was investigated in California for allegedly colluding with at least two other power sellers in 2000 to obtain excess profits by submitting false information to the manager of California's electricity grid. In 2005 Enron agreed to pay California $47 million for taking advantage of California consumers during an energy shortage.

LEARNING FROM ENRON

Enron was the biggest business scandal of its time, and legislation like the Sarbanes–Oxley Act was passed to prevent future business fraud. But did the business world truly learn its lesson from Enron's collapse? Greed and corporate misconduct continued to be a problem throughout the first decade of the twenty-first century, culminating in the 2008–2009 global recession. Corporations praised high performance at any cost, even when employees cut ethical corners. In the mortgage market, companies like Countrywide rewarded their sales force for making risky subprime loans, even going so far as to turn their back on loans that they knew contained falsified information in order to make a quick profit. Other companies traded in risky financial instruments like credit default swaps (CDSs) when they knew that buyers did not have a clear understanding of the risks of such instruments. Although they promised to insure against default of these instruments, the companies did not have enough funds to cover the losses after the housing bubble burst. The resulting recession affected the entire world, bankrupting such established companies as Lehman Brothers and requiring government intervention in the amount of nearly $1 trillion in TARP (Troubled Asset Referendum Program) funds to salvage numerous financial firms. The economic meltdown inspired a new wave of legislation designed to prevent corporate misconduct, including the Dodd–Frank Wall Street Reform and Consumer Protection Act.

> "Enron was the biggest business scandal of its time, and legislation like the Sarbanes–Oxley Act was passed to prevent future business fraud."

It is unfortunate that the Enron scandal did not hinder corporate misconduct. However, Enron still has lessons to teach us. Along with the business scandals of the financial crisis, Enron demonstrates that, first, regulatory agencies must be improved so as to better detect corporate misconduct. Second, companies and regulatory authorities should pay attention to the warnings of concerned employees and "whistle-blowers" like Sherron Watkins. Third, executives should understand the risks and rewards of the financial instruments their companies use and maintain a thorough knowledge of the inner workings of their companies (something that Ken Lay claimed he did not have). These conditions are crucial to preventing similar business fraud in the future.

CONCLUSION

The example of Enron shows how an aggressive corporate culture that rewards high performance and gets rid of the "weak links" can backfire. Enron's culture encouraged intense competition, not only among employees from rival firms, but also among Enron employees themselves. Such behavior creates a culture where loyalty and ethics are cast aside in favor of high performance. The arrogant tactics of Jeffrey Skilling and the apparent ignorance of Ken Lay further contributed to an unhealthy corporate culture that encouraged cutting corners and falsifying information to inflate earnings.

The allegations surrounding Merrill Lynch's and Arthur Andersen's involvement in the debacle demonstrate that rarely does any scandal of such magnitude involve only one company. Whether a company or regulatory body participates directly in a scandal or whether it refuses to act by looking the other way, the result can be further perpetuation of fraud. This fact was emphasized during the 2008–2009 financial crisis, in which the misconduct of several major companies and the failure of monitoring efforts by regulatory bodies contributed to the worst financial crisis since the Great Depression. With the country recovering from widespread corporate corruption, the story of Enron is once again at the forefront of people's minds.

The Enron scandal has become legendary. In 2005, four years after the scandal, a movie was made about the collapse of Enron called *Enron: The Smartest Guys in the Room*. To this day, Jeffrey Skilling continues to maintain his innocence and appeal his case. Enron's auditor, Arthur Andersen, faced over 40 shareholder lawsuits claiming damages of more than $32 billion. In 2009 the defunct company agreed to pay $16 million to Enron creditors. Enron itself faced many civil actions, and a number of Enron executives faced federal investigations, criminal actions, and civil lawsuits. As for the giant tilted "E" logo so proudly displayed outside of corporate headquarters, it was auctioned off for $44,000.

QUESTIONS

1. How did the corporate culture of Enron contribute to its bankruptcy?

2. Did Enron's bankers, auditors, and attorneys contribute to Enron's demise? If so, how?

3. What role did the company's chief financial officer play in creating the problems that led to Enron's financial problems?

SOURCES

Aldrick, Philip. "NatWest Three Return to U.K." *Telegraph.co.uk,* November 7, 2008, http://www.telegraph.co.uk/news/worldnews/northamerica/usa/3394139/NatWest-Three-return-to-UK.html (accessed September 7, 2009); Associated Press. "Merrill Lynch Settles an Enron Lawsuit." *The New York Times,* July 7, 2006, http://www.nytimes.com/2006/07/07/business/07enron.html?scp=3&sq=%22merrill%20lynch%22%20enron&st=cse (accessed September 7, 2009); Associated Press. "Two Enron Traders Avoid Prison Sentences." *The New York Times,* February 15, 2007, http://www.nytimes.com/2007/02/15/business/15enron.html?ex=1329195600&en=0f87e8ca8 3a557ed&ei=50 90&partner=rssuserland&emc=rss (accessed September 7, 2009); Barrionuevo, Alexei. "Fastow Gets His Moment in the Sun." *The New York Times,* November 10, 2006, http://www.nytimes.com/2006/11/10/business/10fastow.html (accessed September 7, 2009); Barrionuevo, Alexei, Jonathan Weil, and John R. Wilke. "Enron's Fastow Charged with Fraud." *The Wall Street Journal,* October 3, 2002, A3–A4; Berger, Eric. "Report Details Enron's Deception." *The Houston Chronicle,* March 6, 2003, 1B, 11B; CBCNews.ca. "Enron Settles California Price-Gouging Claim." http://www.cbc.ca/money/story/2005/07/15/enron-gouge050715.html July 15, 2005 (accessed September 7, 2009); Chen, Christine Y. "When Good Firms Get Bad Chi." *Fortune,* November 11, 2002, 56; Eichenwald, Kurt. "Enron Founder, Awaiting Prison, Dies in Colorado." *The New York Times,* July 6, 2006, http://www.nytimes.com/2006/07/06/business/06enron.html (accessed September 7, 2009); Elkind, Peter, and Bethany McLean. "Feds Move up Enron Food Chain." *Fortune,* December 30, 2002, 43–44; Enron Creditors Recovery Co. "Enron Announces Completed Sale of Prisma Energy International, Inc." September 7, 2006, http://www.enron.com/index.php?option=com_content&task=view&id=94&Itemid=34 (accessed September 7, 2009); Enron Creditors Recovery Co. "FAQs." http://www.enron.com/index. php?option=com_content&task=view&id=17&Itemid=27 (accessed September 7, 2009); Enron. http://www.enron.com/ (accessed September 7, 2009); Associated Press, "Ex-Enron CFO Fastow Indicted on 78 Counts." *The Los Angeles Times,* November 1, 2002, http://articles.latimes.com/2002/nov/01/business/fi-fastow1 (accessed July 6, 2011); Farrell, Greg. "Former Enron CFO Charged." *USA Today,* October 3, 2002, B1; Farrell, Greg, Edward Iwata, and Thor Valdmanis. "Prosecutors Are Far from Finished." *USA Today,* October 3, 2002, 1–2B; Felsenthal, Mark, and Lillia Zuill. "AIG Gets $150 Billion Government Bailout; Posts Huge Losses." *Reuters,* November 10, 2008, http://www.reuters.com/article/topNews/idUSTRE4A92FM20081110?feedType=RSS&feedName=topNews

(accessed September 7, 2009); Ferrell, O. C. "Ethics." *BizEd,* May/June 2002, 43–45; Ferrell, O. C., and Linda Ferrell. "The Responsibility and Accountability of CEOs: The Last Interview with Ken Lay." *Journal of Business Ethics,* November 11, 2010; Ferrell, O. C., and Linda Ferrell. *Examining Systemic Issues That Created Enron and the Latest Global Financial Industry Crisis* (2009). White paper; Ferrell, O. C., and Linda Ferrell. "Understanding the Importance of Business Ethics in the 2008–2009 Financial Crisis." In Ferrell, Fraedrich, Ferrell, *Business Ethics,* 7th ed. (Boston: Houghton Mifflin, 2009); Fick, Jeffrey A. "Report: Merrill Replaced Enron Analyst." *USA Today,* July 30, 2002, B1; IBD's Washington Bureau. "Finger-Pointing Starts as Congress Examines Enron's Fast Collapse." *Investor's Business Daily,* February 8, 2002, A1; Fonda, Daren. "Enron: Picking over the Carcass." *Fortune,* December 30, 2002–January 6, 2003, 56; France, Mike. "One Big Client, One Big Hassle." *BusinessWeek,* January 28, 2002, 38–39; Gruley, Bryan, and Rebecca Smith. "Keys to Success Left Kenneth Lay Open to Disaster." *The Wall Street Journal,* April 26, 2002, A1, A5; Hamburger, Tom. "Enron CEO Declines to Testify at Hearing." *The Wall Street Journal,* December 12, 2001, B2; HighBeam Research. "British Bankers Indicted in Enron Case: Three Men Accused of Siphoning Off $7.3 Million Owed to Their Employer." *The Washington Post,* September 13, 2002, http://www.highbeam.com/doc/1P2-369257.html (accessed September 7, 2009); Kadlec, Daniel. "Power Failure." *Time,* December 2, 2001, http://www.time.com/time/ magazine/article/0,9171,1101011210-186639,00.html#ixzz0updcIQaT (accessed July 29, 2010); Kadlec, Daniel. "Enron: Who's Accountable?" *Time,* January 13, 2002, http://www.time.com/time/business/article/0,8599,193520,00. html#ixzz0v0Yku2MF (accessed July 29, 2010); Kahn, Jeremy. "The Chief Freaked Out Officer." *Fortune,* December 9, 2002, 197–198, 202; Karnitschnig, Matthew, Carrick Mollenkamp, and Dan Fitzpatrick. "Bank of America to Buy Merrill." *The Wall Street Journal,* September 15, 2008, http://online.wsj.com/article/SB122142278543033525. html?mod=special_coverage (accessed April 4, 2011); Kranhold, Kathryn, and Rebecca Smith. "Two Other Firms in Enron Scheme, Documents Say." *The Wall Street Journal,* May 9, 2002, C1, C12; Lanman, Scott, and Craig Torres. "Republican Staff Says Fed Overstepped on Merrill Deal (Update 1)." *Bloomberg,* June 10, 2009, http://www.bloomberg. com/apps/news?pid=newsarchive&sid=a5A4F5W_PygQ (accessed April 4, 2011); Lozano, Juan A. "U.S. Court Orders Skilling Resentenced." *The Washington Post,* January 7, 2009, http://www.washingtonpost.com/wp-dyn/content/ article/2009/01/06/AR2009010603214.html (accessed July 6, 2011); McLean, Bethany. "Why Enron Went Bust." *Fortune,* December 24, 2001, 58, 60–62, 66, 68; Morse, Jodie, and Amanda Bower. "The Party Crasher." *Fortune,* December 30, 2002–January 6, 2003, 53–56; Needles, Belverd E., Jr., and Marian Powers. "Accounting for Enron." *Houghton Mifflin's Guide to the Enron Crisis* (Boston: Houghton Mifflin, 2003), 3–6; Norris, Floyd. "Ruling Could Open Door to New Trial in Enron Case." *The New York Times,* January 6, 2009, http://www.nytimes.com/2009/01/07/ business/07enron.html?scp=3&sq=skilling&st=nyt (accessed September 7, 2009); "Playing the Blame Game." *Time,* January 20, 2002, http://www.time.com/time/2002/enron/collapse (accessed July 29, 2010); Ross, Brian, and Alice Gomstyn. "Lehman Brothers Boss Defends $484 Million in Salary, Bonus." ABC News, October 6, 2008, http://www. abcnews.go.com/Blotter/Story?id=5965360&page=1 (accessed September 7, 2009); Schulman, Miriam. "Enron: Whatever Happened to Going Down with the Ship?" Markkula Center for Applied Ethics, www.scu.edu/ethics/ publications/ethicalperspectives/schulman0302.html (accessed September 7, 2009); Sigismond, William. "The Enron Case from a Legal Perspective." *Houghton Mifflin's Guide to Enron,* 11–13; Smith, Rebecca, and Kathryn Kranhold. "Enron Knew Portfolio's Value." *The Wall Street Journal,* May 6, 2002, C1, C20; Smith, Rebecca, and Mitchell Pacelle. "Enron Plans Return to Its Roots." *The Wall Street Journal,* May 2, 2002, A1; Sorkin, Andrew Ross. "Ex-Enron Chief Skilling Appeals to Supreme Court." DealBook Blog, *The New York Times,* March 12, 2009, http://dealbook.blogs. nytimes.com/2009/05/12/former-enron-chiefskilling- appeals-to-supreme-court/?scp=1-b&sq=skilling&st= nyt (accessed September 7, 2009); "Times Topics: Enron." *The New York Times,* http://topics.nytimes.com/top/news/ business/companies/enron/index.html?scp=1-spot&sq=Enron&st=cse (accessed September 7, 2009); Ulick, Jake. "Enron: A Year Later." CNN Money, December 2, 2002, http://money.cnn.com/2002/11/26/news/companies/enron_ anniversary/index.htm (accessed September 7, 2009); Ungagged.net. "The Other Side of the Enron Story." http:// ungagged.net (accessed July 29, 2010); Weber, Joseph. "Can Andersen Survive?" *BusinessWeek,* January 28, 2002, 39–40; Weidlich, Thomas. "Arthur Andersen Settles Enron Suit for $16 Million." Bloomberg.com, April 28, 2009, http://www.bloomberg.com/apps/news?pid=20601072&sid=avopmnT7eWjs (accessed September 7, 2009); Winthrop Corporation. "Epigraph." *Houghton Mifflin's Guide to Enron,* 1; Zellner, Wendy. "A Hero—and a Smoking-Gun Letter." *Business Week,* January 28, 2002, 34–35.

CASE 10

Home Depot Implements Stakeholder Orientation*

When Bernie Marcus and Arthur Blank opened the first Home Depot store in Atlanta in 1979, they forever changed the hardware and home-improvement retailing industry. Marcus and Blank envisioned huge warehouse-style stores stocked with an extensive selection of products offered at the lowest prices. Today, 22 million customers visit Home Depot every week. Do-it-yourselfers and building contractors can browse among 40,000 different products for the home and yard, from kitchen and bathroom fixtures to carpeting, lumber, paint, tools, and plant and landscaping items. If a product is not provided in one of the stores, Home Depot offers 250,000 products that can be special ordered. Some Home Depot stores are open twenty-four hours a day, but customers can also order products online. Additionally, the company offers free home-improvement clinics to teach customers how to tackle everyday projects like tiling a bathroom. For those customers who prefer not to "do it yourself," most stores offer installation services. Knowledgeable employees, recognizable by their orange aprons, are on hand to help customers find items or to demonstrate the proper use of a particular tool.

Currently, Home Depot employs more than 300,000 people and operates over 2,200 Home Depot stores in the United States, Mexico, Puerto Rico, China, the Virgin Islands, Guam, and Canada. It also operates four wholly owned subsidiaries: Apex Supply Company, Georgia Lighting, Maintenance Warehouse, and National Blinds and Wallpaper. The company is the largest home-improvement retailer in the world, with $66 billion in revenues. Home Depot continues to do things on a grand scale, including putting its corporate muscle behind a tightly focused social responsibility agenda.

MANAGING CUSTOMER RELATIONSHIPS

In 2006 John Costello was the chief marketing officer, or "chief customer officer," as he refers to the position. Costello consolidated marketing and merchandising functions to help consumers achieve their goals in home-improvement projects more effectively and efficiently. According to Costello, "Above all else, a brand is a promise. It says here's what you can expect if you do business with us. Our mission is to empower our customers to achieve the home or condo of their dreams." When Costello arrived in 2002 Home Depot's reputation was faltering. His plan called for overhauling the Home Depot website as well as integrating

*This case was developed by Jennifer Sawayda and Melanie Drever for and under the direction of O. C. Ferrell and Linda Ferrell. We appreciate the previous editorial assistance of Jennifer Jackson. This case was prepared for classroom discussion rather than to illustrate either effective or ineffective handling of an administrative, ethical, or legal decision by management. All sources used for this case were obtained through publicly available material.

mass marketing and direct marketing with in-store experience. The new philosophy was expressed by the new Home Depot mantra: "You can do it. We can help." Teams of people from merchandising, marketing, visual merchandising, and operations attempted to provide the very best shopping experience. The idea was simple. Home Depot believed that customers should be able to read and understand how one ceiling fan is different from another, and associates (employees) should be able to offer installation and design advice.

In 2008 Frank Bifulco took over as new chief marketing officer and senior vice president. It was a tough time for Home Depot. Because of the 2008–2009 recession, consumers were spending less on their homes. Home Depot's new marketing strategy was to emphasize the store's everyday low prices, high product value, and quality energy-saving products. At the same time, the company cut back on special offers like discounts and promotions.

Despite Home Depot's proactive approach to customer issues, the company has had its share of challenges, even before the onset of the recession. The company was forced to deal with negative publicity associated with customer-satisfaction measures published by outside sources. The University of Michigan's annual American Customer Satisfaction Index in 2006 showed Home Depot slipping to last place among major U.S. retailers. "This is not competitive and too low to be sustainable. It's very serious," wrote Claes Fornell, professor of business at the University of Michigan. Fornell believed that the drop in satisfaction was one reason why Home Depot's stock was stagnant.

> "Despite Home Depot's proactive approach to customer issues, the company has had its share of challenges."

Robert Nardelli, the Home Depot CEO during that time, said that the survey was a "sham." Nardelli pointed out that Fornell had created his own ethical concerns when he shorted Home Depot stock before the survey came out (purchase options that would cause Fornell to profit from Home Depot's stock price decreasing). Fornell defended himself by saying that the trades were part of research into a correlation between companies' customer-satisfaction scores and stock price performance, but the University of Michigan banned the practice anyway.

Some former managers at Home Depot have blamed the company's service issues on a culture that operated under principles reminiscent of the military. Under Nardelli, some employees feared being terminated unless they followed directions to a tee. Harris Interactive's 2005 Reputation Quotient Survey ranked Home Depot number 12 among major companies and said that customers appreciated Home Depot's quality services. However, two years later the company had fallen to number 27 on the list. Nardelli was ousted and replaced by Frank Blake in January 2007. The start of 2008 seemed more auspicious for Home Depot, as it was listed as number six on *Fortune*'s Most Admired Companies (still trailing behind Lowe's), up from 13 in 2006. Home Depot also bounced back up on the American Customer Satisfaction Index. Although it still trails behind Lowe's, Home Depot ranked 72 percent in 2009 (versus 5 percent at its lowest point).

One way in which Home Depot attempts to practice good customer service and simultaneously act in a socially responsible manner is through its program designed to teach children basic carpentry skills. Home Depot provides a free program called the Kids Workshop available at all its stores. The workshops are for children ages five through twelve, available on the first Saturday of each month between 9 A.M. and noon. During the workshops, children learn to create objects that can be used around their homes or neighborhoods. Projects include toolboxes, mail organizers, and window birdhouses and bughouses. An average of 75 children attend Kids Workshops per store, while some stores have as many as 200 children. Home Depot also offers free workshops especially designed for women and for new homeowners.

ENVIRONMENTAL INITIATIVES

Cofounders Marcus and Blank nurtured a corporate culture that emphasizes social responsibility, especially with regard to the company's impact on the natural environment. Home Depot began its environmental program on the twentieth anniversary of Earth Day in 1990 by adopting a set of Environmental Principles (see Table 1). These principles have since been adopted by the National Retail Hardware Association and Home Center Institute, which represents more than 46,000 retail hardware stores and home centers.

Guided by these principles, Home Depot has initiated a number of programs to minimize the firm's—and its customers'—impact on the environment. In 1991 the retailer began using store and office supplies, advertising, signs, and shopping bags made with recycled content. It also established a process for evaluating the environmental claims made by suppliers. The following year the firm launched a program to recycle wallboard shipping packaging, which became the industry's first "reverse distribution" program. In addition, it was the first retailer in the world to combine a drive-through recycling center with one of its Georgia stores in 1993. One year later Home Depot became the first home-improvement retailer to offer wood products from tropical and temperate forests that were certified as "well-managed" by the Scientific Certification System's Forest Conservation Program. The company also began to replace its hardwood wooden shipping pallets with reusable "slip sheets" to minimize waste and energy usage and to decrease pressure on hardwood resources.

TABLE 1 Home Depot's Environmental Principles

The Home Depot acknowledges the importance of conservation. The following principles are Home Depot's response:

- We are committed to improving the environment by selling products that are manufactured, packaged and labeled in a responsible manner, that take the environment into consideration and that provide greater value to our customers.

- We will support efforts to provide accurate, informative product labeling of environmental marketing claims.

- We will strive to eliminate unnecessary packaging.

- We will recycle and encourage the use of materials and products with recycled content.

- We will conserve natural resources by using energy and water wisely and seek further opportunities to improve the resource efficiency of our stores.

- We will comply with environmental laws and will maintain programs and procedures to ensure compliance.

- We are committed to minimizing the environmental health and safety risk for our associates and our customers.

- We will train our employees to enhance understanding of environmental issues and policies and to promote excellence in job performance and all environmental matters.

- We will encourage our customers to become environmentally conscious shoppers.

Source: "The Home Depot Environmental Principles," Home Depot, http://corporate.homedepot.com/wps/portal/Environmental_Principles (accessed May 13, 2009).

In 1999 Home Depot announced that it would endorse independent, third-party forest certification and wood from certified forests. The company joined the Certified Forests Products Council, a nonprofit organization that promotes responsible forest product buying practices and the sale of wood from Certified Well-Managed Forests. Yet the company continued to sell products made from wood harvested from old growth forests. Protesters led by the Rainforest Action Network, an environmental group, had picketed Home Depot and other home center stores for years in an effort to stop the destruction of old growth forests, of which less than 20 percent still survive. Later that year, during Home Depot's twentieth anniversary celebration, Arthur Blank announced that Home Depot would stop selling products made from wood harvested in environmentally sensitive areas.

To be certified by the Forest Stewardship Council (FSC), a supplier's wood products must be tracked from the forest, through manufacturing and distribution, to the customer. Harvesting, manufacturing, and distribution practices must ensure a balance of social, economic, and environmental factors. Blank challenged competitors to follow Home Depot's lead, and within two years several had met that challenge, including Lowe's, the number-two home-improvement retailer; Wickes, a lumber company; and Andersen Corporation, a window manufacturer. By 2003 Home Depot reported that it had reduced its purchases of Indonesian lauan, a tropical rainforest hardwood used in door components, by 70 percent, and it continued to increase its purchases of certified sustainable wood products. In addition to sustainable wood products, Home Depot offers compact fluorescent light bulbs (CFLs) in its stores and has even introduced an in-store recycling program for CFL bulbs. Customers can drop off their used bulbs in stores, and Home Depot works with an environmental management company to recycle the bulbs safely and responsibly. The company has managed to reduce its energy use by 16 percent between 2004 and 2010. It hopes to reach 20 percent within the next five years. Home Depot's reduction in energy thus far has equaled a savings of 2.6 billion kilowatt hours, which is enough to power over 200,000 homes for one year.

Home Depot believes that it has a philanthropic responsibility to improve the communities in which it operates. In 2002 the company founded the Home Depot Foundation, which provides additional resources to assist nonprofits in the United States and Canada. The Foundation awards grants to eligible nonprofits three times per year and partners with innovative nonprofits across the country that are working to increase awareness and successfully demonstrate the connection between housing, the urban forest, and the overall health and economic success of their communities. In 2007 the Foundation pledged to invest $400 million over the next decade to create 100,000 affordable, sustainable homes and plant three million "community trees" in communities nationwide.

These efforts have yielded many rewards in addition to improved relations with environmental stakeholders. Home Depot's environmental programs have earned the company an A on the Council on Economic Priorities Corporate Report Card, a Vision of America Award from Keep America Beautiful, and a President's Council for Sustainable Development Award. The company has also been recognized by the U.S. Environmental Protection Agency with its Energy Star Award for Excellence.

Home Depot has established better relations with some environmental activists, but not all are satisfied that the company is doing everything it can to help the environment. In 2008 Home Depot came under controversy for doing business with two Chilean wood suppliers that supported the building of a dam in the Chilean region of Patagonia, a project that would cause irreparable harm to a fragile ecosystem. An environmental institution known as International Rivers demanded that Home Depot pull its contracts with the suppliers if they refused to abandon the dam project. However, Home Depot's environmental chief Ron Jarvis said that the two suppliers were obeying the 2003 agreement not to cut down endangered forests for tree farms. Since they were also not supplying Home Depot with wood products from native forests, Home Depot had no legitimate reason to cancel the contracts. Additionally, Jarvis maintained that the two Chilean suppliers were only minor players in the dam project and that the company's pull-out would not have much of an effect.

This example demonstrates the type of ethical dilemma that all companies have to manage in balancing their economic interests and potential environmental damage. There will always be debatable areas because some stakeholders have less concern about the economic success of a company and are only concerned about environmental impact. Shareholders are a highly relevant stakeholder and corporations are obligated to make decisions that are in their interests. Some environmental special interest groups will always target companies like Home Depot no matter how hard they try to make decisions that support sustainability while maintaining their economic viability. The role of top management at Home Depot is to make informed decisions that balance stakeholder interests.

CORPORATE PHILANTHROPY

"Home Depot focuses corporate social responsibility efforts on affordable housing and disaster relief."

In addition to its environmental initiatives, Home Depot focuses corporate social responsibility efforts on affordable housing and disaster relief. For instance, Home Depot works with more than 350 affiliates of Habitat for Humanity, a nonprofit organization that constructs and repairs homes for qualified low-income families. In March 2008 Home Depot and Habitat for Humanity announced a five-year initiative to provide funding for creating at least 5,000 energy-efficient homes. The Home Depot Foundation will provide $30 million in support of this program. Home Depot also awards grants to housing projects throughout the nation.

Additionally, Home Depot addresses the growing needs for relief from disasters such as hurricanes, tornadoes, and earthquakes. After the 9/11 terrorist attacks in 2001, the company set up three command centers with more than 200 associates to help coordinate relief supplies such as dust masks, gloves, batteries, and tools to victims and rescue workers. After the 2010 Haitian earthquake, Home Depot Mexico donated $30,000 to Habitat for Humanity to assist in Haiti's recovery efforts in addition to launching a fundraising program for its Mexican associates. Home Depot pledged to double the resources that its Mexican associates raised to aid in the relief effort. U.S. Home Depot and The Home Depot Foundation also donated $100,000 to the Red Cross, while The Home Depot Canada Foundation pledged to donate $50,000.

EMPLOYEE AND SUPPLIER RELATIONS

Home Depot encourages employees to become involved in the community through volunteer and civic activities. With more than 300,000 employees, the company provides about 2 million volunteer service hours each year. Home Depot also strives to apply social responsibility to its employment practices, with the goal of assembling a diverse workforce that reflects the population of the markets it serves. However, in 1997 the company settled a class-action lawsuit brought by female employees who alleged that they were paid less than male employees, awarded fewer pay raises, and promoted less often. The $87.5 million settlement represented one of the largest settlements in a gender discrimination lawsuit in U.S. history at the time. In announcing the settlement, the company emphasized that it was not admitting to wrongdoing and defended its record, saying that it "provides opportunities for all of its associates to develop successful professional careers and is proud of its strong track record of having successful women involved in all areas of the company."

Since the lawsuit, Home Depot has worked to show that it appreciates workforce diversity and seeks to give all its associates an equal chance to be employed and advance in its stores. In 2005 Home Depot formed partnerships with the ASPIRA Association, Inc., the Hispanic Association of Colleges and Universities, and the National Council of La Raza to recruit Hispanic candidates for part-time and full-time positions. Also in 2005 Home Depot became a major member of the American Association of Retired Persons' (AARP) Featured Retirement Program, which helps connect employees 50 years or older with companies that value their experience. Home Depot also has a strong diversity supplier program. As a member of the Women's Business Enterprise National Council and the National Minority Suppliers Development Council, Home Depot has come into contact and done business with a diverse range of suppliers, including many minority- and women-owned businesses. In 2005 the company became a founding member of The Resource Institute, whose mission is to help small minority- and women-owned businesses by providing them with resources and training. Home Depot's supplier diversity program has won it numerous recognitions. It ranked number thirteen for the Top 50 American Organizations for Multicultural Business Opportunities in 2010 and was named the Georgia Minority Supplier Development Council (GMSDC) George Lottier Rising Star of the Year in 2009.

HOME DEPOT'S RESPONSE TO THE RECESSION

Home Depot's emphasis on expansion has changed drastically in light of the 2008–2009 recession. CEO Frank Blake decided to halt expansion and focus on improving existing stores. Blake saw the warning signs of the impending crisis and began halting expansion in early 2007, reducing new store openings from around two a week to five a year, a strategy that represented a major shift after a decade of aggressive expansion. In early 2009 Blake shut down Home Depot's EXPO stores, which largely catered to the wealthier class, estimating that they would lose millions each year. While Home Depot's 2007 revenue was over $80 billion, its revenue in 2009 fell to around $65 billion. That year the company was forced to cut 7,000 jobs.

Home Depot's reaction to the crisis was swift and decisive. As the crisis worsened in September 2008, Home Depot managers transferred all extra cash to Home Depot headquarters, cut capital spending, and suspended a stock buy-back program in order to avoid losses and prevent having to borrow. For the first time, Home Depot is paying all its expenses from its own revenue. This fiscally conservative strategy is aimed at stemming future losses and reducing risk, yet it limits Home Depot's ability to grow and adapt quickly. Home Depot may need to develop new strategies in the future if revenues continue to fall.

Home Depot's tactic may put it at a disadvantage in relation to competitors who have chosen the opposite approach such as Lowe's, which has continued to expand, taking advantage of the new low costs of land and labor. Such an approach is risky, but may prove profitable in the long run. Lowe's expansion could have one of two consequences: (1) overexpansion at a bad time might result in losses, or (2) its aggressive approach might pay off and make it an even more formidable foe for Home Depot. As consumers begin to take on more home-improvement projects, Home Depot's store revenues are expected to rise by single digits. Home Depot has begun to expand once again, but at a slower pace this time. The company announced plans to open 10 new stores in 2011.

NEW TECHNOLOGY INITIATIVES

While Home Depot has begun to slow its rate of expansion, the company is turning toward technology to improve customer service and become more efficient. Compared to its rivals, Home Depot has lagged behind technologically. For instance, employees were using computers powered by motorboard batteries and stocking shelves in the same way as they had done for the past 15 years. Unlike its rival Lowe's, Home Depot did not allow customers to order products online and then pick them up at the stores. As more and more consumers choose to complete their transactions on the web, this represented a weakness for Home Depot. In 2010 Home Depot's online sales constituted only 1.5 percent of overall sales. Although its rapid expansion had increased its reach, Home Depot was not adapting as quickly to the fast-paced world of technology.

After recognizing its limitations in this field, Home Depot has embarked upon several technology initiatives. These initiatives are intended to improve both its customer service and Home Depot's daily operations. One small victory that Home Depot has achieved is beating Lowe's in unleashing a mobile app that enables consumers to order Home Depot products. Additionally, Home Depot has invested $64 million to create First Phone, a device that will replace the old computers on associates' carts. By December 2010 Home Depot had distributed 30,000 of these devices in over 1,900 of its stores. The device allows associates to communicate with other associates, print labels, process credit and debit card transactions, and manage inventory, among other functions. According to CEO Frank Blake, the purpose of First Phone is to help associates spend less time on routine tasks and more on customer service. Home Depot also redesigned its website to improve navigation and communication channels. The company provided upgrades such as live chat and plans to include a buy online pickup option. Home Depot has managed to reduce response time to customer emails from 24 hours to one hour or less. Additionally, Home Depot is improving its logistics. Whereas before the company had its suppliers send trucks of merchandise directly to the stores, where associates would then unload them, Home Depot has created 19 distribution centers to make operations run more smoothly. This change will also enable its associates to devote more time to customer service.

These are just a few of the steps that Home Depot is taking to adopt a more proactive stance toward technological innovation. By concentrating on innovations that will increase customer service, the retailer is attempting to advance its stakeholder orientation into all aspects of its operations.

A STRATEGIC COMMITMENT TO SOCIAL RESPONSIBILITY

Home Depot has strived to secure a socially responsible reputation with stakeholders. Although it received low scores in the past on customer surveys and the American Customer Satisfaction Index, it has worked hard to bring those scores back up. It has responded to concerns about its environmental impact by creating new standards and principles to govern its relationship with its suppliers. Despite Home Depot's success, however, the company does face challenges in the future. Though it remains the world's largest home retailer, its main competitor Lowe's is picking up the pace, and the company is still trying to recover from the recession. Still, Home Depot's philanthropic endeavors and its promotion of its products' low prices and high value continue to make it a popular shopping destination.

Knowing that stakeholders, especially customers, feel good about a company that actively commits resources to environmental and social issues, Home Depot executives have committed to social responsibility as a strategic component of the company's business operations. The company should remain committed to its focused strategy of philanthropy, volunteerism, and environmental initiatives. Customers' concerns over social responsibility and green products have not abated, and Home Depot's sales of green products are strong. Its commitment to social responsibility extends throughout the company, fueled by top-level support from its cofounders and reinforced by a corporate culture that places great value on playing a responsible role within the communities it serves.

QUESTIONS

1. On the basis of Home Depot's response to environmental issues, describe the attributes (power, legitimacy, urgency) of this stakeholder. Assess the company's strategy and performance with environmental and employee stakeholders.

2. As a publicly traded corporation, how can Home Depot justify budgeting so much money for philanthropy? What areas other than the environment, disaster relief, affordable housing, and at-risk youth might be appropriate for strategic philanthropy by Home Depot?

3. Is Home Depot's recessionary strategy of eliminating debt and halting growth a wise one? What would you recommend to the CEO?

SOURCES

American Customer Satisfaction Index. "Fourth Quarter, 2009." February 16, 2010, http://www.theacsi.org/index.php?Itemid=214&id=203&option=com_content&task=view (accessed February 6, 2011); Blair, Adam. "Home Depot's $64 Million Mobile Investment Rolls Out to 1,970 Stores." RIS, December 7, 2010, http://risnews.edgl.com/store-systems/Home-Depot-s-$64-Million-Mobile-Investment-Rolls-Out-to-1,600-Stores56966 (accessed January 31, 2011); Bloomberg Businessweek. "HOME DEPOT INC (HD: New York)." http://www.usatoday.com/money/industries/retail/2010-12-08-home-depot-outlook_N.htm, February 5, 2011 (accessed February 6, 2011); Burritt, Chris. "Home Depot's Fix-It Lady." Bloomberg BusinessWeek, January 17–23, 2011, 65–67; Bustillo, Miguel. "For Lowe's, Landscape Begins to Shift." The Wall Street Journal, February 24, 2011, B3; Carlton, Jim. "How Home Depot and Activists Joined to Cut Logging Abuse." The Wall Street Journal, September 26, 2000, A1; Common Dreams Newswire. "Home Depot Announces Commitment to Stop Selling Old Growth Wood; Announcement Validates Two-Year Grassroots Environmental Campaign." http://www.commondreams.org/pressreleases/august99/082699c.htm, August 26, 1999 (accessed September 8, 2009); CNBC. "Home Depot vs. Lowe's." http://www.cnbc.com/id/26406040/?__source=aol|headline|quote|text|&par=aol, August 26, 2008 (accessed September 8, 2009); Daniels, Cora. "To Hire a Lumber Expert, Click Here." Fortune, April 3, 2000, 267–270; Demaster, Sarah.

"Use proper lumber, demand protesters." *BNet,* April 5, 1999, http://findarticles.com/p/articles/mi_m0VCW/is_7_25/ai_54373184/ (accessed September 8, 2009); Energy Star. "Profiles in Leadership: 2008 ENERGY STAR Award Winners." http://www.energystar.gov/ia/partners/pt_awards/2008_profiles_in_leadership.pdf (accessed September 8, 2009); *Fortune.* "World's Most Admired Companies: Home Depot." http://money.cnn.com/magazines/fortune/globalmostadmired/2008/snapshots/2968.html (accessed September 8, 2009); *Fortune.* "America's Most Admired Companies." http://money.cnn.com/magazines/fortune/mostadmired/2008/industries/11.html (accessed September 8, 2009); Grimsley, Kirstin Downey. "Home Depot Settles Gender Bias Lawsuit." *The Washington Post,* September 20, 1997, D1; Grow, Brian, Diane Brady, and Michael Arndt. "Renovating Home Depot." *Business Week,* March 6, 2006, http://www.businessweek.com/print/magazine/content/06_10/b3974001.htm?chan=gl (accessed September 8, 2009); Habitat for Humanity. "Habitat for Humanity and the Home Depot Foundation Announce National Green Building Effort." http://www.habitat.org/newsroom/2008archive/03_21_08_Home_Depot.aspx, March 20, 2008 (accessed September 8, 2009); Habitat for Humanity. "Habitat for Humanity and The Home Depot Mexico partner to help rebuild Haiti." http://www.habitat.org/lac_eng/newsroom/2010/02_08_2010_homedepot_eng.aspx?tgs=Mi81LzIwMTEgMTI6NDg6NTYgUE0%3d, February 8, 2010 (accessed February 6, 2011); Harris Interactive. "The Annual RQ 2007: The Reputations of the Most Visible Companies." Marketing Charts, http://www.marketingcharts.com/direct/corporate-reputation-in-decline-but-top-companies-buck-trend-5129/harris-corporate-reputation-2007-most-visible-companiesjpg/ (accessed July 6, 2011); Heher, Ashley M. "Home Depot Reports Loss of $54M, but Beats Estimates." *USA Today,* February 24, 2009, http://www.usatoday.com/money/companies/earnings/2009-02-24-home-depot_N.htm (accessed September 8, 2009); Hincha-Ownby, Melissa. "Home Depot Shrinks Energy Bill." *Forbes,* March 11, 2010, http://www.forbes.com/2010/03/10/energy-efficiency-lighting-technology-ecotech-home-depot.html (accessed February 6, 2011); Home Depot. "2008 Annual Report." http://www.homedepot.com/ (accessed September 8, 2009); Home Depot. "CFL Recycling Program." http://www6.homedepot.com/ecooptions/index.html?MAINSECTION=cflrecycling (accessed September 8, 2009); Home Depot. "Corporate Financial Review." http://corporate.homedepot.com/en_US/Corporate/Public_Relations/Online_Press_Kit/Docs/Corp_Financial_Overview.pdf (accessed September 8, 2009); Home Depot. "The Home Depot and the Environment." http://corporate.homedepot.com/wps/portal/Environmental_Principles (accessed September 8, 2009); Home Depot. "Message from the Supplier Diversity Director." http://corporate.homedepot.com/wps/portal/SupplierDiversity (accessed February 6, 2011); Home Depot. "Our History." http://corporate.homedepot.com/wps/portal/!ut/p/c1/04_SB8K8xLLM9MSSzPy8xBz9CPoos3gDdwNHHotDU1M3g1APRoN31xBjAwgAykfC5H1MzNoMzDycDANMYdIGBHT7eeTnpuoX5EaUAwDOvP5h/dl2/d1/L2dJQSEvUUt3QS9ZQnB3LzZfMEcwQUw5TDQ3RjA2SEIxUEY5MDAwMDAwMDA!/ (accessed September 8, 2009); Home Depot. "Our Mission and Outreach Efforts." http://corporate.homedepot.com/wps/portal/!ut/p/c1/04_SB8K8xLLM9MSSzPy8xBz9CPoos3gDdwNHHosfE3M3AzMPJ8MAfzcDKADKR2LKmxrD5fHr9v PIzo3VL8iNKAcAC4X4Kg!!/dl2/d1/L2dJQSEvUUt3QS9ZQnB3LzZfMEcwQUw5TDQ3RjA2SEIxUFBGMDAwMDAwMDA!/ (accessed September 8, 2009); Home Depot. "United We Can—Take on Challenges, Shape Careers and Improve Communities." https://careers.homedepot.com/cg/content.do?p=/united (accessed May 21, 2009); Home Depot. "We Build Community: Team Depot." http://corporate.homedepot.com/wps/portal/!ut/p/c1/04_SB8K8xLLM9MSSzPy8xBz9CPoos3gDdwNHHosfE3M3AzMPJ8MALxcDKADKR2LKmxrD5fHr9vPIzo3VL8iNKAcAbzcnOw!!/dl2/d1/L2dJQSEvUUt3QS9ZQnB3LzZfMEcwQUw5TDQ3RjA2SEIxUE1EMDAwMDAwMDA!/ (accessed March 12, 2009); Home Depot Foundation. "What We Do." http://www.homedepotfoundation.org/what.html (accessed September 8, 2009); Home Depot Foundation. "Our Pledge." http://www.homedepotfoundation.org/what-we-do/pledge.html (accessed February 6, 2011); Home Depot Foundation. "Building a Home, Building a Community." http://www.homedepotfoundation.org/ (accessed September 8, 2009); "Home Depot Retools Timber Policy." *Memphis Business Journal,* January 2, 2003, www.bizjournals.com/memphis/stories/2002/12/30/daily12.html (accessed September 8, 2009); "Home Depot ups 2010 outlook on strong sales, will hire." *Bloomberg Businessweek,* December 8, 2010, http://investing.businessweek.com/research/stocks/earnings/earnings.asp?ticker=HD:US (accessed February 6, 2010); Internet Retailer. "Home Depot builds out its online customer service." www.internetretailer.com/2010/06/04/home-depot-builds-out-its-online-customer-service, June 4, 2010 (accessed January 31, 2011); *PR Newswire.* "The Home Depot Launches Environmental Wood Purchasing Policy." http://www.prnewswire.com/cgi-bin/stories.pl?ACCT=104&STORY=/www/story/08-26-1999/0001010227&EDATE=, August 26, 1999 (accessed September 8, 2009); Jackson, Susan, and Tim Smart. "Mom and Pop Fight Back." *Business Week,* April 14, 1997, 46; Jacobs, Karen. "Home Depot Pushes Low Prices, Energy Savings." *Reuters,* September 10, 2008, http://www.reuters.com/article/ousiv/idUSN1051947020080910 (accessed September 8, 2009); Lloyd, Mary Ellen. "Home Improvement Spending Remains Tight." *The Wall Street Journal,* May 6, 2009, http://online.wsj.com/article/SB124162405957992133.html (accessed September 8, 2009); McGregor, Jena. "Home Depot Sheds Units." *Business Week,* January 26, 2009, http://www.businessweek.com/bwdaily/dnflash/content/jan2009/db20090126_454995.htm (accessed September 8, 2009); MSNBC. "Home Depot CEO Nardelli Quits." January 3, 2007, http://www.msnbc.msn.com/id/16451112/ (accessed March September 8, 2009); *PR Newswire.* "The Home Depot Forms Unprecedented Partnership with Four Leading National Hispanic Organizations." HispanicBusiness.com, February 15, 2005, http://www.hispanicbusiness.com/news/newsbyid.asp?idx=20997&page=1&cat=&more= (accessed September 8, 2009); Ramos, Rachel Tobin. "Home Depot in Middle of Patagonian Dam Debate." International Rivers, May 18, 2008, http://internationalrivers.org/en/node/2828 (accessed September 8, 2009); Scelfo, Julie. "The Meltdown in Home Furnishings." *The New York Times,* January 28, 2009, http://www.nytimes.com/2009/01/29/garden/29industry.html (accessed September 8, 2009); Swanekamp, Kelsey. "Home Depot Cuts Jobs." *Forbes,* January 26, 2010, http://www.forbes.com/2010/01/26/home-depot-jobs-markets-equities-cuts.html (accessed February 6, 2011); Uchitelle, Louis. "Home Depot Girds for Continued Weakness." *The New York Times,* May 18, 2009, http://www.nytimes.com/2009/05/19/business/19depot.html (accessed September 8, 2009); Zimmerman, Ann. "Home Depot Spanish Site Is Shuttered," *The Wall Street Journal,* May 2, 2009, http://online.wsj.com/article/SB124122625291179435.html (accessed September 8, 2009).

CASE 11

The Fraud of the Century: The Case of Bernard Madoff*

The fraud perpetrated by Bernard Madoff that was discovered in December 2008 was what is known as a Ponzi scheme. A Ponzi scheme works in a way that is similar to a pyramid scheme. Madoff took money from new investors to pay earnings for existing customers without ever actually investing the money. In order to keep making payouts to older clients, Madoff had to continually attract new investors. The Ponzi scheme was named after Charles Ponzi, who in the early twentieth century saw a way to profit from international reply coupons. An international reply coupon was a guarantee of return postage in response to an international letter. Ponzi determined that he could make money by swapping out these coupons for more expensive postage stamps in countries where the stamps were of higher value. Ponzi convinced investors to provide him with capital to trade coupons for higher-priced postage stamps. His promise to investors who joined in his scheme was a 50 percent profit in a few days.

Touted as a financial wizard, Ponzi lived a fairly opulent life outside of Boston. He would often bring in as much as $250,000 a day. Part of Ponzi's success came from his personal charisma and ability to con even savvy investors. People trusted Ponzi because he created an image of power, trust, and responsibility—much as Bernard Madoff did a century later. The largest problem with his scheme was that in order to keep giving earlier investors their promised return, Ponzi had to continually draw new people into the scheme. In July of 1920 the *Boston Post* ran an article exposing the scheme, and soon after that regulators raided Ponzi's offices and charged him with mail fraud, knowing that his fabricated investment reports were mailed to his clients. Most Ponzi schemes self-destruct fairly quickly as the ability to keep attracting new investors dwindles. Bernard Madoff's case was unusual because he was able to continue his fraud for many years.

BERNARD L. MADOFF INVESTMENT SECURITIES LLC: "ALL IN THE FAMILY"

Bernard Madoff was not merely a criminal. He was also a highly successful, legitimate businessperson. He started a legal investment business in 1960 buying and selling over-the-counter stocks that were not listed on the New York Stock Exchange (NYSE). These stocks were traded via telephone with no automation. This meant that an in-the-know individual

*This case was prepared by Linda Ferrell with editorial assistance from Jennifer Sawayda and Jennifer Jackson. It was prepared for classroom discussion rather than to illustrate either effective or ineffective handling of an administrative, ethical, or legal decision by management. All sources used for this case were obtained through publicly available material.

such as Madoff could profit from variations between different quotes. Basically, he served as a "wholesaler" between institutional investors. In the early days, working with investment firms such as A. G. Edwards, Charles Schwab, and others, Madoff made his money on the variance between the offer price and sales price of stocks.

In the 1990s Madoff Securities was trading up to 10 percent of the NASDAQ (National Association of Securities Dealers Automated Quotations) shares on certain days. Early success and competitive advantage came from Madoff working with his brother Peter (the first of several family members to join his firm), who after graduating from law school joined Madoff's company and developed superior technology for trading, buying, and selling at the best prices. Madoff controlled the funds in-house and made his money in this division from commissions on sales and profits. The profits were not based on fraud; however, there is evidence that Madoff occasionally injected funds from his illegal business into his legal one during times of low revenues.

As Madoff became more successful, he moved the company's headquarters from Wall Street to the famous "Lipstick Building" on Third Avenue. Madoff also became more involved in lobbying for regulatory changes that would make it easier to trade electronically. Peter Madoff took on more oversight of the firm's securities business while Bernard Madoff served as chair of the NASDAQ in 1990, 1991, and 1993. In addition, he held a seat on the government advisory board on stock market regulation, served on charitable boards, and started his own foundation, all of which added to his credibility. He developed respectability and trust as a highly knowledgeable investment specialist.

For years Madoff had been using his legitimate success and high visibility to start a second business managing money. He seemed trustworthy and promised consistent returns of 10 to 12 percent, attracting billions of dollars from hundreds of investors. Part of the appeal of investing with Bernie was the appeal of exclusivity. Madoff made every client feel like he or she was his only client. His inaccessibility and "invitation only" approach to new investors created an air of exclusivity. His wife Ruth Madoff also worked at the firm for a time, and served as a friendly face for the companies.

Peter Madoff's daughter Shana Madoff was a rules and compliance officer at Madoff's legitimate firm and worked under her father, who was head of compliance in the market-making arm (not the firm's money management business). Shana is married to Eric Swanson, a former Securities and Exchange Commission (SEC) compliance lawyer. Shana Madoff has a respected career and was honored by the Girl Scouts of America as a "woman of distinction." Although she has not been charged with any crimes, she and other members of Madoff's family are fighting a $200 million lawsuit filed by Bernie Madoff bankruptcy trustee Irving Picard.

Although also under investigation, neither of Madoff's sons, Mark and Andrew, were charged with any wrongdoing. It was to them that Madoff confessed his crime, and they were responsible for turning in their father to the authorities. The two denied any knowledge of the fraud and refused to speak to their parents for years after Madoff's arrest. The family emphasizes that the legitimate, stock-trading business (run on the nineteenth floor) was distinct from the illegitimate, investment management business (run by Madoff on the seventeenth floor).

In March 2009, when Bernard Madoff stated his guilt in court, he never indicated the involvement of any other company employees or family members. "I want to emphasize today that while my investment advisory business—the vehicle of my wrongdoing—was part of Bernard L. Madoff Securities," he stated, "the other businesses that my firm engaged in, proprietary trading and market making, were legitimate, profitable and successful in all respects. Those businesses were managed by my brother and two sons." Further investigation will determine the extent and level of external support that Madoff had in defrauding thousands. Madoff chose to hire inexperienced, sometimes uneducated individuals with no background in finance to work in his investment management business. Some speculate that he did this so as to surround himself with unknowing participants.

EXPLAINING THE GROWTH NUMBERS

Madoff staked his investment business on claims that he could consistently generate 10 to 12 percent returns for investors, no matter what the economic climate. Many of his clients were already wealthy and just looking for a stable and constant rate of return. To these people, his friends at the Palm Beach Country Club, for example, reliable constant returns managed by one of their own seemed like the perfect way to invest. His stated strategy was to buy stocks while also trading options on those stocks as a way to limit the potential losses. His market timing strategy was called the "split-strike conversion." With the large financial portfolio Madoff managed, many indicate at least one "red flag" would have been the fact that he would have had to make more trades than the market would physically allow just to meet his everyday financial goals. Shocking his clients, Madoff confessed in his Plea Allocation that he never invested any of his client's funds. All of the money was deposited in banks, and Madoff simply moved money between Chase Manhattan Bank in New York and Madoff Securities International Ltd., a U.K. Corporation. In the confession Madoff stated that his fraud began in the early 1990s.

To help continuously draw in new clients, Madoff developed relationships with intermediaries, also known as "feeders." These feeders were other investment managers who trusted Madoff to take care of their clients' money, and it does not appear that they were integrally involved in the fraud. Many of them had themselves invested money with Madoff. One such intermediary, René-Thierry Magon de la Villehuchet, committed suicide after losing his life savings to Madoff. These feeders profited by receiving fees and ensuring that Madoff had a stream of money flowing into his operation. Robert Jaffe operated as a middleperson for Madoff starting in 1989 when he became the manager of Boston-based Cohmad Securities, a firm co-owned by Madoff that he used as a means of attracting investors. Jaffe was the son-in-law of one of Madoff's earliest investors and was a member of the Palm Beach Country Club. Jaffe earned a small commission whenever Madoff took on an investor introduced to him by Jaffe.

FINANCIAL SUPPORT NEAR THE END AND THE ARREST

Toward the end of Madoff's fraud, he was becoming desperate for funds. As the economy collapsed in late 2008, more and more clients were requesting their deposits back. In order to pay them and not become exposed, Madoff needed more cash quickly. He resorted to soliciting, and sometimes subtly threatening, clients for more deposits—making them feel guilty for not being better clients of such a distinguished investment firm.

A week and a half before Madoff admitted to his sons that he was operating a Ponzi scheme, 95-year-old Palm Beach philanthropist and entrepreneur Carl Shapiro gave Madoff $250 million. Shapiro lost that money, as well as $100 million in additional funds that had belonged to a charitable organization. Martin Rosenman, the president of a fuel company in New York, also provided an additional $10 million in deposits just a few days before Madoff's Ponzi scheme collapsed. He sued to get his lost money back, but in December 2009 a federal judge upheld a bankruptcy court filing that Rosenman was not entitled to any special treatment in the case.

Of course, even these hundreds of millions in additional deposits would not have been enough to cover Madoff's losses. Possibly because he knew that the game was up, he turned himself in to his sons. Madoff was arrested on December 11. The official charge was criminal securities fraud. Madoff declared to his sons that he had roughly $200–300 million left in the business and that he wanted to provide the money to employees before turning himself over to authorities. This was news to his sons; they thought the investment arm of the business held between $8 billion and $15 billion in assets. The SEC records showed that the firm had $17 billion in assets at the beginning of 2008.

THE INVESTIGATION AND CHARGES

Investigators in this case included the SEC, FBI, federal prosecutors from the U.S. Attorney's Office for the Southern District of New York, and the Financial Industry Regulatory Authority. Forensic accountants will try to follow the trail of investments and spending to determine where the money went. Perhaps multiple offshore funds were created by Madoff to shelter assets prior to the collapse of the firm. Madoff's business was not registered with the SEC until 2006, after an SEC investigation. Investigators are now evaluating documents dating back to 2000. The charges did not come as a surprise to the SEC when Madoff was finally exposed; beginning in 1992, federal regulators had been investigating allegations of wrongdoing by Madoff. Table 1 provides a summary of the nature of these investigations.

TABLE 1 Government and Regulatory Investigations of Bernard Madoff

Year	Nature of Investigation
1992	Bernard Madoff's name came to the attention of the SEC during an investigation into the conduct of some Florida accountants
1999	SEC reviewed Madoff's trading practices
2001	Securities industry executive Harry Markopolos provided information to the SEC that generated questions regarding Madoff's returns
2004	SEC reviewed allegations of improper trading practices
2005	SEC interviewed Madoff and family but found no improper trading activities
2005	Industry-based regulatory group found no improper trading activities
2005	SEC met with Harry Markopolos, who claimed Madoff was operating the world's largest Ponzi scheme

(continued)

TABLE 1 Government and Regulatory Investigations of Bernard Madoff (*continued*)

2006	An SEC enforcement investigation found misleading behavior, and Madoff subsequently registered as an investment advisor
2007	Financial Industry Regulatory Authority investigated Madoff, but no regulatory action was taken
2008	Enforcement staff was alerted to possible corruption regarding Bernard Madoff's records, but the complaint was sent back with a note stating that allegations would not be pursued
2009	The United States SEC Office of Inspector General concluded that the SEC had received enough evidence to justify a thorough investigation of Madoff's practices; two Madoff victims file a lawsuit against the SEC
2011	A top lawyer from the SEC was sued in a Madoff "clawback" case

Source: Associated Press, "The Many Fruitless Probes into Bernie Madoff," APNewswire, January 5, 2009, http://news.moneycentral.msn.com/provider/providerarticle.aspx?feed=AP&date=20090105&id=9486677, accessed January 5, 2009. Used with permission of The Associated Press Copyright© 2011. All rights reserved.; Investigation Failure of the SEC to Uncover Bernard Madoff's Ponzi Scheme, http://www.cbsnews.com/htdocs/pdf/Report_Summary.pdf?tag=contentMain;contentBody, accessed March 7, 2011; Chad Bray and Jean Eaglesham, "SEC's Top Lawyer Sued in Madoff 'Clawback' Case," The Wall Street Journal, February 24, 2011, http://online.wsj.com/article/SB10001424052748704520504576162230809781862.html, accessed March 7, 2011; Tom Hals, "Two Madoff victims file lawsuit against the SEC," Reuters, October 14, 2009, http://www.reuters.com/article/2009/10/14/us-madoff-sec-idUSTRE59D43320091014, accessed March 7, 2011.

It is believed that much of the money invested with Madoff went either to offset losses in his legal business or to fund the Madoff family's lavish lifestyle. There is growing evidence that although family members may not have known that Madoff was running a Ponzi scheme, they thought nothing of treating his businesses like their personal piggybanks.

INVESTORS IMPACTED

The long list of Madoff clients reads like a who's who of organizations, nonprofits, successful entrepreneurs, and businesspeople, as well as celebrities such as Steven Spielberg. The Fairfield Greenwich Group, one of Madoff's largest feeder funds, had around $7.5 billion, or more than half of its assets, invested in the firm. The Noel family, owners of Fairfield Greenwich, has been so disgraced by its association with the Madoffs that their membership to the Round Hill Country Club in Greenwich, Connecticut, was revoked. Tremont Group Holdings, owned by Oppenheimer, had $3.3 billion invested. Ezra Merkin, head of a GMAC-operated hedge fund, lost $1.8 billion to Madoff. Merkin also faced civil suits after allegedly funneling more than $2 billion of charity and investor funds into Madoff's business.

Several victims have shared information about their history and relationship with Madoff, information that may provide valuable insight into how the Madoff scheme lasted so long. Richard Sonking met with Madoff in the mid-1990s after his father, who had an account with Madoff, recommended the investment firm for its steady 8–14 percent returns. Sonking pulled together the minimum $100,000 required for investment at that time, feeling confident that he was joining a highly select group of investors. Sonking continued to place money in Madoff's hands as he accumulated greater wealth. As with all of Madoff's clients, he was happy with the constant returns and with the detailed statements that were mailed to him each month. Like others, he never questioned why Madoff did not make online records available, nor did he question the secrecy to which Madoff swore his investors. Upon retiring in 2005, Sonking requested quarterly distributions from his account. As with most of Madoff's loyal investors, Sonking received no warnings of fraudulent activity until he heard the news of Madoff's arrest.

Loretta Weinberg, a New Jersey state senator, was a conservative investor who embraced her late husband's philosophy that you should live on half of what you make and save the rest. She had no investments with Madoff, but she did place money in the hands of Stanley Chais, a Los Angeles money manager who provided quarterly investment reports and a 10–14 percent annual return. It just so happened that Chais was a feeder with Madoff, funneling much of his clients' money Madoff's way. Until the Madoff scandal hit the press, Weinberg had not even heard of Madoff. As a 73-year-old state senator making $49,000/year, she is coming to terms with what it means to have lost her life savings, $1.3 million.

Joseph Gurwin, who died Sept. 24, 2009, at age 89, lived in Palm Beach. Like many others, he came to know Madoff and became his friend through the local social and philanthropic community. Madoff had a tremendous reputation for secure and conservative financial management, and it was considered a huge honor among the elites in Palm Beach to be invested with him. Gurwin's foundation (The J. Gurwin Foundation, Inc.), operating with around $28 million in assets, donated $1.2 million annually to Jewish health care, services, and programs for frail, elderly, or disabled younger adults. After investing heavily with Madoff, Gurwin's charitable foundation lost all of its assets when the Ponzi scheme crashed.

> "Madoff had a tremendous reputation for secure and conservative financial management."

Law firms in Florida represented clients who believed they were investing with Westport National Bank (a regulated banking institution in Connecticut), and not with Madoff, but who had received a letter from Westport National indicating that they had a custodial agreement giving full discretionary authority to Bernard L. Madoff Investment Securities. As these cases demonstrate, Madoff's sweep went far beyond his immediate circle.

LAWSUITS AND RESTITUTION

So far thousands of people have submitted claims for restitution in the Madoff case. However, paying back all these investors will be a difficult task. Although Madoff's fraud is billed as a $65 billion Ponzi scheme, Madoff never had anywhere near that amount of money. The figure of $65 billion is the total amount Madoff told people they had invested and earned with him. The actual amount may be well below $10 billion.

In 2008 Irving Picard was appointed the trustee for the liquidation of Bernard L. Madoff Investment Securities LLC. Under federal law, the trustee for the Madoff bankruptcy suit can sue to retrieve money in what are called "clawback" suits. Picard has unleashed a number of lawsuits against both individuals and institutions that he believes directly or indirectly contributed to the fraud. Picard is seeking over $34 billion from banks, feeder funds, investors, and other institutions. Table 2 lists some of the individuals and organizations named in the lawsuits. Picard believes the defendants knew or should have known about the fraud that Madoff was committing. For instance, in the lawsuit filed against JP Morgan Chase, Picard claims that the company had discussed warning signs that Madoff might be committing fraud but chose not to act. JP Morgan Chase denied the charges.

TABLE 2 Defendants Named in Madoff Lawsuits

Name	Damages Sought
Citigroup	$425 million
Merrill Lynch	$16 million
Fred Wilpon and Saul Katz, owner of Mets	$1 billion
Sonja Kohn	$19.6 billion
Jeffrey Picower	Widow settled for $7.2 billion
Madoff Family	$200 million
JP Morgan Chase	$6.4 billion
David Becker	$1.5 million

©Cengage Learning 2013

Another issue that regulators face involves calculating the losses from the Madoff fraud and prioritizing the victims. Financially speaking, the Madoff fraud has resulted in two types of victims: net losers and net winners. Net losers are those who put in more money initially than they ended up receiving—they lost money. This is the case with thousands of Madoff investors who lost their life savings and retirement money in the fraud. Net winners are those who recouped their original investment and additional profits— profits which turned out to be fictional, as Madoff never invested the money but instead used the cash from new investors to pay returns. Part of the dispute involves whether net winners like Mets owners Fred Wilpon and Saul Katz should be forced to return these fictional profits. Picard and the SEC also argue that net losers should be first in line to receive compensation from the bankruptcy proceedings. Net winners can collect money from whatever is left over. Finally, the formula proposed by Picard for recouping the investments of net losers stipulates that the money net losers are owed is the difference between what the investors put in and what they took out. The problem is that this formula does not account for the loss of value that might have occurred naturally due to market forces. There is no easy solution to this matter, and the fraud has made it very difficult to determine who is owed what.

The Madoff family in particular has been forced to deal with the consequences of Bernard Madoff's wrongdoing. Madoff's wife Ruth gave up claims to $80 million in assets to federal prosecutors. The couple's sons Mark and Andrew suffered possibly irrecoverable damage to their reputations, prompting Mark Madoff's wife and their two young sons to change their last names. Tragically, Mark Madoff committed suicide on December 11, 2010, the two-year anniversary of Bernard Madoff's arrest, while his son slept in the next bedroom. Although he expressed condolences, Picard continued the lawsuit against Mark Madoff's estate, as he believed that the family received tens of millions of dollars from the fraud.

Investigators are also looking into potential misconduct on the part of some of Madoff's clients. For example, Picard alleges that Austrian banker Sonja Kohn used feeder funds to invest her clients' money with Madoff in exchange for kickbacks (Ms. Kohn's lawyers call the suit "groundless"). According to investigations, Madoff feeder funds withdrew over $12 billion in 2008, with half of that money being withdrawn in the three months leading up to his arrest—a huge sum that probably led to Madoff's confession when he could no longer pull together cash to make payments. The argument is that the $12 billion was essentially "stolen" from other investors who actually owned the money. Hence, to protect their assets from seizure, many who received payout funds from Madoff are transferring the money to irrevocable trusts, homes, annuities, or life insurance policies.

One of Picard's lawsuits sought remuneration from a prominent Madoff client and Palm Beach investor named Jeffry Picower. Although Picower's charitable fund was one of the highest-profile victims of the Madoff downfall, investigators suspect some foul play. Part of the concern is that as a professional investor, Picower should have known that the profits he was getting from Madoff were too high. The accusations further state that Picower was getting payments from Madoff to help perpetuate the Ponzi scheme, which means that Picower would have known about the scheme all along. After Picower passed away, his widow agreed to pay $7.2 billion without admitting any wrongdoing on her husband's part. Other people who chose to settle claims include Maurice Cohn and his daughter Marcia of Cohmad Securities Corp., who received over $100 million for referring investors to Madoff. The SEC had accused the Cohns of negligence in communicating with potential Madoff investors and with not keeping accurate financial records (they too have denied any wrongdoing). These are only a few of what will surely amount to dozens of lawsuits and settlements related to the attempt to recover and redistribute funds from Madoff clients. Undoubtedly this web will take years to untangle as investigators seek to learn who knew about Madoff's scheme and are therefore guilty of complicity.

Finally, some investors are suing the SEC for negligence in its regulatory capacity for not identifying the fraud. Such attempts represent the first time investors have sought restitution from a regulatory agency. Christopher Cox, SEC chair at the start of the fraud investigation, has indicated that the SEC examiners missed "red flags" in reviewing the Madoff firm. Allegations of wrongdoing started in the early 1990s, and Madoff confirms fraud dating back to that time. Repeated investigations and examinations by the SEC showed no investment fraud. In 2001 Harry Markopolos, a security industry executive, raised concerns about Madoff's activities. Once again the SEC did not find evidence of improper practices. Because many SEC employees have ended up working in the investment business on Wall Street, there has been speculation that an overall lack of objectivity clouded these investigations. In the wake of the Madoff fallout, it has become clear that some SEC investigators were sufficiently knowledgeable about the kinds of complex financial instruments used on Wall Street. Thus, they should have been knowledgeable enough to be able to detect the fraud.

> "Some investors are suing the SEC for negligence in its regulatory capacity for not identifying the fraud."

Additionally, the SEC has been criticized for potential conflict of interest. The issue first came into the public consciousness after former SEC general counsel David Becker and his brother were sued by Irving Picard for $1.5 million. Picard claimed that the money, which was part of an inheritance from Becker's mother, was generated from investments with Bernard Madoff. The issue generated controversy because Becker had not removed himself from decisions related to the Madoff fraud during his time as SEC legal counsel. Some regulators believe that because Becker indirectly profited from a Madoff investment, his participation in decisions concerning the fraud violated the agency's conflict-of-interest policies. Although SEC Chairwoman Mary Schapiro remarked that she did not view this as a violation, she agreed to launch a review of the agency's policies.

Perhaps the greatest restitution for some investors came as Bernard Madoff was handcuffed and taken to prison after his twelve-minute confession of guilt in a Lower Manhattan courthouse. Some victims asked the judge Denny Chin for a trial to uncover more about this extensive fraud and to determine why the government regulatory system failed so many investors. Judge Chin indicated there would be no trial since Madoff had pleaded guilty and there was an ongoing investigation. On June 29, 2009, Madoff was sentenced to 150 years in prison.

So what does Bernard Madoff think about his fraud? During a prison interview, he explained that when he first started committing fraud in the 1990s, he thought he could get back on track. However, everything spiraled out of control. Although he claimed full responsibility for the fraud and for ruining the lives of his family members, he also said that his reason for starting the fraud was pressure from his four largest investors. He maintained that the majority of people who invested with him should have had suspicions. Additionally, he said, banks and hedge funds should have known that fraud was taking place. Thus, he appeared to try to shift the blame for the fiasco onto others.

THE FUTURE OF CHARITABLE GIVING

The Madoff fraud affected charities, nonprofits, and educational institutions including the Elie Wiesel Foundation for Humanity, Yeshiva University, and Wunderkinder Foundation (Steven Spielberg's fund). The vast majority of nonprofits indicated that the economy had had a negative impact on fundraising even before the Madoff scandal was exposed. In the future, it is certain that charities and donors alike will approach the donation process with greater care.

CONCLUSION

Bernard Madoff, who is serving his sentence at the Butner Federal Correctional Complex near Raleigh, N.C., is accused of creating a Ponzi scheme that lost $65 billion in investments. From an ethical perspective, this would be an example of white-collar crime. White-collar criminals dupe their victims by establishing themselves as trustworthy and respectable figures. As in this case, victims of white-collar crime are trusting clients who believe there are sufficient checks and balances to certify that an operation is legitimate. Madoff was an educated and experienced individual in a position of power, trust, respectability, and responsibility who abused his trust for personal gains. From the inception of his investment business, he knew that he was operating a Ponzi scheme and defrauding his clients. In the end, he said he "knew this day would come."

An important question is how one individual could deceive so many intelligent people and officials who certified his operation as legitimate. Madoff's accountants, family, and other employees will have to answer to authorities about their knowledge of the operations. Seven people have been criminally charged, including Madoff's key lieutenant Frank DiPascali, who confessed to lying to investigators and helping to fabricate documents. David Friehling, a New York accountant who audited Madoff's financial statements, also confessed to securities fraud but denied knowledge of the Ponzi scheme.

White-collar crime is unique in that it is often perpetrated by a rogue individual who knowingly steals, cheats, or manipulates in order to damage others. Often, the only way to prevent white-collar crime is to have internal controls and compliance standards that detect misconduct. In the Madoff case, the opportunity existed to deceive others without effective audits, transparency, or understanding of the true nature of the operation. As a result of this case, individual investors, institutions, and hopefully regulators will exert more diligence in demanding transparency and honesty from those who manage investments.

QUESTIONS

1. What are the ethical issues involved in the Madoff case?

2. Do you believe that Bernard Madoff worked alone, or do you think he had help in creating and sustaining his Ponzi scheme?

3. What should be done to help ensure that Ponzi schemes like Madoff's do not happen in the future?

SOURCES

Bandler, James, and Nicholas Varchaver with Doris Burke. "How Bernie Did It." *Fortune,* May 11, 2009, 50–71; "Bernard L. Madoff." *The New York Times,* December 18, 2010, http://topics.nytimes.com/top/reference/timestopics/people/m/bernard_l_madoff/index.html (accessed February 11, 2011); Bernard L. Madoff Investment Securities LLC Liquidation Proceeding website, http://www.madofftrustee.com/ (accessed February 2, 2011); Bernstein, Elizabeth. "After Madoff, Donors Grow Wary of Giving." *The Wall Street Journal,* December 23, 2008, http://online.wsj.com/article/SB122999068109728409.html (accessed September 2, 2009); Bray, Chad. "Kohn's Lawyer Calls Madoff Suit Groundless." *The Wall Street Journal,* December 13, 2010, http://online.wsj.com/article/SB10001424052748704681804576017522481432448.html (accessed February 2, 2011); Bray, Chad. "Madoff Trustee: Mets Owners Ignored Ponzi Warning Signs." *The Wall Street Journal,* February 4, 2011, http://online.wsj.com/article/SB10001424052748704709304576124104225741650.html?mod=djemalertNEWS (accessed February 5, 2011); Bray, Chad, and Michael Rothfeld. "Two Ex-Madoff Employees Indicted." *The Wall Street Journal,* November 19, 2010, http://topics.wsj.com/article/SB20001424052748704104104575622301407122546.html (accessed February 2, 2011); Bryan-Low, Cassel. "Inside a Swiss Bank, Madoff Warnings." *The Wall Street Journal,* January 14, 2009, 1A; Catan, Thomas, Christopher Bjork, and Jose De Cordoba. "Giant Bank Probe over Ties to Madoff." *The Wall Street Journal,* January 13, 2009, http://online.wsj.com/article/SB123179728255974859.html (accessed September 2, 2009); CBS News. "Madoff: Pressure from big clients led to scam." April 9, 2011, http://www.cbsnews.com/stories/2011/04/09/earlyshow/saturday/main20052422.shtml (accessed May 11, 2011); Eaglesham, Jean, and Jessica Holzer. "Schapiro Defends against GOP Fire." *The Wall Street Journal,* March 10, 2011, C1; Efrati, Amir. "Q&A on the Madoff Case." *The Wall Street Journal,* March 12, 2009, http://online.wsj.com/article/SB123005811322430633.html (accessed September 2, 2009); Efrati, Amir. "Scope of Alleged Fraud Is Still Being Assessed." *The Wall Street Journal,* December 18, 2008, http://online.wsj.com/article/SB122953110854314501.html (accessed September 2, 2009); Efrati, Amir, and Chad Bray. "U.S.: Madoff Had $173 Million in Checks." *The Wall Street Journal,* January 9, 2009, http://online.wsj.com/article/SB123143634250464871.html (accessed September 2, 2009); Efrati, Amir, Aaron Luccchetti, and Tom Lauricella. "Probe Eyes Audit Files, Role of Aide to Madoff." *The Wall Street Journal,* September 2, 2009, http://online.wsj.com/article/SB122999256957528605.html (accessed December 23, 2008); Frank, Robert, and Amir Efrati. "Madoff Tried to Stave off Firm's Crash before Arrest." *The Wall Street Journal,* January 7, 2009, http://online.wsj.com/article/SB123129835145559987.html (accessed September 2, 2009); Frank, Robert, and Tom Lauricella. "Madoff Created Air of Mystery." *The Wall Street Journal,* December 20, 2008, http://online.wsj.com/article/SB122973208705022949.html (accessed September 2, 2009); Goldfarb, Zachary. "Investment Advisors Would Face More Scrutiny under SEC Proposal." *The Washington Post*, May 15, 2009, http://www.washingtonpost.com/wp-dyn/content/article/2009/05/14/AR2009051403970.html?hpid=topnews (accessed September 2, 2009); Hays, Tom. "Trustee: Nearly 9,000 claims in Madoff scam." *The San Francisco Chronicle*, May 14, 2009, http://www.sfgate.com/cgi-bin/article.cgi?f=/n/a/2009/05/14/financial/f090030D98.DTL&feed=rss.business (accessed September 2, 2009); Heller, Jamie, and Joanna Chung. "Life after Madoff's 'Big Lie.'" *The Wall Street Journal*, December 11, 2010, http://online.wsj.com/article/SB10001424052748703727804576011451297639480.html (accessed February 2, 2011); Henriques, Diana B. "From Prison, Madoff Says Banks 'Had to Know' of Fraud." *The New York Times*, February 15, 2011, http://www.nytimes.com/2011/02/16/business/madoff-prison-interview.html (accessed May 11, 2011); Henriques, Diana B. "Madoff Victims Have Their Day in Appeals Court." *The New York Times*, March 3, 2011, http://www.nytimes.com/2011/03/04/business/04madoff.html (accessed March 4, 2011); Henriques, Diana B., and Zachery Kouwe. "Billions Withdrawn before Madoff Arrest." *The New York Times*, May 12, 2009, http://www.nytimes.com/2009/05/13/business/13madoff.html?_r=1&scp=1&sq=madoff%20%2412%20billion&st=cse (accessedSeptember 2, 2009); Kim, Jane J. "As 'Clawback' Suits Loom, Some Investors Seek Cover." *The Wall Street Journal*, March 12, 2009, C3. Lenzner, Robert. "JP Morgan Chase May Be Complicit in Madoff Scandal." *Forbes*, February 4, 2011, http://blogs.forbes.com/robertlenzner/2011/02/04/j-p-morgan-chase-may-be-complicit-in-madoff-scandal/ (accessed May 11, 2011); Lucchetti, Aaron. "Victims Welcome Madoff Imprisonment." *The Wall Street Journal*, March 13, 2009, http://online.wsj.com/article/SB123687992688609801.html (accessed September 2, 2009); Madoff, Bernard. "Plea Allocution of Bernard L. Madoff." *The Wall Street Journal*, March 12, 2009, http://online.wsj.com/public/resources/documents/20090315madoffall.pdf (accessed September 2, 2009); "Madoff's Victims." *The Wall Street Journal*, March 6, 2009, http://s.wsj.net/public/resources/documents/st_madoff_victims_20081215.html (accessed September 2, 2009); Pettersson, Edvard, and Bob Van Voris. "Citigroup, Bank of America Sued by Madoff Trustee." *Bloomberg Businessweek*, December 9, 2010, http://www.businessweek.com/news/2010-12-09/citigroup-bank-of-america-sued-by-madoff-trustee.html (accessed February 2, 2011); Rieker, Matthias. "Victims of Scandal Reflect on Shocking Turnabout." *The Wall Street Journal*, December 23, 2008, http://online.wsj.com/article/SB122972955226822819.html (accessed September 2, 2009); Ross, Brian, Anna Schecter, and Mark Schone. "Mark Madoff Wore 'Heart His Heart on His Sleeve.'" ABC News, December13,2010,http://abcnews.go.com/Blotter/mark-madoff-suicide-stop-lawsuits/story?id=12379077&page=1 (accessed February 2, 2011); Rothfeld, Michael. "U.S. Eyes Madoff Kin as Probe Grinds On." *The Wall Street Journal*, December 11, 2010, http://online.wsj.com/article/SB10001424052748703727804576011852515747500.html (accessed February 2, 2010); Rothfeld, Michael, and Chad Bray. "Widow to Return $7.2 Billion." *The Wall Street Journal*, December 17, 2010, http://online.wsj.com/article/SB10001424052748704034804576025392596402176.html (accessed February 11, 2011); Rubin, Adam. "Picard amends suit against Wilpons." ESPN New York, March 18, 2011, http://espn.go.com/blog/new-york/mets/post/_/id/17066/picard-amends-suit-against-wilpons (accessed May 11, 2011); Scannell, Kara. "Investor Who Lost Money in Alleged Scheme Seeks Relief from SEC." *The Wall Street Journal*, December 23, 2008, http://online.wsj.com/article/SB122999646876429063.html (accessed September 2, 2009); Strasburg, Jenny. "Madoff 'Feeders' under Focus." *The Wall Street Journal*, December 27–28, 2008, A1, A8; Stapleton, Christine. "Madoff scandal ripples among Palm Beach county foundations." *The Palm Beach Post*, February 8, 2009, http://www.palmbeachpost.com/localnews/content/local_news/epaper/2009/02/08/a1b_foundations_0209.html (accessed September 2, 2009); Strasburg, Jenny. "Mass Mutual Burned by Madoff." *The Wall Street Journal*, December 22, 2008, C1; Trex, Ethan. "Who Was Ponzi—What the Heck Was His Scheme?" CNN.com, December 23, 2008, http://www.cnn.com/2008/LIVING/wayoflife/12/23/mf.ponzi.scheme/index.html (accessed September 2, 2009); Van Voris, Bob. "Madoff Trustee Told Mets' Owners They Should Have Known of Ponzi Scheme." *Bloomberg*, February 2, 2011, http://www.bloomberg.com/news/2011-02-01/madoff-trustee-told-mets-they-should-have-known-of-ponzi-scheme.html (accessed February 2, 2011); Williamson, Elizabeth. "Shana Madoff's Ties to Uncle Probed." *The Wall Street Journal*, December 22, 2008, http://online.wsj.com/article/SB122991035662025577.html (accessed September 2, 2009).

CASE 12

Insider Trading at the Galleon Group*

The Galleon Group was a privately owned hedge fund firm that provided services and information about investments such as stocks, bonds, and other financial instruments. Galleon made money for itself and others by picking stocks and managing portfolios and hedge funds for investors. At its peak, Galleon was responsible for more than $7 billion in investor income. The company's philosophy was that it was possible to deliver superior returns to investors without employing leverage or timing tactics. Founded in 1997, Galleon attracted employees from firms such as Goldman Sachs, Needham & Co., and ING Barings. Every month, the company held meetings in which executives explained the status and strategy of each fund to investors. In addition, Galleon told investors that no employee would be personally trading in any stock or fund that the investors held.

In 2009 Raj Rajaratnam, the head of Galleon, was indicted on 14 counts of securities fraud and conspiracy. He and five others were accused of insider trading related to using nonpublic information from company insiders and consultants to make millions in personal profits. Rajaratnam's trial began in 2011, and he pleaded not guilty.

RAJ RAJARATNAM

Rajaratnam, born in Sri Lanka to a middle-class family, received his bachelor's degree in engineering from the University of Sussex in England. In 1983 he earned his MBA from the University of Pennsylvania's Wharton School of Business. With a focus on the computer chip industry, he meticulously developed contacts. He went to manufacturing plants, talked to employees, and connected with executives who would later work with Galleon on their IPOs.

In 1985 the investment banking boutique Needham & Co. hired Rajaratnam as an analyst. The corporate culture at Needham & Co. profoundly influenced Rajaratnam and his business philosophy. George Needham was obsessive about minimizing expenses, making employees stay in budget hotel rooms and take midnight flights to and from meetings. The company also urged analysts to gather as much information as possible. Analysts were encouraged to sift through garbage, question disgruntled employees, and even place people in jobs in the target industries. They went to professional meetings, questioned academics doing research and consulting, and set up clandestine agencies that collected information. At Needham & Co., Rajaratnam developed an aggressive networking and note-taking research strategy that enabled him to make very accurate predictions about companies' financial situations.

*This case was prepared by John Fraedrich and Harper Baird. It was prepared for classroom discussion rather than to illustrate either effective or ineffective handling of an administrative, ethical, or legal decision by management. All sources used for this case were obtained through publicly available material.

After a while at Needham, Rajaratnam's personality began to impact the company's culture. Rajaratnam once told a new analyst that Needham's name was on the company, but he was the boss. He began to push ethical limits when gathering information about companies. For example, concerns about Rajaratnam's activities ended Paine Webber's interest in buying Needham. Soon, similar worries spurred complaints from some inside Needham. By 1996 at least five Needham executives were worried about Rajaratnam's conduct. Additionally, many of Needham's clients complained that Rajaratnam had potentially conflicting roles in the firm as president, fund manager, and sometime stock analyst. Normally, investment banks keep those areas separate to prevent clients' interests from clashing with the interests of bank-run funds. In 1996, after 11 years at Needham, Rajaratnam left the company and started the Galleon Group, taking several Needham employees with him.

ACCUSATIONS OF INSIDER TRADING AT GALLEON

At Galleon, Rajaratnam developed a flamboyant leadership style. During one meeting, Rajaratnam hired a dwarf to act as an analyst hired to cover "small-cap" stocks. At another meeting, when executives from stun-gun maker Taser International, Inc., came to make an investment pitch, Rajaratnam offered $5,000 to anyone who'd agree to be shocked. One trader, Keryn Limmer, volunteered to be tased and went unconscious. Rajaratnam also used his wealth to grow Galleon's business. He held a Super Bowl party in a $250,000-a-week mansion on a man-made island in Biscayne Bay for wealthy investors and executives.

At the same time, Rajaratnam also contributed to various causes that promoted development in the Indian subcontinent, as well as programs that benefited lower-income South Asian youths in the New York area. He joined the board of the Harlem Children's Zone, an education nonprofit, and later raised about $7.5 million for victims of the South Asian tsunami. He was acknowledged as a celebrity donor and was even honored with a symphony performance at Lincoln Center.

However, Rajaratnam was already in trouble with the government. In 2005 he paid over $20 million to settle a federal investigation into a fake tax shelter to hide $52 million. Rajaratnam and his business partner then sued their lawyers, claiming that they had no idea the shelter was illegal; the pair was awarded $10 million in damages. Galleon also paid $2 million in 2005 to settle an SEC investigation into its stock trading practices. In addition, Intel discovered in 2001 that Roomy Khan, an Intel employee, had leaked information about sales and production to Rajaratnam. When Khan left Intel, she took a job with Galleon. Although Intel reported the incidents to the authorities, no one could prove that Rajaratnam had actually made trades based on the inside information about Intel.

> "There is a constant struggle to gather key information that can predict changes in stock prices, quarterly reports, and revenue."

Analysts live or die on the information they can acquire on publicly traded firms. As such, there is a constant struggle to gather key information that can predict changes in stock prices, quarterly reports, and revenue. Rajaratnam had a deep network of acquaintances, including employees at Goldman Sachs Group, Intel Corp., McKinsey & Co., and Applied Materials, Inc. Federal investigators grew more suspicious that the networking and research at Galleon involved illegal activities, however. In 2007 SEC lawyers discovered a new text message from Roomy Khan advising Rajaratnam to "wait for guidance" before buying a stock. The SEC had convinced Khan to cooperate in their investigation and allow them to record her conversations with Rajaratnam. This single wiretap eventually led to the discovery of several insider trading rings as investigators persuaded more people to participate in the investigation over the course of two years. More than 40 people are mentioned in the criminal complaint from the FBI, and 26 people (including hedge fund managers, lawyers, executives, and analysts) were eventually charged with crimes. Table 1 describes the central players.

TABLE 1 Central Players in the Galleon Information Network

Player and employer	Shared insider information about	Charges
Raj Rajaratnam Galleon		At the center of the insider trading network; pled not guilty to 14 charges of insider trading and fraud
Danielle Chiesi New Castle/Bear Stearns	IBM, Sun Microsystems, and AMD	Pled guilty to charges of insider trading
Roomy Khan Intel, Galleon	Intel, Hilton, Google, Kronos	Pled guilty to charges of securities and conspiracy fraud and agreed to the government's request to use wiretaps
Anil Kumar McKinsey & Co.	AMD	Pled guilty to passing inside information to Rajaratnam in exchange for $1.75 million
Rajiv Goel Intel	Intel	Pled guilty to passing inside information
Rajat K. Gupta Goldman Sachs	Goldman Sachs, Procter & Gamble, McKinsey	Accused by the SEC of passing insider tips to Rajaratnam
Adam Smith Galleon	Galleon, ATI, AMD	Pled guilty to giving inside information directly to Rajaratnam over a six-year period
Michael Cardillo Galleon	Axcan Pharma, Procter & Gamble	Pled guilty to receiving tips indirectly from Rajaratnam; allegedly has evidence about Rajaratnam's trades based on insider information
Zvi Goffer, a.k.a. the "Octopussy" Schottenfeld Group, Galleon	Hilton, several others	Had a reputation for having multiple sources of inside information; allegedly paid others and gave them prepaid mobile phones to avoid detection

©Cengage Learning 2013

THE TRIAL

In October 2009 Raj Rajaratnam was arrested on 14 charges of securities and wire fraud and accused of gaining over $63.8 million from insider tips. Rajaratnam was released on a $100 million bond and immediately hired several top defense attorneys and public relations specialists. His trial began in March 2011.

The laws on insider trading are vague, which often makes it difficult to convict white-collar criminals. Prosecutors had to prove that Rajaratnam not only traded on information that he knew was confidential but also that the information was important enough to affect the price of a company's stock. The government's main evidence was 45 recorded phone calls between individuals suspected of insider trading, including six witnesses who had already pled guilty and were aiding federal investigators. In many of these phone calls, Raj Rajaratnam discussed confidential information with investors and insiders before the information was released to the public. In one recording, Rajaratnam told employees to cover up evidence of insider trading. Another recording suggests that Rajaratnam received a tip from someone on Goldman Sach's board that the company's stock price was going to decrease. He was recorded as saying, "I heard yesterday from somebody who is on the board of Goldman Sachs that they are going to lose $2 per share." That information had been talked about during a confidential Goldman Sachs board meeting only a day earlier.

The challenge for the prosecution was to prove that Rajaratnam used these tips to make illicit trades. Wiretaps of conversations between Goldman Sachs board member Rajat Gupta and Rajaratnam, along with Rajaratnam's subsequent actions, implies that this occurred. For instance, during a board meeting on September 23, 2008, Goldman board members discussed a $5 billion preferred stock investment in Goldman Sachs by Berkshire Hathaway along with a public equity offering. According to the prosecution, a few minutes after the meeting Gupta called Rajaratnam. That same day, right before the market closed, Galleon bought 175,000 shares in Goldman. The announcement about Berkshire Hathaway was announced after the market closed, and the next morning the stock had gone from $125.05 to $128.44. Galleon liquidated the stock and generated a profit of $900,000.

The government also has several key witnesses from the insider trading rings who are cooperating with investigators. Before the start of Rajaratnam's trial, 19 members of the Galleon network pled guilty to charges of insider trading, and some agreed to testify against Rajaratnam. Anil Kumar, who pleaded guilty to providing insider information in exchange for over $1.75 million wired to a secret offshore account, told the jury that Rajaratnam offered to hire him as a consultant but told him that traditional industry research "wasn't really what I [Rajaratnam] want." Kumar says Rajaratnam also told him, "You have such great ideas. It's worth a lot of money."

> "The prosecution argued that Rajaratnam corrupted his friends and employees in order to make profits for himself and for Galleon."

The prosecution argued that Rajaratnam corrupted his friends and employees in order to make profits for himself and for Galleon. In his closing argument, Assistant U.S. Attorney Reed Brodsky said, "Getting information that others didn't have was very valuable. In a world of uncertainty, he had certainty because he had insiders who knew tomorrow's news today."

In order to convict Rajaratnam of insider trading, the government had to prove that the information he had received could only have been acquired via inside sources. Rajaratnam's defense maintained that some of the information Rajaratnam used was publicly available and that he was not aware that other information had not been publicly disclosed. The defense argued that Galleon's public announcements, press releases, investor meetings, government filings, and additional sources showed that the information had appeared days and weeks before Rajaratnam and others had used that information. Good investment advisors are in the business of acquiring, analyzing, and making calculated predictions so that their clients' investments increase. The defense attorneys argued that Rajaratnam's access to corporate executives was the reason his investors hired him. The defense also claimed that these same executives were aware of the law and of their own duties to their employers and shareholders; that they ought to have known what they could and could not say about their businesses, whereas Rajaratnam's obligations were to his investors.

Rajaratnam lost money on some of the trades that the government said were based on inside information. The defense argued that if he had had insider information, the opposite should be true. The defense maintained that Galleon's analysts were right about half of the time, and that if they were cheating, then they should have been right all the time. The defense also questioned the validity of some of the prosecution's witnesses. For example, one witness confessed to the fabrication of a false affidavit, a false doctor's letter, false tax forms, and false bank letters, allegedly to protect his original statements to the prosecution. The defense argued that many of the prosecution's witnesses lied to save themselves from heavier prison terms for unrelated misdeeds. Anil Kumar testified that, between 2004 and 2009, he gave material nonpublic information about several companies to Rajaratnam. Galleon's records show that Kumar was paid consulting fees for his advice and guidance but that he never shared these consulting fees with his McKinsey partners. Instead, he hid them in shell companies in overseas bank accounts and failed to report these consulting fees on his tax returns. Then there is Rajiv Goel, who allegedly gave Rajaratnam material nonpublic information he obtained from his employer, Intel. The defense argues that Goel filed false tax returns unrelated to Rajaratnam and now is facing 25 years in prison. The only way out was for him to testify against Rajaratnam.

THE VERDICT

After 12 days of deliberation, the jury declared Raj Rajaratnam guilty of all 14 counts of securities fraud and conspiracy. In total, the counts carried a potential sentence of 205 years in prison, although Rajaratnam will likely get a much lighter sentence. One juror said later, "We all wanted to give Raj the benefit of the doubt. I wanted to believe he was an honest man. How could someone so smart and rich already be involved in something so horrendous?" Jurors cited the recorded conversations between Rajaratnam and his trading network as some of the most convincing evidence. In addition to collecting insider information, Rajaratnam seemed to treat his informants and employees with apathy and sometimes animosity. Rajaratnam and his defense team plan to appeal the decision.

THE IMPACT OF THE GALLEON CASE

The Galleon case is the largest investigation into insider trading within hedge funds. Twenty-six people were charged with fraud and conspiracy. Galleon closed in 2009 after investors quickly withdrew over $4 billion in investments from the company. In addition, over a dozen companies' stocks were traded based on allegedly nonpublic information (see Table 2). These trades could have affected the financial status of the companies, their stock prices, and their shareholders.

TABLE 2. Companies Affected by Galleon's Alleged Insider Information Network

3Com Corp
Advanced Micro Devices
Akamai Technologies
Atheros
Axcan Pharma
Goldman Sachs
Google
Hilton Hotels
IBM
Intel
Kronos
Marvell Technology Group
Polycom
Procter & Gamble
Sun Microsystems

©Cengage Learning 2013

The Galleon insider trading investigation was the first to use techniques usually used to convict people of involvement in terrorism, drugs, and organized crime. Former federal prosecutor Robert Mintz said, "This is a landmark case in that it is the first time prosecutors used wiretap evidence in an insider-trading case. This conviction will undoubtedly embolden prosecutors, and we can expect more of these cases in the future." Because investment firms rely on email, phone calls, and other digital information, electronic surveillance will likely become the technique of choice for white collar crime investigators. Federal authorities also hope that the Galleon convictions will deter other powerful investment managers from engaging in insider trading. Manhattan U.S. Attorney Preet Bharara said, "Unlawful insider trading should be offensive to everyone who believes in, and relies on, the market. It cheats the ordinary investor. ... We will continue to pursue and prosecute those who believe they are both above the law and too smart to get caught."

QUESTIONS

1. Are information gathering techniques like Rajaratnam's common on Wall Street? If so, what could regulators, investors, and executives do to reduce the practice?

2. What are the implications of sharing confidential material information? Is it something that would affect your decision about how to trade a stock if you knew about it?

3. Do you think the secret investigation and conviction of Rajaratnam and other people in the Galleon network will deter other fund managers and investors from sharing non-public information?

SOURCES

Andrews, Suzanna. "How Gupta Came Undone." *Bloomberg Businessweek,* May 23-May 29, 2011, pp. 56-63; Berenson, Alex. "For Galleon Executive, Swagger in the Spotlight." *The New York Times,* November 1, 2009, http://www.nytimes.com/2009/11/02/business/02insider.html (accessed April 22, 2011); Dealbook. "Timeline of Key Events in the Galleon Case." *The New York Times Dealbook,* March 7, 2011, http://dealbook.nytimes.com/2011/03/07/timeline-of-key-events-in-the-galleon-case (accessed April 22, 2011); "The Defense of Raj Rajaratnam." http://rajdefense.org (accessed April 18, 2011); Dowd, John. "Defense Attorney's Opening Statement, *United States of America vs. Raj Rajaratnam.*" RajDefense.org, March 9, 2011, http://rajdefense.org/wp-content/uploads/2011.03.09-Opening-Statement-by-John-Dowd.pdf (accessed April 18, 2011); "Galleon's Web." *The Wall Street Journal,* March 10, 2011, http://online.wsj.com/article/SB10001424052748703386704576186592268116056.html (accessed April 18, 2011); Glovin, David, Patricia Hurtado, and Bob Van Voris. "Galleon's Rajaratnam Talked on Tape About Goldman Board Source." *Bloomberg Businessweek,* March 31, 2011, http://www.businessweek.com/news/2011-03-31/galleon-s-rajaratnam-talked-on-tape-about-goldman-board-source.html (accessed July 7, 2011); Glovin, David, Patricia Hurtado, and Bob Van Voris. "Rajaratnam Sought to 'Conquer' Wall Street, U.S. Tells Jurors." *Bloomberg Businessweek,* April 21, 2011, http://www.businessweek.com/news/2011-04-21/rajaratnam-sought-to-conquer-wall-street-u-s-tells-jurors.html (accessed April 25, 2011); Guth, Robert A., and Justin Scheck. "The Man Who Wired Silicon Valley." *The Wall Street Journal,* December 30, 2009, http://online.wsj.com/article/SB126204917965408363.html (accessed April 18, 2011); Kouwe, Zachery, and Michael J. De la Merced. "Galleon Chief and Associate Indicted in Insider Case." *The New York Times,* December 15, 2009, http://www.nytimes.com/2009/12/16/business/16insider.html?_r=1 (accessed April 15, 2011); Susan Pulliam. "Fund Chief Snared by Taps, Turncoats." *The Wall Street Journal,* December 30, 2009, http://online.wsj.com/article/SB126213287690309579.html (accessed March 20, 2011); Pulliam, Susan, and Chad Bray. "Galleon Chief Seen Testifying at Trial." *The Wall Street Journal,* March 5, 2011, http://online.wsj.com/article/SB10001424052748704076804576180803410903550.html (accessed April 18, 2011); Pulliam, Susan, and Chad Bray. "Jury Hears Galleon Wiretaps." *The Wall Street Journal,* March 11, 2011, A1; Pulliam, Susan, and Chad Bray. "Seasoned Prosecutors Prep for 'War.'" *The Wall Street Journal,* March 9, 2011, http://online.wsj.com/article/SB10001424052748703662804576188960685479264.html (accessed April 18, 2011); Pulliam, Susan, and Michael Rothfeld. "Trial Win Adds to Momentum." *The Wall Street Journal,* May 12, 2011, A7; Pulliam, Susan, and Michael Siconolfi. "Wiretapped Voice Spoke Volumes." *The Wall Street Journal,* May 12, 2011, A7; Rothfeld, Michael, Susan Pulliam, and Chad Bray. "Fund Titan Found Guilty." *The Wall Street Journal,* May 12, 2011, A1, A6; Shell, Adam. "Jury Finds Rajaratnam Guilty." *USA Today,* May 12, 2011, B1, B2; Strasburg, Jenny, Jessica Silver-Greenberg, and Jeannette Neumann. "Inside the Galleon Jury Room." *The Wall Street Journal,* May 14, 2011, A1, A2; Van Voris, Bob. "Galleon Scandal Scorecard: Hedge Funds, Lawyers and 'Octopussy.'" *Bloomberg.com,* November 7, 2009, http://www.bloomberg.com/apps/news?pid=newsarchive&sid=aRqWWXi06f4Y (accessed April 18, 2011).

CASE 13

GlaxoSmithKline Experiences High Costs of Product Quality Issues*

GlaxoSmithKline (GSK) is a global leader in the pharmaceutical industry. The diversity of products that the company offers can be traced back to a number of smaller businesses, including laxative pill manufacturer Beecham Pills; Smith, Kline & Co.; Burroughs Wellcome & Co.; and Glaxo (which was originally registered as the name of a dried milk product). After several mergers, these companies combined to form a pharmaceutical giant with operations in over 100 countries and annual sales of over $25 billion. Its products include such well-known brand names as Avandia, Wellbutrin, and Paxil. GSK is focused on increasing growth, reducing risk, and improving its long-term financial performance.

To gain a better understanding of the nature of the pharmaceutical industry, including the major ethical issues common to this field, we will provide a brief overview of the pharmaceutical industry. Next, we discuss GSK's background along with its leadership and structure. We follow with an examination of GSK's corporate responsibility initiatives. Finally, we discuss the ethical issues that have plagued GSK, causing major losses and potential damage to its corporate reputation.

INDUSTRY BACKGROUND

The global pharmaceutical industry is enormous. In the United States alone, drugs comprise 10 percent of medical costs and are the fastest growing segment of the nation's $1.3 trillion health care bill. Sales revenues have tripled over the last decade, with price increases of 150 percent. Fewer than 100 companies comprise more than 90 percent of the global market. The industry spends more than $15 billion each year to advertise its drugs to physicians and consumers.

The 1970s saw a shift in the industry from relatively small companies to giant multinational corporations. Additional patent legislation passed during this time gave pharmaceutical companies more control over the types of drugs they could sell. Through the 1980s and 1990s many pharmaceutical companies became involved with DNA chemistries and bioengineering. The need for more research and development funding resulted in mergers and acquisitions. Pharmaceutical manufacturing became more concentrated, with a few large companies dominating the industry (see Table 1). Markets became larger, and cooperation between companies began to increase. Because medicines are, for the most part,

*This case was prepared by John Fraedrich with the editorial assistance of Jennifer Sawayda. It was prepared for classroom discussion rather than to illustrate either effective or ineffective handling of an administrative, ethical, or legal decision by management. All sources used for this case were obtained through publicly available material.

TABLE 1 Top 20 Global Pharmaceutical Companies, Total Audited Markets (in millions of $)

	2010 rank (US$)	2010 Sales (US$ MN)	2009 Sales (US$ MN)	2008 Sales (U3$ MN)	2007 Sales (US$ MN)	2006 Sales (US$ MN)
Global Market	0	$ 791,449	$ 752,022	$ 727,067	$ 671,164	$ 609,614
PFIZER	1	$ 55,602	$ 57,024	$ 58,677	$ 59,909	$ 59,415
NOVARTIS	2	$ 46,806	$ 38,460	$ 36,684	$ 34,479	$ 31,653
MERCK & CO	3	$ 38,468	$ 38,963	$ 39,488	$ 39,365	$ 35,965
SANOFI-AVENTIS	4	$ 35,875	$ 35,524	$ 36,437	$ 34,390	$ 31,843
ASTRAZENECA	5	$ 35,535	$ 34,434	$ 32,498	$ 29,999	$ 27,311
GLAXOSMITHKLINE	6	$ 33,664	$ 34,973	$ 36,736	$ 37,620	$ 36,212
ROCHE	7	$ 32,693	$ 32,763	$ 30,285	$ 27,232	$ 23,168
JOHNSON & JOHNSON	8	$ 26,773	$ 26,783	$ 29,638	$ 29,010	$ 27,615
ABBOTT	9	$ 23,833	$ 19,840	$ 19,401	$ 17,359	$ 15,971
LILLY	10	$ 22,113	$ 20,310	$ 19,042	$ 17,177	$ 15,176
TEVA	11	$ 21,064	$ 15,947	$ 15,143	$ 13,295	$ 11,664
BAYER	12	$ 15,656	$ 15,711	$ 15,887	$ 14,103	$ 12,329
AMGEN	13	$ 15,531	$ 15,038	$ 15,281	$ 15,900	$ 15,932
BRISTOL-MYERS SQB.	14	$ 14,977	$ 14,110	$ 13,559	$ 12,021	$ 11,348
BOEHRINGER INGEL	15	$ 14,591	$ 15,275	$ 14,109	$ 12,556	$ 11,320
TAKEDA	16	$ 12,983	$ 14,338	$ 13,833	$ 12,748	$ 11,783
DAIICHI SANKYO	17	$ 9,797	$ 8,773	$ 8,149	$ 7,180	$ 6,752
NOVO NORDISK	18	$ 9,719	$ 8,594	$ 7,941	$ 6,740	$ 5,762
EISAI	19	$ 8,757	$ 8,130	$ 7,109	$ 6,294	$ 5,798
OTSUKA	20	$ 8,732	$ 7,878	$ 6,456	$ 5,294	$ 4,643

Sales and rank are in US$ with quarterly exchange rates.

Sales cover direct and indirect pharmaceutical channel wholesalers and manufacturers. The figures above include prescription and certain over-the-counter data and represent manufacturer prices.

Source: IMS Health Midas, December 2010, http://www.imshealth.com/deployedfiles/imshealth/Global/Content/StaticFile/Top_Line_Data/Top_20_Global_Companies.pdf (accessed May 31, 2011).

needs goods and in many cases relate directly to life or death, or at least quality of life, countries were amenable toward this reduced form of competition. Large multinational corporations now often dominate the entire drug process, including discovery and development, manufacturing, quality control, marketing, sales, and distribution. Smaller companies tend to focus on specific areas of the drug process, such as discovering new drugs or specializing in medicines for rare diseases. Research organizations, physicians, universities, and large pharmaceutical companies collaborate to explore and develop new drugs. One study suggests that it costs a company about $1.8 billion to market one unique drug.

Interestingly, regulations that are meant to encourage the development of drugs to combat deadly diseases have also resulted in a significant ethical issue. Since drugs for heart disease and AIDS were being pushed by governments to stave off an epidemic, regulatory bodies began to loosen restrictions to achieve a faster approval process. Yet without thorough oversight, some drugs may have been brought too quickly to market. This fast approval system led to unanticipated problems that took the form of side effects or even death.

Beginning in the twenty-first century, a number of countries began to question drug prices because these prices directly affected their citizens as well as their gross domestic products (GDPs). As a result, countries began to pressure pharmaceutical companies to reduce their prices. Some governments dedicated resources to manufacturing generic forms of patented drugs. In other words, although the drugs were protected by patents, governments began to support the creation of cheaper generic drugs that were more affordable. The first country to do this was India. Strategic government policies transformed the Indian pharmaceutical industry from an importer of drugs to an innovation-driven, cost-effective producer of quality drugs. Other governments have tried to do the same. Drug companies have tried to counter this trend through lawsuits, including one filed against the South African government for passing laws to make it easier to produce generics of patented drugs. Public outcry caused the companies to drop the suit.

Pharmaceutical companies consider actions such as those of the South African and Indian governments to be akin to the theft of their legally protected property. From the corporations' perspective, they should have a right to protect their investment and recoup the heavy costs of researching and developing the product, as well as make a profit. On the other hand, developing countries whose populations are threatened with deadly diseases believe they have the right to use medicines to save peoples' lives—even if these medicines are patent-protected.

> "The marketing of drugs has also changed dramatically in the last few decades, partly because of new strategies within the industry."

The marketing of drugs has also changed dramatically in the last few decades, partly because of new strategies within the industry. This change primarily occurred within the U.S. market but has spread around the world. Pharmaceutical companies used to market drugs to physicians, who in turn would prescribe them to their patients. But with U.S. consumers becoming more educated, the industry began to use a "pull" strategy for their products. Companies began marketing their medicines to consumers, and consumers, in turn, started to request them from their physicians. The strategy began when the FDA allowed direct-to-consumer advertising. This strategy was a huge success with drugs that increased libido, dealt with depression, or helped curb eating. To gain more sales, companies began to market these drugs for "off-label" uses. Off-label use occurs when a medicine is prescribed for something that the drug was not approved to treat. The Food and Drug Administration can approve a drug for prescription use, but it does not have the authority to regulate the way a physician prescribes the drug to his or her patients. One study found that off-label use in cardiac medications and anticonvulsants was very common, even though no scientific support existed for its use. Pharmaceutical companies were accused of "disease mongering," or over-prescribing medications for non-medical issues such as social problems.

Ethical considerations concerning drug safety have also come to the forefront. Some argue that the approval processes used by regulatory bodies such as the FDA are flawed. The approval mechanism is driven by the submission of evidence selected by the pharmaceutical

industry. There are no independent clinical trials, and an increasing body of evidence suggests that pharmaceutical companies are highly selective in submitting evidence, choosing to suppress inadequate or potentially dangerous features of their new products. Additionally, there is no positive monitoring procedure for verifying safety in use following approval. It all depends on the motivation of individual physicians to report adverse events.

THE MERGERS

At the end of the twentieth century, the pharmaceutical industry experienced a variety of mergers that resulted in a few dominant players in the market. One important merger was between Glaxo Wellcome and SmithKline Beecham. Talk of a merger began in 1998. Jan Leschly, SmithKline Beecham's chief executive officer, was set to be the chief executive for the newly merged company, with Glaxo chief executive Richard Sykes as the new chair. Yet to everyone's surprise, the original deal was called off. Publicly, Glaxo Wellcome indicated it was not prepared to proceed on the agreed-upon basis. Privately, SmithKline directors claimed that Glaxo Wellcome had reneged on the original agreement that Leschly would be the company's leader. Glaxo executives never challenged this version of events.

Part of the reason that the merger initially failed could have been a conflict between the management styles of Leschly and Sykes. Leschly's stern management style and SmithKline's performance-based culture appeared to conflict with Sykes' fervent belief in science and Glaxo's traditional management style. While Leschly feared that he would be forced to give up the chief executive position, Sykes and his management board feared the merger would end up as a takeover by SmithKline people. After Leschly retired, talks of a merger resumed. Interest in the merger might also have been affected by the announcement that Pfizer, the U.S. drug giant, had begun negotiations with Warner-Lambert, another U.S. competitor. The merger eventually occurred, and Jean-Paul Garnier emerged as chief executive of the new GlaxoSmithKline.

GSK'S STRUCTURE AND LEADERSHIP

Jean-Paul Garnier had a rocky road ahead of him when he assumed the position of CEO in 2000. He had to reconcile two different corporate cultures, criticism from both consumers and shareholders, and some of the worst "pipelines" of drugs in the pharmaceutical industry. GSK adopted a corporate structure that combined traditional activities with innovative strategies. While the company has centralized certain functions, such as clinical trials and marketing, GSK also wanted to remain flexible enough to grasp new opportunities and remain competitive. Under Garnier's leadership, GSK's pipeline of drugs also became one of the best in the industry.

In 2007 a significant power shift occurred within the executive ranks. Garnier was ready to retire, but was unsure about who should replace him. He devised a competition to test three possible candidates: David Stout, the Philadelphia-based chief of the American division; Chris Viehbacher, head of the U.S. pharmaceuticals division; and Andrew Witty, president of the pharmaceuticals division in Europe. The competition ended with Witty as the new GSK chief executive. When Stout was told of the decision, Garnier offered him and Chris Viehbacher approximately $4 million in stock and cash and board seats. Viehbacher took the board seat, while Stout chose to resign.

Andrew Witty had his work cut out for him. As the years passed, GSK was hit with a string of lawsuits that cost the company money, sales, and reputational benefits. The price of GSK shares had declined 50 percent since 2005. Witty announced that an overhaul was needed. He proposed breaking into new fields, such as drugs that had largely been ignored by other large companies, along with expanding into emerging markets. He believed that an emphasis on corporate social responsibility might also help to boost GSK's reputation in the eyes of stakeholders.

CORPORATE SOCIAL RESPONSIBILITY

GlaxoSmithKline's policy statement includes the following:

> Being a responsible business means operating in a way that reflects our values, treating our stakeholders with respect, and connecting our business decisions to society's health care needs. Our business makes a valuable contribution to society. However, we know that the research and development, manufacture and sale of our medicines, vaccines and consumer products raise ethical issues, and we aim to be open and transparent about how we tackle them. We seek to minimize the negative impacts and maximize the benefits of our business, and our approach is guided by our corporate responsibility principles.

Over the years, GSK's efforts have included contributions to global health. GSK also uses preferential pricing arrangements in addition to voluntary licenses for certain drugs targeted toward tropical diseases for the impoverished. The company charges impoverished countries 75 percent less for its patented medicines than it does developed nations.

In addition to an Employee Guide to Business Conduct, GSK has a Corporate Ethics and Compliance intranet for employees that contains details of employee training, company policies, and the phone numbers of the company's Global Confidential Reporting line and U.S. Integrity Helpline. The company's Corporate Ethics and Compliance department is in charge of ensuring that company members comply with GSK's code of conduct and all aspects of the law. GSK has also introduced a Third Party Code of Conduct for its suppliers to ensure that suppliers meet GSK standards regarding ethics, management, and human rights.

GSK has set several ambitious goals for its environmental policy, some of which it has already fulfilled. For instance, GSK has exceeded its goals for water reduction, waste water quality, and emissions of volatile compounds, and has met its goal of reducing its greenhouse gas emissions by 5 percent by 2010. The company continues to update its environmental goals. The company wants to eliminate its waste from operations to landfills by 2020 and obtain carbon neutrality by 2050. The company also adheres to the UN Universal Declaration of Human Rights; the OECD Guidelines for Multinational Enterprises, the core labor standards set by the International Labor Organization; and the UN Global Compact, a voluntary global standard on human rights, labor, the environment, and anticorruption practices.

GSK's global CSR investment in 2010 was $345 million, which was 36 percent higher than its 2009 investment. GSK has expanded several philanthropic programs, including its African Malaria Partnership and its commitment toward eliminating lymphatic filariasis, a disease caused by parasites. Since 2008 the company's product donations have been valued at cost (average cost of goods) rather than wholesale price (WAC). GSK believes that this is a more accurate reflection of the cost of its donated goods and is the first pharmaceutical company to adopt this practice.

Additionally, GSK is committed to discovering groundbreaking medications to combat diseases that currently have no cure. The company is working on a malaria vaccine that, if successful, would be the first vaccine available against malaria. GSK also expressed its intention of keeping the price of the drug from preventing people from gaining access to this potentially life-saving vaccine.

ETHICAL AND LEGAL ISSUES

GSK has faced several lawsuits over the years regarding product liability, marketing, and quality control. GSK has been highly criticized for selling drugs to the public when it knew or suspected that these drugs could be detrimental to patients' health. In 2011 the company announced that it would record a $3.49 billion charge on its fourth-quarter earnings to deal with litigation against the company regarding its marketing practices and Avandia lawsuits. The year before, the company had paid $2.59 billion to settle lawsuits concerning Avandia and Paxil as well as charges stemming from investigations into its plant in Cidra, Puerto Rico.

> "GSK has been highly criticized for selling drugs to the public when it knewor suspected that these drugs could be detrimental to patients' health."

Paxil

Paxil is an antidepressant commonly prescribed to patients with depression or anxiety disorders. Although the drug has effectively relieved symptoms in many cases, Paxil has also been accused of generating severe side effects such as addictive behavior, birth defects, withdrawal symptoms, and even suicidal tendencies. Research has suggested that these side effects are worse in children. A class-action lawsuit was filed against GSK claiming that the company had marketed Paxil for children and purposefully hid the fact that the drug was unsafe and ineffective for patients at that age. GSK denied any wrongdoing but agreed to settle for more than $60 million. One year later, GSK agreed to pay $40 million after British authorities accused the company of knowing that Paxil could cause depressive behavior in patients under 18. But GSK's ordeal with Paxil was not over. GSK also faced lawsuits alleging that Paxil caused birth defects. The company agreed to settle for more than $1 billion. In 2010 Maria Carmen Palazzo, a psychiatrist on the payroll of GlaxoSmithKline, was sentenced to 13 months in prison after admitting to committing research fraud in trials of the antidepressant Paxil on children. Palazzo enrolled children in a clinical trial who did not suffer from major depressive or obsessive-compulsive disorders. Palazzo also falsified records and psychiatric diagnoses to cover up her crime. GSK had paid Palazzo $5,000 for every child she enrolled.

Avandia

In 2007 a class-action suit was filed against GlaxoSmithKline claiming that its diabetes drug Avandia increased the risk of heart attacks. One study conducted by *The New England Journal of Medicine* reported that consumers who took Avandia were 43 percent more likely to suffer from heart attacks than consumers taking alternative diabetes medications. The lawsuit alleged that the company knew about the risks but had failed to properly disclose them to the public. Indeed, GSK had conducted an analysis that showed such a risk existed but argued that because similar studies did not show a significant risk, the company found the analysis to be "unpersuasive." The lawsuit thus alleged that not only did GSK fail to disclose the risks of Avandia, it also artificially inflated the drug's price by portraying it as less risky than it really is.

GSK denied the allegations and took a proactive stance to demonstrate that the results of the studies were misleading. The company accused lawyers of running false Avandia advertisements to drum up business and sent letters to plaintiff lawyers with these complaints. However, the lawsuits only gained momentum. A former manager in the FDA's drug-safety unit alleged that the drug did carry a higher risk of heart attacks than alternative diabetes drugs and testified that GSK had refused to disclose an email from researchers explaining that such risks existed (GSK denied the allegations). One study estimated that more than 47,000 people taking Avandia had suffered from strokes or heart trouble during a ten-year period. In 2010 the FDA determined that the risks of Avandia outweighed the benefits. The agency severely restricted sales of Avandia. As a result of the decision, GSK can no longer promote the drug and doctors can only prescribe Avandia if no other diabetes medication is working for the patient. Those already taking Avandia can continue to use it. The European Union went a step further, banning Avandia outright. Such restrictions were a severe blow for GSK, which had been making more than $1 billion from Avandia sales annually.

Marketing and Sales Litigation

GSK has also faced litigation associated with its marketing and sales activities. In particular, the U.S. government has inquired about the alleged promotion of many drugs for off-label uses. Although the FDA has limited control over how a doctor prescribes medications, it is illegal for pharmaceutical companies to promote medications for uses not approved by the FDA. Off-label drug marketing has serious ethical implications. It has the potential to lead to consumer misuse of medications, which could cause harm to the individual. In this case, the U.S. government accused GSK of promoting the drug Wellbutrin, an antidepressant, for weight loss. The Department of Justice filed criminal charges against Lauren C. Stevens, a former vice president and associate general counsel for GSK, for allegedly trying to cover up GSK's use of off-label marketing. The charges alleged that Stevens lied to the FDA by saying that GSK did not promote Wellbutrin for off-label uses, and failed to turn over promotional slides that the FDA had requested. Stevens was later acquitted of all charges, but the government has continued to investigate GSK over its Wellbutrin marketing claims.

> "Off-label drug marketing has the potential to lead to consumer misuse of medications."

Another marketing ethics issue is GSK's use of promotions such as sponsored continuing medical education programs, speaker events, advisory boards, and grants. The U.S. Senate Finance Committee sent letters to pharmaceutical companies expressing concern that grants were being improperly (and illegally) used to promote drug products. The committee requested that the companies provide information about their use of educational grants. As a result of the information provided by GSK, the committee believed that misconduct has occurred. Several physicians and GSK representatives now face criminal charges. GSK has also faced legal repercussions concerning its average wholesale pricing, including allegations that the company violated federal fraud and abuse laws such as the

Federal False Claims Act as it relates to Medicare and Medicaid drug payments. GSK has agreed to pay $70 million to settle these claims.

QUALITY CONTROL ISSUES

Another lawsuit against GSK regarded quality control at a Cidra, Puerto Rico, manufacturing site. The suit alleged that GSK sold over 20 drugs with potential safety issues, including Paxil, Paxil CR, Coreg, Avandia, Avandamet, and the ointment Bactroban, all manufactured at Cidra. Although safety issues at pharmaceutical plants are nothing new, this was the first case in which it was determined that a company knowingly sold contaminated drugs. The FDA discovered deficiencies at the plant, and GSK agreed to close Cidra.

A lawsuit was also filed by Cheryl D. Eckard, GSK's former quality-control manager at the Cidra plant. Eckard described the use of bacteria-tainted water and the contamination of raw materials by employees allowed to stick their bare hands and arms into sterile control tanks. Eckard also claimed that some of the medications were made too strong, while others were too weak. Because employees were not cleaning the machines, medications would get mixed up. The impact of this protocol violation was highlighted when a pharmacist wrote a letter to GSK stating that 25-milligram Paxil tablets were being delivered in bottles labeled 10 milligrams. Eckard told her superiors about the problems, but nothing was done. Finally, she sent a summary to seven executives detailing the high risks at the plant. Weeks later, GSK "downsized" her; she was out of a job. Because of her allegations, the FDA investigated the plant and seized defective drugs worth millions. GlaxoSmithKline pleaded guilty to a felony and paid $750 million in fees and penalties, $96 million of which went to Eckard under a federal whistle-blower law. Although GSK admits the plant was not following compliance procedures, it maintains that it had been working on the problems at the Cidra plant since 2001 and that the company has a strict nonretaliation policy for whistle-blowers.

CONCLUSIONS

Although GSK has made great strides in social responsibility and business conduct, it is apparent that its stated values have not been fully implemented in its operations. The company's failure to disclose the risks and side effects of some of its drugs indicates a lack of the transparency that is necessary in an ethical corporation. To restore its reputation, GSK will have to institute additional controls that will ensure the quality of its products and manufacturing processes. Despite the company's ethical controls and its Corporate Ethics and Compliance department, serious misconduct has occurred. Defective medicinal products go beyond a mere inconvenience for the consumer. They can make the difference between life and death. As a result, the Obama administration has begun to crack down harder on the pharmaceutical industry, imposing heavy fines on those caught committing misconduct. Since GSK likely cannot afford to make any more mistakes, it must reinforce compliance procedures across the company. CEO Andrew Witty has announced plans to revamp operations through expansion and other methods. However, in light of the problems facing GSK, the company may need major revisions in its oversight mechanisms, code of conduct, and compliance procedures.

QUESTIONS

1. Identify ethical lapses that may have impacted product quality at GSK.
2. What caused GSK's leadership to fail in preventing ethical issues related to integrity failures?
3. What can GSK do to prevent future ethical dilemmas and reputational damage from failures in product quality?

SOURCES

Avert. "Reducing the price of HIV/AIDS treatment." http://www.avert.org/generic.htm (accessed April 22, 2011); Bain & Co. "Has the Pharmaceutical Blockbuster Model Gone Bust?" December 8, 2003, http://www.bain.com/about/press/press-releases/has-the-pharmaceutical-blockbuster-model-gone-bust.aspx (accessed July 7, 2011); Bátiz-Lazo, Bernardo. "GSK—A Case Study on the Strategy of 'Merger with Equals' in Ethical Pharmaceuticals." Open University Business School, http://www.scribd.com/doc/15925536/GSK-Merger (accessed April 22, 2011); Blackden, Richard, and Rachel Cooper. "Avandia Lawsuit Settled on Eve of Trial." *The Telegraph,* January 31, 2011, http://www.telegraph.co.uk/finance/newsbysector/pharmaceuticalsandchemicals/8293684/GlaxoSmithKline-settles-Avandia-lawsuit-on-eve-of-trial.html (accessed April 22, 2011); Carmel Engineering College, Department of Management Studies. "Organizational Study at Cachet Pharmaceuticals Pvt. Ltd, Bhiwadi." http://www.scribd.com/doc/36130378/Cachet (accessed April 22, 2011); Clark, Andrew. "Andrew Witty of GSK: 'Big firms have allowed themselves to be seen as detached from society.'" *The Observer,* March 20, 2011, http://www.wikinvest.com/wikinvest/api.php?action=viewNews&aid=2437747&page=Stock%3AGlaxoSmithKline_%28GSK%29&format=html&comments=0 (accessed April 22, 2011); Company Thumbs. "Answering the Questions That Matter: Annual Report 2007." http://www.companythumbs.com/ReportByCompanyUK100.asp?lc=G&arYear=2007 (accessed April 22, 2011); Donohoe, Martin. "The Pharmaceutical Industry: Facts, Fiction, Policy and Ethics." http://docs.google.com/viewer?a=v&q=cache:7vfUySn5tTwJ:phsj.org/files/Pharmaceutical%2520Industry/Pharmaceutical%2520Industry%2520Ethics.ppt+drugs,+Sales+revenues+have+tripled+over+the+last+decade,+with+price+increases+of+150+percent&hl=en&gl=us&pid=bl&srcid=ADGEESjINFFBcAzndn6YwQVHRcrMwVyMKvKiesoj49rKpsgDcqbyImfM6aKudm2t7_hKw2lrFXoRFY2B-PUl5UCuSQG6P5dWFbSgLUV9pj_EUbQc_EGlmbn_JDRRGjdNCfwp8BfeoR6i&sig=AHIEtbT34aQzYzW3x2WgYL_fplITjtWPeA (accessed April 22, 2011); Feeley, Jef, and Trista Kelley. "Glaxo Said to Pay $460 Million to End Avandia Suits." *Bloomberg Businessweek,* July 13, 2010, http://www.businessweek.com/news/2010-07-13/glaxo-said-to-pay-460-million-to-end-avandia-suits.html (accessed April 25, 2011); Fiercepharma.com. "Musical chairs at GSK leaves Stout out." http://www.fiercepharma.com/story/musical-chairs-gsk-leaves-stout-out/2007-12-07?utm_medium=rss&utm_source=rss&cmp-id=OTC-RSS-FP0, December 7, 2007 (accessed April 22, 2011); GlaxoSmithKline. "2005 Corporate Responsibility Report." http://www.gsk.com/responsibility/downloads/CR-Report-2005.pdf; GlaxoSmithKline. "Corporate Responsibility Review 2010." http://www.gsk.com/responsibility/downloads/GSK-CR-2010-Review.pdf (accessed April 25, 2011); GlaxoSmithKline. "Corporate responsibility." March 16, 2011, http://www.gsk.com/careers/corp-responsibility.htm (accessed April 4, 2011); GlaxoSmithKline. "Corporate Responsibility Report." http://www.gsk.com/responsibility/downloads/GSK-CR-2008-full.pdf (accessed April 22, 2011);

GlaxoSmithKline. "Human Being: Annual Report 2005." http://www.gsk.com/investors/reps05/annual-report-2005.pdf (accessed April 22, 2011); GlaxoSmithKline. "Human Race: Annual Report 2006." http://www.gsk.com/investors/reps06/annual-report-2006.pdf (accessed April 22, 2011); GlaxoSmithKline. "Human Race: Corporate Responsibility Report 2006." http://www.gsk.com/responsibility/downloads/CR-Report-2006.pdf (accessed April 22, 2011); GlaxoSmithKline. "Grow, Deliver, Simplify: Annual Report 2008." http://www.gsk.com/investors/reps08/GSK-Report-2008-full.pdf (accessed April 22, 2011); GlaxoSmithKline. "Grow, Simplify, Deliver: 2009 Annual Report." http://www.gsk.com/investors/reps09/GSK-Report-2009-full.pdf (accessed April 22, 2011); GlaxoSmithKline. "The Impact of Medicine: Annual Report 2002." http://www.gsk.com/investors/reps02/annual-report-2002.pdf (accessed April 22, 2011); GlaxoSmithKline. "The Impact of Medicine: Sustainability in Environment, Health and Safety 2002." http://www.gsk.com/responsibility/downloads/gsk_ehs_2002.pdf (accessed April 22, 2011); GlaxoSmithKline. "Improving Performance Every day: Annual Report 2003." http://www.gsk.com/investors/reps03/annual_report2003.pdf (accessed April 22, 2011); GlaxoSmithKline. "Making a Difference Every Day: Sustainability in Environment, Health & Safety Report 2003." http://www.gsk.com/responsibility/downloads/EHS-2003.pdf (accessed April 22, 2011); GlaxoSmithKline. "New Challenges, New Thinking: Annual Report 2004." http://www.gsk.com/investors/reps04/annual-report-2004.pdf (accessed April 22, 2011); GlaxoSmithKline. "Our History." http://www.gsk.com/about/history.htm (accessed April 4, 2011); GlaxoSmithKline. "Responsibility." http://www.gsk.com/responsibility/ (accessed April 22, 2011); GlaxoSmithKline. "Sustainability in Environment, Health and Safety: Report 2004." http://www.gsk.com/responsibility/downloads/EHS-2004.pdf (accessed April 22, 2011); GlaxoSmithKline Settlement. "Welcome to the GSK Settlement Website." http://www.gsksettlement.com/glaxo/welcome.htm (accessed April 25, 2011); Goldstein, Jacob. "An Avandia Lawsuit Emerges, Inevitably." *The Wall Street Journal,* June 12, 2007, http://blogs.wsj.com/health/2007/06/12/avandia-lawsuits-emerge-inevitably/ (accessed April 25, 2011); Goldstein, Jacob. "Glaxo Pays $40 Million in (Another) Paxil Settlement." *The Wall Street Journal,* October 2, 2008, http://blogs.wsj.com/health/2008/10/02/glaxo-pays-40-million-in-another-paxil-settlement/ (accessed April 4, 2011); Gutierrez, David. "Psychiatrist on Payroll of Glaxo Pleads Guilty to Research Fraud." *NaturalNews,* November 29, 2010, http://www.naturalnews.com/030557_psychiatry_fraud.html (accessed April 22, 2011); Harris, Gardiner. "Glaxo Memo on Avandia Is Questioned." *The New York Times,* August 19, 2010, http://www.nytimes.com/2010/08/20/health/policy/20fda.html?ref=glaxosmithklineplc&pagewanted=print (April 22, 2011); Harris, Gardiner. "FDA to Restrict Avandia, Citing Heart Risk." *The New York Times,* September 23, 2010, http://www.nytimes.com/2010/09/24/health/policy/24avandia.html (accessed April 25, 2011); Harris, Gardiner, and Duff Wilson. "Glaxo to Pay $750 Million for Sale of Bad Products." *The New York Times,* October 26, 2010, http://www.nytimes.com/2010/10/27/business/27drug.html?ref=glaxosmithklineplc (accessed April 22, 2011); Huber, Nick. "JP Garnier leaves bitter-sweet pill for Glaxo to swallow." Guardian.co.uk, May 20, 2008, http://www.guardian.co.uk/business/2008/may/20/glaxosmithklinebusiness.pharmaceuticals (accessed April 22, 2011); IMS. "IMS Forecasts Global Pharmaceutical Market Growth of 4–6% in 2010; Predicts 4–7% Expansion through 2013." http://www.imshealth.com/portal/site/imshealth/menuitem.a46c6d4df3db4b3d88f611019418c22a/?vgnextoid=500e8fabedf24210VgnVCM100000ed152ca2RCRD (accessed April 22, 2011); Jolly, David, and Gardiner Harris. "Glaxo Plans $2.3 Billion Liability Charge." *The New York Times,* July 15, 2010, http://www.nytimes.com/2010/07/16/business/global/16avandia.html?fta=y&pagewanted=print (accessed April 22, 2011); Langreth, Robert. "Shrink It, Cure It." *Forbes,* http://www.forbes.com/forbes/2011/0117/features-glaxosmithkline-andrew-witty-shrink-it-cure-it.html (accessed April 22, 2011); Langreth, Robert. "Will Glaxo's Legal Woes Ever End?" January 17, 2011, http://blogs.forbes.com/robertlangreth/2011/01/17/will-glaxos-legal-woes-ever-end (accessed April 22, 2011); Lattman, Peter. "Glaxo Trying to Nip Avandia Litigation in the Bud." *The Wall Street Journal,* July 17, 2007, http://blogs.wsj.com/law/2007/07/17/glaxo-trying-to-nip-avandia-litigation-in-the-bud/ (accessed April 25, 2011); Moynihan, Ray, and Alan Cassels. *Selling Sickness: How Drug Companies Are Turning Us All into Patients.* New York: Allen & Unwin, 2005; Mundy, Alicia, and Brent Kendall. "U.S. Rebuffed in Glaxo Misconduct Case." *The Wall Street Journal,* May 11, 2011, B1; Pelley, Scott. "Glaxo Whistle-Blower Lawsuit: Bad Medicine." CBSNews.com, January 2, 2011, http://www.cbsnews.com/stories/2010/12/29/60minutes/main7195247.shtml (accessed April 22, 2011); Phillyinc.biz.

"Stout Snubs $4 Million." December 10, 2007, http://blogs.phillynews.com/inquirer/phillyinc/2007/12/stout.html (accessed April 22, 2011); Radley, David C., Stan N. Finkelstein, and Randall S. Stafford. "Off-label Prescribing among Office-Based Physicians." *Archives of Internal Medicine* 166, no. 9, (May 8, 2006 1021–26, http://archinte. ama-assn.org/cgi/content/full/166/9/1021 (accessed April 22, 2011); Rosenberg, Martha. "Posts Tagged 'criminal charges.'" Citizen's Commission on Human Rights International, December 31, 2010, http://www.cchrint.org/tag/ criminal-charges/ (accessed April 22, 2011); Silverman, Ed. "Glaxo Receives Federal Subpoena about Avandia." Pharmalot.com, October 21, 2010, http://www.pharmalot.com/2010/10/glaxo-receives-federal-subpoena-about-avandia (accessed April 22, 2011); Silverman, Ed. "David Who? A Glaxo Exec and Manufacturing Fraud." Pharmalot.com, October 29, 2010, http://www.pharmalot.com/2010/10/david-who-a-glaxo-exec-and-manufacturing-fraud (accessed April 22, 2011); Silverman, Ed. "Former Glaxo Lawyer Points Finger at Big Law Firm." Pharmalot.com, December 22, 2010, http://www.pharmalot.com/2010/12/former-glaxo-lawyer-points-finger-at-big-law-firm (accessed April 22, 2011); Silverman, Ed. "Now Glaxo Takes a $3.4 Billion Charge for Avandia." Pharmalot.com, January 18, 2011, http://www.pharmalot.com/2011/01/now-glaxo-takes-a-34-billion-charge-for-avandia (accessed April 22, 2011); Silverman, Ed. "Glaxo Exec Wants to Know What Went Wrong." Pharmalot.com, January 25, 2011, http://www.pharmalot.com/2011/01/glaxo-exec-wants-to-know-what-went-wrong (accessed April 22, 2011); Stovall, Sten. "Glaxo Settles Some Paxil Lawsuits." *The Wall Street Journal,* July 20, 2010, http://online.wsj.com/article/SB10001424052748703724104575379080064038098.html (accessed April 22, 2011); Whalen, Jeanne. "Glaxo to Take $3.49 Billion Litigation Charge." *The Wall Street Journal,* January 18, 2011, B3; Wilson, Duff. "Ex-Glaxo Executive Is Charged in Drug Fraud." *The New York Times,* November 9, 2010, http://www.nytimes.com/2010/11/10/health/10glaxo.html?ref=glaxosmithklineplc&pagewanted=print (accessed April 22, 2011); Wilson, Duff. "Former Glaxo Lawyer Indicted." *The New York Times,* November 9, 2010, http://prescriptions. blogs.nytimes.com/2010/11/09/former-glaxo-lawyer-indicted (accessed April 22, 2011); Times Online and Agencies. "GSK also-ran to leave as rival joins board." *Times online*, December 7, 2007, http://business.timesonline. co.uk/tol/business/industry_sectors/health/article3018239.ece (accessed April 22, 2011); HealthCare.gov. "New Tools to Fight Fraud, Strengthen Medicare and Protect Taxpayer Dollars." January 24, 2011, http://www.healthcare. gov/news/factsheets/new_tools_to_fight_fraud.html (accessed July 7, 2011); "Glaxo Smith Kline to axe 4,000 jobs." *Deccan Herald,* January 31, 2011, http://www.deccanherald.com/content/50004/glaxo-smith-kline-axe-4000.html (accessed April 22, 2011); Wikinvest. "GlaxoSmithKline (GSK)." http://www.wikinvest.com/stock/GlaxoSmithKlin e_%28GSK%29#Comparison_to_Competitors (accessed April 22, 2011).

CASE 14

Hospital Corporation of America: Learning from Past Mistakes?*

In 1968 Dr. Thomas Frist, Sr., Jack C. Massey, and Dr. Thomas Frist, Jr., founded the Hospital Corporation of America (HCA) to manage Park View Hospital in Nashville, Tennessee. The firm grew rapidly over the next two decades by acquiring and building new hospitals and contracting to manage additional facilities for their owners. In 1994 it merged with Columbia Hospital Corporation to become Columbia/HCA Healthcare Corporation, and Columbia founder Richard Scott became chair and CEO of the combined companies. Scott, a lawyer specializing in hospital mergers, had created Columbia in 1987 when he purchased two troubled hospitals in El Paso, Texas, before expanding across Texas and Florida.

By 1997 Columbia/HCA had grown to become one of the largest for-profit healthcare services company in the United States, operating 343 hospitals, 136 outpatient surgery centers, and approximately 550 home-health locations. It also provided extensive outpatient and ancillary services in 37 states, as well as in the United Kingdom and Switzerland. The firm's comprehensive network included more than 285,000 employees and used economies of scale to increase profits. Richard Scott was named one of *Time* magazine's most influential people in 1996, and *Fortune* magazine named Columbia/HCA as the most admired healthcare company in 1997.

However, the success of Columbia/HCA came at a price. In 1997 the federal government launched an investigation into the company's business practices. Columbia/HCA eventually pleaded guilty to 14 felonies and paid over $1.7 billion in fines for committing fraud, falsely billing Medicare, and violating federal antikickback laws. It was the largest healthcare fraud case ever prosecuted in America.

CORPORATE CULTURE AT COLUMBIA/HCA

Scott's management philosophy at Columbia/HCA was based on creating a competitive environment while cutting costs at the company's facilities. Columbia/HCA capitalized on its size and created economies of scale in the internal control of its costs and sales activities. The focus was on bottom-line performance and new business acquisitions. This strategy proved to be very successful. Columbia/HCA generated $19 billion in annual profits and was the ninth largest employer in America.

A number of critics have charged that healthcare services and staffing at Columbia/HCA often took a back seat to the focus on profits. For example, the company provided shorter training periods than competing hospitals. One former administrator reported that

*This case was prepared by Harper Baird for and under the direction of O. C. Ferrell and Linda Ferrell. It was prepared for classroom discussion rather than to illustrate either effective or ineffective handling of an administrative, ethical, or legal decision by management. All sources used for this case were obtained through publicly available material.

training that typically took six months was sometimes accomplished in as little as two weeks at a Columbia/HCA hospital. In addition, the company was accused of "patient dumping," which refers to discharging emergency room patients or transferring them to other hospitals when they are not yet in stable condition. In 1997 officials at the Department of Health and Human Services Inspector General's Office indicated that they were considering imposing fines on Columbia/HCA for an unspecified number of patient-dumping cases. Additionally, the corporate watch dog INFACT publicly challenged the company's practices, inducting Columbia/HCA into its "Hall of Shame" of corporations that manipulate public policy to the detriment of public health.

In order to expand, the company targeted poorly performing and nonprofit hospitals. Columbia/HCA negotiations with these hospitals were often secret and not disclosed to hospital staff or to the public. The company also routinely threatened to open competing hospitals near the hospitals they wished to acquire. Additionally, Columbia/HCA often worked with hospitals during negotiations to eliminate community services; the hospital would not be required to provide these services once it became for-profit.

Columbia/HCA relied on patient referrals from local doctors in order to increase revenues. In order to encourage referrals, Columbia/HCA provided doctors with incentives such as reduced or free rent, high-paid consulting jobs, free vacations, low-cost pharmaceuticals, and free stock in local hospitals.

Columbia/HCA also passed several of their costs on to Medicare in order to increase profits. The company routinely engaged in a practice known as "upcoding," exaggerating patient illnesses on Medicare claims. Additionally, Columbia/HCA filed false cost reports in order to generate more federal reimbursements for overhead such as interest and depreciation. In case Medicare contested these charges, Columbia/HCA created a reserve account that held as much as $1 billion. When Medicare did not question the charges, the cash in the reserve account became profit. Reserves accounted for over 25 percent of Columbia/HCA's profits.

> "The highest-performing managers were rewarded with large bonuses while the lowest-performing managers lost their jobs."

Employee performance was critical to success at Columbia/HCA. The highest-performing managers were rewarded with large bonuses while the lowest-performing managers lost their jobs. Because the company's expansion strategy relied on the purchase of poorly performing hospitals, executives with less profitable hospitals were under intense pressure to increase profits. Some managers viewed Columbia/HCA's corporate culture as so unethical that they resigned. Moreover, Columbia/HCA did not have a compliance department. Jerre Frazier, a lawyer called in to investigate compliance issues at the company, said, "I don't think Rick Scott had given a thought about focusing on compliance." Over 30 whistle-blowers associated with Columbia/HCA had filed complaints against the company between 1993 and 1997, and some even lost their jobs when they attempted to share their concerns with their supervisors.

LEGAL PROBLEMS BEGIN

In March 1997 the FBI investigated Columbia/HCA's El Paso offices; the investigation moved on to the company's other locations in July. Federal investigators accused Columbia/HCA of engaging in a "systematic effort to defraud government healthcare programs." The investigation resulted in the indictment of three mid-level Columbia/HCA Healthcare Corporation executives for filing false cost reports that resulted in losses of more than $4.4 million from government programs. The government alleged that Columbia/HCA had gained at least part of its profit by overcharging Medicare and other federal health programs; that is, executives had billed the government for nonreimbursable interest expenses. In a 74-page document, federal investigators quoted confidential witnesses who stated that the company's CEO, Scott, and its president, David Vandewater, were briefed routinely on issues relating to Medicare reimbursement claims that the government had charged were fraudulent. Samuel Greco, Columbia/HCA's chief of operations, was also implicated in the scandal.

Other concerns for investigators were the incentives to physicians and the possible overuse of home health services. Investigators found that the physician referral kickback scheme had been a corporate policy from Columbia's inception, even after company lawyers had warned executives that it could be a violation of federal antikickback laws. Using this strategy, Columbia had paid doctors off in the amount of $6.9 million, thus generating over $103 million in Medicare business in El Paso alone.

Additionally, federal investigators discovered that Columbia/HCA had fraudulently overstated home healthcare laboratory-test expenses and knowingly miscategorized other expenditures so as to inflate the amounts for which it sought reimbursement. For example, Columbia/HCA's Southwest Florida Regional Medical Center in Fort Myers reportedly claimed $68,000 more in property taxes than it paid. Moreover, documents showed that the hospital had set aside money to return to the government in case auditors caught the inflated figure. Technically, expenses claimed on cost reports must be related to patient care and fall within the realm of allowable Medicare reimbursements. However, medical billing can be confusing, chaotic, imprecise, and subject to interpretation. It is not unusual for hospitals to keep two sets of accounting books. One set is provided to Medicare, and the other set, which includes records for set-aside money, is held in case auditors interpret the Medicare cost report differently than the hospital does. Some believe it is appropriate for a hospital to set aside money to return to the government if the hospital in good faith believes that its Medicare cost claims are legitimate. However, if administrators believe strongly or know that certain claims are not allowable, yet still file the claims and note them in the second set of books, they are guilty of fraud.

Confidential witnesses said that Columbia/HCA had made an effort to hide internal documents from federal regulators, documents that could have disclosed the alleged fraud. In addition, Columbia/HCA's top executive in charge of internal audits had instructed employees to soften language used in internal financial audits that was critical of Columbia/HCA's practices. According to FBI agent Joseph Ford, "investigation by the [FBI and the Defense Criminal Investigative Service] has uncovered a systematic corporate scheme perpetrated by corporate officers and managers of Columbia/HCA's hospitals, home health agencies, and other facilities in the states of Tennessee, Florida, Georgia, Texas, and elsewhere to defraud Medicare, Medicaid, and the [Civilian Health and Medical Program of the Uniformed Services]." Indicted Columbia/HCA officials pled not guilty, and defense lawyers for Columbia/HCA tried to diminish the importance of the allegations contained in the government's affidavits.

DEVELOPING A NEW ETHICAL CLIMATE AT COLUMBIA/HCA

Richard Scott resigned as CEO in July 1997. He received a substantial benefits package, including $5.1 million in cash, two years of office and secretarial expenses, $300 million in stock and options, and a five-year consulting job with Columbia/HCA that was worth

$950,000 annually. Scott says he resigned because he believed that Columbia/HCA should contest the charges, while the board believed settling was the best option.

Following Scott's resignation, Dr. Thomas Frist, Jr., became chair and CEO of the company. Frist, who had been president of HCA before it merged with Columbia, vowed to cooperate fully with the government and to develop a plan to change the troubled firm's corporate culture. Under the Federal Sentencing Guidelines for Organizations (FSGO), companies that have effective due diligence compliance programs can reduce their fines if they are convicted of fraud. For penalties to be reduced, however, an effective compliance program must be in place before misconduct occurs. Although the FSGO requires that a senior executive be in charge of the due diligence compliance program, Columbia/HCA's general counsel had been designated to take charge of the program.

> "Columbia/HCA's new mission statement emphasized a commitment to quality medical care and honesty in business practices."

After 100 days as chairman and CEO of Columbia/HCA, Frist outlined changes that would reshape the company. His reforms included a new mission statement as well as plans to create a new senior executive position to oversee ethical compliance and quality issues. Columbia/HCA's new mission statement emphasized a commitment to quality medical care and honesty in business practices. It did not, however, mention financial performance. "We have to take the company in a new direction," Frist said. "The days when Columbia/HCA was seen as an adversarial or in your face, a behind-closed-doors kind of place, is [sic] a thing of the past."

Columbia/HCA hired Alan Yuspeh as the senior executive to oversee ethical compliance and quality issues. As Senior Vice President of Ethics, Compliance, and Corporate Responsibility, Yuspeh was given a staff of 12 at the corporate headquarters and assigned to work with group, division, and facility presidents to create a "corporate culture where Columbia workers feel compelled to do what is right." Yuspeh's first initiatives were to refine monitoring techniques, boost workers' ethics and compliance training, develop a code of conduct for employees, and create an internal mechanism for workers to report any wrongdoing.

COLUMBIA/HCA LAUNCHES AN ETHICS, COMPLIANCE, AND CORPORATE RESPONSIBILITY PROGRAM

Under Yuspeh's leadership, Columbia/HCA announced that it was taking a critical step in developing a company-wide ethics, compliance, and corporate responsibility program. To initiate the program, the company designated more than 500 employees as facility ethics and compliance officers (ECOs). The new ECOs began their roles with a two-day training session in Nashville. The local leadership provided by these facility ECOs was thought to be the key link in ensuring that the company continued to develop a culture of ethical conduct and corporate responsibility.

As part of the program, Yuspeh made a 15-minute videotape that was sent to managers throughout the Columbia/HCA system. The tape announced the launch of the compliance-training program and the unveiling of a code of ethics that was designed to effectively communicate Columbia/HCA's new emphasis on compliance, integrity, and social responsibility. Frist stated, "We are making a substantial investment in our ethics and compliance program in order to ensure its success," and "Instituting a values-based culture throughout this company is something our employees have told us is critical to forming our future. The ethics and compliance initiative is a key part of that effort."

Training seminars for all employees, conducted by each facility's ECO, included introductions to the training program, the Columbia/HCA code of conduct, and the company's overall ethics and compliance program. The training seminars also included presentations by members of senior management and small-group discussions in which participants discussed how to apply the new Columbia/HCA code of conduct in ethics-related scenarios.

The purpose of the program was to help employees understand the company's strict definition of ethical behavior rather than to change their personal values. Columbia/HCA's ethical guidelines tackled basic issues such as whether nurses can accept $100 tips (they cannot), as well as complicated topics such as what constitutes Medicare fraud. In addition, the company developed certification tests for the employees who determined billing codes. In 1998 a 40-minute training video was shown to all of the firm's employees; it featured three ethical scenarios for employees to consider.

RESOLVING THE CHARGES

In 1997–1998 Columbia/HCA Healthcare settled with the Internal Revenue Service (IRS) for $71 million over allegations that it had made excessive compensation and "golden parachute" payments to over 100 executives. As a result of the settlement, the IRS, which had sought $276 million in taxes and interest, agreed to drop its charges that Columbia/HCA had awarded excessive compensation by allowing the executives to exercise stock options after a new public offering of Columbia/HCA stock. Frist had reportedly earned about $125 million by exercising stock options after that public offering, and 17 other top executives each made millions on the deals.

In August 2000 Columbia/HCA became the first corporation ever to be removed from INFACT's Hall of Shame. The executive director of INFACT announced that Columbia/HCA had drastically reduced its political activity and influence. For example, the corporation has no active federal lobbyists and has a registered lobbying presence in only twelve states. According to INFACT's executive director, "This response to grassroots pressure constitutes a landmark development in business ethics overall and challenges prevailing practices among for-profit healthcare corporations."

In December 2000 Columbia/HCA announced that it would pay the federal government more than $840 million in criminal fines and civil penalties. In June 2003 the company agreed to pay $631 million to settle the last of the government's charges that it had filed false Medicare claims, paid kickbacks to doctors, and overcharged at wound-care centers.

No senior executives at Columbia/HCA have ever been charged with a crime. However, the company has paid a total of $1.7 billion in fines, refunds, and lawsuit settlements after admitting that it had, through two subsidiaries, offered financial incentives to doctors in violation of antikickback laws, falsified records to generate higher payments for minor treatments or treatments that never occurred, charged for laboratory tests that were never ordered, charged for home health care for patients who did not qualify for it, and falsely labeled advertisements as "community education." KPMG, the firm's auditor, denied any wrongdoing on its part but agreed to pay $9 million to settle a whistle-blower lawsuit related to the charges. Columbia/HCA also signed a "Corporate Integrity Agreement" in 2000 that subjected the firm to intense scrutiny until 2009. In the same year, the company was officially renamed HCA—The Healthcare Company.

In January 2001 Frist relinquished the title of CEO to focus on other interests, but remained involved in corporate strategy as chairman of HCA's board of directors. Jack Bovender, Jr. (formerly CFO), replaced him. Of the fraud investigation, Bovender said, "We think the major issues have been settled," but he admitted that the company still had some "physician relations issues and cost report issues" to resolve in civil actions involving individual hospitals.

HCA'S ETHICS PROGRAM AT WORK

Today HCA's ethics program includes an ethics and compliance committee of independent board directors, two separate corporate committees that draft ethics policy and monitor its use, and a 20-member department that implements the program. In all, 26 executives oversee ethics and compliance for a variety of issues, ranging from taxes to pollution to the Americans with Disabilities Act.

The ethics compliance program established by Alan Yuspeh includes seven components: (1) articulating ethics through a code of conduct and a series of company policies and procedures; (2) creating awareness of these standards of compliance and promoting ethical conduct among everyone in the company through ethics training, compliance training, and other ongoing communication efforts; (3) providing a 24-hour, toll-free telephone hotline to report possible misconduct; (4) monitoring and auditing employees' performance in areas of compliance risk to ensure that established policies and procedures are being followed and are effective; (5) establishing organizational supports for the ethics compliance effort; (6) overseeing the company's implementation of and adherence to the Corporate Integrity Agreement; and (7) undertaking other efforts such as clinical ethics and pastoral services.

Training continues to play a major role in helping employees understand HCA's new focus on ethics and legal compliance. Every new employee is required to undergo two hours of orientation on the firm's code of conduct within 30 days of employment. During that time, new employees receive a copy of the code of conduct, participate in training using videotapes and games, and sign an acknowledgment card. All employees complete one hour of refresher training on the firm's code of conduct every year.

"HCA's new ethics hot line helps the firm identify misconduct and take corrective action where necessary."

HCA's new ethics hotline helps the firm identify misconduct and take corrective action where necessary. For example, in 2002 an anonymous caller to the toll-free line accused a hospital supply clerk of stealing medical gear and reselling it online through eBay. After investigators verified the complaint, the clerk was fired. Since its inception, the ethics program has fielded hundreds of such ethics-related complaints.

HCA's effort to change its corporate culture quickly and become a model corporate citizen in the healthcare industry was a real challenge. This healthcare provider learned the hard way that maintaining an organizational ethical climate is the responsibility of top management. As Bovender says, "Internal controls can always be corrupted. We've tried to come up with a system that would require a lot of people to conspire. It would be very hard for Tyco-type things to happen here." HCA seems to have recovered well from all of its problems, and in 2011 a number of companies were trying to acquire it, an indication that they view it as a great business opportunity.

HCA TODAY

Today HCA is comprised of over 160 locally managed hospitals and 105 surgery centers across the United States and the United Kingdom. In November 2006 HCA became a private company when it was purchased by a private equity group for $33 billion, which was the largest leveraged buyout in American history at the time. In March 2011 HCA became a public company once more. HCA's initial public offering (IPO) raised $3.79 billion through the sale of 126.2 million shares. Its IPO is the largest by a private equity-backed company in the United States.

Thanks to the Columbia/HCA fraud case, many health care companies implemented plans to ensure that they comply with governmental regulations and act ethically. Codes of conduct help hospitals and health care groups to improve the quality of patient care while continuing to reduce costs. Legal and compliance departments often conduct audits of hospital operations and make reports to boards of directors. These audits ensure that employees are aware of company policies, that internal controls are working, and that the corporate culture remains focused on ethical behavior.

GOVERNOR RICHARD SCOTT

After leaving Columbia/HCA, in 2001 Richard Scott cofounded Solantic, a chain of Florida walk-in clinics. Famous for its "Starbucks-like" transparent pricing, Solantic also faced legal issues, including false Medicare claims, providing false medical licensing information, and accusations of employment discrimination.

Scott entered the political arena in 2009 when he created a nonprofit political organization called Conservatives for Patients' Rights to oppose healthcare reform. In 2010 Scott announced his campaign to run for the governor of Florida. Scott portrayed himself as a government outsider, saying, "There's going to be a clear choice between career politicians with their old ideas and stuck in the status quo, and a complete outsider with fresh ideas.... I've built companies, I've created jobs, I know the frustration of small businesses with higher taxes."

Scott won the election and became the governor of Florida in January 2011. He plans to apply his cost-cutting management style to the governorship. He announced plans to donate his $133,000 salary to charity or return it to the state treasury despite spending over $3 million in corporate and lobbyist donations on his inaugural celebrations. Additionally, in March 2011 he signed an executive order requiring all state workers to undergo drug testing. These tests could cost taxpayers over $3.5 million, and Solantic clinics could be one of the major providers. Although Scott no longer has any Solantic holdings, his wife is the controlling investor of the company, which creates a major conflict of interest. As governor, Scott faces many challenges. Florida is $26 billion in debt, with another $3.5 billion deficit projected for 2011 and a 12 percent unemployment rate. Scott says, "I learned very hard lessons from what happened [at Columbia/HCA], and those lessons have helped me become a better businessman and leader."

QUESTIONS

1. What were the organizational ethical leadership problems that resulted in Columbia/HCA's misconduct?

2. Discuss the strengths and weaknesses of HCA's current ethics program. Does this program appear to satisfy the provisions of the Federal Sentencing Guidelines for Organizations and the Sarbanes–Oxley Act?

3. What other suggestions could Columbia/HCA have implemented to sensitize its employees to ethical issues?

SOURCES

Allen, Greg. "Gov. Scott, Ex-CEO, Aims to Run Fla. Like a Business." January 6, 2011, http://www.npr.org/2011/01/06/132684525/rick-scott-floridas-outsider-is-now-in-office (accessed January 10, 2011); AOL News. "Columbia/HCA Launches Ethics and Compliance Training Program." February 12, 1998, http://cbs.aol.com (access date unknown); Barry, Megan. "Compliance in Healthcare GPOs." *Ethisphere,* Q1 2010, 22–23; Caputo, Mark. "Few details emerge from suits against Rick Scott's chain of clinics." *The Miami Herald,* August 5, 2010, http://www.miamiherald.com/2010/08/05/1761961/few-details-emerge-from-suits.html (accessed January 10, 2011); Columbia/HCA Healthcare Corporation. "1996 Annual Report to Stockholders." "Columbia/HCA to Sell Part of Business." *Commercial Appeal,* June 3, 1998, B8; Eichenwald, Kurt. "Reshaping the Culture at Columbia/HCA." *The New York Times,* November 4, 1997, C2; Eichenwald, Kurt, and N. R. Kleinfeld. "At Columbia/HCA, Scandal Hurts." *Commercial Appeal,* December 21, 1997, C1, C3; "HCA again a public company." March 10, 2011, South Florida Business Journal, http://www.bizjournals.com/southflorida/news/2011/03/10/hca-a-public-company-again.html (accessed June 4, 2011); "HCA Tentatively Agrees to Multimillion Fraud Settlement." *American Medical News,* January 27, 2003, http://www.ama-assn.org/sci-pubs/amnews/pick_03/gvbf0127.htm (accessed April 24, 2003); Hiaasen, Scott, and John Dorschner. "Rick Scott and his role in Columbia/HCA scandal." *The Miami Herald,* June 26, 2010, http://www.miamiherald.com/2010/06/26/v-fullstory/1703036/rick-scott-and-his-role-in-columbiahca.html (accessed January 6, 2011); Hospital Corporation of America. "About Our Company." http://hcahealthcare.com/about (accessed January 6, 2011); Hospital Corporation of America. "Ethics, Compliance, and Corporate Responsibility: Introduction." http://ec.hcahealthcare.com (accessed April 24, 2003); Hospital Corporation of America. "History." http://hca.hcahealthcare.com/CustomPage.asp?guidCustomContentID=C2E6928A-D8B1-42AF-BA44-6C2B591282D5 (accessed April 24, 2003); Lagnado, Lucette. "Columbia Taps Lawyer for Ethics Post: Yuspeh Led Defense Initiative of 1980s." *The Wall Street Journal,* October 14, 1997, B6; Lowry, Tom. "Columbia/HCA Hires Ethics Expert." *USA Today,* October 14, 1997, 4B; Lowry, Tom. "Loss Warning Hits Columbia/HCA Stock." *USA Today,* February 9, 1998, 2B; Mansfield, Duncan. "HCA Names Bovender Chief Executive." January 8, 2001, Yahoo! News, http://biz.yahoo.com/apf/010108/hca_change_2. html (accessed January 16, 2001); Ornstein, Charles. "Columbia/HCA Prescribes Employee Ethics Program." *The Tampa Tribune,* February 20,

1998, 4; *PR Newswire.* "Corporate Influence Curtailed." August 2, 2000; *PR Newswire.* "INFACT Urges Columbia/HCA to Remove Itself from the Hall of Shame." http://www.prnewswire.com (accessed May 27, 1999); Queisser, Lori. "Healthcare Compliance: A Pharmactical Perspective." *Ethisphere,* Quarter 01 2010, 24–25; Rick Scott for Governor, 2010. "The Truth about Rick Scott." http://www.truthaboutrickscott.com (accessed January 6, 2011); Rodriguez, Eva M. "Columbia/HCA Probe Turns to Marketing Billing." *The Wall Street Journal,* August 21, 1997, A2; "Rick Scott: Now the hard part." *The Florida Times-Union,* January 5, 2011, http://jacksonville.com/opinion/editorials/2011-01-05/story/rick-scott-now-hard-part (accessed January 10, 2011); Sharockman, Aaron, and Marc Caputo. "Gov. Rick Scott orders random drug tests for state workers." *The Miami Herald,* March 23, 2011, http://www.miamiherald.com/2011/03/23/2130397/gov-rick-scott-orders-random-drug.html#ixzz1IZgtVZxf (accessed April 4, 2011); Singer, Stacey. "Gov. Rick Scott's drug testing policy stirs suspicion." *The Palm Beach Post,* March 26, 2011, http://www.palmbeachpost.com/money/gov-rick-scotts-drug-testing-policy-stirs-suspicion-1350922.html?viewAsSinglePage=true (accessed April 4, 2011); Smith, Adam C. "Rick Scott, multimillionaire political rookie, gunning to be governor of Florida." *The St. Petersburg Times,* May 7, 2010, http://www.tampabay.com/news/politics/elections/rick-scott-multimillionaire-political-rookie-gunning-to-be-governor-of/1093234 (accessed January 10, 2011); Terry, Ken. "IPO on Hold, HCA Owners Pile More Debt on Hospital Chain." December 6, 2010, http://www.bnet.com/blog/healthcare-business/ipo-on-hold-hca-owners-pile-more-debt-on-hospital-chain/2198 (accessed January 6, 2011); Weinberg, Neil. "Healing Thyself." *Forbes* online, March 17, 2003, http://www.forbes.com/forbes/2003/0317/064.html (accessed April 24, 2003); Woodyard, Chris. "FBI Alleges Systemic Fraud at Columbia." *USA Today,* October 7, 1997, 1B; U.S. Department of Justice. "Largest Health Care Fraud Case in U.S. History Settled: HCA Investigation Nets Record Total of $1.7 Billion (Press Release)." http://www.justice.gov/opa/pr/2003/June/03_civ_386.htm, June 26, 2003 (accessed January 6, 2011); Wynne, Michael. "Columbia/HCA." University of Wollongong, 2000–2007, http://www.uow.edu.au/~bmartin/dissent/documents/health/access_columbia_hca.html (accessed January 7, 2011).

CASE 15

The Coca-Cola Company Struggles with Ethical Crises*

As one of the most valuable brand names worldwide, Coca-Cola has generally excelled as a business over its long history. However, in recent decades the company has had difficulty meeting its financial objectives and has been associated with a number of ethical crises. As a result, some investors have lost faith in the company. For example, Warren Buffet (board member and strong supporter of and investor in Coca-Cola) resigned from the board in 2006 after years of frustration over Coca-Cola's failure to overcome its challenges.

Since the 1990s Coca-Cola has been accused of unethical behavior in a number of areas, including product safety, anticompetitiveness, racial discrimination, channel stuffing, distributor conflicts, intimidation of union workers, pollution, depletion of natural resources, and health concerns. The company has dealt with a number of these issues, some via private settlements and some via court battles, while others remain unresolved. Although its handling of different ethical situations has not always been lauded, Coca-Cola has generally responded by seeking to improve its detection and compliance systems. However, it remains to be seen whether the company can permanently rise above its ethical problems, learn from its mistakes, make necessary changes, avoid further problems, and still emerge as a leader among beverage companies.

HISTORY OF THE COCA-COLA COMPANY

Founded in 1886, the Coca-Cola Company is the world's largest beverage company. In addition to Coca-Cola and Diet Coke, it sells other profitable brands including Powerade, Minute Maid, and Dasani water. To service global demand, the company has the world's largest distribution system, which reaches customers and businesses in nearly every country on the planet.

Until the mid-twentieth century Coca-Cola focused on expanding market share within the United States. After World War II, however, the company began to recognize the opportunity in global sales. In the last part of the twentieth century Coca-Cola extended this global push, taking advantage of international revenue opportunities and fierce soft drink competition in an effort to dominate the global soft drink industry. By the late 1990s Coca-Cola had gained more than 50 percent global market share in the soft drink industry, while PepsiCo, Coke's greatest rival, stood around 15 to 20 percent. Coca-Cola remains

*This case was prepared by Jennifer Sawayda, Kevin Sample, and Rob Boostrum under the direction of Debbie Thorne, O. C. Ferrell, and Linda Ferrell. It was prepared for classroom discussion rather than to illustrate either effective or ineffective handling of an administrative, ethical, or legal decision by management. All sources used for this case were obtained through publicly available material.

largely focused on beverages, while PepsiCo has diversified into snack foods and drinks such as waters, teas, and fruit juices. While Pepsi has tended to focus more on American markets, the largest portion of Coca-Cola's sales now come from outside the United States. As the late Roberto Goizueta, former CEO of Coca-Cola, once said, "Coca-Cola used to be an American company with a large international business. Now we are a large international company with a sizable American business."

In spite of international recognition and a strong brand, Coca-Cola has run into numerous difficulties. The company's problems began in the mid-1990s at the executive level. In 1997 Doug Ivester became CEO. Ivester, heralded for his ability to handle the company's complex finances, had been groomed for the position by Goizueta. However, Ivester's tenure as CEO was short. He was not well equipped to handle the tough competition from Pepsi combined with the many ethical disasters Coke faced throughout the 1990s. Some people even began to doubt "Big Red's" reputation and its future prospects. Ivester's departure in 1999 represented a high-profile aberration in a relatively strong 100-year record.

In 2000 Doug Daft, the company's former president and chief operating officer (COO), replaced Ivester as CEO. Daft's tenure too was rocky, and the company continued to have problems throughout the early 2000s. For example, the company was allegedly involved in racial discrimination, misrepresentations of market tests, manipulation of earnings, and the disruption of long-term contractual arrangements with distributors.

By 2004 Neville Isdell, former chairman and CEO of Coca-Cola Beverages Plc in Great Britain, was called out of retirement to improve Coca-Cola's reputation; however, the company continued to face ethical crises. These problems aside, Coca-Cola's overall performance seemed to improve under Isdell's tenure. In 2008 Isdell relinquished the role of CEO to then-president and COO Muhtar Kent. Isdell also decided to step down as chair of the board in order to return to retirement. Under Kent's leadership, Coca-Cola is seeking to revise its strategy through social responsibility initiatives and brand expansion.

PEPSICO: SERIOUS COMPETITION

Coca-Cola has been a success for more than 120 years. In contrast, PepsiCo (founded at roughly the same time) did not become a serious competitor until after World War II, when it came up with the idea to sell its product in larger portions for the same price as Coke. The "cola wars" picked up speed in the mid-1960s and have not abated since. Today the two American companies wage war primarily on international fronts. While the fight occasionally grows ugly, with accusations of anticompetitive behavior, generally the two companies remain civil.

In early 2006 PepsiCo enjoyed a market value greater than Coca-Cola for the first time. Pepsi's strategy of focusing on snack foods and innovative approaches in the noncola beverage market has helped the company gain market share and surpass Coca-Cola in overall performance. During the 2008–2009 recession PepsiCo's diversification strategy continued to pay off. On the other hand, some investors fear for Coca-Cola's long-term prospects because of the company dependence on international sales and a strong dollar. Combined with the recent global recession, these are liabilities that may hurt Coca-Cola's long-term profitability. Because PepsiCo does 60 percent of its business in North America, a strong dollar does not adversely affect the company as much as it does Coca-Cola. These factors may give PepsiCo more of an upper-hand over Coca-Cola in the future.

COCA-COLA'S REPUTATION

Coca-Cola remains one of the most recognized brand names in the world today, worth more than $73 billion in 2011. The company has always demonstrated strong market orientation, making strategic decisions and taking action to attract, satisfy, and retain customers. During World War II, for example, then-president Robert Woodruff distributed Coke around the world to sell to members of the armed services for a nickel a bottle. This strategy gave soldiers an affordable taste of home, created lifelong loyal customers, and increased global brand recognition. The presence of Coca-Cola products in almost every corner of the globe today shows how successful the company's international marketing strategy has been. Savvy marketing and a reputation for quality have always been hallmarks of Coca-Cola and have helped to make the product ubiquitous.

However, in the 1990s and 2000s poor decisions, mismanagement, and alleged misconduct cast a shadow over the company. In 2000 Coca-Cola failed to make the top ten of *Fortune*'s annual "America's Most Admired Companies" list for the first time in ten years. By 2010 Coca-Cola was in tenth place. Leadership issues, disappointing economic performance, and other upheavals likely affected its standing on the *Fortune* list. In 2001 the company disappeared from the top 100 of *Business Ethics* magazine's annual list of "100 Best Corporate Citizens." For a company that had been on both lists for years, this was disappointing but not unexpected given its recent ethical crises. However, there are signs that Coca-Cola is bouncing back. In 2010 Coca-Cola ranked number eight in *Corporate Responsibility* Magazine's "100 Best Corporate Citizens" list, while PepsiCo was number 13.

CRISIS SITUATIONS

In 1996 Coca-Cola traded just below $50 a share. In 2010 it ranged between $46 and $59. This slow growth may be attributed to various internal problems associated with top management turnover and departure of key investors, as well as external problems that have led to a loss of reputation. The following incidents exemplify some of the key crises Coca-Cola has faced in the last several years.

Contamination Scare

Perhaps the most damaging of Coca-Cola's crises—and a situation dreaded by every company—began in June 1999 when about thirty Belgian children became ill after consuming Coke products. Although the company issued an isolated product recall, the problem escalated. The Belgian government eventually ordered the recall of all Coca-Cola products, which prompted officials in Luxembourg and the Netherlands to recall Coke products as well. Coca-Cola finally determined that the illnesses were the result of an improperly processed batch of carbon dioxide. Coca-Cola was slow to issue a response to the problem, taking several days to address the media. The company had initially judged the problem to be minor and did not immediately investigate the extent of the issue. The slow response time led to a public relations nightmare. France soon reported more than 100 people sick from bad Coke and temporarily banned all Coca-Cola products as well. Soon thereafter, a shipment of Bonaqua, a new Coca-Cola water product, arrived in Poland contaminated with mold. In each of these instances, the company's slow responses and failure to acknowledge the severity of the situation harmed its reputation and cast doubt on then-CEO Ivester's ability to successfully lead.

The contamination crisis was exacerbated in December 1999 when Belgium ordered Coca-Cola to halt the "Restore" marketing campaign it had launched in order to regain consumer trust and sales in Belgium. A rival firm claimed that the campaign strategy—which included free cases of the product, discounts to wholesalers and retailers, and extra promotion personnel—was unlawful. The claim was upheld under Belgium's strict anti-trust laws, and Coca-Cola was forced to abandon the campaign. This decision, following the previous crisis, further reduced Coca-Cola's market standing in Europe.

Competitive Issues

In the late 1990s, government inquiries into the company's marketing tactics plagued the company throughout Europe. Because EU countries have strict antitrust laws, all firms must pay close attention to market share and position when considering joint ventures, mergers, and acquisitions. During the summer of 1999 Coca-Cola began an aggressive expansion push in France, and the French government responded by refusing Coca-Cola's bid to purchase Orangina, a French beverage company. French authorities also forced Coca-Cola to scale back its acquisition of Cadbury Schweppes, maker of Dr. Pepper.

Moreover, in late 1999 Italy successfully won a court case against Coca-Cola over anticompetitive prices, prompting the European Commission to launch a full-scale probe into the company's competitive practices. In addition, PepsiCo and Virgin Cola accused Coca-Cola of using rebates and discounts to crowd their products off the shelves. Coca-Cola's strong-arm tactics were found to be in violation of European laws, once again demonstrating the company's lack of awareness of European culture and laws.

> "Coca-Cola's strong-arm tactics were found to be in violation of European laws."

Despite these legal tangles, Coca-Cola products, along with many other U.S. products, dominate foreign markets worldwide. The growing omnipresence of U.S. products, especially in highly competitive markets, makes corporate reputation, both perceived and actual, essential to building relationships with business partners, government officials, and other stakeholders.

Allegations of Racial Discrimination

In 1999 Coca-Cola's reputation was dealt another blow when 1,500 African American employees sued for racial discrimination. The lawsuit, which eventually grew to include 2,000 current and former employees, accused the company of discriminating in areas of pay, promotion, and performance evaluation. Plaintiffs charged that the company grouped African American workers at the bottom of the pay scale and that they earned around $26,000 a year less than Caucasian employees in comparable jobs. The suit also alleged that top management had known about companywide discrimination since 1995 but had done nothing about it. In 1992 Coca-Cola had pledged to spend $1 billion on goods and services from minority vendors, an action designed to show the public that Coca-Cola did not discriminate, but the lawsuit from its own employees painted a different picture. Although Coca-Cola strongly denied the allegations, the lawsuit provoked unrest within the company. In response, Coca-Cola created a diversity council and the company paid $193 million to settle the claims.

Inflated Earnings Related to Channel Stuffing

Coca-Cola was also accused of channel stuffing during the early 2000s. Channel stuffing is the practice of shipping extra, unrequested inventory to wholesalers and retailers before the end of a quarter. A company counts the shipments as sales although the product often remains in warehouses or is later returned. Because the goods have been shipped, the company counts them as revenue at the end of the quarter. Channel stuffing creates the appearance of strong demand (or conceals declining demand) and results in inflated financial statement earnings and the subsequent misleading of investors.

In 2004 Coca-Cola was accused of sending extra concentrate to Japanese bottlers between 1997 and 1999 in an effort to inflate its profits. The company was already under investigation; in 2000 a former employee had filed a lawsuit accusing the company of fraud and improper business practices. The company settled the allegations, but the Securities and Exchange Commission (SEC) did find that channel stuffing had occurred. Coca-Cola had pressured bottlers into buying additional concentrate in exchange for extended credit.

Trouble with Distributors

In early 2006 Coca-Cola once again faced problems—this time on its home front. Fifty-four of its U.S. bottlers filed lawsuits against Coke and the company's largest bottler, Coca-Cola Enterprises (CCE). The suit sought to block Coke and CCE, both based in Atlanta, from expanding delivery of Powerade sports drinks directly to Walmart warehouses instead of to individual stores. Bottlers alleged that the Powerade bottler contract did not permit warehouse delivery to large retailers. They claimed that Coke breached the agreement by committing to provide warehouse delivery of Powerade to Walmart and by proposing to use CCE as its agent for delivery. The main problem was that Coke was attempting to step away from the century-old tradition of direct-store delivery (DSD), in which bottlers deposit drinks at individual stores, stock shelves, and build merchandising displays. Bottlers claimed that if Coke and CCE went forward with their plan, it would greatly diminish the value of their businesses.

In their defense, Coke and CCE asserted that they were simply trying to accommodate a request from Walmart for warehouse delivery (which is how PepsiCo distributes its Gatorade brand). CCE had also proposed making payments to other bottlers in return for taking over Powerade distribution in their territories. However, bottlers feared such an arrangement violated antitrust laws. The bottlers and Coca-Cola reached an undisclosed agreement in 2007. As part of the settlement, warehouse deliveries were deemed acceptable in some situations, and guidelines were developed for assessing those situations.

When addressing problems faced by Coca-Cola, the media tends to focus primarily on the company's reputation rather than on its relations with bottlers, distributors, suppliers, and other partners. Without these strategic partnerships, Coca-Cola would not be where it is today. Such partnerships involve sharing in risks and rewards. Issues such as the contamination scare and racial discrimination allegations, especially when handled poorly, can reflect on business relationships beyond the key company's business. When the reputation of one company suffers, all those within the supply chain suffer in some way. This is especially true because Coca-Cola adopted an enterprise-resource system that linked Coca-Cola's once highly secret information to a host of partners. The company's crises also harmed Coke's partner companies, their stakeholders, and eventually their bottom lines.

> "When the reputation of one company suffers, all those within the supply chain suffer in some way."

International Problems Related to Unions

More sinister accusations against Coca-Cola have surfaced in Colombia and Guatemala. Since 1989 eight unionized workers employed at the Coca-Cola bottling plant in Colombia had been killed, 48 had been forced into hiding, and 65 had received death threats. Many believe the deaths and threats were the results of intimidation against union workers. The union, which alleged that Coke and its local bottler were complicit in the intimidation and the deaths, sought reparations for the families of the slain and displaced workers. Coke denied the allegations and noted that only one of the eight workers was killed on the bottling plant premises. Also, the company maintains that the other deaths were byproducts of Colombia's four-decades-long civil war. As a result of the problems in Colombia, among other concerns, in 2007 a group of hundreds of people including Teamsters, environmentalists, human rights proponents, and student activists gathered in New York City to protest Coca-Cola.

Coca-Cola was later sued by Guatemalan workers alleging that they and their families at the Coke-owned bottling plant Incasa had been victims of violence after the workers decided to join unions. The plaintiffs accuse Coke of knowing about the retaliation that unionized workers face in Guatemala but doing little to prevent it. A Coca-Cola spokeswoman has stated that although the company has a minority stake in Incasa, the Guatemalan plant is independently owned.

Issues Regarding Water Usage and Pollution

Coca-Cola has also encountered trouble at its bottling plants in India, fielding accusations of both groundwater depletion and contamination. In 2003 the Centre for Science and Environment (CSE) tested soft drinks produced in India by Coca-Cola and other companies; findings indicated extreme levels of pesticides from using contaminated groundwater. In 2004 the first set of standards for pesticides in soft drinks was developed, supported by an Indian parliamentary committee. Although Coca-Cola denied the allegations, stating that its water is filtered and its final products are tested before being released, sales dropped temporarily by 15 percent.

In the Indian city of Varanasi, Coca-Cola was also accused of contaminating the groundwater with wastewater. Officials at the company admitted that the plant did have a wastewater issue but insisted that a new pipeline had been built to eliminate the problem. However, during the early 2000s a number of tests were conducted regarding "sludge" produced at Coca-Cola's Indian plants. These tests, conducted by the Central Pollution Control Board of India and the British Broadcasting Corporation, came up with toxic results.

The company runs bottling plants in a handful of drought-plagued areas around India, and groups of officials blame the plants for a dramatic decline in available water. In 2004 local officials closed a Coca-Cola plant in the Indian state of Kerala; however, the closure was overturned by Kerala's court. Although the court agreed that Coca-Cola's presence contributed to water depletion, it stated the company was not solely to blame. Nonetheless, farmers and local residents, forced to vie with Coca-Cola for water, have protested Coca-Cola's presence both there and throughout India.

As a result of these accusations, the University of Michigan requested that the Energy and Resources Institute in New Delhi research the issues. The university had suspended its contracts with Coca-Cola until the company hired third parties to investigate the claims. The Energy and Resources Institutes's findings indicated that Coca-Cola's soda did not contain higher-than-normal levels of pesticides. However, the report did indicate that the company's bottling plants were stressing water resources and suggested that the company do a better job of considering a plant's location based on resources and future impact.

Coca-Cola's Impact on Health

For years Coca-Cola has been battling consumer perceptions that its soft drinks contribute to obesity. In 2008 Coca-Cola launched a "Motherhood and Myth-Busting" campaign in Australia, attempting to convince the public that a diet including soda was healthy for children. The Australian Competition and Consumer Commission promptly took Coca-Cola to court after the Obesity Policy Coalition, the Parents' Jury, and the Australian Dental Association all filed complaints. As a result, in 2009 the company was forced to release new advertisements in a number of Australian newspapers correcting information such as the amount of caffeine found in Diet Coke. Coca-Cola admits that it did not supply consumers with detailed information during its campaign. Also in 2008 the FDA declared that the company had violated the Federal Food, Drug, and Cosmetic Act when naming the Coca-Cola Diet Plus beverage. Using "plus" in the name indicated an unsubstantiated nutritional claim.

The next year Coca-Cola was sued by the Center for Science in the Public Interest regarding misleading marketing that concerned the contents of its VitaminWater. Although the beverage is marketed as healthy, it contains a high amount of sugar. (One television advertisement featured a woman describing how VitaminWater has allowed her to use so few sick days she could "play hooky" at home with her boyfriend.) Coca-Cola tried to have the lawsuit dismissed, but a judge ruled that it could continue after determining that Vitamin-Water lacked the nutritional requirements needed to make certain health claims.

As concerns over obesity escalate, the U.S. government is considering imposing a tax on soft drinks. The massive national deficit has added fuel to the fire, with some lawmakers recommending a soda tax as a way to reduce the deficit. Coca-Cola and similar companies vehemently oppose such a tax and accuse the government of unfairly targeting its industry. CEO Muhtar Kent believes the problem of obesity stems more from a "sedentary lifestyle" than from sugary beverages. He also points to the fact that the average caloric content in soft drinks has dropped 25 percent over the last two decades through the adoption of diet beverages. The trade group for Coca-Cola and other soft-drink makers is spending millions of dollars in lobbying efforts and has run advertisements encouraging consumers to oppose the tax.

Another possible challenge for Coca-Cola involves claims that certain ingredients in its products could contribute to cancer. In 2011 the Center for Science in the Public Interest (CSPI) wrote a letter to the Food and Drug Administration urging the agency to institute a ban against caramel coloring in soda drinks and other products. CSPI maintains that the caramel coloring contains two cancer-causing ingredients. The American Beverage Association has denied this view, claiming that there is no evidence that shows caramel coloring causes cancer in humans. However, California subsequently made plans to consider labeling products that contain caramel coloring. If other states follow California's lead, this could negatively impact sales of Coca-Cola and other soft drinks.

RECOVERY FROM ETHICAL CRISES

Following the health scare in Belgium, Belgian officials closed their investigation involving Coca-Cola and announced that no charges would be filed. A Belgian health report indicated that no toxic contamination had been found inside Coke bottles. The bottles did contain tiny traces of carbonyl sulfide, producing a rotten-egg smell, but it was not nearly enough to be toxic. Officials also reported no structural problems within Coca-Cola's production plant.

The racial discrimination lawsuit, along with the threat of a boycott by the National Association for the Advancement of Colored People (NAACP), led Coca-Cola to address its diversity issues. When the company settled the racial discrimination lawsuit, the agreement stipulated that Coke would donate $50 million to a foundation supporting programs in minority communities, hire an ombudsman reporting directly to the CEO to investigate complaints of discrimination and harassment, and set aside $36 million to form a seven-person task force with authority to oversee the company's employment practices. The task force, which includes business and civil rights experts, has unprecedented power to dictate company policy regarding the hiring, compensation, and promotion of women and minorities.

In response to the SEC's findings regarding channel stuffing, Coca-Cola created an ethics and compliance office, and the company is required to verify quarterly that it has not altered the terms of payment or extended special credit. Additionally, the company agreed to work to reduce the amount of concentrate held by international bottlers.

Coca-Cola has defended itself against allegations of violence in Colombia, and the Colombian court and the Colombian attorney generally support the company. The Eleventh Circuit Court of Appeals in Florida dismissed the lawsuit after concluding that the plaintiffs had not presented sufficient evidence of wrongdoing.

Although Coca-Cola's issues in India did cause a temporary dip in sales and ongoing protests, the company insists that it has taken measures to ensure safety and quality. Coca-Cola has partnered with local governments, NGOs, schools, and communities to establish rainwater-collection facilities across India. The goal is to work toward renewing and returning all groundwater. In addition, the company is strengthening its plant requirements and working with local communities to ensure the sustainability of local water resources. As a result, Coca-Cola has received several corporate social responsibility awards in areas such as water conservation, management, and community development initiatives.

> "Coca-Cola has received several corporate social responsibility awards in areas such as water conservation, management, and community development initiatives."

Despite its global work in water sustainability, groundwater-depletion issues continue to plague Coca-Cola in India. The state of Kerala has passed a law that allows individuals to seek compensation from the company. The government claims that Coca-Cola "over-extracted" groundwater and improperly disposed of sludge, causing damages to the environment and local populations. Coca-Cola has countered that the decision was not based on facts and claims that studies have failed to find a link between Coca-Cola's bottling operations and environmental damage. This situation could partially undermine Coca-Cola's sustainability image in India.

Responding to health issues related to Coca-Cola's products is a more complex process. The company itself cannot be held responsible for how many sugary or artificially sweetened beverages the public consumes. Ultimately, Coca-Cola's responsibility is to disclose honest, detailed information regarding its products so that consumers may make educated beverage choices. Coca-Cola has also begun researching healthier products, both as a way to enhance its reputation and increase profits. To make its soft drinks healthier, Coca-Cola is investigating no-calorie sweeteners like stevia as future product ingredients. Coca-Cola is also creating smaller-sized soft drinks. The new "Coke Mini" product is only 7.5 ounces and contains 90 calories. Additionally, Coca-Cola is making an effort to encourage consumers to exercise and embrace a healthy lifestyle through nutritional education and partnerships with governments, NGOs, and public health representatives. For instance, the company awarded a grant to the American Academy of Family Physicians to create educational content regarding soft drinks and sweeteners on AAFP's health and wellness website. Although critics accuse AAFP of selling out, the AAFP has assured the public that it will not endorse the brands or products of any of its partners.

SOCIAL RESPONSIBILITY FOCUS

Because Coca-Cola is a globally recognized brand and has a strong history of market orientation, the company has developed a number of social responsibility initiatives to further enhance its business. These initiatives are guided by the company's core beliefs in marketplace, workplace, community, and environment. As stated in its Mission and Vision & Values statements, Coca-Cola wants to "Inspire Moments of Optimism" through brands and actions as well as to create value and to make a positive difference in the countries in which it does business. For instance, Coca-Cola is joining former U.S. Secretary of State Madeleine Albright and The Aspen Institute President and CEO Walter Isaacson on an initiative to provide assistance to entrepreneurs in Muslim-majority countries. The organization Partners for a New Beginning (PNB), with Albright as chair and Muhtar Kent and Issacson as vice chairs, is working to encourage businesses, universities, NGOs, and other organizations to help Muslim entrepreneurs through investments and/or contributions of technology and equipment. PNB also vowed to increase access to finance, education, and other areas of business for Muslim entrepreneurs. According to CEO Muhtar Kent, Coca-Cola's participation in this initiative will help to "build a strong bridge of understanding and respect between the U.S. and the Muslim world."

Coca-Cola also offers grants to various colleges and universities, both nationally and internationally. In addition to grants, Coca-Cola provides scholarships to hundreds of colleges, including thirty tribal colleges belonging to the American Indian College Fund. Such initiatives help enhance the Coca-Cola name, and ultimately benefit shareholders. Through the Coca-Cola Scholars Foundation, 250 new Coca-Cola Scholars are named each year and brought to Atlanta for interviews. Fifty students are then designated National Scholars, receiving awards of $20,000 for college; the remaining 200 are designated Regional Scholars, receiving $10,000 awards.

Like many other companies, Coca-Cola is addressing the issues of recycling and climate change. In 2007 Coca-Cola signed the UN Global Compact's "Caring for Climate: The Business Leadership Platform." In doing so, the company pledged to increase energy efficiency and reduce emissions. In 2009 Coca-Cola released the PlantBottle™. This new bottle, made from 30 percent plant-based material, is fully recyclable and reduces use of nonrenewable resources and production of carbon emissions. Coca-Cola has partnered with the Heinz Co. to extend Coke's PlantBottle packaging to Heinz ketchup bottles. Coca-Cola also used the PlantBottle when it sponsored the 2010 Olympics in Vancouver. In fact, Coca-Cola vowed to produce zero waste during the games, one of the first times such a major marketer has embarked on this initiative. Some of the other ways that Coca-Cola went "green" during the Olympics included its use of diesel-electric hybrid delivery trucks, staff uniforms made out of recycled bottles, and carbon offsets for air travel.

In addition, Coca-Cola has taken action to improve communities, both nationally and on a global scale. For instance, Coca-Cola's Sprite business partnered with Miami Heat forward LeBron James on the Sprite Spark Parks Project. Sprite announced plans to contribute

$2 million into the building or restoration of over 150 basketball courts, athletic fields, community spaces, and playgrounds in a minimum of 40 cities. In terms of its global responsibilities, the company remains proactive on issues such as the HIV/AIDS epidemic in Africa. Coca-Cola has partnered with UNAIDS and other NGOs to put in place important initiatives and programs to help combat the threat of HIV/AIDS.

Because consumers generally respect Coca-Cola, trust its products, and have strong attachments through brand recognition and product loyalty, Coca-Cola's actions foster relationship marketing. Because of this sense of relationship with the Coca-Cola brand, problems at the company can stir the emotions of stakeholders.

THE CURRENT SITUATION AT COCA-COLA

In the early part of the twenty-first century, Coca-Cola's financial performance was positive, with the company maintaining a sound balance sheet. However, earnings across the soft drink industry have been on a slow decline because of decreased consumption, increased competition, and the 2008–2009 global recession. Nevertheless, Coca-Cola is confident of its long-term viability and remains strong in the belief that the company is well positioned to succeed.

> "Organizations like the World Health Organization are criticizing such an expansion as they believe it is unethical to introduce a product with no nutritional benefits into impoverished countries."

In an attempt to regain growth, Coca-Cola is expanding globally. With Coke reaching market saturation in developed countries, the company is looking to gain a foothold in emerging economies. In 2010 the company announced plans to undergo a major expansion in Africa, with plans to invest $12 billion into the continent within the next 10 years. Such a plan has both positive and negative aspects. On the negative side, organizations like the World Health Organization are criticizing such an expansion as they believe it is unethical to introduce a product with no nutritional benefits into impoverished countries. On the other hand, Coke employs approximately 65,000 Africans and encourages entrepreneurship. Success in emerging economies may be the push that Coca-Cola needs to jumpstart growth.

CONCLUSION

For more than a decade Coca-Cola has been fighting allegations of a lack of health and safety of its products, unlawful competitive practices, racial discrimination and employee intimidation, channel stuffing, unfair distributor treatment, and the pollution and pillaging of natural resources, but under Neville Isdell and Muhtar Kent's leadership, the company appears to have rebounded and begun to take strides toward improving its image. The company is focusing more on environmental stewardship, for example. However, the company's critics say that Coca-Cola is not doing enough—that its efforts are merely window dressing to hide its corruption. Case in point: Although the company claims to have addressed all its issues in India and says it is making an effort to aid the country's population, both the government and the citizens of Kerala maintain that the company has decreased the area's groundwater. Shareholder reactions have altered many times over the company's history, but the company has retained a large loyal base. The company hopes that its current leadership is strong enough to move Coca-Cola past this focus on ethics and into a profitable start to the twenty-first century.

QUESTIONS

1. What role does corporate reputation play within organizational performance and social responsibility? Develop a list of factors or characteristics that different stakeholders may use in assessing corporate reputation. Are these factors consistent across stakeholders? Why or why not?

2. Assume you have just become CEO at Coca-Cola. Outline the strategic steps you would take to remedy the concerns emanating from the company's board of directors, consumers, employees, business partners, governments, and the media. What elements of social responsibility would you draw from in responding to these stakeholder issues?

3. What do you think of Coca-Cola's environmental initiatives? Are they just window dressing, or does the company seem to be sincere in its efforts?

SOURCES

AAFP. "Coca-Cola Grant Launches AAFP Consumer Alliance Program." October 6, 2009, http://www.aafp.org/online/en/home/publications/news/news-now/inside-aafp/20091006cons-alli-coke.html (accessed February 25, 2011); Ames, Paul. "Case Closed on Coke Health Scare." Associated Press, April 22, 2000, HighBeam Research, http://www.highbeam.com/doc/ 1P1-26137611.html (accessed September 4, 2009); "Another Coke Plant, More Pollution Dumping." *South Asian,* June 10, 2007, http://www.thesouthasian.org/archives/2007/another_coke_plant_more_pollut.html (accessed September 4, 2009); Beucke, Dan. "Coke Promises a Probe in Colombia." *BusinessWeek,* February 6, 2006, 11; Brooker, Katrina. "The Pepsi Machine." *Fortune,* February 6, 2006, 68–72; Burke, Kelly. "Coca-Cola Busted for Big Fat Rotten Lies." *The Sydney Morning Herald,* April 2, 2009, http://www.smh.com.au/national/cocacolabusted-for-big-fat-rotten-lies-20090402-9kn6.html?page=1 (accessed September 4, 2009); Chase, Randall. "Judge Dismisses Shareholder Suit against Coca-Cola." Associated Press via SignonSanDiego.com, October 22, 2007, http://www.signonsandiego.com/news/business/20071022-1441-coca-cola-lawsuit.html (accessed September 8, 2009); CNN Money. "Most Admired Companies 2010." http://money.cnn.com/magazines/fortune/mostadmired/2010/ (accessed February 18, 2011); "Coca-Cola Appears to Have Settled Lawsuit over Distribution to Retail Distribution Centers." *Supply Chain Digest,* February 14, 2007, http://www.scdigest.com/assets/newsViews/07-02-14-2.cfm?cid=896&ctype=content (accessed September 4, 2009); *CR (Corporate Responsibility) Magazine.* "CR's 100 Best Corporate Citizens 2010." http://www.thecro.com/files/CR100Best.pdf (accessed January 6, 2011); Coca-Cola Company. http://www.thecoca-colacompany.com (accessed May 16, 2009); Coca-Cola Company. "Coca-Cola Commits to Advancing Opportunity in the Muslim World, Helping End Child Hunger." http://www.thecoca-colacompany.com/citizenship/news_pnb.html, September 24, 2010 (accessed February 25, 2011); Doyle, T. C. "Channel Stuffing Rears Its Ugly Head." *VARBusiness,* May 6, 2003, http://www.crn.com/ it-channel/18823602;jsessionid=TC1LHY0F4LAXYQSNDLPSKHSCJUNN2JVN (accessed September 4, 2009); Drawbaugh, Kevin. "Soda pop, sales tax targeted to cut deficit." *Reuters,* http://www.reuters.com/article/2010/11/17/us-usa-deficit-domenici-rivlin-idUSTRE6AG31U20101117?pageNumber=1 (accessed February 25, 2011); Foust, Dean, and Geri Smith. "'Killer Coke' or Innocent Abroad? Controversy over Anti-Union Violence in Colombia Has Colleges Banning Coca-Cola." *BusinessWeek,* January 23, 2006, 46–48; Fredrix, Emily. "Coca-Cola Says Industry Must Fight Soda Taxes." Manufacturing.Net, June 14, 2010, http://www.manufacturing.net/News-Coca-Cola-Says-Industry-Must-Fight-Soda-Taxes-061410.aspx (accessed February 25, 2011); Gaouette,

Nicole. "Clinton Says Intel, Coca-Cola Will Assist Muslim Entrepreneurs." *Bloomberg Businessweek,* April 28, 2010, http://www.businessweek.com/news/2010-04-28/clinton-says-intel-coca-cola-will-assist-muslim-entrepreneurs.html (accessed February 25, 2011); Glovin, David, and Duane D. Stanford. "PepsiCo Sues Coca-Cola over Powerade Advertisements (Update3)." *Bloomberg.com,* April 13, 2009, http://www.bloomberg.com/apps/news?pid=20601110&sid=aYXG QIH6Hisk (accessed September 4, 2009); "Grand Jury to Investigate Coke on Channel Stuffing Allegations." *Atlanta Business Chronicle,* May 3, 2004, atlanta.bizjournals.com/atlanta/stories/2004/05/03/daily2.html (accessed September 4, 2009); "Heinz to use Coca-Cola PlantBottle technology." *Atlanta Business Chronicle,* February 23, 2011, http://www.bizjournals.com/atlanta/news/2011/02/23/heinz-to-use-coca-cola-plantbottle.html (accessed February 25, 2011); Hobson, Katherine. "What Do Jelly Beans Have to Do with Coke's VitaminWater?" *The Wall Street Journal,* July 26, 2010, http://blogs.wsj.com/health/2010/07/26/what-do-jelly-beans-have-to-dowith-cokes-vitaminwater/ (accessed February 25, 2011); Hoffman, Andrew J. and Sarah Howie. "Coke in the Cross Hairs: Water, India and the University of Michigan." Globalens, July 25, 2010, http://globalens.com/DocFiles/PDF/cases/inspection/GL1429098I.pdf (accessed July 7, 2011); Hurtado, Patricia. "Coca-Cola Sued in U.S. by Guatemalans over Anti-Union Violence." *Bloomberg Businessweek,* February 27, 2010, http://www.businessweek.com/news/2010-02-27/coca-cola-sued-in-u-s-by-guatemalans-over-anti-union-violence.html (accessed February 25, 2011); Kelly, Marjorie. "100 Best Corporate Citizens." *Business Ethics* (Spring 2007): 23–24; Kent, Muhtar. "Coke Didn't Make America Fat." *The Wall Street Journal,* October 7, 2009, http://online.wsj.com/article/SB10001424052748703298004574455464120581696.html (accessed February 25, 2011); Milward Brown Optimor. ""Brandz Top 100 Most Valuable Global Brands 2011." http://www.millwardbrown.com/libraries/optimor_brandz_files/2011_brandz_top100_chart.sflb.ashx (accessed July 7, 2011); Morran, Chris. "Consumers Group Asks FTC to Stop Misleading VitaminWater Marketing." *Consumerist,* February 2, 2011, http://consumerist.com/2011/02/consumers-group-asks-ftc-to-stop-misleading-vitaminwater-marketing.html (accessed May 10, 2011); Peer, Melinda. "In Downturn, Pepsi May Beat Coke." *Forbes,* February 19, 2009, http://www. forbes.com/2009/02/19/coca-cola-pepsico-markets-equity_dividend_outlook_49.html (accessed September 4, 2009); Peterson, Kristina. "Court Cites Iqbal Ruling to Dismiss Coca-Cola Case." *The Wall Street Journal,* August 14, 2009, http://online.wsj.com/article/SB125029795346133593.html (accessed February 25, 2011); *PR Wire.* "Teamsters Converge on Times Square to Protest Coke's Anti-Worker Tactics; Teamsters Put Coke on Notice for Possible Job Actions over Worker Abuses." http:// www.prnewswire.com/cgi-bin/stories.pl?ACCT=104&STORY=/www/story/04-02-2007/0004557941&EDATE=, April 2, 2007 (accessed September 4, 2009); *Reuters.* "Coca-Cola Unveils Sleek, New 90-Calorie Mini Can." http://www.reuters.com/article/2009/10/14/idUS153812+14-Oct-2009+BW20091014, October 14, 2009 (accessed February 25, 2011); Simons, Craig. "Report Examines Coke Water Use in India." Cox News Service, January 15, 2008, http://www.statesman.com/business/content/shared/money/stories/2008/01/COKE_INDIA15_1STLD_COX_ F4362_1.html (accessed September 4, 2009); Singh, Jyotsna. "India Coca-Cola compensation law is passed in Kerala." BBC News, February 24, 2011, http://www.bbc.co.uk/news/world-south-asia-12567542 (accessed February 25, 2011); "Sprite and LeBron James Pump New Life into Neighborhood Basketball Courts around the Country." *Reuters,* February 18, 2011, http://www.reuters.com/article/2011/02/18/idUS202128+18-Feb-2011+BW20110218 (accessed July 7, 2011); Srivastava, Amit. "Reality Check for Coca-Cola's Public Relations." India Resource Center, April 16, 2009, http://www.indiaresource.org/campaigns/coke/2009/realitycheck.html (accessed September 4, 2009); Stanford, Duane D. "Coke's Last Round." *Bloomberg Businessweek,* November 1–7, 2010, 54-61; Terhune, Chad. "Bottlers' Suit Challenges Coke Distribution Plan." *The Wall Street Journal,* February 18–19, 2006, A5; Terhune, Chad. "A Suit by Coke Bottlers Exposes Cracks in a Century-Old System." *The Wall Street Journal,* March 13, 2006, A1; Waldman, Amy. "India Tries to Contain Tempest over Soft Drink Safety." *The New York Times,* August 23, 2003, http://query.nytimes.com/gst/fullpage.html?res=9A04E 6DC1439F930A1575BC0A9659C8B63 (accessed September 4, 2009); Weise, Elizabeth. "Group urges caramel coloring in colas be banned." *USA Today,* http://www.usatoday.com/money/industries/food/2011-02-21-colacolor21_ST_N.htm (accessed February 25, 2011); Yahoo! Finance. "Coca-Cola Bottling Co. Consolidated (COKE)." http://finance.yahoo.com/q/hp?s=COKE&a=00&b=1&c=2010&d=00&e=8&f=2011&g=w (accessed February 25, 2011); Zmuda, Natalie. "Big Red goes completely green at Olympics." *Advertising Age,* February 1, 2010, 2.

CASE 16

Recreational Equipment Incorporated (REI): A Responsible Retail Cooperative*

Recreational Equipment Incorporated (REI) is a national retail cooperative famous for its outdoor apparel and equipment. A cooperative consists of individuals who have joined together to secure the benefits of a larger organization. In the case of REI, the company is organized as a consumer cooperative. Members of the cooperative receive a portion of the organization's profits annually based on a percentage of their eligible purchases. As a result, REI maintains a strong focus on customers, an emphasis that has encouraged the organization to offer superior goods and services in areas such as mountain climbing, camping, and other outdoor activities.

This case will discuss REI's social responsibility initiatives and business framework. We begin by analyzing REI's background and business structure. Next, we examine REI's emphasis on employees, the environment, and the community. We then touch upon REI's advocacy efforts and the REI Foundation. The case concludes by looking at some problematic areas that the company must address.

HISTORY AND BACKGROUND

The concept of REI originated due to a need that could not be met locally. During the 1930s Lloyd Anderson, a member of the Pacific Northwest Mountaineers, was looking for a high-quality ice ax at a reasonable cost. After searching without success, Anderson found what he needed in an Austrian Alpine Gear catalog for $3.50. His find excited the climbing community around Seattle, prompting Anderson to envision a local business that would carry items for mountain climbers at reasonable prices. In 1938 Lloyd Anderson and his wife Mary, along with 21 fellow climbers, founded an outdoor gear consumer cooperative. At first the cooperative was focused specifically on mountain climbing. In fact, its first full-time employee and eventual CEO was John Whittaker, the first American to successfully climb Mt. Everest. Yet over the years REI grew to include gear for camping and hiking, bicycling, fitness, paddling, and more. Today it is the largest consumer cooperative in the United States.

REI is not a publicly traded company. Anyone can shop at REI, but those who wish to become members of the co-op pay $20 for a lifetime membership. REI members are eligible to receive annual dividends consisting of member rebates and REI Visa card rebates. The more each member purchases from REI, the bigger his or her dividend, which is applied to future purchases. Cooperative members can also receive member discounts on products

*This case was prepared by Debbie Acosta, Michael Trujillo, and Jennifer Sawayda for and under the direction of O.C. Ferrell and Linda Ferrell. This case was prepared for classroom discussion rather than to illustrate either effective or ineffective handling of an administrative, ethical, or legal decision by management. All sources used for this case were obtained through publicly available material and the REI website

and vote for REI's board of directors. Thus far, this business model has appeared to work for REI. It has 4.4 million active members and generated revenues of $1.7 billion in 2010.

BUSINESS STRUCTURE AND PRODUCTS

REI operates more than 100 retail stores in 27 states. To help customers choose the right product, REI retail locations contain features like bike trails and rock climbing walls that allow customers to test the gear. In addition, to make sure that customers purchase products that meet their needs, REI allows customers to return any item purchased from REI if they are dissatisfied, regardless of whether or not it has been used. REI retailers also have Internet kiosks to educate consumers about the brands and products it sells.

Although 80 percent of REI sales come from its retail stores, the company has also invested in online technology, direct sales, and mobile apps. REI developed its own iPhone and Android apps to help consumers in their purchasing decisions. Consumers who have these apps can research REI products, make purchases, and, if they are members, check their dividends. REI decided to embark on this new channel due to the immense popularity of mobile applications. The company wants to offer consumers superior services outside as well as inside the store.

REI also owns successful brands of apparel and equipment that are only available in REI stores. Products developed under the REI brands are designed and tested by REI's quality assurance teams in laboratory settings as well as in the field by REI employees. Several organizations have recognized REI Gear and Apparel for its high quality. For instance, REI's Half Dome 2 Tent won the "2010 Editors' Choice Gold" in *Backpacker* magazine and "2010 Gear of the Year" in *Outside* magazine. REI also makes its own brand of bicycles, "Novara," which includes mountain, touring, recreational, and road bikes.

In addition to its outdoor products, REI also provides services to its customers. A newer program that REI offers in select cities is Outdoor School programs. Customers can attend free or low-cost classes for beginners all the way up to experts in climbing, cycling, hiking and camping, navigation, outdoor fitness, outdoor photography, paddling, snow sports, stewardship, and wilderness medicine. REI's Outdoor Schools provide equipment and professional instruction for those who want to increase their outdoor skills. REI also offers a service called REI Adventures. Customers can choose from a number of different trips that REI Adventures puts together. The trips are ranked by the location, type of physical activity, and fitness level. REI Adventures often employs local guides to enhance the travelers' sightseeing experience.

MANAGEMENT STRUCTURE

Although consumer members essentially own the company, REI has a system of management in place to oversee its day-to-day decisions and risks. REI's board of directors can consist of up to 13 directors. Ten of those 13 board directors must be elected by REI members, and one is the REI President and CEO. The board is legally responsible for generating policy and overseeing the performance of REI. Business risk management, compliance, and corporate governance fall under the realm of the Audit and Finance Committee and the Nominating and Governance Committee. While the former manages business risk and compliance, these risks are more financial in nature. The Nominating and Governance Committee recommends nominees for director positions and oversees corporate governance policies. The two other board committees are the Compensation Committee and the Executive Committee.

The board encourages REI members to contact them directly. Members are allowed to attend annual meetings to gain a better understanding of company policy and offer feedback. Figure 1 provides a glimpse of how the board and corporate officer positions are organized. As the figure demonstrates, REI has corporate officers specifically for areas such as gear and apparel, stores and real estate, and customer experience.

Employee relations, consumer safety, supplier relationships, financial status, and community relations all have their own sets of risks. Despite REI's unique business model, a consumer cooperative, the company faces the same risks as any other retailer. For instance, in terms of customer risk, REI stores allow customers to test and experiment with different gear. At the same time, this feature also introduces the risks of potential injury. Managers must be vigilant in mitigating risk through training and protection such as liability insurance. With effective mechanisms in place, REI executives can reduce, if not eliminate, the chance of mishaps.

FIGURE 1 Board and Corporate Officer Organizational Structure

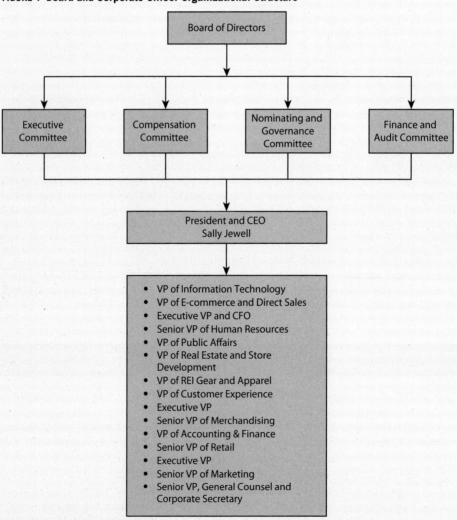

Sources: "Corporate Officer," REI, http://www.rei.com/aboutrei/officers.html; "Board of Directors," REI, http://www.rei.com/aboutrei/directors.html (accessed June 2, 2011).

CORPORATE CULTURE AND VALUES

In its quest to satisfy customers, REI recognizes that its employees are integral to its success as an organization. REI products require a skilled staff that is knowledgeable about outdoor gear. Therefore, REI tries to hire employees who are passionate about the outdoors and who are willing to learn about the products they are selling to consumers. Furthermore, REI prides itself on creating a culture of trust, inclusion, and social responsibility. The company has developed standards for itself and its vendors to ensure that it complies with best industry practices.

To demonstrate its commitment to socially responsible practices, REI releases an annual stewardship report. This report highlights not only the organization's social and environmental progress but also major challenges for that year. REI's stewardship report is one way that the organization is able to demonstrate transparency to its stakeholders—a value that the company views as key to being a responsible citizen. REI's annual stewardship report focuses on three stakeholders integral to company success: employees, the environment, and the community. The following sections will describe REI's relationships with these stakeholders in more detail.

EMPLOYEE STAKEHOLDER RELATIONSHIPS

REI recognizes employees as the glue that holds the organization together. With more than 8,000 employees in the United States, REI must manage a complex network of employee relationships, yet it has consistently been recognized as a top employer. The organization has earned a spot on *Fortune* magazine's "100 Best Companies to Work for" every year since 1998. One reason why employees remain loyal to REI is its extensive benefits package. In addition to traditional benefits, REI offers perks that are unique to the company. For instance, employees receive a 50 to 75 percent discount on REI brand products, along with free rentals of certain equipment and a yearly gift of gear. This unique perk makes employees feel valued and familiarizes them with REI products. Other REI benefits include a four-week paid sabbatical after 15 years of employment and a special program called the Challenge Grant, which encourages employees to spend time outdoors. The Challenge Grant awards $300 in REI gear to employees who participate in challenging outdoor activities.

REI also offers a Pay for Performance compensation package. This package includes an employee incentive plan called Xcels. Xcels rewards employees and departments for reaching individual, department, and company goals. Although such an incentive plan is a good motivator for employees to strive to meet firm-specific goals, REI must be careful to exert oversight in how these goals are reached. A plan like Xcels could become problematic if employees take ethical short cuts to reach their targets.

REI's employee initiatives and benefits have shown promise. The organization's turnover rate went from 51.5 percent in 2001 to 28.5 percent in 2009. The average employee turnover rate for the retail industry is 47 percent. To ensure that employees are satisfied with REI operations, REI surveys their employees every year. These anonymous surveys measure employee engagement. REI believes that the more employees feel engaged in the firm, the more loyal and satisfied they will be. The survey asks employees questions such as whether the employees support REI values and whether they would recommend the organization to others. For the majority of the questions, 90 percent or more of respondents viewed the company favorably.

> "REI has made diversity and inclusion an important company value."

Additionally, REI has made diversity and inclusion an important company value. A diverse workforce has the advantage of reaching a wider array of diverse customers. One way in which REI seeks to increase workforce diversity is by utilizing nontraditional recruiting sources to locate prospective employees from diverse backgrounds. Retail managers and staff are provided with diversity training to help them to create a more inclusive environment for all employees.

Finally, REI recognizes its responsibilities toward the workers in the factories from which it sources. The company has expressed its commitment to go above and beyond local laws in ensuring fair treatment for factory workers. In 1993 REI modeled its factory Code of Conduct after guidelines set forth by the International Labor Organization, a UN agency committed toward establishing fair international labor standards.

Since REI partners with third parties to create the products it sells, the organization has less control over the practices occurring within the factories. It therefore performs visits and social audits to make certain that these manufacturers are complying with REI's factory Code of Conduct. Factory audits are performed by a third party to guarantee the credibility of the audit. The challenge for REI is to balance profitability and long-term supplier relationships with responsible sourcing. REI has therefore partnered with other companies and industry groups to create industry-wide compliance programs and expectations for factories.

As part of this collaboration, REI embarked upon a partnership with the Outdoor Industry Association (OIA) in 2006. Together, the partners created the Fair Labor Toolkit to provide advice for companies and point out ethical issues in labor compliance. REI also joined the Fair Factories Clearinghouse (FFC) in 2009. The FFC is a nonprofit organization dedicated to using software to improve workplaces and business transactions. The partnership between REI and FFC seeks to facilitate collaboration across industries.

Challenges in Employee Stakeholder Relationships

REI faces many challenges in managing its employee stakeholders, particularly after the last economic recession. Like many businesses, REI suffered from decreased sales. This forced REI to lay off some of its workforce and reduce the number of hours worked for its retail employees. Employee and managerial benefits, such as pay increases and bonuses, were also decreased.

REI believes that it continues to offer a competitive benefits package in spite of cutbacks. The company still contributes to the retirement of eligible employees, although the contribution has decreased to 10 percent. Additionally, REI began a company examination of its benefits and asked for employee feedback. Although REI's cutbacks might be difficult for its workforce, its emphasis on employee satisfaction has enabled it to maintain its high employee retention rates.

REI has also encountered workforce diversity challenges. Approximately 87 percent of the REI workforce describes themselves as white non-Hispanic. This fact could be problematic considering REI's values toward employee diversity as well as in reaching new markets. As a result, REI has stepped up its efforts to create brand awareness among diverse populations through community outreach. It also created a new Diversity and Inclusion Awareness and Skills Training for company leaders.

Perhaps the biggest challenge in terms of ethical lapses involves the labor conditions in factories from which REI sources. An independent audit of these factories revealed some violations of REI's factory Code of Conduct. Many of these violations were relatively minor in nature but still call for improvement. The majority of violations dealt with health and safety, followed by fair wages. This is a very important issue for REI, as unsafe working conditions—should they escalate—can create reputational harm for the company. Some of the violations included blocked aisles in factories (which could cause problems during emergencies), failure to wear safety equipment, and making employees work seven-day weeks. The reported violations also came with recommendations from the independent auditor, such as the suggestion to create more independence between compliance and business teams as well as to use technology to report audit results more efficiently. The board at REI agreed to accept these recommendations.

ENVIRONMENTAL STAKEHOLDERS

While it may seem unusual to regard the environment as a critical stakeholder, the impact that businesses have upon the natural environment is becoming increasingly important. Climate change, waste management, and pollution concerns affect how businesses conduct their operations. By including the environment as an important stakeholder in its stewardship report, REI acknowledges the importance of sustainability in its daily activities. Its strategic focus on environmental responsibility has enabled REI to reduce its environmental footprint.

The strategic focus REI uses is centered on five environmental priorities: (1) greenhouse gas emissions and energy use, (2) green building, (3) paper sourcing, (4) reducing waste and recycling, and (5) responsible product stewardship. REI's sustainability mission is to "use the power of innovation and collaboration with our industry peers to create positive change that is beneficial not only to REI but manufacturers and other consumer outdoor brands and retailers." REI aspires to create effective change in the areas of sustainability throughout the industry through the following steps.

Reducing Gas Emissions/Energy Usage

A major priority in REI's sustainability strategy is to find ways to grow while minimizing greenhouse gas emissions. With climate change at the forefront of environmental concerns, REI has been reducing the impact of its greenhouse gas emissions through methods such as the purchase of carbon offsets. During a one-year period, REI reduced its emissions by ten percent, even as the company added more stores.

Since the majority of greenhouse gas emissions come from transportation, REI has begun promoting responsible transportation whenever possible, including alternative approaches such as subsidizing vanpools and offering incentives for public transportation. Corporate travel at REI has been reduced while video conferencing has increased.

The challenge of decreasing greenhouse gas emissions while simultaneously increasing REI business operations will require REI to do more with less energy. Success in this area will benefit not only the environment, through lower carbon emissions, but also the company, through additional energy savings.

Increase Investment in Green Building

Another priority for REI is green—or ecofriendly—buildings. Using ecofriendly materials to construct buildings reduces energy usage, and REI seeks to capitalize on this opportunity. Prototype stores, which are designed using REI's new standards for sustainability, emphasize energy efficiency, renewable energy, and waste reduction. REI has six green building facilities that are LEED-certified. LEED, which stands for Leadership in Energy and Environmental Design, is an internationally recognized rating system for sustainable building. Buildings that receive certification have attained a high level of sustainability in their construction. REI's prototype stores meet these standards, and the company has even won awards for its innovative use of sustainable construction techniques. For instance, the organization's prototype store in Round Rock, Texas, which earned the Association for Retail Environments' project of the year award in 2009, features a rooftop solar power array, solar thermal water system, natural lighting, and recyclable carpet.

Increase Ecofriendly Paper Sourcing

REI wants to ensure that the paper it uses is sourced responsibly. It is impossible for REI to completely eliminate its use of paper, but the company's paper policy encourages the purchase of paper products sourced from post-consumer waste or virgin fiber harvested from forests certified by the Forest Stewardship Council (FSC). Certification implies that the paper-based products have been responsibly sourced. In 2009 REI was able to decrease its overall paper usage while increasing its usage of FSC-certified paper to 38.2 percent of the total.

Decreasing Waste and Increasing Recycling

> "REI has set the impressive goal of becoming a zero waste-to-landfill company by 2020."

REI has set the impressive goal of becoming a zero waste-to-landfill company by 2020. The organization is therefore seeking innovative ways to generate less waste and recycle the waste it does generate. These efforts are focused on the entire supply chain. The idea is to reduce waste before it gets to the retail level. Some of REI's methods include redesigning packaging to reduce packaging waste, increasing recycling programs for items such as paper products and rechargeable batteries, and composting organic waste. REI was able to recycle over 80 percent of its operational waste by volume. Currently, the majority of waste from REI that ends up in landfills comes from the company's retail stores.

Increasing Responsible Product Stewardship

Environmental stewardship does not stop after a company sells a product. Some companies believe that once a customer has purchased a product, that product and its subsequent disposal are the consumer's responsibility. However, REI makes product stewardship a key tenet of its sustainability goals. One way in which it promotes responsible product stewardship is by selling items made from ecofriendly materials. These products do not use as much waste during production and/or degrade more easily. REI has therefore branded an environmentally responsible label called "ecoSensitive." This label identifies products that contain a high percentage of recycled, rapidly renewable, and/or organic fibers. The company now sells over 300 ecoSensitive products.

COMMUNITY STAKEHOLDERS

Each year REI supports many local programs to further conservation and outdoor recreation. In order to make the biggest impact, REI invites and engages its members, customers, and entire communities. REI also encourages its employees to volunteer in improving and protecting the outdoors. A primary focus for REI is youth. REI seeks to inspire and educate the younger generation about the outdoors. The company's Promoting Environmental Awareness in Kids (PEAK) program is one step toward youth engagement. PEAK is a result of the collaboration between REI and the Leave No Trace Center for Outdoor Ethics. This program teaches kids about outdoor ethics—such as cleaning up waste materials and respecting wildlife—while having fun outdoors. PEAK has two goals: to introduce youth to the wonders of the outdoors, and to practice responsible "No Trace" principles.

REI sets aside three percent of its previous year's operating budget to support nonprofits and other causes that promote outdoor stewardship. In addition to supporting diversity in its workforce, REI encourages diversity in the outdoors. REI has participated in a number of endeavors supporting minority groups, including sponsoring the Atlanta conference entitled, "Breaking the Color Barrier in the Great Outdoors" in 2009.

ADVOCACY EFFORTS AND THE REI FOUNDATION

REI's advocacy efforts center on its desire to protect the environment and promote outdoor recreation. The company has lobbied and continues to lobby for public lands and environmental causes. More specifically, the organization has supported the Land and Water Conservation Fund, the Omnibus Public Lands Bill, and the Outdoor Industry Association. Additionally, REI is involved with the Washington Wildlife and Recreation Coalition. REI CEO Sally Jewell, who serves on the board of the National Parks and Conservation Association (NPCA), even testified before the House Subcommittee on the National Parks, Forests, and Public Lands on behalf of NPCA.

In 1993 REI founded the REI Foundation, with the mission of encouraging and supporting youth participation in the outdoors. The Foundation has awarded grants to support programs implemented by the National Audubon Society, the NYC Green Stops Partnership, the EarthTeam Environmental Network, Outdoor Outreach, and YMCA Camp Surf. Sometimes REI works outside the foundation; for example, in 2010 it gave $3.7 million to nonprofit organizations whose activities aligned with REI's mission.

CONCLUSION

REI has experienced great success since its founding in 1938. Its unique consumer cooperative business model increases member commitment, and the company has been able to gain a loyal customer following. Moreover, employees give the company consistently high ratings as an employer. REI has backed up its stated commitment toward youth, communities, and the outdoors through philanthropic and sustainability initiatives to improve the lives of its stakeholders.

At the same time, REI will face obstacles in maintaining its current status. The last recession introduced difficulties for REI regarding its employee stakeholders when the company was forced to make cutbacks. REI appears to have handled these cutbacks relatively well as it continues to be voted as one of the best companies to work for. REI must also continue to overcome environmental challenges. The company admits that there is room for improvement and has set high goals for itself. But there are few standards for measuring sustainability, which can be an issue since REI sells many items that it categorizes as ecofriendly. Since there is no standard by which to measure this label, companies like REI must exert caution when promoting a product as green. REI also continues to have waste issues at its retail locations. REI will have to expend resources and adopt innovative solutions in order to be zero-waste by 2020.

Despite these challenges, REI remains a good example of corporate social responsibility. Its stewardship report reflects a stakeholder orientation, or a perspective that encompasses all the different company constituents rather than just investors or customers. The REI has proven that ethics, social responsibility, and a powerful vision can help a company to thrive.

QUESTIONS

1. Is REI successful because it is a consumer cooperative or because of effective stakeholder orientation?
2. Who is responsible for managing ethics and social responsibility at REI?
3. Assess REI's ethical and social responsibility risks and suggest how these risks can be managed effectively.

SOURCES

Burke, Monte. "A Conversation with REI Chief Executive Sally Jewell." *Forbes,* May 19, 2011, http://blogs.forbes.com/monteburke/2011/05/19/a-conversation-with-rei-chief-executive-sally-jewell/ (accessed May 31, 2011); CNN Money. "100 Best Companies to Work for." http://money.cnn.com/magazines/fortune/bestcompanies/2011/snapshots/9.html (accessed May 31, 2011); Fair Factories Clearinghouse. "Streamlining Business Practices." http://www.fairfactories.org/Main/Index.aspx (accessed May 31, 2011); Ferrell, O. C., Geoffrey A. Hirt, and Linda Ferrell. *Business: A Changing World,* 8th ed. New York, NY: McGraw-Hill Irwin, 2011, 138; Frey, Christine. "Product-testing REI employees take the scrapes for buyers." *Seattle PI,* October 18, 2002, http://www.seattlepi.com/default/article/Product-testing-REI-employees-take-the-scrapes-1098834.php (accessed June 1, 2011); FSC. "FSC Certification." http://www.fsc.org/certification.html (accessed June 1, 2011); Global Foresight. "Advisory Board." http://www.global-foresight.net/about/about-who.html (accessed May 31, 2011); Goodwin, Michael. "REI 2010 Sales Up 14%." *Transworld Business,* March 29, 2011, http://business.transworld.net/60259/news/rei-2010-sales-up-14/ (accessed June 1, 2011); GreenBiz.com. "REI Prototype Store Lands Top Sustainable Design Award." July 6, 2009, http://www.greenbiz.com/news/2009/07/06/rei-prototype-store-lands-top-sustainable-design-award (accessed May 31, 2011); International Labour Organization. "About the ILO." http://www.ilo.org/global/about-the-ilo/lang--en/index.htm (accessed May 31, 2011); Leave No Trace Website. http://www.lnt.org/programs/peak/index.html (accessed June 1, 2011); National Parks Conservation Association. "Testimony of Sally Jewell, Trustee, National Parks Conservation Association." http://www.npca.org/media_center/testimonies/jewellservice_040209.html, April 2, 2009 (accessed June 1, 2011); New York Job Source. "Recreation Equipment Inc." October 6, 2010, http://nyjobsource.com/rei.

html (accessed May 31, 2011); REI. "Advocacy for the Outdoors: 2009 Stewardship Report." http://www.rei.com/aboutrei/csr/2009/advocacy-for-the-outdoors.html (accessed June 1, 2011); REI. "Being an REI Member Just Got Better: REI Introduces Free Shipping Exclusively for Members." http://www.rei.com/aboutrei/releases/10free_shipping.html (accessed May 31, 2011); REI. "Board of Directors." http://www.rei.com/aboutrei/directors.html (accessed June 2, 2011); REI. "Community." http://www.rei.com/aboutrei/stewardship_community.html (accessed June 1, 2011); REI. "Diversity and Inclusion: 2009 Stewardship Report." http://www.rei.com/aboutrei/csr/2009/diversity-inclusion.html (accessed June 1, 2011); REI. "Employee Engagement & Retention: 2009 Stewardship Report." http://www.rei.com/aboutrei/csr/2009/employee-engagement-retention.html (accessed June 1, 2011); REI. "Employee Pay & Benefits: 2009 Stewardship Report." http://www.rei.com/aboutrei/csr/2009/employee-pay-benefits.html (accessed June 1, 2011); REI. "Factory & Labor Compliance: 2009 Stewardship Report." http://www.rei.com/aboutrei/csr/2009/factory-labor.html (accessed June 1, 2011); REI. "Giving Philosophy: 2009 Stewardship Report." http://www.rei.com/aboutrei/csr/2009/giving-philosophy.html (accessed June 1, 2011); REI. "Governing Documents of Recreational Equipment, Inc.: Charter of the Nominating and Corporate Governance Committee." http://www.rei.com/pdf/aboutrei/nomgovcharter09.pdf (accessed June 2, 2011); REI. "Governing Documents of Recreational Equipment, Inc.: Charter of the Audit and Finance Committee." May 20, 2010, http://www.rei.com/pdf/aboutrei/afcmtecharter.pdf (accessed June 2, 2011); REI. "Green Building: 2009 Stewardship Report." http://www.rei.com/aboutrei/csr/2009/green-building.html (accessed June 1, 2011); REI. "Greenhouse (GHG) Emissions: 2009 Stewardship Report." http://www.rei.com/aboutrei/csr/2009/greenhouse-gas-emissions.html (accessed June 1, 2011); REI. "Overview." http://www.rei.com/aboutrei/business.html (accessed May 31, 2011); REI. "Paper Usage: 2009 Stewardship Report." http://www.rei.com/aboutrei/csr/2009/paper-usage.html (accessed June 1, 2011); REI. "Product Stewardship: 2009 Stewardship Report: Product Stewardship." http://www.rei.com/aboutrei/csr/2009/product-stewardship.html (accessed June 1, 2011); REI. "REI and Youth." http://www.rei.com/aboutrei/reikids02.html (accessed June 1, 2011); REI. "The REI Member Dividend." https://www.rei.com/membership/dividend (accessed May 31, 2011); REI. "The REI Story." http://www.rei.com/jobs/story.html (accessed June 1, 2011); REI. "REI Foundation," http://www.rei.com/aboutrei/csr/2009/rei-foundation.html (accessed June 1, 2011); REI. "REI Outdoor School Classes and Outings." http://www.rei.com/outdoorschool (accessed June 1, 2011); REI. "REI Outdoor School Facts." http://www.rei.com/outdoorschool/faqs.html (accessed June 1, 2011); REI. "REI's 2009 Stewardship Report Highlights Environmental Sustainability, Community Connections and Workplace Engagement." September 8, 2010, http://www.rei.com/aboutrei/releases/10stewardship.html (accessed June 1, 2011); REI. "REI's Culture & Values." http://www.rei.com/jobs/culture.html (accessed June 1, 2011); REI. "Waste and Recycling: 2009 Stewardship Report." http://www.rei.com/aboutrei/csr/2009/waste.html (accessed June 1, 2011); REI. "Workforce Diversity." http://www.rei.com/jobs/diversity.html (accessed June 1, 2011); REI. "Workplace." http://www.rei.com/stewardship/rei_workplace (accessed June 1, 2011); REI Adventures. http://www.rei.com/adventures (accessed June 1, 2011); REI Adventures. "Our Trips Include Living Guidebooks." http://www.rei.com/adventures/resources/guides.html (accessed June 1, 2011); Tsirulnik, Giselle. "REI app purpose is twofold: sales and service." *Mobile Commerce Daily,* March 25, 2011, http://www.mobilecommercedaily.com/2011/03/25/rei-app-purpose-is-twofold-sales-and-service (accessed June 1, 2011); U.S. Green Building Council. "What LEED Is." http://www.usgbc.org/DisplayPage.aspx?CMSPageID=1988 (accessed May 31, 2011).

CASE 17

Better Business Bureau: Protecting Consumers and Dealing with Organizational Ethics Challenges*

The Better Business Bureau (BBB) is one of the best known self-regulatory trade associations in the United States. Self-regulation expresses a commitment on a company's part to adhere to certain rules that demonstrate best practices and social responsibility. Although their pledges do not have the force of law, companies that engage in self-regulation agree to go beyond what is legally required. Trade associations such as the Better Business Bureau create self-regulatory programs for their members. The BBB uses its website, newspapers, and the media to inform consumers of businesses who have violated these standards. They may also receive low ratings in BBB reliability reports, and accredited members can be expelled from the association.

While many self-regulatory programs encompass a specific field such as direct selling, the BBB encompasses all businesses. Its purpose is to create an environment of trust between buyers and sellers. The BBB consists of hundreds of local BBB chapters spread out across the United States and Canada, which operate independently but work together through the umbrella organization Council of Better Business Bureaus (CBBB). The BBB provides important resources for both businesses and consumers, including dispute and complaint resolution services, reliability reports, and arbitration. Although the BBB does not recommend businesses to consumers, it does provide information about an organization's practices through reliability reports and ratings.

Over time the BBB has become a credible resource for consumers. The goal of the BBB is to foster transparency between businesses and consumers. It has helped many consumers avoid falling prey to scams, and it provides important information on the ethical practices of an organization. Those companies failing to resolve consumer complaints often have their ratings downgraded, a practice that alerts consumers to exert caution in dealing with them. Conversely, accredited members of the BBB or nonaccredited members with high ratings are generally perceived to be more credible.

The BBB also offers accreditation to businesses that wish to become members. Membership in the BBB indicates that an organization has agreed to comply with a set of eight ethical principles to promote trust in the marketplace. Those that become accredited members gain access to BBB services and gain a reputation for following best practices. Accredited members must pay a fee to secure their membership.

*This case was prepared by Richard Alano, Erica Talley, and Jennifer Sawayda for and under the direction of O. C. Ferrell and Linda Ferrell. It was prepared for classroom discussion rather than to illustrate either effective or ineffective handling of an administrative, ethical, or legal decision by management. All sources used for this case were obtained through publicly available material.

reporting of the organization's accomplishments, failures, and opportunities for improvement in disaster response activities.

The ARC must also address the ethical risks specific to a disaster-relief organization. Clear and efficient communications with federal and local government agencies is a challenge. The ARC must develop strategic plans to better accomplish disaster response goals. These plans must include how to respond to organizational missteps and failures. Transparent, honest reporting of the ARC's goals, accomplishments, opportunities for improvement, and mistakes would go a long way toward restoring the country's trust in the organization.

In short, the American Red Cross has a stakeholder obligation to fulfill its charter's expectations effectively and efficiently. Charitable donations fund the nonprofit's operations, and volunteers comprise 95 percent of its workers. The ARC staff and volunteers need to be managed by capable directors and executives within ARC. Improvements to the ARC as an organization must begin with executive leadership and flow downward to every level of the group. Congressional oversight and interaction with federal, state, and local organizations must continue to be reviewed and modified to suit current needs.

Disaster relief cooperation in the form of partnering with private corporations to provide efficient and effective responses to victims of disasters should be continued. Joint marketing practices between the ARC and private businesses should also continue, as long as unethical interactions or associations do not compromise the mission of the ARC. The many stakeholders of the ARC, including donors, staff, volunteers, and society, must continue to monitor the American Red Cross in order to ensure its long-term success.

QUESTIONS

1. Explain the possible problems in the ethical culture of the Red Cross that created the issues discussed in this case.

2. Name some of the problems the ARC has encountered with handling donation money.

3. What are some of the reasons for the ARC's ethical dilemmas, and how can the organization guarantee that these problems will not recur in the future?

4. What effect do organizational structure and compensation have on ethical behavior among chief executives at ARC?

SOURCES

Abbott Laboratories. "Abbott to Provide $1 Million in Funding, Products to Help Address Health Needs in Haiti." January 13, 2010, http://www.abbott.com/global/url/pressRelease/en_US/Press_Release_0811.htm (accessed February 25, 2011); American Red Cross. "About Us." http://www.redcross.org/aboutus (accessed February 10, 2011); American Red Cross. "Ethics Rules and Policies." http://www.redcross.org/www-files/Documents/Governance/file_cont5874_lango_2226.pdf, 7–8; American Red Cross. "Governance." http://www.redcross.org/portal/site/en/menuitem.d8aaecf214c576bf971e4cfe43181aa0/?vgnextoid=d18859f392ce8110VgnVCM10000030f3870aRCRD&vgnextfmt=default (accessed February 25, 2011); American Red Cross. "Overview of Red Cross Services 2008." http://www.redcross.org/portal/site/en/menuitem.86f46a12f382290517a8f210b80f78a0/?vgnextoid=1aa644e75215b110VgnVCM10000089f0870aRCRD&vgnextfmt=default, 3; Archibold, Randal C. "California: Ex-Executive at

Red Cross Pleads Guilty." *The New York Times,* May 26, 2007, http://www.nytimes.com/2007/05/26/us/26brfs-EXEXECUTIVEA_BRF.html?_r=1 (accessed December 22, 2008); Attkisson, Sharyl. "Disaster Strikes in Red Cross Backyard." CBS Evening News, July 29, 2002, http://www.cbsnews.com/stories/2002/07/29/eveningnews/main516700.shtml (accessed April 21, 2008); "The Battle Stations of the Cross." *Modern Healthcare* 36 (August 20, 2007); Breitkopf, David. "Stored-Value Cards for Katrina Victims." *American Banker* 170, no. 173 (2005): 20; "Caveat, Donor." *Searcher* 15, no. 2 (2007): 14; "Discrimination in Disasters." *Time,* December 31, 2007, 31; "Red Cross Does Not Mark the Spot." *The Economist,* December 2, 2006, 47; Dreazen, Yochi. "More Katrina Woes: Incidents of Fraud at Red Cross Centers." *The Wall Street Journal,* October 14, 2005, B1; Hackl, Franz, and Gerald Josef Pruckner. "Demand and Supply of Emergency Help: An Economic Analysis of Red Cross Services." *Health Policy* 77, no. 3 (2006): 338; Fox Business Online. "Johnson and Johnson and American Red Cross Announce Resolution to Lawsuit." http://www.foxbusiness.com/story/markets/industries/health-care/johnson--johnson-american-red-cross-announce-resolution-lawsuit, June 17, 2008 (accessed December 22, 2008); Mullman, Jeremy. "Shoe on the Other Foot for Marin Institute." *Advertising Age* 77, no. 20 (2006): 8; National Center for Charitable Statistics. "Number of Nonprofit Organizations in the United States, 1999–2009." http://nccsdataweb.urban.org/PubApps/profile1.php (accessed February 25, 2011); Nobel, Carmen. "Donations Test Red Cross Staff." *Eweek* 22, no. 37 (2005): 23; "Red Crossing the Line." *Brandweek,* September 3, 2007, 38; Salmon, Jacqueline L. "Red Cross Gave Ousted Executive $780,000 Deal." *The Washington Post,* March 4, 2006, A9; Sontag, Deborah. "What Brought Bernadine Healy Down?" *The New York Times,* December 21, 2001, http://query.nytimes.com/gst/fullpage.html?res=9C02EEDC173EF930A15751C1A9679C8B63 (accessed December 22, 2008); Spector, Mike. "Red Cross CEO Shuffles Executive Ranks." *The Wall Street Journal,* September 23, 2008, http://online.wsj.com/article/SB122220688507068655.html (accessed October 21, 2008); Strom, Stephanie. "Bill Would Restructure Red Cross." *The New York Times,* December 5, 2006, http://www.nytimes.com/2006/12/05/washington/05cross.html (accessed April 17, 2008); Strom, Stephanie. "Firing Stirs New Debate over Red Cross." *The New York Times,* November 29, 2007, http://www.nytimes.com/2007/11/29/us/29cross.html?ref=us (accessed April 14, 2008); Strom, Stephanie. "Nonprofits Rush to Solicit Donations via Text, but the System Is Flawed." *The New York Times,* October 31, 2010, http://www.nytimes.com/2010/11/01/business/01text.html?_r=1&ref=americanredcross&pagewanted=all (accessed February 25, 2011); Strom, Stephanie. "President of Red Cross Resigns: Board Woes, Not Katrina, Cited." *The New York Times,* December 14, 2005, http://www.nytimes.com/2005/12/14/politics/14redcross.html (accessed December 22, 2008); Strom, Stephanie. "Problems Persist with Red Cross Blood Services." *The New York Times,* July 17, 2008, http://www.nytimes.com/2008/07/17/us/17cross.html?pagewanted=1&_r=1 (accessed February 25, 2011); Strom, Stephanie. "Red Cross Sifting Internal Charges over Katrina Aid." *The New York Times,* March 24, 2006, A2; Suarez, Ray. "Red Cross Woes." The NewsHour with Jim Lehrer, December 19, 2001; Thomas, Anisya, and Lynn Fritz. "Disaster Relief, Inc." *Harvard Business Review* 84, no. 11 (2006): 121; U.S. Government Accountability Office. "Coordination between FEMA and the Red Cross Should Be Improved for the 2006 Hurricane Season." Report to Congressional Committees: Hurricanes Katrina and Rita, June 2006, 2.

CASE 19

Nike: Managing Ethical Missteps—Sweatshops to Leadership in Employment Practices*

Phil Knight and his University of Oregon track coach Bill Bowerman founded Blue Ribbon Sports, later renamed Nike, in 1964. The idea, born as a result of a paper written by Knight during his Stanford MBA program, was to import athletic shoes from Japan into the U.S. market, which was otherwise dominated by German competitors Puma and Adidas. The company began as a distributor for a Japanese athletic shoe company, Onitsuka Tiger, but also developed its own brand of athletic footwear to promote in the American market. The company's relationship with Onitsuka Tiger ended in 1971, and the Nike brand was created in 1972 (named "Nike" after the Greek goddess of victory). The company as a whole was renamed Nike in 1978, and has since grown to be the largest worldwide seller of athletic goods, with approximately 168 Nike stores in the United States and a presence in about 160 countries.

Nike was publicized by celebrity athlete sponsors. As the popularity of the Nike product grew, so did the company's manufacturing demands. In contrast to its meteoric rise in the 1980s after going public, the late 1990s began a period of combating allegations about labor and human rights violations in Third World countries in which manufacturing had been subcontracted. Nike's response to this issue has been considered by critics to be more focused on damage control than on a sincere attempt at labor reform.

CRITICISMS OF NIKE'S MANUFACTURING PRACTICES

In order to remain competitive and keep manufacturing costs low, athletic footwear production has moved to areas of the world with low labor costs. Assembly of shoes (as well as low-cost apparel, footwear, radios, TVs, toys, sporting goods equipment, and consumer electronics) began shifting offshore in the 1960s, first to Japan, then to Korea and Taiwan, and then, beginning in the 1980s, to Southern China. By the mid-1980s Taiwan and Korea supplied 45 percent of the world's footwear exports, and production has continually shifted to other Asian nations where the cost of manufacturing is lower still.

Because of its history and experience with Japanese manufacturing and production, Nike was a pioneer in overseas manufacturing as a way to cut costs on sports gear

*This case was prepared by O. C. Ferrell, Jennifer Jackson, and Jennifer Sawayda. Melanie Drever and Alexi Sherrill assisted on the previous edition. This case was prepared for classroom discussion rather than to illustrate either effective or ineffective handling of an administrative, ethical, or legal decision by management. All sources used for this case were obtained through publicly available material.

manufacturing. When Japan became too expensive, Nike shifted its contracts to Vietnam, Indonesia, and China. The working conditions in these factories have been a source of controversy. Allegations of poor conditions, child labor, widespread harassment, and abuse have all been issues for the company. Because the Asian factories have further subcontracted out the work, it has become increasingly difficult for Nike to keep track of and regulate the working conditions and wages in these factories.

Sweatshop labor is not merely an issue for Nike. It permeates the public consciousness across all manufacturing. Perhaps the incident that brought sweatshop labor to the forefront of American consciousness was the Kathy Lee Gifford debacle in 1996 when the human rights group the National Labor Committee uncovered that Gifford's clothing line was made in Honduran sweatshops that used child labor. As an industry leader, Nike's high visibility made it ripe for attack when labor rights violations were uncovered.

Since the mid-1990s, Nike has faced a barrage of criticism from labor rights activists, the mainstream media, and others for human and labor rights violations in its factories. The accusations have included deficiencies in health and safety conditions, extremely low wages, and indiscriminate hiring and firing practices. While much of the firestorm has died down as Nike and other athletic wear manufacturers have sought to clean up their images, the criticism has damaged the company's reputation.

In Indonesia, where Korean suppliers owned a majority of Nike factories, reports by labor activists and other nongovernmental organizations revealed several cases of human rights abuses and labor violations. These conditions came to the attention of the general public through stories such as Roberta Baskin's CBS report on the conditions in Nike's manufacturing facilities in Indonesia in 1993.

In 1996 *Life* magazine published an exposé complete with photos of Pakistani children stitching soccer balls for Nike, Adidas AG, and other companies. The images of these children had a devastating impact on Nike's sales and corporate reputation. Customers who had previously held the American athletics brand in high regard began to develop a lower opinion of the company. Bob Herbert's op-ed article in *The New York Times* in 1996 led to further public interest in this issue, and protests and demonstrations were held all over the United States. Several demonstrations occurred at "Nike Towns," the Nike retail megastores.

Nike also experienced problems with factory conditions in Vietnam. A private report on one of its factories commissioned by Nike as part of an audit by Ernst and Young was leaked to the press, and *The New York Times* ran it as a front-page article. The audit reported unacceptable levels of exposure to chemicals in the factory and documented cases of resulting employee health problems, as well as other infringements of the established code of conduct.

In response to the criticisms raised during the 1990s, Nike had to take rapid measures not only to redeem its reputation, but also to rectify problematic policies and lack of international oversight of its operations. Nike's new priorities became to make certain that its factories were not taking advantage of its workers and to ensure that each worker had a safe work environment and competitive wage.

ENVIRONMENTAL PROBLEMS RELATED TO THE TEXTILE INDUSTRY

Because of the nature of the textile industry, Nike faces numerous challenges and potentially critical problems. The textile industry negatively impacts the environment wherever manufacturing is located. Problems generated by the textile industry in general, and Nike specifically, include increased water deficits; climate change; pollution of land, air, and waterways; and large fossil fuel and raw material consumption. In addition to these environmental hazards, today's electronic textile plants expend significant amounts of energy. All of these issues are exacerbated by Western culture, where fashions are popular for only a few months before being discarded.

In addition to environmental considerations, textile manufacturers must consider their employees' working conditions. The demand for cheap labor and lax labor laws in developing countries such as Vietnam, China, and Indonesia have led to an increased prevalence of child labor and abusive practices. In her book *No Logo,* Naomi Klein claims that Nike abandons manufacturing sites when countries begin to work toward developing better pay and employment rights. Nike's critics believe the company should improve transparency measures in its factories, allow independent inspection to verify conditions, and disclose all audits to the public. Nike has complied with these demands to a limited extent. For example, audits of Nike generally have determined that Nike pays wages above the legal minimum. Critics are not satisfied, however, arguing that in most cases the wages still do not constitute a fair living wage.

In response, Nike claimed that sharing factory locations with independent third parties on a confidential basis enables the company to monitor its supply chain properly. It stated that disclosure of the factory names, plus details of audits of those factories, would be used by NGOs simply to make further attacks rather than as a way to help the company address and resolve problems. Nike also stated that establishing what constitutes a "fair" wage is difficult given the fact that costs of living and economic conditions vary from country to country.

NIKE RESPONDS TO CHALLENGES

Public protests against Nike have taken the form of boycotts and picketing of Nike stores. Universities have cancelled their deals with Nike to produce branded athletic goods. In 1998 Nike revenues and stock prices decreased by approximately 50 percent, and the company laid off 1,600 workers. Nike launched a large public relations campaign to combat the damaging allegations of child labor, inhospitable working conditions, and low or nonexistent wages. In an effort to directly address the concerns of student activists, Nike visited several college campuses, opening dialogue with students and university administrations about its manufacturing policies. Nike even invited teams of Dartmouth graduate students to tour the Indonesian and Vietnamese factories for three weeks at Nike's expense.

The company has spent considerable resources focusing on improving the labor standards in each of its factories. It must weigh the expense of labor in nations where product manufacturing is available. However, because these factories subcontract out to the local workforce, it is difficult for Nike to regulate the working environment. Nike must take extra measures to ensure that the independent subcontractors used to supply the workforce in their factories do not engage in any illegal activities such as child labor, excessive work hours, hostile work environments, or inappropriate payments.

Nike also has implemented a code of conduct for all of its suppliers, and has been working with the Global Alliance to help review its factories. In August 1996 Nike Corporation joined the Apparel Industry Partnership, a coalition of companies and labor and human rights groups assembled by the Clinton administration, to draft an industry-wide code of conduct.

Since universities form a core segment of Nike's market and the company felt the repercussions of its manufacturing practices in the form of several canceled university contracts,

Nike sent letters detailing the acceptable conditions in its factories and stressing its commitment to corporate responsibility to universities around the country. Representatives from Nike also visited campuses and spoke to students, assuring them of Nike's intention to be a responsible corporate citizen. Phil Knight himself visited the campus of the University of North Carolina at Chapel Hill. Nike also launched a public relations campaign that included writing op-ed pieces, letters to the editor, and press releases to defend its reputation and to refute critics' claims.

However, Marc Kasky, a California activist, maintained that Nike's claims were misleading and deceptive to the public. He filed a lawsuit claiming that Nike's actions should be classified as commercial speech that violated California's unfair competition and advertising laws. The legal controversy culminated in the California Supreme Court's decision in *Kasky v. Nike.* The court determined that public relations communications may constitute "commercial speech" that can be interpreted as "false advertising." As commercial speech is afforded less protection under the First Amendment, Nike would be liable for any claims under its public relations campaign that could be construed as misleading the public. After the ruling, Nike settled the lawsuit at approximately $2 million.

NIKE'S CORPORATE SOCIAL RESPONSIBILITY

"Nike has increased its efforts to be more ethical in its manufacturing practices and has become something of an industry leader in certain areas."

Nike's corporate social responsibility (CSR) practices have been evolving since 1991. At first, Nike's approach to CSR could be characterized as insufficient and generally lacking in any true forms of regulation and implementation throughout its global supply chain. Manufacturers in foreign locations were simply trying to comply with the minimal contract requirements, while at times overlooking fair labor practices in order to perform as low-cost suppliers. Nike's initial response to criticism was reputation management rather than wide-scale changes in its practices. However, as more and more issues have surfaced and been brought to the attention of both the corporation and its consumers, Nike has increased its efforts to be more ethical in its manufacturing practices and has become something of an industry leader in certain areas.

According to Harvard University senior fellow Simon Zadek, corporate responsibility evolves through five stages:

1. Defensive: "It's not our fault."
2. Compliance: "We'll do only what we have to."
3. Managerial: "It's the business."
4. Strategic: "It gives us a competitive edge."
5. Civil: "We need to make sure everybody does it."

Nike could be classified as having evolved from the defensive stage through the compliance stage to the managerial stage. The company's first CSR report demonstrated how Nike had handled complaints from stakeholders who wanted to see better working conditions at Nike's contract factories. In its 2005 report, the company provided the names and locations of factories that produced its products for the first time ever. In its third CSR report, Nike officials said they were moving away from using corporate responsibility as a crisis-management tool and would instead be using it as an opportunity for innovation and growth.

Nike must now grow fully into the fourth and fifth CSR stages. The company must continue to develop its corporate responsibility strategies and increase enforcement of its policies in its factories to ensure its market share dominance in the footwear industry. With its new emphasis on corporate responsibility as an innovative tool, Nike is implementing further CSR initiatives to make the company an industry leader and thus give it a competitive edge in the footwear industry.

The following sections further discuss some of Nike's CSR practices. The areas covered include environmental sustainability, audit tools used to evaluate Nike contractor practices, factory transparency, Nike's corporate responsibility committee, and philanthropy.

Environmental Sustainability

In 1990 Nike began development of the Reuse-A-Shoe Program to reduce the company's environmental footprint (so to speak) and decrease the amount of shoes that end up in landfills. The purpose of the program was to find an environmentally friendly way to dispose of worn-out shoes. The material made from the recycled shoes was called "Nike Grind." In 1995 Reuse-A-Shoe began collecting old shoes in Nike retail stores. In 2002 Nike expanded Reuse-A-Shoe by partnering with the National Recycling Coalition and by beginning plans to go international with drop-off stations in Europe and Australia. Since the program was created, more than 1.5 million pairs of used shoes have been collected for recycling each year. Nike has collected more than 25 million pairs of used athletic shoes since 1995.

Nike has also crafted a sustainability philosophy called Considered Design in its step toward creating a closed-loop business. A closed-loop business occurs when waste at all levels of the operation can be recycled. According to Nike, Considered Design is "a companywide ethos built around designing the best products for the best athletes while using the most sustainable methods possible." To make Considered Design a reality, Nike has set forth a variety of baseline standards that its products must meet or exceed. Its goal is to have all of its products from all over the world meet these standards by 2020.

Audit Tools

In 1998 Nike developed auditing tools to help provide increasing transparency and insight into the manner in which Nike contract factories are evaluated for compliance with company standards. Management Audit Verification (MAV) combines audit and verification into one tool. It helps to identify issues related to work hours, wages and benefits, freedom of association, and grievance systems, as well as to follow up on these issues and to create an action plan to correct them according to local law and Nike's Code Leadership Standards. The Environment, Safety and Health (ESH) audit is an in-depth audit tool used by Nike compliance teams to determine compliance with Nike's Code Leadership Standards. In addition to its own auditing tools, external organizations such as NGOs frequently audit Nike. Until recently, Nike also employed a Safety, Health, Attitude of Management, People and Environment (SHAPE) tool used quarterly by contract factories to determine their compliance with Nike's Code Leadership Standards. In 2007 the tool was changed to a factory self-evaluation as Nike felt that a numeric score by itself was insufficient. Nike estimates that it visits its factories an average of 1.77 times per year.

Factory Transparency

> "Nike became the first company to respond to student requests to publicly disclose the names and locations of its contracted factories that produced licensed collegiate products."

In 2000 Nike became the first company to respond to student requests to publicly disclose the names and locations of its contracted factories that produced licensed collegiate products. A contract factory making Nike products could be producing for as many as thirty different schools. By disclosing its supply chain, Nike believes it can be more successful at monitoring and making changes once issues have been uncovered not only in its own factories, but also on an industry-wide basis. The company hopes that by disclosing its own supply chain, it can encourage other companies to do the same. The company also feels that transparency should work as a motivator for contract factories. Those with high compliance rankings can be confident that business will come their way.

With multiple brands, and many universities represented, contract factories must decide which company's code(s) of conduct to follow. This task is not an easy one, as standards for the varying corporate codes of conduct can contradict each other. Nike has attempted to make it easier for contract factories to comply with its code of conduct by guaranteeing that its code aligns with that of the Fair Labor Association. The company hopes that eventually a standardized code of conduct followed by all companies in the industry can be implemented, creating widespread compliance and better working conditions. Even as Nike has taken dramatic steps to increase its transparency and accountability, activists have continued to put pressure on the company to improve its standards and practices.

Nike also has implemented a program it calls the Balanced Scorecard for its suppliers. The Balanced Scorecard is a lettered grading system used to better assess factory compliance with the code of conduct. Rather than simply assessing financial factors, the Balanced Scorecard also measures labor, health, and environmental standards of factories. This system gives the company a reliable method for rewarding high-performance, compliant factories. The card measures cost, delivery, and quality, all of which need to be addressed equally for the work in factories to flow smoothly. The Balanced Scorecard gives factories incentives to improve working conditions, and Nike rewards those that show improvement.

Corporate Responsibility Committee

In order to become a leader in corporate responsibility, Nike established a Corporate Responsibility (CR) Committee to review policies and activities and to make recommendations to the board of directors regarding labor and environmental practices, community affairs, philanthropy, diversity and equal opportunity, and environmental and sustainability initiatives. The board is actively involved on the committee; at least two committee members must be from the board of directors. Nike expects corporate responsibility to be integrated into the executive level as well. Nike's Vice President of Corporate Responsibility, for example, reports directly to the CEO of Nike. These leaders help to ensure that corporate responsibility is considered at every level of the company.

Philanthropy

One of Nike's newest goals to increase its CSR is by building a social network "where innovations are shared, new funds are mobilized and human and social capital is exchanged in support of a global movement based on the power of sport to unleash human potential." Nike's goal is to encourage the use of sports as a means of empowering individuals and building skills such as leadership, conflict resolution, equity, and trauma relief. Nike partners with various groups that work with low-income youth, minorities, and young women who live in conflict situations across the world. Because sports require access to safe spaces, good coaches, safe equipment, and education, Nike is forming partnerships in these areas. The company awarded $315 million in grants, product donations, and other support through 2011 to give underprivileged youth greater access to sport programs. While contributing to the global community, the company also strives to invest in its own local communities of Portland, Oregon; Memphis, Tennessee; Hilversum, Holland; Laakdal, Belgium; and other places around the world where Nike corporate offices are located. With a continued focus on corporate responsibility, Nike strives to build and improve its relationships with consumers, to achieve a high-quality supply chain, and to create top-quality, innovative products.

NEW CHALLENGES IN THE FUTURE

So far Nike's efforts have seemed to pay off, as it has seen considerable improvement in its reputation and corporate image in the past few years. As a result of its positive changes, Nike appeared in *Fortune*'s 2010 list of "The World's Most Admired Companies" as the number one most admired apparel company and was ranked 24 overall. Nike was also listed at number 23 in *CR (Corporate Responsibility)* magazine's "Best Corporate Citizens" in 2010.

The news has not all been good for Nike, however. In 2010 several universities threatened to cancel their contracts with Nike over labor concerns among Honduran factory workers. A year earlier, two of Nike's subcontractors had closed without notice, laying off 1,800 workers. Under Honduran labor law, the workers were owed over $2 million in severance pay along with other unemployment aid. Although Nike agreed to provide the workers with training and give them priority jobs at other factories, the company stated that the responsibility for the situation rested with the suppliers, not Nike. One could argue that Nike was reverting back to the defensive stage of corporate responsibility. Nike's actions did not go far enough to please the Worker Rights Consortium, who began urging universities to cancel their contracts with Nike until the labor dispute was settled. Other labor watchdogs staged demonstrations outside Nike shops, changing Nike's slogan from "Just Do It" to "Just Pay It." The University of Wisconsin–Madison was the first to cancel its licensing agreement with Nike, stating that its code of conduct requires companies that make products carrying the university name to assume responsibility for their suppliers. Nike eventually capitulated and set aside a $1.54 million fund to aid the laid-off Honduran workers. Although Nike experienced bad publicity over the event, labor activists see its actions as a positive deviation from industry standards. They hope that this step will set a precedent for other companies to follow.

This incident reveals that there are still flaws in Nike's supply chain, both in contract negotiation and supplier oversight. Although some experts herald Nike as a leader in CSR, its use of hundreds of international contractors makes detection and enforcement of abuses incredibly difficult. Nike plans to pursue an accelerated growth strategy in foreign markets, particularly in emerging economies, which makes increased oversight of its factories even more of an imperative.

Indeed, Nike sees international expansion as essential for its continued profitability. About one-fourth of Nike's sales come from developing countries. China in particular represents a lucrative market for Nike, with profit margins of 37 percent compared to 23 percent in North America. As a result of this high growth potential, Nike has announced plans to increase its sales in emerging economies from $3 billion to $3.5 billion by 2015. Nike is also taking steps to portray itself as a socially responsible company and increase its visibility; during the 2010 World Cup, for example, Nike opened a facility in a low-income South African township that doubled as both a football training center and a clinic for AIDS testing and awareness.

Corporate and social responsibility are not only changing Nike's image; they can also be good for its bottom line in a highly competitive industry. Nike's target audience has broadened from mainly male athletes to female athletes and children as well. As Nike's target audience widens, being perceived as an ethical company will help attract and retain new customers.

Such an approach is requiring Nike to undertake socially responsible initiatives and develop more sustainable products. For instance, Nike celebrated the World Cup while simultaneously embracing sustainability with a new product: World Cup shirts made from recycled bottles. According to Nike, each shirt requires less material and consists of recycled polyester and eight recycled bottles. It is estimated that Nike's recycled shirts kept over 550,000 pounds of polyester out of landfills. Nike is also creating innovative products to increase consumers' healthy living (as well as the bottom line). Its Nike$^+$ shoes contain sensors that can communicate with the wearer's iPod to track the person's consumption of calories. Nike plans to develop more innovative and sustainable products in the future.

Nike itself admits that it has a long way to go in the area of corporate responsibility, including continuing to improve its monitoring systems. However, the company is being rewarded for its efforts toward improvement thus far.

QUESTIONS

1. Why did Nike fail to address corporate social responsibility early on?
2. Evaluate Nike's response to societal and consumer concerns about its contract manufacturing.
3. What are the challenges facing Nike in the future?

SOURCES

Balfour, Frederick. "Acting Globally but Selling Locally: Chinese Athletic Wear Maker Li Ning Is Raising Its International Profile to Win over Shoppers at Home." *BusinessWeek*, May 12, 2008, 27–29; Associated Press. "Wisconsin cuts ties with Nike over labor concerns in Honduras." *USA Today*, April 10, 2010, http://www.usatoday.com/sports/college/2010-04-09-wisconsin-nike-honduras_N.htm (accessed February 9, 2011); B & T Marketing. "Nike Answers Critics on Corporate Responsibility." http://www.bandt.com.au/news/25/0c00d225.asp (accessed September 3, 2009); Branding Strategy. "Social Responsibility: The Nike Story." http://www.brandingstrategyinsider.com/2008/07/social-responsi.html (accessed September 3, 2009); Canizares, Kristina. "NIKE Failed on Sweatshop Reform Promises." *Albion Monitor*, June 1, 2001, http://www.albionmonitor.com/0105b/copyright/nikereport.html

(accessed July 8, 2011); Collins, E. L., L. M. Zoch, and C. S. McDonald. "A Crisis in Reputation Management: The Implications of *Kasky v. Nike*." Paper presented at the meeting of the International Communication Association, May 27, 2004, New Orleans Sheraton, New Orleans, LA, http://www.allacademic.com/meta/p113246_index. html (accessed September 3, 2009); *CR (Corporate Responsibility) Magazine*. "CR's 100 Best Corporate Citizens 2010." http://www.thecro.com/files/CR100Best.pdf (accessed February 8, 2011); CSR Wire. "Corporate Social Responsibility Profile—Nike." http://www.csrwire.com/profile/1262.html (accessed September 3, 2009); DeTienne, Kristen B., and Lee W. Lewis. "The Pragmatic and Ethical Barriers to Corporate Social Responsibility Disclosure: The Nike Case." *Journal of Business Ethics* 60, no. 4 (2005): 359–376; Elsasser, John. "Watching Nike Sweat." *Public Relations Tactics* 6 (1998): 1–4; *Ethics Newsline*. "Nike-Funded Study Claims Workers at Nike's Indonesian Factories Are Subject to Abuse and Harassment." February 26, 2001, http://www.globalethics.org/newsline/2001/02/26/ nike-funded-study-claims-workers-at-nikes-indonesian-factories-are-subject-to-abuse-and-harassment, (accessed September 3, 2009); Foreign Policy Centre. "Corporate Social Responsibility in Emerging Markets: The Role of Multinational Corporations." http://fpc.org.uk/fsblob/919.pdf (accessed September 3, 2009); *Fortune*. "The World's Most Admired Companies." February 7, 2011, 23; Klein, Naomi. *No Logo*. New York: Riemann Verlag, 2002; Krentzman, Jackie. "The Force behind the Nike Empire." *Stanford Magazine*, http://www.stanfordalumni.org/news/ magazine/1997/janfeb/articles/knight.html (accessed September 3, 2009); Levenson, Eugenia. "Citizen Nike." *CNN Money*, November 17, 2008, http://money.cnn.com/2008/11/17/news/companies/levenson_nike.fortune.index. htm (accessed July 8, 2011); Nike. "Considered Design." http://www.nike.com/nikeos/p/gamechangers/en_US/ considered (accessed February 8, 2011); Nike. "Charter of the Corporate Responsibility Committee." http://invest. nike.com/phoenix.zhtml?c=100529&p=irol-govCommittee&Committee=7452 (accessed February 8, 2011); Nike. "FY05–06 Corporate Responsibility Report, 2005–2006." http://www.nikebiz.com/responsibility/documents/Nike_ FY05_06_CR_Report_C.pdf (accessed September 8, 2009); Nike. "Innovate for a Better World," Nike FY05–06 Corporate Responsibility Report, 2005–2006. http://www.nikebiz.com/responsibility/documents/Nike_FY05_06_ CR_Report_C.pdf (accessed September 3, 2009); Nike. "Our Community Programs: Reuse-A-Shoe & Nike Grind." October 28, 2008, http://www.nikebiz.com/responsibility/community_programs/reuse_a_shoe.html (accessed September 3, 2009); Nike. "Our Mission: Considered Design & Nike Corporate Social Responsibility." http://www. nikereuseashoe.com/the-impact/our-mission (accessed February 8, 2011); Nike. "Responsibility Governance." http://www.nikebiz.com/responsibility/cr_governance.html#operational_integration, accessed February 8, 2011; Nike. "Workers and Factories," Corporate Responsibility Report. http://www.nikebiz.com/crreport/content/ workers-and-factories/3-2-2-factory-monitoring-and-results.php?cat=profiles (accessed February 8, 2011); Padgett, Tim. "Just Pay It: Nike Creates Funds for Honduran Workers." *Time*, July 27, 2010, http://www.time.com/time/ business/article/0,8599,2006646,00.html (accessed February 9, 2011); PBS. "Labors' Pains." http://www.pbs.org/ newshour/bb/business/jan-june97/sweatshops_4-14.html, April 14, 1997 (accessed September 3, 2009); Perspectives in Responsible Sourcing. "Nike's New CSR Report: They Just Did It—Again." http://cscc.typepad. com/responsiblesourcing/2007/06/nikes_new_csr_r.html (accessed September 3, 2009); Schwartz, Ariel. "World Cup Shirts to Be Made out of Recycled Plastic Bottles." *Fast Company*, February 25, 2010, http://www.fastcompany. com/1563572/world-cup-shirts-to-be-made-out-of-recycled-plastic-bottles (accessed February 9, 2011); Seeking Alpha. "The Long Case for Nike—'Just Do It'" http://seekingalpha.com/article/23192-the-longcase- for-nike-just-do-it (accessed September 3, 2009); Speaks, Jonathon. "Nike University: Hooked on Sweatshops." *Irregular Times*, http://irregulartimes.com/nike.html (accessed July 8, 2011); World Bank. "Nike in Vietnam: The Tae Kwang Vina Factory." http://siteresources.worldbank.org/INTEMPOWERMENT/Resources/14826_Nike-web.pdf (accessed April 11, 2009); The World Is Green. "Nike's Corporate Social Responsibility Efforts Falling Short?" http:// worldisgreen.com/2007/06/05/csr-and-business-startegywith- nike/ (accessed September 3, 2009); Zadek, Simon. "The Path to Corporate Responsibility." *Harvard Business Review*, 82, no. 12 (December 2004); Zwolinski, Matt. "The Promise and Perils of Globalization: The Case of Nike." In James Ciment, ed., *Social Issues in America: An Encyclopedia*. Armonk, NY: M. E. Sharpe, 2006; "Shoes Sought in Recycling Project." *Wicked Local Lexington*, April 29, 2008, http://www.wickedlocal.com/lexington/news/business/x883026486 (accessed July 8, 2011); "The swoosh heard around the world," *The Economist*, July 3, 2010, 62–63.

CASE 20

Best Buy Fights Against Electronic Waste*

Although Best Buy has not been in business as long as other established brands, the company is becoming a well-known name both within and outside the United States. This consumer electronics retailer is the largest specialty retailer within its sector throughout the United States with 21 percent of the market. To maintain its competitive advantage against rivals in specialty electronics, Best Buy has begun investigating competitive pricing strategies, international expansion, and the targeting of a younger demographic.

In addition to its discounted and high-quality products, Best Buy has become known for its customer-centered approach and sustainable outreach. After realizing the importance of sustainability to its customers, Best Buy has implemented an extensive recycling program. In the process, Best Buy has earned itself a name as a socially responsible company. The company has also adopted programs and systems, including the ROWE system, to provide flexibility and aid to its employees. As a result of its corporate and social responsibility initiatives Best Buy has been awarded numerous honors, including a spot on *Ethisphere*'s 2010 World's Most Ethical Companies and *Forbes*' America's Most Reputable Companies.

This case will provide a brief history of Best Buy, including details on its expansion and the models it has implemented to become the success it is today. Next, we will discuss Best Buy's vision, along with the actions the company is taking to turn its vision into a reality. We will also briefly analyze Best Buy's community outreach programs. We will look at Best Buy's large-scale environmental initiatives, particularly those regarding energy savings and recycling. Finally, we will examine some of the challenges that Best Buy is encountering as it struggles to maintain its dominance in the consumer electronics market.

HISTORY

Best Buy, Inc., has undergone a number of changes over the course of its 40-year history. The company was founded by Richard Schulze, who had worked as a representative for a consumer-electronics manufacturer. Schulze recognized that a demand existed among college-age consumers for audio equipment, and in 1966 he opened an audio specialty store called Sound of Music in the Twin Cities (Minnesota) area. A year later, the company acquired the Kencraft Hi-Fi Company. Schulze opened two additional stores and began earning a yearly income of $173,000. The company would continue to grow and flourish over the next few years, hitting $1 million in annual revenue by 1970. Best Buy's equipment was originally targeted toward college students who wanted electronic goods at the higher

*This case was developed by Jennifer Sawayda, Amanda Solosky, and Shelby Peters for and under the direction of O. C. Ferrell and Linda Ferrell. It was prepared for classroom discussion rather than to illustrate effective or ineffective handling of an administrative, ethical, or legal decision by management. All sources used for this case were obtained through publicly available material.

end of the spectrum. However, due to increasing competition in the consumer electronics industry during the 1970s, Schulze realized his stores would have to adapt to compete effectively.

In 1983 Schulze decided to convert his Sound of Music stores into a high-volume discount chain selling electronics, consumer appliances, and videocassettes and records. He renamed this chain Best Buy. Yet competition remained fierce from companies such as Sears and Wards, and Schulze was once against forced to innovate. He came up with an entirely new model that would end up revolutionizing the retail industry as a whole. The changes that Schulze implemented included eliminating the backrooms of stores and bringing all merchandise onto the sales floor, paying salespeople hourly wages rather than commissions, and retraining salespeople to become more customer-focused.

Best Buy, Inc., also embarked upon partnerships and acquisitions to increase its market share, such as acquiring the computer repair service the Geek Squad along with Magnolia Audio Video and Pacific Sales. With the downward trend in computer sales in the 2000s, Best Buy embraced what it calls Concept 5 stores—companies that would not only sell products but also teach consumers how to use them. With the acquisition of the Geek Squad, Best Buy furthered this goal and significantly reduced its service turnaround time, leading to higher customer satisfaction and a new chapter in the consumer electronics industry.

Best Buy operates businesses in several countries outside of the United States as well, including stores in Canada, Mexico, and subsidiaries in China. In 2009 the company opened its first stores based in the United Kingdom. The company began by acquiring a 50 percent stake in the U.K.-based mobile phone company known as the Carphone Warehouse. Best Buy began opening branded Best Buy stores in the U.K. in 2010. The company also discussed the possibility of acquiring Kesa Electricals and DSG International, both of which are rival retail electronics outlets in the United Kingdom. DSG International is responding to the rising threat of Best Buy stores by conducting an overhaul of its own retail outlets.

Today, Best Buy, Inc. is a leading provider of consumer electronics with a presence in U.S., Canadian, British, Chinese, and Mexican markets. In March of 2009 the company became the primary online and brick and mortar provider for the eastern United States after its rival Circuit City closed its doors. Unlike Best Buy, Circuit City had failed to adapt to a fast-paced marketplace; it chose to hire workers at lower wages and encountered severe inventory backlogs, which resulted in less loyal employees, greater inefficiencies, and customer dissatisfaction. With annual revenues of more than $49 billion, Best Buy now dominates the marketplace. The company currently employs about 155,000 people.

VISION

"People. Technology. And the pursuit of happiness." This is the corporate vision that Best Buy strives to achieve. The company is attempting to apply best practices in every facet of its operations. To meet the needs of its customers, employees, vendors, and stockholders, Best Buy has adopted a stakeholder orientation that focuses on quality relationships with these various groups. Technology is an inextricable part of this orientation, as the company prides itself on selling quality technological products and services that meet its customers' varied needs. Best Buy also wants to create

> "Best Buy has adopted a stakeholder orientation that focuses on quality relationships with these various groups."

a satisfying work environment and give back to the communities in which it operates. The company feels that happy employees and communities translate into happy customers. The following sections will describe the initiatives that Best Buy has implemented to fulfill its vision.

Consumer Engagement

Best Buy views itself as a customer-centered organization and aims to achieve better customer relationships, a greater understanding of customer needs and preferences, and continual engagement in customer dialogue. Under CEO Brian Dunn's leadership, Best Buy focuses on listening to consumers, and the company utilizes various channels to gather their feedback. For instance, Best Buy has participated in forums like Facebook, Twitter, and blogs. Best Buy also encourages its customers to rate their experiences and products on www.BestBuy.com. The company has even invited customers to leadership meetings in order to gain a better outlook on their needs. In this way, Best Buy hopes to create a better fit between the company and its customers.

Best Buy takes the concerns of its customers seriously. In 2007 the company published its first Corporate Social Responsibility Report (CSR) in response to consumers' demands to know what Best Buy is doing in the area of sustainability. Electronic waste has been rapidly accumulating in landfills, and society has become increasingly concerned with how to reduce this waste. Best Buy's surveys revealed that its customers wanted the company to find ways to recycle electronics and use less energy. Best Buy answered this call through its implementation of a wide-scale electronics recycling program. Best Buy's recycling program will be discussed in more detail later in the case.

Best Buy is also working to continually improve its customer service. Its subsidiary, the Geek Squad, provides 24-hour service on-site, at home, or through the Internet. The Squad's Agents—wearing their signature white shirts, black ties, and black trousers and sporting Geek Squad logos, complete with black and white cars for at-home services—are often able to make repairs in a matter of hours (versus days or weeks for many other computer repair services). This feature of the company has served to increase Best Buy's customer satisfaction. Best Buy also provides customer service tailored to small or medium-sized businesses through its brand Speakeasy. Speakeasy provides broadband voice, IT, and data services to Best Buy's business customers. Speakeasy's technical staff is available 24 hours a day to answer callers' questions. The service consistently scores between 85 and 90 percent in customer approval ratings. Overall, Best Buy's customer satisfaction ratings have displayed an upward trend in the past few years as the company's customer-centered focus has provided it with an advantage in the marketplace and enabled it to grab market share from its competitors.

Employee Engagement

Employees are an integral part of Best Buy's vision. Best Buy requires a talented, dedicated staff to solve technical problems and demonstrate exemplary customer service. Best Buy's corporate culture emphasizes listening to employees as well as customers. Employees are able to post their thoughts on online forums such as the Watercooler and on an internal news site. The company's Chief Ethics Officer Kathleen Edmond demonstrated the importance of communication to the company when she created the Chief Ethics Officer Blog for employees to view. Edmond used cases of unethical events that took place within the company in order to teach employees about ethical conduct. Her actions caused her to be listed in *Ethisphere*'s Most Influential People in Business Ethics for 2009 and 2010.

Best Buy also encourages employees to participate in Employee Business Networks such as Wolf@Best Buy: Women's Leadership Forum. Through its Wolf program, Best Buy hopes to improve the experiences of both its female employees and its female customers. Between 2007 and 2008 recruitment and hiring of female employees jumped from 31 percent to 35 percent. Best Buy's share of the female electronics market improved from 14.3 percent in 2007 to 15.7 percent in 2008.

Best Buy also takes a stand on diversity training for its employees. Every year Best Buy holds a Cultural Immersion program for its employees at the Lorraine Hotel in Memphis. The hotel was the site where Dr. Martin Luther King, Jr., was assassinated in 1968; in 1991 it was converted into the National Civil Rights Museum. It is Best Buy's goal to encourage its employees to practice inclusion and awareness of different cultures.

Best Buy embraces a decentralized structure in which employees are provided with greater flexibility and the opportunity to engage in company operations. The company has adopted work approaches to encourage dedication on the part of its employees, including what the company calls its "open source" approach and the ROWE work system.

> "Best Buy embraces a decentralized structure in which employees are provided with greater flexibility and the opportunity to engage in company operations."

OPEN SOURCE APPROACH   Best Buy classifies its open source approach as a "way of opening the door for employees to modify or enhance a program or initiative based on their first-hand experience or innovative nature." In other words, employees have the ability to engage in projects to improve the company's products and operations. For instance, several of Best Buy's employees have created groups to develop social responsibility initiatives for the company. One of the company's achievements was initiated by members of Best Buy's Geek Squad who banded together to work on reducing the packaging waste of HDMI cables. Together the team created a new design that would decrease 30 percent of the plastic in the packaging content. By adopting the open source approach, Best Buy seeks not only to encourage its employees to participate in the company, but also to create innovative inventions to increase the company's bottom line.

ROWE SYSTEM   ROWE is short for Results Only Work Environment. This system is a nontraditional approach that allows employees to choose when and where to work. Best Buy implemented this system after surveys revealed that employees felt too micromanaged, which in turn was creating higher turnover rates. Under ROWE, employees are judged for their productivity; if they can be more productive outside of the workplace, ROWE gives them that opportunity. Employees under ROWE are paid for completed tasks, not for the hours it takes to obtain them. For instance, employees can choose their own work schedules or work from home as long as they obtain the desired work results. As a result of this system, employee satisfaction has grown, coinciding with a one-third increase in overall employee productivity. These two components landed Best Buy onto the "World's Most Admired Companies" 2010 list. The successful adoption of ROWE demonstrates that Best Buy's innovative approaches are not limited to its product lines but to all aspects of operations.

Community Engagement

Best Buy adheres to the belief that being a socially responsible company requires contributing to the communities in which it operates. Thus, Best Buy frequently engages with stakeholders in these communities, particularly in the areas of education and technology.

While Best Buy's community programs give back to the communities in which it does business, they also provide the company with a chance to create long-lasting relationships with consumers, employees, and other stakeholders. Best Buy supports corporate philanthropy through programs such as @15, volunteerism, Tag Team Awards, Local Giving programs, and disaster relief funds.

@15 PROGRAM   @15 is a program started by Best Buy to build relationships with one of its largest stakeholder groups—teenagers. The @15 program empowers teenagers to become involved in civic engagement, encouraging them to develop and share their points of views on issues that matter to them along with recommendations on how to stimulate positive change. These comments are posted on the @15 website, www.at15.com. Starting in 2009 Best Buy launched the @15 Challenge to reward youth teams for their proposals. These Youth Venture Teams were provided with $10,000 each to support their programs for positive change. Two other @15 programs deal specifically with education. Best Buy's @15 Scholarship Program has awarded nearly $17.5 million in scholarships since it was implemented in 1999. The Teach@15 Awards give teenagers the ability to designate the awards by nominating their own school and then casting votes.

TAG TEAM AWARDS   The Tag Team Awards program depends upon employees to determine the amount of awards the company will give to nonprofit organizations, providing them with a philanthropic incentive to volunteer. When employees volunteer their skills or time, the Best Buy Children's Foundation provides cash awards to qualified nonprofit organizations. The Best Buy Children's Foundation contributes to organizations that utilize interactive technology to engage children in learning. Best Buy estimates that the value of their employee's time is $18.77 an hour. Therefore, the more time employees volunteer for certain causes, the more Best Buy Children's Foundation will award to qualified nonprofits. In 2010 the Best Buy Children's Foundation awarded almost $2.5 million to local nonprofit organizations. Employees themselves can also win awards for exceeding volunteer service expectations through the President's Volunteer Service Award.

LOCAL GIVING PROGRAM   In addition to allowing employees to take on project responsibilities, the company also gives employees a say in how the money from the Best Buy Children's Foundation is allocated among local organizations. In the process, the company hopes to increase employee philanthropy and morale. In 2010 the Local Giving program awarded 193 grants amounting to $1.1 million. Local giving programs are also available for Best Buy stores in Mexico, Canada, and China. Employees from Best Buy's Chinese subsidiary Five Star chose to create a scholarship program to provide college funds for 100 students affected by the 2008 Sichuan earthquake.

DISASTER RELIEF   Best Buy partners with disaster relief organizations to donate money and aid to hard-hit areas around the world. For example, after the 2008 Sichuan earthquake, Best Buy China donated over $1 million to aid victims. The company also contributed walkie-talkies, and Best Buy's subsidiary Jiangsu Five Star contributed tents and other materials. More recently Best Buy donated $200,000 for disaster relief in Haiti after the devastating earthquake in 2010.

Best Buy also supports employees who live in areas affected by natural disasters. If the Best Buy store in the area is forced to close, employees are paid until the store reopens or are given the opportunity to work at another Best Buy if the store remains closed. Hotlines, counseling services, and employee assistance programs are also available for employees impacted by natural disasters.

BECOMING MORE SUSTAINABLE

Becoming more sustainable goes hand in hand with Best Buy's business model and strategy. Best Buy has incorporated ecofriendly practices into several facets of its operations, from reduced energy consumption to recycling of electronic waste (e-waste). The company is also incorporating innovative ecofriendly inventions into its product line. For instance, Best Buy has begun selling electric bicycles and providing charging stations for Ford Motor Company's electric cars. To reduce its environmental footprint, Best Buy is also forming partnerships with other companies such as Energy Star. Best Buy has joined with SmartWay Transport to create a partnership to reduce greenhouse gas emissions. SmartWay Transport is a collaboration between the Environmental Protection Agency and the freight industry with the goal of reducing waste and becoming more energy efficient.

> "Becoming more sustainable goes hand in hand with Best Buy's business model and strategy."

Best Buy has also begun to enforce ethical and sustainable practices among its vendors. Suppliers must adhere to the company's Supplier Compliance Standards, and to ensure compliance, Best Buy audits its various suppliers each year. Factories that are found to have violations are dealt with accordingly; those that do not improve sufficiently in the designated time frame may be dropped. To ensure that their suppliers are not abusing worker rights, Best Buy conducts ongoing human rights audits.

CONSERVING ENERGY ONE STORE AT A TIME

One area of particular concern to Best Buy is energy consumption. Realizing that its many stores consume large quantities of energy—some of which could be conserved through more sustainable practices—Best Buy joined the Business for Innovative Climate and Energy (BICEP) in February 2010. BICEP is a coalition of companies who want to advance climate and energy policies within the United States. The focus of BICEP is on embracing innovation in sustainability. Other BICEP members include Starbucks and Nike. According to Best Buy Senior Director of Government Relations, this is one step toward Best Buy's commitment "to building sustainable business practices and helping our customers realize ways to live more sustainable lives."

As part of Best Buy's energy conservation program, the company set the goal of reducing operation emissions 8 percent per square foot by 2012. It achieved this goal three years ahead of schedule. The company's action plan includes improving lighting in its stores through skylights, implementing a "no-idling" policy that prohibits trucks from idling their engines outside Best Buy locations, and investigating new energy-saving technologies such as virtual servers and surge protectors/power bars. Additionally, in 2010 Best Buy created an everyday in-store recycling program in its U.S. stores with the goal of increasing its recycling rate to 1 billion consumer products in five to six years. In 2010 Best Buy collected more than 75 million pounds of electronic waste for recycling. These changes have improved Best Buy's ability to become more sustainable through energy conservation and recycling.

ENVIRONMENTAL SUSTAINABILITY— ENERGY STAR PRODUCTS

In addition to saving energy in its operations, Best Buy also sells energy-saving products. Best Buy has an extensive partnership with Energy Star to save its customers money on energy costs and help the environment by selling energy-efficient items. Energy Star–qualified products have met strict efficiency guidelines set by the U.S. Department of Energy and the Environmental Protection Agency. During 2008 Best Buy employees underwent Energy Star training so that they could provide consumers with detailed information on Energy Star products. In 2009 Best Buy won the Energy Star Excellence in Electronic and Appliance Retailing award for its commitment to saving energy. Best Buy offers everything from refrigerators to laptops to printers that are Energy Star–qualified. In 2010 Best Buy estimated that its sales of Energy Star products saved consumers over $91 million overall in utility bills.

COMBATING E-WASTE

As the world moves toward sustainability, the issue of e-waste has taken on an increased importance among consumers. Best Buy surveys revealed that both its employees and consumers were concerned about the growing amount of electronic waste that occurs after an item breaks or, more frequently, becomes obsolete. Without any clear idea of how to recycle these electronic items, consumers were often forced to throw them away—contributing to a greater amount of e-waste in landfills. Stakeholders desired programs that could help them figure out how to recycle their used electronics, and Best Buy decided to meet that demand with its "Greener Together" initiative. Greener Together includes a recycling program that has brought the recycling of electronic waste to a whole new level. Consumers can drop off their used electronics and Best Buy will recycle them regardless of their condition or brand. If Best Buy doesn't recycle a specific product, it will help the customer find a way to recycle it. Best Buy offers information on how to recycle items that it does not accept on its website and in stores. The tech trade-in service even prints out a shipping label so customers can send their unwanted products to places that will recycle the item. The Greener Together program allows consumers to recycle two electronics per day, per household, at all of its stores. The stores take cell phones, DVD players, and most other electronic products. Electronics that are over 32 inches in size cost $10 to recycle. These types of products often include electronic waste like old laptops, monitors, CRTs, and TVs. The $10 fee is used to offset the cost of dealing with these heavier recyclables. However, to encourage consumers to recycle these items, customers are given a $10 Best Buy gift card to replace the money spent on recycling them. Best Buy can then make money from these reusable items and at the same time encourage consumers to purchase products from the store with their gift cards. Best Buy monitors the gift cards' usage to see if the recycling program is bringing in new business. The company hopes that by encouraging purchases, consumers will shop from Best Buy again in the future.

Other resources that Best Buy utilizes in its large-scale recycling initiatives are its trade-in program, recycling kiosks, and TV and appliance pickup service. The trade-in program offers consumers two options: trading electronics online or in-store. The online system accepts a wider variety of product trade-ins and allows more flexibility in where the products were purchased. After inputting the product information, consumers are provided with a trade-in value and can either accept or decline the value offered. If they accept, consumers print a prepaid shipping label and ship the item in. They receive a Best Buy gift card or check within 14 days after Best Buy receives the item. The trade-in system allows consumers to trade an item in and use the store credit to buy a newer model of a similar item. The in-store option follows similar steps, although it only allows trade-ins of iPods, mobile phones, and laptops.

Recycling kiosks have become a familiar site at Best Buy stores. Every Best Buy in the United States now has recycling kiosks located near the front entrance. The kiosks are used to recycle small items including rechargeable batteries, cell phones, and ink cartridges. During 2009 Best Buy installed recycling kiosks across its stores in Canada as well.

> "Recycling kiosks have become a familiar site at Best Buy stores."

Best Buy also offers haul-away services for large items. If a customer buys a television from Best Buy and has it delivered, Best Buy offers to haul their old television away and recycle it for free. If consumers want to hire Best Buy to haul a large item off without a purchase, Best Buy charges a $100 fee. This is Best Buy's attempt to gain environmentally conscious customers. The company is dedicated to its mission of recycling unwanted materials and, if possible, giving these products a second life. As part of this mission, since 2003 Best Buy has been a member of the Environmental Protection Agency's Plug Into eCycling program, which is committed to increasing consumer awareness about the importance of recycling.

Managing such an extensive recycling program requires that Best Buy collaborate with other organizations committed to the same cause. As a result, Best Buy has partnered with various recycling companies, many of which attempt to give used electronics a "second life." Several of Best Buy's recycling partners take the items apart and organize them into plastics, metals, glass, etc. Then they decide whether the products can be repaired before recycling the parts for other uses. To ensure that its partners are acting in a socially responsible manner, Best Buy monitors its recyclers to make sure they are following safe recycling practices. These partnerships serve to reduce pollution by keeping items out of landfills.

RECYCLING PROGRAM BENEFITS

The environmental benefits of recycling are quite clear—reduction in waste, decreased gas emissions, energy-savings, and more. However, as Best Buy demonstrates, recycling can have positive implications for the business world as well. For example, if a product like a cell phone can be fixed, it can be sent to outlets like eBay who can resell the product. If not, the products are taken apart so the materials used to make it can be reused. Best Buy splits the profit made from recycled products with its partners.

Recycling programs also encourage manufacturers to take greater responsibility in product design. With the growing demand for sustainability, many manufacturing companies have begun to embark upon new and innovative designs to make their products more recyclable. For example, Dell has begun using fewer screws in its computers to make them easier to recycle. Best Buy is supporting this movement toward lighter recyclable electronics, as demonstrated by product offerings like its organic LED (OLED) televisions that are lighter and easier to recycle.

Of course, with the benefits of recycling come some costs as well. For example, televisions are heavy to handle and are not as recyclable as other goods. Dealing with them costs companies like Best Buy time and money. However, CEO Brian Dunn feels that the connections developed between Best Buy and its community makes the company's effort worth the cost. Best Buy hopes that its status as a sustainable and ethical company will attract more loyal customers, aiding both its reputation and its bottom line.

CHALLENGES FOR BEST BUY

Although the closure of top competitor Circuit City bodes well for Best Buy, the company is facing new competition from retailers such as Amazon and Apple. Whereas Amazon's electronic and nonmedia revenue rose 66 percent in 2010, Best Buy's market share has begun to drop. Analysts believe the reason for this loss is due to pricing considerations. It has become more common for consumers to visit Best Buy stores, find items they want, and shop for those items on Amazon or other e-commerce sites at lower prices. This trend is causing Best Buy to consider investigating more aggressive pricing strategies as a way to compete.

Best Buy is also having trouble with its Chinese stores. The company's big-box retailers did not perform well in the Chinese market, causing Best Buy to abandon its nine branded stores in that country. Once again, price may have been a primary factor. Chinese consumers have indicated that although the environment of Best Buy was much nicer than comparable retailers, the prices were too high. However, Best Buy is not abandoning China entirely. While it is shutting down its branded stores, the company plans to expand its Chinese subsidiary Five Star by 40 to 50 stores. As China's economy continues to progress, Best Buy is confident these stores will continue to profit.

Another way in which Best Buy is rising to its challenges is by appealing to a younger market. In 2011 the big-box retailer partnered with teen sensation Justin Bieber to feature Bieber in advertisements and Facebook updates. With 20 million Bieber Facebook followers, Best Buy has the potential to reach a massive teenage audience using social media. Best Buy also ran an ad featuring Bieber and rock legend Ozzie Osbourne in its first-ever Super Bowl commercial. If successful, Best Buy's techniques to regain customers and expand its customer base might enable it to recapture market share.

CONCLUSION

Best Buy occupies an important link in the supply chain of electronic products that reach consumers. In many ways, Best Buy can influence producers and suppliers to become more sustainable by encouraging products that reduce waste and are more efficient to use. Its recent initiatives to help consumers recycle old electronic devices provide an incredible opportunity to deal with a significant sustainability problem. Its approach to social responsibility has been to identify key stakeholders and to incorporate important ethical and social concerns in its overall business strategy.

Best Buy's continuous efforts toward sustainability and ethical practices earned it a place among *Ethisphere*'s 2010 list of Most Ethical Companies for a second year in a row.

The Ethisphere Institute has described Best Buy as "operating under the highest standards for business behavior." While the company will have to overcome obstacles to retain its competitive edge, Best Buy is a shining example of how a company can use social responsibility and a strong stakeholder orientation to prosper in both reputational and financial areas. In order to retain this image, Best Buy must continue to maintain high ethical standards regarding its customers, employees, vendors, and the environment.

QUESTIONS

1. Why do you think Best Buy has been able to gain competitive advantage in the retail electronics market while also driving many initiatives to support sustainability?

2. Do you think the resources that Best Buy is dedicating to help consumers recycle their old electronic devices represent a good investment for Best Buy?

3. How do Best Buy's social responsibility efforts impact key stakeholders such as employees, shareholders, consumers, and suppliers?

REFERENCES

Best Buy. "About Best Buy." http://www.bby.com/about/ (accessed August 18, 2010); Best Buy. Annual Sustainability Report Fiscal 2010. http://www.bby.com/cmn/files/Best-Buy-2010-Sustainability-Report.pdf (accessed March 10, 2011); Best Buy. "Fiscal 2009 Climate and Energy Policy (CEP) Report, March 2010." http://www.bby.com/wp-content/uploads/2010/03/Climate-Change-Policy-BBY-3.18.10.pdf (accessed August 18, 2010); Best Buy. "2009 Corporate Social Responsibility (CSR) Report." http://www.bby.com/cmn/files/BBY_CSR_2009.pdf (accessed March 10, 2011); Bissonenette, Zac. "Best Buy Workers Make a Serious Commitment to Diversity." *BloggingStocks*, April 6, 2008, http://www.bloggingstocks.com/2008/04/06/best-buy-workers-makes-a-serious-commitment-to-diversity (accessed May 9, 2008); BBC News. "Carphone in £1.1bn US partnership." May 8, 2008. http://news.bbc.co.uk/2/hi/business/7389291.stm (accessed August 17, 2010); Best Buy. "e-cycle." http://www.bestbuy.com/recycling (accessed August 18, 2010); Best Buy. "From Coast to Coast, More People Recycle Their Electronics With Best Buy Than Any Other Retailer." April 14, 2011, http://www.bby.com/phoenix.zhtml?c=244152&p=irol-newsArticle&ID=1550976&highlight= (accessed July 8, 2011); Best Buy. "Energy Star." http://www.bestbuy.com/site/null/null/pcmcat149900050024.c?id=pcmcat149900050024 (accessed August 18, 2010); Best Buy. "Greener Together." http://www.bestbuy.com/site/null/Best+Buy/pcmcat149900050023.c?id=pcmcat149900050023&DCMP=rdr0001424 (accessed August 13, 2010); Best Buy. "Our Foundation." http://communications.bestbuy.com/communityrelations/our_foundation.asp (accessed August 13, 2010); Best Buy. "Trade-in." https://www.bestbuytradein.com/bb/ (accessed August 16, 2010); Best Buy Career Center. "Culture." http://69.12.100/CareerCenter/Culture.asp (accessed May 9, 2008); Best Buy Career Center. "Diversity." http://69.12.100/CareerCenter/Diversity.asp (accessed May 9, 2008); Best Buy Company News. "Ethisphere Names Best Buy to 2010 List of World's Most Ethical Companies." http://www.bby.com/2010/03/24/ethisphere-names-best-buy-to-2010-list-of-worlds-most-ethical-companies/, March 24, 2010 (accessed August 18, 2010); EPA. "Best Buy Ramps up Recycling." http://www.epa.gov/waste/inforesources/news/2009news/03-bestbuy.htm, March 31, 2010 (accessed August 18, 2010); EPA. "SmartWay Transport." http://www.epa.gov/smartway/transport/index.htm (accessed October 13, 2010); *Ethisphere*. "2010 World's Most Ethical Companies." Q1, 30–31; *Ethisphere*. "2010's 100 Most Influential People in Business Ethics." http://ethisphere.com/2010s-100-most-influential-people-in-business-ethics/#28, January 31, 2011 (accessed March 10, 2011); *Forbes*. "America's Most Reputable Companies." April 20, 2010, http://www.forbes.com/2010/04/19/kraft-microsoft-google-pepsi-disney-kellogg-cmo-network-america-least-reputable-companies_3.html (accessed March 10, 2011); Gunther, Marc. "Best Buy Wants Your Electronic Junk." *Fortune,* December 1, 2009; Hamilton, Anita. "Why Circuit City Busted While Best Buy Boomed." *Time,* November 11, 2008. http://www.time.com/time/business/article/0,8599,1858079,00.html (accessed August 12, 2010); Horovitz, Bruce. "Bieber teams with Best Buy for Bowl ad." *USA Today,* January 26, 2011, 1B; Inman, Phillip. "Best Buy to battle DSG International with launch of UK stores." guardian.co.uk, March 28, 2010, http://www.guardian.co.uk/business/2010/mar/28/best-buy-electronics-retailer-launch-uk-stores (accessed August 18, 2010); Jannarone, John. "Forecast for Best Buy: Worst Is Yet to Come." *The Wall Street Journal,* March 4, 2011, C8; Kilger, Patrick J. "Throwing Out the Rules of Work." Workforce Management, www.workforce.com/section/09/feature/24/54/28 (accessed April 28, 2010); Ludden, Jennifer. "The End of 9-to-5: When Work Time Is Anytime." *NPR,* March 16, 2010. www.npr.org/templates/story/story.php?storyId = 124705801 (accessed April 29, 2010); MacLeod, Calum. "Best Buy, Home Depot find China market a tough sell." *USA Today,* February 23, 2011, 5B; Malik, Naureen S. "Best Buy to Sell Ford's Electric Charging Stations." *The Wall Street Journal,* January 7, 2011, http://blogs.wsj.com/digits/2011/01/07/best-buy-to-sell-fords-electric-charging-stations/ (accessed March 10, 2011); Minnesota Council of Foundations. "Responses by Minnesota Foundations & Corporation to 2008 Disasters." http://www.mcf.org/disasters/international08.htm (accessed August 13, 2010); Morris, Scott. "Best Buy Joins BICEP Coalition Advocating for Strong Climate and Energy Policy in the United States." Best Buy Sustainability, February 4, 2010. http://www.bby.com/2010/02/24/best-buy-joins-bicep-coalition-advocating-for-strong-climate-and-energy-policy-in-the-united-states/ (accessed August 18, 2010); MSN Money. "Best BUY Company Inc—Company Financial Statements (BBY): Annual Income Statement." http://moneycentral.msn.com/investor/invsub/results/statemnt.aspx?symbol=BBY (accessed March 10, 2011); Norman, Jason. "Best Buy to Stock E-Bikes in Select Stores." *Bicycle Retailer,* April 29, 2009. http://www.bicycleretailer.com/news/newsDetail/2648.html (accessed February 26, 2010); *TwinCities Business.* "2003 Minnesota Business Hall of Fame." http://www.tcbmag.com/halloffame/minnesotabusinesshalloffame/104304p1.aspx, July 2003 (accessed August 12, 2010); Wolf @ Best Buy. "Haiti Earthquake Relief Efforts." http://www.wolfatbestbuy.com/news/haiti-earthquake-relief-efforts (accessed August 13, 2010); Thomson Financial. "Best Buy may make offers for International, Kesa—report." *Forbes,* May 11, 2008. http://www.forbes.com/feeds/afx/2008/05/11/afx4994500.html (accessed August 17, 2010); "Smashing the Clock." *Business Week,* December 11, 2006, http://www.businessweek.com/magazine/content/06_50/b4013001.htm (accessed May 1, 2010); Speakeasy. "Speakeasy Customer Service Standard Helps Drive Growth." February 11, 2009, http://www.speakeasy.net/press/pr/pro21109.php (accessed July 8, 2011).

SUSTAINABILITY: ETHICAL AND SOCIAL RESPONSIBILITY DIMENSIONS

INTRODUCTION

Business ethics comprises the principles, values, and standards that guide behavior in the world of business. Some ethical decisions have consequences for society. In the case of the natural environment, there are many decisions that not only have social responsibility implications, but also reflect the ethical culture of the organization. For many organizations, the collective participation of employees in making sustainable decisions can result in business success and at the same time contribute to finding positive solutions to questions about the use of natural resources and the well-being of society.

The purpose of this appendix is to outline key issues and risks in making business decisions that impact the natural environment. Identifying issues and risks provides opportunities for responsible individual and organizational responses to promote sustainability. We examine the concept of sustainability and the concerns of various stakeholders about our future. Next, we look at some of the major issues that relate to ethical and socially responsible conduct. The first topic we address is atmospheric issues including air pollution and global warming. Next, we look at water issues such as water pollution and water quality. Land pollution issues relate to waste management, deforestation, urban sprawl, and biodiversity. Related to land pollution and biodiversity is the issue of genetically modified organisms. We look at business response to sustainability issues, including positive actions such as green marketing and the ethical issues associated with greenwashing. Finally, we link sustainability to a stakeholder orientation that considers the ethical and financial performance of organizations. Firms that adopt a stakeholder orientation in their sustainability initiatives will need to conduct a stakeholder assessment and environmental audit to ensure they are meeting stakeholder needs while not overlooking financial performance.

Sustainability issues fit into our stakeholder model addressed in Chapter 2. Because most stakeholders have concerns about some aspects of the natural environment, organizations should respond to those issues in their strategies, policies, and operations. Businesses that show concern for the natural environment are achieving a citizenship level that is consistent with a positive ethical culture. A corporate culture strengthened by ethical values and positive business practices, such as a sustainability agenda, can create favorable employee work responses.[1] In addition, corporate social responsibility performance has been found to increase employees' company identification and commitment.[2]

DEFINING SUSTAINABILITY

Sustainability from a strategic business perspective is the potential for the long-term well-being of the natural environment, including all biological entities, as well as the mutually beneficial interactions among nature and individuals, organizations, and business strategies. Sustainability includes the assessment and improvement of business strategies, economic sectors, work practices, technologies, and lifestyles while maintaining the natural environment. In recent years, business has played a significant role in adapting, using, and maintaining the quality of sustainability.

The protection of air, water, land, biodiversity, and renewable natural resources emerged as a major issue in the twentieth century in the face of increasing evidence that mankind was putting pressure on the long-term sustainability of these resources. As the environmental movement sounded the alarm over these issues, governments around the globe responded with environmental protection laws during the 1970s. In recent years, companies have been increasingly incorporating these issues into their overall business strategies. By being proactive in addressing these issues, companies can reduce their environmental impact and generate a reputation as an eco-responsible company.

ATMOSPHERIC ISSUES

Air Pollution

As emerging economies become more industrialized, air pollution is becoming an increasingly serious issue. While not all air pollution comes from man-made sources, the pollution emitted by factories, power plants, cars, trucks, planes, and trains is having a detrimental effect on the quality of the air we breathe. Such conditions can cause markedly shorter life spans, along with chronic respiratory problems (e.g., asthma, bronchitis, and allergies) in humans and animals. Some of the chemicals associated with air pollution may contribute to birth defects, cancer, and brain, nerve, and respiratory system damage. Air pollution can harm plants, animals, and water bodies. It also causes haze, which can reduce visibility and interfere with traveling.

Global Warming

When carbon dioxide and other gases collect in Earth's atmosphere, they trap the sun's heat like a greenhouse and prevent Earth's surface from cooling. Without this process, the planet would become too cold to sustain life. However, during the twentieth century, the burning of fossil fuels—gasoline, natural gas, oil, and coal—accelerated dramatically, increasing the concentration of "greenhouse" gases like carbon dioxide and methane in Earth's atmosphere. Chlorofluorocarbons—from refrigerants, coolants, and aerosol cans—also harm Earth's ozone layer, which filters out the sun's harmful ultraviolet light. While the United States and China give off the most greenhouse gases, developing nations like India are going to make up an increasing percentage of overall emissions. Emerging economies are also more likely to use coal, which is the dirtiest of all fossil fuels in terms of emissions.

Most scientists believe that concentrations of greenhouse gases like methane and carbon dioxide in the atmosphere are accelerating a warming of the planet. Accumulations of greenhouse gases have increased dramatically in the past century, with some of the hottest years on record occurring within the last two decades. The accumulation of gases appears to have increased average temperatures by over 1°Fahrenheit over the last century. This is sufficient to increase the rate of polar ice sheet melting. For the first time in thousands of years, ships are able to cross through areas of the North Pole that were previously covered with ice. Climate change is also affecting weather. For instance, climate change has been blamed for making northern countries more prone to flooding and southern countries more drought-ridden. As the polar icecaps melt, scientists fear that rising sea levels will flood many coastal areas and even submerge low-lying island nations.

The Kyoto Protocol created in 1997 was an international treaty meant to curb global greenhouse gas emissions. With the Kyoto Protocol commitment period expiring in 2012, countries are debating about whether to extend the protocol or adopt new global environmental initiatives. Whereas many countries want to extend the protocol, Russia, Japan, and Canada announced they would not agree to extend emission cuts. These countries want to create a climate treaty that would include all of the world's top emitters of carbon dioxide, particularly the U.S. and China. Japan has also expressed doubts concerning certain provisions of the Kyoto Protocol intended to help developing countries cut their carbon emissions. As a result, Japan implemented its own carbon trading system with developing nations, investing in clean energy technology and low carbon initiatives within these countries in exchange for carbon credits.[3] The expiration of the first stage of the Kyoto Protocol will likely inspire a new global debate about the next steps to take in combating global warming.

Many U.S. businesses are responding to stakeholder pressure and are committing to self-regulatory standards with respect to global warming and related areas, even in the absence of federal mandates. For instance, several utility companies are in the process of embedding climate change strategies into their operations. Many aspects of the process would be similar in other industries.

WATER ISSUES

Water Pollution

Water pollution is one of the biggest contributors to illnesses in developing countries, with over a billion people lacking access to clean water. Chemicals found in commonly used fertilizers and pesticides can drain into water supplies with each rainfall. Mercury, a common chemical found in batteries and some household products is another concern as it contaminates oceans and therefore human food supplies. Even in the United States, which has one of the safest drinking water supplies in the world, pollution remains a problem. Pollutants can come from a wide variety of sources in today's industrialized world, and many of them have unknown side effects on

people and wildlife. Pharmaceutical products have been found in water sources in North America, Europe, Asia, and Australia. Fish and frogs are highly susceptible to living in and near water tainted with drugs. Agricultural operations, including animal-feeding, pesticide use, and plowing, are also a major source of pollution in the nation's lakes and rivers.

The 2010 BP oil spill in the Gulf of Mexico brought water pollution issues to the forefront. Known as the worst oil spill in U.S. waters to date, the disaster prompted the Obama administration to impose a six-month moratorium on deep-sea drilling. In addition to killing many marine animals, oil from the leak settled onto the sea floor of the Gulf. It could take years before we can understand the full extent of this environmental catastrophe. Another problem affecting ocean waters involves carbon emissions. A large amount of the carbon in the atmosphere is absorbed into the ocean, which is a naturally occurring process. However, the increasing release of carbon emissions from manmade sources has boosted the amount of carbon absorbed into the ocean. Too much carbon buildup could heat up the ocean's temperatures, causing the potential flooding of coastal cities.[4]

The Environmental Protection Agency has also expressed concerns over certain exemptions in federal environmental laws that apply to natural gas drillers. Natural gas drilling is exempt from parts of seven out of 15 laws regulating air and water pollution. According to the E.P.A., these exemptions are allowing drilling waste to be released into the water supply. Although there have been calls to halt such drilling until proper controls are in place, some believe that a serious conflict of interest exists among government officials as many are heavily supported by the oil and gas industry.[5]

While environmental groups in the United States criticize U.S. water policy, special interests make it even more difficult to regulate water pollution in other parts of the world. Tougher regulations are needed globally to address pollution from activities such as the dumping of waste into the ocean, large animal-feeding operations, logging sites, public roads, parking lots, oil spills, and industrial waste created by production operations.

Water Quantity

In addition to concerns about the quality of water, some parts of the globe are increasingly worried about its quantity. Water use has increased dramatically in the last two decades, creating serious consequences for the global water supply. Not only is water needed for drinking, but reduced water availability will lead to lower food crops and will affect businesses as well. It is estimated that by 2030, almost half of the world's population will live in areas with major water stress. After several of the hottest years on record and below average precipitation across most of the nation, water fears have hit home. To combat this impending water crisis, both companies and individuals must take steps to reduce their impact. Even small actions, such as switching to low-flow toilets and watering yards only during certain periods of the day, can help to mitigate the problem.

LAND ISSUES

Waste Management

One of the biggest factors in land pollution is the dumping of waste into landfills. American consumers are by far the world's biggest wasters. The nation has up to 40,000 abandoned landfills, which are often left untreated and are filled with plastics and other materials that can take 1,000 years to degrade. Electronic waste is becoming a big problem as it can release harmful toxins into the air and water. Increasingly, electronics firms are being pressured to take back used electronics for recycling. Large chains such as Best Buy now offer e-recycling to keep this waste out of landfills. Other organizations like Terracycle have organized a business around turning trash into sellable products. Many stakeholders believe that companies that produce the goods should be responsible for their proper disposal and recycling. Companies, on the other hand, argue that this practice would be too expensive and argue for greater responsibility on the part of individuals. Perhaps a more suitable solution would be to balance environmental responsibility between companies, governments, and individuals.

Deforestation

Rain forests are being destroyed at a rate of nearly 50,000 square miles. The reasons for this wide-scale destruction are varied. Because of the boom in biofuels, Southeast Asia and the Pacific regions have been cutting down trees to make room for palm oil plantations. Brazil has long cut down the Amazon for farming or for raising sugarcane. On a more optimistic note, in 2010 deforestation of the Brazilian rainforest hit its lowest rate in 22 years. The Brazilian government credits improved oversight and police monitoring for the reduction in deforestation and hopes to reach its goal of decreasing deforestation to 5,000 square kilometers (1930.5 miles) per year by 2017. However, even at its lowest peak, the amount of deforestation in Brazil in a one year period was greater than half the size of Jamaica.[6]

A competitive global economy drives the need for money in economically challenged tropical countries. In the short term, logging and converting forestlands to other uses seems the profitable thing to do. However, the profits from deforestation for farmers are usually short-lived as rainforest soil is of poor quality. This prompts low-income farmers to destroy more forest to eke out a living. Unless this cycle of poverty is stopped, the destruction of forests is likely to continue.

Companies are now adopting designations like that granted by the Forest Stewardship Council, a nonprofit organization comprised of loggers, environmentalists, and sociologists. The FSC seeks to coordinate forest management around the world and to develop a uniform set of standards. Being FSC-certified can help companies indicate to consumers and stakeholders that they are committed to preserving forest resources, that they are a socially responsible, and that they take a long-term view of environmental management. Table A.1 lists some facts about the harmful effects of global deforestation.

Urban Sprawl

Urban sprawl began in the United States with the post–World War II building boom. This boom transformed the nation from primarily low-density communities designed to accommodate one-

TABLE A.1 Facts about Global Deforestation

- Almost 20 percent of all global CO_2 emissions are caused by deforestation.

- People who are cutting down trees (i.e., illegal loggers in Borneo, soy growers in Brazil, subsistence farmers in Laos) together send as much carbon into the atmosphere as do all the activities of the entire U.S. (factories, vehicles, buildings, farming, power plants, etc.).

- Every four hours the world loses tropical forest equivalent in size to the island of Manhattan.

- By conserving just *one* acre of threatened tropical forest, the yearly emissions of 40 cars, trucks, and SUVs can be offset.

- Burning and clearing forest costs the global economy 2 trillion dollars per year, as valued through lost fresh water, food, timber, and carbon reduction.

NOTE: Adapted from Alan Grey, "Tropical Deforestation and Global Warming Linkage," News Blaze, June 25, 2009, http://newsblaze.com/story/20090625101021zzzz.nb/topstory.html, (accessed August 26, 2011)

car households, bicyclists, and pedestrians to large-scale suburban developments at the edges of established towns and cities. Downtowns and inner cities deteriorated as shopping malls, office parks, corporate campuses, and residential developments sprang up on what was once forest, prairie, or farmland. As the places where people live, work, and shop grew further apart, people began spending more time in automobiles driving greater distances. Urban sprawl has not only consumed wildlife habitat, wetlands, and farmland, but it has also contributed to land, water, and especially air pollution. Lack of urban planning means that these places grow without reason. In an age of erratic gas prices, traffic congestion, and obesity, it has become increasingly expensive in terms of dollars and health to live in sprawling cities.

Some urban areas are fighting to limit sprawl. Portland, Oregon, for example, has established an Urban Growth Boundary to restrict growth and preserve open space and rural land around the city. Adding to the appeal of returning to cities is a movement to increase urban parks. Rather than allowing loggers to profit off of forests, more and more cities are buying forested land to convert to park space. Stemming sprawl preserves natural spaces outside of the city. People are also beginning to realize that living near where they work is more convenient, cheaper, and better for their health. Although limiting urban sprawl may create disadvantages for car and oil companies, many businesses can benefit from urban renewal movements that reduce sprawl.

Biodiversity

Deforestation, pollution, development, and urban sprawl have put increasing pressure on wildlife, plants, and their habitats. Many plants and animals have become extinct, and thousands more are threatened. The Yangtze River Dolphin is one of the more recent extinctions, and thousands of more animals, including the Florida panther, the tiger, and most lemurs, are facing the same fate.

Experts fear that overutilization of natural resources will cause catastrophic imbalances in the environment. Because each biological species plays a unique role in its ecosystem and is part of a complex chain of events, the loss of any one of them may threaten the entire ecosystem. Pollinators, for example, play a significant role in that they help fruits and vegetables to grow by spreading pollen from plant to plant. Increasing development and widespread use of pesticides have reduced the populations of bees, insects, and bats that help plants reproduce. Without these species, the world's food supply would be seriously jeopardized. People and businesses must use resources more carefully in order to maintain a livable world for many generations to come.

Genetically Modified Organisms

Depending on whom you ask, genetically modified foods are either going to save impoverished areas from starvation and revolutionize agriculture, or they will destroy biodiversity and make us all sick. Genetically modified (GM) organisms are created through manipulating plant and animal genes so as to produce a desired effect like resistance to pests and viruses, drought resistance, or high crop yield. This process generally involves transferring genes from one organism to another in a way that would never occur naturally to create a new life form that has unique traits. Companies like Monsanto and DuPont develop genetically modified corn, soybeans, potatoes, canola oil seeds, and cotton plants that they claim are more pest and insecticide resistant and have higher yields. Many people fear that these unnatural genes will have negative effects on nature, somewhat like how invader species of plants and animals can wipe out native ones, or that GM produce may have negative effects on humans. Even so, a lot of interest in GM products remains. In countries where malnutrition is a problem, the idea of higher yields is very appealing, even if the seed itself is more expensive. Over 280 million acres worldwide are devoted to genetically modified crops. Their use has doubled corn crop yields in some parts of the world.

The long-term impact of this genetic tinkering is not known, although the Food and Drug Administration has deemed GM food safe to consume. Today, as much as 75 percent of all processed food contains GM ingredients—and the United States does not require these products to be labeled as such. This has caused many consumers to turn toward organic foods, creating a market opportunity for organic and all-natural grocery chains like Whole Foods. Other parts of the world boycott products made from GM crops. For instance, it is illegal to grow GM crops in Thailand, and only one type of GM corn is allowed to be grown in the European Union.

As with GM plants, the problem with the genetic engineering of animals or animal products is that the long-run effects are unknown. Large numbers of genetically altered animals could upset the balance in relationships among various species with undetermined effects, such as the ability to reproduce or fight diseases and pests. Additionally, if genetically modified plant seeds are carried by wind or pollinators to areas with native plants, it is possible that genetic contamination could take place among native plants, thus reducing biological diversity. Further research is needed to address public concerns about the safety and long-term environmental effects of these technologies.

ALTERNATIVE ENERGY SOURCES

In Chapter 3 of this book, we discussed some alternative sources of energy that could supplement or take the place of fossil fuels. This appendix will provide further detail regarding these alternative energy sources.

Wind Power

Wind power holds great promise for the United States, particularly as it is home to one of the world's greatest wind corridors: the Great Plains. However, restructuring the nation's power grids to efficiently transmit wind will take much investment. Widespread adoption of wind power has been slowed by the high cost of the turbines as well as limitations on an outdated national power grid. Despite these roadblocks, many people believe that the United States will be a wind power hot spot in the future. The United States is one of the largest producers of wind power in the world. Wind power also offers opportunities for businesses, even those for whom alternative energy might otherwise be perceived as a threat. BP, for example, has invested in several wind farms in North America and in other parts of the globe.

Geothermal Power

Geothermal power has significant advantages and disadvantages, which may either advance or limit its adoption. On the one hand, geothermal energy provides a constant source of heat. It is subsequently a more dependable energy source than some of the other forms of alternative energy. Geothermal plants also emits fewer carbon emissions than do coal power plants. On the other hand, geothermal energy is expensive, and geothermal drilling sites are not readily available everywhere. However, in spite of these initial costs, those who utilize geothermal energy have reported a savings in overall energy costs. Due to its reliability, geothermal power could be a good substitute for natural gas in powering buildings and homes.

Solar Power

Solar power is 100 percent renewable energy that can be converted into electricity through the use of either photovoltaic cells (solar cells) on homes and other structures or solar power plants. The major disadvantages of solar power are that the technology remains expensive and inefficient compared to traditional fossil fuel-generated energy, and that the infrastructure for mass production of solar panels is not in place in many locations. However, cloudy days are not necessarily a problem as the UV rays needed to generate power filter through clouds.

Given the strong sunshine in places like the U.S. Southwest and California, solar power has gained a lot of support in the United States. The administration is attempting to lead by example through the installation of solar panels around the White House. For instance, President Obama announced plans to install solar panels on top of the White House along with a solar water heater in 2011. Solar power was also implemented during the Bush administration to heat the pool and power a maintenance building on the grounds.[7] These actions at the top levels of government might spur more businesses and individuals to invest in alternative energy like solar power.

Nuclear Power

Countries throughout Europe have managed to greatly reduce their emissions through the implementation of nuclear power plants, yet this form of power remains controversial. Because of the danger associated with nuclear meltdowns and radioactive waste disposal, nuclear power has earned a bad reputation in the United States. On the one hand, nuclear power is pollution-free and cost-competitive. Uranium is abundant enough that generating even 60 times more energy than what is produced today would not be a problem. On the other hand, critics are concerned with the safety of nuclear power plants and the disposal of waste. As the production of nuclear power gives off radiation, the safety of workers and the transport of nuclear waste is a prime concern. The Chernobyl nuclear disaster in the Ukraine, which resulted in deaths, sicknesses, and birth defects, has made this a viable concern. Yet with careful oversight, nuclear energy could change the world's dependence on oil. The nuclear plant crisis that occurred in Japan after several of the country's nuclear reactors were "damaged in the 2011 earthquake and tsunami further decreased support for nuclear energy.

Biofuels

Perhaps the most controversial form of alternative energy after nuclear power is ethanol. Critics argue that ethanol takes lots of energy and thus is not much more sustainable than oil. Carmakers have said that the models they currently manufacture are not calibrated to handle greater amounts of ethanol. Finally, because ethanol in the United States is made from corn, opponents believe that ethanol is decreasing the world's food supply and increasing food prices. This has prompted some companies to begin looking at alternatives to corn ethanol.

However, ethanol has taken off in countries like Brazil, leading to legal mandates to incorporate biofuels as a substitute for fossil fuels. In 1976, for example, the Brazilian government made it a requirement to blend gasoline with ethanol. As a result, Brazil currently is the largest exporter of bioethanol. Biofuel production in other countries like the Philippines has been criticized because it has contributed to rapid deforestation of ecologically sensitive areas—companies in a rush to create profits from the popularity of biofuels have installed plantations on former jungle land, for example.

To solve these problems and take advantage of the benefits of ethanol, scientists are researching alternative sources for this fuel. Algae and nonedible plants such as grasses are currently being explored. Since grass and algae are not food sources and do not require the destruction of trees, ethanol proponents are excited to see whether these alternatives will become adopted.

Hydropower

Throughout history, people have used water as a power source and a means of transportation. From the water-powered mills of centuries past to modern hydroelectric dams, water is a powerful renewable energy source. Although in the United States, hydroelectric power only provides 7 percent of total output, hydroelectric provides 19 percent of total electricity production worldwide, making it the largest form of renewable energy.

As with all other forms of energy production, hydropower has benefits and downsides. One of the major downsides is the destruction of wildlife habitats, and sometimes even human habitations, when valleys are flooded using dams. Hydroelectricity also disrupts the lifecycles of aquatic life. However, hydroelectric power decreases greenhouse gas emissions and air pollution. To be a suitable eco-friendly alternative to fossil fuels, hydroelectric facilities should be built to minimize negative environmental impacts.

BUSINESS RESPONSE TO SUSTAINABILITY ISSUES

Partly in response to federal legislation and partly due to stakeholder concerns, businesses are applying creativity, technology, and business resources to respond to environmental issues. Many businesses have adopted a triple-bottom line approach. With this strategy, businesses take into consideration social and environmental performance in addition to economic performance. Many firms are learning that being environmentally friendly and sustainable has numerous benefits—including increased goodwill from stakeholders and even money savings from being more efficient and less wasteful. Several companies even have a vice president of environmental affairs, including Staples, Disney, and Hyatt Hotels & Resorts. This position is designed to help companies achieve their business goals in an environmentally responsible manner. Businesses like Walmart and IBM have also developed environmental scorecards for their suppliers.[8] Corporate efforts to respond to environmental issues focus on green marketing, recycling, emissions reductions, and socially responsible buying.

Yet despite the importance of the environment, companies are in business to make a profit. Economic performance is still a necessary bottom line for most businesses. Studies suggest that improving a company's environmental performance can in fact increase revenues and reduce costs. Figure A.1 suggests mechanisms through which this can occur.

As shown in the figure, better environmental performance can increase revenue in three ways: through better access to certain markets, differentiation of products, and the sale of pollution-control technology. A firm's innovation in sustainability can be based on applying existing knowledge and technology or creating a completely new approach. Improving a firm's reputation for environmental stewardship may help companies capture a growing market niche. Since even large companies like Walmart are requiring their suppliers to be more environmentally friendly, improving a supply chain's environmental performance may be key to attracting more business from the retail industry. Going green may also help firms to differentiate their products from competitors. Whole Foods, a natural foods retailer, has made being environmentally friendly part of its image from the start. Finally, going green has opened up a whole new industry referred to as the eco-industry, where some firms have actually discovered pollution-control technology and are now able to sell this technology to other firms.

Better environmental performance can also reduce costs by improving risk management and stakeholder relationships, reducing the amount of materials and energy used, and reducing capital and labor costs. Improved environmental standards should help prevent some major environmental disasters in the future. For those disasters that cannot be avoided, the firm can at least show that it applied due diligence with its environmental performance, which may reduce the company's culpability in the public's eye. Companies can also decrease the costs of compliance with governmental regulations and reduce fines if they become more energy efficient.

Today's greener firms may also find that they have better access to capital. Banks often have environmental experts evaluate the environmental

FIGURE A.1 Positive Links Between Environmental and Economic Performance

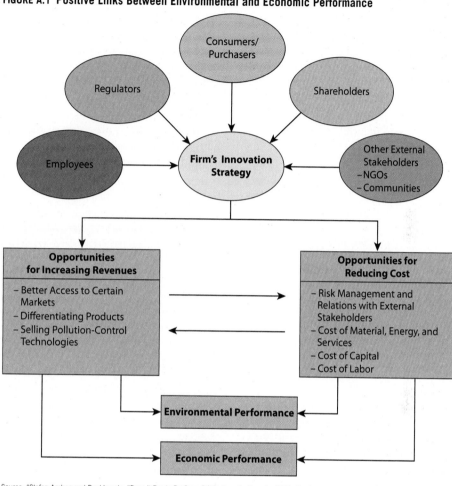

Source: "Stefan Ambec and Paul Lanoie, "Does It Pay to Be Green? A Systematic Overview," *The Academy of Management Perspectives*, **22**(4), November 2008, p. 47

performance of potential borrowers to determine whether to grant bank loans. They have begun to recognize poor environmental management as an increased liability. Finally, labor surveys have shown that even workers care about the environmental impact of the firms for which they work. Clearly, company environmental performance is ceasing to be simply an environmental matter and also influences the bottom line.

Green Marketing

Green marketing is a strategic process involving stakeholder assessment to create meaningful long-term relationships with customers, while maintaining, supporting, and enhancing the natural environment. One company that is known for its commitment to being green is New Belgium Brewery in Fort Collins, Colorado. From its conception, New Belgium has been a company committed to sustainability. Much of its energy comes from wind power, its facilities use natural lighting, and it provides its employees with bikes so they can travel to work and reduce fossil fuel usage. Even some real estate developers are attempting to integrate environmental concerns into new communities to protect the land. Buildings produce around 40 percent of all greenhouse gas emissions in the world, and developers are realizing that a way to gain a competitive edge is through being green. As environmental mandates on emissions and waste become stricter, it will become an important way for real estate developers to cut costs and increase compliance by utilizing green technology and materials as much as possible.

Many products are certified as "green" by environmental organizations such as Green Seal and carry a special logo identifying them as such. In Europe, companies can voluntarily apply for an Eco-label to indicate that their product is less harmful to the environment than competing products, based on scientifically determined criteria. The European Union supports the Eco-label program, which has been utilized in product categories as diverse as refrigerators, mattresses, vacuum cleaners, footwear, and televisions.[9]

Greenwashing

However, as green products become more popular, greenwashing is increasingly becoming an ethical issue. **Greenwashing** involves misleading a consumer into thinking that a product or service is more environmentally friendly than it really is. It can range from making environmental claims that are required by law and are therefore irrelevant (CFC-free) to puffery, or exaggerating environmental claims, to fraud. Researchers compared claims on products sold in ten countries, including the United States, to labeling guidelines established by the International Organization for Standardization (ISO), which prohibit vague and misleading claims as well as unverifiable ones such as "environmentally friendly" and "nonpolluting." The study found that many products' claims are too vague or misleading to meet ISO standards.[10] For example, some products will be labeled as "chemical-free," when in fact everything contains chemicals, including plants and animals. Among the products with the highest number of misleading or unverifiable claims were laundry detergents, household cleaners, and paints. Environmental advocates agree that there is still a long way to go to ensure that shoppers are adequately informed about the environmental impact of the products they buy.[11]

Although environmentalists and businesses are often at odds, there is growing agreement between them that companies should work to protect and preserve sustainability by implementing a number of goals. First, companies should strive to eliminate waste. Because pollution and waste usually stem from inefficiency, the issue should not be what to do with waste, but rather how to make things more efficiently so that no waste is produced. Second, companies should rethink the concept of a product. Products can be classified as consumables, which are eaten or biodegradable; durable goods, such as cars, televisions, computers, and refrigerators; and unsalables, including

---

DEBATE ISSUE   TAKE A STAND

Issue: Is it acceptable for companies to exaggerate environmental claims in order to sell products?

Being perceived as "green" can help firms create a competitive advantage. However, greenwashing has become a problem as more companies seek to profit from this claim. Although the Federal Trade Commission can prosecute and fine firms that ignore "green guides," most greenwashers do not face legal repercussions.

The current administration has taken a tougher stand on environmental issues, and as greenwashing becomes more prevalent, legal action will likely increase. Some organizations have begun developing a certification system to help consumers make informed decisions when buying green products. For example, the Carbon Trust offers a certification that validates claims about reducing carbon output. However, certification organizations are not always trustworthy. Some of them will certify products simply in exchange for a fee. The best way for consumers to be informed about eco-friendly products is to conduct research before shopping.

1. Companies should be held to rigorous standards before being able to advertise their products as "green."

2. Imposing strict green standards on businesses is too burdensome, particularly as the term "green" does not have a clear definition.

such undesirable byproducts as radioactive materials, heavy metals, and toxins. The design of durable goods should utilize a closed loop system of manufacture and use, and a return to the manufacturing process that allows products and resources to be disassembled and recycled while minimizing the disposal of unsalables. Third, the price of products should reflect their true costs, including the costs of replenishing natural resources that are utilized or damaged during the production process. Finally, businesses should seek ways to make their commitment to the environment profitable.[12]

STRATEGIC IMPLEMENTATION OF ENVIRONMENTAL RESPONSIBILITY

Businesses have responded to the opportunities and threats created by environmental issues with varying levels of commitment. Some companies, like New Belgium Brewing, consider sustainability a core component of the business. Other companies engage in greenwashing and do not actively seek to be more sustainable. As Figure A.2 indicates, a low-commitment business attempts to avoid dealing with environmental issues and hopes that nothing bad will happen or that no one will ever find out about an environmental accident or abuse. Such firms may try to protect themselves against lawsuits. After the *Deepwater Horizon* oil leak in the Gulf of Mexico, BP faced a number of lawsuits, including one filed by the U.S. Justice Department, due to the subsequent environmental damage. Other firms are more proactive in anticipating risks and environmental issues. Such firms develop strategic management programs, which view the environment as an opportunity for advancing organizational interests. These companies respond to stakeholder interests, assess risks, and develop a comprehensive environmental strategy. Home Depot, for example, has established a set of environmental principles that include selling responsibly marketed products, eliminating unnecessary packaging, recycling and encouraging the use of products with recycled content, and conserving natural resources by using them wisely.

Stakeholder Assessment

Stakeholder assessment is an important part of a high-commitment approach to environmental issues. This process requires acknowledging and actively monitoring the environmental concerns of all legitimate stakeholders. Thus, a company must have a process in place for identifying and prioritizing the many claims and stakes on its business and

FIGURE A.2 Strategic Approaches to Environmental Issues

Low Commitment	Medium Commitment	High Commitment
Deals only with existing problems	Attempts to comply with environmental laws	Has strategic programs to address environmental issues
Makes only limited plans for anticipated problems	Deals with issues that could cause public relations problems	Views environment as an opportunity to advance the business strategy
Fails to consider stakeholder environmental issues	Views environmental issues from a tactical, not a strategic, perspective	Consults with stakeholders about their environmental concerns
Operates without concern for long-term environmental impact	Views environment as more of a threat than an opportunity	Conducts an environmental audit to assess performance and adopts international standards

©Cengage Learning 2013

for dealing with trade-offs related to the impact on different stakeholders. Although no company can satisfy every claim, all risk-related claims should be evaluated before a firm decides to take action on or ignore a particular issue. To make accurate assumptions about stakeholder interests, managers need to conduct research, assess risks, and communicate with stakeholders about their respective concerns.

However, not all stakeholders are equal. There are specific regulations and legal requirements that govern some aspects of stakeholder relationships, such as air and water quality. A business cannot knowingly harm the water quality of other stakeholders in order to generate a profit. Additionally, some special-interest groups take extreme positions that, if adopted, would undermine the economic base of many other stakeholders (e.g., fishing rights, logging, and hunting). Regardless of the final decision a company makes with regard to particular environmental issues, information should be communicated consistently across all stakeholders. This is especially important when a company faces a crisis or negative publicity about a decision. Another aspect of strong relationships with stakeholders is the willingness to acknowledge and openly address potential conflicts. Some degree of negotiation and conciliation will be necessary to align a company's decisions and strategies with stakeholder interests.

Risk Analysis

The next step in a high-commitment response to environmental concerns is assessing risk. Through industry and government research, an organization can usually identify environmental issues that relate to manufacturing, marketing, and consumption and use patterns associated with its products. Through risk analysis, it is possible to assess the environmental risks associated with business decisions. The real difficulty is measuring the costs and benefits of environmental decisions, especially in the eyes of interested stakeholders. Research studies often conflict, which only adds to the confusion and controversy over sustainability.

Debate surrounding environmental issues will force corporate decision makers to weigh the evidence and take some risks in final decisions. The important point for high-commitment organizations is to continue to evaluate the latest information and to maintain communication with all stakeholders. For example, if all of the millions of sport utility vehicles (SUVs) on U.S. roads today were replaced with fuel-efficient electric-powered cars and trucks, there would be a tremendous reduction of greenhouse gas emissions. However, the cooperation and commitment needed to gain the support of government, manufacturers, consumers, and other stakeholders to accomplish this would be almost impossible to achieve. Although SUVs may harm the environment, many of their owners have prioritized other concerns, such as protection in case of an accident.

This issue illustrates that many environmental decisions involve trade-offs for various stakeholders' risks. Through risk management, it is possible to quantify these trade-offs in determining whether to accept or reject environmentally related activities and programs. Usually, the key decision is between the amount of investment required to reduce the risk of damage and the amount of risk acceptable in stakeholder relationships. A company should assess these relationships on an ongoing basis. Both formal and informal methods are needed to get feedback from stakeholders. For example, the employees of a firm can use formal methods such as exit interviews, an open-door policy, and toll-free telephone hot lines. Conversations between employees could provide informal feedback. But it is ultimately the responsibility of the organization's management to make the best decision possible after processing all available research and information. Then, if it is later discovered that a mistake has been made, change is still possible through open disclosure and thoughtful reasoning. Finally, a high-commitment organization will incorporate new information and insights into the strategic planning process.

The Strategic Environmental Audit

Organizations that are highly committed to environmental responsibility may conduct an audit of their efforts and report the results to all interested

TABLE A.2 Strategic Sustainability Audit

Yes	No	Checklist
O	O	Does the organization show a high commitment to a strategic environmental policy?
O	O	Do employees know the environmental compliance policies of the organization?
O	O	Do suppliers and customers recognize the organization's stand on environmental issues?
O	O	Are managers familiar with the environmental strategies of other organizations in the industry?
O	O	Has the organization compared its environmental initiatives with those of other firms?
O	O	Is the company aware of the best practices in environmental management regardless of industry?
O	O	Has the organization developed measurable performance standards for environmental compliance?
O	O	Does the firm reconcile the need for consistent responsible values with the needs of various stakeholders?
O	O	Do the organization's philanthropic efforts consider environmental issues?
O	O	Does the organization comply with all laws and regulations that relate to environmental impact?

©Cengage Learning 2013

stakeholders. Table A.2 provides a starting point for examining environmental sensitivity. Such organizations may also wish to use globally accepted standards, such as ISO 14000, as benchmarks in a strategic environmental audit. The International Organization for Standardization developed ISO 14000 as a comprehensive set of environmental standards that encourage a cleaner, safer, and healthier world. There is currently considerable variation among the environmental laws and regulations of nations and regions, making it difficult for high-commitment organizations to find acceptable solutions on a global scale. The goal of the ISO 14000 standard is to promote a common approach to environmental management and to help companies attain and measure improvements in environmental performance. Companies that choose to abide by the ISO standards must review their environmental management systems periodically and identify all aspects of their operations that could impact the environment.[13] Other performance benchmarks available for use in environmental audits come from nonprofit organizations such as CERES, which has also developed standards for reporting information about environmental performance to interested stakeholders.

As this appendix has demonstrated, social responsibility entails responding to stakeholder concerns about the environment, and many firms are finding creative ways to address environmental challenges. Although many of the companies mentioned in this chapter have chosen to implement strategic environmental initiatives to capitalize on opportunities and achieve greater efficiency and cost savings, most also believe that responding to stakeholders' concerns about environmental issues will both improve relationships with stakeholders and make the world a better place.

NOTES

Chapter 1

1. "The Ethics of American Youth: 2010," Josephson Institute Center for Youth Ethics, February 10, 2011, http://charactercounts.org/programs/reportcard/2010/installment02_report-card_honesty-integrity.html (accessed February 15, 2011).

2. Jodi Upton, Denise Amos, and Anne Ryman, "For teachers, many ways and reasons to cheat on tests," *USA Today,* March 10, 2011, 1A.

3. Paul W. Taylor, *Principles of Ethics: An Introduction to Ethics,* 2nd ed. (Encino, CA: Dickenson, 1975), 1.

4. Adapted and reproduced from *The American Heritage Dictionary of the English Language,* 4th ed. Copyright © 2002 by Houghton Mifflin Company.

5. Wroe Alderson, *Dynamic Marketing Behavior* (Homewood, IL: Irwin, 1965), 320.

6. Amir Efrati, "Google Says Bing Cheated," *The Wall Street Journal,* February 2, 2011, http://online.wsj.com/article/SB10001424052748704124504576118510340787364.html (accessed February 15, 2011); Nick Wingfield, "Microsoft 'Insulted' by Google's Copying Claims," *The Wall Street Journal,* February 3, 2011, B3.

7. Ethics Resource Center, *2009 National Business Ethics Survey,* p. 9.

8. Associated Press, "Investors allege massive fraud by Countrywide," *The Wall Street Journal,* January 25, 2011, http://online.wsj.com/article/AP0cb3b6db114a4a93b2ff62d19a9bd363.html (accessed February 15, 2011).

9. *2011 Edelman Trust Barometer,* January 26, 2011, http://www.edelman.com/trust/2011/ (accessed March 15, 2011).

10. James Herron, "BP Rapped over North Sea Rig Safety," February 2, 2011, http://online.wsj.com/public/page/news-economy.html (accessed February 15, 2011).

11. Mike Esterl, "Walmart Retreats from Civil War Site," *The Wall Street Journal,* January 27, 2011, http://online.wsj.com/article/SB10001424052748703293204576105981421547732.html (accessed February 15, 2011).

12. Catalina Camia, "DeLay gets 3-year sentence for corruption," *USA Today,* January 11, 2011, 2A.

13. The Associated Press, "Justice investigation shows FBI agents cheated on test," *USA Today,* September 28, 2010, 10A; James Vicini, "FBI employees reportedly cheated on security test," Reuters, September 27, 2010, http://www.reuters.com/article/2010/09/27/us-usa-security-fbi-idUSTRE68Q32O20100927 (accessed February 15, 2010).

14. Adam Schefter and the Associated Press, "Vick eligible to play after third week," September 4, 2009, ESPN NFL, http://sports.espn.go.com/nfl/news/story?id=4442627 (accessed February 15, 2011); Pat Yasinskas and the Associated Press, "Unable to make trade, Falcons cut Vick," June 12, 2009, ESPN NFL, http://sports.espn.go.com/nfl/news/story?id=4253231 (accessed February 15, 2010).

15. Mariko Sanchanta, "Match-Fixing Claims Hit Sumo Wrestlers," *The Wall Street Journal,* February 3, 2011, A8.

16. Sandra Block, "Jackson Hewitt sues over Block ads," *USA Today,* February 1, 2011, 5B.

17. Archie B. Carroll and Ann K. Buchholtz, *Business and Society: Ethics and Stakeholder Management* (Cincinnati: South-Western, 2006), 452–455.

18. Alan R. Yuspeh, "Development of Corporate Compliance Programs: Lessons Learned from the DII Experience," in *Corporate Crime in America: Strengthening the "Good Citizenship" Corporation* (Washington, DC: U.S. Sentencing Commission, 1995), 71–79.

19. Eleanor Hill, "Coordinating Enforcement under the Department of Defense Voluntary Disclosure Program," in *Corporate Crime in America: Strengthening the "Good Citizenship" Corporation* (Washington, DC: U.S. Sentencing Commission, 1995), 287–294.

20. "Huffing and Puffing in Washington: Can Clinton's Plan Curb Teen Smoking?" *Consumer Reports* 60 (1995): 637.

21. Arthur Levitt with Paula Dwyer, *Take on the Street* (New York: Pantheon Books, 2002).

22. Hill, "Coordinating Enforcement."

23. Richard P. Conaboy, "Corporate Crime in America: Strengthening the Good Citizen Corporation," in *Corporate Crime in America: Strengthening the "Good Citizenship" Corporation* (Washington, DC: U.S. Sentencing Commission, 1995), 1–2.

24. *United States Code Service* (Lawyers' Edition), 18 U.S.C.S. Appendix, Sentencing Guidelines for the United States Courts (Rochester, NY: Lawyers Cooperative Publishing, 1995), sec. 8A.1.

25. "Fraud Inc.," CNN/Money, http://money.cnn.com/news/specials/corruption/ (accessed February 5, 2002); "SEC Formalizes Investigation into Halliburton Accounting," *The Wall Street Journal* online, December 20, 2002, http://online.wsj.com; "WorldCom CEO Slaps Arthur Andersen," CNN, July 8, 2002, www.cnn.com.

26. "Corporate Reform Bill Passed," CNN, July 25, 2002, www.cnn.com.

27. Muel Kaptein, "From Inaction to External Whistleblowing: The Influence of the Ethical Culture of Organizations on Employee Responses to Observed Wrongdoing," *Journal of Business Ethics,* (2011) 98: 513–530.

28. "Global Sullivan Principles of Social Responsibility," Leon H. Sullivan Foundation, http://www.thesullivanfoundation.org/about/global_sullivan_principles (accessed November 22, 2010).

29. "About Us," CERES Principles, http://www.ceres.org/Page.aspx?pid=416 (accessed November 22, 2010).

30. United Nations, "Global Compact: Corporate Citizenship in the World Economy," http://www.unglobalcompact.org/docs/news_events/8.1/GC_brochure_FINAL.pdf (accessed February 15, 2011).

31. "The 2010 World's Most Ethical Companies—Company Profile: Granite Construction," *Ethisphere*, Q1, 33; "Granite Construction Named to *Ethisphere*'s 2011 "World's Most Ethical Companies" for 2nd Year in a Row," Granite, http://www.graniteconstruction.com/investor-relations/release_detail.cfm?printpage=1&ReleaseID=558348 (accessed April 27, 2011).

32. Bernard J. Jaworski and Ajay K. Kohli, "Market Orientation: Antecedents and Consequences," *Journal of Marketing* 57 (1993): 53–70.

33. Michael Lee Stallard, "Has SAS chairman Jim Goodnight cracked the code of corporate culture?" *The Economic Times*, June 18, 2010, http://economictimes.indiatimes.com/features/corporate-dossier/has-sas-chairman-jim-goodnight-cracked-the-code-of-corporate-culture/articleshow/6060110.cms (accessed February 15, 2011); "100 Best Companies to Work For: SAS," CNNMoney, http://money.cnn.com/magazines/fortune/bestcompanies/2011/snapshots/1.html (accessed February 15, 2011).

34. Terry W. Loe, "The Role of Ethical Culture in Developing Trust, Market Orientation and Commitment to Quality" (PhD diss., University of Memphis, 1996).

35. Sean Valentine, Lynn Godkin, Gary M. Fleischman, and Rolan Kidwell, "Corporate Ethical Values, Group Creativity, Job Satisfaction and Turnover Intention: The Impact of Work Context on Work Response," *Journal of Business Ethics*, (2011) 98: 353–572.

36. Ethics Resource Center, *2000 National Business Ethics Survey*, 5.

37. John Galvin, "The New Business Ethics," *SmartBusinessMag.com*, June 2000, 99.

38. "How Ethics Influence Future Profitability—Walmart's Way," May 20, 2009,http://www.insideretailing.com.au/Default.aspx?articleId=5395&articleType=ArticleView&tabid=53 (accessed June 3, 2009).

39. "Biz Deans Talk—Business Management Education Blog," January 2, 2009, http://www.deanstalk.net/deanstalk/2009/01/warren-buffetts.html (accessed May 27, 2009).

40. Serena Ng and Erik Holm, "Buffett Jolted as Aide Quits," *The Wall Street Journal*, March 31, 2011, A1–A2; Gina Chon and Serena Ng, "Mixed Signals Marked Sokol Meeting," *The Wall Street Journal*, April 2–3, 2011, B1–B2.

41. "Investors Prefer Ethics over High Return," *USA Today*, January 16, 2006, B1.

42. Conservacion Patagonica, http://www.conservacionpatagonica.org/index.htm (accessed February 16, 2011); Patagonia Homepage, http://www.patagonia.com/us/home (accessed February 16, 2011).

43. "Trend Watch," *Business Ethics*, March/April 2000, 8.

44. Marjorie Kelly, "Holy Grail Found. Absolute, Definitive Proof that Responsible Companies Perform Better Financially," *Business Ethics*, Winter 2004.

45. "Google's Corporate Culture," http://www.google.com/intl/en/corporate/culture.html (accessed May 27, 2009).

46. O. C. Ferrell, Isabelle Maignan, and Terry W. Loe, "The Relationship between Corporate Citizenship and Competitive Advantage," in *Rights, Relationships, and Responsibilities*, ed. O. C. Ferrell, Lou Pelton, and Sheb L. True (Kennesaw, GA: Kennesaw State University, 2003).

47. Don Clark and Shara Tibken, "Intel Finds Chip-Design Flaw," *The Wall Street Journal*, February 1, 2011, http://online.wsj.com/article/SB10001424052748703439504576115992660815876.html (accessed February 15, 2011).

48. Galvin, "The New Business Ethics."

Chapter 2

1. Vikas Anand, Blake E. Ashforth, and Mahendra Joshi, "Business as Usual: The Acceptance and Perpetuation of Corruption in Organizations," *Academy of Management Executive* 18, no. 2 (2004): 39–53.

2. Debbie Thorne, O. C. Ferrell, and Linda Ferrell, *Business and Society* (Boston: Houghton Mifflin, 2003), 64–65.

3. Elena Conis, "Breakfast Just Got a Little Less Sweet," February 6, 2011, http://articles.latimes.com/2011/feb/06/health/la-he-breakfast-cereals-20110206 (accessed February 14, 2011).

4. Lynn Brewer, Robert Chandler, and O. C. Ferrell, "Managing Risks for Corporate Integrity: How to Survive an Ethical Misconduct Disaster," (Mason, OH: Texere/Thomson, 2006), 11.

5. Dana Mattioli, "Crisis Trigger Dramatic Departures," *The Wall Street Journal*, December 26, 2010, http://online.wsj.com/article/SB10001424052748704259704576033483108595762.html (accessed February 14, 2011).

6. *2011 Edelman Trust Barometer*, January 26, 2011, http://www.edelman.com/trust/2011/ (accessed March 15, 2011).

7. Josh Mitchell, Mike Ramsey, and Chester Dawson, "U.S. Blames Drivers, Not Toyota," *The Wall Street Journal*, February 9, 2011, http://online.wsj.com/article/SB10001424052748704422204576131311592922574.html?KEYWORDS=Toyota (accessed February 14, 2011).

8. Ana Campoy, "Dallas Cabbies Play Political Football with City Leaders," *The Wall Street Journal*, January 27, 2011, http://online.wsj.com/article/SB10001424052748704013604576104441185099396.html?KEYWORDS=boycott#printMode (accessed February 14, 2011).

9. Adapted from Isabelle Maignan, O. C. Ferrell, and Linda Ferrell, "A Stakeholder Model for Implementing Social Responsibility in Marketing," *European Journal of Marketing* 39 (2005): 956–977.

10. Ibid.

11. Ibid.

12. Thorne, Ferrell, and Ferrell, *Business and Society*.

13. Sharon C. Bolton, Rebecca Chung-hee Kim, and Kevin D. O'Gorman, "Corporate Social Responsibility as a Dynamic Internal Organizational Process: A Case Study," *Journal of Business Ethics*, published online, January 7, 2011.

14. Isabelle Maignan and O. C. Ferrell, "Corporate Social Responsibility: Toward a Marketing Conceptualization," *Journal of the Academy of Marketing Science* 32 (2004): 3–19.

15. "Buy Back Program," Best Buy, http://www.bestbuy.com/site/Misc/Buy-Back-Program/pcmcat230000050010.c?id=pcmcat230000050010&searchresults=1&searchterm=buy+back&ref=30&loc=KW-3455&s_kwcid=TC|8063|buy%20back%20program||S|b|6981861039 (accessed February 14, 2011).

16. Ibid.

17. Wenlong Yuan, Yongjian Bao, and Alain Verbeke, "Integrating CSR Initiatives in Business: An Organizing Framework," *Journal of Business Ethics*, published online, January 8, 2011.

18. Ibid.

19. Joseph A. McKinney, Tisha L. Emerson, and Mitchell J. Neubert, "The Effects of Ethical Codes on Ethical Perceptions of Actions toward Stakeholders," *Journal of Business Ethics*, (2010) 97: 505–516.

20. Roger Bate, "China's Bad Medicine," *The Wall Street Journal*, May 5, 2009, http://online.wsj.com/article/SB124146383501884323.html (accessed April 14, 2011).

21. Maignan and Ferrell, "Corporate Social Responsibility."

22. G. A. Steiner and J. F. Steiner, *Business, Government, and Society* (New York: Random House, 1988).

23. Milton Friedman, "Social Responsibility of Business Is to Increase Its Profits," *The New York Times Magazine*, September 13, 1970, 122–126.

24. "Business Leaders, Politicians and Academics Dub Corporate Irresponsibility 'An Attack on America from Within,'" *Business Wire*, November 7, 2002, via America Online.

25. Adam Smith, *The Theory of Moral Sentiments*, Vol. 2. (New York: Prometheus, 2000).

26. Sheelah Kolhatkar, "Cheating, Incorporated," *Bloomberg Businessweek*, February 14–February 20, 2011, 60–66; "Brands," Avid Life Media, http://www.avidlifemedia.com/brands.html (accessed February 21, 2011).

27. Theodore Levitt, *The Marketing Imagination* (New York: Free Press, 1983).

28. Norman Bowie, "Empowering People as an End for Business," in *People in Corporations: Ethical Responsibilities and Corporate Effectiveness*, ed. Georges Enderle, Brenda Almond, and Antonio Argandona (Dordrecht, Netherlands: Kluwer Academic Press, 1990), 105–112.

29. Randall Braaksma, "How Often Do Competitors Agree?," Herman Miller, http://www.hermanmiller.com/discover/tag/bifma-level/ (accessed February 14, 2011).

30. Stephanie Strom and Miguel Helft, "Google Finds It Hard to Reinvent Philanthropy," *The New York Times*, January 29, 2011, http://www.nytimes.com/2011/01/30/business/30charity.html (accessed February 14, 2011).

31. Paige Brady, "Walking the Walk," Whole Foods Market Blog, April 23, 2009, http://blog.wholefoodsmarket.com/2009/04/walking-the-walk/ (accessed April 14, 2011).

32. *Walmart 2009 Global Sustainability Report*, 20–34.

33. "ISO 26000:2010," International Organization for Standardization, http://www.iso.org/iso/catalogue_detail?csnumber=42546 (accessed February 16, 2011).

34. ISO Standards Catalogue, http://www.iso.org/iso/iso_catalogue.htm (accessed April 14, 2011).

35. Anne Carey and Keith Simmons, "USA Leads in Wind Power," American Wind Energy Association and the Global Wind Energy Council, printed in *USA Today*, February 17, 2009, A1; Rikki Stancich, "Wind energy markets buck the trend—with the right incentives," Wind Energy Update, February 6, 2011, http://social.windenergyupdate.com/industry-insight/wind-energy-markets-buck-trend-right-incentives (accessed February 16, 2011); "United States," Global Wind Energy Council, http://dev6.semaforce.be/index.php?id=121&L=0 (accessed February 16, 2011).

36. Tobias Webb, James Rose, and Peter Davis, "ISO 26000 Indicates Immaturity: If Corporate Responsibility Is to Be Effective, Prominence Has to Be Given to Both Quantitative and Qualitative Analyses," *Ethical Corporation* (December 2005): 9.

37. Archie B. Carroll, "The Pyramid of Corporate Social Responsibility: Toward the Moral Management of Organizational Stakeholders," *Business Horizons* 34 (1991): 42.

38. Isabelle Maignan, O. C. Ferrell, and G. Tomas M. Hult, "Corporate Citizenship: Cultural Antecedents and Business Benefits," *Journal of the Academy of Marketing Science* 27 (1999): 457.

39. *Dodge v. Ford Motor Co.*, 204 Mich.459, 179 N.W. 668, 3 A.L.R. 413 (1919).

40. "The Moral Hazards of Managing Other People's Money," *The Wall Street Journal*, April 29, 2009, http://online.wsj.com/article/SB124087477951861329.html (accessed April 14, 2011).

41. Alfred Marcus and Sheryl Kaiser, "Managing beyond Compliance: The Ethical and Legal Dimensions of Corporate Responsibility," *North Coast Publishers*, 2006, 79.

42. Joann S. Lublin, "Corporate Directors' Group Gives Repair Plan to Boards," *The Wall Street Journal*, March 24, 2009, http://online.wsj.com/article/SB123784649341118187.html (accessed April 14, 2011).

43. Aaron Smith, "GM Bonuses to Exceed 50% of Some Salaries," February 11, 2011, http://money.cnn.com/2011/02/11/news/companies/gm_bonus/ (accessed February 15, 2011).

44. Les Coleman, "Losses from Failure of Stakeholder Sensitive Processes: Financial Consequences for Large U.S. Companies from Breakdowns in Product, Environmental, and Accounting Standards," *Journal of Business Ethics*, (2011) 98: 247–258.

45. Ben W. Heineman, Jr., "Are You a Good Corporate Citizen?," *The Wall Street Journal*, June 28, 2005, B2.

46. Phred Dvorak, "Poor Year Doesn't Stop CEO Bonuses," *The Wall Street Journal*, March 18, 2009, http://online.wsj.com/article/SB123698866439126029.html (accessed April 14, 2011).

47. Darryl Reed, "Corporate Governance Reforms in Developing Countries," *Journal of Business Ethics* 37 (2002): 223–247.

48. Maria Maher and Thomas Anderson, *Corporate Governance: Effects on Firm Performance and Economic Growth* (Paris: Organisation for Economic Co-operation and Development, 1999).

49. A. Demb and F. F. Neubauer, *The Corporate Board: Confronting the Paradoxes* (Oxford: Oxford University Press, 1992).

50. Maher and Anderson, *Corporate Governance*.

51. Organisation for Economic Co-operation and Development, *The OECD Principles of Corporate Governance* (Paris: Organisation for Economic Co-operation and Development, 1999).

52. Louis Lavelle, "The Best and Worst Boards," *BusinessWeek*, October 7, 2002, 104–114.

53. Floyd Norris, "For Boards, S.E.C. Keeps the Bar Low," *The New York Times*, March 3, 2011, http://www.nytimes.com/2011/03/04/business/04norris.html?pagewanted=1&_r=1&src=busln (accessed March 4, 2011).

54. Melvin A. Eisenberg, "Corporate Governance: The Board of Directors and Internal Control," *Cordoza Law Review* 19 (1997): 237.

55. S. Trevis Certo, Catherine Dalton, Dan Dalton, and Richard Lester, "Boards of Directors' Self-Interest: Expanding for Pay in Corporate Acquisitions?," *Journal of Business Ethics* 77, no. 2 (January 2008): 219–230.

56. Gary Strauss, "$228,000 for a part-time job? Apparently, that's not enough," *USA Today*, March 4–6, 2011, 1A.

57. Business Dictionary, http://www.businessdictionary.com/definition/interlocking-directorate.html, (accessed February 15, 2011).

58. Amy Borrus, "Should Directors Be Nervous?," *BusinessWeek* online, March 6, 2006 http://www.businessweek.com/magazine/content/06_10/b3974062.htm (accessed April 14, 2011).

59. John A. Byrne with Louis Lavelle, Nanette Byrnes, Marcia Vickers, and Amy Borrus, "How to Fix Corporate Governance," *BusinessWeek*, May 6, 2002, 69–78.

60. Catherine Dodge, "Banning Big Wall Street Bonus Favored by 70% of Americans in National Poll," *Bloomberg*, December 12, 2010, http://www.bloomberg.com/news/2010-12-13/banning-big-wall-street-bonus-favored-by-70-of-americans-in-national-poll.html (accessed February 16, 2011).

61. American International Group, Inc., "*The New York Times*, December 9, 2010, http://topics.nytimes.com/top/news/business/companies/american_international_group/index.html (accessed February 16, 2011); David Goldman, "AIG overhauls bonus system," CNNMoney, February 10, 2010, http://money.cnn.com/2010/02/10/news/companies/aig_bonuses/index.htm (accessed March 15, 2011).

62. "Executive PayWatch 2010," AFL-CIO, http://www.aflcio.org/corporatewatch/paywatch/ / (accessed February 16, 2011).

63. Sarah Anderson, John Cavanagh, Ralph Estes, Chuck Collins, and Chris Hartman, *A Decade of Executive Excess: The 1990s Sixth Annual Executive.* Boston: United for a Fair Economy, 1999, online, June 30, 2006, http://www.faireconomy.org/press_room/1999/a_decade_of_executive_excess_the_1990s (accessed April 14, 2011).

64. Louis Lavelle, "CEO Pay, The More Things Change . . . ," *BusinessWeek,* October 16, 2000, 106–108.

65. Scott Thurm, "Options Given During Crisis Spell Large Gains for CEOs," *The Wall Street Journal,* April 26, 2011, http://online.wsj.com/article/SB10001424052748703789104576273042510527896.html (accessed April 27, 2011).

66. Kara Scanell, "SEC Ready to Require More Pay Disclosures," *The Wall Street Journal,* June 3, 2009, http://online.wsj.com/article/SB124397831899078781.html (accessed April 14, 2011).

67. Gary Strauss, "America's Corporate Meltdown," *USA Today,* June 27, 2002, 1A, 2A.

68. Li-Chiu Chi, "Do transparency and performance predict firm performance? Evidence from the Taiwan Market," *Expert Systems with Applications,* Vol. 36, Issue 8, October 2009, http://www.sciencedirect.com/science?_ob=ArticleURL&_udi=B6V03-4VTVPW4-1&_user=10&_rdoc=1&_fmt=&_orig=search&_sort=d&_docanchor=&view=c&_acct=C000050221&_version=1&_urlVersion=0&_userid=10&md5=3b7a30dbefb291c4c56f3a5f3a62d859 (accessed April 14, 2011).

69. Ilan Brat, "Start-Up Seeks Profits in Mounds of Garbage," *The Wall Street Journal,* May 3, 2010, http://online.wsj.com/article/SB10001424052748703572504575214431306540058.html (accessed February 16, 2011); "Announcing the 2010 Best New Product Winners," Edison Awards, http://www.edisonawards.com/Winners2010.php (accessed February 16, 2011); Eco Huddler, "Always stay true to your mission," Yahoo! Green, September 4, 2008, http://green.yahoo.com/blog/huddlergreenhome/13/always-stay-true-to-your-mission.html (accessed February 16, 2011).

70. "Obesity Issue Looms Large," Washington Wire, *The Wall Street Journal* online, March 3, 2006, http://blogs.wsj.com/washwire/2006/03/03/obesity-issue-looms-large/ (accessed April 14, 2011).

71. "Six in Ten Say Family Put Off Medical Care Due to Cost," Kaiser Family Foundation, April 23, 2009, http://www.kff.org/kaiserpolls/pomr042309nr.cfm (accessed April 14, 2011); Stephanie Condon, "Poll: Most Oppose Cutting Funding for Healthcare Reforms," *CBS News,* February 15, 2011, http://www.cbsnews.com/8301-503544_162-20032114-503544.html (accessed February 16, 2011).

72. "Being a Responsible Company," http://www.starbucks.com/aboutus/csr.asp (accessed April 14, 2011).

73. Jessica E. Vascellero, "Facebook Grapples with Privacy Issues," *The Wall Street Journal,* May 19, 2010, http://online.wsj.com/article/SB10001424052748704912004575252723109845974.html (accessed February 16, 2011); Rob Pegoraro, "Facebook founder Zuckerberg's not-quite-apology," *The Washington Post,* May 24, 2010, http://voices.washingtonpost.com/fasterforward/2010/05/facebook_founder_zuckerbergs_n.html (accessed February 16, 2011).

74. Jon Swartz, "Facebook changes its status in Washington," *USA Today,* January 13, 2011, 1B–2B; "Details of 100 million Facebook users published online," MSNBC.com, July 29, 2010, http://www.msnbc.msn.com/id/38463013/ns/technology_and_science/?GT1=43001 (accessed April 14, 2011).

75. "Consumer Watchdog Welcomes Larry Page as Google's CEO," Consumer Watchdog, January 20, 2011, http://www.consumerwatchdog.org/newsrelease/consumer-watchdog-welcomes-larry-page-googles-ceo (accessed February 16, 2011).

76. Alex Taylor III, "Tata Takes on the World Building an Auto Empire in India," *Fortune,* May 2, 2011, 92.

Chapter 3

1. Michael Carolan, "U.K. lawmakers blast Kraft over Cadbury plant closing," *The Wall Street Journal,* April 7, 2010, http://online.wsj.com/article/SB20001424052702303493904575167464 (accessed February 11, 2011).

2. Peter Elkind, David Whitford, and Doris Burke, "'An Accident Waiting to Happen,'" *Fortune,* February 7, 2011, 106–132.

3. Ben Casselman, Isabel Ordonez, and Angel Gonzalez, "Chevron Hit with Record Judgment," *The Wall Street Journal,* February 15, 2011, http://online.wsj.com/article/SB10001424052748703584804576144464044068664.html (accessed February 16, 2011).

4. Eric H. Beversluis, "Is There No Such Thing as Business Ethics?," *Journal of Business Ethics* 6 (1987): 81–88. Reprinted with permission of Kluwer Academic Publishers, Dordrecht, Holland.

5. Carolyn Said, "Ellison Hones His 'Art of War' Tactics," *San Francisco Chronicle,* June 10, 2003, A1.

6. Michael Liedtke, "Oracle CEO to Pay $122M to Settle Lawsuit," Associated Press, *The Washington Post* online, November 22, 2005, http://www.accessmylibrary.com/coms2/summary_0286-12061795_ITM (accessed August 5, 2009).

7. Sarah Anderson, Chuck Collins, Sam Pizzigati, and Kevin Shih, "Executive Excess 2010: CEO Pay and the Great Recession," Institute for Policy Studies, September 1, 2010, http://www.ips-dc.org/reports/executive_excess_2010 (accessed February 16, 2011).

8. Vernon R. Loucks, Jr., "A CEO Looks at Ethics," *Business Horizons* 30 (1987): 4.

9. William Atkinson, "Stealing time," BNet, November 2006, http://findarticles.com/p/articles/mi_qa5332/is_11_53/ai_n29304996/?tag=content;col1 (accessed February 17, 2011).

10. "Proper Use of Company, Customer, and Supplier Resources," Boeing, November 19, 2009, http://www.boeing.com/companyoffices/aboutus/ethics/pro10pdf (accessed January 28, 2010).

11. I. Niedhammer, S. David, S. Degioanni, A. Drummond, and P. Philip, "Workplace bullying and sleep disturbances: Findings from a large-scale cross-sectional survey in the French working population," *Sleep* (2009) 32 (9): 1211–1219.

12. Isiah Carey, "Corporate Bullying Affects 1 in 3: Stats," Fox News Houston, November 18, 2010, http://www.myfoxdetroit.com/dpp/news/national/corporate-bullying-affects-1-in-3-stats-20101118-wpms (accessed February 11, 2011).

13. Lisa Broadt, "Proposed Laws Could Send Firms to Court for 'Abusive' Behavior," *Washington Business Journal,* http://www.bizjournals.com/washington/stories/2008/09/29/smallb8.html (accessed February 2, 2009).

14. Barbara Safani, "Bullying at Work a Growing Trend," AOL Jobs, January 24, 2011, http://jobs.aol.com/articles/2011/01/24/bullying-at-work-a-growing-trend/ (accessed April 27, 2011).

15. Associated Press, "Intel to pay AMD $1.25 billion to settle lawsuits," MSNBC, November 12, 2009, http://www.msnbc.msn.com/id/33882559/ns/business-us_business (accessed February 17, 2011).

16. James Kanter, "Europe Fines Intel $1.45 Billion in Antitrust Case," *The New York Times,* May 13, 2009, http://www.nytimes.com/2009/05/14/business/global/14compete.html (accessed February 17, 2011).

17. "GAO Document B-295402," Lockheed Martin Corporation, February 18, 2005, http://www.gao.gov/decisions/bidpro/295402.htm (accessed August 5, 2009).

18. Maurice Kenton and Tim Strong, "United Kingdom: The Bribery Act 2010—What does it mean for your business?" *Mondaq Criminal Law,* May 21, 2010, http://www.mondaq.com/article.asp?articleid=101060 (accessed February 11, 2011).

19. United States Department of Justice, "Foreign Corrupt Practices Act Antibribery Provisions," http://www.justice.gov/criminal/fraud/fcpa/docs/lay-persons-guide.pdf (accessed February 17, 2011).

20. Jamila Trindle, "Alcatel-Lucent Settles U.S. Bribery Charges, *The Wall Street Journal*, December 28, 2010, B3.

21. Ira Winkler, *Corporate Espionage: What It Is, Why It's Happening in Your Company, What You Must Do about It* (New York: Prima, 1997).

22. Almelin, Snyder, Sapoznikow, McCollum, and Weader, "United States, intellectual property, a statistical analysis of trade secret litigation in federal courts," April 1, 2010 (originally published in the *Gonzaga Law Review*, March 2010), http://www.tradesecretsblog.info/2010/04 (accessed February 14, 2011).

23. Ben Klayman, "Ex-Ford engineer sentenced for trade secrets theft," *Reuters*, April 13, 2011, http://www.reuters.com/article/2011/04/13/us-djc-ford-tradesecrets-idUSTRE73C3FG20110413 (accessed April 27, 2011).

24. Develin Barrett, "Hackers Penetrate Nasdaq Computers," *The Wall Street Journal*, February 5, 2011, http://online.wsj.com/article/SB10001424052748704709304576124502351634690.html (accessed February 10, 2011).

25. "Charge Statistics," http://www.eeoc.gov/eeoc/statistics/enforcement/charges.cfm (accessed February 17, 2011).

26. "African American CEOs of Fortune 500 Companies," Black Profiles, http://www.blackentrepreneurprofile.com/fortune-500-ceos (accessed February 17, 2011).

27. Nancy Cook, "Keep Young and Beautiful—Especially at Work," *Newsweek*, April 7, 2010, http://www.newsweek.com/blogs/jobbed/2010/04/17/keep-young-and-beautiful-especially-at-work.html (accessed February 18, 2011).

28. "AARP Best Employers for Workers over 50: About the Program," AARP, September 2009, http://www.aarp.org/work/employee-benefits/info-09-2009/about_the_best_employers_program.html (accessed February 18, 2011).

29. "What Is Affirmative Action?," HR Content Library, October 12, 2001, http://www.hrnext.com/content/view.cfm?articles_id=2007&subs_id=32 (accessed August 5, 2009).

30. "What Affirmative Action Is (and What It Is Not)," National Partnership for Women & Families, http://www.nationalpartnership.org/site/DocServer/AffirmativeActionFacts.pdf?docID=861 (accessed August 5, 2009).

31. Debbie M. Thorne, O. C. Ferrell, and Linda Ferrell, *Business and Society: A Strategic Approach to Social Responsibility and Ethics*, 4th ed. (Mason, OH: South-Western Cengage Learning, 2011), 182.

32. Joe Millman, "Delayed Recognition; Arab Americans Haven't Put Much Effort into Advancing Their Rights as a Minority. Until Relatively Recently, That Is." *The Wall Street Journal*, November 14, 2005, R8.

33. Paula N. Rubin, "Civil Rights and Criminal Justice: Primer on Sexual Harassment Series: NIJ Research in Action," October 1995, http://www.ncjrs.org/txtfiles/harass.txt (accessed August 5, 2009).

34. "Sexual Harassment Charges," EEOC, http://www.eeoc.gov/eeoc/statistics/enforcement/sexual_harassment.cfm (accessed February 18, 2011).

35. Steve Stecklow, "Sexual Harassment Cases Plague UN," *The Wall Street Journal*, May 21, 2009, http://online.wsj.com/article/SB124233350385520879.html (accessed June 11, 2009).

36. *Zabkowicz v. West Bend Co.*, 589 F. Supp. 780, 784, 35 EPD Par.34, 766 (E.D. Wis.1984).

37. Iddo Landau, "The Law and Sexual Harassment," *Business Ethics Quarterly* 15, no. 2 (2005): 531–536.

38. "Enhancements and Justice: Problems in Determining the Requirements of Justice in a Genetically Transformed Society," *Kennedy Institute Ethics Journal* 15, no. 1 (2005): 3–38.

39. Alex Frangos, "Timber Backs a New 'Green' Standard," *The Wall Street Journal*, March 29, 2006, B6.

40. Ibid.

41. Matthew Dalton, "European Farmers Turn to Biogas Plants," *The Wall Street Journal*, June 18, 2009, http://online.wsj.com/article/SB124527861144324987.html (accessed February 21, 2011).

42. Bertrand d'Armagnac, "Danish wind farms show sustainable attitude toward renewable energy," guardian.co.uk, August 10, 2010, http://www.guardian.co.uk/world/2010/aug/10/denmark-renewable-wind-farm-energy (accessed January 25, 2011).

43. Wendy Koch, "Here comes the sun: White House to install solar panels," *The Wall Street Journal*, October 6, 2010, 10A.

44. Chen Jialu, "Three Gorges Dam champions clean energy program," *China Daily*, February 23, 2010, http://www.chinadaily.com.cn/cndy/2010-02/23/content_9486733.htm (accessed February 21, 2011).

45. Ami Cholia, "Top Ten Green Countries," *The Huffington Post*, August 21, 2009, http://www.huffingtonpost.com/2009/07/21/top-10-green-countries-ph_n_241867.html?slidenumber=7 (accessed January 25, 2011).

46. Russell Gold and Ian Talley, "Exxon CEO Advocates Emissions Tax," *The Wall Street Journal*, January 9, 2009, http://online.wsj.com/article/SB123146091530566335.html (accessed June 4, 2009).

47. Association of Certified Fraud Examiners, *Report to the Nations on Occupational Fraud and Abuse: 2010 Global Fraud Study*, 3.

48. Justin Scheck and Kara Scannell, "SEC: Intel cash inflated Dell," July 23, 2010, *The Wall Street Journal*, http://online.wsj.com/article/SB10001424052748703467304575383470750065524.html (accessed February 14, 2011).

49. Cassell Bryan-Low, "Accounting Firms Face Backlash over the Tax Shelters They Sold," *The Wall Street Journal* online, February 7, 2003, http://online.wsj.com/article/SB1044568358985594893.html?mod=googlewsj (accessed August 5, 2009).

50. Jean Eaglesham, "SEC Levels Case against Ex-Officers of IndyMac," *The Wall Street Journal*, February 12, 2011, http://online.wsj.com/article/SB10001424052748703786804576138621943426058.html (accessed February 15, 2011).

51. *Gillette Co. v. Wilkinson Sword, Inc.*, 89-CV-3586, 1991 U.S. Dist. Lexis 21006, *6 (S.D.N.Y. January 9, 1991).

52. Archie B. Carroll, *Business and Society: Ethics and Stakeholder Management* (Cincinnati: South-Western, 1989), 228–230.

53. Barry Newman, "With ban on clove cigarettes, importer claims its product is all stogie," October 28, 2009, *The Wall Street Journal*, p. A30.

54. "Retail Fraud, Shoplifting Rates Decrease, According to National Retail Security Survey," National Retail Federation, June 15, 2010, http://www.nrf.com/modules.php?name=News&op=viewlive&sp_id=945 (accessed February 21, 2011).

55. Richard Esposito, "Thain Tells All on Merrill Lynch Bonuses," ABC News, February 25, 2009, http://abcnews.go.com/Blotter/WallStreet/story?id=6959962&page=1 (accessed February 21, 2011).

56. Damian Paletta, Maya Jackson Randall, and Michael R. Crittenden, "Geithner Calls for Tougher Standards on Risk," *The Wall Street Journal*, March 25, 2009, http://online.wsj.com/article/SB123807231255147603.html (accessed April 14, 2011).

57. Jennifer Liberto and David Ellis, "Wall Street reform: What's in the bill," CNNMoney.com, June 30, 2010, http://money.cnn.com/2010/06/25/news/economy/whats_in_the_reform_bill/index.htm (accessed February 14, 2011).

58. Jason Zweig, "Insider Trading: Why We Can't Help Ourselves," *The Wall Street Journal,* April 2, 2011, http://online.wsj.com/article/SB10001424052748704530204576236922024758718.html (accessed April 27, 2011); Michael Rothfeld, Susan Pulliam, and Vanessa O'Connell, "The Confessions of an Inside Trader," *The Wall Street Journal,* April 16, 2011, http://online.wsj.com/article/SB10001424052748703983104576262921972017168.html (accessed April 27, 2011).

59. Anna Wilde Mathews, "Copyrights on Web Content Are Backed," *The Wall Street Journal,* October 27, 2000, B10.

60. Jennifer Martinez, "Report: One-fourth of web traffic is pirated content," Politico.com, February 21, 2011, http://hamptonroads.com/2011/02/report-onefourth-web-traffic-pirated-content (accessed February 21, 2011).

61. Roger Bate, "China's Bad Medicine," *The Wall Street Journal,* May 5, 2009, http://online.wsj.com/article/SB124146383501884323.html (accessed August 5, 2009); "Chinese Intellectual Property Violations," Idea Buyer, http://www.ideabuyer.com/news/chinese-intellectual-property-violations/ (accessed August 5, 2009).

62. Deli Yang, Mahmut Sonmez, Derek Bosworth, and Gerald Fryzell, "Global Software Piracy: Searching for Further Explanations," *Journal of Business Ethics,* September 2008.

63. Nora J. Rifon, Robert LaRose, and Sejung Marina Choi, "Your Privacy Is Sealed: Effects of Web Privacy Seals on Trust and Personal Disclosures," *Journal of Consumer Affairs* 39, no. 2 (2002): 339–362.

64. "2005 Electronic Monitoring and Surveillance Survey: Many Companies Monitoring, Recording, Videotaping—and Firing—Employees," *The New York Times,* May 18, 2005, via http://www.amanet.org/press/amanews/ems05.htm (accessed August 5, 2009).

65. Ruth Mantell, "Watch Your E-mails. Your Boss Is," *The Wall Street Journal,* May 2, 2010, http://online.wsj.com/article/SB127277297445285515.html (accessed February 14, 2011).

66. Mitch Wagner, "Google's Pixie Dust," *Information Week,* Issue 1061 (2005): 98.

67. Stephenie Steitzer, "Commercial Web Sites Cut Back on Collections of Personal Data," *Wall Street Journal,* March 28, 2002, http://online.wsj.com/article/SB1017247161553469240.html?mod=googlewsj (accessed August 5, 2009).

68. Ben Worthen, "Hackers Aren't Only Threat to Privacy," *Wall Street Journal,* June 22, 2010, http://online.wsj.com/article/SB10001424052748704122904575314703487356896.html (accessed February 14, 2011).

69. Morgan Downs (Producer), *Inside the Mind of Google* [DVD], United States: CNBC Originals, 2010.

70. "Obesity and Overweight," Centers for Disease Control, June 18, 2010, http://www.cdc.gov/nchs/fastats/overwt.htm (accessed February 21, 2011).

71. Cynthia Ogden, Ph.D., and Margaret Carroll, M.S.P.H., "Prevalence of Obesity among Children and Adolescents: United States, Trends 1963–1965 through 2007–2008," CDC Division of Health and Nutrition Examination Surveys, June 2010, http://www.cdc.gov/nchs/data/hestat/obesity_child_07_08/obesity_child_07_08.pdf (accessed February 21, 2011).

Chapter 4

1. "Corporate Information: Corporate Culture," Google, http://www.google.com/corporate/culture.html (accessed March 15, 2011).

2. Paul K. Shum and Sharon L. Yam, "Ethics and Law: Guiding the Invisible Hand to Correct Corporate Social Responsibility Externalities," *Journal of Business Ethics,* 98 (2011): 549–571.

3. Don Clark and Shayndi Raice, "Tech Firms Intensify Clashes over Patents," *The Wall Street Journal,* October 4, 2010, B3.

4. John Jannarone, "Starbucks May Spill Kraft's Coffee," *The Wall Street Journal,* November 29, 2010, C8.

5. Alessandro Torello, "UPDATE: Google Antitrust Investigation Still Ongoing, EU Says," *The Wall Street Journal,* February 8, 2011, http://online.wsj.com/article/BT-CO-20110208-704805.html (accessed February 21, 2011).

6. Aaron Back, "China Acts to Prevent Collusion on Prices," *The Wall Street Journal,* January 5, 2011, http://online.wsj.com/article/SB10001424052748704723104576061160620783364.html (accessed February 21, 2011).

7. Dionne Searcy, "U.K. Laws on Bribes Has Firms In a Sweat," *The Wall Street Journal,* December 28, 2010, B1.

8. Gregory T. Gundlach, "Price Predation: Legal Limits and Antitrust Considerations," *Journal of Public Policy & Marketing* 14 (1995): 278.

9. David Goldman, "Obama Vows Antitrust Crackdown," *CNN Money,* May 11, 2009, http://money.cnn.com/2009/05/11/news/economy/antitrust/index.htm (accessed March 15, 2011).

10. Steve Lohr, "High-Tech Antitrust Cases: The Road Ahead," *The New York Times,* May 13, 2009, http://bits.blogs.nytimes.com/2009/05/13/high-tech-antitrust-the-road-ahead/?scp=1&sq=high-tech%20antitrust&st=cse (accessed March 15, 2011).

11. "10 Ways to Combat Corporate Espionage," Data Destruction News, http://www.imakenews.com/accushred/e_article001225805.cfm?x=bdtNVCP,bbGvRs5c,w (accessed March 15, 2011).

12. Berman, Dennis K., "Big Lots Settles Suit with Researcher," *The Wall Street Journal,* February 18, 2011, http://online.wsj.com/article/SB10001424052748704546704576150894015891156.html (accessed March 4, 2011).

13. "Baseball's Antitrust Exemption: Q&A," ESPN, December 5, 2001, http://sports.espn.go.com/espn/print?id=1290707&type=story (accessed March 15, 2011).

14. "A Child Shall Lead the Way: Marketing to Youths," *Credit Union Executive,* May–June 1993, 6–8.

15. Julia Angwin, "How to Keep Kids Safe Online," *The Wall Street Journal,* January 22, 2009, http://online.wsj.com/article/SB123238632055894993.html (accessed March 15, 2011).

16. Jennifer Levitz, "Laws Take on Financial Scams against Seniors," *The Wall Street Journal,* May 19, 2009, http://online.wsj.com/article/SB124269210323932723.html (accessed March 15, 2011).

17. "What We Do," U.S. Food and Drug Administration, http://www.fda.gov/AboutFDA/WhatWeDo/default.htm (accessed February 21, 2011).

18. David Kesmodel, "FDA: Last Call for Drinks Mixing Stimulants, Alcohol," *The Wall Street Journal,* November 17, 2010, B1–B2; "Update on Caffeinated Alcoholic Beverages," U.S. Food and Drug Administration, November 24, 2010, http://www.fda.gov/NewsEvents/PublicHealthFocus/ucm234900.htm (accessed February 21, 2011); "Video: Four Loko a Dangerous Alcoholic Energy Drink," *The Wall Street Journal,* November 16, 2010, http://online.wsj.com/video/four-loko-a-dangerous-alcoholic-energy-drink/245600EB-99AE-44A3-B2F8-1818386C3161.html (accessed February 21, 2011).

19. "Women's Bureau Priority Issues," United States Department of Labor, http://www.dol.gov/wb/programs/four_priorities_2010.htm (accessed February 24, 2011).

20. Lee Tae-hoon, "Overworked, drowsy cab drivers pose danger," *The Korea Times,* July 19, 2010, http://www.koreatimes.co.kr/www/news/special/2010/11/180_69764.html (accessed February 21, 2011).

21. "United Nations General Assembly Report," http://www.un.org/documents/ga/res/42/ares42-187.htm (accessed March 15, 2011).

22. "Consumer Interest in Environmental Purchasing Not Eclipsed by Poor Economy," Cone 2009 Environmental Survey, http://coneinc.com/content2032 (accessed March 15, 2011).

23. "Cone LLC Releases the 2010 Cone Cause Evolution Study," Cone, September 15, 2010, http://www.coneinc.com/cause-grows-consumers-want-more (accessed February 24, 2011).

24. Michael Arndt, Wendy Zellner, and Peter Coy, "Too Much Corporate Power," *Business Week,* September 11, 2000, 149.

25. Associated Press, "Chevron asks court to block $9.5B Ecuadorian award," *The Wall Street Journal,* February 18, 2011, http://online.wsj.com/article/AP9feedefd566647f98c76c9c2111578f3.html?KEYWORDS=Chevron+Ecuador (accessed February 24, 2011); Ben Casselman, Isabel Ordonez, and Angel Gonzalez, "Chevron Hit with Record Judgment," *The Wall Street Journal,* February 15, 2011, A1, A2.

26. "Electronics Recycling Is Making Gains, Says EPA," *PC World,* January 8, 2009, http://www.pcworld.com/businesscenter/article/156721/article.html?tk=nl_bnxnws (accessed March 15, 2011).

27. VikasBajas, "At Moody's, Some Debt was Rated Incorrectly," *New York Times,* July 2, 2008, http://query.nytimes.com/gst/fullpage.html?res=9505E3DB173DF931A35754C0A96E9C8B63 (accessed September 27, 2011).

28. Sarah Lynch, "Schapiro: More Oversight Needed for Credit-Rating Firms," *The Wall Street Examiner,* April 15, 2009, http://forums.wallstreetexaminer.com/index.php?showtopic=807630 (accessed March 15, 2011).

29. Mike Spector and Shelly Banjo, "Pay at Nonprofits Gets a Closer Look," *The Wall Street Journal,* March 27, 2009, http://online.wsj.com/article/SB123811160845153093.html (accessed March 15, 2011).

30. Floyd Norris and Adam Liptak, "Justices Uphold Sarbanes-Oxley Act," *The New York Times,* June 28, 2010, http://www.nytimes.com/2010/06/29/business/29accounting.html?pagewanted=1&_r=1 (accessed February 22, 2011).

31. Tim Elfrink, "The Rise and Fall of the Stanford Financial Group," *Houston Press,* April 9, 2009, http://www.houstonpress.com/content/printVersion/1173931/ (accessed February 22, 2011); ShiraOvide, "Lehman Brothers Whistle-blower Matthew Lee Again in Spotlight," *The Wall Street Journal,* December 21, 2010, http://blogs.wsj.com/deals/2010/12/21/lehman-brothers-whistle-blower-matthew-lee-again-in-spotlight/ (accessed February 22, 2011).

32. Tricia Bisoux, "The Sarbanes–Oxley Effect," *BizEd,* July/August 2005, 24–29.

33. 2010 *Sarbanes-Oxley Compliance Survey,* http://www.auditnet.org/articles/KL201010.pdf (accessed February 22, 2011).

34. President Barack Obama, "Remarks by the President on 21st Century Financial Regulatory Reform," The White House, June 17, 2009, http://www.whitehouse.gov/the_press_office/Remarks-of-the-President-on-Regulatory-Reform/ (accessed February 22, 2011).

35. Ibid.

36. Joshua Gallu, "Dodd-Frank May Cost $6.5 Billion and 5,000 Workers," *Bloomberg,* February 14, 2011, http://www.bloomberg.com/news/2011-02-14/dodd-frank-s-implementation-calls-for-6-5-billion-5-000-staff-in-budget.html (accessed February 22, 2011); Binyamin Appelbaum and Brady Dennis, "Dodd's overhaul goes well beyond other plans," *The Washington Post,* November 11, 2009, http://www.washingtonpost.com/wp-dyn/content/article/2009/11/09/AR2009110901935.html?hpid=topnews&sid=ST2009111003729 (accessed February 22, 2011).

37. Maria Bartiromo, "JPMorgan CEO Jamie Dimon sees good times in 2011," *USA Today,* February 21, 2011, http://www.usatoday.com/money/companies/management/bartiromo/2011-02-21-bartiromo21_CV_N.htm (accessed February 22, 2011).

38. "Office of Financial Research," *U.S. Department of Treasury,* http://www.treasury.gov/initiatives/Pages/ofr.aspx (accessed February 22, 2011).

39. "Initiatives: Financial Stability Oversight Council," *U.S. Department of Treasury,* http://www.treasury.gov/initiatives/Pages/FSOC-index.aspx (accessed February 22, 2011).

40. *Financial Stability Oversight Council Created Under the Dodd-Frank Wall Street Reform and Consumer Protection Act: Frequently Asked Questions,* October 2010, http://www.treasury.gov/initiatives/wsr/Documents/FAQs%20-%20Financial%20Stability%20Oversight%20Council%20-%20October%202010%20FINAL%20v2.pdf (accessed February 22, 2011).

41. "Subtitle A—Bureau of Consumer Financial Protection," *One Hundred Eleventh Congress of the United States of America,* p. 589.

42. "Wall Street Reform: Bureau of Consumer Financial Protection (CFPB)," *U.S. Treasury,* http://www.treasury.gov/initiatives/Pages/cfpb.aspx (accessed February 22, 2011).

43. "Wall Street Reform: Bureau of Consumer Financial Protection (CFPB)," *U.S. Treasury,* http://www.treasury.gov/initiatives/Pages/cfpb.aspx (accessed February 22, 2011); Sudeep Reddy, "Elizabeth Warren's Early Words on a Consumer Financial Protection Bureau," *The Wall Street Journal,* September 17, 2010, http://blogs.wsj.com/economics/2010/09/17/elizabeth-warrens-early-words-on-a-consumer-financial-protection-bureau/ (accessed November 5, 2010); Jennifer Liberto & David Ellis, "Wall Street reform: What's in the bill," CNN, June 30, 2010); http://money.cnn.com/2010/06/25/news/economy/whats_in_the_reform_bill/index.htm (accessed November 5, 2010).

44. Jean Eaglesham, "Warning Shot on Financial Protection," *The Wall Street Journal,* February 9, 2011, http://online.wsj.com/article/SB10001424052748703507804576130370862263258.html?mod=googlenews_wsj (accessed February 22, 2011).

45. Gary Langer, "ABC News Poll: Two-thirds Back Financial Reform; The Question: How Far to Go," ABC News, April 26, 2010, http://abcnews.go.com/PollingUnit/abc-news-poll-two-thirds-back-financial-reform/story?id=10476079 (accessed February 22, 2011).

46. Jean Eaglesham, "Warning Shot on Financial Protection."

47. Jean Eaglesham and Ashby Jones, "Whistle-blower Bounties Pose Challenges," *The Wall Street Journal,* December 13, 2010, C1, C3.

48. Ibid.

49. Win Swenson, "The Organizational Guidelines' 'Carrot and Stick' Philosophy, and Their Focus on 'Effective' Compliance," in *Corporate Crime in America: Strengthening the "Good Citizenship"-Corporation* (Washington, DC: U.S. Sentencing Commission, 1995), 17–26.

50. *United States Code Service* (Lawyers' Edition), 18 U.S.C.S. Appendix, Sentencing Guidelines for the United States Courts (Rochester, NY: Lawyers Cooperative Publishing, 1995), sec. 8A.1.

51. O. C Ferrell and Linda Ferrell, "Current Developments in Managing Organizational Ethics and Compliance Initiatives," University of Wyoming, white paper, Bill Daniels Business Ethics Initiative 2006.

52. Open Compliance Ethics Group 2005 Benchmarking Study Key Findings, http://www.oceg.org/view/Benchmarking2005 (accessed June 12, 2009).

53. "US Sentences Guidelines Changes Become Effective November 1," FCPA Compliance and Ethics Blog, November 2, 2010, http://tfoxlaw.wordpress.com/2010/11/02/us-sentencing-guidelines-changes-become-effective-november-1/ (accessed March 15, 2011).

54. Ferrell and Ferrell, "Current Developments in Managing Organizational Ethics and Compliance Initiatives."

55. Lynn Brewer, "Capitalizing on the Value of Integrity: An Integrated Model to Standardize the Measure of Non-financial Performance as an Assessment of Corporate Integrity," in *Managing Risks for Corporate Integrity. How to Survive an Ethical Misconduct Disaster,* ed. Lynn Brewer, Robert Chandler, and O. C. Ferrell (Mason, OH: Thomson/Texere, 2006), 233–277.

56. "McDonald's Launches 'Balanced, Active Lifestyles' Campaign," Consumer Affairs, http://www.consumeraffairs.com/news04/2005/mcdonalds_ads.html (accessed March 15, 2011).

57. Ingrid MurroBotero, "Charitable Giving Has 4 Big Benefits," *Business Journal of Phoenix online*, January 1, 1999, www.bizjournals.com/phoenix/stories/1999/01/04/smallb3.html (accessed March 15, 2011).

58. Haya El Nasser, "Charitable giving shows modest gain," *USA Today*, June 20, 2011, http://yourlife.usatoday.com/mind-soul/doing-good/story/2011/06/Charitable-giving-shows-modest-gain/48631470/1 (accessed September 27, 2011).

59. 2007 Corporate Citizen Report, Wells Fargo, https://www.wellsfargo.com/downloads/pdf/about/csr/reports/wf2007corporate_citizenship.pdf (accessed March 15, 2011).

60. *Walmart: 2010 Annual Report*, http://cdn.walmartstores.com/sites/AnnualReport/2010/PDF/WMT_2010AR_FINAL.pdf (accessed February 23, 2011); "Tracking Big Corporate Donors," *USA Today*, http://www.usatoday.com/money/companies/2010-08-08-corporate-philanthropy-interactive-graphic_N.htm (accessed February 23, 2011).

61. "Walmart Foundation Fact Sheet," Walmartfacts.com, http://walmartstores.com/pressroom/FactSheets/ (accessed February 23, 2011).

62. Susan G. Komen for the Cure, http://ww5.komen.org/AboutUs/AboutUs.html (accessed February 23, 2011); "Save Lids to Save Lives®," Yoplait, http://www.yoplait.com/Slsl/default.aspx (accessed February 23, 2011).

63. "Even as Cause Marketing Grows, 83 Percent of Consumers Still Want to See More," Cone, http://www.coneinc.com/cause-grows-consumers-want-more (accessed February 23, 2011).

64. Leigh Buchanan, "More Than a Moving Company," Inc., December 1, 2010, www.inc.com/magazine/20101201/more-than-a-moving-company.html (accessed December 17, 2010); Gentle Giant Movers website, www.gentlegiant.com (accessed January 12, 2011).

65. "How We're Helping," Home Depot, http://corporate.homedepot.com/wps/portal/!ut/p/c1/04_SB8K8xLLM9MSSzPy8xBz9CP0os3gDdwNHH0sfE3M3AzMPJ8OAEBcDKADKR2LKmxrD5fHr9vPIz03VL8iNKAcAJzsP4g!!/dl2/d1/L2dJQSEvUUt3QS9ZQnB3LzZfMEcwQUw5TDQ3RjA2SEIxUEs5MDAwMDAwMDA1/ (accessed March 15, 2011); "Habitat for Humanity and The Home Depot Mexico partner to help rebuild Haiti," Habitat for Humanity, February 8, 2010, http://www.habitat.org/lac_eng/newsroom/2010/02_08_2010_homedepot_eng.aspx?tgs=Mi81LzIwMTEgMTI6NDg6NTYgUE0%3d (accessed February 6, 2011).

Chapter 5

1. Thomas M. Jones, "Ethical Decision Making by Individuals in Organizations: An Issue-Contingent Model," *Academy of Management Review* 16 (February 1991): 366–395; O. C. Ferrell and Larry G. Gresham, "A Contingency Framework for Understanding Ethical Decision Making in Marketing," *Journal of Marketing* 49 (Summer 1985): 87–96; O. C. Ferrell, Larry G. Gresham, and John Fraedrich, "A Synthesis of Ethical Decision Models for Marketing," *Journal of Macromarketing* 9 (Fall 1989): 55–64; Shelby D. Hunt and Scott Vitell, "A General Theory of Marketing Ethics," *Journal of Macromarketing* 6 (Spring 1986): 5–16; William A. Kahn, "Toward an Agenda for Business Ethics Research," *Academy*

of Management Review 15 (April 1990): 311–328; Linda K. Trevino, "Ethical Decision Making in Organizations: A Person-Situation Interactionist Model," *Academy of Management Review* 11 (March 1986): 601–617.

2. Jones, "Ethical Decision Making," 367, 372.

3. Donald P. Robin, R. Eric Reidenbach, and P. J. Forrest, "The Perceived Importance of an Ethical Issue as an Influence on the Ethical Decision Making of Ad Managers," *Journal of Business Research* 35 (January 1996): 17.

4. Susan Pulliam, Michael Rothfeld, and Jenny Strasburg, "Big Consultants Payouts Hint Insider Probe Will Broaden," *The Wall Street Journal*, January 10, 2011, http://online.wsj.com/article/SB10001424052748704055204576068403964057550.html (accessed February 28, 2011).

5. Jack Beatty, "The Enron Ponzi Scheme," *The Atlantic Monthly*, March 13, 2002, http://www.theatlantic.com/doc/200203u/pp2002-03-13 (accessed August 17, 2009).

6. Roselie McDevitt and Joan Van Hise, "Influences in Ethical Dilemmas of Increasing Intensity," *Journal of Business Ethics* 40 (October 2002): 261–274.

7. Anusorn Singhapakdi, Scott J. Vitell, and George R. Franke, "Antecedents, Consequences, and Mediating Effects of Perceived Moral Intensity and Personal Moral Philosophies," *Journal of the Academy of Marketing Science* 27 (Winter 1999): 19.

8. Ibid.

9. Ibid.

10. Kathy Lund Dean, Jeri Mullins Beggs, and Timothy P. Keane, "Mid-level Managers, Organizational Context, and (Un)ethical Encounters," *Journal of Business Ethics*, 97 (2010): 51–69.

11. Singhapakdi, Vitell, and Franke, 17.

12. Damodar Suar and Rooplekha Khuntia, "Influence of Personal Values and Value Congruence on Unethical Practices and Work Behavior," *Journal of Business Ethics*, 97 (2010): 443–460.

13. "Lead the Way," *Spirit*, February 2011, 41.

14. B. Elango, Karen Paul, Sumit K. Kundu, and Shishir K. Paudel, "Organizational Ethics, Individual Ethics, and Ethical Intentions in International Decision-Making," *Journal of Business Ethics*, 97 (2010): 543–561.

15. T. W. Loe, L. Ferrell, and P. Mansfield, "A Review of Empirical Studies Assessing Ethical Decision Making in Business," *Journal of Business Ethics* 25 (2000): 185–204.

16. Steven Kaplan, Kurt Pany, Janet Samuels, and Jian Zhang, "An Examination of the Association between Gender and Reporting Intentions for Fraudulent Financial Reporting," *Journal of Business Ethics* 87, No. 1 (June 2009): 15–30.

17. Michael J. O'Fallon and Kenneth D. Butterfield, "A Review of the Empirical Ethical Decision-Making Literature: 1996–2003," *Journal of Business Ethics* 59 (July 2005): 375–413; P. M. J. Christie, J. I. G. Kwon, P. A. Stoeberl, and R. Baumhart, "A Cross-Cultural Comparison of Ethical Attitudes of Business Managers: India, Korea and the United States," *Journal of Business Ethics* 46 (September 2003): 263–287; G. Fleischman and S. Valentine, "Professionals' Tax Liability and Ethical Evaluations in an Equitable Relief Innocent Spouse Case," *Journal of Business Ethics* 42 (January 2003): 27–44; A. Singhapakdi, K. Karande, C. P. Rao, and S. J. Vitell, "How Important Are Ethics and Social Responsibility? A Multinational Study of Marketing Professionals," *European Journal of Marketing* 35 (2001): 133–152.

18. R. W. Armstrong, "The Relationship between Culture and Perception of Ethical Problems in International Marketing," *Journal of Business Ethics* 15 (November 1996): 1199–1208; J. Cherry, M. Lee, and C. S. Chien, "A Cross-Cultural Application of a Theoretical Model of Business Ethics: Bridging the Gap between Theory and Data," *Journal of Business Ethics* 44 (June 2003): 359–376; B. Kracher, A. Chatterjee,

and A. R. Lundquist, "Factors Related to the Cognitive Moral Development of Business Students and Business Professionals in India and the United States: Nationality, Education, Sex and Gender," *Journal of Business Ethics* 35 (February 2002): 255–268.

19. J. M. Larkin, "The Ability of Internal Auditors to Identify Ethical Dilemmas," *Journal of Business Ethics* 23 (February 2000): 401–409; D. Peterson, A. Rhoads, and B. C. Vaught, "Ethical Beliefs of Business Professionals: A Study of Gender, Age and External Factors," *Journal of Business Ethics* 31 (June 2001): 225–232; M. A. Razzaque and T. P. Hwee, "Ethics and Purchasing Dilemma: A Singaporean View," *Journal of Business Ethics* 35 (February 2002): 307–326.

20. B. Elango, Karen Paul, Sumit K. Kundu, Shishir K. Paudel, "Organizational Ethics, Individual Ethics, and Ethical Intentions in International Decision-Making," *Journal of Business Ethics*, 97 (2010): 543–561.

21. J. Cherry and J. Fraedrich, "An Empirical Investigation of Locus of Control and the Structure of Moral Reasoning: Examining the Ethical Decision-Making Processes of Sales Managers," *Journal of Personal Selling and Sales Management* 20 (Summer 2000): 173–188; M. C. Reiss and K. Mitra, "The Effects of Individual Difference Factors on the Acceptability of Ethical and Unethical Workplace Behaviors," *Journal of Business Ethics* 17 (October 1998): 1581–1593.

22. O. C. Ferrell and Linda Ferrell, "Role of Ethical Leadership in Organizational Performance," *Journal of Management Systems* 13 (2001): 64–78.

23. Barry Z. Posner, "Another Look at the Impact of Personal and Organizational Values Congruency," *Journal of Business Ethics*, 97 (2010): 535–541.

24. K. Praveen Parboteeah, Hsien Chun Chen, Ying-Tzu Lin, I-Heng Chen, Amber Y-P Lee, and Anyi Chung, "Establishing Organizational Ethical Climates: How Do Managerial Practices Work?" *Journal of Business Ethics*, 97 (2010): 599–611.

25. James Weber and Julie E. Seger, "Influences upon Organizational Ethical Subclimates: A Replication Study of a Single Firm at Two Points in Time," *Journal of Business Ethics* 41 (November 2002): 69–84.

26. Sean Valentine, Lynn Godkin, and Margaret Lucero, "Ethical Context, Organizational Commitment, and Person-Organization Fit," *Journal of Business Ethics* 41 (December 2002): 349–360.

27. Bruce H. Drake, Mark Meckler, and Debra Stephens, "Transitional Ethics: Responsibilities of Supervisors for Supporting Employee Development," *Journal of Business Ethics* 38 (June 2002): 141–155.

28. Ferrell and Gresham, "A Contingency Framework," 87–96.

29. R. C. Ford and W. D. Richardson, "Ethical Decision Making: A Review of the Empirical Literature," *Journal of Business Ethics* 13 (March 1994): 205–221; Loe, Ferrell, and Mansfield, "A Review of Empirical Studies."

30. National Business Ethics Survey, *How Employees Perceive Ethics at Work* (Washington, DC: Ethics Resource Center, 2000), 30.

31. "Employee Theft Solutions," The Shulman Center, http://www.employeetheftsolutions.com/ (accessed January 14, 2009).

32. Justin Lahart and Mark Whitehouse, "Economists' Group May Revamp Ethical Guide," *The Wall Street Journal*, January 7, 2011, http://online.wsj.com/article/SB10001424052748704415104576066 611532847124.html (accessed March 1, 2011).

33. Matthew Rosenberg and Maria Abi-Habib, "Afghan Officials Probed over Bank," *The Wall Street Journal*, February 1, 2011, http://online.wsj.com/article/SB10001424052748704254304576761 15780302300212.html (accessed March 1, 2011); Alissa J. Rubin and James Risen, "Losses at Afghan Bank Could Be $900 Billion," *The New York Times*, http://www.nytimes.com/2011/01/31/world/asia/31kabul.html?pagewanted=1&_r=1 (accessed March 1, 2011).

34. National Business Ethics Survey, 30.

35. Peter Verhezen, "Giving Voice in a Culture of Silence: From a Culture of Compliance to a Culture of Integrity," *Journal of Business Ethics* 96 (2010): 187–206.

36. R. Eric Reidenbach and Donald P. Robin, *Ethics and Profits* (Englewood Cliffs, NJ: Prentice-Hall, 1989), 92.

37. James B. Avey, Michael E. Palanski, and Fred O. Walumbwa, "When Leadership Goes Unnoticed: The Moderating Role of Follower Self-Esteem on the Relationship between Ethical Leadership and Follower Behavior," *Journal of Business Ethics* 98 (2011): 573–582.

38. Constance E. Bagley, "The Ethical Leader's Decision Tree," *Harvard Business Review*, January–February 2003, 18.

39. Serena Ng and Erik Holm, "Buffett Jolted as Aide Quits," *The Wall Street Journal*, March 31, 2011, A1–A2; Gina Chon and Serena Ng, "Mixed Signals Marked Sokol Meeting," *The Wall Street Journal*, April 2–3, 2011, B1–B2.

40. Choe San-hun, "Samsung Chairman Resigns," *The New York Times*, April 23, 2008, http://www.nytimes.com/2008/04/23/business/worldbusiness/23samsung.html?scp=1&sq=samsung%20lee&st=cse (accessed June 5, 2009); "About Samsung," http://www.samsung.com/us/aboutsamsung/index.html (accessed June 5, 2009).

41. Daniel J. Brass, Kenneth D. Butterfield, and Bruce C. Skaggs, "Relationship and Unethical Behavior: A Social Science Perspective," *Academy of Management Review* 23 (January 1998): 14–31.

42. Cam Caldwell, Linda A. Hayes, and Do Tien Long, "Leadership, Trustworthiness, and Ethical Stewardship," *Journal of Business Ethics* 96 (2010): 497–512.

43. From *Managing Risks for Corporate Integrity: How to Survive an Ethical Misconduct Disaster*, 1st edition, by Brewer, Chandler, and Ferrell. Copyright © 2006. Reprinted with permission of South-Western, a division of Thomson Learning.

44. J. M. Burns, *Leadership* (New York: Harper & Row, 1985).

45. Royston Greenwood, Roy Suddaby, and C. R. Hinings, "Theorizing Change: The Role of Professional Associations in the Transformation of Institutionalized Fields," *Academy of Management Journal* 45 (January 2002): 58–80.

46. Eric Pillmore, "How Tyco International Remade its Corporate Governance," speech at Wharton Business School, September 2006.

47. Stephen R. Covey, *The 7 Habits of Highly Effective People* (New York: Simon & Schuster, 1989).

48. Archie B. Carroll, "Ethical Leadership: From Moral Managers to Moral Leaders," in *Rights, Relationships and Responsibilities*, Vol. 1, ed. O. C. Ferrell, Sheb True, and Lou Pelton (Kennesaw, GA: Kennesaw State University, 2003), 7–17.

49. Andy Serwer, "Walmart: Bruised in Bentonville," *Fortune* online, April 4, 2005, http://money.cnn.com/magazines/fortune/fortune_archive/2005/04/18/8257005/index.htm (accessed August 17, 2009).

50. Thomas I. White, "Character Development and Business Ethics Education," in *Rights, Relationships and Responsibilities*, Vol. 1, ed. O. C. Ferrell, Sheb True, and Lou Pelton (Kennesaw, GA: Kennesaw State University, 2003), 137–166.

51. Carroll, "Ethical Leadership," 11.

52. Keith H. Hammonds, "Harry Kraemer's Moment of Truth," *Fast Company* online, December 19, 2007, www.fastcompany.com/online/64/kraemer.html (accessed August 17, 2009).

53. Carroll, "Ethical Leadership," 11.

54. "100 Best Companies to Work for: DreamWorks Animation SKG," *Fortune*, http://money.cnn.com/magazines/fortune/bestcompanies/2011/snapshots/10.html (accessed March 1, 2011).

55. Carroll, "Ethical Leadership," 12.

56. "Waste Management Named One of the World's Most Ethical Companies by Ethisphere Institute," Waste Management, March 22, 2010, http://www.wm.com/about/press-room/pr2010/20100322_WM_Named_One_of_the_Worlds_Most_Ethical_Companies_By_Ethisphere_Institute.pdf (accessed March 1, 2011); Marc Gunther,

"Waste Management's New Direction," *Fortune*, December 6, 2010, 103–108.

57. Brent Smith, Michael W. Grojean, Christian Resick, and Marcus Dickson, "Leaders, Values and Organizational Climate: Examining Leadership Strategies for Establishing an Organizational Climate Regarding Ethics," *Journal of Business Ethics*, as reported at "Research @ Rice: Lessons from Enron—Ethical Conduct Begins at the Top," Rice University, June 15, 2005, www.explore.rice.edu/explore/NewsBot.asp?MODE=VIEW&ID=7478&SnID=878108660 (accessed August 17, 2009)

58. "Our Core Values," Whole Foods, http://www.wholefoodsmarket.com/company/corevalues.php (accessed March 1, 2011).

59. Herb Baum and Tammy Kling, "Book Review: The Transparent Leader," in *Leadership Now*, http://www.leadershipnow.com/leadershop/0060565470.html (accessed August 17, 2009).

60. "2010's 100 Most Influential People in Business Ethics," *Ethisphere*, January 31, 2011, http://ethisphere.com/2010s-100-most-influential-people-in-business-ethics/ (accessed March 1, 2011).

61. "The 100 Most Influential People in Business Ethics," *Ethisphere*, Q4 2010, 36; "Retailer's Ethics Blog: 'A Remarkable Exercise in Transparency,'" *Ethikos*, September/October 2009, http://www.ethikospublication.com/html/bestbuy.html (accessed April 29 2011).

62. David Voreacos, Alex Nussbaum, and Greg Farrell, "Johnson and Johnson's Bitter Pills," *Bloomberg Businessweek*, April 4–April 10, 2011, 64–71.

Chapter 6

1. James R. Rest, *Moral Development Advances in Research and Theory* (New York: Praeger, 1986), 1.

2. "Business Leaders, Politicians and Academics Dub Corporate Irresponsibility 'An Attack on America from within,'" *Business Wire*, November 7, 2002, via Find Articles, http://findarticles.com/p/articles/mi_m0EIN/is_2002_Nov_7/ai_94631434 (accessed March 30, 2011).

3. "Let a million flowers bloom," *The Economist*, March 12, 2011, 80.

4. A. C. Ahuvia, "If Money Doesn't Make Us Happy, Why Do We Act as If It Does?," *Journal of Economic Psychology* 29 (2008): 491–507.

5. Abhijit Biswas, Jane W. Licata, Daryl McKee, Chris Pullig, and Christopher Daughtridge, "The Recycling Cycle: An Empirical Examination of Consumer Waste Recycling and Recycling Shopping Behaviors," *Journal of Public Policy & Marketing* 19 (2000): 93; Miguel Bastons, "The Role of Virtues in the Framing of Decisions," *Journal of Business Ethics* (2008): 395.

6. Miquel Bastons, "The Role of Virtues in the Framing of Decisions," *Journal of Business Ethics* (2008): 395.

7. "Court Says Businesses Liable for Harassing on the Job," *Commercial Appeal*, June 27, 1998, A1; Richard Brandt, *Ethical Theory* (Englewood Cliffs, NJ: Prentice-Hall, 1959), 253–254.

8. Harris Gardiner and Walt Bogdanich, "Drug tied to China had contaminant, FDA says," *The New York Times*, March 6, 2008, http://www.nytimes.com/2008/03/06/health/06heparin.html (accessed March 10, 2011).

9. J. J. C. Smart and B. Williams, *Utilitarianism: For and Against* (Cambridge, UK: Cambridge University Press, 1973), 4.

10. C. E. Harris, Jr., *Applying Moral Theories* (Belmont, CA: Wadsworth, 1986), 127–128.

11. Jessica Holzer and Shayndi Raice, "IBM Settles Bribery Charges," *The Wall Street Journal*, March 19, 2011, http://online.wsj.com/article/SB10001424052748704608504576208634150691292.html (accessed March 25, 2011).

12. Example adapted from Harris, *Applying Moral Theories*, 128–129.

13. Gerald F. Cavanaugh, Dennis J. Moberg, and Manuel Velasquez, "The Ethics of Organizational Politics," *Academy of Management Review* 6 (1981): 363–374; U.S. Bill of Rights, http://www.law.cornell.edu/constitution/constitution.billofrights.html (accessed August 18, 2009).

14. U.S. Bill of Rights, http://www.law.cornell.edu/constitution/constitution.billofrights.html (accessed August 18, 2009).

15. Marie Brenner, "The Man Who Knew Too Much," *Vanity Fair*, May 1996, available at http://www.jeffreywigand.com/vanityfair.php (accessed March 30, 2011).

16. Norman E. Bowie and Thomas W. Dunfee, "Confronting Morality in Markets," *Journal of Business Ethics* 38 (2002): 381–393.

17. "JetBlue cancels flights, to present 'Bill of Rights,'" CNN, February 19, 2007, http://money.cnn.com/2007/02/19/news/companies/jetblue/index.htm?postversion=2007021917&iid=EL (accessed March 23, 2011).

18. Immanuel Kant, "Fundamental Principles," 229.

19. Thomas E. Weber, "To Opt In or Opt Out: That Is the Question When Mulling Privacy," *The Wall Street Journal*, October 23, 2000, B1; Eric Markowitz, "Is 2011 the Year of a Digital Privacy Revolution?" *Inc.*, January 21, 2011, http://www.inc.com/articles/201101/is-2011-the-year-of-the-digital-privacy-revolution.html (accessed May 2, 2011).

20. R. Bateman, J. P. Fraedrich, and R. Iyer, "The Integration and Testing of the Janus-Headed Model within Marketing," *Journal of Business Research* 56 (2003): 587–596; J. B. DeConinck and W. F. Lewis, "The Influence of Deontological and Teleological Considerations and Ethical Culture on Sales Managers' Intentions to Reward or Punish Sales Force Behavior," *Journal of Business Ethics* 16 (1997): 497–506; J. Kujala, "A Multidimensional Approach to Finnish Managers' Moral Decision Making," *Journal of Business Ethics* 34 (2001): 231–254; K. C. Rallapalli, S. J. Vitell, and J. H. Barnes, "The Influence of Norms on Ethical Judgments and Intentions: An Empirical Study of Marketing Professionals," *Journal of Business Research* 43 (1998): 157–168; M. Shapeero, H. C. Koh, and L. N. Killough, "Underreporting and Premature Sign-Off in Public Accounting," *Managerial Auditing Journal* 18 (2003): 478–489.

21. William K. Frankena, *Ethics* (Englewood Cliffs: Prentice-Hall, 1963).

22. R. E. Reidenbach and D. P. Robin, "Toward the Development of a Multidimensional Scale for Improving Evaluations of Business Ethics," *Journal of Business Ethics* 9, no. 8 (1980): 639–653.

23. Patrick E. Murphy and Gene R. Laczniak, "Emerging Ethical Issues Facing Marketing Researchers," *Marketing Research* 4, no. 2 (1992): 6–11.

24. T. K. Bass and Barnett G. Brown, "Religiosity, Ethical Ideology, and Intentions to Report a Peer's Wrongdoing," *Journal of Business Ethics* 15, no. 11 (1996): 1161–1174; R. Z. Elias, "Determinants of Earnings Management Ethics among Accountants," *Journal of Business Ethics* 40, no. 1 (2002): 33–45; Y. Kim, "Ethical Standards and Ideology among Korean Public Relations Practitioners," *Journal of Business Ethics* 42, no. 3 (2003): 209–223; E. Sivadas, S. B. Kleiser, J. Kellaris, and R. Dahlstrom, "Moral Philosophy, Ethical Evaluations, and Sales Manager Hiring Intentions," *Journal of Personal Selling & Sales Management* 23, no. 1 (2003): 7–21.

25. Cheng-Li Huang and Bau-Guang Chang, "The Effects of Managers' Moral Philosophy on Project Decision under Agency Problem Conditions," *Journal of Business Ethics* (2010) 94: 595–611.

26. Manuel G. Velasquez, *Business Ethics Concepts and Cases*, 5th ed. (Upper Saddle River, NJ: Prentice-Hall, 2002), 135–136.

27. Ibid.

28. Adapted from Robert C. Solomon, "Victims of Circumstances? A Defense of Virtue Ethics in Business," *Business Ethics Quarterly* 13, no. 1 (2003): 43–62.

29. Ian Maitland, "Virtuous Markets: The Market as School of the Virtues," *Business Ethics Quarterly* (January 1997): 97.

30. Ibid.

31. Stefanie E. Naumann and Nathan Bennett, "A Case for Procedural Justice Climate: Development and Test of a Multilevel Model," *Academy of Management Journal* 43 (2000): 881–889.

32. Joel Brockner, "Making Sense of Procedural Fairness: How High Procedural Fairness Can Reduce or Heighten the Influence of Outcome Favorability," *Academy of Management Review* 27 (2002): 58–76.

33. "Nugget Markets Named #8 in *Fortune Magazine's* "100 Best Companies to Work for," January 20, 2011, http://www.nuggetmarket.com/press-release/100 (accessed March 10, 2011); "100 Best Companies to Work for 2010," *Fortune,* http://money.cnn.com/magazines/fortune/bestcompanies/2010/snapshots/5.html (accessed March 10, 2011).

34. John Fraedrich and O. C. Ferrell, "Cognitive Consistency of Marketing Managers in Ethical Situations," *Journal of the Academy of Marketing Science* 20 (1992): 245–252.

35. Manuel Velasquez, Claire Andre, Thomas Shanks, S. J. and Michael J. Meyer, "Thinking Ethically: A Framework for Moral Decision Making," *Issues in Ethics* (Winter 1996): 2–5.

36. Lawrence Kohlberg, "Stage and Sequence: The Cognitive Developmental Approach to Socialization," in *Handbook of Socialization Theory and Research,* ed. D. A. Goslin (Chicago: Rand McNally, 1969), 347–480.

37. Adapted from Kohlberg, "Stage and Sequence."

38. Clare M. Pennino, "Is Decision Style Related to Moral Development among Managers in the U.S.?," *Journal of Business Ethics* 41 (2002): 337–347.

39. K. M. Au and D. S. N. Wong, "The Impact of Guanxi on the Ethical Decision-Making Process of Auditors: An Exploratory Study on Chinese CPA's in Hong Kong," *Journal of Business Ethics* 28, no. 1 (2000): 87–93; D. P. Robin, G. Gordon, C. Jordan, and E. Reidenback, "The Empirical Performance of Cognitive Moral Development in Predicating Behavioral Intent," *Business Ethics Quarterly* 6, no. 4 (1996): 493–515; M. Shapeero, H. C. Koh, and L. N. Killough, "Underreporting and Premature Sign-Off in Public Accounting," *Managerial Auditing Journal* 18, no. 6 (1996): 478–489; N. Uddin and P. R. Gillett, "The Effects of Moral Reasoning and Self-Monitoring on CFO Intentions to Report Fraudulently on Financial Statements," *Journal of Business Ethics* 40, no. 1 (2002): 15–32.

40. Robbie Whelan, "Minkow to Plead Guilty in Lennar Insider-Trading Case," *The Wall Street Journal,* March 17, 2011, http://online.wsj.com/article/SB10001424052748703899704576204582698571822.html?mod=djem_jiewr_BE_domainid (accessed March 23, 2011).

41. "The Influence of Corporate Psychopaths on Corporate Social Responsibility and Organizational Commitment to Employees," *Journal of Business Ethics* (2010) 97: 1–19; Clive R. Boddy, Richard K. Ladyshewsley, and Peter Galvin, "The Implications of Corporate Psychopaths for Business and Society: An Initial Examination and a Call to Arms," *AJBBS* 1, no. 2 (2005): 30–40, http://www.mtpinnacle.com/pdfs/Psychopath.pdf (accessed May 3, 2011).

42. KPMG, "Fraud contagion shows no sign of abating," *Fraud Barometer,* June 2010, http://www.kpmg.com/AU/en/IssuesAndInsights/ArticlesPublications/Fraud-Barometer/Documents/Fraud-Barometer-June-2010-Readings.pdf (accessed March 23, 2011).

43. Eysenck, "Personality and Crime: Where Do We Stand?" *Psychology, Crime & Law* 2, no. 3 (1996): 143–152; Shelley Johnson Listwan, *Personality and Criminal Behavior: Reconsidering the Individual,* University of Cincinnati, Division of Criminal Justice, 2001, http://criminaljustice.cech.uc.edu/docs/dissertations/ShelleyJohnson.pdf (accessed August 18, 2009).

44. "The Influence of Corporate Psychopaths on Corporate Social Responsibility and Organizational Commitment to Employees," *Journal of Business Ethics.*

45. J. M. Rayburn and L. G. Rayburn, "Relationship between Machiavellianism and Type A Personality and Ethical-Orientation," *Journal of Business Ethics* 15, no. 11 (1996): 1209–1219.

46. Quoted in Marjorie Kelly, "The Ethics Revolution," *Business Ethics* (Summer 2005): 6.

47. O. C. Ferrell and Larry G. Gresham, "A Contingency Framework for Understanding Ethical Decision Making in Marketing," *Journal of Marketing* 49 (2002): 261–274.

48. Thomas I. White, "Character Development and Business Ethics Education," in *Fulfilling Our Obligation: Perspectives on Teaching Business Ethics,* ed. Sheb L. True, Linda Ferrell, and O. C. Ferrell (Kennesaw, GA: Kennesaw State University Press, 2005), 165.

49. Ibid., 165–166.

Chapter 7

1. J. W. Lorsch, "Managing Culture: The Invisible Barrier to Strategic Change," *California Management Review* 28 (1986): 95–109.

2. "Diversity and Inclusion," Mutual of Omaha, http://www.mutualofomaha.com/about/company/diversity/ (accessed March 7, 2011).

3. Richard L. Daft, *Organizational Theory and Design* (Cincinnati: South-Western, 2007).

4. Stanley M. Davis, quoted in Alyse Lynn Booth, "Who Are We?" *Public Relations Journal* (July 1985): 13–18.

5. SWAMEDIA, Southwest Airlines Story Leads, http://www.swamedia.com/ (accessed March 15, 2011).

6. "A Study of the Ford Motor Co. Turnaround 2010," Business Value Group LLC, September 2010, http://www.bvgintl.com/wp-content/uploads/2010/10/FordMotorCoWhitePaperI.pdf (accessed March 15, 2011); "GM and Ford: Roadmaps for Recovery," *BusinessWeek* online, March 14, 2006, http://www.businessweek.com/print/investor/content/mar2006/pi20060314_416862.htm (accessed March 15, 2011).

7. Ariel Schwartz, "Ford Gives Dealers a Blueprint for Sustainability," *Fast Company,* February 16, 2010, http://www.fastcompany.com/1551705/ford-gives-dealerships-a-blueprint-for-sustainability (accessed March 7, 2011).

8. Abstracted from "Enhancing Compliance with Sarbanes–Oxley 404," Quantisoft, http://www.quantisoft.com/Industries/Ethics.htm (accessed March 15, 2011).

9. Taras Vasyl, Julie Rowney, and Piers Steel, "Half a Century of Measuring Culture: Approaches, Challenges, Limitations, and Suggestions Based on the Analysis of 121 Instruments for Quantifying Culture," white paper, 2008, Haskayne School of Business, University of Calgary, http://www.ucalgary.ca/~taras/_private/Half_a_Century_of_Measuring_Culture.pdf (accessed March 15, 2011).

10. Ibid.

11. Geert Hofstede, Bram Neuijen, Denise Daval Ohayv, and Geert Sanders, "Measuring Organizational Cultures: A Qualitative and Quantitative Study across Twenty Cases," *Administrative Science Quarterly* 35, no. 2 (1990): 286–316.

12. "Culture of trust," IBM, http://www.ibm.com/ibm/responsibility/trust.shtml (accessed March 8, 2011); IBM, *Basic Conduct*

Guidelines, http://www.ibm.com/investor/pdf/BCG_Feb_2011_ English_CE.pdf (accessed March 8, 2011).

13. Cam Caldwell, Linda A. Hayes, and Do Tien Long, "Leadership, Trustworthiness, and Ethical Stewardship," *Journal of Business Ethics* 96 (2010): 497–512.

14. N. K. Sethia and M. A. Von Glinow, "Arriving at Four Cultures by Managing the Reward System," in *Gaining Control of the Corporate Culture* (San Francisco: Jossey-Bass, 1985), 409.

15. "UPS Fact Sheet," UPS, http://www.pressroom.ups.com/ Fact+Sheets/UPS+Fact+Sheet (accessed March 8, 2011).

16. "UPS deeply rooted in going green: Some of the many ways UPS conserves," UPS, May 2008, http://compass.ups.com/article. aspx?id=153 (accessed March 15, 2011); "UPS Fact Sheet," UPS, http://www.pressroom.ups.com/Fact+Sheets/UPS+Fact+Sheet (accessed March 8, 2011).

17. "100 Best Companies to Work for," *Fortune,* February 7, 2011, 91–101.

18. *2005 National Business Ethics Survey: How Employees Perceive Ethics at Work,* 20. Copyright © 2006, Ethics Resource Center (ERC). Used with permission of the ERC, 1747 Pennsylvania Ave. NW, Suite 400, Washington, DC 2006, www.ethics.org.

19. Cassandra Sweet and Guy Chazan, "BP Faces New Hit over Spill in Alaska," *The Wall Street Journal,* November 20–21, 2011, B1.

20. Susan M. Heathfield, "Five Tips for Effective Employee Recognition," http://humanresources.about.com/od/ rewardrecognition/a/recognition_tip.htm (accessed March 15, 2011).

21. "Recognition Programs," FedEx, http://about.fedex.designcdt. com/corporate_responsibility/our_people/recognition_programs (accessed March 8, 2011).

22. Isabelle Maignan, O. C. Ferrell, and Thomas Hult, "Corporate Citizenship, Cultural Antecedents and Business Benefit," *Journal of the Academy of Marketing Science* 27 (1999): 455–469.

23. Susanne Arvidsson, "Communication of Corporate Social Responsibility: A Study of the Views of Management Teams in Large Companies," *Journal of Business Ethics* 96 (2010): 339–354.

24. R. Eric Reidenbach and Donald P. Robin, *Ethics and Profits* (Englewood Cliffs, NJ: Prentice-Hall, 1989), 92.

25. "IKEA Named as One of the 'World's Most Ethical Companies' for Fourth Consecutive Year in 2010," *PRNewswire,* March 29, 2010, http://www.prnewswire.com/news-releases/ikea-named-as-one- of-the-worlds-most-ethical-companies-for-fourth-consecutive- year-in-2010-89384407.html (accessed March 8, 2011); "IKEA U.S. Community Relations guidelines," http://www.ikea.com/ms/ en_US/ikea_near_you/woodbridge/new_wood_app.pdf (accessed March 8, 2011).

26. E. Sutherland and D. R. Cressey, *Principles of Criminology,* 8th ed. (Chicago: Lippincott, 1970), 114.

27. O. C. Ferrell and Larry G. Gresham, "A Contingency Framework for Understanding Ethical Decision Making in Marketing," *Journal of Marketing* 49 (1985): 90–91.

28. Edward Wong, "Some at Shuttle Fuel Tank Plant See Quality Control Problems," *The New York Times,* February 18, 2003, http:// www.nytimes.com/2003/02/18/national/nationalspecial/18ORLE. html (accessed March 8, 2011); *Columbia Crew Survival Investigation Report,* NASA, http://www.nasa.gov/pdf/298870main_ SP-2008-565.pdf (accessed March 8, 2011).

29. "Ethics and Nonprofits," *Stanford Social Innovation Review* (Summer 2009), http://www.ssireview.org/articles/entry/ethics_ and_nonprofits (accessed March 15, 2011).

30. "Whistle-blower Debate Heats up," *CFO,* February 11, 2011, http:// www.cfo.com/article.cfm/14554934/c_14556017 (accessed March 8, 2011).

31. Matthew Goldstein, "Ex-Employees at Heart of Stanford Financial Probe," *BusinessWeek,* February 13, 2009, http://www.businessweek. com/bwdaily/dnflash/content/feb2009/db20090213_848258.htm (accessed March 15, 2011).

32. Thomas S. Mulligan, "Whistle-Blower Recounts Enron Tale," *The Los Angeles Times,* March 16, 2006, via http://www.whistleblowers. org/storage/whistleblowers/documents/whistle_blower_-_la_times. pdf (accessed March 15, 2011).

33. John W. Schoen, "Split CEO-Chairman Job, Says Panel," MSNBC. com, January 9, 2003, http://www.msnbc.com/news/857171.asp (accessed June 27, 2006).

34. Michael Barbaro, "Walmart Says Official Misused Company Funds," *The Washington Post,* July 15, 2005, http://www. washingtonpost.com/wp-dyn/content/article/2005/07/14/ AR2005071402055.html (accessed March 15, 2011).

35. "Qui Tam Tips: How to File a Whistle-blower Complaint," http:// www.jameshoyer.com/practice_qui_tam.html?se= Overture (accessed March 15, 2011).

36. James Sandler, "The war on whistle-blowers," *Salon,* November 1, 2007, http://www.salon.com/news/ feature/2007/11/01/whistleblowers (accessed March 8, 2011).

37. Wim Vandekerckhove and Eva E. Tsahuridu, "Risky Rescues and the Duty to Blow the Whistle," *Journal of Business Ethics* 97 (2010): 365–380.

38. Ethics Resource Center, *2009 National Business Ethics Survey,* 36.

39. Paula Dwyer and Dan Carney, with Amy Borrus, Lorraine Woellert, and Christopher Palmeri, "Year of the Whistle-blower," *BusinessWeek,* December 16, 2002, 106–110.

40. Paula J. Desiom, "Federal Whistle-blower Rights Increase under the Stimulus Law," *Ethics Today,* February 18, 2009, http://www.ethics. org/ethics-today/0209/policy-report3.html (accessed March 15, 2011).

41. Darren Dahl, "Learning to Love Whistle-blowers," *Inc.,* March 2006, 21–23.

42. Muel Kaptein, "From Inaction to External Whistle-blowing: The Influence of the Ethical Culture of Organizations on Employee Responses to Observed Wrongdoing," *Journal of Business Ethics* 98 (2011): 513–530.

43. Alan Yuspeh, "Speaking up: Letter from the Editor," *Ethisphere,* Q1, 2010, 6.

44. John R. P. French and Bertram Ravin, "The Bases of Social Power," in *Group Dynamics: Research and Theory,* ed. Dorwin Cartwright (Evanston, IL: Row, Peterson, 1962), 607–623.

45. Frank Reynolds, "Ex-WorldCom CFO Gets Five Years for Role in $11 B Fraud," Findlaw, August 19, 2005, http://news.findlaw.com/ andrews/bf/cod/20050819/20050819sullivan.html (accessed August 20, 2009).

46. Cam Caldwell and Mayra Canuto-Carranco, "'Organizational Terrorism' and Moral Choices: Exercising Voice When the Leader Is the Problem," *Journal of Business Ethics* 97 (2010): 159–171.

47. Clayton Alderfer, *Existence, Relatedness, and Growth* (New York: Free Press, 1972), 42–44.

48. Pablo Zoghbi-Manrique-de-Lara, "Do Unfair Procedures Predict Employees' Ethical Behavior by Deactivating Formal Regulations?" *Journal of Business Ethics* 94 (2010): 411–425.

49. International Labor Conference, *The cost of coercion: Global Report under the follow-up to the ILO Declaration on Fundamental Principles and Rights at Work,* 98th session, Report I(B) (Geneva: International Labor Office, 2009), 42.

50. Kathy Lund Dean, Jeri Mullins Beggs, and Timothy P. Keane, "Mid-level Managers, Organizational Context, and (Un)ethical Encounters," *Journal of Business Ethics* 97 (2010): 51–69.

51. Stanley Holmes, "Cleaning up Boeing," *BusinessWeek* online, March 13, 2006, http://www.businessweek.com/print/magazine/content/06_11/b3975088.htm?chan=gl (accessed March 15, 2011).

52. Joseph A. Belizzi and Ronald W. Hasty, "Supervising Unethical Sales Force Behavior: How Strong Is the Tendency to Treat Top Sales Performers Leniently?" *Journal of Business Ethics* 43 (2003): 337–351.

53. John Fraedrich and O. C. Ferrell, "Cognitive Consistency of Marketing Managers in Ethical Situations," *Journal of the Academy of Marketing Science* 20 (1992): 243–252.

54. B. Elango, Karen Paul, Sumit K. Kundu, and Shishir K. Paudel, "Organizational Ethics, Individual Ethics, and Ethical Intentions in International Decision Making," *Journal of Business Ethics* 97 (2010): 543–561.

55. Damodar Suar and Rooplekha Khuntia, "Influence of Personal Values and Value Congruence on Unethical Practices and Work Behavior," *Journal of Business Ethics* 97 (2010): 443–460.

56. Michael Martinez, "San Francisco bans Happy Meals with toys," CNN, November 9, 2010, http://articles.cnn.com/2010-11-09/us/california.fast.food.ban_1_meal-combinations-apple-dippers-yale-university-s-rudd-center?_s=PM:US (accessed March 8, 2011); "Where Happy Meals Are Illegal," ABC News, April 28, 2010, http://abcnews.go.com/Business/video/happy-meals-illegal-in-california-county-10497027 (accessed March 8, 2011).

57. Sora Song, "School's out for soda," *Time*, May 8, 2010, http://www.time.com/time/question/sora_song_060504.html (accessed March 8, 2011).

Chapter 8

1. Bob Lewis, "Survival Guide: The Moral Compass—Corporations Aren't Moral Agents, Creating Interesting Dilemmas for Business Leaders," *InfoWorld*, March 11, 2002, http://www.findarticles.com (accessed March 15, 2011).

2. "2010 World's Most Ethical Companies," *Ethisphere*, Q4, 30–31.

3. Jean Eaglesham and Jessica Holzer, "Schapiro Defends against GOP Fire," *The Wall Street Journal*, March 10, 2011, C1; Carla Main, "Hedge-Fund Survey, Popcorn, Energy Bill: Compliance," *Bloomberg Businessweek*, March 11, 2011, http://www.businessweek.com/news/2011-03-11/hedge-fund-survey-popcorn-energy-bill-compliance.html (accessed March 14, 2011).

4. Indra Nooyi, "Business Has a Job to Do: Rebuild Trust," April 22, 2009, http://www.money.cnn.tv/2009/04/19/news/companies/nooyi.fortune/index.htm (accessed March 15, 2011).

5. Linda K. Trevino and Stuart Youngblood, "Bad Apples in Bad Barrels: Causal Analysis of Ethical Decision Making Behavior," *Journal of Applied Psychology* 75 (1990): 378–385.

6. Caroline Winter, David Glovin, and Jennifer Daniel, "A Guide to the Galleon Case," *Bloomberg Businessweek*, March 10, 2011, http://www.businessweek.com/magazine/content/11_12/b4220079522428.htm (accessed March 14, 2011); Ashby Jones, "Raj Opening Statements: 'Tomorrow's Trades Today' vs. 'Shoe-Leather Research,'" *The Wall Street Journal*, March 9, 2011, http://blogs.wsj.com/law/2011/03/09/raj-opening-statements-tomorrows-trades-today-vs-shoe-leather-research/?KEYWORDS=rajaratnam (accessed March 14, 2011).

7. Trevino and Youngblood, "Bad Apples in Bad Barrels."

8. Ibid.

9. Brad Stone and Bruce Einhorn, "Baidu China," *Bloomberg Businessweek*, November 15–21, 2010, 60–67.

10. Constance E. Bagley, "The Ethical Leader's Decision Tree," *Harvard Business Review* (February 2003): 18–19.

11. Bella L. Galperin, Rebecca J. Bennett, and Karl Aquino, "Status Differentiation and the Protean Self: A Social-Cognitive Model of Unethical Behavior in Organizations," *Journal of Business Ethics* 98 (2011): 407–424.

12. "Warren Buffett's Berkshire Hathaway Letter to Shareholders," http://www.berkshirehathaway.com/letters/2010ltr.pdf (accessed March 14, 2011).

13. "Trust in the workplace: 2010 Ethics & Workplace Survey," Deloitte, http://www.deloitte.com/assets/Dcom-UnitedStates/Local%20Assets/Documents/us_2010_Ethics_and_Workplace_Survey_report_071910.pdf (accessed March 15, 2011).

14. David Gauthier-Villars, "Rogue French Trader Sentenced to Three Years," *The Wall Street Journal*, October 6, 2010, A1.

15. "Conducting Ourselves Ethically and Transparently," Merck, http://www.merck.com/corporate-responsibility/business-ethics-transparency/approach.html (accessed March 15, 2011).

16. "Limiting Exposure to Fraud and Corporate Wastage with Next Generation GRC Applications," OCEG, http://www.oceg.org/event/limiting-exposure-fraud-and-corporate-wastage-next-generation-grc-applications (accessed March 15, 2011).

17. "Global Survey Shows Business Fraud Up," *Corporate Compliance Insights*, May 19, 2010, http://www.corporatecomplianceinsights.com/2010/global-survey-shows-business-fraud-up-boards-have-increased-concern-about-liability/?pfstyle=wp (accessed March 15, 2011).

18. Barry Z. Posner, "Another Look at the Impact of Personal and Organizational Values Congruency," *Journal of Business Ethics* 97 (2010): 535–541.

19. Frances Chua and Asheq Rahman, "Institutional Pressures and Ethical Reckoning by Business Corporations," *Journal of Business Ethics* 98 (2011): 307–329.

20. KPMG Forensic Integrity Survey 2008–2009, http://www.kpmg.com.br/publicacoes/forensic/Integrity_Survey_2008_2009.pdf (accessed March 15, 2011).

21. Christopher Sindik, "50 Banking & Insurance Industries Companies," *Ethisphere*, Q4, 15–17.

22. Mark S. Schwartz, "A Code of Ethics for Corporate Code of Ethics," *Journal of Business Ethics* 41 (2002): 37.

23. Ibid.

24. Joseph A. McKinney, Tisha L. Emerson, and Mitchell J. Neubert, "The Effects of Ethical Codes on Ethical Perceptions of Actions toward Stakeholders," *Journal of Business Ethics* 97 (2010): 505–516.

25. "Code of Ethics," American Society of Civil Engineers, http://www.asce.org/Leadership-and-Management/Ethics/Code-of-Ethics/ (accessed March 15, 2011).

26. "Kao Named One of the 'World's Most Ethical Companies' for Four Consecutive Years," Kao, March 23, 2010, http://www.kao.com/jp/en/corp_news/2010/20100323_001.html (accessed March 15, 2011); "Kao receives Environmental Technology Award from JCIA," Kao, http://www.kao.com/jp/en/corp_csr/topics/eco_activities_20090617_001.html (accessed March 15, 2011); "Special Advertising Section—Japan 3.0: Serving the Global Community," *Fortune*, S15–S15.

27. *National Business Ethics Survey 2007*, 39.

28. "USSC Commissioner John Steer Joins with Compliance and Ethics Executives from Leading U.S. Companies to Address Key Compliance, Business Conduct and Governance Issues," *Society for Corporate Compliance and Ethics*, PR Newswire, October 31, 2005.

29. "The Power of ECOA Membership," Ethics & Compliance Officer Association, http://www.theecoa.org/imis15/Documents/ECOA-Global-Membership-2010.pdf (accessed March 14, 2011).

30. Jim Nortz, "Compliance and Ethics Officers: A Survival Guide for the Economic Downturn," March 10, 2009, http://www.corporatecomplianceinsights.com/2010/compliance-and-ethics-officers-surviving-economic-downturn/ (accessed March 15, 2011).

31. Anne M. Simmons, "Want to Avoid Unpleasant Compliance Surprises? Embrace a Strong Whistle-Blowing Policy," January 8, 2009, http://ethisphere.com/want-to-avoid-unpleasant-compliance-surprises-embrace-a-strong-whistle-blowing-policy/ (accessed March 15, 2011).

32. "Combat Fraud of Almost $1 Trillion," April 17, 2009, http://ethicaladvocate.blogspot.com/2009_04_01_archive.html (accessed March 15, 2011).

33. Bob Grant, "NSF adopts new ethics rules," *The Scientist*, September 3, 2009, http://www.the-scientist.com/blog/display/55962/ (accessed March 15, 2011); Mackenzie Martin, "National Science Foundation research grants to require ethics training," *The Minnesota Daily*, http://www.mndaily.com/2009/09/27/national-science-foundation-research-grants-require-ethics-training# (accessed March 15, 2011).

34. Tom Parfitt, "Vladimir Putin orders ethics training for drivers with blue flashing lights," guardian.co.uk, December 9, 2010, http://www.guardian.co.uk/world/2010/dec/09/vladimir-putin-blue-flashing-lights-russia (accessed March 15, 2011).

35. Linda Ferrell and O. C. Ferrell, *Ethical Business* (DK Essential Managers Series, May 4, 2009), 1–72.

36. Debbie Thorne LeClair and Linda Ferrell, "Innovation in Experiential Business Ethics Training," *Journal of Business Ethics* 23 (2000): 313–322.

37. David Slovin, "The Case for Anonymous Hotlines," *Risk & Insurance*, April 15, 2007, FindArticles, http://findarticles.com/p/articles/mi_m0BJK/is_5_18/ai_n27221119/ (accessed March 15, 2011).

38. Mael Kaptein, "Guidelines for the Development of an Ethics Safety Net," *Journal of Business Ethics* 41 (2002): 217.

39. Ethics Resource Center, *Research Brief from the 2009 NBES*, 15.

40. *National Business Ethics Survey 2007*, 6.

41. Jess Bravin, "Justices Extend Protection over Workplace Retaliation," *The Wall Street Journal*, January 25, 2011, B1.

42. Curt S. Jordan, "Lessons in Organizational Compliance: A Survey of Government-Imposed Compliance Programs," *Preventive Law Reporter* (Winter 1994): 7.

43. Lori T. Martens and Kristen Day, "Five Common Mistakes in Designing and Implementing a Business Ethics Program," *Business and Society Review* 104 (1999): 163–170.

Chapter 9

1. Muel Kaptein, "Toward Effective Codes: Testing the Relationship with Unethical Behavior," *Journal of Business Ethics* 99 (2011): 233–251.

2. O. C. Ferrell and Michael D. Hartline, *Marketing Strategy*, 5th ed. (Mason, OH: South-Western Cengage Learning, 2011): 324; *CR's 100 Best Corporate Citizens 2010*, http://www.thecro.com/files/CR100Best.pdf (accessed March 22, 2011).

3. Muel Kaptein, "Guidelines for the Development of an Ethics Safety Net," *Journal of Business Ethics* 41 (2002): 217–234.

4. "The 100 Most Influential People in Business Ethics," *Ethisphere*, 2010, Q4, 37; "Green Index," Timberland, http://community.timberland.com/Earthkeeping/Green-Index (accessed March 22, 2011); Andrew Clark, "Timberland boss Jeffrey Swartz puts the boot in—over his own failures," guardian.co.uk, March 18, 2010, http://www.guardian.co.uk/business/2010/mar/18/jeffrey-swartz-timberland (accessed March 22, 2011).

5. John Rosthorn, "Business Ethics Auditing—More Than a Stakeholder's Toy," *Journal of Business Ethics* 27 (2000): 9–19.

6. Debbie Thorne, O. C. Ferrell, and Linda Ferrell, *Business and Society: A Strategic Approach to Corporate Citizenship*, 3rd ed. (Boston: Houghton Mifflin, 2008).

7. Rosthorn, "Business Ethics Auditing."

8. *Walmart 2009 Global Sustainability Report*, http://walmartstores.com/sites/sustainabilityreport/2009/ (accessed September 27, 2011).

9. "Accountability," Business for Social Responsibility, http://www.bsr.org/BSRResources/WhitePaperDetail.cfm?DocumentID=259 (accessed February 13, 2003).

10. Marcy Gordon, "SEC Reaches $25M Fraud Settlement with Diebold," *ABC News*, June 2, 2010, http://abcnews.go.com/Business/wireStory?id=10807747 (accessed March 22, 2011).

11. Marcus Selart and Svein Tvedt Johansen, "Ethical Decision Making in Organizations: The Role of Leadership Stress," *Journal of Business Ethics* 99 (2011): 129–143.

12. Anke Arnaud, "Conceptualizing and Measuring Ethical Work Climate," *Business & Society* 49 (2010): 345–358.

13. Kevin J. Sobnosky, "The Value-Added Benefits of Environmental Auditing," *Environmental Quality Management* 9 (1999): 25–32.

14. "Accountability," Business for Social Responsibility.

15. Trey Buchholz, "Auditing Social Responsibility Reports: The Application of Financial Auditing Standards," Colorado State University, professional paper, November 28, 2000, 3.

16. "Accountability," Business for Social Responsibility.

17. "The World's Most Admired Companies," *Fortune*, March 21, 2011, 139–146.

18. "The 100 Most Influential People in Business Ethics," *Ethisphere*; Stephanie Rosenbloom, "Walmart Unveils Plan to Make Supply Chain Greener," *The New York Times*, February 25, 2010, http://www.nytimes.com/2010/02/26/business/energy-environment/26walmart.html (accessed March 22, 2011).

19. John Pearce, *Measuring Social Wealth* (London: New Economics Foundation, 1996), as reported in Warren Dow and Roy Crowe, *What Social Auditing Can Do for Voluntary Organizations* (Vancouver: Volunteer Vancouver, July 1999), 8.

20. Colin Barr, "Obama Talks Tough on CEO Pay," February 4, 2009, http://money.cnn.com/2009/02/04/news/obama.exec.pay.fortune/index.htm (accessed March 22, 2011); "Executive Comp and Governance Provisions of Dodd–Frank Act," *Business Ethics*, July 22, 2010, http://business-ethics.com/2010/07/22/1640-executive-compensation-and-corporate-governance-provisions-of-the-dodd-frank-act/ (accessed March 22, 2011).

21. "The Effect of Published Reports of Unethical Conduct on Stock Prices," reported in "Business Ethics," Business for Social Responsibility, http://www.bsr.org/BSRResources/WhitePaperDetail.cfm?DocumentID=270 (accessed March 5, 2003).

22. Ellen Byron and Joann S. Lublin, "Probe Fears Hit Avon Shares," *The Wall Street Journal*, April 14, 2010, http://online.wsj.com/article/SB10001424052702304604204575182402303199376.html (accessed March 24, 2011).

23. Penelope Patsuris, "The Corporate Accounting Scandal Sheet," *Forbes* online, August 26, 2002, www.forbes.com/2002/07/25/accountingtracker.html (accessed September 3, 2009).

24. David L. Levy, Halina Szejnwald Brown, and Martin de Jong, "The Contested Politics of Corporate Governance: The Case of the Global Reporting Initiative," *Business & Society* 49 (March 2010): 88–115.

25. "What is GRI," Global Reporting Initiative, http://www.globalreporting.org/AboutGRI/WhatIsGRI/ (accessed March 23, 2011).

26. "FAQS," Global Reporting Initiative, http://www.globalreporting.org/AboutGRI/FAQs/FAQSustainabilityReporting.htm (accessed March 23, 2011).

27. "What is GRI," Global Reporting Initiative.

28. "Burgundy Book (GRC Assessment Tools)," OCEG, http://www.oceg.org/resource/burgundy-book-grc-evaluation-tool (accessed March 23, 2011).

29. "Certification of Capabilities and Individuals," OCEG, http://www.oceg.org/certification (accessed March 23, 2011).

30. Risako Morimoto, John Ash, and Chris Hope, "Corporate Social Responsibility Audit: From Theory to Practice," *Journal of Business Ethics* 62 (2005): 315–325.

31. The methodology in this section was adapted from Thorne, Ferrell, and Ferrell, *Business and Society.*

32. "Audit Committee Charter," The Coca-Cola Company, http://www.thecoca-colacompany.com/investors/governance/audit.html (accessed March 24, 2011).

33. Ethics Resource Center, "Mission and Values," http://www.ethics.org/page/erc-mission-and-values (accessed September 3, 2009).

34. "Verification," Business for Social Responsibility, http://www.bsr.org/BSRResources/White PaperDetail.cfm?DocumentID=440 (accessed February 13, 2003).

35. "Ethical Statement," Social Audit, SocialAudit.org, http://www.socialaudit.org/pages/ethical.htm (accessed March 4, 2003).

36. "Our Five Core Values," Franklin Energy, http://www.franklinenergy.com/corevalues.html (accessed March 24, 2011).

37. "Verification," Business for Social Responsibility.

38. "Audit and Evaluation," Open Compliance and Ethics Group, http://www.oceg.org/view/15839 (accessed September 3, 2009).

39. "Ethical Statement," Social Audit.

40. "About Us: The Environment," National Grid, https://www.nationalgridus.com/niagaramohawk/about_us/environment.asp (accessed March 24, 2011).

41. Judith L. Walls, Phillip H. Phan, and Pascual Berrone, "Measuring Environmental Strategy: Construct Development, Reliability, and Validity," *Business & Society* 50 (2011): 71–115.

42. "Verification," Business for Social Responsibility.

43. Green Mountain Coffee, http://www.greenmountaincoffee.com (accessed June 11, 2009).

44. Buchholz, "Auditing Social Responsibility Reports," 15.

45. Willem Landman, Johann Mouton, and Khanyisa Nevhutalu, "Chris Hani Baragwanath Hospital Ethics Audit," Ethics Institute of South Africa, 2001, http://ethicssa.intoweb.co.za/UserFiles/ethicssa.intoweb.co.za//CHBHFinalReport.pdf (accessed September 3, 2009).

46. "Verification," Business for Social Responsibility.

47. "Introduction to Corporate Social Responsibility," Business for Social Responsibility, http://www.bsr.org/BSRResources/WhitePaperDetail.cfm?Document ID=138 (accessed March 5, 2003).

48. Landman, Mouton, and Nevhutalu, "Chris Hani Baragwanath Hospital Ethics Audit."

49. "Introduction to Corporate Social Responsibility," Business for Social Responsibility.

50. Liz Gunnison, "The Best and Worst CEOs Ever," *Condé Nast Portfolio,* May 9, 2009, 44.

51. "Accountability," Business for Social Responsibility.

52. Ibid.

53. Ethics and Compliance Officer Association, http://www.theecoa.org (accessed June 18, 2009).

54. "Verification," Business for Social Responsibility.

55. Ibid.

56. "Independent Assurance Report," Siemens, http://www.siemens.com/sustainability/report/09/pool/pdf/siemens_sr09_independentassurancereport.pdf (accessed March 23, 2011).

57. Nicole Dando and Tracey Swift, "From Methods to Ideologies," *Journal of Corporate Citizenship,* December 2002, via http://goliath.ecnext.com/coms2/gi_0199-1001798/From-methods-to-ideologies-closing.html (accessed March 24, 2011), 81.

58. Buchholz, "Auditing Social Responsibility Reports," 16–18.

59. Ibid., 19–20.

60. "Accountability," Business for Social Responsibility.

61. Buchholz, "Auditing Social Responsibility Reports," 19–20.

62. Mouton, "Chris Hani Baragwanath Hospital Ethics Audit."

63. "OCEG 2005 Benchmarking Study Key Findings," Open Compliance Ethics Group, http://www.oceg.org/Details/18594 (accessed September 3, 2009).

64. "2010 Award Recipients," BBB, http://www.bbb.org/international-torch-awards/2010-awards.html (accessed March 23, 2011).

65. International Corporate Responsibility Survey, 2008, KPMG, http://www.kpmg.com/SiteCollectionDocuments/International-corporate-responsibility-survey-2008_v2.pdf (accessed June 17, 2009), 28.

66. International Corporate Responsibility Survey, 2008, KPMG, http://www.kpmg.com/SiteCollectionDocuments/International-corporate-responsibility-survey-2008_v2.pdf (accessed June 17, 2009).

67. Buchholz, "Auditing Social Responsibility Reports," 1.

68. Sandra Waddock and Neil Smith, "Corporate Responsibility Audits: Doing Well by Doing Good," *Sloan Management Review* 41 (2000): 75–83.

69. Buchholz, "Auditing Social Responsibility Reports," 1.

70. Waddock and Smith, "Corporate Responsibility Audits."

71. J. C. Collins and J. I. Porras, *Built to Last: Successful Habits of Visionary Companies* (New York: HarperCollins, 1997).

72. Waddock and Smith, "Corporate Responsibility Audits."

Chapter 10

1. Philip R. Cateora, Mary C. Gilly, and John L. Graham, *International Marketing,* 15th ed. (New York: McGraw-Hill Irwin, 2011), 109–110.

2. Linda K. Trevino and Katherine A. Nelson, *Managing Business Ethics,* 3rd ed. (Hoboken, NJ: John Wiley & Sons, Inc., 2004), 319.

3. Cateora, Gilly, and Graham, *International Marketing,* 110–111.

4. Ibid.

5. "Court Rules against Part of Walmart Code," Blog.WakeupWalMart.com, http://blog.wakeupwalmart.com/ufcw/2005/06/court_rules_aga.html (accessed June 22, 2009).

6. The Heart of Hinduism, http://hinduism.iskcon.com/index.htm (accessed March 24, 2011).

7. Mecca Centric Dawa Group, "Islamic virtues from the Quran," http://www.2muslims.com/directory/Detailed/224066.shtml (accessed March 24, 2011).

8. Gordon B. Hinckley, *Standing for Something: Ten Neglected Virtues That Will Heal Our Hearts and Homes,* 1st ed. (New York: Times Books, 2000).

9. Unit Six: The Four Immeasurables, http://www.buddhanet.net/e-learning/buddhism/bs-s15.htm (accessed March 24, 2011).

10. John (Jack) Ruhe and Monle Lee, "Teaching Ethics in International Business Courses: The Impacts of Religions," *Journal of Teaching in International Business* 19, no. 4 (2008); Andrew Wilson, editor, *World Scripture: A Comparative Anthology of Sacred Texts,* A project of the international religious foundation (Paragon House: New York, 1995).

11. "Briefing after Mubarak," *The Economist,* February 19–25, 2011, 47–53.

12. "The autumn of the patriarchs," *The Economist,* February 19, 2011, 47–49; "Calling in the big guns," *The Economist,* March 19, 2011, 56.

13. Nancy Gibbs, "The Day the Earth Moved," *Time,* March 28, 2011, 26; Hannah Beech, "How Japan Will Reawaken," *Time,* March 28, 2011, 42–47.

14. "What Happens When Countries Go Bankrupt?" *TimeTurk: English,* November 5, 2008, http://en.timeturk.com/

What-Happens-when-Countries-Go-Bankrupt-10871-haberi.html (accessed June 13, 2009).

15. Alan S. Blinder, *Keynesian Economics*, Library of Economics and Liberty, http://www.econlib.org/library/Enc/KeynesianEconomics.html (accessed June 1, 2009).

16. Robert L. Formaini, "Milton Friedman—Economist as Public Intellectual," *Economic Insights* 7, no. 2 (2002), Federal Reserve Bank of Dallas, http://www.dallasfed.org/research/ei/ei0202.html (accessed June 5, 2009).

17. E. Roy Wientraub, "Neoclassical Economics," Library of Economics and Liberty, http://www.econlib.org/library/Enc1/NeoclassicalEconomics.html (accessed June 22, 2009).

18. Jose De Cordoba and Nicholas Casey, "Cuba Unveils Huge Layoffs in Tilt toward Free Market," *The Wall Street Journal*, September 14, 2010, A1, A15.

19. David G. Blanchflower and Andrew J. Oswald, "International Happiness: A New View on the Measure of Performance," *The Academy of Management Perspectives* 25 (February 2011): 6–22.

20. Robbie Whelan, "Barry Minkow Charged in Fraud against Lennar," *The Wall Street Journal*, March 25, 2011, http://online.wsj.com/article/SB10001424052748704438104576219662795056534.html (accessed March 25, 2011).

21. Richard Whitely, "U.S. Capitalism: A Tarnished Model?" *The Academy of Management Perspectives* (May 2009): 11–22.

22. Thayer Watkins, "The Economy and the Economic History of Sweden," San Jose State University Department of Economics, http://www.sjsu.edu/faculty/watkins/sweden.htm (accessed June 22, 2009).

23. Tarun Khana, "Learning from Economic Experiments in China and India," *The Academy of Management Perspectives* (May 2009): 36–43.

24. Andrew Monahan, "China Overtakes Japan as World's No. 2 Economy," *The Wall Street Journal*, February 14, 2011, http://online.wsj.com/article/SB100014240527487033619045761428327414394 02.html (accessed March 25, 2011).

25. Timothy M. Devinney, "Is the Socially Responsible Corporation a Myth? The Good, the Bad, and the Ugly of Corporate Social Responsibility," *The Academy of Management Perspectives* (May 2009): 44–56.

26. Peter Waldman, "Unocal to Face Trial over Link to Forced Labor," *The Wall Street Journal*, June 13, 2002, B1, B3.

27. "Case profile: Unocal lawsuit (re Burma)," Business & Human Rights Resource Centre, http://www.business-humanrights.org/Categories/Lawlawsuits/Lawsuitsregulatoryaction/LawsuitsSelectedcases/UnocallawsuitreBurma (accessed March 28, 2011).

28. "Ethics in the global market: 2009 Corporate Citizenship Report," Texas Instruments, http://www.ti.com/corp/docs/csr/corpgov/ethics/global_market.shtml (accessed March 28, 2011).

29. "Ethics in TI," Texas Instruments, http://actrav.itcilo.org/actrav-english/telearn/global/ilo/code/texas.htm (accessed March 28, 2011).

30. Business for Social Responsibility, http://www.bsr.org (accessed June 21, 2009).

31. Mauro F. Guillén and Esteban García-Canal, "The American Model of the Multinational Firm and the "New" Multinationals From Emerging Economies," *The Academy of Management Perspectives* (May 2009): 23–25.

32. "Global Roundup," *International Business Ethics Review* (Spring/Summer 2005): 17.

33. Abigail Moses, "Greek Contagion Concern Spurs European Sovereign Default Risk to Record," *Bloomberg*, April 26, 2010, http://www.bloomberg.com/news/2010-04-26/greek-contagion-concern-spurs-european-sovereign-default-risk-to-record.html

(accessed March 18, 2011); James G. Neuger and Joe Brennan, "Ireland Weighs Aid as EU Spars over Debt-Crisis Remedy," *Bloomberg*, http://www.bloomberg.com/news/2010-11-16/ireland-discusses-financial-bailout-as-eu-struggles-to-defuse-debt-crisis.html (accessed March 18, 2011).

34. "UN at a Glance," UN, http://www.un.org/en/aboutun/index.shtml (accessed March 25, 2011).

35. "Overview of the UN Global Compact," United Nations Global Compact, http://www.unglobalcompact.org/AboutTheGC/index.html (accessed March 25, 2011).

36. Ibid.

37. "About AACSB," AACSB International, http://www.aacsb.edu/about/default.asp (accessed March 25, 2011); "Principles for Responsible Management Education Now Endorsed by over 100 Business Schools," PRME, April 7, 2007, http://www.aacsb.edu/media/releases/2008/4.7.08%20PRME%20First%20100%20-%20AACSB.pdf (accessed March 25, 2011).

38. "The Principles for Responsible Business Education," PRME, http://www.unprme.org/the-6-principles/index.php (accessed March 25, 2011).

39. Bao Chang, "Steel fastener makers hope EU sales can recover on WTO ruling," *China Daily*, December 7, 2010, http://www.chinadaily.com.cn/bizchina/2010-12/07/content_11662675.htm (accessed January 10, 2011).

40. John W. Miller, "WTO Details Rising Protectionism, Pushes Countries to Reverse Course," *The Wall Street Journal*, March 26, 2009, http://online.wsj.com/article/SB123808014186248481.html (accessed March 28, 2011).

41. "Global Village Investment Club," Earthlink, http://home.earthlink.net/~beowulfinvestments/globalvillageinvestmentclubwelcome/id25.html (accessed March 31, 2011).

42. "Global Ethics Corner: 2011 Top Risks and Ethical Decisions," Carnegie Council, January 21, 2011, http://www.carnegiecouncil.org/resources/gec/data/00114 (accessed March 24, 2011); The Eurasia Group, "Top Risks 2011," January 4, 2011.

43. "U.S. Securities and Exchange Commission and Department of Justice Clarify 'Best Practices' for FCPA Compliance," *Mayer Brown*, January 11, 2011, 1; Mike Koehler, "RAE Systems Held Liable for the Acts of Its Subsidiaries' Joint Venture Partners," *Corporate Compliance Insights*, December 13, 2010, http://www.corporatecomplianceinsights.com/2010/rae-systems-held-liable-for-the-acts-of-its-subsidiaries-joint-venture-partners/ (accessed May 4, 2011).

44. "Foreign Corrupt Practices Act's Antibribery Provisions," The 'Lectric Law Library, Excerpted from U.S. Commerce Dept., May 10, 1994, http://www.lectlaw.com/files/bur21.htm (accessed March 28, 2011).

45. "Global Fact Gathering," James Mintz Group, June 2009, http://www.mintzgroup.com/pdf/GFG-Issue4.pdf (accessed March 28, 2011).

46. Dionne Searcey, "U.K. Law on Bribes Has Firms in a Sweat," *The Wall Street Journal*, December 28, 2010, B1.

47. Julius Melnitzer, "U.K. enacts 'far-reaching' antibribery act," *Law Times*, February 13. 2011, http://www.lawtimesnews.com/201102148245/Headline-News/UK-enacts-far-reaching-anti-bribery-act (accessed March 28, 2011).

48. Searcey, "U.K. Law on Bribes Has Firms in a Sweat"; Melnitzer, "U.K. enacts 'far-reaching' anti-bribery act."

49. Searcey, "U.K. Law on Bribes Has Firms in a Sweat."

50. Melnitzer, "U.K. enacts 'far-reaching' anti-bribery act."

51. Michael Volkov, "The U.K. Antibribery Act: Let's Cool Down the Hysteria," http://www.fcpablog.com/blog/2011/1/18/the-uk-anti-bribery-act-lets-cool-down-the-hysteria.html (accessed March 28, 2011).

52. James Kanter, "Europe Fines Intel $1.45 Billion in Antitrust Case," *The New York Times,* May 13, 2009, http://www.nytimes.com/2009/05/14/business/global/14compete.html (accessed March 29, 2011).

53. "Cyber Security," Business Exchange, http://bx.businessweek.com/cyber-security/jobs/ (accessed March 28, 2011).

54. James T. Areddy, "People's Republic of Hacking," *The Wall Street Journal,* February 18, 2010, http://online.wsj.com/article/SB10001424052748704141010457505749034318 3782.html (accessed March 28, 2011).

55. Ashby Jones, "Pentagon Papers II? On WikiLeaks and the First Amendment," *The Wall Street Journal,* July 26, 2010, http://blogs.wsj.com/law/2010/07/26/pentagon-papers-ii-on-wikileaks-and-the-first-amendment/ (accessed March 29, 2011).

56. Jon Swartz, "Facebook changes its status in Washington," *USA Today,* January 13, 2011, 1B–2B.

57. Ibid.

58. Summer Said, "Pact Keeps BlackBerrys Running," *The Wall Street Journal,* August 9, 2010, B3; Loretta Chao and Jason Dean, "China's internet censors thrive by confusing web users," *The Wall Street Journal,* April 1, 2010, A10.

59. Chao and Dean, "China's internet censors thrive by confusing web users"; "China rejects Google accusation on email," *Bloomberg Businessweek,* March 22, 2011, http://www.businessweek.com/ap/financialnews/D9M46A3G0.htm (accessed March 29, 2011).

60. Matt Villano, "The Separation of Church and Job," *The New York Times,* February 5, 2006, http://query.nytimes.com/gst/fullpage.html?res=9C0CE7D8163EF936A35751C0A9609C8B63 (accessed March 29, 2011).

61. Anup Shah, "Health Issues," *Global Issues,* October 27, 2008, http://www.globalissues.org/issue/587/health-issues (accessed March 29, 2011).

62. Jeff Aronson, "Dying for Drugs," *British Medical Journal,* May 3, 2003, http://www.pubmedcentral.nih.gov/articlerender.fcgi?artid=1125906 (accessed June 22, 2009).

63. Katherine Hobson, "Two Surveys Spotlight Health Care Cost Variations," *The Wall Street Journal,* November 22, 2010, http://blogs.wsj.com/health/2010/11/22/two-surveys-spotlight-health-care-cost-variations/ (accessed March 29, 2011).

64. "Law Prompts Some Health Care Plans to Drop Mental Health Benefits: WSJ," Fox Business, December 23, 2010, http://www.foxbusiness.com/markets/2010/12/23/law-prompts-health-care-plans-drop-mental-health-benefits-wsj/ (accessed March 29, 2011).

65. Kate Kelland, January 18, 2010, "Global healthcare fraud costs put at $260 billion," Reuters, http://www.reuters.com/article/2010/01/18/us-healthcare-fraud-idUSTRE60H01620100118?pageNumber=1 (accessed March 29, 2011).

66. Thomas Catan and Avery Johnson, "Michigan's Blue Cross Sued over Pacts with Hospitals," *The Wall Street Journal,* October 19, 2010, http://online.wsj.com/article/SB100014240527023044105045 7556022408657 1764.html (accessed March 29, 2011).

67. "Germany: Development of the Health Care System," Country Database, http://www.country-data.com/cgi-bin/query/r-4924.html (accessed April 1, 2011).

68. United Nations Development Programme, "Power, Voice and Rights," Asia-Pacific Human Development Report, http://hdr.undp.org/en/reports/regional/asiathepacific/RHDR-2010-AsiaPacific.pdf (accessed March 30, 2011).

69. Sangeeta Shastry, "EU to tackle gender pay inequality," *Reuters,* March 8, 2010, http://blogs.reuters.com/global/2010/03/08/eu-to-tackle-gender-pay-inequality/ (accessed March 30, 2011).

70. "2010 annual survey of violations of trade union rights," ITUC, http://survey.ituc-csi.org/+-Whole-World-+.html (accessed March 30, 2011).

71. David Barboza, "McDonald's in China Agrees to Unions," *The New York Times,* April 10, 2007, http://query.nytimes.com/gst/fullpage.html?res=9D00E6DC153FF933A25757C0A9619C8B63&n=Top/Reference/Times%20Topics/Subjects/F/Fringe%20Benefits (accessed March 30, 2011).

72. Lisa Belkin, "The Fight for Paid Maternity Leave," *The New York Times,* February 1, 2010, http://parenting.blogs.nytimes.com/2010/02/01/the-fight-for-paid-maternity-leave/ (accessed March 30, 2011).

73. "Paternity Leave: International Comparisons," emplaw.co.uk, http://www.emplaw.co.uk/lawguide?startpage=data/20033221.htm (accessed March 30, 2011).

74. "Wages," United States Department of Labor, http://www.dol.gov/dol/topic/wages/minimumwage.htm (accessed March 30, 2011); "The National Minimum Wage Rates," Directgov, http://www.direct.gov.uk/en/Employment/Employees/TheNationalMinimumWage/DG_10027201 (accessed March 30, 2011); Ben Schneiders, "Minimum wage lifted to $570 a week," *The Sydney Morning Herald,* June 3, 2010, http://www.smh.com.au/business/minimum-wage-lifted-to-570-a-week-20100603-x1by.html (accessed March 30, 2011).

75. "Corporate Social Responsibility: Companies in the News," Mallenbaker.net, http://www.mallenbaker.net/csr/CSRfiles/nike.html (accessed March 30, 2011).

76. Deborah Ball, "UBS Posts Profit, Cuts Bonuses," *The Wall Street Journal,* February 9, 2011, http://online.wsj.com/article/SB1000142405274870442220457613133 1167797372.html?KEYWORDS=UBS+Cuts+Bonus+Pool (accessed March 30, 2011).

77. "China bosses told to cut salaries," BBC News, April 09, 2009, http://news.bbc.co.uk/2/hi/7993377.stm (accessed March 30, 2011).

78. Anup Shah, "Consumption and Consumerism," *Global Issues,* September 3, 2008, http://www.globalissues.org/issue/235/consumption-and-consumerism (accessed March 30, 2011).

79. Ibid.

80. Keith Bradsher, "China Fears Consumer Impact on Global Warming," *The New York Times,* July 4, 2010, http://www.nytimes.com/2010/07/05/business/global/05warm.html?_r=1&ref=business (accessed March 30, 2011).

81. Subhash Agrawal, "India's Premature Exuberance," *The Wall Street Journal,* June 16, 2009, http://online.wsj.com/article/SB124513568534118169.html (accessed March 30, 2011).

82. "India's greenhouse gas emissions rise by 58%," guardian.co.uk, May 12, 2010, http://www.guardian.co.uk/environment/2010/may/12/india-greenhouse-gas-emissions-rise (accessed March 30, 2011).

83. Sarita Agrawal, "Globalisation, consumption and green consumerism," HighBeam Research, originally published in *Political Economy Journal of India,* January 1, 2010, http://www.highbeam.com/doc/1G1-227797569.html (March 30, 2011).

84. "How Much of the World's Resource Consumption Occurs in Rich Countries?" Earth Trends, http://earthtrends.wri.org/updates/node/236 (accessed April 1, 2011); "The Global Sustainability Challenge," http://www.globalsustainabilitychallenge.com/ (accessed April 1, 2011).

85. "Global Ethics Office," Walmart Corporate, http://walmartstores.com/aboutus/280.aspx (accessed March 31, 2011).

86. "As GM Struggles, Its Ethics and Compliance Office Moves On," *Ethikos and Corporate Conduct Quarterly,* September/October 2008, http://www.ethikospublication.com/html/generalmotors.html (accessed March 31, 2011).

87. Mary Swanton, "Combating Corruption: GCs Aim to Establish Global Ethics Codes," InsideCounsel, January 1, 2011, http://www.insidecounsel.com/Issues/2011/January/Pages/

Combating-Corruption-GCs-Aim-to-Establish-Global-Ethics-Codes.aspx?page=3 (accessed March 31, 2011).

Appendix

1. Sean Valentine, Lynn Godkin, Gary M. Fleischman, and Roland Kidwell, "Corporate Ethical Values, Group Creativity, Job Satisfaction and Turnover Intention: The Impact of Work Context on Work Response," *Journal of Business Ethics* 98 (2011): 353–372.

2. "Corporate Social Responsibility and Employee-Company Identification," *Journal of Business Ethics* 95 (2010): 557–569.

3. Mathew Carr and Tsuyoshi Inajima, "Kyoto Doubts Prompts Japan to Hedge its CO_2 Bets: Energy Bets," *Bloomberg Businessweek,* November 10, 2010, http://www.businessweek.com/news/2010-11-10/kyoto-doubts-prompt-japan-to-hedge-its-co2-bets-energy-markets.html (accessed March 3, 2011); Risa Maeda, "UN: work on climate pacts to start next month," *Reuters,* March 3, 2011, http://www.reuters.com/article/2011/03/03/us-climate-un-idUSTRE7221WN20110303?pageNumber=2 (accessed March 3, 2011).

4. Monica Villavicencio, "Is the Ocean's Carbon Sink Getting Too Full?," *NPR,* August 2, 2007, http://www.npr.org/templates/story/story.php?storyId=12431939 (accessed March 3, 2011).

5. Ian Urbina, "Pressure Limits Efforts to Police Drilling for Gas," *The New York Times,* March 3, 2011, http://www.nytimes.com/2011/03/04/us/04gas.html?pagewanted=1&_r=1 (accessed March 7, 2011).

6. "Brazil: Amazon deforestation falls to new low," *BBC,* December 1, 2010, http://www.bbc.co.uk/news/world-latin-america-11888875 (accessed March 3, 2011).

7. Wendy Koch, "Here comes the sun: White House to install solar panels," *USA Today,* October 6, 2010, 10A.

8. Stefan Ambec and Paul Lanoie, "Does It Pay to Be Green? A Systematic Overview," *The Academy of Management Perspectives* 22 (4), November 2008, 45–62.

9. "The EU Eco-label," http://www.eco-label.com/default.htm (accessed July 15, 2009).

10. "The Seven Sins of Greenwashing," Terra Choice, http://sinsofgreenwashing.org/ (accessed July 15, 2009).

11. "Eco-Friendly Product Claims Often Misleading," *NPR,* November 30, 2007, http://www.npr.org/templates/story/story.php?storyId=16754919 (accessed June 25, 2009).

12. Paul Hawken and William McDonough, "Seven Steps to Doing Good Business," *Inc.,* November 1993, 79–90, www.inc.com/magazine/19931101/3770.html, accessed September 11, 2003.

13. "Voluntary Environmental Management Systems/ISO 14001: Frequently Asked Questions," *United States Environmental Protection Agency,* http://www.epa.gov/OWM/iso14001/isofaq.htm (accessed June 26, 2009).

INDEX

Information in figures and tables is indicated by *f* and *t*.